A FREEplace to learn FINANCE

• Excel Spreadsheet Modeling

LEARN TO BUILD YOUR OWN SPREADSHEET MODELS.

A special set of PC Spreadsheet exercises was created by Craig Holden of Indiana University to accompany this textbook. Learn how to build your own Excel templates, using actual examples from the textbook. These templates can be used repeatedly to implement models of professional quality for financial forecasting, discounted–cashflow valuation, option pricing, and more.

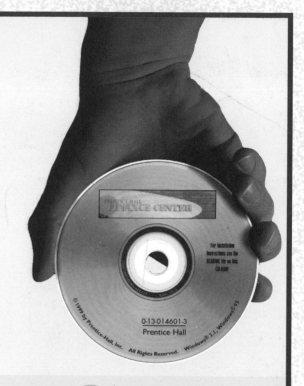

PRENTICE HALL
FINANCE CENTER
For Installation Instructions use the README file on this CD-ROM
© 1999 by Prentice-Hall, Inc. All Rights Reserved. Windows® 3.1, Windows®95
0-13-014601-3
Prentice Hall

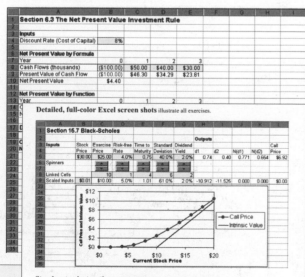

Spreadsheet Modeling: Net Present Value

Problem. A project requires an investment of $100,000 in year 0, but then generate positive cash flows of $50,000, $40,000, and $30,000 in years 1, 2, and 3, respectively. At a discount rate of 8%, should you accept or reject the project?

Solution Strategy. Calculate Net Present Value two different ways. First, use the Time Value of Money *formula* to discount each cash flow back to the present and then sum up the present value terms. Second, use the Time Value of Money *function* =current cash flow+ NPV(discount rate, future cash flow range). See the figure below.

FIGURE 6.3.1 Spreadsheet for Net Present Value.

	A	B	C	D	E	F	G	H	I
1	Section 6.3 The Net Present Value Investment Rule								
3	Inputs								
4	Discount Rate (Cost of Capital)	8%							
6	Net Present Value by Formula								
7	Year		0	1	2	3			
8	Cash Flows (thousands)	($100.00)	$50.00	$40.00	$30.00				
9	Present Value of Cash Flow	($100.00)	$46.30	$34.29	$23.81				
10	Net Present Value	$4.40							
12	Net Present Value by Function								
13	Year		0	1	2	3			

Detailed, full-color Excel screen shots illustrate all exercises.

	A	B	C	D	E	F	G	H	I	J	K	L
1	Section 15.7 Black-Scholes											
							Outputs					
3	Inputs	Stock Price	Exercise Price	Risk-free Rate	Time to Maturity	Standard Deviation	Dividend Yield	d1	d2	N(d1)	N(d2)	Call Price
4		$30.00	$25.00	4.0%	0.75	40.0%	2.0%	0.74	0.40	0.771	0.654	$6.92
5	Spinners											
8	Linked Cells	10	1	4	6	2						
9	Scaled Inputs	$0.01	$10.00	5.0%	1.01	61.0%	2.0%	-10.912	-11.525	0.000	0.000	$0.00

Call Price and Intrinsic Value chart:
$12, $10, $8, $6, $4, $2, $0 — Current Stock Price $0 $5 $10 $15 $20
— Call Price
— Intrinsic Value

Step-by-step instructions teach your students two levels of modeling:
- How to Build Your Own Spreadsheet Model (the basic level) and
- How to Use the Power of Your Spreadsheet Model (the advanced level).

How To Build Your Own Spreadsheet Model.

1. **Inputs.** Enter the inputs described above into the range B5:G5.
2. **d1 and d2 Formulas.** The d_1 formula is $\left(\ln(S/E)+\left(r-d+\sigma^2/2\right)T\right)/\left(\sigma\sqrt{T}\right)$. In cell H5, enter
   =(LN(B5/C5)+(D5-G5+F5^2/2)*E5)/(F5*SQRT(E5))

• Career Center

EXPLORE THE WORKING WORLD OF FINANCE!

"A Day in the Life" profiles how finance professionals use the concepts that students are currently learning to improve personal interviewing skills, survey the job market, and more!

PRENTICE HALL FINANCE CENTER
ONLINE EDITION

SW +1/4 LATEST CAREER UPDATE NEWS: TUNE IN @

FEATURES
resources
in the news
case studies
updates
research

CAREERS
fund mgmt.
investment
banking
commercial
banking
corporate

STRATEGIC PLANNING

Staying on top of the job market and giving you the latest news and updates are our goals here at the PH Finance Center. We've assembled workshops to help you figure out your career path, hone your resume, as well as practice those interviewing skills. Want to know what it's like to

John
Pennella

Put A New Twist On Time-Value-of-Money, And $5 In Your Pocket.

You will learn a great deal in this book about the Time-Value-of-Money. TI wants to help you learn the "value of time and money" with a great offer on the BAII PLUS™ financial calculator.

Save time. The easy-to-use features of the BAII PLUS will speed you through calculations such as net present value, internal rate of return, time-value-of-money, and more. And because the BAII PLUS is available at most stores where calculators are sold, you won't spend time searching for it.

Save money. You don't have to spend a lot of money because the BAII PLUS is priced to fit your budget. Plus, for a limited time, TI will put an extra $5 in your pocket.

Take advantage of this offer on the BAII PLUS today, and get the most value out of your time and money.

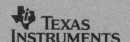
TEXAS INSTRUMENTS

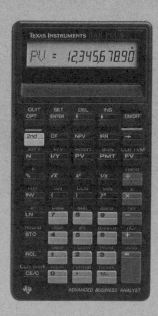

TEXAS INSTRUMENTS

BAII PLUS Rebate Terms and Conditions

This offer is valid only for BAII PLUS purchases between January 1, 1999 and April 30, 2001. All claims must be postmarked by May 31, 2001. Allow 8 to 10 weeks for processing. All purchases must be made in the U.S. or Canada. Rebates will be sent only to addresses in the U.S. and Canada and paid in U.S. dollars. Not redeemable at any store. Send this completed form along with the cash register receipt (original or copy) and the UPC bar code to the address indicated. This original mail-in certificate must accompany your request and may not be duplicated or reproduced. Offer valid only as stated on this form. Offer void where prohibited, taxed, licensed, or restricted. Limit one rebate per household or address. Texas Instruments reserves the right to discontinue this program at any time and without notice.

Yes! I Want $5 Back On My Purchase of the BAII PLUS.

Finance

ZVI BODIE

Professor of Finance
School of Management
Boston University

ROBERT C. MERTON

John and Natty McArthur University Professor
Harvard University

Prentice Hall, Upper Saddle River, New Jersey 07458

Acquisitions Editor: Paul Donnelly
Associate Editor: Gladys Soto
Editorial Director: James C. Boyd
Editor-in-Chief: PJ Boardman
Editorial Assistant: Cheryl Clayton
Marketing Manager: Lori Braumberger
Associate Managing Editor: Cynthia Regan
Manufacturing Buyer: Lisa DiMaulo
Senior Manufacturing Supervisor: Paul Smolenski
Manufacturing Manager: Vincent Scelta
Senior Designer: Kevin Kall
Design Manager: Patricia Smythe
Interior/Cover Design: Karen Quigley
Illustrator (Interior):   Omegatype Typography, Inc.
Cover Illustration/Photo: Burstein Goldman/The Stock Rep., Inc.
Composition: Omegatype Typography, Inc.

Copyright © 2000 by Prentice-Hall, Inc.
Upper Saddle River, New Jersey 07458

Library of Congress Cataloging-in-Publication Data

Bodie, Zvi.
    Finance / Zvi Bodie, Robert C. Merton.
      p. cm.
    Includes index.
    ISBN 0-13-310897-X
      1. Finance. I. Merton, Robert C. II. Title.
    HG173.B58 2000
    658.15—dc21   99-31591
                                 CIP

Prentice-Hall International (UK) Limited, London
Prentice-Hall of Australia Pty. Limited, Sydney
Prentice-Hall Canada, Inc., Toronto
Prentice-Hall Hispanoamericana, S. A., Mexico
Prentice-Hall of India Private Limited, New Delhi
Prentice-Hall of Japan, Inc., Tokyo
Prentice-Hall (Singapore) Pte. Ltd.
Editora Prentice-Hall do Brasil, Ltda., Rio de Janeiro

Printed in the United States of America

10 9 8 7 6 5 4 3 2

I dedicate this book to my wife, Judy, and my daughters,
Lara and Moriya, without whose patient love and encouragement
I could never have brought it to completion.

Zvi Bodie

To Lisa, logophile and chrematist,
and to Samantha, Robert F., and Paul, the ineffable three.

Robert C. Merton

Foreword

Every year dozens of new textbooks are published. No wonder. As Willie Sutton told the judge about why he robbed banks: "That's where the money is." But only every other decade does there arrive an innovative new work that sets a new pattern of excellence and pedagogy. This Bodie-Merton *Finance* has long been expected. And it proves to be well worth the wait. Good teachability, like good wine, requires much deliberate time.

In the meanwhile, Robert Merton shared the 1997 Nobel Prize in Economics. His was never a case of "if" but only a case of "when," for it has been well said that Merton is the Isaac Newton of modern finance theory. And ever since their graduate student days at MIT, Bodie and Merton have made a productive team. Speaking as one of their teachers, I hail their demonstrating that water can indeed rise above its source. The kind of finance that matters for modern experts goes beyond the tools that have been revolutionizing Wall Street: the pricing of options and other contingent derivatives. Yes, all that is important practically and theoretically. But as this book's coverage shows, it is the Main Street economy of production, capital budgeting, personal finance, and rational accounting that is best illuminated by this overdue breakthrough in teaching.

I moan to myself, "Where were these authors back when I was a student?" Well, the future is longer than the past, and future students will reap the harvest that these innovative teachers have sown.

Enjoy!

Paul A Samuelson

Paul A. Samuelson
Massachusetts Institute of Technology

Brief Contents

Contents

Preface

Finance is an introductory text intended for use in the first course at the MBA level. It has a broader scope and a greater emphasis on general principles than most other introductory-level texts in finance, which typically focus exclusively on corporate finance. The preliminary edition of this text, which was published in September 1997, has also proven to be well suited for students of economics, law, mathematics and for business executives seeking a solid understanding and overview of the entire field of finance.

SCOPE OF THE TEXT

In most well-developed fields of study, such as chemistry, the educational norm is for the introductory course to cover general principles and to give the student an appreciation of the scope of the whole discipline's subject matter. It thereby lays the foundation for more specialized courses that have a narrower focus, such as organic or inorganic chemistry. In line with this approach, our text encompasses all of the subfields of finance—corporate finance, investments, and financial institutions—within a single unifying conceptual framework.

CONTENT AND ORGANIZATION

Finance as a scientific discipline is the study of how to allocate scarce resources over time under conditions of uncertainty. There are three analytical "pillars" to finance: optimization over time (the analysis of intertemporal trade-offs), asset valuation, and risk management (including portfolio theory). At the core of each of these pillars are a few basic laws and principles that apply across all of the topical subfields.

The book is divided into six major parts. Part I explains what finance is, gives an overview of the financial system, and reviews the structure and uses of corporate financial statements. Parts II, III, and IV correspond to each of the three conceptual pillars of finance and emphasize the application of finance principles to decision problems faced by households (life-cycle financial planning and investments) and firms (capital budgeting). Part V covers the theory and practice of asset pricing. It explains the Capital Asset Pricing Model, and the pricing of futures, options, and other contingent claims, such as risky corporate debt, loan guarantees, and levered equity. Part VI deals with issues in corporate finance: capital structure, mergers and acquisitions, and real options analysis of investment opportunities.

Finance is intended for use in its current form anywhere in the world. The book is written so that its concepts are as relevant and understandable to a student in Argentina, France, Japan, or China as they are to a student in the United States. The international aspects of finance are integrated throughout the book, not confined to specific, separate "international" chapters.

PEDAGOGICAL FEATURES

- There are many *examples* to illustrate theory at work in making financial decisions.

- There are "Quick Check" *concept questions* at critical points in the text to help students check their understanding of the material just presented. Answers to these questions are provided at the end of the chapter.

- There are *special-interest boxes* inserted throughout the text containing newspaper clippings and applications that encourage students to make active use of the theory in dealing with their own affairs and in interpreting the financial news.

- There are a large number of end-of-chapter *problems,* sorted by topic and level of difficulty. Complete step-by-step solutions for all problems are provided in the *Instructor's Manual* in a format that allows adopters of the text to distribute them to their students.

TEMPLATE
X.X

- A special set of spreadsheet templates, which correspond with selected end-of-chapter problems, was created by Craig Holden of Indiana University to accompany this textbook. They are contained on the Prentice Hall Finance Center CD-ROM found in the inside back cover of each copy of the text.

E-BOOK
X.X

- E-book icons, found adjacent to selected headings in the text, refer to the Spreadsheet Modeling Exercises Handbook. This handbook contains 19 models that demonstrate how students can build their own Excel spreadsheet models. The exercises guide the reader step-by-step through the implementation of models designed to teach the applied aspects of finance. The end result of each exercise is the production of an Excel template that can be used repeatedly to implement models of professional quality for financial forecasting, discounted-cash-flow valuation, option pricing, and more. These same templates were used to create the numerical examples in the textbook itself. The Spreadsheet Modeling Student Handbook is included on the Finance Center CD.

FLEXIBILITY

The text is organized in a way that readily permits an instructor teaching a traditional introductory course in corporate or managerial finance to adopt the book. However, for schools that are currently updating their finance curriculum to reflect advances in the theory and practice of finance, *Finance* provides a flexible alternative to the traditional introductory text. Instead of focusing exclusively on corporate finance, it teaches the conceptual building blocks and applied techniques that are required in *all* areas of finance—investments and financial institutions, as well as corporate finance. Consequently, instructors in subsequent elective courses do not have to develop these fundamentals from scratch, as is often the case now. *Finance*'s broad-based approach thereby eliminates considerable duplication of effort in the elective offerings.

The text is organized to allow instructors considerable latitude in choosing the content and level of detail they wish to deliver to their classes.

One outcome of this flexible structure is that an instructor who wishes to emphasize corporate finance in the introductory course can focus on chapters 3, 6, 13, 16, and 17 and still provide effective coverage of general valuation and risk management by using selected chapters from Parts III and IV. Instructors who instead wish to emphasize investment subjects such as portfolio selection and option pricing in the introductory course can readily do so by covering more chapters from Parts IV and V.

REQUIRED LEVEL OF MATHEMATICS

The level of mathematical sophistication required to understand the text is elementary algebra. We provide many algebraic models in the text, which serve as the foundation for spreadsheet modeling.

SUPPLEMENTS FOR THE INSTRUCTOR

Instructor's Manual with Solutions

The Instructor's Manual includes worked out answers to *all* end-of-chapter questions and problems.

Instructor's Resource CD

This CD, included in every copy of the Instructor's Manual, contains a PowerPoint Lecture Presentation of over 2,000 slides with numerous graphs, tables, and equations as well as an abridged version of approximately 40 slides per chapter with outlines and graphs. The CD also contains the complete Excel program specifically designed for this text by Craig Holden: Excel templates and solutions for selected end-of-chapter problems, the Spreadsheet Modeling Exercises Handbook, and the worked out answers to the modeling exercises.

Test Bank

Written by Bonnie Buchanan of Georgia State University, the test bank contains approximately 1,000 multiple-choice questions, short-answer problems, and a separate section with more analytical, challenging problems.

Test Manager

The new Version 4.1 computerized test bank has added database capabilities. Instructors can store students' grades, export grades to Excel, and archive previous semester grade statistics.

FINCOACH Test Manager and FINCOACH Instructor's Manual

Test Manager software has been developed to allow instructors to generate tests based on FINCOACH—The Financial Management Math Practice Program contained within the Prentice Hall Finance Center CD available to all students using *Finance*. In addition, an Instructor's Manual for using FINCOACH Test Manager and FINCOACH in the course has been developed and is included with the FINCOACH Test Manager software.

PHLIP/CW: Prentice Hall's Learning on the Internet Partnership/Companion Web Site (www.prenhall.com/bodie)

Prentice Hall's Learning on the Internet Partnership/Companion Web site is a content-rich, multidisciplinary business Web site with Internet exercises, activities, and resources related to a specific text. All Internet resources are updated every two weeks, allowing both instructors and students to use a wealth of up-to-date, on-line resources. Instructors will need to acquire a password and user ID code from their local Prentice Hall representative in order to open the faculty site and gain access to the following materials.

- **Downloadable supplements,** including Instructor's Manuals, PowerPoint presentations, and Excel spreadsheet solutions, for selected end-of-chapter problems.
- **On-line faculty support** with additional cases, current event articles, links, and full support for exercises posted on the Student Page.

Visit the Faculty Lounge area to find:

- Talk to Team—Faculty chat room
- Teaching Archive—Resources for enhancing lecture materials and doing research on the Web
- Help with Computers—Provides tips and access to getting answers to tricky computer problems

Companion Web Site (www.prenhall.com/bodie)

Companion Web sites provide an interactive learning environment for students, and supply support resources for instructors. Among other resources, every Companion Web site integrates Syllabus Manager^{TM}, an on-line syllabus creation and management utility. Syllabus Manager^{TM} provides instructors with an easy, step-by-step process to create and revise syllabi, with direct links into Companion Web site and other on-line content. Students access Syllabus Manager^{TM} directly from within the Companion Web site, providing quick access to course assignments. The Companion Web site for *Finance* contains sample syllabi created using Syllabus Manager^{TM}.

FOR THE STUDENT

The Prentice Hall Finance Center CD

Contained in the inside back cover of *Finance* is the *Prentice Hall Finance Center CD*. This all-in-one robust learning tool contains features designed to increase student awareness of what finance professionals do, ensure comprehension and mastery of the financial mathematics contained in the text, provide help for students in building their own Excel spreadsheets, and provide a direct link to PHLIP (Prentice Hall Learning on the Internet Partnership).

    Specifically, the following dynamic tools are found on the Prentice Hall Finance Center CD.

- *Careers Center.* Introduces the student to a vast array of professional opportunities in finance through video interviews with professionals and insights into what they do on the job on an average day. Here the student will meet an options trader, a mutual fund manager, investment analysts, a CFO, and others. Also accessible are features for personal development, résumé writing, interviewing techniques, and career planning information.

- *FINCOACH—The Financial Math Practice Center.* Contains more than 5 million problems and self-tests in virtually all math areas covered in this text. Save problems, review them, and print them. This is a step-by-step guide to solve any finance mathematics problem and allows the student to rapidly gain mastery in all mathematical challenges.

- *PHLIP—Principles and Practice Web Center.* PHLIP (Prentice Hall Learning on the Internet Partnership) can be accessed either directly from the CD or remotely at *http://www.prenhall.com/bodie*. Here's what the student can do on PHLIP:

  - See current news items from the popular business press and directly related to individual chapters. These news items use chapter terminology, provide links to related information, and offer discussion questions and projects for assignment by the instructor.

  - Access additional career information.

  - Learn study and writing skills and engage in conferences with other students studying finance.

  - Access to a free on-line study guide specifically designed for the text

- *Spreadsheet Modeling Exercises.* Spreadsheet modeling is a core skill for real-world finance. Employers want individuals who both understand finance models and can implement them on a spreadsheet. The Spreadsheet Modeling Exercises section of the Prentice Hall Finance Center CD was created by Dr. Craig W. Holden of Indiana University. This dynamic educational tool is based on a hands-on, active-learning paradigm. Starting with a blank spreadsheet, the student follows complete user-friendly instructions and builds spreadsheet models in 30 to 60 minutes. Excel screen shots show what the completed spreadsheet will look like. Each exercise contains two levels: 1) "How to Build Your Own Spreadsheet Model," and 2) "Using the Power of Your Spreadsheet Model," which extends the model to an advanced level. Every important quantitative model in *Finance* is covered. Templates for problems at the end of each chapter are also provided.

- *Companion Web site.* The Companion Web site includes a free on-line study guide that provides various self-assessment exercises and immediate feedback for the student.

CHANGES SINCE THE PRELIMINARY EDITION

In September 1997 Prentice Hall published a preliminary edition of this text with the intention of getting extensive feedback from teachers of finance and other reviewers. To our delight, several universities adopted the preliminary edition, and we were therefore able to benefit from their experiences with it. Here is what we learned from these class testers of the preliminary edition and the way we have responded in this first edition:

- Students liked the emphasis on practical financial decision making, especially the examples drawn from personal finance. We have therefore reorganized the old chapters 4 and 5. The revised chapter 5, Life-Cycle Financial Planning, is now a self-contained primer in personal financial decision making, using time value of money concepts in making saving, borrowing, and investment decisions over the life cycle.

- Readers liked chapter 3 on financial statements, but many thought that it is best to cover financial forecasting and working capital (the old chapter 19) as part of the same unit. In the first edition, these two chapters have been combined into a single revised chapter 3, How to Interpret and Forecast Financial Statements. This is a self-contained primer that requires no prior knowledge of accounting.

- In response to faculty reviewer comments, coverage of corporate finance topics is significantly expanded in the first edition. As already noted, management of working capital and the construction of pro forma statements for forecasting have been incorporated into an expanded chapter 3 on financial statements. Chapter 6, on capital budgeting, now contains a detailed spreadsheet analysis of an investment project, including the calculation of expected cash flows and sensitivity analysis of NPV. This same project appears in the Spreadsheet Modeling Exercises Handbook with step-by-step instructions on how to build the model and to carry out sensitivity analyses using Excel. Chapter 16 now contains the APV, FTE, and WACC approaches to integrating financing considerations into the capital budgeting decision. A detailed analysis and illustration compares the three approaches and demonstrates their mutual consistency. Furthermore, chapter 16 has added a detailed discussion of how a firm's financing mix is chosen in the real world, underscored with several concrete examples.

- In general, reviewers found the second half of the preliminary edition to be more difficult to understand than the first half. We have therefore made the first edition flow more evenly by simplifying the second half, and reviewers of the revised text have unanimously praised the results of that effort. For example, we have simplified and streamlined the presentation of options and contingent claims. Instead of separate chapters on each, there is now a single revised chapter 15, Options and Contingent Claims, and it is full of practical examples of how options and option-pricing concepts can be applied. We have also combined the old chapters 11 and parts of 12 into a single chapter 11, Hedging, Insuring, and Diversifying, to allow more instructors to fit these risk management topics into the introductory course.

- As a result of messages received from several careful readers, we have corrected a number of typographical and numerical errors that crept into the preliminary edition. Nonetheless, despite these efforts, this first edition will almost surely contain some errors, and we ask your help in identifying them. We are committed to correcting all errors as soon as they are discovered. Please notify the authors directly by email sent to zbodie@bu.edu or rmerton@hbs.edu.

ACKNOWLEDGMENTS

We gratefully acknowledge the contributions of our colleagues in the Global Financial System Project at the Harvard Business School to the development, refinement, and enrichment of the functional perspective that serves as the underlying analytical framework of our book. We especially appreciate the opportunity provided by the Project for the two of us to be located together at the Business School during some critical years in the book's formulation.

From the earliest stages, many experienced teachers of finance were involved in the development of this text. They provided feedback and suggestions which were critical to the book's current form and content. We especially thank Craig Holden of Indiana University, expert extraordinaire, who first helped us to design the Excel spreadsheet exercises that accompany the text, and who then, single-handedly, turned that design into a reality. We would like to offer our special thanks to the following colleagues who reviewed the manuscript in whole or in part: Jack Aber (Boston University), James Angel (Georgetown University), Dean Baim (Pepperdine University), Susan Belden (University of Colorado, Colorado Springs), Marc Bertoneche (University of Bordeaux), Paul Bursick (St. Norbert College), George Chacko (Harvard Business School), Ted Chadwick (Boston University), Joseph Cherian (Boston University), William W. Damon (Vanderbilt University), Richard DeFusco (University of Nebraska–Lincoln), Michael Dowd (University of Toledo), Rex DuPont (Boston University), Steven Feinstein (Babson College), Michael Fishman (Northwestern University), Frederick Floss (SUNY Buffalo), Micah Frankel (California State University–Hayward), Thomas Gefzey (Temple University), Raymond Gorman (Miami University of Ohio), Kathryn Griner (Boston University), R. W. Hafer (Southern Illinois University at Edwardsville), Sam Hanna (Boston University), Rex Daniel Harawa (SUNY Geneseo), Craig Holden (Indiana University), Keith Howe (De Paul University), Steve Johnson (University of Texas–El Paso), Elizabeth Sawyer Kelly (University of Wisconsin–Madison), W. Carl Kester (Harvard Business School), Brian Kluger (University of Cincinnati), Glen Larson, Jr. (Univeristy of Tulsa), Jaewoo Lee (University of California at Irvine), Robert Lutz (Weber State University), Matthew Malone (Boston University), Surendra Mansinghka (San Francisco State University), J. Harold McClure (University College–Dublin), Bruce McManis (Nicholls State University), Joseph Messian (San Francisco State University), Lisa Meulbroek (Harvard Business School), John Mitchell (Central Michigan University), Karlyn Mitchell (North Carolina State University), Mark Mitchell (University of Chicago/Harvard Business School), Shahruz Mohtadi (Suffolk University), L. W. Murray (University of San Francisco), Paul Natke (CMU), David Nickerson (American University), John Norstad (Northwestern University), Akorlie Nyatepe-Coo (University of Wisconsin–La Crosse), Coleen Pantalone (Northeastern), George Pennacchi (University of Illinois Urbana-Champaign), Lynn Pi (California State University), Rose Prasad (Central Michigan University), Charles Rayhorn (Northern Michigan University), Asani Sarkar (University of Illinois Urbana-Champaign), Dennis Sheehan (Penn State University), Clemens Sialm (Stanford University), Wonhi Synn (Elon College), Harold Tamule (Providence College), Manuel Tarrazo (University of San Francisco), Peter Tufano (Harvard Business School), S. Venkataraman (Univeristy of Florida), Joseph Walker (University of Alabama–Birmingham), and Laura Wolff (Southern Illinois University).

Capable research assistance was provided by the following graduate students: Noël Ashekian (Boston University), Richard Hanna (Boston University), Rayana Hobballah (Boston University), Li Jin (MIT), Matt Malone (Boston University), Jan Mahrt-Smith (MIT), Bhanu Narasimhan (MIT), and John Neumann (Boston University).

During the development of *Finance* both Prentice Hall and we benefited immensely from feedback we accumulated from many of our colleagues who teach finance. This feedback came in the form of responses from a survey conducted in the fall of 1998 and from personal conversations. We are most appreciative to all of these individuals for sharing their thoughts and their valuable time with regard to our text. They are Saul Adelman (Miami University), Kofi Amoateng (North Carolina Central University), Leslie Anderson (Portland State University), Thomas Anderson (Kennesaw State University), Tony Apap (University of West Florida), David Arnold (College of the Southwest), Leroy Ashorn (Sam Houston State University), Anthony Avallone (Point Loma Nazarene University), Yu-Jong Avis (College of St. Rose), Curtis Bacon (Southern Oregon University), Sung Bae (Bowling Green State University), Bruce Bagamary (Central Washington University), Dean Baim (Pepperdine University), Ray Baker (Rockford College), Sheldon Balbirer (University of North Carolina–Greensboro), Mary Ballantyne (Passaic County Community College), Joel Barber (Florida International University), Marisa Baron (Isothermal Community College), Scottie Barty (Northern Kentucky University), Ron Bealer (Norwalk Community Technical College), Thomas Bear (Stetson University), Kenneth Beller (Washington State University–Tri Cities), Scott Below (East Carolina University), Yvette Bendeck (University of Houston–Clearlake), Gary Benesh (Florida State University), Art Berman (Chemeketa Community College), Robert Berry (University of Houston), Carol Billingham (Central Michigan University), John Bilson (Illinois Institute of Technology), Michael Binder (Buena Vista University), Homer Bonitsis (New Jersey Institute of Technology), John Boos (Ohio Wesleyan University), Brian Boscaljon (Calvin College), Steve Bouchard (Goldey Beacom College), James Boyd (Kent State University), Michael Boyd (Stetson University), William Brent (Howard University), Billie Brotman (Kennesaw State University), William Brown (Claremont McKenna College), Richard Brunell (Concordia University), Paul Bursik (Saint Norbert College), Wayne Buchanan (Alice Lloyd College), Alva Butcher (University of Puget Sound), Kirt Butler (Michigan State University), Robert Butler (Olivet College), Joseph Byers (Community College of Allegheny County), Ezra Byler (Millikin University), Tony Byrd (University of Central Florida), Julie Cagle (Xavier University), Alan Carper (Bob Jones University), David Carter (Abilene Christian University), Steven Carvell (Cornell University), Stephen Cassidy (Howard University), Jennifer Caudill (Auburn University), Karen Chambliss (Florida Institute of Technology), P. Chandy (University of North Texas), Robert Chatfield (University of Nevada Las Vegas), Leo Cheatham (Northeast Louisiana University), Chao Chen (California State University–Northridge), Carl Chen (University of Dayton), Haiyang Chen (Youngstown State University), Yin-Wong Cheung (University of California Santa Cruz), Andreas Christofi (Monmouth University), Bert Connell (Loma Linda University), C. Mitchell Conover (University of North Carolina–Wilmington), Clyde Cooley (Weber State University), Thomas Corrigan (Sacred Heart University), John Cresson (Northeastern State University), Robert Cullen (Mercyhurst College), Tom Curry (Morningside College), Robbie Dail (Beaufort County Community College), Wallace Davidson (Southern Illinois University–Carbondale), Steve Davis (Northwestern College), Dennis Debrecht (Carroll College), Karen Denning (West Virginia University), Anand Desai (Kansas State University), Les Dlabay (Lake Forest College), David Dubofsky (Virginia Commonwealth University), Martine Duchatelet (Barry University), Mary Ducy (Texas Southern University), John Dunkelberg (Wake Forest University), Michael Dunn (California State University–Northridge), Dan Ebels (University of Michigan–Ann Arbor), David Echevarria (St. Joseph's University), Richard Edelman (American University), Al Eferstein (Lindsey Wilson College), Imad Elhaj (Colorado School of Mines), Barry Ellis (Southeastern Oklahoma State University), Ronel Elul (Brown University), Lisa

Fairchild (Loyola College), Hsing Fang (California State University–Los Angeles), Greg Fink (Richard Stockton State College), Peggy Fletcher (Northeastern University), Jennifer Foo (Stetson University), Swint Friday (University of South Alabama), Mark Geiger (William Woods University), Richard Gendreau (Bemidji State University), Tommy Georgiades (Devry Institute of Technology), Bruno Gerard (University of Southern California), John Gerlach (Sacred Heart University), Erika Gilbert (Illinois State University), Preston Gilson (Fort Hays State University), Chris Gingrich (Eastern Mennonite University), Ruth Gitzendanner (Tri State University), Douglas Gordon (Arapahoe Community College), David Gordon (Governors State University), Ray Gorman (Miami University–Oxford), Diane Gregory (Bentley College), Deborah Griest (Lake Tahoe Community College), John Griffith (University of Minnesota–Duluth), Richard Gritta (University of Portland), Russell Grosjean (Erie Community College), Mahmoud Haddad (University of Tennessee–Martin), Richard Halberg (Houghton College), Dan Hall (East Central College), Karen Hallows (George Mason University), Tom Hannen (College of Notre Dame), Robert Hanson (Eastern Michigan University), Eugene Harris (Hanover College), Rick Harvey (Fairmont State College), Ron Heisner (Kishwaukee College), Larry Heldreth (Danville Community College), Glenn Henderson (University of Cincinnati), Helmut Hergeth (North Carolina State University), Linda Herrington (Community College of Allegheny), George Hicks (Muskingum Area Technical College), Pat Hill (University of Alabama–Birmingham), Bob Hoerber (Westminster College), Marion Hoginboom (Elmhurst College), Leonard Hopkins (Central Carolina Technical College), James Horrell (University of Oklahoma), Ronald Horwitz (Oakland University), Sylvia Hudgins (Old Dominion University), Carl Hudson (Auburn University), Jerry Hunt (East Carolina University), Virginia Ingram (Kennesaw State University), Zahid Iqbal (Texas Southern University), Steven Isberg (University of Baltimore), Thomas Jackman (Nebraska Wesleyan University), Katherine Jackson (Indiana University), John Jahera (Auburn University), Terrance Jalbert (University of Hawaii at Hilo), William Jennings (California State University–Northridge), Jeff Jewell (Lipscomb University), Zhenhu Jin (Illinois Wesleyan University), Craig Johnson (California State University Hayward), Steve Johnson (University of Texas–El Paso), Dick Johnston (Monmouth College), Alan Jung (San Francisco State University), Ashok Kapoor (Marist College), Janice Karlen (Laguardia Community College), James Kehr (Miami University–Oxford), Alfred Kelly (Northwest Missouri State University), David Ketcham (Bryant College), James Keys (Florida International University), Kashi Khazeh (Salisbury State University), Brian Kluger (University of Cincinnati), John Knight (University of the Pacific), Barbara Kouskoulas (Lawrence Technological University), Jim Krause (University of Tampa), Duncan Kretovich (Eastern Michigan University), Thomas Krueger (University of Wisconsin–La Crosse), Linda Kuechler (Daemen College), Craig Kuhlemeyer (University of Northern Colorado), George Kutner (Marquette University), Frank Laatsch (Bowling Green State University), Gene Lai (University of Rhode Island), John Lajaunie (Nicholls State University), Douglas Lamdin (University of Maryland–Baltimore), Howard Lanser (University of Notre Dame), Martin Laurence (William Paterson College), Joe Lavely (Longwood College), Rick LeCompte (Wichita State University), Kyoo-hwan Lee (Brooklyn College of CUNY), Youngho Lee (Howard University), Elaine Leff (Laguardia Community College), Steven Lifland (Eastern Connecticut State University), Ralph Lim (Sacred Heart University), J. Barry Lin (Husson College), Kenneth Locke (University of Missouri–St Louis), Raymond Lopez (Pace University), Maria Lorusso (University of Texas–San Antonio), Lynne Luper

(Ocean County College), Thomas Lynch (Hocking College), Paul Maloney (Providence College), George Mangiero (Iona College), Susan Mangiero (Sacred Heart University), Inayat Mangla (Western Michigan University), Surendra Mansinghka (San Francisco State University), Timothy Manuel (University of Montana), Jay Marchand (Westminster College), Paul Marshall (Widener University), Don Materniak (Franciscan University), Judy Matteson (Cleary College), Patricia Matthews (Mount Union College), Thomas Maynard (Converse College), Michael Mazzeo (Michigan State University), Anna Mcaleer (Beaver College), Roger McCallister (Towson General Agency), Joseph McCarthy (Keuka College), Gilbert McKee (Cal State Polytech University), Bruce McManis (Nicholls State University), Kathy McNichol (La Salle University), Gillermo Melendez (Metropolitan University), David Merrifield (Christian Heritage College), Joseph Messina (San Francisco State University), Stuart Michelson (University of Central Florida), David Minars (Brooklyn College of CUNY), John Mitchell (Central Michigan University), Cheryl Mitteness (St. Cloud State University), Naval Modani (University of Central Florida), Timothy Moffitt (Kalamazoo College), Lynn Moller (Kansas Wesleyan University), Robert Monfort (Saint Josephs College), Scott Moore (John Carroll University), Dianne Morrison (University of Wisconsin–La Crosse), Saeed Mortazari (Humboldt State University), Jon Moulton (Oregon State University), David Mullis (University of South Carolina), Laurie Murphy (Flathead Valley Community College), L. William Murray (University of San Francisco), James Nelson (University of Arizona), Randy Nelson (Colby College), William Nelson (Indiana University Northwest), Jeffry Netter (University of Georgia), Chee Ng (Rowan University), Joan Nix (Queens College of CUNY), John Nofsinger (Marquette University), Gary Noreiko (University of Southern Colorado), Jamie O'Brien (South Dakota State University), Oris Odom (University of Texas at Tyler), Jim Owens (West Texas A&M University), R. Daniel Pace (University of West Florida), Therese Pactwa (Florida International University), Roger Palmer (University of St Thomas), Chang Park (Clinch Valley College), Andrew Parkes (East Central University), Sam Penkar (University of Houston–Downtown), Jonathan Peters (Wagner College), Corey Pfaffe (Maranatha Baptist Bible College), Michael Phillips (Austin Peay State University), Jim Philpot (Ouachita Baptist University), Eugene Poindexter (State University of West Georgia), J. C. Poindexter (North Carolina State University), Thomas Potter (University of North Dakota), Annette Poulsen (University of Georgia), Cynthia Powell (Southern Nazarene University), Rose Prasad (Central Michigan University), John Primus (California State University Hayward), Richard Proctor (Siena College), Dennis Proffitt (Grand Canyon University), Frances Quinn (Merrimack College), Ganas Rakes (Ohio University–Athens), Kumoli Ramakrishnan (University of South Dakota), Sanjay Ramchander (Minnesota State University Mankato), Ganga Ramdas (Lincoln University), Robert Rainish (University of New Haven), Linda Ravelle (Moravian College), David Rayome (Northern Michigan University), John Reik (University of Minnesota), Cecilia Ricci (Seton Hall University), Hong Rim (Shippensburg University), Kenneth Roberts (Southwestern University), Georges Rocourt (Barry University), Foster Roden (University of North Texas), Bernard Rose (Rocky Mountain College), Mike Rosen (Pepperdine University), Stan Rosenberg (La Roche College), Herbert Roth (Shippensburg University), Arlyn Rubash (Bradley University), Bruce Rubin (Old Dominion University), Chip Ruscher (James Madison University), Patricia Ryan (Drake University), Robert Saemann (Alverno College), Paul Sarmas (Cal State Polytech University), Vincent Scerbinski (Southampton College), Patricia Schaeff (Miami University–Oxford), Burton Schaffer (California State University–

Sacramento), Michael Schellenger (University Wisconsin–Oshkosh), Stephen Schepman (Central Washington University), Bill Schmidt (Shorter College), Jeffrey Schultz (Christian Brothers University), Robert Schweitzer (University of Delaware), James Seifert (Marquette University), Jimmy Senteza (Washington State University), Rodney Serizawa (San Francisco State University), Edward Shafer (University of Maryland), Dianna Shallenburger (Central Methodist College), Peter Sharp (California State University–Sacramento), Allen Shin (Frostburg State University), Kilman Shin (Ferris State University), Julian Shlager (Plymouth State College), Joseph Shott (Westmoreland County Community College), Connie Shum (Pittsburgh State University), Fred Siegel (University of Louisville), Debra Skaradzinski (Hollins University), Julie Smith (Oral Roberts University), Patricia Smith (North Carolina Wesleyan College), Ronald Smith (St. Thomas Aquinas College), Stephanie Smith (Texas A&M International University), Ira Sohn (Montclair State University), Patricia Sommerville (St. Mary's University), Kean Song (Prairie View A&M University), Austin Spencer (Western Carolina University), Katherine Spiess (University of Notre Dame), Hubert Spraberry (Howard Payne University), Jan Squires (Southwest Missouri State University), Suresh Srivastava (University of Alaska–Anchorage), Marty St. John (Westmoreland County Community College), Richard Stackman (University of Washington Tacoma), Edward Stendardi (St. John Fisher College), Glenn Stevens (Franklin Marshall College), Jerry Stevens (University of Richmond), Eric Stiles (Fordham University), Gabe Stoeppler (Limestone College), Steve Stover (California Maritime Academy), John Stowe (University of Missouri–Columbia), Charles Strang (Western New Mexico University), Robert Stretcher (Hampton University), Jan Strockis (Santa Clara University), Barbara Suleski (Cardinal Stritch College), Mark Sullivan (Wor Wic Community College), Michael Sullivan (University of Nevada Las Vegas), Janice Swain (Regis College), George Swales (Southwest Missouri State University), Wonhi Synn (Elon College), Harry Tamule (Providence College), Amir Tavakkol (Kansas State University), Janet Thatcher (University of Wisconsin–Whitewater), Madeline Thimmes (Utah State University), Bruce Toews (Walla Walla College), José Trinidad (Southwest Texas State University), George Trivoli (Jacksonville State University), C. Joe Ueng (University of St. Thomas), E. Upton (Virginia Commonwealth University), David Vang (University of St. Thomas), Dennis Varin (Southern Oregon University), Sue Visscher (University of Toledo), Ashok Vora (Baruch College of CUNY), Jean Walker (West Texas A&M University), Edward Waller (University of Houston–Clearlake), Stan Warren (Niagara University), Randi Waxman (Columbia Union College), Samuel Weaver (Lehigh University), Marsha Weber (Moorhead State University), Loren Weishaar (Texas Lutheran College), Charles Wellens (Fitchburg State College), Gary Wells (Idaho State University), Peng Wen (Fresno Pacific College), Mark Wencel (Piedmont Community College), John White (Georgia Southern University), Michael White (Bob Jones University), Howard Whitney (Franklin University), Marilyn Wiley (Florida Atlantic University), Gary Wishniewsky (California State University Hayward), Edward Wolfe (Western Kentucky University), Bob Wood (Tennessee Technical University), David Wright (University of Wisconsin), Mark Wrolstad (Winona State University), Jerry Yang (University of Arizona), Richard Yanow (Massachusetts College of Liberal Arts), Philip Young (Southwest Missouri State University), Ken Yung (Old Dominion University), Richard Zock (California State University Hayward), and Thomas Zwirlein (University of Colorado).

We also thank our developmental editor, Jane Tufts, who forced us to clarify our exposition of finance theory and to illustrate every point with real-world examples.

In our current lexicon the verb "to tuft" means to express oneself clearly, concisely, and concretely. We thank Linda Arricale, Harvard Business School, for her help in keeping the two of us organized throughout this book's years of development, and for so much more. The editorial staff at Prentice Hall has been very supportive and patient throughout the long process of developing and writing the many drafts of the text. Our special thanks go to Will Ethridge, who convinced us to publish with Prentice Hall, and to Leah Jewell, who was the book's most enthusiastic, faithful, and hard-working fan at Prentice Hall during the years of development. Our editorial team of Paul Donnelly and Gladys Soto has shown remarkable initiative, imagination, and friendship in working with us during the final stages of writing and bringing the book to market. We thank them for their many contributions.

Zvi Bodie
Robert C. Merton

About the Authors

Zvi Bodie is Professor of Finance at Boston University's School of Management. He received his Ph.D. from the Massachusetts Institute of Technology and has served on the finance faculties of MIT's Sloan School and the Harvard Business School. Bodie has published widely on investing, financial innovation, and pension finance. Currently, he conducts research and lectures on the funding and investment policies of pension plans and on the financial aspects of social security reform. He is currently a member of the Pension Research Council at the Wharton School, and has served as an adviser to the Financial Accounting Standards Board, the OECD, and the World Bank.

Robert C. Merton is the John and Natty McArthur University Professor at the Harvard Business School. After receiving a Ph.D. in Economics from the Massachusetts Institute of Technology in 1970, he served on the finance faculty of MIT's Sloan School of Management until 1988 when he moved to Harvard. Dr. Merton holds honorary degrees from the University of Chicago, Hautes Etudes Commerciales (Paris), University of Lausanne, National Sun Yat-sen University, and University of Paris-Dauphine. A Senior Fellow of the International Association of Financial Engineers, he was the first recipient of its Financial Engineer of the Year Award. He is a past president of the American Finance Association, and a member of the National Academy of Sciences. Dr. Merton received the Alfred Nobel Memorial Prize in Economic Sciences in 1997.

Dr. Merton's research is focused on developing finance theory in the areas of capital markets and financial institutions. He has written extensively on intertemporal portfolio choice, capital asset pricing, the pricing of options, risky corporate debt, loan guarantees, and other complex derivative securities. He has also written on the operation and regulation of financial institutions, including issues of capital budgeting, production, hedging, and risk management.

Before collaborating on *Finance,* Bodie and Merton worked together on several research projects, first at the National Bureau of Economic Research and then at the Harvard Business School. Over the past twenty years, they have coauthored at least ten publications on the theory and practice of finance.

CHAPTER

What Is Finance?

1

OBJECTIVES

- Define finance.
- Explain why finance is worth studying.
- Introduce two of the main players in the world of finance—households and firms—and the kinds of financial decisions they make. The other main players, financial intermediaries and government, are introduced in chapter 2.

CONTENTS

- You have started to save for the future and all of your savings are in a bank account. Should you invest in mutual funds? What kind of mutual funds?
- You have decided to get a car. Should you buy it or lease it?
- You worked as a waiter during your college years and are thinking about starting your own restaurant when you graduate. Is it worth doing? How much money do you need to start? Where can you get the money?
- You are advising the chief financial officer (CFO) of a major computer manufacturer whether to expand into the telecommunications business. It is expected to cost $3 billion over the next few years to enter the business,

and the expected benefits are increased profits of $1 billion per year thereafter. What do you recommend?

- You are part of a team working at the World Bank analyzing an application for a loan to a small country in Latin America to finance a major hydroelectric project. How do you decide what to recommend?

These are all examples of financial decisions. This book will provide you with a way of addressing these and similar questions by exploring the basic principles of finance. In this chapter we define finance and consider why it is worth studying; then we introduce the main players in the world of finance—households and firms—and the kinds of financial decisions they make.

1.1 DEFINING FINANCE

Finance is the study of how people allocate scarce resources *over time*. Two features that distinguish financial decisions from other resource allocation decisions are that the costs and benefits of financial decisions are (1) spread out over time and (2) usually not known with certainty in advance by either the decision makers or anybody else. In deciding whether to start your own restaurant, for example, you must weigh the *costs* (such as the investment in fixing up the place and buying the stoves, tables, chairs, little paper umbrellas for exotic drinks, and other equipment you need) against the uncertain *benefits* (your future profits) that you expect to reap over several years.

In implementing their decisions people make use of the **financial system,** defined as *the set of markets and other institutions used for financial contracting and the exchange of assets and risks.* The financial system includes the markets for stocks, bonds, and other financial instruments, financial intermediaries (such as banks and insurance companies), financial service firms (such as financial advisory firms), and the regulatory bodies that govern all of these institutions. The study of how the financial system evolves over time is an important part of the subject matter of finance.

Finance theory consists of a set of concepts that help you to organize your thinking about how to allocate resources over time and a set of quantitative models to help you evaluate alternatives, make decisions, and implement them. The same basic concepts and quantitative models apply at all levels of decision making, from your decision to lease a car or to start a business, to the decision of the CFO of a major corporation to enter the telecommunications business, to the decision of the World Bank about which development projects to finance.

A basic tenet of finance is that the ultimate function of the system is to satisfy people's *consumption preferences,* including all the basic necessities of life, such as food, clothing, and shelter. Economic organizations such as firms and governments exist in order to facilitate the achievement of that ultimate function.

1.2 WHY STUDY FINANCE?

There are at least five good reasons to study finance:

- to manage your personal resources.
- to deal with the world of business.
- to pursue interesting and rewarding career opportunities.
- to make informed public choices as a citizen.
- to expand your mind.

Let us elaborate on each of these reasons one at a time.

First, knowing some finance helps you to manage your own resources. Can you get along without knowing anything about finance? Perhaps. But if you are completely ignorant, then you are at the mercy of others. Remember the old adage: "A fool and his money are soon parted."

In some cases you will seek the help of experts. There are many finance professionals and financial service firms that provide financial advice—bankers, stockbrokers, insurance brokers, and firms selling mutual funds and other financial products and services. Often the advice is "free" if you are a potential customer. But how do you evaluate the advice you are given? The study of finance provides a conceptual framework for doing so (see Box 1.1).

A second reason to study finance is that a basic understanding of finance is essential in the business world. Even if you do not intend to specialize in finance, you must have a sufficient understanding of the concepts, techniques, and terminology employed by finance specialists to communicate with them and to recognize the limits of what they can do for you.

Third, you may be interested in a career in finance. There are varied and potentially rewarding career opportunities in the field of finance and many possible paths you can follow as a finance professional. Most finance professionals are employed in the financial services sector of the economy—such as banking, insurance,

---

BOX 1.1

Need a Financial Adviser?

Some Helpful Considerations

Let's say you have a portfolio worth $500,000 (including your retirement accounts), a home, the usual debts, and some stock options. You want to know whether your investments make sense, whether you're on track with retirement savings, and whether there's anything else you need to worry about, such as life insurance or buying a long-term-care policy. So, following the brochures, you choose someone who has been in the business for years, has a lot of impressive credentials, hasn't been arrested, and is a really nice person. Now what?

Here's what you could expect: Most financial advisers/planners/consultants (take your pick) are brokers and insurance agents. They have an incentive to get you to change your investments, even if you don't really need to. Some advisers charge an hourly fee like accountants and lawyers. There are some things you can do to sift through all those people out there who call themselves financial advisers:

- *Don't rely on a referral.* Sure, your brother-in-law may gush that his adviser is great, but unless he can tell you what he is invested in and why, and whether the returns are good or bad,

he's like someone who tells you his mechanic is fantastic because the guy has a tow truck. Instead, rely on referrals from friends only if it's clear they know what they're talking about.

- *Don't pay too much attention to credentials.* Professional designations often mean the person is licensed to sell, can pass a multiple-choice exam, or has gone to a lot of conferences in places like Palm Springs, California. Instead, ask advisers what they did before they became advisers. Most will have sales backgrounds, but an increasing number are coming out of other professions such as accounting, engineering, teaching, and law. This can give a different perspective that can benefit you.

- *Beware of these red flags.* Steer clear of any adviser trying to sell penny stocks, tax liens, commodities, coins, art, or racehorses. Someone claiming insider knowledge of the markets or a "secret strategy" is probably either a scoundrel or an idiot.

Source: Adapted from an article by Ellen E. Schultz, *The Wall Street Journal,* May 22, 1998, p. C1. Reprinted by permission of *The Wall Street Journal,* © 1998 Dow Jones & Company, Inc. All Rights Reserved.

or investment management. However, many others work as financial managers in nonfinancial firms or in government. Some even pursue academic careers.

Households, businesses, and government agencies often seek the advice of financial consultants. Moreover, a background in finance provides a good foundation for a career in general management. Many of the chief executives of major corporations around the world started in finance.

Fourth, to make informed public choices as a citizen, you should have a basic understanding of how the financial system works. The financial system is an important part of the infrastructure of any market-oriented society. Indeed, a sound set of financial institutions is believed by many to be an essential element in economic growth and development. As citizens we sometimes must make political choices that affect the functioning of the financial system. For example, do you want to vote for a political candidate who favors abolishing government deposit insurance or one who would impose strict controls on stock-market trading?

Fifth, finance can be a fascinating field of study on purely intellectual grounds. It expands your understanding of how the real world works. The scientific study of

---

BOX 1.2

Nobel Prize in Economics for Work in Finance

In 1990 the Nobel Prize in economics was awarded to three scholars—Harry Markowitz, Merton Miller, and William Sharpe—for scientific contributions that have had a powerful impact on both the theory and practice of finance. Let us briefly explain their contributions.

Harry Markowitz is the father of modern portfolio theory, the scientific study of how to trade off risk and reward in choosing among risky investments. In his seminal article, "Portfolio Selection," which appeared in the *Journal of Finance* in 1952, he developed a mathematical model showing how investors could achieve the lowest possible risk for any given target rate of return. The Markowitz model has been incorporated into basic finance theory and is widely used by practicing investment managers.

William Sharpe took Markowitz's results as his starting point and developed their implications for asset prices. By adding the assumption that at all times asset prices will adjust to equate demand and supply for each risky asset, he showed that a very specific structure must exist among the expected rates of return on risky assets ("Capital Asset Prices: A Theory of Market Equilibrium under Conditions of Risk," *Journal of Finance,* 1964). The structure suggested by Sharpe's theory is widely used today as the basis for making risk adjustments in many areas of finance theory and practice.

Merton Miller has contributed mainly to the theory of corporate finance. He and Franco Modigliani (an earlier recipient of the Nobel Prize in economics) addressed the dividend and borrowing policies of firms in a series of articles, starting with "The Cost of Capital, Corporation Finance, and the Theory of Investment," which appeared in the *American Economic Review* in 1958. Their fundamental contribution was to focus the attention of theorists and practitioners of finance on how corporate dividend and financing policies affect the total value of a firm. The M&M (Modigliani-Miller) propositions developed in their joint papers are among the basic building blocks of modern corporate finance.

Again in 1997 the Nobel Prize in economics was awarded to financial economists. The laureates were Robert C. Merton (one of the authors of this textbook) and Myron Scholes. The prize committee also mentioned a third scholar, Fischer Black, whose untimely death in 1995 at age 57 made him ineligible to share the prize. These three men discovered a mathematical formula for the pricing of options and other derivative securities that has had an enormous impact on both the theory and practice of finance. It is generally known as the Black-Scholes option pricing formula.

finance has a long history. Adam Smith's *The Wealth of Nations,* published in 1776, is widely regarded as the beginning of the science of economics. Finance theorists today are generally economists specializing in financial economics. Indeed, in 1990 and again in 1997, the Nobel Prize in economics was awarded to scholars for their scientific contributions in the field of finance (see Box 1.2).

1.3 FINANCIAL DECISIONS OF HOUSEHOLDS

Most households are families. Families come in many forms and sizes. At one extreme is the *extended family,* which consists of several generations living together under one roof and sharing their economic resources. At the other extreme is the single person living alone, whom most people wouldn't think of as a "family." In finance, however, all are classified as households.

Households face four basic types of financial decisions:

- *Consumption and saving decisions:* How much of their current wealth should they spend on consumption and how much of their current income should they save for the future?
- *Investment decisions:* How should they invest the money they have saved?
- *Financing decisions:* When and how should households use other people's money to implement their consumption and investment plans?
- *Risk-management decisions:* How and on what terms should households seek to reduce the financial uncertainties they face or when should they increase their risks?

As a result of saving part of their income for use in the future, people accumulate a pool of wealth, which can be held in any number of different forms. One form is bank accounts, another might be a piece of real estate or a share in a business venture. All of these are **assets.** *An asset is anything that has economic value.*

When people choose how to hold their pool of accumulated savings, it is called *personal investing* or **asset allocation.** In addition to investing in their own homes, people will often choose to invest in financial assets, such as stocks or bonds.

When people borrow, they incur a **liability,** which is just another word for debt. A household's wealth or **net worth** is measured by the value of its assets minus its liabilities. Say you own a house worth $100,000 and have a $20,000 bank account. You also owe $80,000 to the bank on your home mortgage loan (a liability) and have a $5,000 credit card debt outstanding. Your net worth is $35,000: your total assets ($120,000) minus your total liabilities ($85,000). Ultimately, all of society's resources belong to households because they own the firms (either directly or through their ownership of shares of stock, pension plans, or life insurance policies) and pay the taxes spent by governments.

Finance theory treats people's consumption preferences as given. Although preferences may change over time, how and why they change is not addressed by the theory.[1] People's behavior is explained as an attempt to satisfy those preferences. The behavior of firms and governments is viewed from the perspective of how it affects the welfare of people.

---

[1]Elements of a theory that are not explained by the theory itself are called *exogenous.* In contrast, those elements that are explained by the theory are called *endogenous.* In finance, people's preferences are exogenous to the theory, but the objectives of firms are endogenous.

Quick Check 1-1
What are the four basic types of financial decisions households have to make? Give an example of each.

1.4 FINANCIAL DECISIONS OF FIRMS

By definition, business firms—or simply firms—are entities whose primary function is to produce goods and services. Like households, firms come in many different shapes and sizes. At the one extreme are small workshops, retail outlets, and restaurants owned by a single individual or family. At the other extreme are giant corporations, such as Mitsubishi or General Motors, with a workforce of hundreds of thousands of people and an even greater number of owners. The branch of finance dealing with financial decisions of firms is called *business finance* or *corporate finance.*

In order to produce goods and services, all firms—small and large—need *capital.* The buildings, machinery, and other intermediate inputs used in the production process are called *physical capital.* The stocks, bonds, and loans used to finance the acquisition of the physical capital are called *financial capital.*

The first decision any firm must make is what businesses it wants to be in. This is called *strategic planning.* Because strategic planning involves the evaluation of costs and benefits spread out over time, it is largely a financial decision-making process.

Often a firm will have a core business defined by its main product line, and it may branch out into related lines of business. For example, a firm that produces computer hardware may also choose to produce the software. It may also choose to service computers.

A firm's strategic goals may change over time, sometimes quite dramatically. Some corporations enter into businesses that are seemingly unrelated to each other. They may even abandon their original core business altogether so that the company's name ceases to have any connection with its current business.

For example, ITT Corporation started out as a telephone company in 1920. Its name stood for International Telephone and Telegraph. In the 1970s ITT became a large multinational conglomerate, operating a diverse set of businesses including insurance, munitions, hotels, bakeries, automobile rentals, mining, forest products, and gardening products in addition to telecommunications. During the 1980s, ITT shed many of its businesses and focused on operating hotels and casinos. By 1996 it had abandoned its original core business of producing telephone equipment and telecommunication services.

Once a firm's managers have decided what businesses they are in, they must prepare a plan for acquiring factories, machinery, research laboratories, showrooms, warehouses, and other such long-lived assets and for training the personnel who will operate them all. This is the *capital budgeting process.*

The basic unit of analysis in capital budgeting is an *investment project.* The process of capital budgeting consists of identifying ideas for new investment projects, evaluating them, deciding which ones to undertake, and then implementing them.

Once a firm has decided what projects it wants to undertake, it must figure out how to finance them. Unlike capital budgeting decisions, the unit of analysis in *cap-*

ital structure decisions is *not* the individual investment project but the firm as a whole. The starting point in making capital structure decisions is determining a feasible financing plan for the firm. Once a feasible financing plan has been achieved, the issue of the optimal financing mix can be addressed.

Firms can issue a wide range of financial instruments and claims. Some are standardized securities that can be traded in organized markets, such as common stock, preferred stock, bonds, and convertible securities. Others are nonmarketable claims, such as bank loans, employee stock options, leases, and pension liabilities.

A corporation's capital structure determines who gets what share of its future cash flows. For example, bonds promise fixed cash payments, whereas stocks pay the residual value left over after all other claimants have been paid. Capital structure also partially determines who gets to control the company. In general, shareholders have control through their right to elect the board of directors. But often bonds and other loans include contractual provisions, called *covenants*, restricting the activities of management. These covenant restrictions give the creditors some control over the company's affairs.

Working capital management is extremely important to the success of a firm. The best long-term plans can go awry if the firm's management does not attend to the day-to-day financial affairs of the business. Even in a growing, successful firm, cash flows in and out may not match up exactly in time. Managers must worry about collecting from customers, paying bills as they come due, and generally managing the firm's cash flow to ensure that operating cash-flow deficits are financed and that cash-flow surpluses are efficiently invested to earn a good return.

The choices that a firm makes in all areas of financial decision making—investment, financing, and working capital management—depend on its technology and on the specific regulatory, tax, and competitive environment in which it operates. The policy choices are also highly interdependent.

Quick Check 1-2
What are the basic types of financial decisions firms have to make? Give an example of each.

1.5 FORMS OF BUSINESS ORGANIZATION

There are three basic types of organizational form for a firm: a sole proprietorship, a partnership, and a corporation. A **sole proprietorship** is a firm owned by an individual or a family, in which the assets and liabilities of the firm are the personal assets and liabilities of the proprietor. A sole proprietor has *unlimited liability* for the debts and other liabilities of the firm. This means that if the firm cannot pay its debts, the proprietor's other personal assets can be seized to satisfy the demands of the firm's creditors.

Many firms start out as sole proprietorships and then change their organizational form as they become established and expand. But frequently a business such as a restaurant, a real estate agency, or a small workshop will remain a sole proprietorship throughout its existence.

A **partnership** is a firm with two or more owners, called the partners, who share the equity in the business. A partnership agreement usually stipulates how decisions

---

BOX 1.3

How to Identify That a Firm Is a Corporation

In the United States, corporations are identified by the letters *Inc.* after their name. It stands for the English word *incorporated.* In France the letters are *SA* (Societé Anonime); in Italy *SpA* (Societa per Azioni); in the Netherlands *NV* (Naamloze Vennootschap); and in Sweden *AB* (Aktiebolag).

In Germany, public corporations are called Aktiengesellschaften, identifiable by the letters *AG* after the company name, whereas private corpora-

tions are Gesellschaften mit beschrankter Haftung, denoted by *GmbH*. The parallel designations in the United Kingdom are *PLC* for public limited company, and *LTD* for private corporations.

The earliest known corporations were formed in Amsterdam and in London in the 1600s and were called *joint stock companies* in English. That term has fallen into disuse.

---

are to be made and how profits and losses are to be shared. Unless otherwise specified, all partners have unlimited liability as in the sole proprietorship.

However, it is possible to limit the liability for some partners called *limited partners.* At least one of the partners, called the general partner, has unlimited liability for the debts of the firm. Limited partners typically do not make the day-to-day business decisions of the partnership; the general partner does.

Unlike a sole proprietorship or a partnership, a **corporation** is a firm that is a legal entity distinct from its owners. Corporations can own property, borrow, and enter into contracts. They can sue and be sued. They are usually taxed according to rules that differ from the rules that apply to the other forms of business organization.

The charter of a corporation sets down the rules that govern it. Shareholders are entitled to a share of any distributions from the corporation (e.g., cash dividends) in proportion to the number of shares they own. The shareholders elect a *board of directors,* which in turn selects managers to run the business. Usually there is one vote per share, but sometimes there are different classes of stocks with different voting rights.

An advantage of the corporate form is that ownership shares can usually be transferred without disrupting the business. Another advantage is *limited liability,* which means that if the corporation fails to pay its debts, the creditors can seize the assets of the corporation but have no recourse to the personal assets of the shareholders. In that sense a corporation serves the same function as a general partner in a partnership, and its shareholders are like limited partners.

Around the world, large firms are almost always organized as corporations, although ownership of the corporation may be restricted to a single person or family. In the United States, corporations with broadly dispersed ownership are called *public corporations;* those with concentrated ownership are called *private corporations.*

Laws governing the corporate form of organization differ in their details from country to country, and even within a country they may differ from one jurisdiction to another. In the United States, for example, laws governing corporations are created and administered at the state level (see Box 1.3).

Quick Check 1-3
A corporation owned by a single person is not a sole proprietorship. Why?

1.6 SEPARATION OF OWNERSHIP AND MANAGEMENT

In sole proprietorships and even in many partnerships the owners and the active managers of the business are the same people. But in many firms, especially the large ones, the owners do not themselves manage the business. Instead they delegate that responsibility to professional managers, who may not own any shares in the business. There are at least five reasons for the owners of a firm to turn over the running of the business to others to manage.

First, professional managers may be found who have a superior ability to run the business. This may be because the professional managers have better technological knowledge, more experience, or a more suitable personality to run the business. In a structure in which the owner is also the manager, the owner must have both the talents of a manager and the financial resources necessary to carry out production. In the separated structure, no such coincidence is required.

For example, consider the entertainment industry. The people most qualified to manage a film studio or a television network may not have the financial resources to own the business, and the people with the wealth to own such a business may have no ability to manage it. Therefore, it makes sense for the managerially competent people to produce and distribute the movies and for the wealthy people to simply provide the capital.

Second, to achieve the efficient scale of a business the resources of many households may have to be pooled. For example, the cost of producing a single movie is in the millions of dollars for a low-budget film, and the average feature-length movie costs many millions of dollars to produce. The need to pool resources to achieve an efficient scale of production calls for a structure with many owners, not all of whom can be actively involved in managing the business.

Third, in an uncertain economic environment, owners will want to diversify their risks across many firms. To diversify optimally requires the investor to hold a portfolio of assets, in which each security is but a small part. Such efficient diversification is difficult to achieve without separation of ownership and management.

For example, suppose an investor thinks that firms in the entertainment industry will do well over the next few years and would like to buy a diversified stake in that industry. If the investor had to also manage the firms she invests in, there is no way she could diversify across many firms. The corporate form is especially well suited to facilitating diversification by investor-owners because it allows them to own a relatively small share of each firm.

Fourth, the separated structure allows for savings in the costs of information gathering. Managers can gather the most accurate information available about the firm's production technology, the costs of its inputs, and the demand for its products. The owners of the firm need to know relatively little about the technology of the firm, the intensity at which it is being operated, and the demand for the firm's products.

Again, consider the entertainment industry. The information needed to successfully manage the production and distribution of a movie is substantial. Although information about top actors and directors who might be hired to star in a movie is readily available at low cost, this is not so with respect to other resource inputs to movie production and distribution. Establishing information networks of agents and jobbers is costly and is most efficiently handled by having movie executives specialize in doing it.

Fifth, there is the "learning curve" or "going concern" effect, which favors the separated structure. Suppose the owner wants to sell all or part of his technology either now or at a later date. If the owner must also be the manager, the new owners have to learn the business from the former owner in order to manage it efficiently. However, if the owner does *not* have to be the manager, then when the business is sold, the manager continues in place and works for the new owners. When a company issues shares to the public for the first time, the original owner-managers often continue to manage the business even if they no longer own any shares in the business.

The corporate form is especially well suited to the separation of owners and managers because it allows relatively frequent changes in owners by share transfer without affecting the operations of the firm. Millions of shares in corporations around the world change hands and rarely is there any effect on the management or operations of the business.

> **Quick Check 1-4**
> What are the main reasons for having a separation of management and ownership of firms? How does the corporate form of organization facilitate this separation?

Offsetting all the reasons in favor of a separation of ownership and management, the separated structure creates the potential for a *conflict of interest* between the owners and the managers. Because the owners of a corporation have only incomplete information about whether the managers are serving their interests effectively, managers may neglect their obligations to the shareholders. In extreme cases, managers may even act *contrary* to the interests of their shareholders. Adam Smith, the father of classical economics, summed it up as follows:

> The directors of such [joint-stock] companies, however, being the managers rather of other people's money than of their own, it cannot well be expected, that they should watch over it with the same anxious vigilance with which the partners in a private copartnery frequently watch over their own. Like the stewards of a rich man, they are apt to consider attention to small matters as not for their master's honour, and very easily give themselves a dispensation from having it. Negligence and profusion, therefore, must always prevail, more or less, in the management of the affairs of such a company.[2]

In those business environments in which the potential for conflicts of interest between owners and managers can be resolved at a reasonable cost, we would expect to find that the owners of business firms will not be the managers. And we would expect that the ownership of firms is dispersed among many individuals. Furthermore, we would expect to observe that, over time, the changes in the composition of the ownership would be far more common than the changes in the composition of the management.

1.7 THE GOAL OF MANAGEMENT

Because the managers of corporations are hired by the shareholders (through the board of directors), the managers' primary commitment is to make decisions that are in the best interests of the shareholders. This is not the exclusive goal of man-

---

[2]Adam Smith, *The Wealth of Nations* (Chicago: University of Chicago Press, 1977).

agement. Like everyone else in society, corporate managers must obey the law. They are also expected to respect ethical norms and to promote desirable social goals when it is possible to do so at a reasonable cost to shareholders.[3]

However, even if we restrict the goal of corporate management exclusively to serving the best interests of the shareholders, it is not obvious how managers can achieve this goal. In principle, managers could review each decision with the owners including the production choices, cost of obtaining capital, and so on and ask them which combination they prefer. But, in that case, the owners would have to have the same knowledge and spend essentially the same amount of time as they would if they were managing the business themselves. There would, therefore, be little point in hiring managers to run the business.

Moreover, although this procedure might be feasible when there are a few owners of the firm, it becomes completely impractical as the number of shareholders becomes large. Indeed, for a large multinational corporation, the number of shareholders can exceed a million, and they may reside in many different countries. Hence, it is essential to find a goal or rule to guide managers of the firm without having to "poll" the owners about most decisions.

To be effective, such a rule should not require the managers to know the risk preferences or opinions of the shareholders because such data are virtually impossible to obtain. And even if the data were available at one point in time, they change over time. Indeed, because shares of stock change hands every day, the owners of the corporation change every day. Thus, to be feasible, the right rule should be independent of who the owners are.

If a feasible rule for the managers to follow were found that would lead them to make the same investment and financing decisions that each of the individual owners would have made had they made the decisions themselves, then such a rule would clearly be the right one. To *maximize the wealth of current stockholders* is just such a rule.[4] Let us explain why.

For example, suppose you are the manager of a corporation trying to decide between two alternative investments. The choice is between a very risky investment project and a very safe one. Some shareholders might want to avoid taking these risks, and others might be pessimistic about the future of the investment. Still other shareholders might be risk lovers or might be optimistic about the outcome of the investment. How then can management make a decision in the best interests of all shareholders?

Suppose that undertaking the risky project would increase the market value of the firm's shares more than would the safe project. Even if some shareholders ultimately want to invest their money in safer assets, it would not be in their best interests for you as the firm's manager to choose the safer project.

This is because in well-functioning capital markets shareholders can adjust the riskiness of their personal portfolios by selling some of the shares in the firm you manage and investing the proceeds in safe assets. By your accepting the riskier project, even these risk-averse shareholders will wind up better off. They will have extra dollars today, which they can invest or consume as they see fit.

---

[3]We assume that the goal of maximizing shareholder wealth does not necessarily conflict with other desirable social goals.

[4]This rule, like any all-encompassing dictum, is not always correct. It needs to be qualified in several respects. First, it assumes well-functioning and competitive capital markets. It also assumes that managers do not make decisions that are illegal or unethical.

Thus, we see that individual owners would want managers to choose the investment project that maximizes the market value of their shares. The only risks relevant to the decision by managers are those of the project that affect the market value of the firm's shares.

The shareholder-wealth-maximization rule depends on the firm's production technology, market interest rates, market risk premiums, and security prices. It leads managers to make the same investment decisions that each of the individual owners would have made had they made the decisions themselves. At the same time, it does not depend upon the *risk aversion* or *wealth* of the owners, and so it can be made without any specific information about the owners. Thus, the shareholder-wealth-maximization rule is the "right" rule for managers to follow in running the firm. They can follow it without polling the owners each time a decision arises.

Scholars and other commentators on corporate behavior sometimes assert that the goal of managers is to maximize the firm's *profits*. Under certain specialized conditions, profit maximization and maximizing shareholder wealth lead to the same decisions. But in general there are two fundamental ambiguities with the profit-maximization criterion:

- If the production process requires many periods, then which period's profit is to be maximized?
- If either future revenues or expenses are uncertain, then what is the meaning of "maximize profits" when profits are described by a probability distribution?

Let us illustrate each of these problems with the profit-maximization criterion. First, the problem of many periods.

Suppose the firm faces a choice between two projects, both of which require an initial outlay of $1 million but last for a different number of years. Project A will return $1.05 million one year from now and then is over. Its profit is, therefore, $50,000 ($1.05 million – $1 million). Project B will last for two years, return nothing in the first year, and then $1.1 million two years from now. How do you apply a profit-maximization criterion in this case?

Now let us illustrate the difficulty of using a profit maximization criterion in an uncertain environment. Suppose you are the manager of a firm trying to choose between two investment projects, both of which require an initial outlay of $1 million and produce all of their returns one period from now. As in the previous example, project A will pay $1.05 million with certainty. We can, therefore, say unambiguously that the profit on project A is $50,000 ($1.05 million – $1 million).

Project C has an uncertain return. It will either pay $1.2 million or $0.9 million, each with probability .5. Thus, project C will either produce a profit of $200,000 or a loss of $100,000. What does it mean in this context to say "choose the project that maximizes the firm's profits"?

Unlike profits, it is clear that the current market value of the firm's shareholders' equity is still well defined (e.g., the future cash flows of the IBM corporation are uncertain, but there is a current price for its stock that is not uncertain). Hence, unlike the profit-maximization rule, the shareholder-wealth-maximization rule causes no ambiguities when future cash flows of the firm are uncertain.

Quick Check 1-5

Why is the shareholder-wealth-maximization rule a better one for corporate managers to follow than the profit-maximization rule?

Of course, management still has the difficult task of estimating the impact of its decision on the value of the firm's shares. Thus, in our preceding illustrations, in order to choose between projects A and B, or between A and C, management would have to determine which of them is likely to increase the value of the firm the most. This is not easy, but the criterion for making the decision is unambiguous.

Thus, the goal of management is to make decisions so as to maximize the firm's value to its shareholders. The main challenge in implementing this criterion is to obtain information about the likely impact of its decisions on the firm's value. Management's task is made much easier when it can observe market prices of its own and other firms' shares.

Indeed, in the absence of such market price information, it is difficult to see how they can implement this criterion at all. Although it is reasonable to assume that good managers will have as much information about their firm's production technology as anyone, such *internal* (to the firm) information is not sufficient to make effective decisions. In the absence of a stock market, managers would require *external* (to the firm) information that is costly if not impossible to obtain: namely, the wealth, preferences, and other investment opportunities of the owners.

Thus, the existence of a stock market allows the manager to substitute one set of external information that is relatively easy to obtain—namely, stock prices—for another set that is virtually impossible to obtain—information about the shareholders' wealth, preferences, and other investment opportunities. The existence of a well-functioning stock market, therefore, facilitates the efficient separation of the ownership and management of firms.

Note that in one respect the corporation's own senior managers and outside stock analysts who follow the corporation face a common task. Both groups are concerned with answering the question: How will the actions taken by management affect the market price of the firm's shares? The big difference is that the managers are the ones who actually make the decisions and have responsibility for implementing them.

One place to look for a statement of the goals of a corporation's top managers is the annual report to shareholders. Often the opening letter from the company's chief executive officer states what management's financial goals are and the general strategic plan for achieving them (see Box 1.4).

BOX 1.4

Corporate Financial Goals and the Annual Report

Here is an excerpt from Honeywell Corporation's 1994 annual report to shareholders. Honeywell's chairman and chief executive officer, Michael R. Bonsignore, writes in his letter to the shareholders:

Profitable growth. Delighted customers. Worldwide leadership in control. This is the vision for Honeywell that I and Honeywell people around the world have set for ourselves. It embodies what we want to be. It underpins how we set our goals. And it defines how we will fulfill the purpose of the company—which is to create value for our shareholders. . . .

The company is now poised to achieve our primary financial objective: first-quartile total shareholder returns among our peers. We define total shareholder returns as share price appreciation plus dividends reinvested in the stock.

Our management team is steadfast in achieving this objective. It is a key goal in our long-range incentive system. Our short-term executive compensation program rewards economic value added. We have constructed an integrated financial plan that sets aggressive targets in each driver of shareholder value: sales growth, operating margins, working capital, capital expenditures, and taxes.

> **Quick Check 1-6**
> How does the existence of a well-functioning stock market facilitate the separation of ownership and management of firms?

1.8 MARKET DISCIPLINE: TAKEOVERS

What forces are there to compel managers to act in the best interests of the shareholders? The shareholders could fire the managers by voting them out. But because a major benefit of the separated structure is that the owners can remain relatively uninformed about the operations of the firm, it is not apparent how these owners could know whether their firm is being mismanaged.

The value of voting rights as a means of enforcement is further cast into doubt if ownership of the firm is widely dispersed. If that is the situation, then the holdings of any single owner are likely to be so small that he or she would not incur the expense to become informed and to convey this information to other owners.[5] Thus, voting rights alone can do little to solve this dilemma.

The existence of a competitive stock market offers another important mechanism for aligning the incentives of managers with those of shareholders. It is called the *takeover*.

To see how the threat of a takeover can compel managers to act in the best interests of shareholders, suppose some entity, call it the takeover bidder, has identified a significantly mismanaged firm (i.e., one whose management has chosen an investment plan that leads to a market value that is significantly less than the maximum value that could be achieved from the firm's resources). If the bidder successfully buys enough shares of the undervalued firm to gain control, it replaces the managers with ones who will operate it optimally.

Having announced the change in the firm's investment plans, the bidder now sells the shares of the firm at the new market price for an immediate profit. Note that the bidder did not have to add any tangible resources to the firm to achieve this profit. Hence, the only expenses incurred are the cost of identifying a mismanaged firm and the cost of acquiring the firm's shares.

Although the cost of identifying a mismanaged firm will vary, it can be quite low if the takeover bidder happens to be a supplier, customer, or competitor of the firm because much of the information required may have been gathered for other purposes already. For this reason, the takeover mechanism can work even if resources are not spent for the explicit reason of identifying mismanaged firms.

However, if significant mismanagement of firms were widespread, then it would pay to spend resources in search of such firms in much the same way that resources are spent on research of new physical investment projects. There are indeed firms that specialize in making hostile (to the management) takeovers. Therefore, the threat of a takeover is credible and the subsequent replacement of management

---

[5]This is called the "paradox" of voting. The paradox is that when there are many voters, none of whose individual vote would appreciably affect the final outcome, it does not pay any individual voter to incur the costs of becoming informed and exercising the right to vote.

provides a strong incentive for current managers (acting in their self-interest) to act in the interests of the firm's current shareholders by maximizing market value.

Indeed, even in the absence of any explicit instructions from the shareholders or knowledge of the theory for good management, one might expect managers to move in the direction of value maximization as a matter of self-preservation. Moreover, it should be noted that it does not matter whether the source of the mismanagement is incompetence or the pursuit of different objectives, the takeover mechanism serves equally well to correct either one.

The effectiveness of the takeover mechanism can be reduced by government policies. For example, in an attempt to prevent the formation of monopolies in various product markets, the U.S. Department of Justice will take legal action under the antitrust laws to prevent mergers or acquisitions that might reduce competition. Because it is more likely that a supplier, customer, or competitor will be the takeover bidder who identifies the mismanaged firm, this public policy will tend to reduce the threat of takeover.

> **Quick Check 1-7**
> How does the threat of a takeover serve as a mechanism to deal with the conflict of interest between owners and managers of a corporation?

1.9 THE ROLE OF THE FINANCE SPECIALIST IN A CORPORATION

Virtually all decisions made in a corporation are at least partially financial because they involve making trade-offs between costs and benefits that are spread over time. Therefore, in large corporations virtually all managers from the chief executive at the top down to managers of individual production units, marketing units, research labs, or other departments make use of the services of finance specialists.

The Financial Executives Institute, a voluntary organization of corporate executives who specialize in finance, offers a broad definition of a financial executive as anyone who has authority for one of the functions listed in Table 1.1.

TABLE 1.1   Financial Functions in a Corporation

1. PLANNING
   Establishment, coordination, and administration, as an integral part of management, of an adequate plan for the control of operations. Such a plan, to the extent required in the business, would provide the following:
   a. Long- and short-range financial and corporate planning
   b. Budgeting for capital expenditures and/or operations
   c. Sales forecasting
   d. Performance evaluation
   e. Pricing policies
   f. Economic appraisal
   g. Analysis of acquisitions and divestments

2. PROVISION OF CAPITAL
   Establishment and execution of programs for the provision of the capital required by the business.

3. ADMINISTRATION OF FUNDS
   a. Management of cash
   b. Maintenance of banking arrangements
   c. Receipt, custody, and disbursement of the company's monies and securities
   d. Credit and collection management
   e. Management of pension funds
   f. Management of investments
   g. Custodial responsibilities

(continued)

TABLE 1.1   Financial Functions in a Corporation *(continued)*

4. ACCOUNTING AND CONTROL
   a. Establishment of accounting policies
   b. Development and reporting of accounting data
   c. Cost standards
   d. Internal auditing
   e. Systems and procedures (accounting)
   f. Government reporting
   g. Report and interpretation of results of operations to management
   h. Comparison of performance with operating plans and standards

5. PROTECTION OF ASSETS
   a. Provision of insurance coverage as required
   b. Assure protection of business assets and loss prevention through internal control and internal auditing
   c. Real estate management

6. TAX ADMINISTRATION
   a. Establishment and administration of tax policies and procedures
   b. Relations with taxing agencies
   c. Preparation of tax reports
   d. Tax planning

7. INVESTOR RELATIONS
   a. Establishment and maintenance of liaison with the investment community
   b. Establishment and maintenance of communications with company stockholders
   c. Counseling with analysts—public financial information

8. EVALUATION AND CONSULTING
   Consultation with and advice to other corporate executives on company policy, operations, objectives, and the effectiveness thereof

9. MANAGEMENT INFORMATION SYSTEMS
   a. Development and use of electronic data processing facilities
   b. Development and use of management information systems
   c. Development and use of systems and procedures

Source: Financial Executives Institute.

The organization of the finance function and its relation to other departments vary from company to company, but Figure 1.1 shows a typical organization chart in a large corporation.

At the top is the firm's chief executive officer (CEO) who often is also the president. The chief financial officer (CFO) is a senior vice president with responsibility for all the financial functions in the firm and reports directly to the CEO. The firm also has senior vice presidents in charge of marketing and operations. In large

FIGURE 1.1   Organization Chart for ZYX Corporation

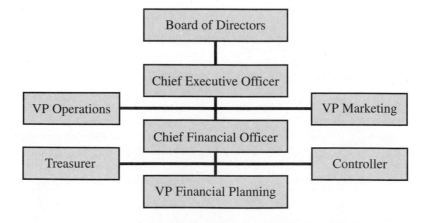

firms, there is sometimes a chief operating officer (COO), who takes responsibility for implementing the CEO's strategy for the firm.

The CFO has three departments reporting to him or her: financial planning, treasury, and control, each headed by a vice president. The vice president for financial planning has responsibility for analyzing major capital expenditures such as proposals to enter new lines of business or to exit existing businesses. This includes analyzing proposed mergers, acquisitions, and spin-offs.

The treasurer has responsibility for managing the financing activities of the firm and for working capital management. The treasurer's job includes managing relations with the external investor community, managing the firm's exposure to currency and interest rate risks, and managing the tax department.

The controller oversees the accounting and auditing activities of the firm. This includes preparation of internal reports comparing planned and actual costs, revenues, and profits from the corporation's various business units. It also includes preparation of financial statements for use by shareholders, creditors, and regulatory authorities.

Summary

Finance is the study of how to allocate scarce resources over time. The two features that distinguish finance are that the costs and benefits of financial decisions are spread out over time and are usually not known with certainty in advance by either the decision maker or anybody else.

A basic tenet of finance is that the ultimate function of the system is to satisfy people's *consumption preferences*. Economic organizations such as firms and governments exist in order to facilitate the achievement of that ultimate function. Many financial decisions can be made strictly on the basis of improving the trade-offs available to people without knowledge of their consumption preferences.

There are at least five good reasons to study finance:

- To manage your personal resources.
- To deal with the world of business.
- To pursue interesting and rewarding career opportunities.
- To make informed public choices as a citizen.
- To expand your mind.

The players in finance theory are households, business firms, financial intermediaries, and governments. Households occupy a special place in the theory because the ultimate function of the system is to satisfy the preferences of people, and the theory treats those preferences as given. Finance theory explains household behavior as an attempt to satisfy those preferences. The behavior of firms is viewed from the perspective of how it affects the welfare of households.

Households face four basic types of financial decisions:

- *Saving decisions:* How much of their current income should they save for the future?
- *Investment decisions:* How should they invest the money they have saved?
- *Financing decisions:* When and how should they use other people's money to satisfy their wants and needs?
- *Risk-management decisions:* How and on what terms should they seek to reduce the economic uncertainties they face or to take calculated risks?

There are three main areas of financial decision making in a business: capital budgeting, capital structure, and working capital management.

There are five reasons for separating the management from the ownership of a business enterprise:

- Professional managers may be found who have a superior ability to run the business.

- To achieve the efficient scale of a business the resources of many households may have to be pooled.

- In an uncertain economic environment, owners will want to diversify their risks across many firms. Such efficient diversification is difficult to achieve without separation of ownership and management.

- To achieve savings in the costs of gathering information.

- The "learning curve" or "going concern" effect: When the owner is also the manager, the new owner has to learn the business from the former owner in order to manage it efficiently. If the owner is not the manager, then when the business is sold, the manager continues in place and works for the new owner.

The corporate form is especially well suited to the separation of ownership and management of firms because it allows relatively frequent changes in owners by share transfer without affecting the operations of the firm.

The primary goal of corporate management is to maximize shareholder wealth. It leads managers to make the same investment decisions that each of the individual owners would have made had they made the decisions themselves.

A competitive stock market imposes a strong discipline on managers to take actions to maximize the market value of the firm's shares.

Key Terms

- finance   2
- financial system   2
- assets   5
- asset allocation   5
- liability   5

- net worth 5
- sole proprietorship   7
- partnership   7
- corporation   8

Answers to Quick Check Questions

Quick Check 1-1   *What are the four basic types of financial decisions households have to make? Give an example of each.*

ANSWER:

- Consumption/saving decisions, such as how much to save for a child's education or for retirement.
- Investment decisions, such as how much to invest in stocks or bonds.
- Financing decisions, such as what type of loan to take to finance the purchase of a home or a car.
- Risk-management decisions, such as whether to buy disability insurance.

Quick Check 1-2 *What are the basic types of financial decisions firms have to make? Give an example of each.*

ANSWER:

- Capital budgeting decisions, such as whether to build a plant to produce a new product.
- Financing decisions, such as how much debt and how much equity it should have in its capital structure.
- Working capital decisions, such as whether it should extend credit to customers or demand cash on delivery.

Quick Check 1-3 *A corporation owned by a single person is not a sole proprietorship. Why?*

ANSWER: In a corporation the liability of the single shareholder would be limited to the assets of the corporation.

Quick Check 1-4 *What are the main reasons for having a separation of management and ownership of firms? How does the corporate form of organization facilitate this separation?*

ANSWER: Five reasons:

- Professional managers may be found who have a superior ability to run the business.
- To achieve the efficient scale of a business the resources of many households may have to be pooled.
- In an uncertain economic environment, owners will want to diversify their risks across many firms. Such efficient diversification is difficult to achieve without separation of ownership and management.
- To achieve savings in the costs of gathering information.
- The "learning curve" or "going concern" effect: When the owner is also the manager, the new owner has to learn the business from the former owner in order to manage it efficiently. If the owner is not the manager, then when the business is sold, the manager continues in place and works for the new owner.

The corporate form is especially well suited to the separation of ownership and management of firms because it allows relatively frequent changes in owners by share transfer without affecting the operations of the firm.

Quick Check 1-5 *Why is the shareholder-wealth-maximization rule a better one for corporate managers to follow than the profit-maximization rule?*

ANSWER: There are two fundamental ambiguities with the profit-maximization criterion:

- If the production process requires many periods, then which period's profit is to be maximized?
- If either future revenues or expenses are uncertain, then what is the meaning of "maximize profits" when profits are described by a probability distribution?

Quick Check 1-6 *How does the existence of a well-functioning stock market facilitate the separation of ownership and management of firms?*

ANSWER: In the absence of a stock market, managers would require information that is costly if not impossible to obtain: namely, the wealth, preferences, and other investment opportunities of the owners.

Quick Check 1-7   *How does the threat of a takeover serve as a mechanism to deal with the conflict of interest between owners and managers of a corporation?*

ANSWER: Managers know that if they fail to maximize the market value of the firm's shares, the firm will be vulnerable to a takeover in which managers might lose their jobs.

Questions and Problems

1. What are your main goals in life? How does finance play a part in achieving those goals? What are the major trade-offs you face?

2. What is your net worth? What have you included among your assets and your liabilities? What have you excluded that you might have included?

3. How are the financial decisions faced by a single person living alone different from those faced by the head of a household with responsibility for several children of school age? Are the trade-offs they have to make different, or will they evaluate the trade-offs differently?

4. Family A and family B both consist of a father, mother, and two children of school age. In family A both spouses have jobs outside the home and earn a combined income of $100,000 per year. In family B, only one spouse works outside the home and earns $100,000 per year. How do the financial circumstances and decisions faced by the two families differ?

5. At what age should children be expected to become financially independent?

6. You are thinking of buying a car. Analyze the decision by addressing the following issues:
   a. Are there other ways to satisfy your transportation requirements besides buying a car? Make a list of all the alternatives and write down the pros and cons for each.
   b. What are the different ways you can finance the purchase of a car?
   c. Obtain information from at least three different providers of automobile financing on the terms they offer.
   d. What criteria should you use in making your decision?

7. You are thinking of starting your own business but have no money.
   a. Think of a business that you could start without having to borrow any money.
   b. Now think of a business that you would want to start if you could borrow any amount of money at the going interest rate.
   c. What are the risks you would face in this business?
   d. Where can you get financing for your new business?

8. Choose an organization that is not a firm, such as a club or church group, and list the most important financial decisions it has to make. What are the key trade-offs the organization faces? What role do preferences play in choosing among alternatives? Interview the financial manager of the organization and check to see if he or she agrees with you.

C H A P T E R

The Financial System

2

OBJECTIVES

- To provide a conceptual framework for understanding how the financial system works and how it changes over time.
- To understand the meaning and determinants of rates of return on different classes of assets.

CONTENTS

Chapter 1 set down the main purpose of this book, which is to help you make better financial decisions. Such decisions are always made within the context of a financial system that both constrains and enables the decision maker. Effective financial decisions thus require an understanding of that system.

Suppose, for example, that you want to further your education, buy a house, or start a new business. Where can you get the funds to do it? The answers to these questions depend very much on where you are located. The roles played by families, governments, and private sector institutions (such as banks and securities markets) in financing economic activities vary considerably among countries. What's more, these roles change over time.

21

This chapter provides a conceptual framework for understanding how the financial system works and how it changes over time. It starts with an overview of the central role played by financial markets and intermediaries in facilitating the flow of funds, the transfer of risk, and several other basic financial functions. The chapter provides a broad overview of the current structure of financial markets and institutions around the world, and it shows that the way the basic financial functions are performed changes over time and differs across borders. Finally, the chapter provides a brief overview of how interest rates and rates of return on risky assets are determined and reviews the history of these rates.

2.1   WHAT IS THE FINANCIAL SYSTEM?

The financial system encompasses the markets, intermediaries, service firms, and other institutions used to carry out the financial decisions of households, business firms, and governments. Sometimes a market for a particular financial instrument has a specific geographic location such as the New York Stock Exchange or the Osaka Options and Futures Exchange, which are institutions housed in buildings in New York City and in Osaka, Japan, respectively. Often, however, the market has no one specific location. Such is the case for the **over-the-counter markets**—or off-exchange markets—in stocks, bonds, and currencies, which are essentially global computer and telecommunications networks linking securities dealers and their customers.

Financial intermediaries are defined as firms whose primary business is to provide financial services and products. They include banks, investment companies, and insurance companies. Their products include checking accounts, commercial loans, mortgages, mutual funds, and a wide range of insurance contracts.

Today's financial system is global in scope. Financial markets and intermediaries are linked through a vast international telecommunications network, so that the transfer of payments and the trading of securities can go on virtually around the clock. If a large corporation based in Germany wants to finance a major new investment, for instance, it will consider a range of international possibilities, including issuing stock and selling it on the New York or London stock exchanges or borrowing from a Japanese pension fund. If it chooses to borrow from the Japanese pension fund, the loan might be denominated in German marks, in Japanese yen, or even in U.S. dollars.

2.2   THE FLOW OF FUNDS

The interactions among the various players in the financial system are shown in Figure 2.1, a flow-of-funds diagram. Funds flow through the financial system from entities that have a surplus of funds (the box on the left) to those that have a deficit (the box on the right).

For example, a household that is saving a portion of its current income for retirement has a surplus of funds whereas another household seeking to buy a house has a deficit. A firm with profits in excess of its need for new investment spending is a surplus unit, whereas another firm that needs to finance a major expansion is a deficit unit.[1]

---

[1] Funds that flow among members of a family or among different units of the same firm are not usually considered part of the flows in the financial system.

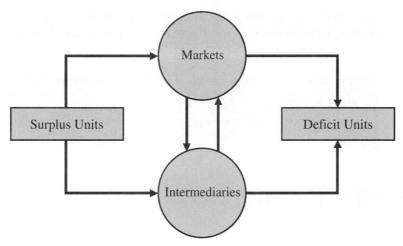

FIGURE 2.1 The Flow of Funds

Figure 2.1 shows that some funds flow from the surplus units to the deficit units through financial intermediaries such as banks (the lower route in Figure 2.1), whereas some funds flow through the financial markets without going through a financial intermediary (the upper route).

To illustrate the **flow of funds** along the upper route, a household (surplus unit) buys shares of stock from a firm (deficit unit) that issues them. In some cases—firms that have dividend reinvestment plans, for example—the household buys the shares directly from the firm issuing them without using a broker. In most cases, however, a broker or a dealer would likely be involved in this flow of funds, collecting the money from the household and transferring it to the issuing firm.

A large part of the funds flowing through the financial system, however, never flow through markets and, therefore, do not follow the upper route in Figure 2.1. Instead, as shown in the lower half of Figure 2.1, they go from the surplus units to the deficit units through financial intermediaries.

To illustrate the flow of funds through intermediaries, suppose you deposit your savings in an account at a bank, and the bank uses the funds to make a loan to a business firm. In this case, you do not own a direct claim on the borrowing firm; instead you have a deposit at the bank. The bank in turn has a claim on the borrowing firm. Your bank deposit has different risk and liquidity characteristics from the loan to the business firm, which is now an asset of the bank. Your deposit is safe and liquid (i.e., you can withdraw the full amount at any time), whereas the loan held as an asset by the bank has some default risk and may be illiquid. Thus, when funds flow from surplus units to deficit units through a bank, the risk and liquidity of the financial instruments created along the way can be substantially altered. Of course, someone has to absorb the risk of the loans—either the bank's owners or the government entity that insures the bank's deposits.

The arrow pointing from the circle labeled *intermediaries* up to the circle labeled *markets* indicates that intermediaries often channel funds into the financial markets. For example, a middle-aged couple saving for retirement (surplus unit) may invest its savings in an insurance company account (intermediary), which then invests its funds in stocks and bonds (markets). Through the insurance company, the couple indirectly provides funds to the firms (deficit units) issuing the stocks and bonds.

The arrow pointing from the *markets* circle down to the *intermediaries* circle indicates that in addition to channeling funds *into* the financial markets, some intermediaries obtain funds *from* the financial markets. A finance company that makes loans to households might, for instance, raise those funds by issuing stocks and bonds in the markets for those securities.

> **Quick Check 2-1**
> A depositor puts $5,000 into a bank account and you take a $5,000 student loan from the bank. Trace this flow of funds in Figure 2.1.

2.3 THE FUNCTIONAL PERSPECTIVE

For a variety of reasons—including differences in size, complexity, and available technology, as well as differences in political, cultural, and historical backgrounds—financial institutions generally differ across borders. They also change over time. Even when the names of institutions are the same, the functions they perform often differ dramatically. For example, banks in the United States today are very different from what they were in 1928 or in 1958, and banks in the United States today are very different from the institutions called banks in Germany or the United Kingdom today.

In this section we try our hand at setting forth a unifying conceptual framework for understanding how and why financial institutions differ across borders and change over time. The key element in the framework is its focus on *functions* rather than on *institutions* as the conceptual "anchor." Hence, we call it the *functional perspective*. It rests on two basic premises:

- Financial functions are more stable than financial institutions—that is, functions change less over time and vary less across borders.

- Institutional form follows function—that is, innovation and competition among institutions ultimately result in greater efficiency in the performance of financial system functions.

From the most aggregated level of the single primary function of efficient resource allocation, we distinguish six basic or core functions performed by the financial system:

- To provide ways to *transfer economic resources* through time, across borders, and among industries.

- To provide ways of *managing risk*.

- To provide ways of *clearing and settling payments* to facilitate trade.

- To provide a mechanism for the *pooling of resources* and for the *subdividing* of ownership in various enterprises.

- To provide *price information* to help coordinate decentralized decision making in various sectors of the economy.

- To provide ways of *dealing with the incentive problems* created when one party to a transaction has information that the other party does not or when one party acts as agent for another.

The rest of this chapter explains these functions of the financial system and illustrates how the performance of each has changed over time.

2.3.1 Function 1: Transferring Resources across Time and Space

A financial system provides ways to transfer economic resources through time, across geographic regions, and among industries.

Many of the funds flows shown in Figure 2.1 involve giving up something now in order to get something in the future, or vice versa. Student loans, borrowing to buy a house, saving for retirement, and investing in production facilities are all actions that shift resources from one point in time to another. The financial system facilitates such *intertemporal* (literally, "between time") transfers of resources.

Without the opportunity to take out a student loan, for example, many young people whose families do not have the means to send them to college might have to forgo a higher education. Similarly, without the ability to raise venture capital from investors, many businesses might never get started.

In addition to facilitating the shifting of resources through time, the financial system plays an important role in shifting resources from one place to another. At times the capital resources available to perform an activity are located far from where they are most efficiently employed. Households in Germany, for example, may be generating capital through saving that could be more efficiently employed in Russia. The financial system provides a variety of mechanisms for facilitating the transfer of capital resources from Germany to Russia. One way is for German citizens to invest in shares issued by firms located in Russia. Another is for German banks to make loans to those firms.

The more complex the economy, the more important is the role of the financial system in providing an efficient means for shifting resources across time and place. Thus, in today's global financial system, a complex network of markets and intermediaries makes it possible for the retirement savings of Japanese workers to be used to finance the house purchased by a young couple in the United States.

Innovation that allows scarce resources to be shifted over time or place from a use with a relatively low benefit to a use offering a higher benefit improves efficiency. For example, suppose that all families were constrained to invest their savings only within the family. In that case, Family A could earn a rate of return of 2% per year on its savings, at the same time that Family B has opportunities to earn a rate of return of 20%. Efficiency is increased by creating an investment company to collect Family A's savings and lend them to Family B.

> **Quick Check 2-2**
> Give an example of a transfer of resources over time that takes place through the financial system. Is there a more efficient way for this transfer of resources to be handled?

2.3.2 Function 2: Managing Risk

A financial system provides ways to manage risk.

Just as funds are transferred through the financial system, so are risks. For example, insurance companies are financial intermediaries that specialize in the activity of risk transfer. They collect premiums from customers who want to reduce their risks and transfer it to investors who are willing to pay the claims and bear the risk in return for some reward.

Often funds and risks are "bundled" together and transferred simultaneously through the financial system so that the flow of *funds* illustrated in Figure 2.1 can also characterize the flow of *risks*. Let us illustrate with the example of business finance and the transfer of business risk.

Suppose you want to start a business and need $100,000 to do so. You have no savings of your own, so you are a deficit unit. Let us assume that you convince a private investor (a surplus unit) to provide you with $70,000 in equity capital in return for a 75% share of the profits of the business, and you convince a bank (a financial intermediary) to lend you the other $30,000 at an interest rate of 6% per year. In Figure 2.1 this flow of $100,000 would appear as a flow of funds from others to you.

But what about the risk of business failure?

In general, it is the equity investors who absorb the risk of business failure. Thus, if your business venture goes sour, the private investor may get none of his or her $70,000 back. However, the bank may also face some risk that it will not get all of its principal and interest. For example, suppose that at the end of a year, the business has a value of only $20,000. Then the equity investors lose all of their investment of $70,000, and the bank loses $10,000 of the $30,000 it has lent to you. *Thus, lenders share some of the business risk of the firm along with the equity investors.*

Although funds and risks often come bundled together, they can be "unbundled." For example, consider the $30,000 loan from the bank to your business. Suppose the bank requires that you get other members of your family to guarantee the loan. The bank thereby transfers the risk of default from itself to your relatives. The bank is now providing you with $30,000 in funds at minimal risk to itself, and the risk of the loan has been transferred to your relatives.

As we will see, many of the financial contracts that we observe in the world of finance serve to transfer risks without transferring funds. This is the case with most insurance contracts and guarantees, and it is also the case with derivatives, such as futures, swaps, and options.

Quick Check 2-3
Give an example of a transfer of risk that takes place through the financial system.

2.3.3 Function 3: Clearing and Settling Payments

A financial system provides ways of clearing and settling payments to facilitate the exchange of goods, services, and assets.

An important function of the financial system is to provide an efficient way for people and businesses to make payments to each other when they wish to buy goods or services. Suppose you live in the United States and are planning a trip around the world. You believe that $5,000 should be enough money to cover your expenses while traveling. In what form should you take the funds? How will you pay for things?

Some hotels, youth hostels, and restaurants will accept U.S. dollars as payment, but others will not. You might be able to pay for everything with a credit card, but some places you're interested in visiting might not accept a credit card. Should you buy traveler's checks? In what currencies should they be denominated? Contemplation of your trip perhaps leads you to think how convenient it would be if every seller in every country were willing to accept the same means of payment.

Imagine instead that you are a wealthy person living in a country whose government limits your access to foreign currency and that you want to travel around the world. Inside your country you can buy whatever you want using the local currency, but outside your country, no one will accept that currency as a means of payment. A shortage of foreign exchange causes your government to prohibit its citizens from purchasing foreign currency or borrowing abroad. What can you do?

One possibility is to buy transportable goods (such as furs or jewelry) in your home country, pack them all in a suitcase, and try to use them to pay for your food and lodging abroad. In other words, you could engage in *barter,* the process of exchanging goods without using money. Needless to say, this would not be a convenient way to see the world. You would need to bring vast amounts of luggage, and instead of enjoying the sights much of your time and energy would be spent in finding a hotel or restaurant that accepts furs or jewelry in exchange for a room or a meal.

As these examples suggest, an important function of the financial system is to provide an efficient payments system, so that households and businesses do not have to waste time and resources in implementing their purchases. The replacement of gold with paper currency as a means of payment is an example of a change that increases efficiency of the payments system. Gold is a scarce resource that is used in medicine and in the production of jewelry. Paper money serves as a superior means of payment. Compared with gold, paper currency is easier to verify (harder to counterfeit) and more convenient to carry around in one's pocket. It doesn't cost as much to make and print currency as it does to mine, refine, and mint gold. The subsequent development of checks, credit cards, and electronic-funds-transfer as alternative means of payment to paper currency has further increased efficiency.

Quick Check 2-4

Would you accept an IOU from me in payment for a good or service that I buy from you? What factors will determine the answer?

2.3.4 Function 4: Pooling Resources and Subdividing Shares

A financial system provides a mechanism for the pooling of funds to undertake large-scale indivisible enterprise or for the subdividing of shares in large enterprises with many owners.

In modern economies, the minimum investment required to run a business is often beyond the means of an individual or even a large family. The financial system provides a variety of mechanisms (such as the stock market or banks) to *pool* or *aggregate* the wealth of households into larger masses of capital for use by business firms.

From the investor's perspective, the financial system provides opportunities for individual households to participate in investments that require large lump sums of money by pooling their funds and then subdividing shares in the investment. For example, suppose you want to invest in a racehorse that costs $100,000, but you only have $10,000 to invest. If there were a way of physically dividing the racehorse into ten pieces, then you could buy one piece. However, in this case the whole is surely worth more than the sum of its parts. A physical splitting of the horse will not do the trick. The financial system solves the problem of how to divide the horse without destroying it. By creating an investment pool and distributing shares to the investors, the $100,000 investment can be divided into $10,000 economic "pieces" without actually cutting up the horse. Any money the horse earns in race winnings or stud fees would, after training and upkeep expenses are taken out, be divided among all the shareholders.

As another example, consider money market funds. Suppose you want to invest in the most secure and liquid dollar-denominated asset, U.S. Treasury bills (T-bills). The minimum denomination is $10,000, and you have only $1,000 to invest. Therefore, the only way you can invest in T-bills is by pooling resources with other investors. In the 1970s, mutual funds that hold U.S. T-bills were developed to facilitate this process.

In a mutual fund, investors' money is pooled, and they are given accounts representing their proportional shares in the fund. The mutual fund frequently posts the price of a share and allows its customers to add or withdraw money at almost any time in almost any amount. Thus, if the price of a share is now $11 and you invest $1,000, the fund will credit your account with 1,000/11, or 90.91 shares. U.S. T-bill mutual funds, thus, improve the performance of Function 4 by transforming large-denomination Treasury bills into almost infinitely divisible securities.

Quick Check 2-5
Give an example of an investment that would not be undertaken if it were not possible to pool the savings of many different households.

2.3.5 Function 5: Providing Information

A financial system provides price information that helps coordinate decentralized decision making in various sectors of the economy.

Every day, newspapers, radio, and television announce stock prices and interest rates. Of the millions of people who receive these news reports, relatively few actually buy and sell securities. Many of those who do not trade securities nevertheless use the information generated from security prices to make other types of decisions. In deciding how much of their current income to save and how to invest it, households make use of information about interest rates and security prices.

An example may help to illustrate how even within families the intertemporal transfer of resources is often facilitated by knowledge of market interest rates. Suppose that you are 30 years old, just got married, and want to buy a house for $100,000. Your local bank will make you a mortgage loan for $80,000 or 80% of the purchase price of the house at an interest rate of 8% per year, but you need to pay 20% down (i.e., $20,000). Your 45-year-old sister has an account at a savings bank with $20,000 in it—just enough for your down payment. She is saving the money for her retirement, which is far in the future, and is currently earning 6% per year. If your sister is willing to lend you her retirement savings for your down payment, how do you decide what a "fair" rate of interest is? Clearly, it is useful to know current market interest rates. You already know that your sister is earning 6% per year on her savings account and that your local bank will charge you 8% per year on the mortgage loan (see Box 2.1).

BOX 2.1

Family Loans

You have a bunch of money in certificates of deposit coming due soon and you can get only about 3% if you roll them over. Your kids are buying a house and need a mortgage. With a little creative thinking and a good lawyer, these two circumstances can be turned into a family loan, and both parties to the loan can benefit from the deal.

Here's how: By lending directly to your children, you eliminate the intermediary. That means the kids can get a mortgage without paying points and application fees. The loan will take less time to process, and the interest rate can be below the 6.75% now commonly available from banks on 30-year, fixed-rate mortgages.

At the same time, you can boost your own return considerably. Rather than the 3% you're earning on CDs, or even the 6% available on a 30-year

Treasury bond, you can get 6.5% and still be offering your kids a bargain.

But this kind of family finance isn't for everyone. Some kids aren't a good credit risk, no matter how much you love them. And there are some parents who after lending the money will find it difficult to collect. That's why some financial advisors recommend putting an independent third party between the family borrowers and lenders. Try to treat it as an arm's-length business deal as much as you can, and don't cut corners just because they are family.

Source: Adapted from Lynn Asinof, "Making Family Loans Can Be a Rewarding Experience," *The Wall Street Journal,* October 10, 1993. Reprinted by permission of *The Wall Street Journal,* © 1993 Dow Jones & Company, Inc. All Rights Reserved Worldwide.

Similarly, knowledge of market prices of assets can be helpful for decision making within families. For example, suppose you and your sister inherit a house or a family business, and it is to be divided equally between you. You don't want to sell it because one of you wants to live in it or continue to operate it. How much should the other sibling receive? Clearly, it would be useful to know the market prices of similar assets to settle on a reasonable price for the inheritance.

Asset prices and interest rates provide critical signals to managers of firms in their selection of investment projects and financing arrangements. Managers of firms with no anticipated need to transact in the financial markets routinely use those markets to provide information for decisions.

For example, a firm earns $10 million in profits in a good year and is faced with deciding whether to reinvest it in the business, pay it out in cash dividends to shareholders, or use it to buy back its own shares. Knowledge of its own and other firm's share prices as well as market interest rates will surely help in deciding what to do.

Whenever a new financial instrument is introduced, new possibilities for information extraction are created as a by-product. For example, the development of trading standardized option contracts on exchanges since 1973 has greatly increased the amount of quantitative information available about the riskiness of economic and financial variables. This information is particularly useful in making risk-management decisions.

Quick Check 2-6
Give an example of a financial transaction that provides important information to parties not involved in the transaction.

2.3.6 Function 6: Dealing with Incentive Problems

A financial system provides ways to deal with the incentive problems when one party to a financial transaction has information that the other party does not, or when one party is an agent that makes decisions for another.

As we discussed, financial markets and intermediaries serve several functions that facilitate the efficient allocation of resources and risks. There are, however, incentive problems that limit their ability to perform some of those functions. Incentive problems arise because parties to contracts often cannot easily monitor or control one another. Incentive problems take a variety of forms—among them, moral hazard, adverse selection, and principal-agent problems.

The **moral hazard** problem exists when having insurance against some risk causes the insured party to take greater risk or to take less care in preventing the event that gives rise to the loss. Moral hazard can lead to unwillingness on the part of insurance companies to insure against certain types of risk. For example, if a warehouse owner buys fire insurance, the existence of the insurance reduces his incentive to spend money to prevent a fire. Failure to take the same precautions makes a warehouse fire a more likely occurrence. In an extreme case, the owner may be tempted to actually start a fire in order to collect the insurance money if the coverage exceeds the market value of the warehouse. Because of this potential moral hazard, insurance companies may limit the amount they will insure or simply refuse to sell fire insurance under certain circumstances.

An example of moral hazard in the realm of contracting is what might happen if I pay you in advance for a job, and you get the same amount of money no matter how good or bad a job you do. There is less of an incentive for you to work hard than would be the case if I pay you after the job is done.

A more subtle example of the moral hazard problem arises in financing business ventures. Suppose you have an idea for a new business venture, and you need startup capital. Where can you get it? The first source you may look to is family and friends. Why? Because you trust them, and they know and trust you. You know your secret plans are safe with them. On the other side, your family believes that you will fully disclose the information you have about the business opportunity, including all of the pitfalls. Moreover, if the business does not immediately prosper and the going gets rough, they know that you will work hard to protect their interests.

What about a bank as a source for the loan? You are perhaps a little uncomfortable about discussing the details of your business plans with the bank loan officer, who is a complete stranger. She might disclose your plans to another customer, who could be a competitor. But even if you can resolve your concerns about the bank, there is the other side. The loan officer is reluctant to lend you the money you want because she knows that you have no incentive to disclose the pitfalls in your plans unless you have to. Thus, there is an imbalance or *asymmetry* in the exchange of information about the business opportunity: You know more about it than the loan officer.

Moreover, the loan officer knows that she is a stranger to you and that the bank is just an impersonal institution to you. Therefore, if the going gets rough, you will not necessarily work as hard to turn it around as you would for your family and friends. Instead, you may decide to walk away from the business and not repay your loan. The reduced incentive for you to work hard when part of the risk of the enterprise has been transferred to an entity whose welfare you do not care much about (such as a bank or an insurance company) is, thus, an example of the problem of moral hazard.

Quick Check 2-7

Give an example of how the problem of moral hazard might prevent you from getting financing for something you want to do. Can you think of a way of overcoming the problem?

Another class of problems caused by asymmetric information is **adverse selection**—those who purchase insurance against risk are more likely than the general population to be at risk. For example, consider **life annuities,** which are contracts that pay a fixed amount of money each month for as long as the purchaser lives. A firm selling such annuities cannot assume that the people who buy them will have the same expected length of life as the general population.

For example, suppose a firm sells life annuities to people retiring at age 65. There are equal numbers of three types of people in the general population: type A live for 10 years, type B for 15 years, and type C for 20 years. On average, people aged 65 live for 15 years. If the firm charges a price that reflects a 15-year life expectancy, however, it will find that the people who buy the annuities are disproportionately of types B and C. Type A people will find that your annuities are not a good deal for them and will not purchase them.

If the annuity firm knew the type of each potential customer, A, B, or C, and could charge a price that reflected the true life expectancy for that type, then there would be no adverse selection problem. But the annuity firm cannot get enough information about customers to know as much about their individual life expectancies as they themselves do. Unless the insurer can charge a price that accurately reflects each person's true life expectancy, a disproportionately large number of the annuities sold will be bought by healthy people who expect to live a long time. In our example, the average life expectancy of buyers of annuities might be 17.5 years, which is 2.5 years longer than in the general population.

Therefore, if annuity firms used life expectancies of the general population to price their annuities without adding an amount to adjust for the adverse selection problem, they would all lose money. As a result, firms in this market charge a price for annuities that is relatively unattractive to people with an average life expectancy, and the market is much smaller than it would be if there were no problem of adverse selection.

Quick Check 2-8

Suppose a bank offered to make loans to potential borrowers without checking their credit history. What would be true of the types of borrowers they would attract compared to banks that did checks of credit history? Would such a bank charge the same interest rate on loans as banks that check credit history?

Another type of incentive problem arises when critical tasks are delegated to others. For example, shareholders in a corporation delegate the running of the firm to its managers, and investors in a mutual fund delegate the authority to select the mix of their security holdings to a portfolio manager. In each case, the individual or organization responsible for the risks associated with a set of decisions gives up or delegates the decision-making authority to another individual or organization. Those who bear the risks associated with the decisions are called the *principals,* and those who assume the decision-making authority are called the *agents.*

The **principal-agent problem** is that agents may not make the same decisions that the principals would have made if the principals knew what the agents know and were making the decisions themselves. There can be a conflict of interest between agents and principals. In extreme cases, agents may even act contrary to the interests of their principals, as when a stockbroker "churns" a client's account only in order to generate commissions for himself.

A well-functioning financial system facilitates the resolution of the problems that arise from all of these incentive problems—moral hazard, adverse selection, and principal-agent—so that the other benefits of the financial system, such as pooling, risk sharing, and specialization, can be achieved. For example, **collateralization** of loans, which means giving the lender the right to seize specific business assets in the event of default, is a widely used device for reducing the incentive problems associated with lending. Collateralization reduces the costs to the lender of monitoring the behavior of the borrower. The lender need only be concerned that the market value of the assets serving as collateral is sufficient to repay the principal and interest due on the loan. Over time, advances in technology have lowered the costs of tracking and valuing certain types of business assets that can serve as collateral—such as goods in inventory—and thereby broadened the range of situations in which collateralized loan agreements are feasible to implement.

Principal-agent problems can be alleviated by using the financial system, too. If the compensation of management depends on the performance of the market value of the firm's shares, the interests of managers and shareholders can be more closely aligned. For example, consider the introduction of "equity-kickers" in loan contracts to help limit possible conflicts of interest between the shareholders and creditors of corporations. An equity-kicker is any provision of the loan contract that allows the lender to share in the benefits accruing to shareholders. One common equity-kicker is a percentage sharing in profits while the loan is outstanding. Another is the right of the lender to convert the loan amount into a prespecified number of shares of stock.

Management is elected by the firm's shareholders. Thus, in cases in which there is a conflict of interest between shareholders and creditors, management has an incentive to take actions that benefit shareholders at the expense of the firm's creditors. The resulting moral hazard problem could prevent an otherwise mutually advantageous loan agreement from taking place. By including an equity-kicker in the loan contract, this problem can be reduced or even eliminated, leaving both the shareholders of the firm and the firm's creditors better off.

Quick Check 2-9

If you get financial planning advice from your insurance agent, how does this give rise to a principal-agent problem? Can you think of a way of overcoming the problem?

2.4 FINANCIAL INNOVATION AND THE "INVISIBLE HAND"

Generally, financial innovations are not planned by any central authority but arise from the individual actions of entrepreneurs and firms. The fundamental economic forces behind financial innovation are essentially the same as for innovation in general. As Adam Smith observed:

> Every individual endeavors to employ his capital so that its produce may be of greatest value. He generally neither intends to promote the public interest, nor knows how much he is promoting it. He intends only his own security, only his own gain. And he is in this led by an **invisible hand** to promote an end which was no part of his intention. By pursuing his own interest he frequently promotes that of society more effectually than when he really intends to promote it.[2]

To illustrate, compare the situation faced by a college graduate traveling around the world in 1965 (when the authors graduated from college) with the one faced by a college graduate undertaking such a journey today. Back then you had the constant worry that you would run out of money in some place where no one could speak your language. If you ran out, then you had to wire home and try to arrange a wire transfer of money from a bank back home to a local bank. The process was costly and time-consuming. Prearranged lines of credit were available only to the wealthiest travelers.

But now, you can pay for almost anything you buy almost anywhere with a credit card. VISA, MasterCard, American Express, and some others are accepted virtually everywhere on the globe. To pay your hotel bill, you simply give the clerk your card, and she slips it into a machine connected to the telephone. Within seconds, she has verified that your credit is good (i.e., that the bank that issued you the card will guarantee payment), and you need only sign the receipt and be on your way to your next destination.

Moreover, you need not worry about your money being lost or stolen. If you cannot find your credit card, you can go to any bank that is connected with your card's network. The bank will help you to cancel the missing card (so no one else can use it) and to get another. The bank will often lend you money in the meantime.

Clearly, world travel has become less costly and more convenient as a result of credit cards. Their invention and dissemination has made millions of people better off and contributed to the "democratization" of finance.

But how has this happened? Let us use the example of credit cards to trace the key factors in the development of a financial innovation.

Technology is an important factor. Credit cards depend on a complex network of telephones, computers, and other more sophisticated telecommunications and information processing hardware and software. But for credit cards to become an important part of the contemporary economic scene, financial service firms looking for profit opportunities had to employ the advanced technology in offering credit card services, and households and businesses had to buy them.

It is not uncommon in the history of innovations (financial or otherwise) that the firm that pioneers a commercially successful innovative idea is not the one to profit the most from it. And so it is here with the credit card. The first firm to offer credit cards to be used by global travelers was Diners Club, which was formed just

---

[2]Adam Smith, *The Wealth of Nations* (Chicago: University of Chicago Press, 1977), p. 408.

after World War II. The initial success of Diners Club led two other firms, American Express and Carte Blanche, to offer similar credit card programs.

Firms in the credit card business earn their revenues from fees paid to them by retailers on credit card purchases (usually a percentage of the purchase price) and from interest paid on loans to credit card customers (on their unpaid balances). Major costs stem from transactions processing, stolen cards, and loan defaults by cardholders.

When commercial banks first tried to enter the credit card business in the 1950s, they found that they could not compete with the established firms because bank operating costs were too high. In the late 1960s, however, advances in computer technology lowered their costs to the point at which they could compete successfully. Today the two big bank networks, VISA and MasterCard, dominate the global credit card business. Diners Club and Carte Blanche account for only a modest share of the business (see Box 2.2).

Thus, competition among the major providers of credit cards keeps their cost comparatively low. For most people traveling today, it is not only more convenient but also less expensive to use a credit card when they travel than to use traveler's checks.

BOX 2.2

How BankAmericard Lost Its Monopoly

For eight years, from 1958 to 1966, Bank of America had the California credit card market entirely to itself. For the last five of those eight years, the card had been an ever-increasing source of profit. But it couldn't last, and it didn't.

Sometime in early 1966, Bank of America's credit card executives began hearing a rumor that four of its biggest California bank rivals were plotting to break jointly into the business; they were going to call their common program Master Charge. Even earlier than that, word had filtered back that First National City Bank of New York (now known as Citibank) was negotiating to buy Carte Blanche, one of the travel and entertainment cards. Such a move would give First National City a web of customers and merchants that would extend nationwide—something no bank in the country could then say—and would pose a different kind of threat to Bank of America. Meanwhile, other banks began hearing rumors that Bank of America was going to push its own program beyond California. After years of relative quiet, the banking industry was awhirl in rumors about credit cards—about possible thrusts and potential parries. For practically the first time since the Depression, banks were contemplating the possibility of openly competing with each other.

The rumors, in turn, helped bring about the next great wave of credit card mailings, a wave that swept the nation in the late 1960s. Fueled by panic and jealousy, bankers jumped into a business about which they knew practically nothing and for which they were utterly unprepared. Large banks and small banks, bank consortiums and single banks, banks that made consumer loans and banks that didn't—in one fell swoop, they all became issuers of credit cards, mailing out such now forgotten labels as Everything Cards, Town & Country Cards, Midwest Bank Cards, Interbank Cards, and dozens more. During a four-year span that ended in 1970, bankers blanketed the nation in credit cards. The country had never seen anything quite like it.

Most credit card veterans now view the late 1960s as a time of madness, culminating in staggering losses to the banks, public embarrassment, and federal legislation. But they also now believe that the madness was necessary. From that chaos emerged the electronic credit card system that now exists. Without it, bank credit cards might never have become what they are today: the plastic symbol of the money revolution.

Source: Adapted from Joseph Nocera, *A Piece of the Action* (New York: Simon and Schuster, 1994). Reprinted by permission of International Creative Management, Inc. Copyright © 1994 Joseph Nocera.

This last observation leads us to another basic point about financial innovation. Analysis of consumer preferences and the forces of competition among financial service providers helps one to make predictions about future changes in the financial system. For example, in light of the advantages of credit cards as a method of making payments, what prediction would you make about the future of traveler's checks? Are traveler's checks destined for the same fate as the slide rule after the invention of the handheld calculator?

Credit cards are only one of a wide array of new financial products developed over the past 30 years that have changed the way we carry on economic activities. Collectively, these innovations have greatly improved the opportunities for people to receive efficient risk-return trade-offs in their personal investments and more effective tailoring to their individual needs over the entire life cycle, including accumulation during the work years and distribution in retirement.

2.5 FINANCIAL MARKETS

The basic types of financial assets are *debt, equity,* and *derivatives.* Debt instruments are issued by anyone who borrows money—firms, governments, and households. The assets traded in debt markets, therefore, include corporate bonds, government bonds, residential and commercial mortgages, and consumer loans. Debt instruments are also called **fixed-income instruments** because they promise to pay fixed sums of cash in the future.

A different classification is by the *maturity* of the claims being traded. The market for short-term debt (less than one year) is called the **money market,** and the one for long-term debt and equity securities is called the **capital market.**

Money market instruments are mostly interest-earning securities issued by governments (such as U.S. Treasury bills) and secure private sector borrowers (such as commercial paper of large corporations). Money markets are today globally integrated and liquid in which **liquidity** is defined by the relative ease, cost, and speed with which an asset can be converted into cash.

Equity is the claim of the *owners* of a firm. Equity securities issued by corporations are called *common stocks* in the United States and *shares* in the United Kingdom. They are bought and sold in the *stock market.* Each share of common stock entitles its holder to an equal share in the ownership of the firm. In typical cases each share is entitled to the same amount of profits and is entitled to one vote on matters of corporate governance. However, some corporations issue two classes of common stock, one with voting rights and the other without.

Common stock represents a **residual claim** on the assets of a corporation. The owners of common stock are entitled to any assets of the firm left over after meeting all of the firm's other financial obligations. If, for example, the firm goes out of business and all of its assets are sold, then common stockholders receive what is left, if anything, after all of the various classes of creditors are paid what they are owed.

Common stock also has the feature of **limited liability.** This means that should the firm be liquidated and the proceeds from the sale of its assets not be sufficient to pay off all the firm's debts, the creditors cannot assess the common stockholders for more money to meet this shortfall. The claims of the creditors of the corporation are limited to the assets of the firm.

Derivatives are financial instruments that derive their value from the prices of one or more other assets such as equity securities, fixed-income securities, foreign currencies, or commodities. Their principal function is to serve as tools for managing exposures to the risks associated with the underlying assets.

Among the most common types of derivatives are *options* and *forward contracts*. A **call option** is an instrument that gives its holder the right to *buy* some asset at a specified price on or before some specified expiration date. A **put option** is an instrument that gives its holder the right to *sell* some asset at a specified price on or before some specified expiration date. When an owner of an asset buys a put option on that asset, he effectively is insuring it against a decline in its price below the price specified in the put-option contract.

Forward contracts are instruments that *oblige* one party to the contract to buy, and the other party to sell, some asset at a specified price on some specified date. They permit buyers and sellers of the asset to eliminate the uncertainty about the future price at which the asset will be exchanged.

Quick Check 2-10
What are the defining features of debt, equity, and derivative securities?

2.6 FINANCIAL MARKET RATES

Every day we are showered with newspaper, television, radio, and on-line computer reports of financial market indicators. These include interest rates, exchange rates, and indicators of stock market performance. In this section we explain the meaning of these rates.

2.6.1 Interest Rates

An interest rate is a *promised* rate of return, and there are as many different interest rates as there are distinct kinds of borrowing and lending. For example, the interest rate that home buyers pay on the loans they take to finance their homes is called the **mortgage rate,** whereas the rate charged by banks on loans made to businesses is called the **commercial loan rate.**

The interest rate on any type of loan or fixed-income instrument depends on a number of factors, but the three most important are its **unit of account,** its **maturity,** and its **default risk.** Let us define each of these factors.

- The *unit of account* is the medium in which payments are denominated. The unit of account is usually a currency, such as dollars, francs, lira, marks, pesos, yen and so on. Sometimes the unit of account is a commodity such as gold or silver or some standard "basket" of goods and services. The interest rate varies depending on the unit of account.
- The *maturity* of a fixed-income instrument is the length of time until repayment of the entire amount borrowed. The interest rate on short-term instruments can be higher, lower, or equal to the interest rate on long-term instruments.
- *Default risk* is the possibility that some portion of the interest or the principal on a fixed-income instrument will not be repaid in full. The greater the default risk, the higher the interest rate the issuer must promise to investors to get them to buy it.

Let us consider how each of these three factors affects interest rates in the real world.

Effect of Unit of Account

A fixed-income instrument is risk free only in terms of its own unit of account, and interest rates vary depending on the unit of account. To see this, consider bonds denominated in different currencies.

Suppose the interest rate on U.K. government bonds is much higher than on Japanese government bonds of comparable maturity. Because these bonds are all free of default risk, shouldn't all investors prefer the U.K. bonds?

The answer is no because the bonds are denominated in different currencies. The U.K. government bonds are denominated in pounds, and the Japanese government bonds are denominated in yen. *Although the bonds offer a risk-free rate of return in their own currency, the rate of return in any other currency is uncertain because it depends on the rate of exchange between the currencies when payments are received in the future.*

Let us illustrate with an example. Suppose you are investing for one year, and the interest rate on a one-year Japanese government bond is 3%, and at the same time it is 9% on a one-year U.K. government bond. The **exchange rate,** which is the price of one currency in terms of the other, is currently 150 yen to the pound.

Suppose you are a Japanese investor, who wants a safe investment in terms of yen. If you buy the Japanese bond, you will earn 3% for sure. If you buy the U.K. government bond, however, your rate of return in yen depends on the yen/pound exchange rate a year from now.

Suppose you invest £100 in a U.K. bond. To do so you will have to convert 15,000 yen into pounds, so your initial investment in yen is 15,000. Because the interest rate on the U.K. bond is 9%, you will receive £109 a year from now. The value of the £109 in yen is not known now because the future yen/pound exchange rate is unknown.

Your realized yen rate of return will be:

$$\text{Yen Rate of Return} = \frac{\text{£109} \times \text{Future Yen Price of the Pound} - 15{,}000}{15{,}000}$$

Suppose the yen price of the pound falls during the year, so that the yen/pound exchange rate is 140 yen to the pound a year from now. What will the realized yen rate of return on the U.K. bond be?

Substituting into the preceding expression we get:

$$\text{Yen Rate of Return} = \frac{\text{£109} \times 140 - 15{,}000}{15{,}000} = 0.017333$$

Thus, your *realized* yen rate of return will be 1.73%, which is less than the 3% risk-free yen interest rate you could have earned on one-year Japanese bonds.

Quick Check 2-11

In the previous example, what does the change in the exchange rate have to be at year's end for the Japanese investor to earn exactly 3% per year on the investment in U.K. bonds?

Effect of Maturity

To illustrate the effect of maturity on interest rates consider Figure 2.2, which shows the U.S. Treasury **yield curve** on June 7, 1999.

The yield curve depicts the relation between interest rates (yields) on fixed-income instruments issued by the U.S. Treasury and the maturity of the instrument at a given moment in time. In Figure 2.2 we see that the annualized yield on one-year Treasury obligations was about 5.25% per year and increased with maturity to about 6.00% per year on 30-year obligations.

Although we do not see this in Figure 2.2, the *shape* and the *level* of the yield curve change significantly over time. At times in the past, short-term rates have been higher than long-term rates, so that the yield curve has been downward sloping.

Quick Check 2-12

Look in the financial pages of today's newspaper and discover what the level and shape of the U.S. Treasury yield curve are. Do the same for the Japanese Treasury yield curve.

Effect of Default Risk

The higher the default risk on fixed-income instruments, the higher the interest rate, holding all other features constant. Table 2.1 shows the interest rates on U.S.-dollar-denominated bonds for issuers with different degrees of default risk. U.S. Treasury bonds have the least default risk, next come high-quality corporate bonds, and then medium-quality corporate bonds.

Consider the difference in yields—called the **yield spread**—between Treasury bonds with maturities greater than 10 years (10 + yr)—6.21% per year and corporate bonds of medium quality (Med Qlty) of the same maturity—7.56% per year. The yield spread is 1.35% per year.

FIGURE 2.2   U.S. Treasury Yield Curve

Source: The Wall Street Journal, June 8, 1999, p. C23. Reprinted by permission of *The Wall Street Journal,* © 1999 Dow Jones & Company, Inc. All Rights Reserved.

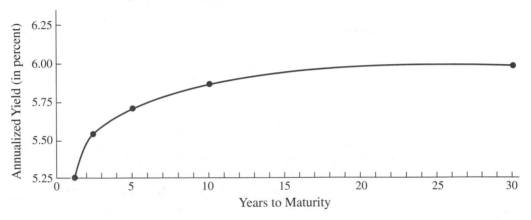

TABLE 2.1 Yield Comparisons	
Treasury 1–10yr	5.70%
10 + yr	6.21
Corporate	
1–10yr High Qlty	6.45
Med Qlty	6.94
10 + yr High Qlty	7.09
Med Qlty	7.56

Based on Merrill Lynch Bond Indexes, priced as of midafternoon Eastern time.

Source: The Wall Street Journal, June 8, 1999, p. C23. Reprinted by permission of *The Wall Street Journal,* © 1999 Dow Jones & Company, Inc.   All Rights Reserved.

Quick Check 2-13
Look in the financial pages of today's newspaper and discover what the yield spreads are between corporate bonds and U.S. Treasury bonds.

2.6.2 Rates of Return on Risky Assets

Interest rates are *promised* rates of return on fixed-income instruments that are a contractual obligation. However, many assets do not carry a promised rate of return. For example, if you invest in real estate, equity securities, or works of art, there is no promise of specified cash payments in the future. Let us now consider how to measure the rate of return on such risky assets.

When you invest in equity securities such as common stocks, the *return* comes from two sources. The first source is the cash dividends paid to the stockholder by the firm that issued the stocks. These dividend payments are not contractually required and, hence, are not called interest payments. Dividends are paid to stockholders at the discretion of the firm's board of directors.

The second source of return to the stockholder is any gain (or loss) in the market price of the stock over the period it is held. This second type of return is called a **capital gain** or **capital loss.** The length of the holding period for measuring returns on stock can be as short as a day or as long as several decades.

To illustrate how returns are measured, suppose you buy shares of stock at a price of $100 per share. One day later the price is $101 per share and you sell. Your *rate of return* for the day is 1%—a capital gain of $1 per share divided by the purchase price of $100.

Suppose you hold the stock for a year. At the end of the year, the stock pays a cash dividend of $5 per share and the price of a share is $105 just after the dividend is paid. The one-year rate of return, *r,* is:

$$r = \frac{\text{Ending Price of a Share} - \text{Beginning Price} + \text{Cash Dividend}}{\text{Beginning Price}}$$

In the example we have:

$$r = \frac{\$105 - \$100 + \$5}{\$100} = 0.10 \text{ or } 10\%$$

Note that we can present the *total* rate of return as the sum of the dividend income component and the price change component:

$$r = \frac{\text{Cash Dividend}}{\text{Beginning Price}} + \frac{\text{Ending Price of a Share} - \text{Beginning Price}}{\text{Beginning Price}}$$

$$r = \text{Dividend Income Component} + \text{Price Change Component}$$

$$r = 5\% + 5\% = 10\%$$

What if you decide *not* to sell your shares at the end of the year—how should we measure your rate of return?

The answer is that *you measure the rate of return exactly the same way whether or not you sell the stock.* The price appreciation of $5 per share is as much a part of your return as is the $5 dividend. That you choose to keep the stock rather than sell it does not alter the fact that you could convert it into $105 of cash at the end of the year. Thus, whether you decide to realize your capital gain by selling the stock or to reinvest it (by not selling), your rate of return is 10%.[3]

Quick Check 2-14

You invest in a stock costing $50. It pays a cash dividend during the year of $1, and you expect its price to be $60 at year's end. What is your expected rate of return?

If the stock's price is actually $40 at year's end, what is your realized rate of return?

2.6.3 Market Indexes and Market Indexing

It is useful for many purposes to have a measure of the overall level of stock prices. For example, people holding stocks might want an indicator of the current value of their investment, or they might want a benchmark against which to measure the performance of their own investment in stocks. Table 2.2 is a list of the stock indexes generally reported in the financial press for the stocks traded on the other major national stock exchanges around the world.

Indexing is an investment strategy that seeks to match the investment returns of a specified stock market index. Indexing is based on a simple truth: It is impossible for all stock investors in the aggregate to outperform the overall stock market. When indexing, an investment manager attempts to replicate the investment results of the target index by holding all—or in the case of very large indexes, a represen-

---

[3]This is only true of your *before-tax* rate of return. Because selling the stock can affect the income taxes you pay, your *after-tax* rate of return may be affected.

TABLE 2.2   Major Stock Indexes around the World

Country	Indexes
United States	DJI, SP500
Japan	Nikkei, Topix
United Kingdom	FT-30, FT-100
Germany	DAX
France	CAC 40
Switzerland	Credit Suisse
Europe, Australia, Far East	MSCI, EAFE

tative sample—of the securities in the index. There is no attempt to use "active" money management or to make "bets" on individual stocks or narrow industry sectors in an attempt to outpace the index. Thus, indexing is a passive investment strategy emphasizing broad diversification and low portfolio trading activity.

Of course, there will always be actively managed funds that outperform index funds. It may just be luck—pure chance would say that some investment managers will provide exceptional returns and they may even have superior performance over lengthy "winning streaks." Or, it may be skill—there may be some investment managers with truly outstanding abilities who can earn superior returns over time. The problem in selecting actively managed funds is how to identify in advance those that will be consistently superior over time.

Indexing's Cost Advantage

Since 1926, the U.S. stock market has provided investors with an average return of about 12% per year. That figure, however, is before costs. These costs come in the form of:

- The fund's expense ratio (including advisory fees, distribution charges, and operating expenses).
- Portfolio transaction costs (brokerage and other trading costs).

The average general equity fund has an annual expense ratio of 1.34% of investor assets. In addition, traditional mutual fund managers have high portfolio activity; the average fund's portfolio turnover rate is 76% per year (Source: Lipper Analytical Services, Inc.). The trading costs of this portfolio turnover may be expected to subtract another 0.5% to 1% annually. Combined, fund expenses and transaction costs for the typical fund take a significant bite out of the investment-return pie. Funds charging sales commissions swallow even more of the returns.

By contrast, one of the key advantages of an index fund is its low cost. An index fund requires only minimal advisory fees, can keep operating expenses at the lowest level, and holds portfolio transaction costs to a minimum. Moreover, because index funds engage in much lower portfolio turnover than actively managed funds, there is a strong (but by no means assured) tendency for index funds to realize and distribute only modest—if any—capital gains to shareholders. Because these distributions are taxable for all shareholders, it is an advantage to defer their realization as long as possible.

Over time, the broad stock market indexes have outperformed the average general equity fund. The following table shows the total return (capital change plus income) of the Wilshire 5000 (a measure of the total U.S. stock market) versus equity funds.

Total Return *(Ten Years Ended September 30, 1996)*		
	Cumulative Rate	*Annual Rate*
Wilshire 5000 Index*	+272.52%	+14.06%
Average General Equity Fund	+237.63%	+12.94%

*The returns of the index have been reduced by 0.3% per year to reflect approximate index fund costs.
Source: Lipper Analytical Services, Inc.

Table 2.3 shows rates of return on different asset classes around the world. Each rate of return is measured in its own currency unit. For example, Table 2.3 shows that stocks in the United States rose on average by 19.6% over the period from March 1998 to March 1999, and in Japan they declined by about 2.1%. To compare performance across the two countries, one must convert to the same currency unit.

The value of the dollar in terms of the yen declined by 9.2% over the same period. So ignoring any cash dividends earned on stocks, those with a portfolio of U.S. stocks worth $1 million in March 1998 would have seen their value increase in dollar terms to $1.196 million by March 1999. The stock portfolio had a value of 130 million yen ($1 million × 130 yen/dollar) in March 1998, and a value of 141.128 million yen ($1.196 million × 118 yen/dollar) in March 1999. So in terms of yen, the value of the U.S. stock market increased by only 8.56%. Thus, the decline in the dollar value of the yen partially offsets the difference in the performance between the U.S. and Japanese stock markets. In the last row of the table we find the percentage

TABLE 2.3   Financial Market Indicators on March 17, 1999

Country	Stock Market 1 Yr % Change	Interest Rates (% per yr) Short Term	Long Term	Currency Unit Per $ Latest	Yr Ago	1 Yr % Change
Australia	+7.5	4.80	5.38	1.59	1.50	+6.0
Britain	+4.0	5.31	4.53	0.61	0.60	+1.7
Canada	-11.2	4.88	5.22	1.52	1.42	+7.0
Denmark	-21.3	3.32	4.29	6.75	6.96	-3.0
Japan	-2.1	0.07	1.81	118.00	130.00	-9.2
Sweden	-3.3	3.17	4.39	8.16	7.95	+2.6
Switzerland	+1.4	1.29	2.54	1.45	1.49	-2.7
United States	+19.6	4.81	5.10	—	—	
Euro-11	+6.2	3.04	3.89	0.91	0.93	-2.2
World	+13.6					

Source: The Economist, March 17, 1999, p. 111. © 1999 The Economist Newspaper Group, Inc. Reprinted with permission. Further reproduction prohibited. www.economist.com.

change in a world stock index, which represents the *dollar* value of the stocks of the different countries combined.[4]

2.6.4 Rates of Return in Historical Perspective

Figure 2.3 and Table 2.4 present the annual total returns on three broad asset classes in the United States for the period 1926–1997. Figure 2.3 gives a graphic representation of the relative volatilities of the three different asset classes. We have plotted the three time series on the same set of axes. Clearly, stocks have the most volatile series.

The first column of Table 2.4 shows the one-year rate of return on a policy of rolling-over 30-day Treasury bills as they mature. As this rate changes from month to month, it is riskless only for a 30-day holding period. The second column presents the annual rate of return an investor would have earned by investing in U.S. Treasury bonds with 20-year maturities. The third column is the rate of return on the Standard & Poor's 500 stock portfolio. Finally, the last column gives the annual inflation rate as measured by the rate of change in the consumer price index.

At the bottom of each column are four descriptive statistics. The first is the arithmetic mean. For bills, it is 3.81%, for bonds 5.58%, and for common stock 8.17%. These numbers imply an average risk premium (the average rate of return less the average risk-free rate of 3.81%) of 1.77% per year on bonds and 4.36% on stocks.

The second statistic reported at the bottom of Table 2.4 is the standard deviation. The higher the standard deviation, the higher the volatility of the rate of return. The standard deviation of stock returns has been 19.66%, compared to 9.27% for bonds, and 3.27% for bills.

FIGURE 2.3   Annual Rates of Return on Stocks, Bonds, and Bills

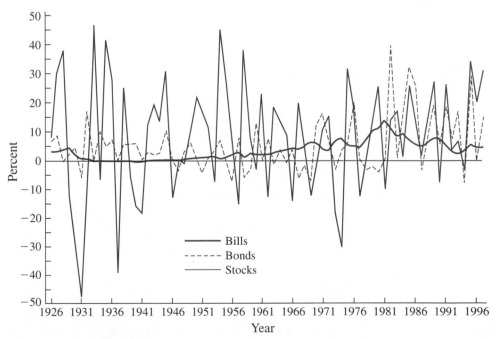

Source: Center for Research in Security Prices.

---

[4]It is the Morgan Stanley Capital International Index (MSCI).

TABLE 2.4   Rates of Return on Bills, Bonds, and Stocks, 1926–1997 (in percent)

Year	Bills	Bonds	Stocks	Inflation	Year	Bills	Bonds	Stocks	Inflation
1926	3.19	7.70	8.27	-1.118	1964	3.52	4.11	12.97	0.972
1927	3.13	8.93	30.91	-2.261	1965	3.97	-0.27	9.06	1.922
1928	3.82	0.10	37.88	-1.155	1966	4.71	3.96	-13.09	3.460
1929	4.74	3.42	-11.91	0.585	1967	4.15	-6.02	20.09	3.040
1930	2.35	4.66	-28.48	-6.393	1968	5.29	-1.20	7.66	4.720
1931	1.02	-5.31	-47.07	-9.316	1969	6.59	-6.52	-11.36	6.195
1932	0.81	16.84	-15.15	-10.275	1970	6.38	12.69	0.10	5.569
1933	0.29	-0.08	46.59	0.764	1971	4.32	16.70	10.79	3.266
1934	0.16	10.02	-5.94	1.516	1972	3.89	5.15	15.63	3.407
1935	0.17	4.98	41.37	2.985	1973	7.06	-2.49	-17.37	8.705
1936	0.18	7.51	27.92	1.449	1974	8.08	3.89	-29.72	12.338
1937	0.32	0.23	-38.59	2.856	1975	5.82	6.10	31.55	6.937
1938	0.04	5.53	25.21	-2.777	1976	5.16	18.18	19.15	4.865
1939	0.01	5.94	-5.45	0.001	1977	5.15	0.90	-11.50	6.701
1940	-0.06	6.09	-15.29	0.714	1978	7.31	-2.93	1.06	9.018
1941	0.04	0.93	-17.86	9.929	1979	10.69	-1.52	12.31	13.294
1942	0.26	3.22	12.43	9.032	1980	11.53	-3.52	25.77	12.517
1943	0.34	2.08	19.45	2.959	1981	14.86	1.16	-9.73	8.923
1944	0.32	2.81	13.80	2.299	1982	10.66	39.74	14.76	3.828
1945	0.32	10.73	30.72	2.247	1983	8.85	1.28	17.27	3.791
1946	0.35	-0.10	-11.87	18.131	1984	9.96	15.81	1.40	3.948
1947	0.46	-2.63	0.00	8.837	1985	7.68	31.96	26.33	3.799
1948	0.98	3.40	-0.65	2.991	1986	6.06	25.79	14.62	1.099
1949	1.11	6.45	10.26	-2.074	1987	5.39	-2.91	2.03	4.434
1950	1.21	0.06	21.78	5.935	1988	6.32	8.71	12.40	4.420
1951	1.48	-3.94	16.46	6.000	1989	8.22	19.23	27.25	4.649
1952	1.64	1.16	11.78	0.755	1990	7.68	6.15	-6.56	6.107
1953	1.78	3.63	-6.62	0.749	1991	5.51	18.59	26.31	3.065
1954	0.86	7.19	45.02	-0.744	1992	3.40	7.95	4.46	2.902
1955	1.56	-0.69	26.40	0.375	1993	2.90	16.91	7.06	2.750
1956	2.42	-6.27	2.62	2.985	1994	3.88	-7.19	-1.54	2.674
1957	3.13	8.22	-14.31	2.898	1995	5.53	30.38	34.11	2.537
1958	1.42	-5.29	38.06	1.759	1996	5.15	-0.35	20.26	3.322
1959	2.82	-2.51	8.48	1.730	1997	5.08	15.46	31.01	1.703
1960	2.58	13.32	-2.97	1.361	**Mean**	3.81	5.58	8.17	3.20
1961	2.16	0.19	23.13	0.671	**Std. Deviation**	3.27	9.27	19.66	4.52
1962	2.72	7.80	-11.81	1.333	**Maximum**	14.86	39.74	46.59	18.13
1963	3.15	-0.79	18.89	1.646	**Minimum**	-0.06	-7.19	-47.07	-10.28

Source: Center for Research in Security Prices.

The other summary measures at the bottom of Table 2.4 show the highest and lowest annual rate of return (the range) for each asset over the 72-year period. The size of this range is another possible measure of the relative riskiness of each asset class. It too confirms the ranking of stocks as the riskiest and bills as the least risky of the three asset classes.

In a recent study comparing international rates of return on stocks, Jeremy Siegel[5] reports the following inflation-adjusted annualized compound real rates of return for the period 1926–1997:

U.S.	7.2%
Germany	6.6%
U.K.	6.2%
Japan	3.4%

The long-term average compound returns for Germany and Japan are surprisingly high, in view of the fact that World War II caused a 90% drop in German stock prices and a 98% drop in Japanese stock prices.

2.6.5 Inflation and Real Interest Rates

People have long recognized that the prices of goods, services, and assets must be corrected for the effects of inflation in order to make meaningful economic comparisons over time. To correct for the effects of inflation, economists distinguish between what they call **nominal prices,** or prices in terms of some currency, and **real prices,** or prices in terms of purchasing power over goods and services.

Just as we distinguish between nominal and real prices, so too we distinguish between *nominal* and *real* interest rates. The **nominal interest rate** on a bond is the promised amount of money you receive per unit you lend. The **real rate of return** is defined as the nominal interest rate you earn corrected for the change in the purchasing power of money. For example, if you earn a nominal interest rate of 8% per year and the rate of price inflation is also 8% per year, then the real rate of return is zero.

What is the unit of account for computing the real rate of return? It is some standardized basket of consumption goods. The real rate of return, therefore, depends on the composition of the basket of consumption goods. In discussions of real rates of return in different countries, the general practice is to take whatever basket is used to compute the national consumer price index (CPI).

What is the real rate of return if the nominal interest rate is 8% per year, and the rate of inflation as measured by the proportional change in the CPI is 5% per year? Intuition suggests that it is simply the difference between the nominal interest rate and the rate of inflation, which is 3% per year in this case. That is approximately correct, but not exactly so.

To see why, let's compute the real rate of return precisely. For every $100 you invest now, you will receive $108 a year from now. But a basket of consumption goods, which now costs $100, will cost $105 a year from now. How much will your future value of $108 be worth in terms of consumption goods? To find the answer we must divide the $108 by the future price of a consumption basket: $108/$105 = 1.02857 baskets. Thus, for every basket you give up now, you will get the equivalent of 1.02857 baskets a year from now. The real rate of return (baskets in the future per basket invested today) is, therefore, 2.857% per year.

---

[5]Jeremy Siegel, *Stocks for the Long Run,* 2nd ed, (New York: McGraw Hill, 1998), p. 19.

The general formula relating the real rate of return to the nominal rate of interest and the rate of inflation is:

$$1 + \text{Real Rate of Return} = \frac{1 + \text{Nominal Interest Rate}}{1 + \text{Rate of Inflation}}$$

or equivalently,

$$\text{Real Rate} = \frac{\text{Nominal Interest Rate} - \text{Rate of Inflation}}{1 + \text{Rate of Inflation}}$$

Substituting into this formula, we can confirm that in our example the real rate works out to be 2.857% per year:

$$\text{Real Rate} = \frac{0.08 - 0.05}{1.05} = 0.02857 = 2.857\%$$

Note that a fixed-income instrument that is risk free in nominal terms will not be risk free in real terms. For example, suppose a bank offers depositors a risk-free dollar interest rate of 8% per year. Because the rate of inflation is not known with certainty in advance, the bank account is risky in real terms.

If the expected rate of inflation is 5% per year, then the expected real rate of return is 2.857% per year. But if the rate of inflation turns out to be higher than 5%, the realized real rate will be less than 2.857%.

Quick Check 2-15

Suppose the risk-free nominal interest rate on a one-year U.S. Treasury bill is 6% per year and the expected rate of inflation is 3% per year. What is the expected real rate of return on the T-bill? Why is the T-bill risky in real terms?

To protect against inflation risk, one can denominate interest rates in terms of real goods and services. For example, one can specify that the unit of account for the fixed-income instrument is some commodity.

Some bonds have their interest and principal denominated in terms of the basket of goods and services used to compute the cost of living in a particular country. For example, the government of the United Kingdom has been issuing such **index-linked bonds** since 1981. The U.S. Treasury started issuing such bonds in January 1997. They are called Treasury Inflation Protected Securities (TIPS). The interest rate on these bonds is a risk-free real rate. In September 1998, the U.S. Treasury added inflation-protected savings bonds (see Box 2.3).

To illustrate how TIPS work, consider one that matures in one year. Assume that it offers a risk-free real rate of interest of 3% per year. The rate of return in dollars is not known with certainty in advance because it depends on the rate of inflation. If the inflation rate turns out to be only 2%, then the realized dollar rate of return will be approximately 5%; if, however, the rate of inflation turns out to be 10%, then the realized dollar rate of return will be approximately 13%.

To summarize, an interest rate is a promised rate of return. Because most bonds offer an interest rate that is denominated in terms of some currency, their real

---

B O X   2 . 3

I Bonds

In September 1998, the U.S. Treasury Department introduced a new type of savings bond, called Series I Savings Bonds or I Bonds. At its web site (www.savingsbonds.gov), the following information is offered about these bonds.

I Bonds are a new type of bond designed for investors seeking to protect the purchasing power of their investment and earn a guaranteed real rate of return. I Bonds are an accrual-type security—meaning interest is added to the bond monthly and paid when the bond is cashed. I Bonds are sold at face value—you pay $50 for a $50 bond—and they grow in value with inflation-indexed earnings for up to 30 years.

Why is the Treasury offering the I Bonds?
The Treasury is offering the I Bond to encourage more Americans to save for the future. We are offering investors a bond with a fixed rate combined with semiannual inflation adjustments that will help protect purchasing power.

How is the earnings rate of an I Bond determined?
The earnings rate of an I Bond is a combination of two separate rates: a fixed rate of return and a variable semiannual inflation rate. The fixed rate remains the same throughout the life of the I Bond, while the semiannual inflation rate can vary every six months. The semiannual inflation rate is combined with the fixed rate of an I Bond to determine the I Bond's earnings rate for the next six months.

What Other Special Features Do I Bonds Have?

• I Bonds are affordable. You can invest as little as $50 or as much as $30,000 per year.

• I Bonds are safe. They're U.S. Treasury securities backed by the full faith and credit of the United States Government.

• I Bonds have tax advantages. You can defer Federal taxes on earnings for up to 30 years, and I Bonds are exempt from state and local income taxes.

• I Bonds will usually increase in value every month, and interest is compounded semiannually.

• I Bonds are liquid. They can be turned into cash any time after six months.

---

rate of return in terms of consumption goods is uncertain. In the case of inflation-indexed bonds the interest rate is denominated in terms of some basket of consumer goods and it is a risk-free real rate for that basket.

Quick Check 2-16
Suppose that the real rate of interest on TIPS is 3.5% per year and the expected rate of inflation in the United States is 4% per year. What is the expected nominal rate of return on these bonds?

2.6.6 Interest Rate Equalization

Competition in financial markets ensures that *interest rates* on equivalent assets are the same. Suppose, for instance, that the interest rate the U.S. Treasury currently pays on its one-year T-bills is 4% per year. What interest rate would you expect a major institution such as the World Bank to pay on its one-year dollar-denominated debt securities (assuming they are virtually free of default risk)?

Your answer should be approximately 4% per year.

To see why, suppose that the World Bank offered significantly *less* than 4% per year. Well-informed investors would not buy the bonds issued by the World Bank; instead they would invest in one-year T-bills. Thus, if the World Bank expects to sell its bonds, it must offer at least as high a rate as the U.S. Treasury.

Would the World Bank offer significantly *more* than 4% per year? Assuming that it wants to minimize its borrowing costs, it would offer no more than is necessary to attract investors. Thus, interest rates on any default-free borrowing and lending denominated in dollars with a maturity of one year will tend to be around the same as the 4% per year interest rate on one-year U.S. T-bills.

If there are entities that have the ability to borrow and lend on the *same* terms (e.g., maturity, default risk) at *different* interest rates, then they can carry out **interest-rate arbitrage:** borrowing at the lower rate and lending at the higher rate. Their attempts to expand their activity will bring about an equalization of interest rates.

Quick Check 2-17

Suppose you have $10,000 in a bank account earning an interest rate of 3% per year. At the same time you have an unpaid balance on your credit card of $5,000 on which you are paying an interest rate of 17% per year. What is the arbitrage opportunity you face?

2.6.7 The Fundamental Determinants of Rates of Return

There are four main factors that determine rates of return in a market economy:

- *productivity of capital goods*—expected rates of return on mines, dams, roads, bridges, factories, machinery, and inventories;
- *degree of uncertainty regarding the productivity of capital goods;*
- *time preferences of people*—the preference of people for consumption now versus consumption in the future; and
- *risk aversion*—the amount people are willing to give up in order to reduce their exposure to risk.

Let us briefly discuss each of the four factors.

The Expected Productivity of Capital Goods

The first determinant of expected rates of return is the **productivity of capital goods.** Recall from chapter 1 that *capital goods* are goods produced in the economy that can be used in the production of other goods. Typical examples of capital goods are mines, roads, canals, dams, power stations, factories, machinery, and inventories. In addition to such physical goods (tangible capital), capital also includes patents, contracts, formulas, brand-name recognition, and production and distribution system designs that contribute to output. Such nonphysical goods (*intangible capital*) are often the result of expenditures on research and development and advertising.

Capital's productivity can be expressed as a percentage per year, called the **rate of return on capital.** This return on capital is the source of the dividends and interest paid to the holders of the stocks, bonds, and other financial instruments issued by firms. These instruments represent claims to the return on capital. The expected rate of return on capital varies over time and place according to the state of technology, the availability of other factors of production such as natural resources and labor, and the demand for the goods and services the capital can produce. *The higher the expected rate of return on capital, the higher the level of interest rates in the economy.*

The Degree of Uncertainty about the Productivity of Capital Goods

The rate of return on capital is always uncertain for a host of reasons. The uncertainties of the weather affect agricultural output; mines and wells often turn out to be "dry"; machines break down from time to time; the demand for a product may change unpredictably due to changing tastes or the development of substitutes; and above all, technological progress that comes from the development of new knowledge is by its nature unpredictable. Even the simple production process of storing goods in inventory for use at a future date is not risk free because an unknown quantity could go bad or become obsolete.

Equity securities represent claims to the profits earned on capital goods. *The greater the degree of uncertainty about the productivity of capital goods, the higher the risk premium on equity securities.*

Time Preferences of People

Another factor determining the level of rates of return is the preferences of people for consumption now versus consumption in the future. Economists generally assume that the rate of interest would still be positive even if there were no capital goods to invest in and the only reason for borrowing and lending was that people wanted to alter their patterns of consumption over time. In general, the greater the preference of people for current consumption over future consumption, the higher the rate of interest in the economy.

One reason people may prefer greater consumption in the present than in the future is uncertainty about their time of death. They know they are alive now to enjoy their consumption spending, but there is some uncertainty about whether they will be around to enjoy it in the future.

Risk Aversion

As discussed, the rate of return on capital is always risky. How then is it possible for people to earn a risk-free rate of interest, and what determines the risk-free rate?

The answer is that the financial system provides contractual mechanisms for people who want to invest in risk-free assets to do so by giving up some of their expected return. People who are more tolerant of risk offer to those who are more averse to risk the opportunity to earn a risk-free rate of interest in return for accepting a rate that is lower than the average expected rate of return on risky assets. The greater the degree of risk aversion of the population, the higher the risk premium required, and the lower will be the risk-free rate of interest.

> **Quick Check 2-18**
> What are the fundamental determinants of the rate of interest?

2.7 FINANCIAL INTERMEDIARIES

Financial intermediaries are firms whose primary business is to provide customers with financial products and services that cannot be obtained more efficiently by transacting directly in securities markets. Among the main types of intermediaries are banks, investment companies, and insurance companies. Their products include checking accounts, loans, mortgages, mutual funds, and a wide range of insurance contracts.

Perhaps the simplest example of a financial intermediary is a mutual fund, which pools the financial resources of many small savers and invests their money in securities. The mutual fund has substantial economies of scale in record keeping and in executing purchases and sales of securities and, therefore, offers its customers a more efficient way of investing in securities than the direct purchase and sale of securities in the markets.

2.7.1 Banks

Banks are today the largest (in terms of assets) and oldest of all financial intermediaries. The earliest banks appeared hundreds of years ago in the towns of Renaissance Italy. Their main function was to serve as a mechanism for clearing and settling payments, thereby facilitating the trade in goods and services that had started to flourish in Italy at that time. The early banks evolved from money changers.[6] Indeed, the word *bank* comes from *banca,* the Italian word for "bench" because money changers worked at benches in converting currencies.

Most firms called banks today, however, perform at least two functions: They take deposits and make loans. In the United States they are called **commercial banks.**

In some countries banks are virtually all-purpose financial intermediaries, offering customers not just transaction services and loans, but also mutual funds and insurance of every kind. In Germany, for example, *universal banks* fulfill virtually all of the functions performed by the more specialized intermediaries to be discussed in the remaining sections of this chapter.

Indeed, it is becoming increasingly difficult to differentiate among the various financial firms doing business around the world on the basis of what type of intermediary or financial service provider they are. Thus, although Deutsche Bank is classified as a universal bank, it performs pretty much the same set of functions around the world as does Merrill Lynch, which is usually classified as a broker/dealer.

2.7.2 Other Depository Savings Institutions

Depository savings institutions, thrift institutions, or simply *thrifts* are the terms used to refer collectively to savings banks, savings and loan associations (S&Ls), and credit unions. In the United States, they compete with commercial banks in both their deposit and lending activities. U.S. thrifts specialize in making home mortgage and consumer loans. In other countries there is a variety of special-purpose savings institutions that are similar to the thrifts and credit unions in the United States.

---

[6]An excellent survey of what historians have discovered about the origins of banking can be found in Raymond de Roover, "New Interpretations of the History of Banking," chapter 5 in *Business, Banking, and Economic Thought in Late Medieval and Early Modern Europe* (Chicago: The University of Chicago Press, 1974).

2.7.3 Insurance Companies

Insurance companies are intermediaries whose primary function is to allow households and businesses to shed specific risks by buying contracts called insurance policies that pay cash compensation if certain specified events occur. Policies that cover accidents, theft, or fire are called *property and casualty* insurance. Policies that cover sickness or the inability to work are called *health and disability* insurance, and policies that cover death are called *life insurance.*

Insurance policies are assets of the households and businesses that buy them, and they are liabilities of the insurance companies that sell them. Payments made to insurance companies for the insurance they provide are called *premiums.* Because customers pay insurance premiums before benefits are received, insurance companies have the use of the funds for periods of time ranging from less than a year to several decades. Insurance companies invest the premiums they collect in assets such as stocks, bonds, and real estate.

2.7.4 Pension and Retirement Funds

The function of a pension plan is to replace a person's preretirement earnings when combined with Social Security retirement benefits and private savings. A pension plan can be sponsored by an employer, a labor union, or an individual.

Pension plans are classified into two types: defined contribution and defined benefit. In a **defined-contribution pension plan,** each employee has an account into which the employer and usually the employee make regular contributions. At retirement, the employee receives a benefit whose size depends on the accumulated value of the funds in the retirement account.

In a **defined-benefit pension plan,** the employee's pension benefit is determined by a formula that takes into account years of service to the employer and, in most cases, wages or salary. A typical benefit formula would be 1% of average retirement salary for each year of service.

The sponsor of a defined-benefit plan or an insurance company hired by the sponsor guarantees the benefits and, thus, absorbs the investment risk. In some countries, such as Germany, Japan, and the United States, a government or quasi-governmental agency backs the sponsor's guarantee of pension benefits up to specified limits.

2.7.5 Mutual Funds

A **mutual fund** is a portfolio of stocks, bonds, or other assets purchased in the name of a group of investors and managed by a professional investment company or other financial institution. Each customer is entitled to a pro rata share of any distributions and can redeem his or her share of the fund at any time at its then current market value.

The company that manages the fund keeps track of how much each investor has and reinvests all distributions received according to the rules of the fund. In addition to divisibility, record keeping, and reinvestment of receipts, mutual funds provide an efficient means of diversification.

There are two types of mutual funds: *open end* and *closed end.* Open-end mutual funds stand ready to redeem or issue shares at their net asset value (NAV), which is the market value of all securities held divided by the number of shares outstanding. The number of shares outstanding of an open-end fund changes daily as investors buy new or redeem old shares.

Closed-end mutual funds do not redeem or issue shares at NAV. Shares of closed-end funds are traded through brokers just like other common stocks, and their prices can, therefore, differ from NAV.

2.7.6 Investment Banks

Investment banks are firms whose primary function is to help businesses, governments, and other entities raise funds to finance their activities by issuing securities. Investment banks also facilitate and sometimes initiate mergers of firms or acquisitions of one firm by another.

Investment banks often *underwrite* the securities they distribute. Underwriting means insuring. In the case of securities, underwriting means committing to buy them at a guaranteed future price.

In many countries, universal banks perform the functions of U.S. investment banks, but in the United States the Glass Steagall Act of 1933 prohibited commercial banks from engaging in most underwriting activities. In recent years, however, commercial banks in the United States have again been permitted to engage in some of these activities.

2.7.7 Venture Capital Firms

Venture capital firms are similar to investment banks, except their clients are startup firms rather than large corporations. Young firms with inexperienced managers often need considerable advice in running their business in addition to financing. Venture capital firms provide both.

Venture capitalists invest their funds in new businesses and help the management team get the firm to the point at which it is ready to "go public"—that is, sell shares of stock to the investing public. Once that point is reached, the venture capital firm will typically sell its stake in the corporation and move on to the next new venture.

2.7.8 Asset Management Firms

Asset management firms are also called *investment management firms*. They advise and often administer mutual funds, pension funds, and other asset pools for individuals, firms, and governments. They may be separate firms or they may be a division within a firm, such as a trust company that is part of a bank, insurance company, or brokerage firm.

2.7.9 Information Services

Many financial service firms provide information as a by-product of their main activities, but there are firms that specialize in providing information. The oldest information service firms are rating agencies, such as Moody's and Standard & Poor's for the securities business and Best's for the insurance industry. A more recent growth sector is the firms or divisions within firms offering analysis of financial data (such as Bloomberg and Reuters) or performance statistics on mutual funds (such as Lipper, Morningstar, and SEI).

2.8 FINANCIAL INFRASTRUCTURE AND REGULATION

All social activity is conducted within the bounds of certain rules of behavior. Some rules are codified in the law and constrain the financial system as they constrain all other realms of economic activity. Prime among these are laws outlawing fraud and enforcing contracts. Moreover, these laws may differ from country to country and change over time. They are part of the legal infrastructure of a society, and we generally treat them as outside the financial system, although changes in the law are sometimes a response to changing needs for the operation of the financial system.

The financial infrastructure consists of the legal and accounting procedures, the organization of trading and clearing facilities, and the regulatory structures that govern the relations among the users of the financial system. Those who take a historical perspective of several centuries have identified the evolution of the infrastructure of the financial system as a key factor in understanding the economic development of nations.

Some regulatory tasks are performed by private sector organizations and some are performed by governmental organizations. The performance of some regulatory tasks that are legally assigned to government are delegated to private sector organizations. This is true in the United States as well as in other countries. Some of these private sector organizations are professional associations with special expertise such as the Financial Accounting Standards Board in the United States, some are securities exchanges, and some are trade associations such as the International Swap Dealers Association (ISDA).

As in other areas of the economic system, so too in the financial system, government can play a useful role in promoting economic efficiency. However, successful public policy depends importantly on recognizing the limits of what government can do to improve efficiency and on recognizing when government *inaction* is the best choice.

2.8.1 Rules for Trading

Rules for trading securities are usually established by organized exchanges and then sometimes given the sanction of law. These rules serve the function of standardizing procedures so that the costs of transacting are kept to a minimum. Ideally, the rules are well thought out to promote low-cost trading, but sometimes they are seemingly arbitrary. Even arbitrary rules, however, are usually preferable to no rules at all.

2.8.2 Accounting Systems

To be useful, financial information must be presented in a standard format. The discipline that studies the reporting of financial information is called *accounting*. Accounting systems are perhaps the most important part of the infrastructure of the financial system.

Not surprisingly, the earliest accounting systems developed in parallel with the development of financial contracting. Archaeologists have found elaborate and detailed accounts of financial transactions dating back to ancient Babylon (around 2000 B.C.). The development of *double-entry bookkeeping*—a major leap forward in accounting systems—occurred in Renaissance Italy in response to the need to keep track of the complex financial transactions arising from trade and banking.

2.9 GOVERNMENTAL AND QUASI-GOVERNMENTAL ORGANIZATIONS

As the maker and enforcer of a society's laws, government is ultimately responsible to regulate the financial system. As demonstrated in the previous section, there are some regulatory tasks that are delegated to private sector organizations such as trade or industry associations or the securities exchanges. This is true in the United States as well as in other countries.

For example, in the United States, the *Securities Exchange Commission* (SEC) establishes the precise disclosure requirements that must be satisfied for a public offering of securities. Other countries have similar regulatory bodies.

However, in addition to their role as regulators of the financial system, governments use the financial system to achieve other public policy goals. An example is the use of monetary policy to achieve national targets for economic growth or employment. In the following sections we describe some of the main governmental organizations that either seek to regulate the operation of some part of the financial system or use the financial system as the principal means of achieving other economic goals.

2.9.1 Central Banks

Central banks are intermediaries whose primary function is to promote public policy objectives by influencing certain financial market parameters such as the supply of the local currency. In some countries the central bank is subject to the direct control of the executive body of government; in others it is semiautonomous.[7]

In many countries the central bank is identifiable through its title: the Bank of England, the Bank of Japan, and so on. But in the United States the central bank is called the *Federal Reserve System* (or the "Fed" for short), and in Germany the *Bundesbank*.

A central bank is usually at the heart of a country's payments system. It provides the supply of local currency and operates the clearing system for the banks. An efficient payments system requires at least a moderate degree of price stability. Central banks, therefore, usually view this as their primary goal. But central banks in many countries are also expected to promote the goals of full employment and economic growth. In these countries, central banks must balance the sometimes conflicting goals of price stability and full employment.

2.9.2 Special-Purpose Intermediaries

This group of organizations includes entities that are set up to encourage specific economic activities by making financing more readily available or by guaranteeing debt instruments of various sorts. Examples are government agencies that make loans or guarantee loans to farmers, students, small businesses, new home buyers, and so on.

A different class of governmental organization is the agencies that are designed to insure bank deposits. Their main function is to promote economic stability by preventing a breakdown in part or all of the financial system.

The worst-case scenario is a banking panic. Depositors are content to leave their deposits in banks as long as they are confident that their money is safe and accessible. However, depositors know that the bank is holding illiquid and risky assets as collateral for its obligation to depositors. If they believe that they will not be able to get back the full value of their deposits, then depositors will race to be first in line to withdraw their money.

---

[7]In the United States, the central bank has a great deal of autonomy from the government. It consists of 12 regional banks and a seven-member board of governors in Washington, DC. All seven members of the board of governors are, however, appointed by the president of the United States and confirmed by the Senate.

This forces the bank into liquidating some of its risky assets. If the collateral assets are illiquid, then being forced to liquidate them quickly means that the bank will have to accept less than full value for them. If one bank does not have sufficient funds to pay off its depositors, then contagion can set in, and other banks are then faced with a run. However, such a contagion problem occurs for the banking system as a whole only if there is a "flight to currency," in which people refuse to hold deposits of *any* bank and insist on having currency.

2.9.3 Regional and World Organizations

Several international bodies currently exist for the purpose of coordinating the financial policies of national governments. Perhaps the most important is the Bank for International Settlements (BIS) in Basel, Switzerland, whose objective is to promote uniformity of banking regulations.

In addition, two official international agencies operate in the international financial markets to promote growth in trade and finance: the International Monetary Fund (IMF) and the International Bank for Reconstruction and Development (World Bank). The IMF monitors economic and financial conditions in member countries, provides technical assistance, establishes rules for international trade and finance, provides a forum for international consultation, and most importantly, provides resources that permit lengthening the time necessary for individual members to correct imbalances in their payments to other countries.

The World Bank finances investment projects in developing countries. It raises funds primarily by selling bonds in developed countries and then makes loans for projects that must meet certain criteria designed to encourage economic development.

Summary

The financial system is the set of markets and intermediaries used by households, firms, and governments to implement their financial decisions. It includes the markets for stocks, bonds, and other securities, as well as financial intermediaries such as banks and insurance companies.

Funds flow through the financial system from entities that have a surplus of funds to those that have a deficit. Often these fund flows take place through a financial intermediary.

There are six core functions performed by the financial system:

- To provide ways to *transfer economic resources* through time, across borders, and among industries.
- To provide ways of *managing risk*.
- To provide ways of *clearing and settling payments* to facilitate trade.
- To provide a mechanism for the *pooling of resources* and for the *subdividing* of shares in various enterprises.
- To provide *price information* to help coordinate decentralized decision making in various sectors of the economy.
- To provide ways of *dealing with the incentive problems* created when one party to a transaction has information that the other party does not or when one party acts as agent for another.

The fundamental economic force behind financial innovation is competition, which generally leads to improvements in the way financial functions are performed.

The basic types of financial assets traded in markets are *debt, equity,* and *derivatives:*

- Debt instruments are issued by anyone who borrows money—firms, governments, and households.
- Equity is the claim of the owners of a firm. Equity securities issued by corporations are called common stocks.
- Derivatives are financial instruments such as options and futures contracts that derive their value from the prices of one or more other assets.

An interest rate is a promised rate of return, and there are as many different interest rates as there are distinct kinds of borrowing and lending. Interest rates vary depending on the unit of account, the maturity, and the default risk of the credit instrument. A *nominal* interest rate is denominated in units of some currency; a *real* interest rate is denominated in units of some commodity or basket of goods and services. Bonds that offer a fixed nominal interest rate have an uncertain real rate of return; and inflation-indexed bonds offering a fixed real interest rate have an uncertain nominal rate of return.

There are four main factors that determine rates of return in a market economy:

- *productivity of capital goods*—expected rates of return on mines, dams, roads, bridges, factories, machinery, and inventories;
- *degree of uncertainty regarding the productivity of capital goods;*
- *time preferences of people*—the preference of people for consumption now versus consumption in the future; and
- *risk aversion*—the amount people are willing to give up in order to reduce their exposure to risk.

Indexing is an investment strategy that seeks to match the returns of a specified stock market index.

Financial intermediaries are firms whose primary business is to provide customers with financial products that cannot be obtained more efficiently by transacting directly in securities markets. Among the main types of intermediaries are banks, investment companies, and insurance companies. Their products include checking accounts, loans, mortgages, mutual funds, and a wide range of insurance contracts.

Key Terms

- over-the-counter markets   22
- flow of funds   23
- moral hazard   30
- adverse selection   31
- life annuities   31
- principal-agent problem   32
- collateralization   32
- fixed-income instruments   35
- money market   35
- capital market   35
- liquidity   35
- residual claim   35
- limited liability   35
- derivatives   35
- call option   36
- put option   36
- forward contracts   36
- mortgage rate   36
- commercial loan rate   36
- unit of account   36
- maturity   36
- default risk   36
- exchange rate   37
- yield curve   38

Answers to Quick Check Questions

Quick Check 2-1   *A depositor puts $5,000 into a bank account and you take a $5,000 student loan from the bank. Trace this flow of funds in Figure 2.1.*

ANSWER: The funds flow from the depositor (a surplus unit) to a financial intermediary, and then from the intermediary to you (a deficit unit).

Quick Check 2-2   *Give an example of a transfer of resources over time that takes place through the financial system. Is there a more efficient way for this transfer of resources to be handled?*

ANSWER: An example would be a young person saving for his or her own retirement by saving money in a bank account. A more efficient way might be for the individual to save for retirement through an insurance company or mutual fund retirement account whose sole function is to provide retirement income.

Quick Check 2-3   *Give an example of a transfer of risk that takes place through the financial system.*

ANSWER: Whenever anyone buys an insurance policy, risk is being transferred.

Quick Check 2-4   *Would you accept an IOU from me in payment for a good or service that I buy from you? What factors will determine the answer?*

ANSWER: The answer depends upon the size of the transaction and the nature of the IOU. If our transaction is very small in size, I will be less concerned with the riskiness of the IOU, as my exposure is small. However, for larger transactions, I would want a guarantee of your IOU from a financial institution. I would accept payment by credit card because I am sure to receive payment from the bank issuing the credit card, but I might not be willing to accept a personal check unless you are a long-standing customer with whom I have done a lot of business.

Quick Check 2-5   *Give an example of an investment that would not be undertaken if it were not possible to pool the savings of many different households.*

ANSWER: Any investment that requires a large minimum investment to complete. One example would be a bridge or a dam.

Quick Check 2-6   *Give an example of a financial transaction that provides important information to parties not involved in the transaction.*

ANSWER: Whenever shares of stock are traded on a competitive stock market, information is being conveyed to everyone who can observe the price about how much investors think the stock is worth.

Quick Check 2-7   *Give an example of how the problem of moral hazard might prevent you from getting financing for something you want to do. Can you think of a way of overcoming the problem?*

ANSWER: If you ask a bank to lend you 100% of the funds you need to enter a certain business venture, the bank may refuse for fear that you will take large risks with its money. One way of overcoming the problem is to offer the bank additional collateral— your own personal assets—or a third-party guarantee of the loan.

Quick Check 2-8   *Suppose a bank offered to make loans to potential borrowers without checking their credit history. What would be true of the types of borrowers they would attract compared with banks that did check credit history? Would such a bank charge the same interest rate on loans as banks that check credit history?*

ANSWER: The bank that did no credit checks would attract borrowers with a higher probability of defaulting on their loans. To survive as a viable business such a bank would have to charge higher interest rates.

Quick Check 2-9   *If you get financial planning advice from your insurance agent, how does this give rise to a principal-agent problem? Can you think of a way of overcoming the problem?*

ANSWER: Insurance agents want you to buy insurance products on which they earn commissions, even if those products are not necessarily in your best interest. To avoid this conflict of interest you should seek financial advice from a qualified adviser who does not profit from selling you a particular financial product other than good advice.

Quick Check 2-10   *What are the defining features of debt, equity, and derivative securities?*

ANSWER: Debt instruments are issued by anyone who borrows money. Equity is the claim of the owners of a firm. Derivatives are financial instruments that derive their value from the prices of one or more other assets such as equity securities, fixed-income securities, foreign currencies, or commodities.

Quick Check 2-11   *In the previous example, what does the change in the exchange rate have to be at year's end for the Japanese investor to earn exactly 3% per year on the investment in U.K. bonds?*

ANSWER:

$$\frac{109 \times \text{Future Yen Price of the Pound} - 15,000}{15,000} = 0.03$$

Future yen price of pound = 141.74 yen per pound

Quick Check 2-12   *Look in the financial pages of today's newspaper and discover what the level and shape of the U.S. Treasury yield curve are. Do the same for the Japanese Treasury yield curve.*

ANSWER: Answers will vary.

Quick Check 2-13   *Look in the financial pages of today's newspaper and discover what the yield spreads are between corporate bonds and U.S. Treasury bonds.*

ANSWER: Answers will vary.

Quick Check 2-14   *You invest in a stock costing $50. It pays a cash dividend during the year of $1, and you expect its price to be $60 at year's end. What is your expected* *rate of return? If the stock's price is actually $40 at year's end, what is your realized rate of return?*

ANSWER:

$$\text{Expected Rate of Return} = \frac{\$1 + \$60 - \$50}{\$50} = 0.22 \text{ or } 22\%$$

$$\text{Realized Rate of Return} = \frac{\$1 + \$40 - \$50}{\$50} = -0.18 \text{ or } -18\%$$

Quick Check 2-15 *Suppose the risk-free nominal interest rate on a one-year U.S. Treasury bill is 6% per year and the expected rate of inflation is 3% per year. What is the expected real rate of return on the T-bill? Why is the T-bill risky in real terms?*

ANSWER: Real interest rate = 2.913%

Because the actual inflation rate is not known when the nominal interest rate is set, investors can never know for certain what their real return will be (it will depend on what inflation actually turns out to be).

Quick Check 2-16 *Suppose that the real rate of interest on TIPS is 3.5% per year and the expected rate of inflation in the United States is 4% per year. What is the expected nominal rate of return on these bonds?*

ANSWER: (1 + nominal rate) = (1 + real rate) × (1 + inflation rate); hence, nominal rate = 1.035 × 1.04 − 1 = 0.0764 or 7.64%

Quick Check 2-17 *Suppose you have $10,000 in a bank account earning an interest rate of 3% per year. At the same time you have an unpaid balance on your credit card of $5,000 on which you are paying an interest rate of 17% per year. What is the arbitrage opportunity you face?*

ANSWER: You could take $5,000 out of your bank account and pay down your credit-card balance. You would give up 3% per year in interest earnings ($150 per year), but you would save 17% per year in interest expenses ($850 per year). So the arbitrage opportunity is worth $700 per year.

Quick Check 2-18 *What are the fundamental determinants of the rate of interest?*

ANSWER:

- The *productivity of capital goods*—expected rates of return on mines, dams, roads, bridges, factories, machinery, and inventories;
- the *degree of uncertainty regarding the productivity of capital goods;*
- *time preferences of people*—the preference of people for consumption now versus consumption in the future; and
- *risk aversion*—the amount people are willing to give up in order to reduce their exposure to risk.

Questions and Problems

1. Do you agree with Adam Smith's view that society can rely more on the "invisible hand" than on government to promote economic prosperity?
2. How does the financial system contribute to economic security and prosperity in a capitalist society?

3. Give an example of how each of the six functions of the financial system are performed more efficiently today than they were in the time of Adam Smith (1776).

4. How does a competitive stock market accomplish the result that Adam Smith describes? Should the stock market be regulated? How and why?

5. Would you be able to get a student loan without someone else offering to guarantee it?

6. Give an example of a new business that would not be able to get financing if insurance against risk were not available.

7. Suppose you invest in a real estate development deal. The total investment is $100,000. You invest $20,000 of your own money and borrow the other $80,000 from a bank. Who bears the risk of this venture and why?

8. You are living in the United States and are thinking of traveling to Germany six months from now. You can purchase an option to buy marks now at a fixed rate of $0.75 per mark six months from now. How is the option like an insurance policy?

9. Give an example of how the problem of moral hazard might prevent you from getting financing for something you want to do. Can you think of a way of overcoming the problem?

10. Give an example of how the problem of adverse selection might prevent you from getting financing for something you want to do. Can you think of a way of overcoming the problem?

11. Give an example of how the principal-agent problem might prevent you from getting financing for something you want to do. Can you think of a way of overcoming the problem?

12. Why is it that a country's postage stamps are not as good a medium of exchange as its paper currency?

13. Who is hurt if I issue counterfeit U.S. dollars and use them to purchase valuable goods and services?

14. Some say the only criterion to use in predicting what will serve as money in the future is the real resource cost of producing it, including the transaction costs of verifying its authenticity. According to this criterion, what do you think will be the money of the future?

15. Should all governments issue debt that is indexed to their domestic price level? Is there a moral hazard problem that citizens face with regard to their public officials when government debt is fixed in units of the domestic currency?

16. Describe your country's system for financing higher education. What are the roles played by households, voluntary nonprofit organizations, businesses, and government?

17. Describe your country's system for financing residential housing. What are the roles played by households, businesses, and government?

18. Describe your country's system for financing new enterprises. What are the roles played by households, businesses, and government?

19. Describe your country's system for financing medical research. What are the roles played by voluntary nonprofit institutions, businesses, and government?

20. Assume there are only two stocks traded in the stock market, and you are trying to construct an index to show what has happened to stock prices. Let us say that in the base year the prices were $20 per share for stock 1 with 100 million shares outstanding and $10 for stock 2 with 50 million shares outstanding. A year later, the

prices are $30 per share for stock 1 and $2 per share for stock 2. Using the two different methods explained in the chapter, compute stock indexes showing what has happened to the overall stock market. Which of the two methods do you prefer and why? (See appendix that follows.)

A P P E N D I X   A

Alternative Stock Market Indexes

In the United States, perhaps the stock index most often cited in the news is the Dow Jones Industrial Index (DJI). It is an index of the prices of 30 stocks of major industrial U.S. corporations. The DJI has two major defects that limit its usefulness as a benchmark for measuring stock performance. One is that it is not broadly diversified enough to accurately reflect the wide spectrum of stocks in the United States. The other is that it corresponds to a portfolio strategy that is unsuitable as a performance benchmark.

Most investment professionals, therefore, prefer to use other indexes such as the Standard and Poor's 500 (S&P 500) as a performance benchmark. The S&P 500 index corresponds to a portfolio of 500 stocks selected from among the largest public corporations in the United States, with dollar amounts invested in each in proportion to their shares of the total market value.

To illustrate the construction of these two types of indexes and to compare them, let us simplify matters by analyzing a hypothetical two-stock index. The two stocks in the index are IBM and DEC. The relevant data on the two stocks are presented in Table 2A.1.

The DJI-type index is computed by taking the average current price of a share, dividing by the average price in the base year, and multiplying the result by 100.

$$\text{DJI-Type Index} = \frac{\text{Average of Current Stock Prices}}{\text{Average of Stock Prices in Base Year}} \times 100$$

Let us say that in the base year the prices were $100 per share for IBM and $50 for DEC. The average price per share, computed by adding the two prices and dividing by 2, is, therefore, $75. A year later, the prices are $50 per share for IBM and $110 per share for DEC, and the average is $80. The DJI-type index would, therefore, show a value of 106.67, indicating an increase of 6.67%.

$$\text{DJI-Type Index} = \frac{(50 + 110)/2}{(100 + 50)/2} \times 100 = \frac{80}{75} \times 100 = 106.67$$

TABLE 2A.1 Data for Constructing Stock Price Indexes

Company	Stock Price		Number of Shares	Market Value	
	Base Year	Now		Base Year	Now
IBM	$100	$50	200 million	$20 billion	$10 billion
DEC	$50	$110	100 million	$5 billion	$11 billion
			Total	$25 billion	$21 billion

The DJI-type index assumes that the benchmark portfolio consists of one share of each stock. Had investors bought one share of IBM stock and one share of DEC in the base year, then their portfolio would have increased in value by 6.67%. Such a portfolio is not a natural benchmark for measuring performance, because the total value of all stocks declined from $25 million to $21 million in our example, which is a 16% decline.

Investment professionals typically use a market-weighted index as a benchmark for measuring the performance of common stock mutual funds. **Market-weighted stock indexes** represent the price performance of a portfolio that holds each stock in proportion to its total market value. In the preceding example, IBM accounted for 80% of the total value of the stock market and DEC for 20%. A market-weighted index gives each stock these weights:

$$\text{S\&P-Type Index} = \left(\text{Weight of IBM} \times \frac{\text{Current Price of IBM}}{\text{IBM's Price in Base Year}} + \right.$$
$$\left. \text{Weight of DEC} \times \frac{\text{Current Price of DEC}}{\text{DEC's Price in Base Year}} \right) \times 100$$
$$= (0.8 \times 0.5 + 0.2 \times 2.2) \times 100 = 84$$

Thus, this index shows a 16% decline, which accurately reflects what has happened to the total market value of all stocks.

APPENDIX B

Sources of Financial Data

Thanks to the Internet, there is a vast amount of free information about the financial system that is accessible at the click of a computer mouse. Our companion website (http://www.prenhall.com/bodie/) has links to many of these online sources of information. Here is a list of some of them:

- Flow of Funds Accounts of the United States
  http://www.bog.frb.fed.us/releases/zl/data.htm
- U.S. and International Government yield curves
  http://www.bloomberg.com/markets/iyc.html
- Craig Holden's interactive yield-curve spreadsheet
  http://www.kelley.iu.edu/finweb/Software.html

CHAPTER 3

Interpreting and Forecasting Financial Statements

OBJECTIVES

- To contrast the economic and accounting models of the firm.
- To show how accounting information can be useful to the financial decision maker when used with care.
- To understand the purpose and process of financial planning.
- To understand why firms need working capital and how to manage it to maximize shareholder value.

CONTENTS

Much of the information about businesses and other organizations available to financial decision makers comes in the form of standard financial statements published in annual and quarterly reports to shareholders. These financial statements—balance sheets, income statements, and statements of cash flow—are prepared according to rules established by the accounting profession, and it is, therefore, important to understand what those rules are. But financial analysts sometimes disagree with how the accounting profession has decided to measure certain key financial variables. The most fundamental disagreement is about how to measure the values of assets and liabilities.

In this chapter we review basic financial statements and show how to use them as templates for financial planning. We begin by reviewing current accounting rules. We then examine how accounting measures of value and income can differ from the underlying economic concepts needed to make good financial decisions. We then construct a financial planning model for a typical manufacturing firm starting from the firm's financial statements for the last few years. Finally, we discuss short-term planning and the management of working capital.

3.1 FUNCTIONS OF FINANCIAL STATEMENTS

Financial statements serve three important economic functions:

- *They provide information to the owners and creditors of the firm about the company's current status and past financial performance.*

Although published financial statements rarely provide enough information to enable one to form conclusive judgments about a company's performance, they can provide important clues about aspects of a firm's operations that should be examined more carefully. Sometimes through a careful audit of financial statements it is possible to detect mismanagement and even fraud. For example, by analyzing financial statements an accounting professor uncovered fraud in one of his university's investments (see Box 3.1).

- *Financial statements provide a convenient way for owners and creditors to set performance targets and to impose restrictions on the managers of the firm.*

Financial statements are used by boards of directors to specify performance targets for management. For example, the board might set targets in terms of a growth rate of accounting earnings or return on equity (*ROE*). Creditors often specify restrictions on management's actions in terms of measures like the ratio of current assets to current liabilities.

- *Financial statements provide convenient templates for financial planning.*

By preparing projections of income statements, balance sheets, and statements of cash flow for the company as a whole, managers can check the overall consistency of separate plans made on a project-by-project basis and estimate the firm's total financing requirements. Although other templates can be substituted for standard financial statements in the planning process, a major advantage of using standard income statements and balance sheets is that the people involved are probably familiar with them from their professional education and training.

Quick Check 3-1
What are the three basic economic functions served by financial statements?

Accountant Blows Lid Off New Era

When Albert J. Meyer moved to Spring Arbor, Michigan, from his native South Africa four years ago, he and his wife came in search of a new cultural experience apart from the hectic pace of major U.S. cities. Settling to teach accounting at Spring Arbor College, a small Christian school in rural Michigan, he wasn't expecting to stir up a hornet's nest over something called Foundation for New Era Philanthropy.

But with a penchant for running down even seemingly innocuous financial details, a characteristic he attributes largely to the training in auditing he underwent to become a chartered accountant, Meyer followed a trail of what he considered suspicious data entries that led him to believe what no one else in his college community at first would believe: that the money Spring Arbor was donating to New Era was possibly supporting a huge Ponzi scheme.

Under a Ponzi scheme, money from new investors is used to pay off old investors, which is how New Era allegedly managed since 1989 to make good on its promise to double whatever money it received on behalf of charities. It claimed to keep the money it received for six months, investing it in Treasury notes to earn interest for paying New Era's operating expenses while it gathered matching donations from so-called anonymous donors. The scheme began to fall apart once incoming funds were insufficient to cover its obligations. New Era's assets are now being liquidated

by a court-appointed trustee, and the SEC has reported evidence that New Era's director, John G. Bennet, Jr., siphoned off millions for his own closely held entity.

Financial smoking gun

Meyer's trail began during his time as a part-time accountant in the college's business office. His first suspicion occurred when he noticed a $296,000 disbursement, which he figured was a material amount for a small college, to the Heritage of Values Foundation. But what sealed the proof for him was when he acquired the financial statement for the year ended December 31, 1993, which was unaudited, on New Era from the Bureau of Charitable Organizations. A careful look made it clear that New Era's numbers just didn't add up. "It treated what I thought were investments as gifts to New Era, so they were shown as revenues and he showed no liabilities," Meyer said.

The financial statement showed that New Era had placed $1.1 million in nonmarketable equity securities, which suggested to Meyer that it had been put into a closely held corporation controlled by Bennett. This suspicion was corroborated by a check with New Era's 990 tax form, which included a reference to a closely held corporation called The Bennett Group International, LTD.

Source: Paul Demery, *The Practical Accountant* (July 1995), pp. 6, 8.

3.2 REVIEW OF FINANCIAL STATEMENTS

To explain the three basic financial statements, we will use the hypothetical example of Generic Products Corporation (GPC). GPC is a company that was founded 10 years ago to manufacture and sell generic products for the consumer market.

Tables 3.1, 3.2, and 3.3 show GPC's balance sheet, income statement, and statement of cash flows. They are fairly typical of a U.S. manufacturing firm. Let us consider each in turn.

3.2.1 The Balance Sheet

A firm's balance sheet shows its assets (what it owns) and its liabilities (what it owes) at a point in time. The difference between assets and liabilities is the firm's net worth, also called owners' equity. For a corporation, net worth is called stockholder's equity.

The values of assets, liabilities, and net worth carried on a company's published balance sheet are measured at historical acquisition costs in accordance with generally accepted accounting principles, otherwise known as GAAP. These rules (GAAP) are determined and modified periodically by the Financial Accounting Standards Board. Any U.S. or non-U.S. corporation that wishes to list its shares on an exchange in the United States must conform with the accounting standards and report regularly on its activities by filing financial statements with the Securities and Exchange Commission.

Table 3.1 presents GPC's balance sheet at two different points in time that bracket the year 20x1. Let us first examine the balance sheet on December 31, 20x0, just before the start of 20x1.

The first section of the balance sheet lists the assets of the firm, beginning with its current assets, defined as cash and other items that will be converted into cash within one year. In GPC's case, cash and marketable securities are valued at $100 million. The other current assets consist of $50 million in receivables, which is the amount owed to GPC by customers, and $150 million in inventories. Inventories consist of raw materials, goods in process of production, and finished goods.

TABLE 3.1   GPC Balance Sheet on December 31

Assets	20x0	20x1	Change
Current assets			
Cash and marketable securities	100	120	20
Receivables	50	60	10
Inventories	150	180	30
Total current assets	300	360	60
Property, plant, and equipment (PP&E)	400	490	90
Accumulated depreciation	100	130	30
Net PP&E	300	360	60
Total assets	600	720	120

Liabilities and Stockholders' Equity			
Current liabilities			
Accounts payable	60.0	72.0	12.0
Short-term debt	90.0	184.6	94.6
Total current liabilities	150.0	256.6	106.6
Long-term debt (8% interest bonds maturing in 20x7)	150.0	150.0	0.0
Stockholders' equity (1 million shares outstanding)	300.0	313.4	13.4
Paid-in capital	200.0	200.0	0.0
Retained earnings	100.0	113.4	13.4
Other data: Market price per common share	$200.00	$187.20	−$12.80

All figures are in millions of U.S. dollars.

Next come GPC's noncurrent assets. These consist of property, plant, and equipment. The reported value of these assets net of depreciation is listed as $300 million. Total assets are $600 million.

Next come GPC's liabilities. Liabilities that must be paid off within a year are called current liabilities. For GPC these consist of $60 million in accounts payable, which is the amount owed to its suppliers, and $90 million in short-term debt.

The difference between a firm's current assets and its current liabilities is called net working capital. It does not explicitly appear as an item on the balance sheet. GPC's net working capital at the end of 20x0 was $150 million: current assets of $300 million less current liabilities of $150 million.

The next liability item on GPC's balance sheet is long-term debt, which consists of bonds with a face value of $150 million maturing in 20x7. The interest rate on these bonds is fixed at 8% per year, which means that each year the interest expense associated with them is $12 million. This interest expense shows up on GPC's income statement.

The final category on GPC's balance sheet is shareholders' equity. The paid-in capital, which is the amount that GPC raised in the past by issuing common stock, is $200 million, and the retained earnings, which is the cumulative amount of past earnings that have been retained in the business, is $100 million.

Let us now consider the changes in GPC's balance sheet between December 31, 20x0 and December 31, 20x1. During the year all assets grew by 20%, as did accounts payable. GPC's short-term debt increased by $94.6 million, and its long-term debt remained fixed at $150 million. Shareholders' equity increased by $13.4 million, which was the net income retained in the business. No new shares were issued, so paid-in capital stayed the same.

Quick Check 3-2

What difference would it have made to the end-of-year balance sheet if GPC had issued an additional $50 million in long-term debt during the year and added that amount to its holdings in cash and marketable securities?

3.2.2 The Income Statement

The income statement summarizes the profitability of the firm over a period of time, in this case a year. Income, profit, and earnings all mean the same thing—the difference between revenues and expenses. The income statement is also known as the statement of earnings or the statement of profit and loss. Table 3.2 shows that in 20x1 GPC had sales revenue of $200 million, and its net income was $23.4 million.

GPC's expenses are broken down into four major categories. The first is cost of goods sold, which was $110 million. This is the expense GPC incurred in producing the products it sold during the year, and includes the materials and labor used to manufacture them. The difference between revenues and cost of goods sold is called gross margin. GPC's gross margin in 20x1 was $90 million.

The second expense category is general, administrative, and selling (GS&A) expense. This represents the expenses incurred in managing the firm (such as the salaries of the managers) and in marketing and distributing the products produced during the year. The difference between gross margin and GS&A expenses is called

TABLE 3.2 GPC Income Statement for 20x1	
Sales revenue	200.0
Cost of goods sold	(110.0)
Gross margin	90.0
General, selling, and administrative expenses	(30.0)
Operating income	60.0
Interest expense	(21.0)
Taxable income	39.0
Income tax	(15.6)
Net income	23.4
Earnings per share (1 million shares outstanding)	23.4
Allocation of net income:	
Dividends	10.0
Change in retained earnings	13.4

All figures are in millions of U.S. dollars.

operating income. GPC's GS&A expenses in 20x1 were $30 million, and its operating income was, therefore, $60 million.

The third category of expense is the interest expense on GPC's debt, and in 20x1 it was $21 million. After deducting interest expense, GPC's taxable income (i.e., its income subject to corporate income tax) was $39 million.

The fourth and last category of expense is corporate income taxes. GPC paid taxes at an average rate of 40% on its taxable income in 20x1 and, therefore, its corporate income tax was $15.6 million. GPC's net income after taxes was, therefore, $23.4 million. Because there were 1 million shares of GPC stock outstanding, the earnings per share were $23.40.

The income statement also shows that GPC paid cash dividends of $10 million in 20x1. This means that $13.4 million of the net income is retained in the business and shows up as an increase in shareholders' equity in the balance sheet at the end of 20x1. It is important to note that this latter figure ($13.4 million) is not an addition to the cash balance of the firm because net income is not the same as cash flow.

> **Quick Check 3-3**
> What difference would it have made to the income statement and the end-of-year balance sheet if GPC had retained all of its net income instead of paying out cash dividends of $10 million?

3.2.3 The Cash Flow Statement

The statement of cash flows shows all of the cash that flowed into and out of the firm during a period of time. It differs from the income statement, which shows the firm's revenues and expenses.

The cash flow statement is a useful supplement to the income statement for two reasons. First, it focuses attention on what is happening to the firm's cash position over time. Even very profitable firms can experience financial distress if they run out of cash. Paying attention to the cash flow statement allows the firm's managers and outsiders to see whether the firm is building up or drawing down its cash and to understand why. Often, for example, rapidly growing, profitable firms run short of cash and have difficulty meeting their financial obligations.

The cash flow statement is also useful because it avoids the judgments about revenue and expense recognition that go into the income statement. The income statement is based on accrual accounting methods according to which not every revenue is an inflow of cash and not every expense is an outflow. A firm's reported net income is affected by many judgments on the part of management about issues such as how to value its inventory and how quickly to depreciate its tangible assets and amortize its intangible assets.

The statement of cash flows is not influenced by these accrual accounting decisions. Therefore, by examining the differences between the firm's cash flow statement and its income statement an analyst is able to determine the impact of these accounting decisions.

Let us illustrate by examining Table 3.3, which presents GPC's cash flow statement for 20x1. It organizes cash flows into three sections: operating activities, investing activities, and financing activities. Let us look at each section in turn.

Cash flow from operating activities (or cash flow from operations) consists of the cash inflows from selling the firm's products less the cash outflows for expenses such as materials and labor. GPC's cash flow from operations in 20xl is $25.4 million, whereas its net income is $23.4 million. Why are these two numbers different?

There are four items that explain the difference between a firm's net income and its cash flow from operations: depreciation charges, the change in accounts receivable, the change in inventories, and the change in accounts payable. Let us consider each of these items for the case of GPC in 20x1.

First, depreciation charges for 19xl were $30 million. This was a noncash expense deducted from revenues in computing net income. The cash outlays for the plant and equipment that gave rise to the depreciation charges occurred when they

TABLE 3.3 GPC Cash Flow Statement for 20x1	
Cash Flow from Operating Activities	
Net income	$23.4
+ Depreciation	+30.0
− Increase in accounts receivable	−10.0
− Increase in inventories	−30.0
+ Increase in accounts payable	+12.0
Total cash flow from operations	25.4
Cash Flow from Investing Activities	
− Investment in plant and equipment	−90.0
Cash Flow from Financing Activities	
− Dividends paid	−10.0
+ Increase in short-term debt	+94.6
Change in cash and marketable securities	20.0

were originally purchased, but the depreciation charges are recognized as an expense in each period over their assumed useful life. Therefore, to get from net income to cash flow from operations, we have to add back the depreciation charges.

The second item is an increase in accounts receivable of $10 million. This is the difference between the revenue recognized during the year and the actual cash collected from customers. The revenue figure of $200 million on the income statement means that $200 million worth of goods and services were shipped and billed to customers in 20x1, but only $190 million in cash was collected. Therefore, to get from net income to cash flow from operations, we have to subtract the $10 million increase in accounts receivable.

The third item is an increase in inventories of $30 million. This means the value of inventories at the end of the year was $30 million more than at the beginning. Thus, $30 million in cash was used to purchase or to produce goods that went into inventory. This cash outlay was not accounted for in computing net income. Therefore, to get from net income to cash flow from operations, we have to subtract the $30 million increase in inventories.

The fourth item is an increase in accounts payable of $12 million. This is the difference between GPC's cost of goods sold during the year ($110 million) and the amount of cash it paid to its suppliers and employees. In computing net income, the full $110 million was deducted, but in computing cash flow from operations only the $98 million in cash that it paid out should be deducted. Therefore, to go from net income to cash flow from operations, $12 million must be added back.

Thus, we can see that there is no reason to expect equality between cash flow from operations and net income. To reconcile the two measures, we must adjust net income for the four items detailed previously. Cash flow statements can be particularly important in making comparisons of companies reporting their net income in different countries that have different accrual accounting standards (see Box 3.2).

The second section of Table 3.3—cash flows from investing activities—shows GPC's $90 million cash outlay on new plant and equipment in 20x1. The third section—cash flows from financing activities—shows that GPC paid out $10 million in cash dividends to shareholders and raised $94.6 million in cash by increasing its short-term debt.

To summarize, the net impact on GPC's cash balances of its operating, investing, and financing activities was to increase cash by $20 million. GPC's operating activities produced $25.4 million in cash, and GPC increased its borrowing by $94.6 million, so a total of $120 million in cash flowed in. Of that amount, $90 million in cash was used to purchase new plant and equipment and $10 million was used to pay dividends.

Quick Check 3-4
What difference would it have made to the cash flow statement if GPC had retained all of its net income instead of paying out cash dividends of $10 million?

Table 3.4 presents a summary of the features of each of the three main financial statements.

BOX 3.2

Standardizing Global Accounting Rules

The London-based International Accounting Standards Committee hopes to achieve a single, unified set of international accounting rules that corporations anywhere can use to list on any stock market on the planet. This fall it will publish a full set of international rules. Market regulators around the world, including the U.S. Securities and Exchange Commission, will then have to decide whether to let foreign companies use the international rules to list on their stock markets.

The economic argument for standardizing global accounting rules is compelling. Right now, the United States blocks foreign companies from using their home countries' accounting rules to list on U.S. stock markets. Instead, foreign corporations have to report profits under U.S. accounting rules before listing their shares here. If a common set of international rules were accepted everywhere, it could help create a smoother jet stream of capital flows around the globe.

Clearly, investors need help cutting through the statistical fog surrounding myriad country-by-country accounting rules, which makes tracking the true earnings power of foreign companies an exercise akin to following gnats in a hurricane. In 1993, for example, British pharmaceuticals giant Smith-Kline Beecham PLC reported about $1.5 billion in profit under U.K. accounting standards. But the company would have reported about $1.2 billion under U.S. accounting rules because of differences in accounting for mergers and acquisitions in each country, according to the Association for Investment Management & Research in Charlottesville, Virginia. That same year, according to the Virginia group, British Airways would have reported about $353 million in profit under U.S. accounting standards, but it booked about $535 million under U. K. rules—a result of differences in accounting for deferred taxes.

China, Australia, and about 50 other countries, most of which have less stringent standards than the United States, welcome the global accounting rules. Gunther Forneck, spokesman for Bayer AG in Germany, says: "We intend to list on the New York Stock Exchange" once the SEC accepts the international rules. He may have a long wait. Although the rest of the world may embrace the new rules, Washington isn't ready to accept them because they create thorny political and regulatory problems.

Edmund Jenkins, chairman of the Financial Accounting Standards Board, the chief U.S. accounting rule maker, which the SEC oversees, says the U.S. rules still "give more information to investors that's of higher quality and greater consistency." U.S. companies, which are held to tougher domestic rules, will likely object if the SEC lets foreign companies list here using gentler international standards. "U.S. companies could rightfully argue why should they have to follow the more detailed, complex U.S. standards," says New York securities lawyer Joseph McLaughlin.

Nevertheless, pressure on the SEC, both here and abroad, to accept the international standards is increasing. The New York Stock Exchange, which stands to profit from additional foreign listings, supports the international effort.

Source: Elizabeth Macdonald, *The Outlook, The Wall Street Journal,* May 11, 1998, p. A1. Reprinted by permission of *The Wall Street Journal,* © 1998 Dow Jones & Company, Inc. All Rights Reserved Worldwide.

3.2.4 Notes to Financial Statements

When a corporation publishes its financial statements, it includes notes providing greater detail about the accounting methods it has used and the financial condition of the company. Frequently there is more information relevant to understanding the true financial condition of the company in the notes to the financial statements than in the statements themselves (see Box 3.3).

TABLE 3.4 Summary of Financial Statements

Balance Sheet

Assets = Liabilities + Stockholders' Equity

- A snapshot at a point in time of the value of the firm's assets and liabilities.
- Long-term assets given at historic cost, depreciated over time.

Income Statement

Net Income = Revenues − Expenses

- A record of the flow of revenues and related expenses over the period.
- Use of accrual principles implies that net income usually does not equal net cash flow.

Statement of Cash Flows

Total Cash Flow = Cash from Operating Activities + Cash from Financing Activities + Cash from Investing Activities

- A flow statement showing how much cash has flowed into and out of the firm over the period.
- Each source and use of cash is placed in one of three categories.

Some of the specific items commonly found in the notes are the following:

- *An explanation of accounting methods used.* Because firms are allowed some latitude in how to report certain costs (e.g., straight-line versus accelerated depreciation charges or LIFO versus FIFO inventory costing methods), the notes must explain which specific methods the company has actually employed. Moreover, accounting standards often change, and companies restate prior year results in the notes using the new standards.
- *Greater detail regarding certain assets or liabilities.* Notes provide details regarding the conditions and expiration dates for long- and short-term debt, leases, and the like.
- *Information regarding the equity structure of the firm.* Notes explain conditions attached to the ownership of shares, and these can be particularly useful for assessing the vulnerability of the firm to takeovers.
- *Documentation of changes in operations.* Two main activities that can have a great impact on financial statements are acquisitions and divestitures, and the notes explain the impact of these.
- *Off-balance-sheet items.* Financial contracts entered into by the firm that do not appear on the balance sheet, but that can profoundly affect its financial condition, are often disclosed in the notes. Among these are derivative contracts such as forward contracts, swaps, and options, which are typically used to reduce certain risk exposures.

Quick Check 3-5

What potentially important information about a firm can be found in the footnotes to its financial statements?

> **B O X   3 . 3**
>
> ## *A Footnote for Employee Stock Options*
>
> Each year, thousands of corporations give their executives and other employees options to buy shares of stock in their company as a reward for good performance or as an incentive to work harder for the company's shareholders. Accounting rules in the United States do not currently require companies to report the value of these options as an expense on their income statement.
>
> From January 1997 to June 1997 Dennis Beresford, now an accounting professor at the University of Georgia, was the chairman of the Financial Accounting Standards Board. During his tenure, FASB tried to figure a better way to account for the costs of burgeoning stock option plans on a company's financial statements. "It's hard to argue that they're any different from cash compensation or any other employee costs," says Beresford. "FASB felt it was a cost."
>
> The board tried to come up with a standard that would require companies to run option costs through their profit and loss statement. But the effort ended after the Big Six accounting firms and much of corporate America lobbied heavily against it. "The argument was: reduced earnings would translate to reduced stock prices," recalls Beresford of the brutal battle that finally buried the idea in 1995. "People said to me, 'If we have to record a reduction in income by 40%, our stock will go down by 40%, our options will be worthless, we won't be able to keep employees. It would destroy all American business and Western civilization,'" he says. The bull market was more important than accurate financial reporting.
>
> What the accounting board did come up with was a way to signal to shareholders the diminishing effect of stock options on earnings. But investors have to comb through the footnotes to a company's financial statements to find the data. There companies now report how their earnings might be affected by options held by employees. But FASB 123, as it's called, leaves lots of room for interpretation. As a result, investors can't be certain that all companies are valuing their options the same way.
>
> A study of the impact of employee stock options on the 100 largest U.S. companies was recently released by economic advisory firm Smithers & Co. in London. The study took six months of sleuthing. "The data were very difficult to get," says Smithers. "It's only in the footnotes to the financials in a company's 10-K. But we found the amount of hidden costs at these companies is significant." Here's their astonishing conclusion: If the 100 companies had charged the costs of option programs to their income statements, their profits in 1995 would have been on average 30% lower than those actually reported. In 1996 full cost accounting for options would have resulted in earnings 36% lower than stated. Eleven companies of the 100 would have shown a loss in 1996 had they run the cost of options through the income statement.
>
> *Source:* Adapted from Gretchen Morgenson, "Stock Options Are Not a Free Lunch," *Forbes,* May 18, 1998, p. 212. Reprinted by Permission of Forbes Magazine © Forbes Inc., 1999.

3.3 MARKET VALUES VERSUS BOOK VALUES

The official accounting values of assets and shareholders' equity are called **book values.** A company's book value per share is the number we get if we divide the total dollar amount in the shareholders' equity account of the firm's official balance sheet by the number of shares of common stock outstanding.[1]

---

[1]Note that shares outstanding do not include Treasury stock, which are shares of stock that the firm has repurchased.

Thus, in Table 3.1 we see that the book value per share of GPC stock at the end of 20x1 was $313.40. But the market price of a share of GPC stock at the end of 20x1 was only $187.50. This was the price that investors were willing to pay for a share of GPC common stock. The market value of the stock does not appear on the official balance sheet.

Why doesn't the market price of a company's stock equal its book value? And which of the two values is more relevant to the financial decision maker? We now turn our attention to these important questions.

There are essentially two reasons why the market price of a company's stock does not necessarily equal its book value:

- The book value does not include all of a firm's assets and liabilities.

- The assets and liabilities included on a firm's official balance sheet are (for the most part) valued at original acquisition cost less depreciation, rather than at current market values.

Let us consider each of these reasons separately.

First, the accounting balance sheet often omits some economically significant assets. For example, if a firm builds up a good reputation for the quality and reliability of its products, this will not appear as an asset on the balance sheet. Similarly, if a firm builds up a knowledge base as the result of past research and development spending or as the result of training its workforce, these too will not appear as assets. These kinds of assets are called **intangible assets,** and clearly they add to the firm's market value and are relevant in decision making.

Accountants do report some intangible assets on the balance sheet, but not at their market values. For example, if a firm buys a patent from another firm, the value of that patent is recorded as an asset and amortized over time. Also, when one firm acquires another firm for a price that exceeds its book value, accountants will record an intangible asset called **goodwill** on the balance sheet of the acquiring firm. The value of goodwill is the difference between the market price of the acquisition and its book value. Despite these cases of intangible assets that are recorded on the accounting balance sheet, many others are not.

The accounting balance sheet also omits some economically significant liabilities. For example, if the firm has lawsuits pending against it, these will not appear on the balance sheet. The existence and amount of such contingent liabilities will at best only be disclosed in the footnotes to the financial statements.

Now let us consider whether it is market value or book value that is relevant for financial decision making. In almost all cases, book values are irrelevant. For example, say three years ago IBM purchased equipment needed for molding computer shells for $3.9 million and today the equipment is carried on its books at $2.6 million, after three years of depreciation. But today, owing to technological change in the manufacture of computer shells, the market value of the machine has fallen to $1.2 million.

Now suppose you are considering replacing the equipment with more modern equipment. What is the relevant value to use to compare the alternatives? If we ignore tax considerations for the moment, we know from first principles in economics that the relevant value is the asset's opportunity cost, which is the asset's value in the best alternative use. Clearly, this value is best approximated by the market value of the equipment of $1.2 million, whereas the book value is essentially irrelevant.

As another example, let us consider your inventory of copper to be used in the manufacturing process of heating furnaces. You paid $29,000 at the beginning of the year for the copper, but today its market value has risen to $60,000. What is the relevant cost to include for the copper in your production decisions? Again, the original cost of $29,000 is not meaningful because the copper could be sold and to replace the inventory will cost $60,000. If you use the copper in production, you are actually using up $60,000 worth of resources.

The difference in value between the two measures can vary drastically depending on the situation. For example, in the case of cash there is literally no difference between book value and market value. In the case of fixed assets, such as specialized plant and equipment, the difference can be, and often is, huge. Thus, the difference between the market and book values of an asset depends on the type of asset. Again, for decision-making purposes, the correct value to use is the market value, whenever available.

It is worth noting that the accounting profession has moved slowly toward market-value–based accounting in an effort to be more relevant to decision makers. For example, assets held by corporations in their pension funds are now reported at current market values rather than acquisition cost. Revaluing and reporting a firm's assets and liabilities at their current market prices is called **marking to market.**

Quick Check 3-6

Why does the market price of a firm's stock usually differ from its book value?

3.4 ACCOUNTING VERSUS ECONOMIC MEASURES OF INCOME

The distinctions made about market values and book values carry over to our notions of income. A commonsense definition of income is the amount that you could spend during the period while maintaining the wealth with which you started the period. That is, what you could spend from incoming cash and still have the amount you started with remaining at the end of the period. Loosely speaking, this is the definition that the English Nobel Prize–winning economist John R. Hicks used in his classic treatise on the subject and the one that is generally used today by economists.[2] The accounting definition of income or earnings or profits (which all mean the same thing) ignores unrealized gains or losses in the market values of assets and liabilities, such as the increase or decrease in value of your shares of stock or the value of your property over the period.

As an example, suppose your net wages over the year were $100,000, which you spent on your family consumption, but your assets overall declined in value by $60,000. Generally speaking, accountants would ignore the decline in the market value of your assets because it is unrealized. The economist, on the other hand, would say that the decline in value must be counted in the income calculation because it affects your consumption possibilities, which are currently $60,000 less than at the beginning of the year. Thus, your income is only $40,000.

One other feature, often overlooked, is that accounting income allows as an income deduction the interest expense for the cost of borrowed funds, but not a

---

[2]J. R. Hicks, *Value and Capital,* 2nd ed. (New York: Oxford University Press, 1946), p. 172.

BOX 3.4

Economic Value Added

A relatively new performance measure adopted by some corporations in the United States is economic value added (EVA). Developed by Stern Stewart and Co., the measure's principal advantage is that it takes into account the imputed cost of equity when calculating EVA. Specifically, EVA is defined as net after-tax operating profit minus a charge for the capital employed to produce those profits. The capital charge is the minimum (required) rate of return needed to compensate the firm's investors, both debt and equity. By identifying equity capital costs explicitly, it may be useful in allocating capital more efficiently and in identifying uneconomic cross-subsidiaries among business units, in which a profitable business unit subsidizes another unit that is unprofitable. It may help corporate managers see where value is being created and thereby allow them to manage more effectively. EVA and its counterpart, *market value added* (MVA), are used to guide acquisitions, divestitures and new-product introductions, among other strategic decisions.

Numerous companies, including AT&T, Quaker Oats, Briggs & Stratton, and Coca-Cola, are now using EVA to evaluate the performance of management. For example, a transportation company, such as CSX Corporation, which had lots of capital employed in fleets of locomotives, trailers, railcars, rights-of-way, and trucks, must recognize that the capital financing of these assets has a cost and must be taken into account when making economic decisions. By recognizing these costs within an EVA framework, CSX reports it was actually able to make decisions such as to sell off certain assets, enhancing efficiency and greatly improving the value of its stock. Although clearly an improvement over EPS growth and return on equity (ROE) as measures of performance, you should recognize that EVA is essentially a modified-accounting–based technique.

comparable deduction for the equity funds employed. For example, if a company earned $2 million but used $50 million in shareholders' equity to finance the firm's assets at an approximate cost of 10% then from an economic perspective the firm incurred a loss of about $3 million (i.e., $2m − $50m × 0.10 = $0.3m). Here is a case in which the accounting profit is positive but the firm is not covering its basic costs, including its costs of capital (see Box 3.4).

3.5 RETURNS TO SHAREHOLDERS VERSUS RETURN ON BOOK EQUITY

When shareholders of a corporation ask how well their company performed in a particular period (a quarter, a year, or several years), they mean by how much did the company add to their personal wealth in that period. A direct way to measure this is to compute the rate of return on an investment in the company's stock over the period. Recall from chapter 2 that we defined the rate of return from investing in a firm's stock as:

$$r = \frac{\text{Ending Price of a Share} - \text{Beginning Price} + \text{Cash Dividend}}{\text{Beginning Price}}$$

This is called **total shareholder returns.**

For example, consider the case of GPC Corp. From observed market data, we know that at the beginning of 20x1 GPC had a market price of $200 per share and at the end of the year after paying dividends the market price was $187.20 per share. Cash dividends for the year were $10; the rate of return on an investment in GPC's stock in 20x1 was, therefore, –1.4% computed as follows:

$$\text{Total Shareholder Returns} = \frac{\$187.20 - \$200 + \$10}{\$200} = -0.014 \text{ or } -1.4\%$$

Traditionally, however, corporate performance has also been measured by looking at a ratio called the *return on equity* (*ROE*). *ROE* is defined as net profit (the bottom line from the company's income statement) divided by the book value of shareholders' equity (the bottom line from the firm's balance sheet).

For GPC's *ROE* we get:

$$ROE = \frac{\text{Net Income}}{\text{Shareholders' Equity}} = \frac{\$23.4 \text{ million}}{\$300 \text{ million}} = 0.078 \text{ or } 7.8\%$$

Thus, we see that there need be no correspondence between a firm's *ROE* in any year and the total rate of return earned by shareholders on their investment in the company's stock.

Quick Check 3-7

In 20x7 VGI Corporation reported earnings per share of $5 and paid a cash dividend to shareholders of $3.00 per share. Its beginning-of-year book value per share was $30, and its market price was $40. At the end of the year, the book value per share was $32 and the market price was $35. Compare VGI's *ROE* and total shareholder returns.

3.6 ANALYSIS USING FINANCIAL RATIOS

Despite the differences between accounting and finance principles and practices listed previously, a firm's published financial statements can often offer some clues about its financial condition and insights into its past performance that may be relevant for the future. In analyzing a firm's performance using its financial statements, it is helpful to define a set of ratios to facilitate comparisons over time and across companies.

We can analyze five main aspects of the firm's performance through ratios: profitability, asset turnover, financial leverage, liquidity, and market value. In Table 3.5 we present these ratios, and calculate them for GPC.

First are *profitability* ratios. Profitability can be measured with respect to sales (return on sales), assets (return on assets), or its equity base (return on equity). Income here is taken as earnings before interest and taxes (*EBIT*) in the case of return on sales and return on assets, but as net income in the case of return on equity. Also, whenever a financial ratio contains one item from the income statement, which covers a period of time, and another from the balance sheet, which is a "snapshot" at a point in time, the practice is to take the average of the beginning and end-of-year balance sheet figures, and use this average as the denominator.

Second are *asset turnover* ratios, which assess the firm's ability to use its assets productively in generating revenue. Asset turnover is a broad measure, whereas

TABLE 3.5   Classification of Financial Ratios

Ratio	Formula	Calculation	
Profitability			
Return on sales (*ROS*)	$\dfrac{EBIT}{\text{Sales}}$	$\dfrac{\$60}{\$200}$	$= 30\%$
Return on assets (*ROA*)	$\dfrac{EBIT}{\text{Average Total Assets}}$	$\dfrac{\$60}{(\$600 + \$720)/2}$	$= 9.1\%$
Return on equity (*ROE*)	$\dfrac{\text{Net Income}}{\text{Stockholders' Equity}}$	$\dfrac{\$23.4}{(\$300 + \$313.4)/2}$	$= 7.6\%$
Asset Turnover			
Receivables turnover	$\dfrac{\text{Sales}}{\text{Average Receivables}}$	$\dfrac{\$200}{(\$50 + \$60)/2}$	$= 3.6 \text{ times}$
Inventory turnover	$\dfrac{\text{Cost of Goods Sold}}{\text{Average Inventory}}$	$\dfrac{\$110}{(\$150 + \$180)/2}$	$= 0.7 \text{ times}$
Asset turnover	$\dfrac{\text{Sales}}{\text{Average Total Assets}}$	$\dfrac{\$200}{(\$600 + \$720)/2}$	$= 0.3 \text{ times}$
Financial Leverage			
Debt	$\dfrac{\text{Total Debt}}{\text{Total Assets}}$	$\dfrac{\$406.6}{\$720}$	$= 57\%$
Times interest earned	$\dfrac{EBIT}{\text{Interest Expense}}$	$\dfrac{\$60}{\$21}$	$= 2.9 \text{ times}$
Liquidity			
Current	$\dfrac{\text{Current Assets}}{\text{Current Liabilities}}$	$\dfrac{\$360}{\$256.6}$	$= 1.4 \text{ times}$
Quick, or acid test	$\dfrac{\text{Cash} + \text{Receivables}}{\text{Current Liabilities}}$	$\dfrac{\$180}{\$256.6}$	$= 0.7 \text{ times}$
Market Value			
Price to earnings	$\dfrac{\text{Price per Share}}{\text{Earnings per Share}}$	$\dfrac{\$187.20}{\$23.4}$	$= 8.0$
Market to book	$\dfrac{\text{Price per Share}}{\text{Book Value per Share}}$	$\dfrac{\$187.20}{\$313.4}$	$= 0.6$

receivable turnover and inventory turnover are specific measures for these particular asset categories.

Third, *financial leverage* ratios highlight the capital structure of the firm, and the extent to which it is burdened with debt. The debt ratio measures the capital structure, and the times interest earned measure indicates the ability of the firm to cover its interest payments.

Fourth, *liquidity* ratios measure the ability of the firm to meet its short-term obligations, or to pay its bills and remain solvent. The main ratios for measuring liquidity are the current ratio and the more stringent quick ratio or acid test, which considers only the most liquid of current assets: cash and marketable securities.

Profit Margin

Fifth are *market value* ratios, which measure the relation between the accounting representation of the firm and the market value of the firm. The two most common ratios are price to earnings (*P/E*) and market to book (*M/B*).[3]

When analyzing a firm's financial ratios, we need first to establish two things:

- whose perspective to adopt—shareholders, creditors, or some other group of stakeholders.
- what standard of comparison to use as a benchmark.

Benchmarks can be of three types:

- financial ratios of other companies for the same period of time.
- financial ratios of the company itself in previous time periods.
- information extracted from financial markets such as asset prices or interest rates.

A variety of sources are available that produce ratios for a number of industries, including (1) Dun & Bradstreet, (2) *Annual Statement Studies* by Robert Morris Associates, (3) the Commerce Department's *Quarterly Financial Report,* and (4) trade associations. Additionally, these data have become available on compact discs and on-line via the Internet.

Quick Check 3-8

What are the five types of financial ratios used to analyze a company's performance?

3.6.1 The Relations among Ratios

It is useful to decompose a firm's *ROA* into the product of two ratios as follows:

$$ROA = \frac{EBIT}{\text{Sales}} \times \frac{\text{Sales}}{\text{Assets}}$$

$$= \text{Return on Sales} \times \text{Asset Turnover}$$

$$= ROS \times ATO$$

= profit margin

The decomposition of *ROA* into *ROS* and *ATO* highlights the fact that firms in different industries can have vastly different *ROS* and turnover ratios yet the same return on assets. Thus, a supermarket typically has a low profit margin on sales and a high asset turnover, whereas a high-priced jewelry store typically has a high profit margin and a low turnover. Both may have the same *ROA*.

To illustrate, let us take two firms with the same *ROA* of 10% per year. The first is a supermarket chain, the second a public utility company. As Table 3.6 shows, the supermarket chain has a "low" *ROS* of 2% and achieves a 10% *ROA* by "turning over" its assets five times per year. The capital-intensive utility, on the other hand, has a "low" *ATO* of only 0.5 times per year and achieves its 10% *ROA* by having an *ROS* of 20%.

---

[3]A measure similar to the market to book (M/B) ratio is Tobin's *Q* ratio, which is named for the American Nobel Prize–winning economist, James Tobin. The ratio is defined as:

$$Q = \text{Market Value of Assets/Replacement Cost}$$

The denominator includes an adjustment to the original cost of assets for inflation.

TABLE 3.6   Differences between *ROS* and *ATO* across Industries

	ROS	×	ATO	=	ROA
Supermarket chain	0.02		5.0		0.10
Public utility	0.20		0.5		0.10

The point here is that a "low" *ROS* or *ATO* ratio need not be a sign of a troubled firm. Each of these ratios must be interpreted in light of industry norms. Even in the same industry systematic differences may exist. For example, a Rolls Royce dealership will almost certainly have a higher margin and lower turnover than a Chevrolet dealership, even though both may have the same *ROA*.

> **Quick Check 3-9**
> If firm A has a higher *ROA* than firm B but the same *ATO*, what must be true of its *ROS*?

3.6.2 The Effect of Financial Leverage

Financial leverage simply means the use of borrowed money. The shareholders of a firm use financial leverage in order to boost their *ROE,* but in so doing they increase the sensitivity of *ROE* to fluctuations in the firm's underlying operating profitability as measured by its *ROA*. In other words, by making use of financial leverage, the firm's shareholders are subjected to financial risk as well as to the operating risk of the firm.

An increase in a firm's financial leverage will increase its *ROE* if and only if its *ROA* exceeds the interest rate on the borrowed funds. This makes intuitive sense. If *ROA* exceeds the borrowing rate, then the firm earns more on the capital it employs than it pays to its creditors. The surplus is thus available to the firm's shareholders, and so raises *ROE*. If, on the other hand, *ROA* is less than the interest rate, the shareholders would have been better off not borrowing at all.

For example, Halfdebt Co. uses financial leverage, whereas Nodebt Co. does not. Let us compare their *ROE* under two different assumptions about the interest rate: (1) 10% per year, and (2) 15% per year. The results are given in Table 3.7.

Increased financial leverage magnifies the variability that firms experience in their *ROE* over the business cycle and increases the likelihood of bankruptcy. Table 3.8 illustrates the behavior of *ROA* and *ROE* under three scenarios, representing phases of the business cycle. We assume that the interest rate on Halfdebt's debt is 10% per year.

The exact relationship between *ROE, ROA,* and leverage can be summarized in the following equation:

$$ROE = (1 - \text{Tax Rate}) \times [ROA + \text{Debt/Equity} \times (ROA - \text{Interest Rate})]$$

This equation has the following implications. If a firm's *ROA* exceeds the interest rate that it pays to its creditors, then its *ROE* will exceed (1 − tax rate) times *ROA* by an amount that will be greater the higher the debt/equity ratio.

TABLE 3.7 Effect of Interest Rate on *ROE*

	Nodebt	*Halfdebt*
Total Assets	$1,000,000	$1,000,000
Equity	1,000,000	500,000
Debt	0	500,000
EBIT	120,000	120,000
ROA (*EBIT/ASSETS*)	12.0%	12.0%
Case (1): Borrowing at an interest rate of 10% per year		
EBIT	120,000	120,000
Interest Expense	0	50,000
Taxable Income	120,000	70,000
Taxes (@ 40%)	48,000	28,000
Net Income	72,000	42,000
Equity	1,000,000	500,000
ROE	7.2%	8.4%
Case (2): Borrowing at an interest rate of 15% per year		
EBIT	120,000	120,000
Interest Expense	0	75,000
Taxable Income	120,000	45,000
Taxes (@ 40%)	48,000	18,000
Net Income	72,000	27,000
Equity	1,000,000	500,000
ROE	7.2%	5.4%

From the perspective of a creditor, an increase in a firm's debt ratio is generally a negative sign. Bond-rating agencies, such as Moody's and Standard and Poors Corporation, will often downgrade a firm's securities if its debt ratio goes up. But from the shareholder's perspective, it might be positive for the firm to increase its debt ratio.

> **Quick Check 3-10**
> What is the effect of increased leverage on a firm's *ROE* if the interest rate on its debt is equal to its *ROA*?

TABLE 3.8 Effect of Business Cycle on *ROE*

Economic Conditions	*ROA*	*ROE*	
		Nodebt	*Halfdebt*
Bad year	1%	0.6%	−4.8%
Normal year	12	7.2	8.4
Good year	30	18.0	30.0

3.6.3 Limitations of Ratio Analysis

Finally, the user of ratios must be aware of their limitations. The basic problem is there is no absolute standard by which to judge whether the ratios are too high or too low. Moreover, ratios are comprised of accounting numbers, often calculated in arbitrary ways. Furthermore, it is difficult to define a set of comparable firms because firms, even within the same industry, are often quite different. For example, firms vary in their level of diversification, in their size, in their age, in the extent to which they are international, and in the accounting methods used (e.g., their inventory and depreciation methods may differ). The punch line of financial ratio analysis, then, is that it may provide a rough guide that should not be relied upon exclusively for decisions.

3.7 THE FINANCIAL PLANNING PROCESS

Financial planning is a dynamic process that follows a cycle of making plans, implementing them, and revising them in the light of actual results. The starting point in developing a financial plan is the firm's strategic plan. Strategy guides the financial planning process by establishing overall business development guidelines and growth targets. Which lines of business does the firm want to expand, which to contract, and how quickly?

For example, ITT Corporation decided in 1995 to quit the insurance business and to concentrate on expanding its gaming and resort businesses. This decision meant that its financial plans starting in that year would be based on redeploying its assets. For several years there would not be any growth in total sales at the corporate level. Indeed, there would be significant "downsizing."[4]

The length of the *planning horizon* is another important element in financial planning. In general, the longer the horizon, the less detailed the financial plan. A five-year financial plan will typically consist of a set of forecasted income statements and balance sheets showing only general categories with few details. On the other hand, a financial plan for next month will show detailed forecasts of revenues and expenses for specific product lines and detailed projections of cash inflows and outflows. Multiyear plans are usually revised on an annual basis, and annual plans on a quarterly basis.

The financial planning cycle can be broken down into several steps:

1. Managers forecast the key external factors that determine the demand for the firm's products and its production costs. These factors include the level of economic activity in the markets in which the firm sells its products, inflation, exchange rates, interest rates, and the output and prices charged by the firm's competitors.

2. Based on these external factors and their own tentative decisions regarding investment outlays, production levels, research and marketing expenditures, and dividend payments, managers forecast the firm's revenues, expenses, and cash flows, and estimate the implied need for external financing. They check that the firm's likely future financial results are consistent with their strategic plan for creating value for shareholders and that financing is available to implement the plan. If there are any inconsistencies, then managers revise their decisions until they come up with a workable plan, which becomes a blueprint for the firm's

---

[4]The stock market reacted quite favorably to this shift in strategy. ITT's stock price rose dramatically compared to the change in the S&P 500 index. ITT's stock price tripled over the period from 1991 to 1995, during which its new strategy was formulated and ultimately implemented.

operating decisions during the year. It is good practice to make contingency plans in case some of the forecasts turn out to be wrong.

3. Based on the plan, senior managers establish specific performance targets for themselves and their subordinates.

4. Actual performance is measured at regular intervals (either monthly or quarterly), compared to the targets set in the plan, and corrective actions are taken as needed. Management may adjust targets during the year to take into account large deviations from forecast values.

5. At the end of each year, rewards (e.g., bonuses or raises) are distributed and the planning cycle starts again.

3.8 CONSTRUCTING A FINANCIAL PLANNING MODEL

E-BOOK

3.8

Financial plans are usually embodied in quantitative models derived in whole or in part from a firm's financial statements. For example, let us construct a one-year financial plan for Generic Products Corporation (GPC), the same hypothetical firm whose financial statements we analyzed earlier in this chapter. GPC is a company that was founded 10 years ago to manufacture and sell generic products for the consumer market. Table 3.9 shows GPC's income statements and balance sheets for the last three years.

TABLE 3.9 GPC Financial Statements: 20x1–20x3

Income Statement	20x1	20x2	20x3
Sales	$200.00	$240.00	$288.00
Cost of goods sold	110.00	132.00	158.40
Gross margin	90.00	108.00	129.60
Selling, general, and administrative expenses	30.00	36.00	43.20
EBIT	60.00	72.00	86.40
Interest expense	30.00	45.21	64.04
Taxes	12.00	10.72	8.94
Net income	18.00	16.07	13.41
Dividends	5.40	4.82	4.02
Change in shareholders' equity	12.60	11.25	9.39

Balance Sheet	20x0	20x1	20x2	20x3
Assets	$600.00	$720.00	$864.00	$1,036.80
Cash and equivalents	10.00	12.00	14.40	17.28
Receivables	40.00	48.00	57.60	69.12
Inventories	50.00	60.00	72.00	86.40
Property, plant, and equipment	500.00	600.00	720.00	864.00
Liabilities	300.00	407.40	540.15	703.56
Payables	30.00	36.00	43.20	51.84
Short-term debt	120.00	221.40	346.95	501.72
Long-term debt	150.00	150.00	150.00	150.00
Shareholders' equity	300.00	312.60	323.85	333.24

In millions of U.S. dollars.

Let us assume that these financial statements are the only information about the company available. How could one formulate a plan for the coming year? The simplest approach is to make a forecast of sales for the next year and assume that most of the items on the income statement and balance sheet will maintain the same ratio to sales as in the previous year. This is called the **percent-of-sales method.** Let us illustrate the method with GPC.

The first step is an examination of past financial data to determine which items on the income statement and balance sheet have maintained a fixed ratio to sales. This enables us to decide which items can be forecast strictly on the basis of our projected sales and which have to be forecast on some other basis. In the case of GPC, it is clear from the record that costs, *EBIT,* and assets have maintained fixed ratios to sales. However, interest expense, taxes, net income, and most liabilities (with the exception of payables) have not. This is shown in Table 3.10.

The second step is to forecast sales. Because so many items are linked to sales, it is important to have an accurate sales forecast and later to test the sensitivity of the plan to variations in sales. For GPC we will assume that sales will continue to grow by 20% next year, so that sales for 20x4 are forecast to be $345.6 million.

The third step is to forecast those items on the income statement and balance sheet that are assumed to maintain a constant ratio to sales. Thus, because cost of

TABLE 3.10   GPC Common-Size Financial Statements: 20x1–20x3

Income Statement	20x1	20x2	20x3
Sales	100.0%	100.0%	100.0%
Cost of goods sold	55.0	55.0	55.0
Gross margin	45.0	45.0	45.0
Selling, general, and adminstrative expenses	15.0	15.0	15.0
EBIT	30.0	30.0	30.0
Interest expense	15.0	18.8	22.2
Taxes	6.0	4.5	3.1
Net income	9.0	6.7	4.7
Dividends	2.7	2.0	1.4
Change in shareholders' equity	6.3	4.7	3.3

Balance Sheet	20x1	20x2	20x3
Assets	360.0%	360.0%	360.0%
Cash and equivalents	6.0	6.0	6.0
Receivables	24.0	24.0	24.0
Inventories	30.0	30.0	30.0
Property, plant, and equipment	300.0	300.0	300.0
Liabilities	203.7	225.1	244.3
Payables	18.0	18.0	18.0
Short-term debt	110.7	144.6	174.2
Long-term debt	75.0	62.5	52.1
Shareholders' equity	156.3	134.9	115.7

goods sold has historically been 55% of sales, the 20x4 forecast is 0.55 × $345.6 million, which is $190.08 million. Because total assets at the end of the year have been three times annual sales, the total asset figure forecast for the end of 20x4 is $1,244.16 million.

The final step is to fill in the missing items in the income statement and balance sheet (i.e., the items that do not maintain a fixed ratio to sales). Let us assume that the interest rate on the long-term debt is 8% per year and on the short-term debt 15% per year. Then our forecast for interest expense is 8% times the amount of long-term debt plus 15% times the amount of short-term debt outstanding at the beginning of the year (i.e., at the end of 20x3). Thus, total interest expense for 20x4 will be $87.26 million. Taxes are assumed to be 40% of income after interest expense, or $6.57 million. Net income after taxes is, therefore, $9.85 million. The income statement for 20x4 will be as shown in the last column of Table 3.11.

Now let us consider the balance sheet at the end of 20x4. Because GPC will pay out 30% of net income as dividends, shareholders' equity will increase by $6.9 million (from $333.24 million to $340.14 million). Total assets will increase by $207.36 million, and payables will increase by $10.37 million. To find the total need for additional funds to be raised either by issuing new stock or by increased

TABLE 3.11 GPC Forecast Income Statement and Balance Sheet for 20x4

Income Statement		20x1	20x2	20x3	20x4e
Sales		$200.00	$240.00	$288.00	$345.60
Cost of goods sold		110.00	132.00	158.40	190.08
Gross margin		90.00	108.00	129.60	155.52
Selling, general, and administrative expenses		30.00	36.00	43.20	51.84
EBIT		60.00	72.00	86.40	103.68
Interest expense		30.00	45.21	64.04	87.26
Taxes		12.00	10.72	8.94	6.57
Net income		18.00	16.07	13.41	9.85
Dividends		5.40	4.82	4.02	2.96
Change in equity		12.60	11.25	9.39	6.90

Balance Sheet	20x0	20x1	20x2	20x3	20x4e
Assets	$600.00	$720.00	$864.00	$1,036.80	$1,244.16
Cash and equivalents	10.00	12.00	14.40	17.28	20.74
Receivables	40.00	48.00	57.60	69.12	82.94
Inventories	50.00	60.00	72.00	86.40	103.68
Property, plant, and equipment	500.00	600.00	720.00	864.00	1,036.80
Liabilities	300.00	407.40	540.15	703.56	904.02
Payables	30.00	36.00	43.20	51.84	62.21
Short-term debt	120.00	221.40	346.95	501.72	691.81
Long-term debt	150.00	150.00	150.00	150.00	150.00
Equity	300.00	312.60	323.85	333.24	340.14

In millions of U.S. dollars.

borrowing, we subtract the increase in retained earnings and the increase in payables from the change in assets as follows:

Additional Financing Needed
= Change in Assets – Increase in Retained Earnings – Increase in Payables
= \$207.36 million – \$6.9 million – \$10.37 million = 190.09 million

Thus, there will be a need for an additional \$190.09 million in external financing. In the balance sheet data of Table 3.11, we have assumed that all of this financing will be in the form of an increase in short-term debt, which therefore increases from \$501.72 million to \$691.81 million.

Quick Check 3-11

If the sales revenue forecast for 20x4 is \$360 million instead of \$345.60, what will be the need for additional external financing?

3.9 GROWTH AND THE NEED FOR EXTERNAL FINANCING

We now know that if GPC's sales grow by 20% during 20x4, it will need to raise an additional \$190.09 million in funds from external sources. Management may decide to raise this money either by increasing its short-term borrowing (as assumed in Table 3.11), by increasing its long-term debt, or by issuing new stock. Let us now see how sensitive this external financing need is to the assumed growth rate of sales.

One way to carry out such a sensitivity analysis is to repeat the procedure we just did in the previous section using different growth rates of sales. This can easily be done by creating an automated spreadsheet model with a computer program such as the one at this textbook's companion website.[5] The result is shown in Figure 3.1.

3.9.1 The Firm's Sustainable Growth Rate

Figure 3.1 tells us the amount of external financing the firm needs in order to achieve a certain targeted growth rate of sales. But we can ask the reverse question: How fast can a firm grow if it is constrained in the amount of external financing available to it?

To address this question we assume that the financing constraint takes the following form:

- The firm will not issue any new equity shares, so that growth in equity capital occurs only through the retention of earnings.
- The firm will not increase its ratio of debt to equity, so that external debt financing will grow at the same rate as equity grows through retained earnings.

Under these circumstances, the firm cannot grow any faster than the growth rate in owners' equity, which is called the firm's **sustainable growth rate.** The formula for the sustainable growth rate is:

Sustainable Growth Rate = Earnings Retention Rate × *ROE*

---

[5]See www.prenhall.com/bodie.

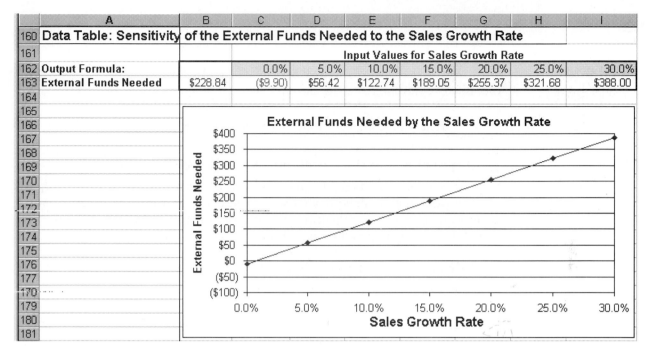

	A	B	C	D	E	F	G	H	I
160	Data Table: Sensitivity of the External Funds Needed to the Sales Growth Rate								
161			Input Values for Sales Growth Rate						
162	Output Formula:		0.0%	5.0%	10.0%	15.0%	20.0%	25.0%	30.0%
163	External Funds Needed	$228.84	($9.90)	$56.42	$122.74	$189.05	$255.37	$321.68	$388.00
164									
165									
166									
167									
168									
169									
170									
171									
172									
173									
174									
175									
176									
177									
178									
179									
180									
181									

FIGURE 3.1   External Funds Needed as a Function of the Growth Rate

Derivation of the Sustainable Growth Equation

Sustainable Growth Rate = Growth Rate of Shareholders' Equity

Without the issuance of new shares, the rate of growth in shareholders' equity is just the increase in retained earnings divided by the beginning-of-year shareholders' equity:

Growth Rate of Shareholders' Equity =
Increase in Retained Earnings ÷ Shareholders' Equity at Beginning of Year

But:

Increase in Retained Earnings =
Earnings Retention Rate × Net Income

The earnings retention rate is the proportion of net income not paid out in dividends or used to repurchase outstanding shares of stock. By definition it is equal to:

Earnings Retention Rate =
1 − Dividend Payout Ratio − Share Repurchase Rate

Therefore, by substitution:

Growth Rate of Shareholders' Equity =
Earnings Retention Rate × Net Income ÷ Shareholders' Equity

or in other words:

Growth Rate of Shareholders' Equity = Earnings Retention Rate × *ROE*

And, thus, we have derived the sustainable growth equation:

Sustainable Growth Rate = Earnings Retention Rate × *ROE*

Implications of the Sustainable Growth Equation

The maximum sustainable growth rate is equal to the firm's *ROE,* and it is achieved when the dividend payout ratio is zero, that is, when all of net income is retained and reinvested in the firm. If a firm tries to grow faster than this rate, then it will have to issue new shares and/or increase its debt ratio.

Example of Sustainable Growth

Rapid Industries (RI) has the following fixed ratios:

Asset Turnover = 0.5 Times per Year
Debt/Equity Ratio = 1.0
Dividend Payout Ratio = 0.4
ROE = 20% per Year

Last year sales were $1 million. That means that assets were $2 million, and debt and shareholders' equity were $1 million each. Because *ROE* was 20%, net income must have been $200,000, of which $80,000 was paid out in dividends and $120,000 retained as new equity capital. With a debt/equity ratio of 1, RI could increase its assets by $240,000 and its sales by as much as $120,000.

The sustainable growth rate of sales is, therefore:

$$g = \frac{\$120,000}{\$1 \text{ million}} = 0.12 \text{ or } 12\%$$

~ Shareholder's equity

We get the same answer by applying the formula:

$$g = ROE \times (1 - \text{Dividend Payout Ratio})$$
$$= 20\% \times (1 - 0.4)$$
$$= 12\%$$

The financial statements of Rapid Industries for three years of sustainable growth are shown in Table 3.12.

Quick Check 3-12
What are the implications for financing if a firm grew at a rate less than its sustainable rate?

TABLE 3.12	Rapid Industries Financial Statements for 20x1–20x3		

Income Statements		20x1	20x2	20x3
Sales		$1,000,000	$1,120,000	$1,254,400
Net income		200,000	224,000	250,880
Dividends		80,000	89,600	100,352
Increase in retained earnings		120,000	134,400	150,528
Balance Sheets	20x0	20x1	20x2	20x3
Assets	$2,000,000	$2,240,000	$2,508,800	$2,809,856
Debt	1,000,000	1,120,000	1,254,400	1,404,928
Equity	1,000,000	1,120,000	1,254,400	1,404,928

3.10 WORKING CAPITAL MANAGEMENT

In most businesses cash must be paid out to cover expenses before any cash is collected from the sale of the firm's products. As a result, a typical firm's investment in assets such as inventories and accounts receivable exceeds its liabilities such as accrued expenses and accounts payable. The difference between these current assets and current liabilities is called **working capital.** If a firm's need for working capital is permanent rather than seasonal, it usually seeks long-term financing for it. Seasonal financing needs are met through short-term financing arrangements, such as a loan from a bank.

The main principle behind the efficient management of a firm's working capital is to minimize the amount of the firm's investment in nonearning assets such as receivables and inventories and maximize the use of "free" credit such as prepayments by customers, accrued wages, and accounts payable. These three sources of funds are free to the firm in the sense that they usually bear no explicit interest charge.[6]

Policies and procedures that shorten the lag between the time that the firm sells a product and the time that it collects cash from its customers reduce the need for working capital. Ideally, the firm would like its customers to pay in advance. The firm can also reduce its need for working capital by extending the time between when it purchases its inputs and when it pays cash for them.

To gain a clearer understanding of the relation between these time lags and the firm's investment in working capital, consider Figure 3.2.

The **cash cycle time** is the number of days between the date the firm must start to pay cash to its suppliers and the date it begins to receive cash from its customers. From Figure 3.2, we see that the cash cycle time is the difference between the sum of the inventory and receivables periods on the one hand and the payables period on the other.

Cash Cycle Time = Inventory Period + Receivables Period − Payables Period

---

[6]If, however, the firm gives price discounts on its products to customers who pay in advance, then the size of this discount represents an implicit interest charge. Similarly, if the firm forgoes a discount from its suppliers by delaying payment to them, this forgone discount represents an implicit interest charge.

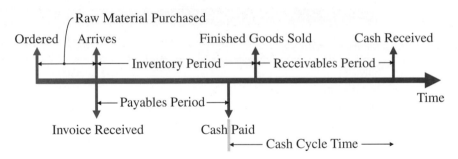

FIGURE 3.2   The Cash Flow Cycle

The firm's required investment in working capital is directly related to the length of its cash cycle time. If the payables period is long enough to cover the sum of the inventory and receivables periods, then the firm needs no working capital at all.

What kinds of actions can a firm take to reduce its need for working capital? From the equation for cash cycle time, we can see that a firm can reduce its need for working capital by:

- *reducing the amount of time that goods are held in inventory.* This can be accomplished by improving the inventory control process or by having suppliers deliver raw materials exactly when they are needed in the production process.

- *collecting accounts receivable more quickly.* Among the methods available to speed up the collection process are improving the efficiency of the collection process, offering discounts to customers who pay faster, and charging interest on accounts that are overdue.

- *paying its own bills more slowly.*

Quick Check 3-13

How can a firm reduce its need for working capital?

3.11 LIQUIDITY AND CASH BUDGETING

There is an apocryphal story about how the billionaire Howard Hughes found himself without any cash or credit cards in a place where no one recognized him. Without any means to pay for food, drink, shelter, or transportation, the billionaire nearly died of starvation and exposure. The same point applies to corporations: A firm that is profitable in the long run can experience serious difficulties and even fail if it runs out of cash or credit in the short run. Rarely does a firm become spectacularly successful simply by managing well the short-term flows of cash into and out of the business, but failure to manage them properly can lead to ruin.

Howard Hughes's problem was that he became temporarily illiquid. **Liquidity** means that one has the means to make *immediate* payment for some purchase or to settle a debt that has come due. *Illiquidity* is a situation in which one has sufficient wealth to afford the purchase or to settle the debt, but one does not have the means to pay immediately.[7]

To avoid the difficulties caused by illiquidity, firms need to forecast their cash outflows and inflows carefully. A plan that shows these forecasts is called a **cash budget.**

Quick Check 3-14
Why is liquidity important to a firm?

Summary

Financial statements serve three important economic functions:

- They provide information to the owners and creditors of the firm about the company's current status and past financial performance.
- They provide a convenient way for owners and creditors to set performance targets and impose restrictions on the managers of the firm.
- They provide convenient templates for financial planning.

The basic accounting statements reviewed are the income statement, the balance sheet, and the statement of cash flows. The *income statement* reports the results of operations over the period and is based on the model of revenues minus costs (including depreciation and taxes) equals net income or earnings. The *balance sheet* shows the assets (both current and long-term or fixed assets) on the one hand, and the claims against them (i.e., the liabilities and equity) on the other. The *statement of cash flows* gives a summary of cash flows from operating, investing, and financing activities for the period.

A firm's accounting balance sheet differs from an economic balance sheet because:

- it omits some economically significant assets and liabilities, and
- it does not report all assets and liabilities at their current market values.

Analysts use financial ratios as one mode of analysis to better understand the company's strengths and weaknesses, whether its fortunes are improving, and what its prospects are. These ratios are often compared with the ratios of a comparable set of companies and to ratios of recent past periods. The five types of ratios are profitability, turnover, financial leverage, liquidity, and market value ratios. Finally, it is helpful to organize the analysis of these ratios in a way that reveals the logical connections among them and their relation to the underlying operations of the firm.

The purpose of financial planning is to assemble the firm's separate divisional plans into a consistent whole, to establish concrete targets for measuring success,

---

[7]The liquidity of an asset can be defined as one's ability to immediately convert it into cash at full value. A good measure of an asset's liquidity is the cost of buying it and then immediately reselling it. Thus, the liquidity of a new car that you buy is the gap between the price you paid for it and the price you could get for it if you sold it to someone else the next instant. For an asset that is traded in a dealer market this cost is its bid-asked spread. Cash is defined as the asset with a zero bid-asked spread.

and to create incentives for achieving the firm's goals. The tangible outcome of the financial planning process is a set of "blueprints" in the form of projected financial statements and budgets. The longer the time horizon, the less detailed the financial plan.

In the short run, financial planning is concerned primarily with the management of working capital. The need for working capital arises because for many firms cash needed to conduct production and selling activities starts to flow out before cash flows in. The longer this time lag, which is called the length of the cash flow cycle, the more the amount of working capital the firm needs.

A firm's need for working capital is measured as the sum of cash equivalents, prepaid expenses, receivables, and inventories minus the sum of customer advances, payables, and accrued expenses. The main principle behind the efficient management of a firm's working capital is to minimize the amount of the firm's investment in low-earning current assets such as receivables and inventories and maximize the use of low-cost financing through current liabilities such as customer advances and accounts payable.

Cash management is important because even a profitable firm can get into financial distress or even go bankrupt if it becomes illiquid.

Key Terms

- book values   73
- intangible assets   74
- goodwill   74
- marking to market   75
- total shareholder returns   76
- percent-of-sales method   84
- sustainable growth rate   86
- working capital   89
- cash cycle time   89
- liquidity   90
- cash budget   91

Answers to Quick Check Questions

Quick Check 3-1 *What are the three basic economic functions served by financial statements?*

ANSWER:

- They provide information to the owners and creditors of the firm about the company's current status and past financial performance.
- They provide a convenient way for owners and creditors to set performance targets and to impose restrictions on the managers of the firm.
- Financial statements provide convenient templates for financial planning.

Quick Check 3-2 *What difference would it have made to the end-of-year balance sheet if GPC had issued an additional $50 million of long-term debt during the year and added that amount to its holdings of cash and marketable securities?*

ANSWER: The liability, long-term debt, and the asset, cash and marketable securities, would both have increased by $50 million, and shareholder's equity would have remained unchanged.

Quick Check 3-3 *What difference would it have made to the income statement and the end-of-year balance sheet if GPC had retained all of its net income instead of paying out cash dividends of $10 million?*

ANSWER: Net income would have been the same. The end-of-year balance sheet, however, would have shown an increase of $10 million in cash and in shareholders' equity.

Quick Check 3-4   *What difference would it have made to the cash flow statement if GPC had retained all of its net income instead of paying out cash dividends of $10 million?*

ANSWER: If GPC had not paid a cash dividend of $10 million, it could have borrowed $10 million less. Therefore, the cash flow statement would have showed no dividend and an increase in debt of only $84.6 million.

Quick Check 3-5   *What potentially important information about a firm can be found in the footnotes to its financial statements?*

ANSWER:

- An explanation of accounting methods used.
- Greater detail regarding certain assets or liabilities.
- Information regarding the equity structure of the firm.
- Documentation of changes in operations.
- Off-balance-sheet items.

Quick Check 3-6   *Why does the market price of a firm's stock usually differ from its book value?*

ANSWER: The book value does not include all of a firm's assets and liabilities. The assets and liabilities included on a firm's official balance sheet are not marked to market.

Quick Check 3-7   *In 20x7 VGI corporation reported earnings per share of $5 and paid a cash dividend to shareholders of $3.00 per share. Its beginning-of-year book value per share was $30, and its market price was $40. At the end of the year, the book value per share was $32 and the market price was $35. Compare VGI's ROE and total shareholder returns (TSR).*

ANSWER:

$$ROE = 5/30 = 16.67\%$$

$$TSR = (3 + 35 - 40)/40 = 5\%$$

Quick Check 3-8   *What are the five types of financial ratios used to analyze a company?*

ANSWER: The five ratios are profitability, activity, financial leverage, liquidity, and market price ratios.

Quick Check 3-9   *If firm A has a higher ROA than firm B but the same ATO, what must be true of its ROS?*

ANSWER: Firm A's *ROS* must be higher than B's.

Quick Check 3-10   *What is the effect of increased leverage on a firm's ROE if the interest rate on its debt is equal to its ROA?*

ANSWER: The firm's *ROE* will not change.

Quick Check 3-11   *If the sales revenue forecast for 20x4 is $360 million instead of $345.60, what will be the need for additional external financing?*

ANSWER: The total asset figure forecast for the end of 20x4 is now 3.6 × $360 million, which is $1,296 million. So the change in assets for the year is $1,296 − $1,036.8, which is $259.20. This growth in assets will be partially financed from the increase in retained earnings and the growth in payables, but the rest of the financing needed will have to come from external sources. Payables will increase by 18% (the ratio of payables to sales) times the increase in sales, which is 0.18 × $72 million or $12.96 million. Now let us forecast the firm's net income. *EBIT* is 0.3 × $360 million, which is $108 million. Total interest expense is unchanged at $87.26 million. Taxes are 40% of income after interest expense: Taxes = 0.4 × (108 − 87.26) = $8.296 million. Net income after taxes is, therefore, 0.6 × (108 − 87.26) = $12.444 million. Because GPC will pay out 30% of net income as dividends, the increase in retained earnings will be 0.7 × $12.444 = $8.711 million.

Additional Financing Needed =
Change in Assets Increase in Retained Earnings Increase in Payables =
$259.2 million − $8.711 million − $12.96 million = $237.529 million

Quick Check 3-12 *What are the implications for financing if a firm grows at a rate less than its sustainable rate?*

ANSWER: The firm will be able to lower its debt ratio or repurchase its own shares.

Quick Check 3-13 *How can a firm reduce its need for working capital?*

ANSWER: By either reducing inventories, speeding up collections, or slowing down the payment of its own bills.

Quick Check 3-14 *Why is liquidity important to a firm?*

ANSWER: A firm that is profitable in the long run can experience serious difficulties and even fail if it runs out of cash or credit in the short run.

Questions and Problems

TEMPLATE

3.11–3.13

Problems 3.1 through 3.8 are based on the following information: The Ruffy Stuffed Toy Company's balance sheet at the end of 20x7 was as follows:

Assets

Cash	$27,300
Accounts receivable	35,000
Inventory	57,000
Total current assets	119,300
Property, plant, and equipment	
Equipment	25,000
Less accumulated depreciation	(2,500)
Net equipment	22,500
Furniture	16,000
Less accumulated depreciation	(2,000)
Net furniture	14,000
Total property, plant, and equipment	36,500
Total assets	155,800

Liabilities and Shareholders' Equity

Payables	
Accounts payable	65,000
Salary payable	3,000
Utilities payable	1,500
Loans (long-term debt)	25,000
Total liabilities	94,500
Common stock	45,000
Retained earnings	16,300
Total shareholders' equity	61,300
Total liabilities and shareholders' equity	155,800

During 20x8, the Ruffy Stuffed Toy Company recorded the following transactions:

a. Early in the year, purchased a new toy stuffing machine for $9,000 cash and signed a three-year note for the balance of $12,000.

b. Had cash sales of $115,000 and sales on credit of $316,000.

c. Purchased inventory and raw materials from suppliers for $207,000.

d. Made payments of $225,000 to its inventory and raw materials suppliers.

e. Paid rent expenses totaling $43,000.

f. Paid insurance expenses totaling $23,000.

g. Paid utility bills totaling $7,500; $1,500 of this amount reversed the existing payable from 20x7.

h. Paid wages and salaries totaling $79,000; $3,000 of this amount reversed the payable from 20x7.

i. Paid other miscellaneous operating expenses totaling $4,000.

j. Collected $270,000 from customers who made purchases on credit.

k. The interest rate on the loan payable is 10% per year. Interest was paid on 12/31/20x8.

Other information:

a. The equipment has been estimated to have a useful life of 20 years, with no salvage value. Two years have been depreciated through 20x7.

b. The existing furniture has been estimated to have a useful life of eight years (no salvage value), of which one year has been depreciated through 20x7.

c. The new stuffing machine has been estimated to have a useful life of seven years, and will probably have no salvage value.

d. The tax rate is 35%, and assume that taxes are paid on 12/31/20x8.

e. Dividend payout, if possible, will be 10% of net income.

f. Cost of goods sold for the year's sales was $250,000.

g. Ending Balance in Accounts Receivable = Beginning Balance – Cash Received from Credit Customers + Sales on Credit.

h. Ending Balance in Accounts Payable = Beginning Balance + Purchases – Cash Payments to Suppliers

i. Ending Balance in Inventory = Beginning Balance + Purchases of Raw Materials – Cost of Goods Sold

j. The company's stock price at market close on 12/31/20x8 was $4\frac{5}{8}$. It has 20,000 shares outstanding.

3.1 Construct the balance sheet for the Ruffy Stuffed Toy Company as of 12/31/20x8.

3.2 Construct the income statement for operations during the year 20x8.

3.3 Construct a cash flow statement for the year 20x8.

3.4 Calculate the following profitability ratios: return on sales, return on assets, return on equity.

3.5 Calculate the following asset turnover ratios: receivables turnover, inventory turnover, asset turnover.

3.6 Calculate the following financial leverage and liquidity ratios: debt, times interest earned, current ratio, quick (acid) test.

3.7 What is the Ruffy's book value per share at the end of 20x8?

3.8 Calculate the firm's price to earnings ratio and the ratio of its market share price to its book value per share.

3.9 You have the following information taken from the 1996 financial statements of Computronics Corporation and Digitek Corporation (all figures are in $ millions except per share amounts):

	Computronix	*Digitek*
Net income	153.7	239.0
Dividend payout ratio	40.0%	20.0%
EBIT	317.6	403.1
Interest expense	54.7	4.8
Average assets	2,457.9	3,459.7
Sales	3,379.3	4,537.0
Average shareholders' equity	1,113.3	2,347.3
Market price of the common stock:		
at beginning of year	$15.0	$38.0
at end of year	$12.0	$40.0
Shares of common stock outstanding	200.0 million	100.0 million

Compare and contrast the financial performance of the two companies using the financial ratios discussed in this chapter.

3.10 Refer to the following financial statements:

Income Statement	*20x6*	*20x7*	*20x8e*
Sales	$1,200,000	$1,500,000	
Cost of goods sold	750,000	937,500	
Gross margin	450,000	562,500	
Operating expenses			
Advertising expense	50,000	62,500	
Rent expense	72,000	90,000	
Salesperson commission expense	48,000	60,000	
Utilities expense	15,000	18,750	
EBIT	265,000	331,250	
Interest expense	106,000	113,000	
Taxable income	159,000	218,250	
Taxes (35%)	55,650	76,388	
Net income	103,350	141,863	
Dividends (40% payout)	41,340	56,745	
Change in retained earnings	62,010	85,118	

Balance Sheet

Assets		
Cash	$300,000	$375,000
Receivables	200,000	250,000
Inventory	700,000	875,000
Property, plant, and equipment	1,800,000	2,250,000
Total assets	$3,000,000	$3,750,000
Liabilities and shareholders' equity		
Liabilities		
Payables	300,000	375,000
Short-term debt (10% interest)	500,000	989,882
Long-term debt (7% interest)	800,000	900,000
Shareholders' equity		
Common stock	1,100,000	1,100,000
Retained earnings	300,000	385,118
Total liabilities and equity	$3,000,000	$3,750,000

a. Determine which items varied in constant proportion to sales between 20x6 and 20x7.

b. Determine the rate of growth in sales that was achieved from 20x6 to 20x7.

c. What was the firm's return on equity for 20x7? Can you calculate it for 20x6?

d. What was the firm's external (additional) funding requirement determined to be for 20x7? How was the funding obtained?

e. Prepare *pro forma* statements for 20x8 with the following assumptions:
Rate of growth in sales = 15%.

The firm intends to pay down $100,000 of its short-term debt on January 1, 20x8.

Interest rates on debt are as stated in the balance sheet, and are applied to the the start-of-year (20x8) balances for short-term and long-term debt. Remember that the firm intends to pay down part of the short-term loan on 1/1/20x8.

The firm's dividend payout in 20x8 will be reduced to 30%.

1) What would be the firm's forecasted return on equity for 20x8?

2) How much additional funding will the firm need for 20x8?

3) The firm will close 40% of any additional funding gap by issuing new stock. It will then use up to $100,000 of long-term debt, with the remainder coming from short-term borrowing. Complete the *pro forma* balance sheet for 20x8.

f. Suppose the firm anticipates an increase in the corporate tax rate to 38%. Determine the amount of additional funding that would be required if this change comes to pass.

3.11 Take the *pro forma* statements (with tax rate = 0.35) developed in problem 3.10, and:

a. Revise them assuming a growth rate in sales from 20x7 to 20x8 of 10%. What is the additional funding required for 20x8 under this scenario?

b. Now develop *pro forma* statements for 20x9 assuming a growth rate in sales of 20% from 20x8 to 20x9. What is the additional funding needed for 20x9? The firm plans to use short-term debt to cover this entire amount.

3.12 Suppose that after analyzing the results of 20x8 and preparing pro forma statements for 20x9, the Give Me Debt Company anticipates an increase in total assets of $50, an increase in retained earnings of $25, and an increase in payables of $40. Assume that other than the payables, the firm's liabilities include short-term and long-term debt, and that its equity includes common stock and retained earnings.

a. The chief financial officer of the company asks you to determine the required amount of external funding in 20x9. What do you tell the CFO?

b. What actions can Give Me Debt Co. undertake to address the situation you have found?

3.13 Place the following planning events in their likely order of occurrence within the planning cycle:

____ Funding needs for implementation of tactical plans are estimated.

____ The final firmwide plan and budgets are completed.

____ CEO and top-management team establish strategic objectives for the firm (e.g., increase market share from 10% to 12%).

____ Line managers devise action plans to support strategic objectives.

____ Revisions are made to the strategic plan and divisional budgets based on feedback from divisional managers with regard to resource (money, people) requirements.

____ Decisions are made as to which sources of external financing to tap.

____ CEO and top management team integrate divisional budgets into a preliminary firm-wide budget.

____ The firm determines the amount of required external financing.

____ Tactical plans and budgets are reviewed with division management; priorities are assigned to planned activities.

____ Division managers review the strategic objectives with their line (or tactical) management.

3.14 Suppose that the sharply abbreviated actual 20x8 and *pro forma* 20x9 income statement and balance sheet for Cones 'R' Us, an ice-cream retailer, appear as follows:

Income Statement	20x8	20x9e
EBIT		$100
Interest expense		25
Taxable income		75
Net income (after taxes of 33%)		50
Dividends		20
Change in retained earnings		30
Balance Sheet		
Assets	$800	$1,000
Liabilities		
Payables	80	100
Debt	300	450
Shareholders' equity	420	450

The $25 interest expense projected for 20x9 is based on a rate of 8.33% applied to the outstanding debt balance of $300 at the end of 20x8. Debt increases from $300 to $450 because of external financing that is obtained to close the gap exhibited in the relation:

$$\text{Additional Financing Needed} = \text{Change in Assets} -$$
$$\text{Increase in Retained Earnings} - \text{Increase in Payables}$$

a. What problems are created in using the *pro forma* statements to determine the required amount of additional (external) financing if the debt that will be used to satisfy the funding need is acquired in total at the beginning of 20x9, rather than at the end of 20x9 as is implied in these statements?

b. Is this problem likely to be significant? Why?

3.15 Assume a firm has net income in 20x9 of $20 and its end-of-year 20x8 total assets were $450. Further assume that the firm has a standing requirement to maintain a debt/equity ratio of 0.8, and that its managers are prohibited from further borrowing or stock issuance.

a. What is this firm's maximum sustainable growth rate?

b. If the firm pays $6 of the $20 net income as a dividend, and plans to maintain this payout ratio into the future, now what is its maximum sustainable growth rate?

c. If the firm uses $12 of the $20 net income to repurchase some of its outstanding shares, now what is its maximum sustainable growth rate?

d. If the firm takes action as described in parts b *and* c, what would its maximum sustainable growth rate be?

3.16 Working capital management questions:

a. Suppose you own a firm that manufactures pool tables. Thirty days ago, you hired a consultant to examine your business and suggest improvements. The consultant's proposal, if implemented, would allow your firm to shorten the time between each sale and the subsequent cash collection by 20 days, slightly lengthen the time between inventory purchase and sale by only five days, but shorten the time between inventory purchase and your firm's payment of the bill by 15 days. Would you implement the consultant's proposal? Why?

b. In general, the principles of cash cycle time management call for a firm to shorten (minimize) the time it takes to collect receivables and lengthen (maximize) the time it takes to pay amounts it owes to suppliers. Explain what trade-offs need to be managed if the firm offers discounts to customers who pay early, and the firm also forgoes discounts offered by its suppliers by extending the time until it pays invoices.

c. Suppose it is 3/13/x2, and you just received your monthly credit card statement with a new balance of $2,000. The payment is due on 4/5/x2, but your spouse panics at the sight (and size) of the balance and wants to pay it immediately. If you practice the principles of cash cycle time management in your personal finances, when would you make the payment? Why? What danger exists in adopting this strategy?

d. Some furniture companies conduct highly advertised annual sale events in which customers can either take an up-front discount for a cash (or credit card) purchase, or defer finance charges for up to one year on their purchases by charging it to the *company's* credit account. Assume that the two options do not present a time value of money advantage for the company. In terms of cash cycle management: (1) Why does the company offer the discount? (2) Why might the company be willing to forgo cash collection for one year if a customer chooses to defer? What risk does the company assume in the deferment case that it does not assume in the discount case?

e. Compare the frequency with which you think a firm may monitor its working capital situation, and move to correct a problem, with the frequency of the firm's planning exercise in forecasting future sales and determining the need for additional financing.

f. If a firm were to monitor its working capital situation closely, what problem might it be looking to avoid?

3.17 How would the following assets and liabilities be recorded on the balance sheets of their owners?

a. a lottery ticket

b. a successful song

c. an unsuccessful movie

3.18 Personal accounting

Show how the following events and transactions should appear on your personal income statement, balance sheet, and cash flow statement.

a. On July 1, 200x, you receive $20,000 in gifts upon graduating from school and pay off a $10,000 student loan.

b. On August 1, 200x, you get a job as a finance intern at General Financial Services Inc. You are promised a salary of $4,000 per month, payable on the last day of each month.

c. On August 31, you receive your first statement of GFS salary and benefits showing the following items:

Gross salary	$4,000
Income tax withholding	1,400
Social Security and Medicare tax	500
Health insurance premium	150
Contribution to pension plan	200
Employer Social Security tax	300
Employer contribution to pension plan	200
Employer contribution to health insurance	150
Amount credited to employee's checking account at GFS Bank	1,750
Total employer benefits	650

d. On September 1, you purchase a new car for $20,000. You make a downpayment of $5,000 and borrow the remaining $15,000 from GFS bank at a monthly interest rate of 1%. Your monthly payment is $498.21 for 36 months.

e. As an individual or household, why might you want to maintain a balance sheet? How often should you replace it? Should you mark-to-market or leave your assets and liabilities at their historical cost?

3.19 Uses of accounting information

You are thinking of taking a trip to Florida for your spring vacation, which begins two months from now. You use Excite's free Preview Travel service on the Web to find the cheapest round-trip fare from Boston to Fort Lauderdale. It tells you that the cheapest airline is AirTran. You have never heard of this airline before and are concerned that it may go out of business before you can use your tickets two months from now. How can you use financial data available on the Web (e.g., at www.quicken.com) to investigate the risk to you of buying an AirTran ticket? Which firms are in the relevant "benchmark" group for your purposes?

CHAPTER

The Time Value of Money and Discounted Cash Flow Analysis

4

OBJECTIVES

- To explain the concepts of compounding and discounting, and future value and present value.
- To show how these concepts are applied in making financial decisions.

CONTENTS

As we saw in chapter 1, financial decisions involve costs and benefits that are spread over time. Financial decision makers in households and firms all have to evaluate whether investing money today is justified by the expected benefits in the future. They must, therefore, compare the values of sums of money at different dates. To do so requires a thorough understanding of the **time value of money** concepts and **discounted cash flow** techniques presented in this chapter.

The time value of money (*TVM*) refers to the fact that money (a dollar, a mark, or a yen) in hand today is worth more than the expectation of the same

101

amount to be received in the future. There are at least three reasons why this is true. The first is that you can invest it, earn interest, and end up with more in the future. The second is that the purchasing power of money can change over time because of inflation. The third is that the receipt of money expected in the future is, in general, uncertain.

In this chapter we study how to take account of the first of these: interest. We leave the study of how to deal with inflation and uncertainty to later chapters.

4.1 COMPOUNDING

We begin our study of the time value of money and discounted cash flow analysis with the concept of **compounding**—the process of going from today's value, or **present value** (*PV*), to **future value** (*FV*). Future value is the amount of money an investment will grow to at some date in the future by earning interest at some compound rate. For example, suppose you put $1,000 (the *PV*) into an account earning an interest rate of 10% per year. The amount you will have in five years, assuming you take nothing out of the account before then, is called the future value of $1,000 at an interest rate of 10% per year for five years.

Let us define our terms more precisely:

PV = present value or beginning amount in your account. Here it is $1,000.

   i = interest rate, usually expressed in percent per year. Here it is 10% (or 0.10 as a decimal).

  n = number of years the account will earn interest.

FV = future value at the end of *n* years.

Now let's calculate the future value in this example one step at a time. First, how much will you have after the first year? You will have your original $1,000 plus interest of $100 (10% of $1,000 or 0.1 × $1,000). Your future value at the end of year 1 will, therefore, be $1,100:

$$FV = \$1,000 \times 1.10 = \$1,100$$

If you redeposit this entire sum of $1,100 for another year, how much will you have at the end of year 2? During year 2 you will earn 10% interest on the entire $1,100. The interest earned is, thus, 0.10 × $1,100 or $110. You will, therefore, have $1,210 at the end of year 2.

To gain a good understanding of the nature of compound interest, we can break this future value of $1,210 into its three components. First, there is the original principal of $1,000. Next, there is the interest on this principal—$100 in the first year and another $100 in the second year. The interest on the original principal is called **simple interest** ($200 in our example). Finally, there is $10 of interest earned in the second year on the $100 of interest earned in the first year. Interest earned on interest already paid is called **compound interest.** The total interest earned ($210) is the sum of the simple interest ($200) plus the compound interest ($10).

Practically speaking, you do not care how much of your total interest of $210 is simple interest and how much is compound interest. All you really care about is how much you will have in your account in the future, that is, the future value. The most direct way to calculate the future value at the end of year 2 is to recognize that it is the original principal multiplied by 1.1 (here we drop the zero from 1.10 to shorten our equations) and then multiplied by 1.1 again:

$$FV = \$1,000 \times 1.1 \times 1.1 = \$1,000 \times 1.1^2 = \$1,210$$

After three years you will have:

$$FV = \$1,000 \times 1.1 \times 1.1 \times 1.1 = \$1,000 \times 1.1^3 = \$1,331$$

By this chain of reasoning, we can find future value after five years by repeated multiplication:

$$\$1,000 \times 1.1 \times 1.1 \times 1.1 \times 1.1 \times 1.1 = \$1,000 \times 1.1^5 = \$1,610.51$$

Thus, we have our answer to the original question. The future value of $1,000 at an interest rate of 10% per year for five years is $1,610.51. The total interest earned over the five years is $610.51, of which $500 is simple interest and $110.51 is compound interest.

Quick Check 4-1

If the interest rate is only 5% per year in the previous example, what is the future value? What are the simple interest and the compound interest?

To help in understanding the effect of compounding, look at Table 4.1, which shows the growth of the amount in your account over the five-year period. The table shows clearly that the total interest earned each year is equal to the beginning amount multiplied by the interest rate of 10%. When the information in the table is graphed in Figure 4.1, it shows the part of the growth in the account that is due to simple interest and the part that is due to compound interest. Although the cumulative total of simple interest grows each year by the same $100, the cumulative total of compound interest grows by larger and larger amounts each year. This is because the compound interest is 10% of the sum of all previous interest earned.

TABLE 4.1 Future Value and Compound Interest

Year	Beginning Amount	Interest Earned	Ending Amount
1	$1,000.00	$100.00	$1,100.00
2	1,100.00	110.00	1,210.00
3	1,210.00	121.00	1,331.00
4	1,331.00	133.10	1,464.10
5	1,464.10	146.41	1,610.51
	Total Interest Earned	$610.51	

Note: Table 4.1 and Figure 4.1 show the future value of $1,000 at 10% per year. Simple interest in the graph is the cumulative total of $100 per year. Compound interest in the graph is the cumulative total of all compound interest earned up to that point.

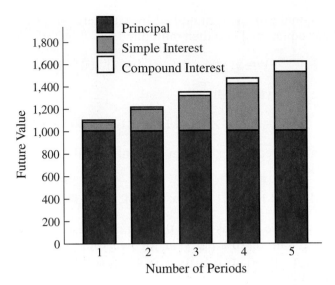

FIGURE 4.1 A Graph of Future Value and Compound Interest

More generally, if i is the interest rate and n is the number of years, the future value of the $1,000 is given by the formula:

$$FV = 1,000(1 + i)^n \qquad (4.1)$$

The expression multiplying the *PV* of $1,000 is the future value of $1 and is known as the **future value factor.** In our example it is 1.61051. The formula for the future value factor is simply:

$$\text{Future Value Factor} = (1 + i)^n$$

The future value of any amount invested at 10% per year for five years is just the amount times the same future value factor of 1.61051. Thus, the future value of $500 invested at 10% per year for five years is $500 × 1.61051 = $804.254. The future value factor is greater the higher the interest rate and the longer the time the investment is held. Table 4.2 and the graph in Figure 4.2 illustrate this relationship for various interest rates and holding periods.

4.1.1 Calculating Future Values

In practice, there is a variety of ways to calculate future values, which we can illustrate with the example of calculating the future value of $1,000 at an interest rate of 10% per year for five years.

1. We could simply multiply 1,000 by 1.1 five times:

$$\$1,000 \times 1.1 \times 1.1 \times 1.1 \times 1.1 \times 1.1 = \$1,610.51$$

This method is fine if the holding period is not too long. But when the number of periods, *n,* gets large, this method becomes tedious. If we have a calculator with a key labeled y^x, we can directly compute:

$$\$1,000 \times 1.1^5 = \$1,610.51$$

TABLE 4.2 Future Value of $1 for Different Periods and Interest Rates

Number of Periods, n	Interest Rate, i					
	2%	4%	6%	8%	10%	12%
1	1.0200	1.0400	1.0600	1.0800	1.1000	1.1200
2	1.0404	1.0816	1.1236	1.1664	1.2100	1.2544
3	1.0612	1.1249	1.1910	1.2597	1.3310	1.4049
4	1.0824	1.1699	1.2625	1.3605	1.4641	1.5735
5	1.1041	1.2167	1.3382	1.4693	1.6105	1.7623
10	1.2190	1.4802	1.7908	2.1589	2.5937	3.1058
15	1.3459	1.8009	2.3966	3.1722	4.1772	4.4736
20	1.4859	2.1911	3.2071	4.6610	6.7275	9.6463

Note: Table 4.2 and Figure 4.3 show the future value of $1 for different holding periods at various interest rates. The higher the interest rate, the faster the future value grows.

The general formula for the future value of $1 is:

$$FV = (1 + i)^n$$

where i is the interest rate expressed as a decimal fraction and n is the number of periods.

There are also special-purpose financial calculators available designed to make doing the calculations even easier. Figure 4.3 shows the keyboard of a typical financial calculator. By pressing the appropriately labeled keys, you enter (in any order you please) the values for the number of periods (n), the interest rate (i), and the amount of the investment (PV), and then compute future value (FV). Like magic, the answer appears in the calculator's display. Similarly, spreadsheet programs for personal computers, such as Lotus and Excel, all have a simple and convenient way to compute future values as a built-in feature.

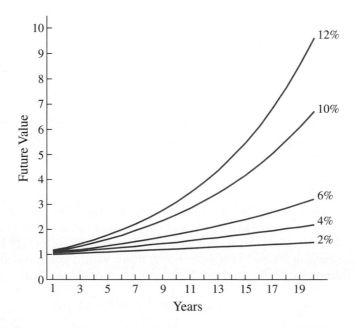

FIGURE 4.2 Future Value of $1 for Different Periods and Interest Rates

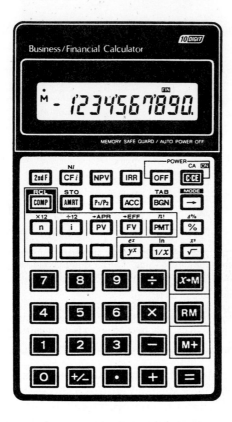

FIGURE 4.3   Financial Calculator

2. We can use tables of future value factors, such as those in Table 4.2, to compute future values. In our example, we would look for the factor corresponding to *n* of 5 and an interest rate of 10%. The table shows 1.6105 as the appropriate factor. We then multiply our $1,000 by this factor.

3. Finally, there is a handy rule of thumb that can help you estimate future values when you do not have your calculator or a table available. It is called the **Rule of 72.** This rule says that the number of years it takes for a sum of money to double in value (the "doubling time") is approximately equal to the number 72 divided by the interest rate expressed in percent per year:

$$\text{Doubling Time} = \frac{72}{\text{Interest Rate}}$$

So at an interest rate of 10% per year, it should take approximately 7.2 years to double your money. If you start with $1,000, you will have $2,000 after 7.2 years, $4,000 after 14.4 years, $8,000 after 21.6 years, and so on.

4.1.2 Saving for Old Age

You are 20 years old and are considering putting $100 into an account paying 8% per year for 45 years. How much will you have in the account at age 65? How much of it will be simple interest, and how much compound interest? If you could find an account paying 9% per year, how much more would you have at age 65?

Using any of the methods discussed previously, we find:

$$FV = \$100 \times 1.08^{45} = \$3,192$$

Because the original principal is $100, total interest earned is $3,092. The simple interest is $45 \times 0.08 \times \$100$ or $360, whereas the compound interest is $2,732.

At an interest rate of 9% per year, we find:

$$FV = \$100 \times 1.09^{45} = \$4,833$$

Thus, a seemingly small increase of 1% in the interest rate results in an extra $1,641 ($4,833 − $3,192) at age 65. This is more than a 50% increase ($1,641/$3,192 = 0.514). The general point of this example is that a small difference in interest rates can make a big difference in future values over long periods of time.

Note that the *Rule of 72* can help us to find a pretty good approximate answer to our questions. At an interest rate of 8% per year, your $100 would double about every nine years. Thus, after 45 years, it would double five times, giving an approximate future value of $3,200:

$$\$100 \times 2 \times 2 \times 2 \times 2 \times 2 = \$100 \times 2^5 = \$100 \times 32 = \$3,200$$

which is not too far from the exact answer of $3,192.

At an interest rate of 9% per year, your money would double about every eight years. In 45 years it would double about 5.5 times (45/8 = 5.625). Therefore, the future value should be about 50% greater than when the interest rate is 8% per year: $1.5 \times \$3,200 = \$4,800$. Again, this is not too far from the exact answer of $4,833.

4.1.3 Reinvesting at a Different Rate

You are faced with the following investment decision. You have $10,000 to invest for two years. You have decided to invest your money in bank certificates of deposit (CDs). Two-year CDs are paying 7% per year and one-year CDs are paying 6%. What should you do?

To make this decision you must first decide what you think the interest rate on one-year CDs will be next year. This is called the **reinvestment rate,** that is, the interest rate at which money received before the end of your planning horizon can be reinvested. Suppose you are sure that it will be 8% per year.

Now you can use the concept of future value to make this investment decision. You compute the future value under each investment alternative and choose the one giving the most money at the end of two years. With the two-year CD, the future value will be:

$$FV = \$10,000 \times 1.07^2 = \$11,449$$

With the sequence of two one-year CDs, the future value will be:

$$FV = \$10,000 \times 1.06 \times 1.08 = \$11,448$$

Thus, you are slightly better off if you invest in the two-year CD.

4.1.4 Paying Back a Loan

Fifty years after graduation, you get a letter from your college notifying you that they have just discovered that you failed to pay your last student activities fee of $100. Because it was your college's oversight, it has decided to charge you an interest rate of only 6% per year. Your college would like you to pay it back at the coming fiftieth reunion of your graduating class. As a loyal alumnus, you feel obliged to pay. How much do you owe them?

Using any of the methods discussed earlier, we find:

$$FV = \$100 \times 1.06^{50} = \$1,842$$

Quick Check 4-2

In 1626 Peter Minuit purchased Manhattan Island from the Native Americans for about $24 worth of trinkets. If the tribe had taken cash instead and invested it to earn 6% per year compounded annually, how much would the tribe have had in 1996, 370 years later?

4.2 THE FREQUENCY OF COMPOUNDING

Interest rates on loans and saving accounts are usually stated in the form of an **annual percentage rate** (*APR*), (e.g., 6% per year) with a certain frequency of compounding (e.g., monthly). Because the frequency of compounding can differ, it is important to have a way of making interest rates comparable. This is done by computing an **effective annual rate** (*EFF*), defined as the equivalent interest rate, *if compounding were only once per year*.

For example, suppose your money earns interest at a stated annual percentage rate (*APR*) of 6% per year compounded monthly. This means that interest is credited to your account every month at 1/12th the stated *APR*. Thus, the true interest rate is actually ½% per month (or 0.005 per month as a decimal.)

We find the *EFF* by computing the future value at the end of the year per dollar invested at the beginning of the year. In this example we get:

$$FV = (1.005)^{12} = 1.0616778$$

The effective annual rate is just this number minus one.

$$EFF = 1.0616778 - 1 = 0.0616778 \text{ or } 6.16778\% \text{ per year}$$

The general formula for the effective annual rate is:

$$EFF = \left(1 + \frac{APR}{m}\right)^m - 1 \tag{4.2}$$

where *APR* is the annual percentage rate, and *m* the number of compounding periods per year. Table 4.3 presents the effective annual rates corresponding to an annual percentage rate of 6% per year for different compounding frequencies.

If compounding is done once per year, then the effective annual rate is the same as the annual percentage rate. As the compounding frequency increases, the effective annual rate gets larger and larger but approaches a limit. As *m* grows without limit, $(1 + APR/m)^m$ gets closer and closer to e^{APR} where *e* is the number 2.71828 (rounded off to the fifth decimal place). In our example, $e^{0.06} = 1.0618364$. Therefore, if interest is continuously compounded, *EFF* = 0.0618365 or 6.18365% per year.

TABLE 4.3   Effective Annual Rates for an *APR* of 6%

Compounding Frequency	m	Effective Annual Rate
Annually	1	6.00000%
Semiannually	2	6.09000%
Quarterly	4	6.13614%
Monthly	12	6.16778%
Weekly	52	6.17998%
Daily	365	6.18313%
Continuous	limit	6.18365%

Quick Check 4-3
You take out a loan at an *APR* of 12% with monthly compounding. What is the effective annual rate on your loan?

4.3 PRESENT VALUE AND DISCOUNTING

E-BOOK

4.3–4.6

When we compute future values, we are asking questions like "How much will we have in 10 years if we invest $1,000 today at an interest rate of 8% per year?" (The answer is: *FV* = $2,159. Check it!)

But suppose we want to know how much to invest today in order to reach some target amount at a date in the future. For example, if we need to have $15,000 for a child's college education eight years from now, how much do we have to invest now? To find the answer to this kind of question, we need to calculate the present value of a given future amount.

Calculating present values is the reverse of calculating future values. That is, it tells us the amount you would have to invest today to have a certain amount in the future. Let's take a look at calculating *PV* step by step.

Suppose we want to have $1,000 one year from now and can earn 10% interest per year. The amount we must invest now is the present value of $1,000. Because the interest rate is 10%, we know that for every dollar we invest now we will have a future value of $1.1. Therefore, we can write:

$$\text{Present Value} \times 1.1 = \$1{,}000$$

Then the present value is given by:

$$\text{Present Value} = \$1{,}000/1.1 = \$909.09$$

So if the interest rate is 10% per year, we need to invest $909.09 in order to have $1,000 a year from now.

Now suppose the $1,000 is not needed until two years from now. Clearly, the amount we need to invest today at an interest rate of 10% is less than $909.09, because it will earn interest at the rate of 10% per year for two years. To find the present value, we use our knowledge of how to find future values:

$$\$1,000 = PV \times 1.1^2 = PV \times 1.21$$

In our example the present value is:

$$PV = \$1,000/1.1^2 = \$826.45$$

Thus, $826.45 invested now at an interest rate of 10% per year will grow to $1,000 in two years.

Calculating present values is called *discounting,* and the interest rate used in the calculation is often referred to as the *discount rate.* Thus, discounting in finance is very different from discounting in retailing. In retailing it means reducing the price in order to sell more goods; in finance it means computing the present value of a future sum of money. To distinguish the two kinds of discounting in the world of business, the calculation of present values is called *discounted cash flow* (*DCF*) analysis.

The general formula for the present value of $1 to be received *n* periods from now at a discount rate of *i* (per period) is:

$$PV = \frac{1}{(1 + i)^n} \qquad (4.3)$$

This is called the present value factor of $1 at an interest rate of *i* for *n* periods.

The present value of $1 to be received five years from now at an interest rate of 10% per year is:

$$PV = \frac{1}{1.1^5} = 0.62092$$

To find the present value of $1,000 to be received in five years at 10%, we simply multiply this factor by $1,000 to get $620.92.

Because discounting is just the reverse of compounding, we could use the same table (see Table 4.2) that we used before for future value factors to find present values. Instead of multiplying by the factor, however, we would divide by it. Thus, we can find the present value of $1,000 to be received in five years at 10% by looking up the future value factor of 1.6105 in Table 4.2 and dividing $1,000 by it:

$$\$1,000/1.6105 = \$620.92$$

For convenience, there are tables of present value factors such as the one shown as Table 4.4 containing the reciprocals of the factors in Table 4.2. Look in Table 4.4 for the present value factor for an interest rate of 10% and five periods, and verify that it is 0.6209.

The general formula for the present value of $1 is:

$$PV = 1/(1 + i)^n$$

where *i* is the interest rate expressed as a decimal fraction and *n* is the number of periods.

TABLE 4.4   Present Value of $1.00 for Different Periods and Rates

Number of periods, n	Interest Rate, i				
	2%	*4%*	*6%*	*8%*	*10%*
1	0.9804	0.9615	0.9434	0.9259	0.9091
2	0.9612	0.9246	0.8890	0.8573	0.8264
3	0.9423	0.8890	0.8396	0.7938	0.7513
4	0.9238	0.8548	0.7921	0.7350	0.6830
5	0.9057	0.8219	0.7473	0.6806	0.6209

By going down any column in Table 4.4, note how present values decline the further in the future the $1 is to be taken out of the account. At an interest rate of 10%, for example, the present value of $1 to be received in one year is $0.9091, but the present value of $1 to be received in 20 years is only $0.1486.

4.3.1 When a $100 Gift Is Not Really $100

It is your brother's tenth birthday, and he receives a $100 savings bond maturing in five years. This type of bond pays nothing until its maturity date. In adding up the value of his birthday "loot," he mistakenly writes down $100 for this bond. How much is it really worth if the discount rate is 8% per year and the bond does not mature for another five years? How could you explain your brother's mistake to him, so that he would understand?

We are looking for the present value of $100 to be received in five years at a discount rate of 8% per year. There are several ways we could compute it. The formula is:

$$PV = \$100/1.08^5$$

On an ordinary calculator, we could find this present value by dividing 100 by 1.08 five times to find that it is 68. On a financial calculator (such as the one pictured in Figure 4.3), we would enter the values for *n, i,* and *FV,* and then compute the present value by pressing the key labeled *PV.* Or we could use the present value factor of $1 in Table 4.4. The table entry corresponding to an interest rate of 8% and five periods is 0.6806. Multiply this factor by $100 to find the present value of $68.

Explaining the answer to your brother is a tough assignment. Probably the best way to do it is to use the idea of future value rather than present value. You could explain to him that his $100 savings bond is worth only $68 because all he has to do to get $100 five years from now is to put $68 into a savings account paying interest of 8% per year.

Quick Check 4-4
What is the present value of $100 to be received in four years at an interest rate of 6% per year?

4.4 ALTERNATIVE DISCOUNTED CASH FLOW DECISION RULES

E-BOOK

4.3–4.6

The discounted cash flow concepts that we have studied so far in this chapter provide a powerful set of tools for making investment decisions. The essential ideas are captured in the equation relating future value, present value, the interest rate, and the number of periods:

$$FV = PV(1 + i)^n \tag{4.4}$$

Given any three of the variables in this equation, we can find the fourth and formulate an investment decision rule based on it. The most common decision rule is the net present value (*NPV*) rule. This rule is not only widely used and universally applicable (i.e., correctly used it never leads to the wrong decision), but it is also very intuitive. Simply put, the *NPV* rule sounds almost obvious: *Accept any project with a present value of future cash flows that exceed the initial investment.* The only trick is to make sure that one does not compare apples to oranges. Thus, when calculating the future cash flows (which happens some time from now), we must use their present value in order to make them comparable.

Formally, the *NPV* rule says the following:

> The *NPV* is the difference between the present value of all future cash inflows minus the present value of all current and future cash outflows. Accept a project if its *NPV* is positive. Reject a project if its *NPV* is negative.

For example, suppose that a $100 savings bond is selling for a price of $75. Your next best alternative for investing is an 8% bank account. Is the savings bond a good investment? Let's show how to use the *NPV* decision rule in evaluating this investment. The initial investment for the savings bond is $75 (this happens today, no discounting necessary). What is the present value of the cash inflows that the bond generates? It is simply the present value of $100 to be received in five years from now. The relevant interest rate is the rate that the money could earn if it were not invested in the bond.

In general, for the *NPV* calculation of any investment, we use the **opportunity cost of capital** (also called the *market capitalization rate*) as the interest rate. The opportunity cost of capital is simply the rate that we could earn somewhere else if we did not invest it in the project under evaluation. In this example, the opportunity cost of capital of investing in the savings bond is the rate that we could earn if we put our money in a bank instead—8% per year in this case. Because it is not always clear where the opportunity cost of capital comes from, the issue is clarified in the appendix to this chapter.

For convenience in keeping track of the calculations (especially if they are being done on a financial calculator), we organize our information in the following table:

Time Value of Money (*TVM*) Calculation Table				
n	*i*	*PV*	*FV*	*Result*
5	8	?	100	*PV* = 68.06

A question mark indicates the variable that has to be computed.

In this case we use three of the variables, *FV, n,* and *i,* to compute the fourth, *PV.* We then compare this computed present value to the known initial investment of the savings bond. Using the formula, we find:

$$PV = \frac{\$100}{1.08^5} = \$68.06$$

Comparing the $68.06 to the $75 necessary to obtain the bond, we conclude that investing in the bond is not worthwhile. In other words, the *NPV* of the investment, $68.06 − $75 = -$6.94, is negative.

The *NPV* is a measure of how much your *current* wealth changes as a result of your choice. Clearly, if the *NPV* is negative, it does not pay to undertake the investment. In this case, if you choose to invest in the bond, your current wealth decreases by approximately $7.

Another way to arrive at the same conclusion is to use a slightly different rule known as the *future value rule.* Simply stated, it says to *invest in the project if its future value is greater than the future value that will obtain in the next best alternative.* This rule is actually slightly more intuitive (and leads to the same decision as the *NPV* rule). The reason it is not used as often in practice is that in many circumstances (as will be shown later in the book) the future value of an investment cannot be computed whereas the *NPV* rule can still be used. Let us illustrate how the future value rule would have worked in the same example just used to illustrate the *NPV* rule.

Investing in a savings bond (initial investment $75, future value of cash flows $100 in five years) clearly leads to a future value of $100. Putting the money into a bank at 8% is the next best thing we can do with the money. Does the savings bond have a higher future value than we could get from the bank? Again, we organize our information in the table:

n	i	PV	FV	Result
5	8	75	?	FV = 110.20

Using the formula, we get that the future value from the bank account is given by

$$FV = \$75 \times 1.08^5 = \$110.20$$

This is clearly better than the $100 future value of the savings bond. Again, we find that the savings bond is an inferior investment.

There are other decision rules that are also used in practice. Each has its own intuition and each is useful for certain problems. It should be noted, however, that none of the rules are as universally applicable as the *NPV* rule. Here is another widely used rule, which in many circumstances is also equivalent to the *NPV* rule:

Accept an investment if its return is greater than the opportunity cost of capital.

This rule is (clearly) based on the concept of rate of return. Recall that in our example the opportunity cost of capital from putting the money into the bank is 8% per year. By investing $75 in the savings bond today, you can get $100 in five years from now. What interest rate would you be earning? In other words, we want to find *i* that solves the equation:

$$\$75 = \$100/(1 + i)^5$$

This is called the bond's **yield to maturity** or **internal rate of return** (*IRR*). The internal rate of return is the discount rate that makes the present value of the future cash inflows equal to the present value of cash outflows. In other words, the *IRR* is exactly that interest rate at which the *NPV* is equal to zero. Thus, if the rate at which the *NPV* is zero (the *IRR*) is higher than the opportunity cost of capital, then we know that the *NPV* at the opportunity cost of capital itself must be positive. In other words, if the *IRR* is (say) 10% (i.e. the *NPV* at 10% is zero), then the *NPV* at the opportunity cost of capital (say) 8% must be positive. Why? We know that the *NPV* calculation discounts future cash flows. We also know that the present value of future cash flows is greater when the discount rate is small. Thus, if the *NPV* is zero at 10%, it will be positive at 8%. Hence, having a 10% *IRR* and an 8% opportunity cost of capital is equivalent to saying that the *NPV* must be positive.[1]

To find i (the *IRR*) on a financial calculator, enter *PV, FV,* and *n* and compute *i:*

n	*i*	*PV*	*FV*	*Result*
5	?	–75	100	$i = 5.92\%$

We have put a negative sign in front of the $75 in the table column labeled *PV* because it signifies an investment (that is, a cash outflow). Most financial calculators require you to enter the initial investment as negative. It should not be surprising that the calculator assumes that an investment (negative cash flow) is needed in order to earn a positive cash flow in the future. If all cash flows were positive, we would have created a money machine and that, sadly, is an impossibility.

If you don't have a financial calculator, you can solve for i using some algebra:

$$100 = 75 \times (1 + i)^5$$
$$(1 + i)^5 = 100/75$$
$$i = (100/75)^{1/5} - 1 = 5.92\%$$

Thus, the yield to maturity (*IRR*) on the bond is 5.92% per year. This should be compared to the 8% per year you could earn by putting your money in the bank. Clearly, you are better off putting your money in the bank.

The rate of return decision rule is equivalent to the *NPV* rule in evaluating a single investment for which there are no negative future cash flows. Even with that condition, it will not in general produce the same rankings from best to worst among several investment opportunities.

> When you have to choose among several alternative investments, choose the one with the highest NPV.

There is one more variable in this example for which we can solve with our calculator in order to arrive at a decision: n (the number of years). Let us do this for the savings bond. We know that the *FV* is $100, the *PV* is $75, the opportunity cost of capital is 8%, what is n?

$$\$75 = \$100/1.08^n$$

---

[1]This conclusion applies only if all future cash flows are positive.

On the financial calculator we input *PV, FV,* and *i* and compute *n:*

n	i	PV	FV	Result
?	8	−75	100	n = 3.74

We find that *n* is 3.74 years. Now, what does this mean? It means that if we put the money into the bank (at 8%), it would take 3.74 years for $75 to grow to $100. With the savings bond, it takes five years for the $75 to grow to $100. This observation has suggested to some the following rule:

> Choose the investment alternative with the shortest payback period.

In other words, choose the investment in which you can "get your money back" (i.e. turn the $75 investment into $100) in the shortest period of time.

This rule, however, applies only in special cases. As with the IRR rule, the "payback" rule is not a reliable one for general investment choice purposes. Although these alternative rules are sometimes used in practice, stick with the *NPV* rule as the safe and universal rule of choice.

4.4.1 Investing in Land

You have the opportunity to buy a piece of land for $10,000. You are sure that five years from now it will be worth $20,000. If you can earn 8% per year by investing your money in the bank, is this investment in the land worthwhile?

> Invest in a project if its net present value (NPV) is positive. Do not invest if the NPV is negative.

What is the present value of having $20,000 (the future cash flow) in five years from now? In this case we input *FV, n,* and *i,* and compute *PV.* We then compare this computed present value to the $10,000 initial outlay, and make our decision based on which one is greater.

n	i	PV	FV	Result
5	8	?	20,000	PV = 13,612

Thus, the investment in the land has a present value of $13,612. Comparing this to the $10,000 cost of the land, it clearly seems like a bargain. Its *NPV* is $3,612.

Quick Check 4-5
Show that the alternative decision criteria presented previously lead to the same result—that the investment is worthwhile.

4.4.2 Other People's Money

In the preceding example, we considered an investment in which you are required to lay out money in the present and receive cash at some future date. But often financial decisions involve just the reverse. For example, suppose that you need to borrow $5,000 to buy a car. You go to a bank and they offer you a loan at an interest rate of 12% per year. You then go to a friend who says he will lend you the $5,000 if you pay him $9,000 in four years. What should you do?

First, let's identify the project that you need to evaluate. The cash flow that you want to evaluate is the $5,000 (today) you can borrow from your friend (a cash inflow). The investment you must make is the present value of the $9,000 repayment (a cash outflow) after four years.

The way to proceed is to calculate the *NPV* of the project. The opportunity cost of capital is 12% (the bank's rate, your next best alternative). The cash flows are given. What is the *NPV*?

n	i	PV	FV	Result
4	12	?	−9,000	PV = 5,719.66

We find that the present value of the cash outflow is $5,719.66. Thus, the *NPV* of the project is $5,000 − $5,719.66 = −719.66 < 0. Hence, the project of borrowing from your friend is not worthwhile. You are better off borrowing from the bank.

What is the implied interest rate that your friend is charging you? The answer is to solve the present value equation for *i*:

$$\$5,000 = \$9,000/(1 + i)^5$$

Using a financial calculator:

n	i	PV	FV	Result
4	?	5,000	−9,000	i = 15.83%

We find that $i = 15.83\%$ per year. You are better off borrowing from the bank.

Note that the rate you have just computed is the *IRR* of borrowing from your friend. It is 15.83%. Now, in the previous examples we stated that the *IRR* rule works as follows: *Invest* in a project if the *IRR* is *greater* than the opportunity cost of capital. This rule works for projects that have the feature of a one-time investment (i.e., the initial cash flow is negative and the future cash flows are positive).

However, it should be clear that for projects that have the feature of borrowing (i.e., the initial cash flow is positive and the future repayment cash flow is negative) the rule must be turned on its head: *Borrow* from a source if the *IRR* of the loan is *less* than the opportunity cost of capital.

As noted previously, a major potential problem with the *IRR* rule rears its head whenever there are multiple cash inflows. In such cases the *IRR* may not be unique (e.g., there are many) or the *IRR* may not exist at all. More on this problem later.

4.5 MULTIPLE CASH FLOWS

E-BOOK

4.3–4.6

So far we have considered situations in which there is a single cash flow in the future. What happens if there is more than one? For example, suppose you want to save for a child's college education or for your own retirement by putting a certain amount each year into an interest-bearing account; or you are evaluating an investment such as a bond that offers a stream of future payments; or you are considering taking a loan that requires you to make periodic installment payments. To deal with all of these more complicated situations we need only extend the concepts already presented.

4.5.1 Time Lines

A useful tool in analyzing the timing of cash flows is a diagram known as a **time line.** It is illustrated in Figure 4.4.

A negative sign in front of a cash flow means that you put in that amount of money (a cash *outflow* from you), whereas no sign means that you take out that amount (cash *inflow* to you). In our example, you put in 100 at time 0 and take out 20 at the end of the first period, 50 at the end of the second, and 60 at the end of the third.

4.5.2 Future Value of a Stream of Cash Flows

We begin with a savings decision and the concept of future value. Each year you deposit $1,000 into an account paying an interest rate of 10% per year starting immediately. How much will you have after two years if you do not withdraw any money before then?

The original $1,000 grows to $1,100 at the end of the first year. Then you add another $1,000, so there is $2,100 in the account at the beginning of the second year. By the end of the second year there is $1.1 \times \$2,100$ or $2,310 in the account.

An alternative way to find this future value of $2,310 is to calculate the future values of each of the two $1,000 deposits separately and then add them together. The future value of the first deposit is:

$$\$1,000 \times 1.1^2 = \$1,210$$

The future value of the second deposit will be:

$$\$1,000 \times 1.1 = \$1,100$$

Adding the two together, we get the same $2,310 that we found by multiplying each year's accumulation by 1.1.

Quick Check 4-6

Suppose you deposit $1,000 now and then $2,000 a year from now. How much will you have two years from now, if the interest rate is 10% per year?

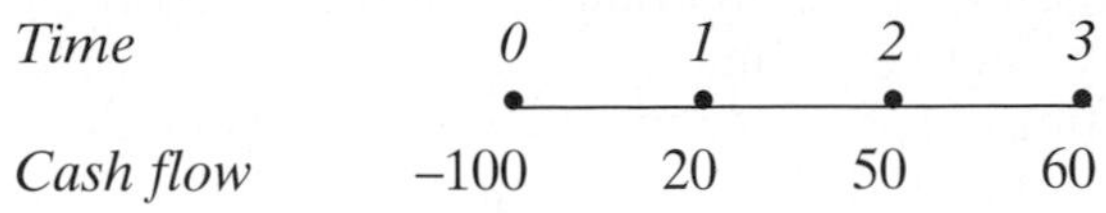

Time	0	1	2	3
Cash flow	−100	20	50	60

FIGURE 4.4   Time Line

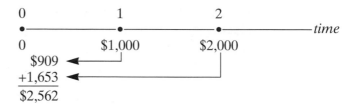

FIGURE 4.5   Present Value of Multiple Cash Flows

4.5.3 Present Value of a Stream of Cash Flows

Often we need to compute the present value rather than the future value of a series of cash flows. For example, suppose you want to have $1,000 one year from now and then $2,000 in two years. If the interest rate is 10% per year, how much would you have to put into an account today in order to satisfy your requirement?

In this case we have to compute the present value of the two cash flows depicted in Figure 4.5. Just as the future value of a stream of cash flows is the sum of the future values of each, so too with the present value.

4.5.4 Investing with Multiple Cash Flows

Suppose you are offered an opportunity to invest in a project that will pay you $1,000 a year from now and another $2,000 two years from now. The project requires you to invest $2,500 now. You are convinced that the project is completely free of risk. Is it a worthwhile investment if you can earn 10% per year on your money by leaving it in the bank?

Note that this problem bears a striking resemblance to the previous one. The cash flows that this project will generate are the same as depicted in Figure 4.5— $1,000 a year from now and $2,000 two years from now. We already know that if you put your money in the bank, it would take $2,562 to generate the same future cash flows. Because the outlay required on the project is only $2,500, it has a net present value of $62. As we saw earlier in this chapter, an investment with a positive *NPV* should be undertaken.

4.6 ANNUITIES

E-BOOK

4.3–4.6

Often the future cash flows in a savings plan, an investment project, or a loan repayment schedule are the same each year. We call such a level stream of cash flows or payments an **annuity.** The term comes from the life insurance business, in which an annuity contract is one that promises a stream of payments to the purchaser for some period of time. In finance it is applied more generally and applies to any level stream of cash flows. Thus, the stream of payments on an installment loan or a mortgage is called an annuity, too.

If the cash flows start immediately, as in a savings plan or a lease, it is called an **immediate annuity.** If the cash flows start at the end of the current period rather than immediately, it is called an **ordinary annuity.** A mortgage is an example of an ordinary annuity. There are some convenient formulas, tables, and calculator functions for computing the present and future values of annuities, which come in handy when the stream of cash flows lasts for many periods.

4.6.1 Future Value of Annuities

For example, suppose that you intend to save $100 each year for the next three years. How much will you have accumulated at the end of that time if the interest rate is 10% per year? If you start saving immediately, you will have:

$$FV = \$100 \times 1.1^3 + \$100 \times 1.1^2 + \$100 \times 1.1$$

Factoring out the constant annual cash flow of $100, we get:

$$FV = \$100 \times (1.1 + 1.1^2 + 1.1^3)$$

The result is a future value of $364.10. The factor multiplying the $100 is the future value of a $1 payment per year for three years. Although tables containing such future value factors for various interest rates and numbers of periods are available, most people today use financial calculators. The calculator key used to input the periodic contribution is labeled *PMT* (short for *payment*) on most models.

In our example, we know *i*, *n*, and *PMT*, and want to compute *PV*. We enter the givens in the appropriate cells of the table and insert a ? (question mark) for the entry that we want to compute.

n	i	PV	FV	PMT	Result
3	10	0	?	100	PV = $8,559.48

In computing the future value of an annuity it matters, of course, whether it is an immediate annuity, as in our current example, or whether it is an ordinary annuity. In the case of an ordinary annuity, the first $100 contribution is made at the end of the first period. Figure 4.6 shows a time line that contrasts the two situations.

Although in both cases there are the same number of payments, under the immediate annuity pattern the entire amount earns interest for an additional year. Thus, an immediate annuity would have an *FV* equal to that of the ordinary annuity multiplied by 1 + *i*. For an ordinary annuity of $1 per year the formula for future value is:

$$FV = \frac{(1 + i)^n - 1}{i}$$

We find that the future value of our savings plan of $100 per year for three years is $364.10 if the first deposit is made immediately (an immediate annuity), and $331 if delayed until the end of the first year (an ordinary annuity).

Some financial calculators have a special key to press to let the calculator know whether the annuity payments start at the beginning or end of the first period. On the calculator displayed in Figure 4.3 this key is labeled *BGN*.

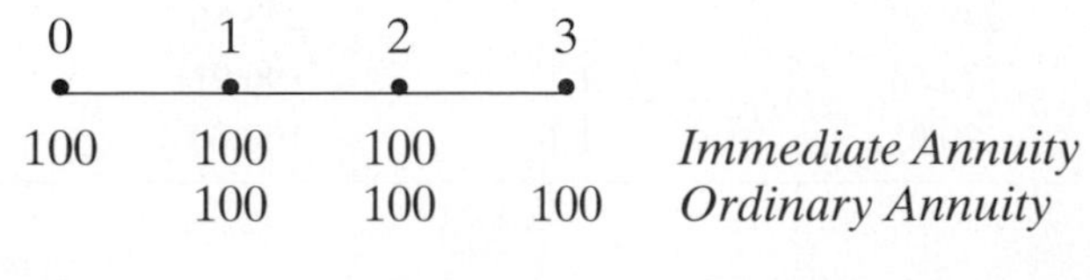

0	1	2	3
100	100	100	
	100	100	100

Immediate Annuity
Ordinary Annuity

FIGURE 4.6 Cash Flow Diagram of Annuities

4.6.2 Present Value of Annuities

Often we want to compute the present value rather than the future value of an annuity stream. For example, how much would you have to put into a fund earning an interest rate of 10% per year to be able to take out $100 per year for the next three years? The answer is the present value of the three cash flows.

The present value of the annuity is the sum of the present values of each of the three payments of $100:

$$PV = \$100/1.1 + \$100/1.1^2 + \$100/1.1^3$$

Factoring out the constant payment of $100 per year, we get:

$$PV = \$100 \times (1/1.1 + 1/1.1^2 + 1/1.1^3)$$

The result is a present value of $248.69. The factor multiplying the $100 payment is the present value of an ordinary annuity of $1 for three years at an interest rate of 10%.

Table 4.5 verifies that indeed $248.69 is all you would have to put in the account to be able to take out $100 each year for the next three years.

The formula for the present value of an ordinary annuity of $1 per period for *n* periods at an interest rate of *i* is:

$$PV = \frac{1 - (1 + i)^{-n}}{i}$$

On a financial calculator, we would enter the values for *n, i,* and *PMT,* and compute the *PV.*

n	i	PV	FV	PMT	Result
3	10	?	0	100	PV = 248.69

4.6.3 Buying an Annuity

You are 65 years old and are considering whether it pays to buy an annuity from an insurance company. For a cost of $10,000 the insurance company will pay you $1,000 per year for the rest of your life. If you can earn 8% per year on your money in a bank account and expect to live until age 80, is it worth buying the annuity? What

TABLE 4.5	Proof That Putting in $248.69 Allows You to Take Out $100 per Year for 3 Years			
Year	Amount at Beginning of Year	Multiply by	Amount at End of Year	Subtract $100
1	248.69	1.1	273.56	173.56
2	173.56	1.1	190.91	90.91
3	90.91	1.1	100.00	0.00

implied interest rate is the insurance company paying you? How long must you live for the annuity to be worthwhile?

The most direct way to make this investment decision is to compute the present value of the payments from the annuity and compare it to the annuity's $10,000 cost. Assuming it is an ordinary annuity, then it is expected to make 15 payments of $1,000 each starting at age 66 and ending at age 80. The present value of these 15 payments at a discount rate of 8% per year is $8,559.48.

n	*i*	*PV*	*FV*	*PMT*	*Result*
15	8	?	0	1,000	$PV = \$8,559.48$

In other words, to generate the same 15 annual payments of $1,000 each, it would be enough to invest $8,559.48 in a bank account paying 8% interest per year. Therefore, the net present value of the investment in the annuity is:

$$NPV = \$8,559.48 - \$10,000 = -\$1,440.52$$

and it is not worth buying.

To compute the implied interest rate on the annuity, we need to find the discount rate that makes the *NPV* of the investment zero. The correct answer is 5.56% per year. On a financial calculator we find it by entering the values for *n, PMT,* and *PV,* and computing *i*.

n	*i*	*PV*	*FV*	*PMT*	*Result*
15	?	−10,000	0	1,000	$i = 5.56\%$

In other words, if a bank were offering you an interest rate of 5.56% per year, you could deposit $10,000 now and be able to withdraw $1,000 per year for the next 15 years.

To find the number of years one would have to live to make this annuity worthwhile, we must ask what value of *n* would make the *NPV* of the investment zero. The correct answer is 21 years. On a financial calculator we find it by entering the values for *i, PMT,* and *PV,* and computing *n*.

n	*i*	*PV*	*FV*	*PMT*	*Result*
?	8	−10,000	0	1,000	$n = 21$

Looking at it differently, if you live for 21 years rather than 15, the insurance company would wind up paying you an implied interest rate of 8% per year.

4.6.4 Taking a Mortgage Loan

Now let's look at an example of a financing decision. You have just decided to buy a house and need to borrow $100,000. One bank offers you a mortgage loan to be repaid over 30 years in 360 monthly payments. If the interest rate is 12% per year, what is the amount of the monthly payment? (Although the interest rate is quoted as an annual percentage rate, the rate is actually 1% per month.) Another bank offers you a 15-year mortgage loan with a monthly payment of $1,100. Which loan is the better deal?

The monthly payment on the 30-year mortgage is computed by using a monthly period ($n = 360$ months) and a monthly interest rate of 1%. The payment is $1,028.61 per month. It is calculated as follows:

n	i	PV	FV	PMT	Result
360	1	−100,000	0	?	$PMT = \$1,028.61$

At first glance, it might seem as if the 30-year mortgage is a better deal because the $1,028.61 monthly payment is less than the $1,100 for the 15-year mortgage. But the 15-year mortgage is finished after only 180 payments. The monthly interest rate is 0.8677%, or an annual percentage rate of 10.4%. To find this rate:

n	i	PV	FV	PMT	Result
360	?	100,000	0	−$1,100	$i = 0.8677\%$

The 15-year mortgage is, therefore, the better deal in this case.

4.7 PERPETUAL ANNUITIES

An important, special type of annuity is a perpetual annuity or **perpetuity.** A perpetuity is a stream of cash flows that lasts forever. The classic example is the "consol" bonds issued by the British government in the nineteenth century, which pay interest each year on the stated face value of the bonds but have no maturity date. Another example, and perhaps a more relevant one, is a share of preferred stock that pays a fixed cash dividend each period (usually every quarter year) and never matures.

A disturbing feature of any perpetual annuity is that you cannot compute the future value of its cash flows because it is infinite. Nevertheless, it has a perfectly well-defined and determinable present value. It might at first seem paradoxical that a series of cash flows that lasts forever can have a finite value today. But consider a perpetual stream of $100 per year. If the interest rate is 10% per year, how much is this perpetuity worth today?

The answer is $1,000. To see why, consider how much money you would have to put into a bank account offering interest of 10% per year in order to be able to take out $100 every year forever. If you put in $1,000, then at the end of the first year you would have $1,100 in the account. You would take out $100, leaving $1,000 for the second year. Clearly, if the interest rate stayed at 10% per year, and you had a fountain of youth nearby, you could go on doing this forever.

More generally, the formula for the present value of a level perpetuity is:

$$PV \text{ of a Level Perpetuity} = \frac{C}{i}$$

where C is the periodic payment and i is the interest rate expressed as a decimal fraction. This is the present value of an ordinary annuity with $n = \infty$.

4.7.1 Investing in Preferred Stock

Suppose you are currently earning a nominal interest rate of 8% per year on your money. The preferred stock of Boston Gas and Electric Co. offers a cash dividend of $10 per year, and it is selling at a price of $100 per share. Should you invest some of your money in BG&E preferred stock?

The first step is to compute the yield on the preferred stock. To do so, we need only divide the cash dividend of $10 per share by the price of $100:

$$\text{Yield on Preferred Stock} = \text{Annual Dividend/Price}$$

In this case the yield is 10% per year (i.e., $10/$100). The 10% yield on the preferred stock exceeds the 8% interest rate you are currently earning. To make your investment decision, however, you must also consider risk, a subject we will consider in detail later in the text.

Often one encounters situations in which the cash flows from an investment grow at a constant rate. For example, suppose that you are considering investing in a property for which you expect the first year's cash flow to be $1,000, and you expect it to grow by 4% each year in perpetuity. To evaluate such an investment you need a formula for computing the present value of a **growth annuity.** That formula is:

$$PV = \frac{C_1}{i - g}$$

where C_1 is the first year's cash flow and g is the growth rate.

In the example at hand suppose that the discount rate i is 9%. Then the present value of the property would be:

$$PV = \$1,000/(0.09 - 0.04)$$
$$= \$1,000/0.05$$
$$= \$20,000$$

If you can purchase the property for less than $20,000, it would be a worthwhile investment.

4.7.2 Investing in Common Stock

You have the opportunity to buy stock in a company that is known to pay a cash dividend that grows by 3% every year. The next dividend will be $1 per share, and is to be paid a year from now. If you require a 10% per year rate of return, how much should you be willing to pay for the stock?

The answer is that you should be willing to pay the *PV* of the expected future cash flows discounted at 10% per year. The stream of expected future cash dividends is a growth annuity. Using the formula for a growth annuity:

$$PV = \$1/(0.10 - 0.03)$$
$$= \$1/0.07$$
$$= \$14.29$$

4.8 LOAN AMORTIZATION

E-BOOK

4.8

Many loans, such as home mortgage loans and car loans, are repaid in equal periodic installments. Part of each payment is interest on the outstanding balance of the loan and part is repayment of principal. After each payment, the outstanding balance is reduced by the amount of principal repaid. Therefore, the portion of the payment that goes toward the payment of interest is lower than the previous period's interest and the portion going towards repayment of principal is greater than the previous period's principal payment.

For example, let us assume you take a $100,000 home mortgage loan at an interest rate of 9% per year to be repaid with interest in three annual installments. First, we calculate the annual payment by finding the *PMT* that has a *PV* of $100,000 when discounted at 9% for three years:

n	i	PV	FV	PMT	Result
3	9	−100,000	0	?	$PMT = \$39{,}504.48$

So the annual payment is $39,504.48. In the first year, how much of the $39,504.48 is interest and how much is repayment of principal? Because the interest rate is 9% per year, the interest portion of the first payment must be $0.09 \times \$100{,}000$ or $9,000. The remainder of the $39,504.48, or $30,504.48, is repayment of the original $100,000 principal. The remaining balance after the first payment is, therefore, $100,000 − $30,504.48 or $69,494.52. The process of paying off a loan's principal gradually over its term is called loan **amortization.**

In the second year, how much of the $39,504.48 is interest and how much is repayment of principal? Because the interest rate is 9% per year, the interest portion of the second payment must be $0.09 \times \$69{,}494.52$, or $6,254.51. The remainder of the $39,504.48, or $33,250.97, is repayment of the outstanding $69,494.52 balance remaining after the first payment. The remaining balance after the second payment is, therefore, $69,494.52 − $33,250.97, or $36,243.54.

The third and final payment covers both interest and principal on this remaining $36,243.55 (i.e., $1.09 \times \$36{,}243.55 = \$39{,}504.47$). Table 4.6 contains all of this information in what is called an **amortization schedule** for the mortgage loan. Its breakdown shows how with each successive payment of $39,504.48, the portion that pays interest declines and the portion that repays principal increases.

TABLE 4.6 Amortization Schedule for 3-Year-Loan at 9%

Year	Beginning Balance	Total Payment	Interest Paid	Principal Paid	Remaining Balance
1	100,000	39,505	9,000	30,505	69,495
2	69,495	39,505	6,255	33,251	36,244
3	36,244	39,505	3,262	36,244	0
	Totals	118,515	18,515	100,000	

TABLE 4.7 Amortization Schedule for 12-Month Loan at 1% per Month

Month	Beginning Balance	Total Payment	Interest Paid	Principal Paid	Remaining Balance
1	1,000.00	88.85	10.00	78.85	921.15
2	921.15	88.85	9.21	79.64	841.51
3	841.51	88.85	8.42	80.43	761.08
4	761.08	88.85	7.61	81.24	679.84
5	679.84	88.85	6.80	82.05	597.79
6	597.79	88.85	4.98	82.87	514.92
7	514.92	88.85	4.15	83.70	431.22
8	431.22	88.85	4.31	84.54	346.68
9	346.68	88.85	3.47	84.38	261.30
10	261.30	88.85	2.61	86.24	174.07
11	174.07	88.85	1.75	87.10	87.97
12	87.97	88.85	0.88	87.97	0
	Totals	1,066.20	66.20	1,000.00	

4.8.1 A Bargain Car Loan?

You are buying a car and thinking of taking a one-year installment loan of $1,000 at an *APR* of 12% per year (1% per month) to be repaid in 12 equal monthly payments. The monthly payment is $88.84.

The salesperson trying to sell you the car makes the following pitch:

> Although the *APR* on this loan is 12% per year, in fact it really works out to be a much lower rate. Because the total interest payments over the year are only $66.19, and the loan is for $1,000, you will only be paying a "true" interest rate of 6.62%.

What is the fallacy in the salesperson's reasoning?

The fallacy is that with your first monthly payment (and each subsequent payment) you are paying not only interest on the outstanding balance, you are also repaying part of the principal. The interest payment due at the end of the first month is 1% of $1,000, or $10. Because your monthly payment is $88.85, the other $78.85 is repayment of principal. The full amortization schedule is presented in Table 4.7.

4.9 EXCHANGE RATES AND TIME VALUE OF MONEY

Suppose you are considering investing $10,000 either in dollar-denominated bonds offering an interest rate of 10% per year or in yen-denominated bonds offering 3% per year. Which is the better investment for the next year and why?

The answer depends on how much the dollar/yen exchange rate will change during the year. Suppose that the exchange rate is now 100 yen per dollar and, therefore, your $10,000 is now worth 1 million yen. If you invest in yen-bonds, you will have 1,030,000 yen a year from now (i.e., 1.03 × 1 million). If you invest in dollar-bonds, you will have $11,000 (i.e., 1.1 × $10,000). Which will be worth more?

If the dollar falls in yen value by 8% per year, then the exchange rate a year from now will be 92 yen per dollar. The yen-bond will have a dollar value of $11,196 (i.e., 1,030,000/92), which is $196 more than the $11,000 you would have from the dollar-bond. If, on the other hand, the dollar falls in yen value by only 6% per year, then the exchange rate a year from now will be 94 yen per dollar. The yen-bond will have a dollar value of $10,957 (i.e., 1,030,000/94), which is $43 less than the $11,000 you would have from the dollar-bond.

At what future exchange rate would you be indifferent between the two bonds? To find the break-even exchange rate, divide 1,030,000 yen by $11,000. The result is 93.636 yen/dollar. Thus, we conclude that if the yen value of the dollar falls by more than 6.364% during the year, the yen-bond would be a better investment.[2]

Quick Check 4-7

If the exchange rate between the U.S. dollar and the deutsche mark is $0.50 per deutsche mark, the dollar interest rate is 6% per year, and the deutsche mark interest rate is 4% per year, what is the "break-even" value of the future dollar/deutsche mark exchange rate one year from now?

4.9.1 Computing *NPV* in Different Currencies

To avoid confusion when making financial decisions with different currencies there is a simple rule that one must observe:

> In any time value of money calculation, the cash flows and the interest rate must be denominated in the same currency.

Thus, to compute the present value of cash flows denominated in *yen* you must discount using the *yen* interest rate, and to compute the present value of cash flows denominated in *dollars* you must discount using the *dollar* interest rate. If you compute the present value of payments denominated in yen using the dollar interest rate, you will get a misleading number.

For example, suppose that you are trying to decide if you should invest in a Japanese project or an American project both of which require an initial outlay of $10,000. The Japanese project will pay you ¥575,000 per year for five years, whereas the American one will pay $6,000 per year for five years. The dollar interest rate is 6% per year, the yen interest rate is 4% per year, and the current dollar price of a yen is $0.01 per yen. Which project has the higher *NPV*?

First, we compute the *NPV* of the American project using the dollar interest rate of 6%:

n	i	PV	FV	PMT	Result
5	6	?	0	$6,000	PV = $25,274

Subtracting the $10,000 initial outlay, we find that *NPV* = $15,274.

---

[2]Of course, you do not know in advance how much the exchange rate will change, so there is uncertainty in this investment. We deal with this uncertainty explicitly in later chapters.

Next we compute the *NPV* of the Japanese project using the yen interest rate to find:

n	i	PV	FV	PMT	Result
5	4	?	0	¥575,000	PV = ¥2,559,798

Next we convert the *PV* of the Japanese project from yen into dollars at the current exchange rate of $0.01 per yen to get a *PV* of $25,598. Subtracting the $10,000 initial outlay, we find that the *NPV* is $15,599. Thus, the Japanese project has a higher *NPV* and is the one that you should choose.

Note, however, that if you mistakenly computed the *PV* of the Japanese project using the dollar interest rate of 6% per year, you would get an *NPV* of only $14,221. You would, therefore, be led to choose the American project.

4.10 INFLATION AND DISCOUNTED CASH FLOW ANALYSIS

E-BOOK

4.10

Dealing with inflation leads to a similar set of rules as dealing with different currencies. Let us consider the issue of saving for retirement. At age 20 you save $100 and invest it at a dollar interest rate of 8% per year. The good news is that at age 65 your $100 investment will have grown to $3,192. The bad news is that it will cost a lot more to buy the same things you buy today. For example, if the prices of all the goods and services you want to buy go up at 8% per year for the next 45 years, then your $3,192 will buy no more than your $100 will buy today. In a "real" sense, you will not have earned any interest at all. Thus, to make truly meaningful long-run savings decisions, you must take account of inflation as well as interest.

To take account of both interest and inflation we distinguish between nominal and real interest rates. The *nominal interest rate* is the rate denominated in dollars or in some other currency, and the *real interest rate* is denominated in units of consumer goods. This distinction between real and nominal interest rates was discussed in chapter 2 (see section 2.6.5).

The general formula relating the real rate of interest to the nominal rate of interest and the rate of inflation is:

$$1 + \text{Real Rate} = \frac{1 + \text{Nominal Interest Rate}}{1 + \text{Rate of Inflation}}$$

or equivalently,

$$\text{Real Rate} = \frac{\text{Nominal Interest Rate} - \text{Rate of Inflation}}{1 + \text{Rate of Inflation}}$$

Using *APR*s with continuous compounding simplifies the algebraic relationship between real and nominal rates of return. With continuous compounding, the relation between *APR*s becomes:

$$\text{Real Rate of Interest} = \text{Nominal Rate} - \text{Inflation Rate}$$

So if we assume a nominal *APR* of 6% per year compounded continuously and an inflation rate of 4% per year compounded continuously, the real rate is exactly 2% per year compounded continuously.

4.10.1 Inflation and Future Values

From a financial planning perspective, there is a great advantage to knowing the real interest rate. This is because ultimately it is what you can buy with your accumulated savings in the future that you care about. Returning to our specific example of saving $100 at age 20, not to be taken out until age 65, what we really want to know is how much you will have accumulated in the account when you reach age 65 in terms of real purchasing power. There are two alternative ways of calculating it—a short way and a long way. The short way is to compute the future value of the $100 using the real interest rate of 2.857% per year for 45 years. We define this as the **real future value.**

$$\text{Real Future Value} = \$100 \times 1.02857^{45} = \$355$$

Alternatively, we can arrive at the same number in stages. First, we compute the **nominal future value** by using the nominal interest rate of 8% per year:

$$\text{Nominal FV in 45 Years} = \$100 \times 1.08^{45} = \$3,192$$

Next, we figure out what the price level will be 45 years from now if the inflation rate is 5% per year:

$$\text{Price Level in 45 Years} = 1.05^{45} = 8.985$$

Finally, divide the nominal future value by the future price level to find the real future value:

$$\text{Real } FV = \frac{\text{Nominal Future Value}}{\text{Future Price Level}} = \frac{\$3,192}{8.985} = \$355$$

The end result is the same. We find that by saving $100 today (age 20) and investing it for 45 years, we expect to have enough at age 65 to buy what would cost $355 at today's prices.

Thus, we see that there are two equivalent ways of computing the real future value of $355:

1. Compute the future value using the real rate of interest.
2. Compute the nominal future value using the nominal rate, and then deflate it to find the real future value.

Which of the two equivalent approaches one adopts depends on the particular context.

4.10.2 Saving for College: 1

Your daughter is 10 years old, and you are planning to open an account to provide for her college education. Tuition for a year of college is now $15,000 and is expected to increase at the rate of 5% per year. If you put $8,000 into an account paying an interest rate of 8% per year, will you have enough to pay for her first year's tuition eight years from now? If you compute the future value of the $8,000 at an interest rate of 8% per year for eight years, you find:

$$FV \text{ in 8 Years} = \$8,000 \times 1.08^8 = \$14,807$$

Because $14,807 is very close to $15,000, it might appear that saving $8,000 now is enough to provide for the first year of college tuition. But tuition level is a moving target. College tuition in the past increased at least at the general rate of inflation. For example, if inflation turns out to be 5% per year, the cost of the first year's college tuition will be $15,000 × 1.05^8 or $22,162. So your $14,807 will be short by about one-third.

4.10.3 Investing in Inflation-Proof CDs

You are investing $10,000 for the next year. You face a choice between a conventional, one-year CD paying an interest rate of 8% or a CD that will pay you an interest rate of 3% per year plus the rate of inflation. We will call the former a *nominal CD* and the latter a *real CD*. Which will you choose?

Your choice depends on your forecast for inflation over the next year. If you are sure that the rate of inflation will be greater than 5%, you will prefer the *real CD*. Suppose, for example, that you think the rate of inflation will be 6%. Then your nominal rate of interest on the real CD will be 9%. If, however, you are sure that inflation will be 4% per year, then the nominal rate of interest on the real CD will be only 7%, so you are better off investing in the nominal CD.

Of course, because you do not know with certainty what the inflation rate will be, the decision is more complicated. We will return to this problem later when we discuss how to take account of uncertainty in investment decisions.

4.10.4 Why Debtors Gain from Unanticipated Inflation

Suppose you borrow $1,000 at an interest rate of 8% per year and have to pay back principal and interest one year later. If the rate of inflation turns out to be 8% during the year, the real interest rate on the loan is zero. Although you must pay back $1,080, its *real* value will be only $1,000. The $80 in interest just offsets the decline in the purchasing power of the $1,000 principal. Another way to state this is that you are paying back the loan with "cheaper" dollars than the ones you borrowed. No wonder that when the interest rate on a loan is fixed in advance, debtors like unanticipated inflation and creditors do not.

4.10.5 Inflation and Present Values

In many financial problems in which present values are calculated, the future amount is not fixed in dollars. For example, suppose you plan to buy a car four years from now and want to invest enough money now to pay for it. Say the kind of car you have in mind now costs $10,000, and the interest rate you can earn on your money is 8% per year.

In attempting to figure out the amount to invest now, it is natural to compute the present value of $10,000 to be received in four years at 8%:

$$PV = \$10,000/1.08^4 = \$7,350$$

So you might conclude that investing $7,350 now is adequate to pay for the car four years from now.

But that would be a mistake. Almost surely, if the car you want costs $10,000 today, a similar car will cost more four years from now. How much more? That depends on the rate of inflation. If inflation in car prices is 5% per year, then the car will cost $10,000 × 1.05^4 or $12,155 in four years.

There are two equivalent ways to take account of inflation in problems such as this. The first is to compute the present value of the $10,000 real future amount using the real discount rate. As we saw earlier in this chapter the real discount rate is:

$$\text{Real Rate of Interest} = \frac{\text{Nominal Rate of Interest} - \text{Rate of Inflation}}{1 + \text{Rate of Inflation}}$$

$$\text{Real Rate of Interest} = \frac{0.08 - 0.05}{1.05} = 0.02857 = 2.857\%$$

Using this real rate to compute the present value of the $10,000, we find:

$$PV = \$10,000/1.02857^4 = \$8,934$$

The second way is to compute the present value of the $12,155 nominal future amount using the nominal discount rate of 8% per year:

$$PV = \$12,155/1.08^4 = \$8,934$$

Either way, we get the same result: You must invest $8,934 now in order to pay the car's inflated price in four years. The reason we at first mistakenly computed the amount we needed to invest as only $7,350, was that we discounted a real future amount of $10,000 at a nominal discount rate of 8% per year.

4.10.6 Saving for College: 2

Recall that your daughter is 10 years old, and you are planning to open an account to provide for her college education. Tuition for a year of college is now $15,000. How much must you invest now in order to have enough to pay for her first year's tuition eight years from now, if you think you can earn a rate of interest that is 3% more than the inflation rate?

In this case you do not have an explicit estimate of the rate of inflation. But do you need one to answer the practical question before you? The answer is that you do not, provided you think that college tuition will rise at whatever the general inflation rate is. Under that assumption the real cost of college tuition eight years from now will be the same $15,000 it is today. By assuming that you can earn 3% per year more than the rate of inflation, you are, in effect, saying that the real discount rate is 3% per year. So you should calculate present value by discounting the $15,000 at 3% for eight years:

$$PV = \$15,000/1.03^8 = \$11,841$$

If, by mistake, you were to discount the $15,000 using a nominal rate such as 8% per year, you would get a very different answer:

$$PV = \$15,000/1.08^8 = \$8,104$$

The result is that you would not have enough to pay for tuition in eight years.

Beware: Never use a nominal interest rate when discounting real cash flows or a real interest rate when discounting nominal cash flows.

4.10.7 Inflation and Savings Plans

When considering a plan for long-run savings, it is essential to take account of inflation. The amount of money you can afford to save each year is likely to rise with the general cost of living because your income will probably also be going up. One easy way to take account of this without having to make an explicit forecast of the rate of inflation is to make your plans in terms of constant *real* payments and a *real* rate of interest.

4.10.8 Saving for College: 3

Recall that your daughter is 10 years old, and you are planning to open an account to provide for her college education. Tuition for a year of college is now $15,000. You want to save in equal real annual installments over the next eight years to have enough to pay for her first year's tuition eight years from now. If you think you can earn a real rate of interest of 3% per year, how much must you save each year? How much will you actually put into the account each year (in nominal terms) if the rate of inflation turns out to be 5% per year?

To find the annual real amount to save we first solve for *PMT:*

n	i	PV	FV	PMT	Result
8	3	0	15,000	?	$1,686.85

So the amount to save each year must be the equivalent of $1,686.85 of today's purchasing power. At an inflation rate of 5% per year, the actual amount of dollars that will have to be contributed to the plan each year are as shown in Table 4.8.

With this plan the nominal amount saved each year has to be adjusted upward in accordance with the actual rate of inflation. The result will be that the amount accumulated in the account in eight years will be enough to pay for tuition. Thus, if the rate of inflation turns out to be 5% per year, then the nominal amount in the account eight years from now will turn out to be $15,000 \times 1.05^8$ or $22,162. The tuition required eight years from now is $15,000 in real terms and $22,162 in nominal terms.

To verify that the nominal future value of this saving plan will be $22,162 if the inflation rate is 5% per year, we can compute the future value of the nominal cash

TABLE 4.8 Nominal Dollar Amounts of a Real Annuity

Payment Number	Real Payment	Inflation Factor	Nominal Payment
1	$1,686.85	1.05	$1,771.19
2	$1,686.85	1.05^2	$1,859.75
3	$1,686.85	1.05^3	$1,952.74
4	$1,686.85	1.05^4	$2,050.38
5	$1,686.85	1.05^5	$2,152.90
6	$1,686.85	1.05^6	$2,260.54
7	$1,686.85	1.05^7	$2,373.57
8	$1,686.85	1.05^8	$2,492.25

TABLE 4.9   Computing Nominal Future Value of a Real Annuity

Payment Number	Real Payment	Nominal Payment	Future Value Factor	Nominal Future Value
1	$1,686.85	$1,771.19	$\times\ 1.0815^7$	$3,065.14
2	$1,686.85	$1,859.75	$\times\ 1.0815^6$	$2,975.87
3	$1,686.85	$1,952.74	$\times\ 1.0815^5$	$2,889.20
4	$1,686.85	$2,050.38	$\times\ 1.0815^4$	$2,805.05
5	$1,686.85	$2,152.90	$\times\ 1.0815^3$	$2,723.35
6	$1,686.85	$2,260.54	$\times\ 1.0815^2$	$2,644.02
7	$1,686.85	$2,373.57	$\times\ 1.0815$	$2,567.02
8	$1,686.85	$2,492.25	$\times\ 1$	$2,492.25
		Total nominal future value		$22,161.90

flows in the last column of Table 4.9. First, note that if the real rate of interest is 3% per year, then the nominal rate of interest must be 8.15%:

$$1 + \text{Real Rate of Interest} = \frac{1 + \text{Nominal Rate of Interest}}{1 + \text{Rate of Inflation}}$$

$$1 + \text{Nominal Rate} = (1 + \text{Real Rate}) \times (1 + \text{Inflation})$$

$$\text{Nominal Rate} = \text{Real Rate} + \text{Inflation} + \text{Real Rate} \times \text{Inflation}$$

$$\text{Nominal Rate} = 0.03 + 0.05 + 0.03 \times 0.05 = 0.0815$$

Compounding each year's nominal payment forward at the nominal interest rate of 8.15%, as shown in Table 4.9, we find that the total nominal future value is indeed $22,162.

Note that if your income goes up at 5% per year, then the nominal payment will remain a constant fraction of your income.

If the rate of inflation turns out to be 10% per year, and you increase your nominal payments into the plan at that rate, then the nominal amount in the account eight years from now will turn out to be $15,000 \times 1.1^8$ or $32,154. This will have a real value in today's dollars of $15,000—just enough to pay the tuition.

4.10.9 Inflation and Investment Decisions

It is just as essential to take account of inflation in investment decisions as it is in saving decisions. When investing money in real assets such as real estate or plant and equipment, the future cash flows from the investment are likely to rise in nominal value due to inflation. If you fail to make the appropriate adjustments, you will tend to pass up worthwhile investment opportunities.

To see how important it is to take proper account of inflation, consider the following example. You currently heat your house with oil and your annual heating bill is $2,000. By converting to gas heat you estimate that this year you could cut your heating bill by $500, and you think that the cost differential between gas and oil is likely to remain the same for many years. The cost of installing a gas heating system is $10,000. If your alternative use of the money is to leave it in a bank account earning an interest rate of 8% per year, is the conversion worthwhile?

Note that there is no natural time horizon for this decision. We will, therefore, assume that the $500 cost differential will remain forever. We will also assume that the future outlays on replacement of heating equipment will be the same under both the oil and gas alternatives, so that we can ignore them for purposes of making this decision. Therefore, the investment is a perpetuity—you pay $10,000 now and get $500 per year forever. The internal rate of return on the investment in gas heat is 5% per year (i.e., $500/$10,000).

Comparing this 5% per year rate of return to the 8% per year alternative, you might be inclined to reject the gas investment opportunity. But wait a minute. The 8% per year rate on the bank account is a nominal rate of interest. What about the 5% per year rate of return on the investment in gas heat?

If you think that the $500 cost differential between gas and oil will increase over time with the general rate of inflation, then the 5% rate of return on the investment is a *real* rate of return. You should, therefore, compare it to the expected *real* rate of interest on the bank account. If you expect the rate of inflation to be 5% per year, then the expected real interest rate on the bank account is 2.875% [i.e., $(.08 - 0.05)/1.05$]. The 5% per year real yield on the investment in gas heat exceeds this, so perhaps the investment is worthwhile after all.

This example leads us to the following rule:

> When comparing investment alternatives, never compare a real rate of return to a nominal opportunity cost of money.

This rule is just a slightly different version of the caution we issued earlier in this chapter:

> Never use a nominal interest rate when discounting real cash flows or a real interest rate when discounting nominal cash flows.

4.11 TAXES AND INVESTMENT DECISIONS

Up to this point our discussion has ignored income taxes. But what you have to spend in the future will be what is left after paying income taxes to the government. For example, suppose that you must pay 30% in taxes on any interest that you earn. You put $1,000 into a bank account offering an interest rate of 8% per year. This is the **before-tax interest rate.** Your **after-tax interest rate** is defined as what you earn after paying your income taxes.

Let us compute what it is. The interest income you will have to report on your income tax return is $0.08 \times \$1,000$ or $80.[3] The tax on this interest income is $0.3 \times \$80$, or $24. Thus, you will be left with $56 in interest income after taxes. Your after-tax interest rate is this $56 divided by your original investment of $1,000, or 5.6%. A shortcut way of computing your after-tax interest rate is to multiply the before-tax interest rate by 1 minus your tax rate:

$$\text{After-Tax Interest Rate} = (1 - \text{Tax Rate}) \times \text{Before-Tax Interest Rate}$$

In our example we get:

$$\text{After-Tax Interest Rate} = (1 - 0.3) \times 8\% = 0.7 \times 8\% = 5.6\%$$

---

[3]You had better report it, too! In the United States, your bank informs directly the Internal Revenue Service how much it pays you in interest.

The rule for investing is:

Invest so as to maximize the net present value of your after-tax cash flows.

Note that this is not necessarily the same as investing so as to minimize the taxes you pay. To see this, consider the following example.

4.11.1 Invest in Tax-Exempt Bonds?

In the United States, municipal bonds are exempt from income taxes. If you are in a high enough tax bracket, you might prefer to invest your money in municipal bonds. For example, if the interest rate on municipal bonds is 6% per year, and they are just as safe as the bank account paying an after-tax interest rate of 5.6% per year, then you would prefer to invest in the municipal bonds. The higher your tax bracket the bigger the advantage to you of investing in tax-exempt securities.

Suppose you are in a 20% tax bracket. Would it make sense for you to invest in municipal bonds paying 6% per year, if you can earn 8% per year from the bank? The answer is no, because even after paying income taxes on the interest from the bank, you would still have an after-tax interest rate that is higher than the tax-exempt rate on municipals:

$$\text{After-Tax Interest Rate on Bank Account} = (1 - 0.2) \times 8\% = 6.4\%$$

Therefore, if you followed the rule of minimizing your taxes, you would be led to make the wrong investment!

What is the personal tax bracket at which an individual would be exactly indifferent between investing in taxable and tax-exempt securities? The answer in our example is 25%. At a tax rate of 25%, the after-tax interest rate on the bank account is 6% (i.e., $0.75 \times 8\%$), the same as the rate on tax-exempt municipal bonds.

Summary

- Compounding is the process of going from present value (PV) to future value (FV). The future value of \$1 earning interest at rate i per period for n periods is $(1 + i)n$.

- Discounting is finding the present value of some future amount. The present value of \$1 discounted at rate i per period for n periods is $1/(1 + i)n$.

- One can make financial decisions by comparing the present values of streams of expected future cash flows resulting from alternative courses of action. The present value of cash inflows less the present value of cash outflows is called net present value (NPV). If a course of action has a positive NPV, it is worth undertaking.

- In any time value of money calculation, the cash flows and the interest rate must be denominated in the same currency.

- Never use a nominal interest rate when discounting real cash flows or a real interest rate when discounting nominal cash flows.

- Always compare investment alternatives in terms of their returns net of income taxes.

Key Terms

- time value of money   101
- discounted cash flow   101
- compounding   102
- present value   102
- future value   102
- simple interest   102
- compound interest   102
- future value factor   104
- Rule of 72   106
- reinvestment rate   107
- annual percentage rate   108
- effective annual rate   108
- opportunity cost of capital   112
- yield to maturity   114

- internal rate of return   114
- time line   117
- annuity   118
- immediate annuity   118
- ordinary annuity   118
- perpetuity   122
- growth annuity   123
- amortization   124
- amortization schedule   124
- real future value   128
- nominal future value   128
- before-tax interest rate   133
- after-tax interest rate   133

Answers to Quick Check Questions

Quick Check 4-1   *If the interest rate is only 5% per year in the example on p. 103, what is the future value? What are the simple interest and the compound interest?*

ANSWER: $1,000 \times (1.05)^5 = \$1,276.28$
Simple interest: $\$1,000 \times 0.05 \times 5 = \$250$
Compound interest: $\$276.28 - \$250 = \$26.28$

Quick Check 4-2   *In 1626 Peter Minuit purchased Manhattan Island from the Native Americans for about $24 worth of trinkets. If the tribe had taken cash instead and invested it to earn 6% per year compounded annually, how much would they have had in 1996, 370 years later?*

ANSWER: To answer this question, students can use the following formula (the answer is too large for most calculator displays):

$$\$24 \times (1.06)^{370} = \$55,383,626,000 \text{ (55 billion, 383 million, 626 thousand dollars)}$$

Quick Check 4-3   *You take out a loan at an* APR *of 12% with monthly compounding. What is the effective annual rate on your loan?*

ANSWER: $EFF = (1 + [0.12/12])^{12} - 1$, hence, $EFF = 12.68\%$.

Quick Check 4-4   *What is the present value of $100 to be received in four years at an interest rate of 6% per year?*

ANSWER: $PV = \$100/(1.06)^4 = \$79.21$

Quick Check 4-5   *Show that the alternative decision criteria presented previously lead to the same result—that the investment is worthwhile.*

ANSWER:

1. *Invest if the future value of the investment is larger than the future value that can be obtained from the next best alternative.*
   First, we compute the future value of the $10,000 if invested in the bank.

$$FV = \$10,000 \times 1.08^5 = \$14,693$$

   Comparing the $14,693 computed future value to the $20,000 from the land, we conclude that investing in the land is worthwhile.

2. *Invest if the IRR is greater than the opportunity cost of capital.* Now we are ready to consider the investment's internal rate of return (*IRR*). By investing $10,000 in the land today, you can get $20,000 five years from now. What interest rate are you earning? In other words, we want to find *i* that solves the equation:

$$\$10,000 = \$20,000/(1 + i)^5$$
$$i = 14.87\%$$

   Thus, the internal rate of return on the investment in land is 14.87% per year. This should be compared to the 8% per year you could earn by putting your money in the bank. Clearly, you can earn a higher rate of return by investing in the land.
   Note that because in this problem the $10,000 investment in land is expected to double over the next five years, the Rule of 72 could be applied to get a "quick and dirty" approximation for the *IRR*. By manipulating the Rule of 72 we find that the *IRR* on an investment that doubles in *n* years is approximately equal to the number 72 divided by *n*:

$$\text{Doubling Time} = 72 \,/\, \text{Interest Rate}$$

hence

$$IRR = 72 \,/\, \text{Doubling Time}$$

In our example, the approximate *IRR* would be:

$$IRR = 72 \,/\, 5 = 14.4\% \text{ per year}$$

This is very close to the exact *IRR* of 14.87%. Even though the payback period rule is subject to many potential pitfalls, in this simple example it does work.

3. *Choose the investment alternative with the fastest payback.* We could ask how long it would take for our $10,000 investment to grow to $20,000 if we invested in the bank at 8% per year. To answer this question we are solving the equation for the number of periods, *n*:

$$\$10,000 = \$20,000/1.08n$$

On the financial calculator we input *PV, FV,* and *i* and compute *n*. We find that *n* is nine years. Because it takes only five years to double your money with the investment in land, clearly the land investment is better than putting your money in the bank. Note that using the Rule of 72 to find *n* we get:

$$\text{Doubling Time} = 72/8 = 9 \text{ Years}$$

Quick Check 4-6   *Suppose you deposit $1,000 now and then $2,000 a year from now. How much will you have two years from now, if the interest rate is 10% per year?*

ANSWER: Future Value of the Initial $1,000 = $1,000 × 1.1^2 = $1,210
Future Value of the $2,000 = $2,000 × 1.1 = $2,200
Total Future Value = $3,410

Quick Check 4-7   *If the exchange rate between the U.S. dollar and the deutsche mark is $0.50 per deutsche mark, the dollar interest rate is 6% per year, and the deutsche mark interest rate is 4% per year, what is the "break-even" value of the future dollar/deutsche mark exchange rate one year from now?*

ANSWER: You could invest $1 today in dollar-denominated bonds and have $1.06 one year from now. Or you could convert the dollar today into 2 deutsche marks and invest in deutsche-mark-denominated bonds to have 2.08 deutsche mark one year from now. For you to break even, the 2.08 deutsche mark would have to be worth $1.06 one year from now, so the break-even exchange rate is: $1.06/2.08DM, or $0.509615 per deutsche mark.

Questions and Problems

TEMPLATE

4.1–4.38, 4.41

1. If you invest $1,000 today at an interest rate of 10% per year, how much will you have 20 years from now, assuming no withdrawals in the interim?

2. **a.** If you invest $100 every year for the next 20 years starting one year from today and you earn interest of 10% per year, how much will you have at the end of the 20 years?
    b. How much must you invest each year if you want to have $50,000 at the end of the 20 years?

3. What is the present value of the following cash flows at an interest rate of 10% per year?
    a. $100 received five years from now.
    b. $100 received 60 years from now.
    c. $100 received each year beginning one year from now and ending 10 years from now.
    d. $100 received each year for 10 years beginning now.
    e. $100 each year beginning one year from now and continuing forever. (Hint: You do not need to use the financial keys of your calculator for this, just some common sense.)

4. You want to establish a "wasting" fund, which will provide you with $1,000 per year for four years, at which time the fund will be exhausted. How much must you put in the fund now if you can earn 10% interest per year?

5. You take a one-year installment loan of $1,000 at an interest rate of 12% per year (1% per month) to be repaid in 12 equal monthly payments.
    a. What is the monthly payment?
    b. What is the total amount of interest paid over the 12-month term of the loan?

6. You are taking out a $100,000 mortgage loan to be repaid over 25 years in 300 monthly payments.
    a. If the interest rate is 16% per year, what is the amount of the monthly payment?
    b. If you can only afford to pay $1,000 per month, how large a loan could you take?
    c. If you can afford to pay $1,500 per month and need to borrow $100,000, how many months would it take to pay off the mortgage?
    d. If you can pay $1,500 per month, need to borrow $100,000, and want a 25-year mortgage, what is the highest interest rate you can pay?

7. In 1626 Peter Minuit purchased Manhattan Island from the Native Americans for about $24 worth of trinkets. If the tribe had taken cash instead and invested it to earn 6% per year compounded annually, how much would the Indians have had in 1986, 360 years later?

8. You win a $1 million lottery, which pays you $50,000 per year for 20 years. How much is your prize really worth, assuming an interest rate of 8% per year?

9. Your great aunt left you $20,000 when she died. You can invest the money to earn 12% per year. If you spend $3,540 per year out of this inheritance, how long will the money last?

10. You borrow $100,000 from a bank for 30 years at an *APR* of 10.5%. What is the monthly payment? If you must pay two points up front, meaning that you only get $98,000 from the bank, what is the true *APR* on the mortgage loan?

11. Suppose that the mortgage loan described in question 10 is a one-year adjustable rate mortgage (ARM), which means that the 10.5% interest applies for only the first year. If the interest rate goes up to 12% in the second year of the loan, what will your new monthly payment be?

12. You just received a gift of $500 from your grandmother and you are thinking about saving this money for graduation, which is four years away. You have your choice between Bank A, which is paying 7% for one-year deposits, and Bank B, which is paying 6% on one-year deposits. Each bank compounds interest annually.
    a. What is the future value of your savings one year from today if you save your money in Bank A? Bank B? Which is the better decision?
    b. What savings decision will most individuals make? What likely reaction will Bank B have?

13. Sue Consultant has just been given a bonus of $2,500 by her employer. She is thinking about using the money to start saving for the future. She can invest to earn an annual rate of interest of 10%.
    a. According to the Rule of 72, approximately how long will it take for Sue to increase her wealth to $5,000?
    b. Exactly how long does it actually take?

14. Larry's bank account has a "floating" interest rate on certain deposits. Every year the interest rate is adjusted. Larry deposited $20,000 three years ago, when interest rates were 7% (annual compounding). Last year the rate was only 6%, and this year the rate fell again to 5%. How much will be in his account at the end of this year?

15. You have your choice between investing in a bank savings account, which pays 8% compounded annually (BankAnnual), and one which pays 7.5% compounded daily (BankDaily).
    a. Based on effective annual rates, which bank would you prefer?
    b. Suppose BankAnnual is only offering one-year certificates of deposit and if you withdraw your money early you lose all interest. How would you evaluate this additional piece of information when making your decision?

16. What are the effective annual rates of the following:
    a. 12% *APR* compounded monthly?
    b. 10% *APR* compounded annually?
    c. 6% *APR* compounded daily?

17. Harry promises that an investment in his firm will double in six years. Interest is assumed to be paid quarterly and reinvested. What effective annual yield does this represent?

18. Suppose you know that you will need $2,500 two years from now in order to make a down payment on a car.
    a. BankOne is offering 4% interest (compounded annually) for two-year accounts and BankTwo is offering 4.5% (compounded annually) for two-year accounts. If you know you need $2,500 two years from today, how much will you need to invest in BankOne to reach your goal? Alternatively, how much will you need to invest in BankTwo? Which bank account do you prefer?
    b. Now suppose you do not need the money for three years. How much will you need to deposit today in BankOne? BankTwo?

19. Lucky Lynn has a choice between receiving $1,000 from her great uncle one year from today or $900 from her great aunt today. She believes she could invest the $900 at a one-year return of 12%.
    a. What is the future value of the gift from her great uncle upon receipt? From her great aunt?
    b. Which gift should she choose?
    c. How does your answer change if you believed she could invest the $900 from her great aunt at only 10%? At what rate is she indifferent?

20. As manager of short-term projects, you are trying to decide whether or not to invest in a short-term project that pays one cash flow of $1,000 one year from today. The total cost of the project is $950. Your alternative investment is to deposit the money in a one-year bank certificate of deposit, which will pay 4% compounded annually.
    a. Assuming the cash flow of $1,000 is guaranteed (there is no risk you will not receive it), what would be a logical discount rate to use to determine the present value of the cash flows of the project?
    b. What is the present value of the project if you discount the cash flow at 4% per year? What is the net present value of that investment? Should you invest in the project?
    c. What would you do if the bank increases its quoted rate on one-year CDs to 5.5%?
    d. At what bank one-year CD rate would you be indifferent between the two investments?

21. Calculate the net present value of the following cash flows: You invest $2,000 today and receive $200 one year from now, $800 two years from now, and $1,000 a year for 10 years starting four years from now. Assume that the interest rate is 8%.

22. Your cousin has asked for your advice on whether or not to buy a bond for $995, which will make one payment of $1,200 five years from today, or invest in a local bank account.
    a. What is the internal rate of return on the bond's cash flows? What additional information do you need to make a choice?
    b. What advice would you give her if you learned the bank is paying 3.5% per year for five years (compounded annually)?
    c. How would your advice change if the bank were paying 5% annually for five years? If the price of the bond were $900 and the bank pays 5% annually?

23. You and your sister have just inherited $300 and a savings bond from your great grandfather who had left them in a safe deposit box. Because you are the oldest, you get to choose whether you want the cash or the bond. The bond has only four years left to maturity at which time it will pay the holder $500.
    a. If you took the $300 today and invested it at an interest rate 6% per year, how long (in years) would it take for your $300 to grow to $500? (Hint: You want to solve for *n* or number of periods.) Given these circumstances, which are you going to choose?
    b. Would your answer change if you could invest the $300 at 10% per year? At 15% per year? What other decision rules could you use to analyze this decision?

24. Suppose you have three personal loans outstanding to your friend Elizabeth. A payment of $1,000 is due today, a $500 payment is due one year from now, and a $250 payment is due two years from now. You would like to consolidate the three loans into one, with 36 equal monthly payments, beginning one month from today. Assume the agreed interest rate is 8% (effective annual rate) per year.
    a. What is the annual percentage rate you will be paying?
    b. How large will the new monthly payment be?

25. As CEO of ToysRFun, you are offered the chance to participate, without initial charge, in a project that produces cash flows of $5,000 at the end of the first period, $4,000 at the end of the next period, and a loss of $11,000 at the end of the third and final year.
    a. What is the net present value if the relevant discount rate (the company's cost of capital) is 10%?
    b. Would you accept the offer?
    c. What is the internal rate of return? Can you explain why you would reject a project that has an internal rate of return greater than its cost of capital?

26. You must pay a creditor $6,000 one year from now, $5,000 two years from now, $4,000 three years from now, $2,000 four years from now, and a final $1,000 five years from now. You would like to restructure the loan into five equal annual payments due at the end of each year. If the agreed interest rate is 6% compounded annually, what is the payment?

27. Find the future value of the following ordinary annuities (payments begin one year from today and all interest rates compound annually):
    a. $100 per year for 10 years at 9%.
    b. $500 per year for 8 years at 15%.
    c. $800 per year for 20 years at 7%.
    d. $1,000 per year for 5 years at 0%.
    e. Now find the present values of the annuities in a–d.
    f. What is the relationship between present values and future values?

28. Suppose you will need $50,000 ten years from now. You plan to make seven equal annual deposits beginning three years from today in an account that yields 11% compounded annually. How large should the annual deposit be?

29. Suppose an investment offers $100 per year for five years at 5% beginning one year from today.
    a. What is the present value? How does the present value calculation change if one additional payment is added today?
    b. What is the future value of this ordinary annuity? How does the future value change if one additional payment is added today?

30. You are trying to decide whether to buy a car for 4.0% *APR* for the full $20,000 purchase price over three years or receive $1,500 cash back and finance the rest at a bank rate of 9.5%. Both loans have monthly payments over three years. Which should you choose?

31. You are looking to buy a sports car costing $23,000. One dealer is offering a special reduced financing rate of 2.9% *APR* on new car purchases for three year loans, with monthly payments. A second dealer is offering a cash rebate. Any customer taking the cash rebate would, of course, be ineligible for the special loan rate and would have to borrow the balance of the purchase price from the local bank at the 9% annual rate. How large must the cash rebate be on this $23,000 car to entice a customer away from the dealer who is offering the special 2.9% financing?

32. Show proof that investing $475.48 today at 10% allows you to withdraw $150 at the end of each of the next four years and have nothing remaining.

33. As pension manager, you are considering investing in a preferred stock, which pays $5,000,000 per year *forever* beginning one year from now. If your alternative investment choice is yielding 10% per year, what is the present value of this investment? What is the highest price you would be willing to pay for this investment? If you paid this price, what would be the dividend yield on this investment?

34. A new lottery game offers a choice for the grand prize winner. You can either receive a lump sum of $1,000,000 immediately or an annuity of $100,000 per year forever, with the first payment *today*. (If you die, your estate will still continue to receive payments.) If the relevant interest rate is 9.5% compounded annually, what is the difference in value between the two prizes?

35. Find the future value of a $1,000 lump-sum investment under the following compounding periods: (Hint: Either figure out effective annual rate or change number of periods and interest rate as compounding period shortens.)
    a. 7% compounded annually for 10 years.
    b. 7% compounded semiannually for 10 years.
    c. 7% compounded monthly for 10 years.
    d. 7% compounded daily for 10 years.
    e. 7% compounded continuously for 10 years.

36. Sammy Jo charged $1,000 worth of merchandise one year ago on her MasterCard, which has a stated interest rate of 18% *APR* compounded monthly. She made 12 regular monthly payments of $50, at the end of each month, and refrained from using the card for the past year. How much does she still owe?

37. Suppose you are considering borrowing $120,000 to finance your dream house. The annual percentage rate is 9% and payments are made monthly.
    a. If the mortgage has a 30-year amortization schedule, what are the monthly payments?
    b. What effective annual rate would you be paying?
    c. How do your answers to parts a and b change if the loan amortizes over 15 years rather than 30?

38. Suppose last year you took out the loan described in problem 33a. Now interest rates have declined to 8% per year. Assume there will be no refinancing fees.
    a. What is the remaining balance of your current mortgage after 12 payments? (Hint: Look for future value.)
    b. What would be your payment if you refinanced your mortgage at the lower rate for 29 years?

Exchange Rates and the Time Value of Money
39. The exchange rate between the pound sterling and the dollar is currently $1.50 per pound, the dollar interest rate is 7% per year, and the pound interest rate is 9% per year. You have $100,000 in a one-year account that allows you to choose between either currency, and it pays the corresponding interest rate.
    a. If you expect the dollar/pound exchange rate to be $1.40 per pound a year from now and are indifferent to risk, which currency should you choose?
    b. What is the break-even value of the dollar/pound exchange rate one year from now?

Real versus Nominal Interest Rates
40. The interest rate on conventional 10-year Treasury bonds is 7% per year and the interest rate on 10-year TIPS (Treasury inflation-protected securities) is 3.5% per year. You have $10,000 to invest in one of them.
    a. If you expect the average inflation rate to be 4% per year, which bond offers the higher expected rate of return?
    b. Which would you prefer to invest in?

41. You are 20 years from retirement, and expect to live another 20 years after retirement. If you start saving now, how much will you be able to withdraw *each year* for every dollar *per year* that you save, assuming an effective annual interest rate of:
   a. 0, 1%, 2%, 3%, 3.5%, 4%, 6%, 8%, and 10%?
   b. How would your answer change if you expect the rate of inflation to be 4% per year?

APPENDIX

Adjusting a Mortgage for Points

Many banks offer mortgages that include *points*. Points are essentially an extra fee paid to the bank up front. Thus, if you take out a three-year $10,000 mortgage with two points, you have to pay 2% of the mortgage amount to the bank at inception. In other words, instead of getting $10,000 at the beginning from the bank, you really only get $9,800. Let us see what points do to the actual interest rate on a mortgage. Suppose you take out the three-year, $10,000 (two points) mortgage from the bank at a stated *APR* of 12% with monthly payments. This corresponds to a monthly interest rate of 1%.

The first step is to compute the actual payment that the bank requires each month. This is done based on the total amount of the mortgage, $10,000.

n	i	PV	FV	PMT	Result
36	1	10,000	0	?	*PMT* = $332.14

The *PV* of the mortgage is not really $10,000, but only $9,800. Thus, together with the monthly payments of $332.14, we can compute the monthly interest rate:

n	i	PV	FV	PMT	Result
36	?	9,800	0	−332.14	*i* = 1.11757%

This monthly interest rate corresponds to an *APR* of 12 × 1.11757% = 13.41%.

Thus, when one bank offers you an *APR* of 13% on the preceding three-year mortgage and charges no points and a second bank offers you an *APR* of 12% with two points, you now know which bank offers the better deal. (Hint: It is not the second bank.)

5

Life-Cycle Financial Planning

OBJECTIVES

- Analyze how much to save for retirement.
- Determine whether to defer taxes or pay them now.
- Determine whether to get a professional degree.
- Determine whether to buy or rent an apartment.

CONTENTS

In chapter 4 we explained how to use discounted cash flow analysis in making financial decisions. In this chapter we apply those discounted cash flow concepts to the major financial decisions we all must make at different stages of our lives. Starting with the decision about how much to save for retirement, we develop a life-cycle model for comprehensive financial planning. We then analyze whether you should defer taxes or pay them immediately, whether you should invest in a professional education, and whether you should buy or rent a house.

5.1 A LIFE-CYCLE MODEL OF SAVING

E-BOOK

5.1

Consider the following example. You are currently 35 years old, expect to retire in 30 years at age 65, and then to live for 15 more years until age 80. Your current labor income is $30,000 per year, and you have not yet accumulated any assets.

We simplify the example by ignoring taxes. Also let us assume that your *real* labor income adjusted for inflation remains at $30,000 per year until age 65. In other words, we assume that your income will keep pace with inflation, but not beat it.

How much should you spend for consumption now and how much should you save for retirement?

Every dollar you save will earn interest until you take it out. Of course, the cost of living will be going up, too. We will assume that the interest rate you earn will exceed the rate of inflation by 3% per year. In other words, the real rate of interest is 3% per year.

There are two approaches that you could take to computing how much you should save for your retirement: (1) Aim for a target replacement rate of preretirement income, and (2) aim for maintaining the same level of consumption spending before and after retirement. We will examine both approaches next.

5.1.1 Approach 1: Target Replacement Rate of Preretirement Income

Many experts recommend that in making a savings plan, you should aim for a replacement rate equal to 75% of your preretirement income. Let us apply this rule to our situation. With a real income before retirement of $30,000, the target level of retirement income is $0.75 \times \$30,000$, or $22,500 per year.

The method for computing how much saving is needed to reach the desired target consists of two steps:

- First compute the amount you need to have accumulated in your personal retirement account when you reach retirement age.

- Then compute the annual amount of saving needed to reach that future value.

So, first we compute the amount that you have to have in your retirement fund at age 65 to be able to withdraw $22,500 per year for 15 years:

n	i	PV	FV	PMT	$Result$
15	3	?	0	−22,500	$PV = \$268,604$

Next we compute how much you need to save each year to have $268,604 accumulated 30 years from now:

n	i	PV	FV	PMT	$Result$
30	3	0	$268,604	?	$PMT = \$5,646$

So the conclusion from this procedure is that in order to be able to take out a retirement benefit of $22,500 per year for 15 years, you would need to save $5,646 per year in each of the next 30 years.

Now, let us consider a problem that arises when you use approach 1. Note that this approach does not necessarily result in your having the same consumption level after retirement as you did during your working years. In the preceding example, your consumption spending during the working years when you are saving $5,646 of your $30,000 annual income will be $24,354 per year, but then in retirement you will have only $22,500 to spend each year.

One way to deal with this problem is to redo the calculations using a higher replacement rate than 75%. If that replacement rate turns out to be too high, then try a lower one. You could continue applying this trial-and-error procedure until you find a replacement rate that results in the same consumption spending before and after retirement. Approach 2 addresses the problem directly without resorting to a trial-and-error search.

Quick Check 5-1
Recompute the saving needed in the example if the target replacement rate is 80%. What does the new saving level imply about consumption spending before and after retirement?

5.1.2 Approach 2: Maintain the Same Level of Consumption Spending

Let us now consider how much you need to save if your goal is to spend the same amount on consumption before and after retirement. This implies a constant stream of the same amount in each of the next 45 years, denoted by C. The amount saved each year from age 35 to 65 is $30,000 minus C. At age 65, the total accumulation will be $47.58 \times (\$30,000 - C)$.[1] The amount withdrawn from the retirement account each year after age 65 will be C. Its present value at age 65 is $11.94C$.[2]

To find C we set the two amounts equal to each other:

$$47.58(30,000 - C) = 11.94C$$
$$C = \$23,982$$

So consumption spending is $23,982 per year. Annual savings during the working years must, therefore, be $6,018 per year (i.e., $30,000 − $23,982). The total accumulation at age 65 will be $286,298.

Columns 1 through 4 in Table 5.1 and Figure 5.1 show the time profiles of income, consumption, and saving derived in this example. They demonstrate that income is $30,000 until age 65, and then it drops off to zero. Consumption stays level at $23,982 per year from age 35 until age 80.

The equation that we have solved in order to find C can be written in a slightly different and more general way:

$$\sum_{t=1}^{45} \frac{C}{(1+r)^t} = \sum_{t=1}^{30} \frac{Y_t}{(1+r)^t} \tag{5.1}$$

where r is the interest rate and Y_t is labor income in year t.

---

[1]The computation is:

n	i	PV	FV	PMT	Result
30	3	0	?	1	$FV = \$47.58$

[2]The computation is:

n	i	PV	FV	PMT	Result
15	3	?	0	1	$PV = \$11.94$

TABLE 5.1   Salary, Consumption, and Saving over the Life Cycle

Age (1)	Salary (2)	Consumption (3)	Saving (4)	Human Capital (5)	Retirement Fund (6)
35	$30,000	$23,982	$6,018	$588,013	0
45	30,000	23,982	6,018	446,324	$68,987
55	30,000	23,982	6,018	255,906	161,700
65	30,000	23,982	6,018	0	286,298
66	0	23,982	−23,982	0	270,905
70	0	23,982	−23,982	0	204,573
75	0	23,982	−23,982	0	109,832
80	0	23,982	−23,982	0	0

Equation 5.1 says that the present value of consumption spending over the next 45 years equals the present value of labor income over the next 30 years. Economists call the present value of one's future labor income **human capital,** and they call the constant level of consumption spending that has a present value equal to one's human capital **permanent income.** (See Box 5.1 about the economists who were awarded Nobel Prizes for their contributions to the theory of human capital and consumption spending.)

In our example, with labor income of $30,000 per year for 30 years, your human capital is $588,013 at age 35, and your permanent income is $23,982 per year.[3] As you get older, the *PV* of your remaining labor income declines, so your human capital falls steadily until it reaches zero at age 65.

FIGURE 5.1   Salary, Consumption, and Saving over the Life Cycle

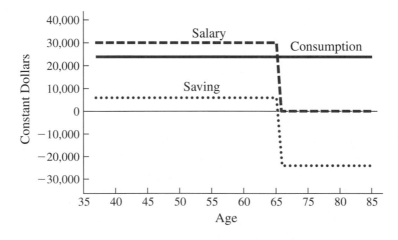

[3]The calculation is:

n	i	PV	FV	PMT
30	3	?	0	30,000

PV = $588,013

n	i	PV	FV	PMT
45	3	588,013	0	?

PMT = $23,982

BOX 5.1

Nobel Prizes for the Theory of Permanent Income, Life-Cycle Saving, and Human Capital

Milton Friedman was awarded the Nobel Prize in economic science in 1976. A contribution cited by the prize committee as being of primary importance was his theory that permanent income and not year-to-year income is the determining factor when assessing total consumption outlays. Friedman demonstrated that a much greater proportion of the former type of income is saved than the latter (Adapted from http://www.nobel.se/laureates/economy-1976-press.html).

Franco Modigliani received the Nobel Prize in 1985 in part for the construction and development of the life-cycle hypothesis of household saving. The underlying idea of the life-cycle hypothesis—that people save for their old age—is, of course, not new; nor is it Modigliani's own. His achievement lies primarily in the rationalization of the idea into a formal model, which he developed in different directions and integrated within a well-defined and established economic theory. The life-cycle model is today the basis of most dynamic

models used for the study of consumption and saving (Adapted from http://www.nobel.se/laureates/economy-1985-press.html).

Gary Becker received the Nobel Prize in 1992 for having extended the domain of microeconomic analysis to a wide range of human behavior. His most noteworthy contribution is in the area of human capital. The theory of human capital is considerably older than Becker's work, but his achievement was to have formulated and formalized the microeconomic foundations of the theory. The theory of human capital has created a uniform analytical framework for studying the return on education and on-the-job training. The human capital approach also helps explain trade patterns across countries; in fact, differences in the supply of human capital among countries have been shown to have more explanatory power than differences in the supply of real capital (Adapted from http://www.nobel.se/laureates/economy-1992-press.html).

Figure 5.2 and columns 5 and 6 in Table 5.1 show the time profiles of human capital and the accumulated amount in the retirement fund implied by the pattern of income and saving in Figure 5.1 and columns 2 and 4 of Table 5.1. The retirement fund starts out at zero at age 35, and it gradually grows to a high of $285,309 at age 65. It then declines to zero at age 80. The individual's total wealth, defined as human capital plus retirement assets, declines continuously between ages 35 and 80.

Quick Check 5-2

Georgette is currently 30 years old, plans to retire at age 65 and expects to live to age 85. Her salary is $25,000 per year, and she intends to maintain a constant level of real consumption spending over the next 55 years. Assume no taxes, no growth in real labor income, and a real interest rate of 3% per year.

a. What is the value of Georgette's human capital?

b. What is her permanent income?

Let us consider what effect a different interest rate would have on both permanent income and human capital. Table 5.2 shows that the higher the interest rate,

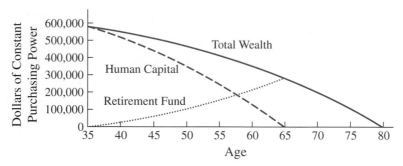

FIGURE 5.2 Human Capital, Retirement Assets, and Total Wealth over the Life Cycle

the lower the value of human capital, but the higher the level of permanent income. Because you save throughout your work years, you are better off with a higher real interest rate, even though the value of your human capital is lower.

Quick Check 5-3

In Table 5.2, what would human capital and permanent income be at a real interest rate of 3.5% per year?

Now suppose that instead of starting out at age 35 with no accumulated assets, you have $10,000 in a savings account. How does that affect the amount you can consume over your lifetime? The answer is that it enables you to increase consumption spending in each of the next 45 years by $407.85, assuming the interest rate is 3% per year.

On the other hand, suppose you wanted to leave a bequest of $10,000 to your children after you die at age 80. With unchanged lifetime income, how does the in-

---

TABLE 5.2 Human Capital and Permanent Income as a Function of the Real Interest Rate

Real Interest Rate (%)	Human Capital	Permanent Income	Saving
0	$900,000	$20,000	$10,000
1	774,231	21,450	8,550
2	671,894	22,784	7,216
3	588,013	23,982	6,018
4	518,761	25,037	4,963
5	461,174	25,946	4,054
6	412,945	26,718	3,282
10	282,807	28,674	1,326

Assumptions: You are currently 35 years old, expect to retire in 30 years at age 65, and then to live for 15 more years until age 80. Your real salary is $30,000 per year, and you have not yet accumulated any assets.

tended bequest affect your lifetime consumption stream? Answer: It would reduce your consumption by $107.85 in each of the next 45 years.

The general formula that expresses the lifetime consumption possibilities open to you as a function of your income, initial wealth, and bequests is:

$$\sum_{t=1}^{T} \frac{C_t}{(1 + r)^t} + \frac{B_t}{(1 + r)^t} = W_0 + \sum_{t=1}^{R} \frac{Y_t}{(1 + r)^t} \tag{5.2}$$

where:

C_t = consumption spending in year t

Y_t = labor income in year t

r = interest rate

R = number of years until retirement

T = number of years of life

W_0 = value of initial wealth

B = bequest

Equation 5.2 says that the present value of your lifetime consumption spending and bequests equals the present value of your lifetime resources—initial wealth and future labor income. This is the **intertemporal budget constraint** that you face in deciding on a lifetime consumption spending plan.

Quick Check 5-4
What effect would a $1 million inheritance that you expect to receive 30 years from now have on your permanent income?

Note that any lifetime consumption spending plan that satisfies your budget constraint (i.e., equation 5.2) is a **feasible plan.** There are many possible feasible plans. To choose among them you must specify a criterion for quantitatively assessing the welfare or satisfaction (economists use the term *utility*) that you receive from each feasible plan. A quantitative model that enables you to choose the best among all feasible plans is called an **optimization model.** Developing optimization models for lifetime financial planning is beyond the scope of this text.[4]

Now let us consider the effect of changes in real income over the life cycle. For example, Dr. Omar Ben Holim has just graduated from medical school at age 30 and has started training to be a surgeon at Mount Heaven Hospital. Omar's real salary for the next five years will be $25,000 per year. After completing his residency, however, Omar expects to earn $300,000 per year in real terms until he retires at age 65. Given his future expectations, he decides to start enjoying a high standard of living immediately. If he wants to maintain the same level of real consumption spending for the rest of his life and his life expectancy is 85 years, how much should he plan to save now and in the future? Assume that the real interest rate is 3% per year, and that Omar can either borrow or lend at that same rate.

Table 5.3 and Figure 5.3 show Omar's expected pattern of salary and planned consumption spending and saving on the assumption that he wants to have the

---

[4]For a review of life-cycle optimization models see R. C. Merton, *Continuous-Time Finance,* chapters 4–6.

TABLE 5.3   Omar's Life-Cycle Saving Plan

Age	Salary	Consumption	Saving	Human Capital	Other Assets or Liabilities
30	0	0	0	5,186,747	0
31	25,000	193,720	−168,720	5,317,349	−168,720
32	25,000	193,720	−168,720	5,451,869	−342,502
33	25,000	193,720	−168,720	5,590,425	−521,497
34	25,000	193,720	−168,720	5,733,138	−705,862
35	25,000	193,720	−168,720	5,880,132	−895,758
36	300,000	193,720	106,280	5,756,536	−816,351
37	300,000	193,720	106,280	5,629,232	−734,562
38	300,000	193,720	106,280	5,498,109	−650,319
39	300,000	193,720	106,280	5,363,053	−563,549
40	300,000	193,720	106,280	5,223,944	−474,175
44	300,000	193,720	106,280	4,624,507	−89,053
45	300,000	193,720	106,280	4,463,242	14,555
65	300,000	193,720	106,280	0	2,882,067
66	0	193,720	−193,720	0	2,774,809
84	0	193,720	−193,720	0	188,078
85	0	193,720	−193,720	0	0

same real consumption every year. His human capital initially is $5,186,747, and his permanent income is $193,720. In order to spend $193,720 per year during the five years of his residency, he will have to borrow ("dissave") $169,720 each year to supplement his $25,000 salary. His total indebtedness will grow to a maximum of $895,758 at age 35, and then decline thereafter as a result of his saving $106,280 every year from age 36 until he retires at age 65. Note that he will not have paid off his debt until age 45. One is never too young to start learning finance (see Box 5.2).

FIGURE 5.3   Omar's Life-Cycle Saving Plan

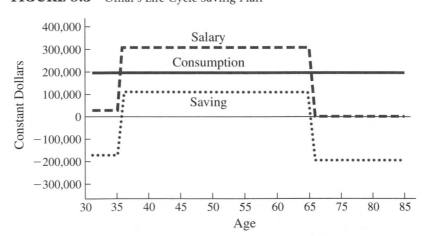

B O X   5 . 2

Kids and Money

Like brushing teeth, financial responsibility is a habit that is easiest to establish when children are young. But teaching kids about money is a long-term project that can take a lot of parental time and patience. It means including kids in financial decisions that involve them and being willing to let them make their own mistakes.

Don't just hand your child a few dollars in weekly allowance and forget about it. Important lessons are taught both in the way the allowance arrives and where it goes. Many parents, for example, tie the weekly payday to family chores; others give a basic allowance but provide extra money in exchange for household responsibilities. The idea is to link work and money.

Once children have money, they have to learn how to handle it, balancing spending and saving. You can divide the allowance into different jars for different purposes or set up a home bank or even a "junior 401(k)" in which you match any amount your child saves. The variations are endless. The important thing is to create a system that both you and your kids like so that you will stick with it.

Source: Adapted from Lynn Asinof, "Kids and Money: Lessons on Dollars and Sense," *The Wall Street Journal,* November 19, 1993, p. C1. Reprinted by permission of *The Wall Street Journal,* © 1993, Dow Jones & Company, Inc. All Rights Reserved Worldwide.

Quick Check 5-5

Suppose that Omar cannot borrow during the next five years. How does that affect his lifetime saving and consumption plan?

5.2 TAKING ACCOUNT OF SOCIAL SECURITY

In many countries the government obliges citizens to participate in a mandatory retirement income system called social security.[5] Under such systems, people pay a tax during their working years and in return qualify for a lifetime annuity in their old age. Such a system of mandatory saving should influence the amount of voluntary saving that we do for retirement. Let us use our life-cycle planning model to examine the right way to take account of social security.

To address this question in the context of our life-cycle discounted cash flow planning model, we first recognize that social security alters the profile of our lifetime net cash inflows. We return to our first example in which you are 35 years old, and your salary will be $30,000 per year for the next 30 years. Your human capital is $588,013—the *PV* of labor income at an interest rate of 3% per year. Suppose the optimal level of consumption spending is a constant $23,982 per year (equal to your permanent income). Annual savings in the preretirement years, must, therefore be $6,018 ($30,000 − $23,982) per year. The total accumulation at age 65 will

---

[5]In the United States, the social security system is called OASDI, which stands for old age, survivors, and disability insurance. As the name implies, it provides not only old age benefits, but also benefits for dependent family members of workers who die during their working years, and benefits to those who can no longer work due to disability.

be $286,309, which is enough to support a retirement income of $23,982 per year for 15 years.

Suppose that social security benefits are equal to what you would have if you had saved each year an amount equal to the amount you pay in social security taxes and earned a real interest rate of 3% per year. Thus, if you pay $2,000 per year in social security taxes for 30 years, you will receive in benefits $7,970 per year for 15 years starting at age 66.[6] What impact will social security have on your savings and your welfare under these circumstances?

The answer is that you will simply reduce your personal voluntary savings by the amount of social security taxes. So your savings will fall from $6,018 per year to $4,018. The difference of $2,000 is the amount you will pay in social security taxes. Thus, you reduce your private saving by an amount equal to the "savings" imposed on you by the social security system. Your pool of private savings will suffice to provide a life annuity of $16,012, which when added to your social security benefit of $7,970 will give you a total retirement income of $23,982 per year.

Thus, if social security pays you the same rate of return you could earn on your private saving, your lifetime consumption plan will not be affected by the existence of social security. There will only be a substitution of forced saving for voluntary private saving.

But what happens if social security pays an implied real interest rate that differs from 3%? If it pays a rate higher than 3%, you will be able to afford a higher lifetime consumption stream than $23,982; if it pays less than 3% per year, your consumption stream will be lower.

In many countries, the social security system offers a higher rate of return to people in the lower end of the income distribution than to those in the upper end. But the fact that benefits are paid in the form of a lifetime annuity implies that no matter how rich or poor you are, the longer you live, the higher your actual rate of return. The effective rate of return earned in the social security system is an important issue (see Box 5.3).

Quick Check 5-6

Suppose that social security offers a 3% real rate of return to someone who pays a 10% tax on a salary of $30,000 per year for 40 years. How large must the annual benefit payment be if it is calculated to last for 20 years?

5.3 DEFERRING TAXES THROUGH VOLUNTARY RETIREMENT PLANS

In many countries governments encourage voluntary saving for retirement through provisions of the tax code. In the United States, people are permitted to establish tax-advantaged accounts, known as individual retirement accounts (IRAs), to which contributions are deductible from current income for tax purposes, and interest on these contributions is not taxed until the money is withdrawn. These plans are called

---

[6]The calculation is:

n	i	PV	FV	PMT
30	3	0	?	2,000

$$FV = \$95,151$$

n	i	PV	FV	PMT
15	3	95,151	0	?

$$PMT = \$7,970$$

The Great Social Security Debate Is Just Beginning. Reform Plans Are Appealing, But Can People Handle the Risk?

By R. A. ZALDIVAR
Herald Washington Bureau

WASHINGTON—When President Franklin D. Roosevelt first proposed Social Security in the 1930s, he told Americans it would serve as "social insurance" against the perils of hunger and homelessness in old age. Now, in the 1990s, reformers are promoting what sounds like a gambler's version of Social Security: personal investment accounts that would let workers put some or all of their Social Security tax dollars in stocks and bonds.

Advocates—including many Republicans and some Democrats—assert that personal accounts would provide many workers with a better payback than vintage, government-run Social Security. But individuals would also have to face the risks of a market downturn, or the consequences of their own misguided investment choices.

This week, at a White House town meeting in Kansas City, Mo., President Clinton will begin a year-long search for consensus on the future of Social Security. Personal accounts are already on the table as the leading alternative to FDR's model. Polls show that Americans are conflicted. They want the choice and sense of ownership of personal accounts, yet the risk gives them pause.

Source: Published Sunday, April 5, 1998, in the *Miami Herald*, http://www.herald.com:80/business/docs/016366.htm. Reprinted with permission of The Miami Herald.

---

tax deferred rather than *tax exempt* because any amounts withdrawn from the plan are taxed at the time of withdrawal.

Some people believe that there is an advantage to such tax deferral only if you will be in a lower tax bracket when you withdraw the money. But that is not correct. Tax deferral is quite advantageous even for people who remain in the same tax bracket after retirement.

To see why, consider the following example, summarized in Figure 5.4. Suppose that you face a tax rate of 20% both before and after retirement. The interest rate is 8% per year. You are 30 years before your retirement date and contribute $1,000 to the plan. Your total before-tax amount accumulated at retirement will be $1,000 \times 1.08^{30}$ = $10,062.65. You will have to pay taxes at the rate of 20% on the entire amount, if you choose to withdraw it at that time. Thus, your taxes will be $0.2 \times \$10,062.65$ = $2,012.53, and you will be left with $8,050.12 after taxes.

If, instead, you choose not to participate in the retirement plan and invest in an ordinary savings plan, you have to pay 20% of the $1,000 or $200 immediately in additional taxes. The remaining $800 will go into the ordinary savings plan, and interest earnings on the $800 will be taxed each year. The after-tax interest rate earned is, therefore, $(1 - 0.2) \times 8\%$ or 6.4%. The amount accumulated at retirement from this ordinary savings plan is 800×1.064^{30} = $5,144.45. Because you have paid the taxes on the original contribution and on the interest along the way, the amount accumulated is not subject to further tax.

Clearly, the tax-deferred savings plan provides a larger after-tax benefit because $8,050.12 is greater than $5,144.45. Thus, even though you remain in the same 20% tax bracket both before and after retirement, the amount you have to spend in the future is almost twice as much under the tax-deferred savings plan.

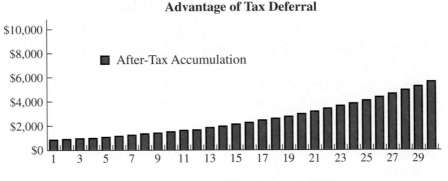

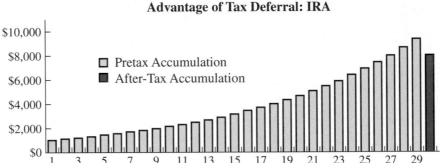

FIGURE 5.4   The Advantage of Tax-Deferred Saving

When your tax rate remains unchanged, the benefit of deferral can be summarized in the rule: *deferral earns you the pretax rate of return after tax.* That is, if you paid the initial tax and invested $800 at the pretax rate of 8%, you would have $800 \times 1.08^{30} = \$8,050.12$.

Quick Check 5-7

Suppose that the investor's tax rate is 30% instead of 20%. How large would be the advantage of tax deferral compared to our example with a 20% tax rate?

5.4 SHOULD YOU INVEST IN A PROFESSIONAL DEGREE?

Education and training can be viewed as an investment in human capital. Although there may be many reasons for acquiring additional schooling, one purpose is to increase people's earning power, that is, increase their human capital.

Let us consider the costs and benefits of additional education. The economic costs consist of *explicit* costs such as tuition and the *implicit* cost of forgone earnings during the time spent in school. The economic benefits consist of the value of the increased stream of earnings attributable to the additional years of education. Like other investment decisions, the investment is worthwhile if the present value of the expected incremental benefits exceeds the present value of the expected incremental costs.

For example, consider Joe Grad who has just graduated from college and is deciding whether to go on for his master's degree. Joe figures that if he takes a job immediately, he can earn $30,000 per year in real terms for the remainder of his working years. If he goes on for two more years of graduate study, however, he can increase his earnings to $35,000 per year. The cost of tuition is $15,000 per year in real terms. Is this a worthwhile investment if the real interest rate is 3% per year?

Ignoring uncertainty, Joe must give up $45,000 (tuition plus forgone earnings) in each of the next two years in order to increase his earnings by $5,000 per year over his remaining career.

Suppose Joe is now 20 years old and expects to retire at age 65. The relevant cash flows for this investment are incremental outflows of $45,000 in each of the next two years and then incremental inflows of $5,000 in each of the succeeding 43 years. The present value of the outflows is $86,106; the present value of the inflows is $113,026. The net present value of the investment in human capital is, therefore, $26,920, and it is worthwhile.[7]

Quick Check 5-8

Suppose that Joe is 30 years old instead of 20. If all the other assumptions remain the same, does the investment in the graduate degree still have a positive *NPV*?

5.5 SHOULD YOU BUY OR RENT?

You are currently renting a house for $10,000 per year and have an option to buy it for $200,000. Property taxes are deductible for income tax purposes, and your tax rate is 30%. The maintenance and property taxes are estimated to be:

Maintenance	$1,200
Property Taxes	$2,400
Total	$3,600

These costs are currently included in the rent.

Let us assume that your objective is to provide yourself with housing at the lowest present value of cost. Should you buy or continue to rent?

The present value of cost equals the discounted value of the after-tax outflows discounted at the after-tax rate of interest. Because property taxes can be deducted from income for federal income tax purposes, the after-tax outflow for property taxes each year is 0.7 × $2,400, or $1,680. Because no date for eventually selling the house has been specified, we will assume for simplicity an infinite horizon.

---

[7]First, compute the present value of the outflows:

n	i	PV	FV	PMT	Result
2	3	?	0	45,000	PV = $86,106

Next compute the *PV* of the inflows:

n	i	PV	FV	PMT	Result
43	3	?	0	5,000	PV = $119,910
2	3	0	119,910	0	PV = $113,026

If you buy the house, then you will have to pay $200,000 immediately, and the expected after-tax cash outflow will consist of the maintenance expenses and property taxes net of the income tax savings from deductibility of the property taxes:

$$\text{Cash Outflow in Year } t = \$1,200 + \$1,680 = \$2,880$$

Letting i be the before-tax discount rate, the present value cost of owning the house is:

$$PV \text{ Cost of Owning} = \$200,000 + \frac{\$2,880}{0.7i}$$

where we have assumed that the properly maintained house continues in perpetuity and have applied the annuity formula. Similarly, the present value cost of renting the house can be written as:

$$PV \text{ Cost of Renting} = \frac{10,000}{0.7i}$$

If PV Cost of Renting $> PV$ Cost of Owning, then it is better to own rather than rent.

Because we are assuming that the maintenance costs and property taxes are fixed in *real* terms, i should be a *real* interest rate. Let us assume no inflation so that the real and nominal before-tax discount rate is 3% per year. Then the real after-tax rate is 2.1% per year.[8] Computing the present value costs under each alternative, we find:

$$PV \text{ Cost of Owning} = \$200,000 + \frac{\$2,880}{0.021} = \$337,143$$

and

$$PV \text{ Cost of Renting} = \frac{10,000}{0.021} = \$476,190$$

Therefore, you would be better off buying the house.

The buy-or-rent decision is really an investment decision. In effect you are laying out $200,000 today in order to receive future cash benefits equal to the after-tax savings in rental costs. In present value terms, you save $139,047 (i.e., $476,190 − $337,143). This is the *NPV* of the investment in the house.

Of course, the relation between *PV* Cost of Renting and *PV* Cost of Owning depends on the rent charged. At what rent would you be indifferent between buying and renting?

This break-even rent (i.e., the annual rental costs at which you would be indifferent between owning or renting) is found by setting *PV* Cost of Owning equal to *PV* Cost of Renting and solving for X:

$$\frac{X}{0.021} = \$200,000 + \frac{\$2,880}{0.021}$$

$$X = 0.021 \times \$200,000 + \$2,880$$

$$X = \$4,200 + \$2,880 = \$7,080$$

---

[8] With no inflation the real after-tax rate equals $(1 - \text{tax rate})$ times the before-tax rate. In this case:

$$(1 - 0.3) \times 3\% = 0.7 \times 3\% = 2.1\%$$

Thus, if the rent is less than $7,080 per year, you would prefer to keep on renting rather than to buy.

Quick Check 5-9
Suppose that the real interest rate before taxes was 4% instead of 3%. What would be the break-even rent?

Summary

- In making lifetime saving/consumption decisions: (1) Do the analysis in real terms (constant dollars) to simplify the calculations and to avoid having to forecast inflation. (2) Start by computing the present value of your lifetime resources. The present value of your lifetime spending cannot exceed this amount.

- Social security or any other forced saving program will offset voluntary saving. It may have a positive or a negative effect on the present value of your total lifetime resources.

- Tax-deferred retirement accounts are advantageous because they allow you to earn a before-tax rate of return until money is withdrawn from the account. They are advantageous if you are in the same tax bracket before and after you retire, and even more so if your tax bracket is lower after you retire.

- Getting a professional degree or other training can be evaluated as an investment in human capital. As such, it should be undertaken if the present value of the benefits (such as increase in your earnings) exceeds the present value of the costs (such as tuition and forgone salary.)

- In deciding whether to buy or rent an apartment or a consumer durable, choose the alternative with the lower present value of costs.

Key Terms

- human capital   146
- permanent income   146
- intertemporal budget constraint   149
- feasible plan   149
- optimization model   149

Answers to Quick Check Questions

Quick Check 5-1   *Recompute the saving needed in the example if the target replacement rate is 80%. What does the new saving level imply about consumption spending before and after retirement?*

ANSWER: The target level of spending in retirement is $0.8 \times \$30,000$, or $24,000 per year. First, we compute the amount that you have to have in your retirement fund at age 65 to be able to withdraw $24,000 per year for 15 years:

n	i	PV	FV	PMT	Result
15	3	?	0	−24,000	PV = $286,510

Next we compute how much we need to save each year to have $286,510 accumulated 30 years from now:

n	i	PV	FV	PMT	Result
30	3	0	$286,510	?	PMT = $6,002

Your consumption spending before retirement will be $23,998 per year, which is very close to the level of $24,000 you will have after retirement. So in this case, aiming for a replacement rate of 80% results in almost the same consumption spending before and after retirement.

Quick Check 5-2   *Georgette is currently 30 years old, plans to retire at age 65 and to live to age 85. Her labor income is $25,000 per year, and she intends to maintain a constant level of real consumption spending over the next 55 years. Assume no taxes, no growth in real salary, and a real interest rate of 3% per year.*
a.   What is the value of Georgette's human capital?
b.   What is her permanent income?

ANSWER:

a.

n	i	PV	FV	PMT	Result
35	3	?	0	25,000	PV = 537,181

b.

n	i	PV	FV	PMT	Result
55	3	537,181	0	?	PMT = 20,062

Quick Check 5-3   *In Table 5.2, what would be human capital and permanent income at a real interest rate of 3.5% per year?*

ANSWER: First compute human capital.

n	i	PV	FV	PMT	Result
30	3.5	?	0	30,000	PV = 551,761

Then compute permanent income.

n	i	PV	FV	PMT	Result
45	3.5	551,761	0	?	PMT = 24,528

Quick Check 5-4   *What effect would a $1 million inheritance that you expect to receive 30 years from now have on your permanent income?*

ANSWER: The present value of your lifetime resources would increase by the *PV* of the expected inheritance and permanent income would increase by the annuitized value of that increase in lifetime resource. Assuming a real interest rate of 3% per year and assuming that the $1 million inheritance is in constant dollars:
First compute the increase in *PV* of your lifetime resources.

n	i	PV	FV	PMT	Result
30	3	?	1,000,000	0	PV = 411,987

Then compute the increase in permanent income

n	i	PV	FV	PMT	Result
45	3	411,987	0	?	PMT = 16,803

So your permanent income increases by $16,803.

Quick Check 5-5   *Suppose that Omar cannot borrow during the next five years. How does that affect his lifetime saving and consumption plan?*

ANSWER: If he cannot borrow, he will only be able to consume what he earns, namely $25,000 per year for five years. At the end of that time he will increase his consumption to equal his permanent income. Let us figure out what his human capital and permanent income will be in another five years.

First compute human capital.

n	i	PV	FV	PMT	Result
30	3	?	0	300,000	PV = 5,880,132

Then compute permanent income

n	i	PV	FV	PMT	Result
50	3	5,880,132	0	?	PMT = 228,534

So starting at age 35, Omar will consume $228,534 per year for the rest of his life.

Quick Check 5-6   *Suppose that social security offers a 3% real rate of return to someone who pays a 10% tax on a salary of $30,000 per year for 40 years. How large must the annual benefit payment be if it is calculated to last for 20 years?*

ANSWER: The future value of the taxes paid over 40 years should equal the present value of the benefits received over the following 20 years when both streams are discounted at 3% per year.

First calculate the *PV* of the taxes:

n	i	PV	FV	PMT	Result
40	3	0	?	3,000	FV = 226,204

Then compute the annual retirement benefit:

n	i	PV	FV	PMT	Result
20	3	226,204	0	?	PMT = 15,204

So the annual benefit payment should be $15,204 in real terms, which is a replacement rate of preretirement income of about 50%.

Quick Check 5-7   *Suppose that the investor's tax rate is 30% instead of 20%. How large would be the advantage of tax deferral compared to our example with a 20% tax rate?*

ANSWER: As in the example in the text, your total before-tax amount accumulated at retirement will still be $1,000 \times 1.08^{30} = \$10,062.65$. You will have to pay taxes at the rate of 30% on the entire amount so your taxes will be $0.3 \times \$10,062.65 = \$3,018.80$, and you will be left with $7,043.85 after taxes. If, instead, you choose not to participate in the retirement plan and invest in an ordinary savings plan, you have to pay 30% of the $1,000 or $300 immediately in additional taxes. The remaining $700 will go into the ordinary savings plan, and interest earnings on the $700 will be taxed each year. The after-tax interest rate earned is, therefore, $(1 - 0.3) \times 8\%$, or 5.6%. The amount accumulated at retirement from this ordinary savings plan is $700 \times 1.056^{30} = \$3,589.35$.

Quick Check 5-8 *Suppose that Joe is 30 years old instead of 20. If all the other assumptions remain the same, does the investment in the graduate degree still have a positive NPV?*

ANSWER: As in the example in the text, Joe must give up $45,000 (tuition plus forgone earnings) in each of the next two years in order to increase his earnings by $10,000 per year over his remaining career. Joe is now 30 years old and expects to retire at age 65. The relevant cash flows for this investment are incremental outflows of $45,000 in each of the next two years and then incremental inflows of $5,000 in each of the succeeding 33 years. The present value of the outflows is $86,106; the present value of the inflows is $97,869. The net present value of the investment in human capital is, therefore, $11,763, and it is still worthwhile.

Quick Check 5-9 *Suppose that the real interest rate before taxes was 4% instead of 3%. What would be the break-even rent?*

ANSWER: The after-tax real discount rate is now $0.7 \times 4\% = 2.8\%$ per year. The annual rental costs at which you would be indifferent between owning or renting, is found by setting *PV* Cost of Owning equal to *PV* Cost of Renting and solving for *X*:

$$\frac{X}{0.028} = \$200,000 + \frac{\$2,880}{0.028}$$

$$X = 0.028 \times \$200,000 + \$2,880$$

$$X = \$5,600 + \$2,880 = \$8,480$$

Questions and Problems

Saving for Retirement

TEMPLATE

5.1, 5.3–5.5

1. Assume that you are 40 years old and wish to retire at age 65. You expect to be able to average a 6% annual rate of interest on your savings over your lifetime (both prior to retirement and after retirement). You would like to save enough money to provide $8,000 per year beginning at age 66 in retirement income to supplement other sources (social security, pension plans, etc.). Suppose you decide that the extra income need be provided for only 15 years (up to age 80). Assume that your first contribution to the savings plan will take place one year from now.
    a. How much must you save each year between now and retirement to achieve your goal?
    b. If the rate of inflation turns out to be 6% per year between now and retirement, how much will your first $8,000 withdrawal be worth in terms of today's purchasing power?

2. You are saving for retirement and you come across the following table. It shows the percentage of your current salary that you should save for your retirement in order to retire with an annuity equal to 70% of your salary if you have not yet saved anything. It assumes that your annual salary will remain constant in real terms until retirement, and that you will live for 25 years after retiring. For instance, if you have 35 years left before you retire and earn 3.5% per year on your investments, then you should save 17.3% of your current salary.

TABLE A Saving Rate Needed to Achieve 70% Replacement Rate			
Real Interest Rate	*Years to Retirement*		
	15	25	35
3.5% per year	59.79%	?	17.30%

a. Fill in the missing number in Table A.

TABLE B Saving to Maintain Constant Lifetime Consumption Spending			
Real Interest Rate	*Years to Retirement*		
	15	25	35
3.5% per year			

b. Now fill in Table B. It assumes that instead of targeting a 70% replacement rate of preretirement income, your goal is to maintain the same level of consumption spending both before and after retirement.

3. You are saving for retirement and you come across the following table. It shows the increase in the annual benefit you can receive in retirement per dollar that you increase your annual retirement saving in the years before retirement. It assumes that you will live for 20 years after retiring. For instance, if you have 35 years left before you retire and earn an interest rate of 3% per year, then you will obtain an increase of $3.20 in your annual retirement benefit for every $1 per year increase in annual saving. Fill in the missing table values.

	Years to Retirement		
Interest Rate	*20*	*25*	*30*
0.0%	$1.00	$1.25	$1.50
0.5%	$1.10	$1.40	$1.70
1.0%	$1.22	$1.57	?
1.5%	$1.35	$1.75	$2.19
2.0%	$1.49	$1.96	$2.48
3.0%	$1.81	?	$3.20
3.5%	?	$2.74	$3.63
4.0%	$2.19	$3.06	$4.13
4.5%	$2.41	$3.43	$4.69
5.0%	$2.65	$3.83	?

4. George Thriftless is 45 years old, earns $50,000 per year, and expects that his future earnings will keep pace with inflation but will not exceed inflation. He has not yet saved anything toward his retirement. His company does not offer any pension plan. George pays social security taxes equal to 7.5% of his salary, and he assumes that when he retires at age 65, he will receive $12,000 per year in inflation-adjusted social security benefits for the rest of his life. His life expectancy is age 85.

George buys a book on retirement planning that recommends saving enough so that when private savings and social security are combined, he can replace 80% of his preretirement salary. George buys a financial calculator and goes through the following calculations.

First, he computes the amount he will need to receive in each year of retirement to replace 80% of his salary:

$$0.8 \times \$50,000 = \$40,000$$

Because he expects to receive $12,000 per year in social security benefits, he calculates that he will have to provide the other $28,000 per year from his own retirement fund.

Using the 8% interest rate on long-term default-free bonds, George computes the amount he will need to have at age 65 as $274,908 (the present value of $28,000 for 20 years at 8% per year). Then he computes the amount he will have to save in each of the next 20 years to reach that future accumulation as $6,007 (the annual payment that will produce a future value of $274,908 at an interest rate of 8% per year). George feels confident that he can save 12% of his salary (i.e., $6,007/$50,000) in order to ensure a comfortable retirement.

a. If the expected long-term *real* interest rate is 3% per year, approximately what is the long-term expected rate of inflation?

b. Has George correctly taken account of inflation in his calculations? If not, how would you correct him?

c. How much should George save in each of the next 20 years (until age 65) if he wants to maintain a constant level of consumption over the remaining 40 years of his life (from age 45 to age 85)? Ignore income taxes.

5. George's company has a defined-benefit pension plan. Suppose the plan pays a benefit equal to 1% of final salary per year of service. George is 40 years old and has worked for the company for 15 years. His last year's salary was $50,000.

a. If normal retirement age is 65, the interest rate is 8%, and George's life expectancy is 80, what is the present value of his accrued pension benefit?

b. If the expected rate of inflation is 4% per year, what effect should his pension benefit have on George's planned saving, assuming he has a 75% target replacement rate?

6. Analyze the "expert's" responses to the following questions:

Question: How early do you recommend people begin saving for retirement? Would it be too early for my 14-year-old to start saving?

Expert: It's never too early.

Question: For a college student, what would you suggest for a savings plan?

Expert: I'd suggest deciding on a specific amount to set aside each month, then making sure you do it, no matter how great the temptations not to.

Investing in Human Capital

7. You are 30 years old and are considering full-time study for an MBA degree. Tuition and other direct costs will be $15,000 per year for two years. In addition you will have to give up a job with a salary of $30,000 per year. Assume tuition is paid and salary received at the *end* of the year. By how much does your salary have to increase (in real terms) as a result of getting your MBA degree to justify the investment? Assume a real interest rate of 3% per year and ignore taxes. Also assume that the salary increase is a constant real amount that starts after you complete your degree (at the end of the year following graduation) and lasts until retirement at age 65.

Buy or Rent an Apartment?

8. Suppose you currently rent an apartment and have an option to buy it for $200,000. Property taxes are $2,000 per year and are deductible for income tax purposes. An-

nual maintenance costs on the property are $1,500 per year and are *not* tax deductible. You expect property taxes and maintenance costs to increase at the rate of inflation. Your income tax rate is 40%, you can earn an *after-tax* real interest rate of 2% per year, and you plan to keep the apartment forever. What is the break-even annual rent such that you would buy it if the rent exceeded this amount?

Buy or Lease a Car?

9. You have decided to acquire a new car that costs $30,000. You are considering whether to lease it for three years or to purchase it and finance the purchase with a three-year installment loan. The lease requires no downpayment and lasts for three years. Lease payments are $400 monthly starting *immediately,* whereas the installment loan will require monthly payments starting a month from now at an annual percentage rate (APR) of 8%.
   a. If you expect the resale value of the car to be $20,000 three years from now, should you buy or lease it?
   b. What is the break-even resale price of the car three years from now, such that you would be indifferent between buying or leasing it?

10. Analyze the following newspaper column:

    Many of us who started families late share a nightmare image: having to pay huge college bills just as we're giving up paychecks and shouldering the steep costs of retirement. In fact, the double whammy might not be so bad, assuming the parents have prepared properly. On the plus side, older parents are likely to have enjoyed their best earning years before the college costs begin, allowing them to put aside more than younger parents can. They've also had more years for investments to compound. In the ideal situation, older parents can avoid borrowing to meet college costs, taking the preferred route of earning interest on investments rather than paying it on student loans. (Excerpted from Jeff Brown's Personal Finance column in the *Philadelphia Inquirer,* May 11, 1998.)

11. Analyze the following newspaper column:

    What's the best age for a person to start collecting Social Security benefits? According to conventional wisdom, retirement starts at age 65. It's true that full benefits don't start until age 65, but 62 year olds can retire and collect 80 percent of their benefits.

    Take the hypothetical cases of John and Mary, who have the same birthday and who are both slated to start drawing $1,000 a month in Social Security benefits at age 65. On his 62nd birthday, John decides to go ahead and start claiming his benefits of $800 a month (80 percent of $1,000). Mary decides to wait until she's 65, when she can claim the full $1,000. Three years later, Mary turns 65 and begins receiving $1,000 a month from the Social Security Administration. John continues to receive $800 a month. But he has already been paid $28,800 while Mary has received nothing.

    Five years go by, with Mary drawing $1,000 a month and John $800 a month. At 70, John has received $76,800, compared with Mary's $60,000. When they reach 77, Mary will pull ahead. So, it seems if a person doesn't live past 76, it would be better to start collecting Social Security benefits at 62. For those who reach their upper 70's, it pays to wait until they are 65 to collect Social Security. (Adapted from *Atlanta Business Chronicle,* Gary Sumner Contributing Writer, June 29, 1998.)

Personal Balance Sheets

12. Using the finance concepts presented in this chapter, construct a personal balance sheet showing your assets, liabilities, and net worth.
    a. Did you value your assets at cost or at current market value? Why?
    b. Did you include your human capital as an asset? Why?
    c. Did you include deferred taxes as a liability? Why?

Home Ownership over the Life Cycle

13. Suppose you buy a house for $200,000 when you are 35 years old. You make a 20% downpayment and borrow the other 80% from a mortgage lender. The mortgage loan is at a fixed interest rate of 8% per year for 30 years and requires level annual payments. At age 65 you plan to take out a "reverse mortgage" loan, which will allow you to borrow a constant annual amount for the rest of your life to be paid off by the sale of your house when you die. Your life expectancy is age 85. The interest rate on both the original mortgage loan and the reverse mortgage will be 8% per year.

    a. Suppose that you expect the inflation rate to be 3% per year and you can rent an equivalent house for $10,000 per year. Is it worth buying the house?

    b. Show how buying the house will affect your assets, liabilities, and cash flow over the next 50 years.

    c. In *Making the Most of Your Money,* J. B. Quinn has written

       Over the long run, the value of homes should follow the inflation rate. But over the time that you own your particular house, its value might rise or fall or stall. You can't predict. But there are reasons other than profit for owning a home.

       • Mortgage payments force you to save, while rental payments don't.

       • You get tax deductions, and can tax-shelter your capital gains.

       • You're landlord-free.

       • You know the deep contentment of holding a spot of ground that others can enter by invitation only.

       • You won't lose your lease.

       • You can renovate to suit.

       • A house is collateral for a loan.

       Comment.

CHAPTER

How to Analyze Investment Projects

6

OBJECTIVES

- To show how to use discounted cash flow analysis to make investment decisions such as whether to enter a new line of business.
- Analyze how to decide whether to invest in equipment to reduce operating costs.

CONTENTS

In the previous chapter we discussed how to apply discounted cash flow analysis to some of the major financial decisions that people face in their personal lives. In this chapter we apply those same techniques to the analysis of investment decisions by business firms, such as whether to launch a new product or to invest in research laboratories, factories, machinery, warehouses, showrooms, marketing campaigns, and training of employees. The process of analyzing such decisions is called *capital budgeting.*

This chapter discusses how businesses handle the capital budgeting process. Although the details vary from firm to firm, any capital budgeting process consists of three elements:

- coming up with proposals for investment projects
- evaluating them
- deciding which ones to accept and which to reject

What criteria should management use in deciding which investment projects to undertake? In chapter 1 we showed that in order to maximize the welfare of its shareholders, the objective of a firm's management is to only undertake those projects that increase—or at least do not decrease—the market value of shareholders' equity. For this, management needs a theory of how the decisions it makes affect the market value of the firm's equity shares. Such a theory was provided in chapter 4: Management should compute the discounted present value of the future expected cash flows from a project and undertake only those projects with positive net present value (*NPV*).

6.1 THE NATURE OF PROJECT ANALYSIS

The basic unit of analysis in the capital budgeting process is the individual investment project. Investment projects start with an idea for increasing shareholder wealth by producing a new product or improving the way an existing product is produced. Investment projects are analyzed as a sequence of decisions and possible events over time starting with the original concept, gathering information relevant to assessing the costs and benefits of implementing it, and devising an optimal strategy for implementing the project over time.

To illustrate the sequence of stages involved in investment project analysis, suppose you are a film industry executive whose job is to come up with proposals for new movies and to analyze their potential value to your company's shareholders. Typically, producing a movie for the mass market involves major outlays of cash over several years before there are any cash inflows from customers who pay to see it. Roughly speaking, the movie will increase shareholder wealth only if the present value of the cash inflows exceeds the present value of the outlays.

Forecasting the likely cash outlays and inflows from the movie is a complicated task. The cash flows will depend on a sequence of decisions and actions that are under your control and on a sequence of events that are not entirely under your control. At each stage in the project's life, from conceiving the idea for the movie's theme to the distribution of the final product to movie theaters and video stores, unpredictable events will occur that affect the stream of cash flows. At each stage you will have to decide whether to continue the project, to discontinue it, to delay it, or to accelerate it. You will also have to decide whether to reduce the level of spending (e.g., by eliminating some costly scenes) or to increase it (e.g., by launching a television advertising campaign).

It is not simply forecasting a project's cash flows that is difficult. Evaluating their likely effect on the market value of shareholders' equity is also complicated. To simplify our exposition of the complicated nature of project analysis in this chapter, we will proceed in stages. In this chapter we will analyze projects as if the future cash flows are known with certainty and use a discounted cash flow valuation procedure similar to the one discussed in chapter 4. Then later in chapter 17 we will consider ways to take account of uncertainty and of the value of managerial options.

6.2 WHERE DO INVESTMENT IDEAS COME FROM?

Most investment projects requiring capital expenditures fall into three categories: new products, cost reduction, and replacement of existing assets. Here are some examples:

- Should the firm start a new-product line that requires investment in plant, equipment, and inventories?
- Should the firm invest in automated equipment that will allow it to reduce its labor costs?
- Should the firm replace an existing plant in order to expand capacity or lower operating costs?

A common source of ideas for investment projects is the firm's existing customers. Surveys of customers, both formal and informal, can suggest new demands that can be met by producing new products and services or by improving existing ones. A firm that manufactures computer equipment, for example, may discover from surveying its customers that providing a repair service for computers might be a profitable new line of business.

Many firms establish a research and development (R&D) department to identify potential new products that are technologically feasible to produce and that seem to satisfy a perceived customer demand. In the pharmaceutical industry, for example, the R&D activity is the source of virtually all new-product ideas.

Another source of project ideas is the competition. For example, if the XYZ software company, which produces a financial planning package for personal computers, knows that a competitor, ABC software company, is working on a new upgrade in its competing product, XYZ may want to consider upgrading its own product. XYZ may want to consider acquiring ABC. Acquisitions of one company by another are capital budgeting projects.

Ideas for capital projects to improve products or reduce costs often come from the production divisions of corporations. For example, engineers, production managers, or other employees who are in close contact with the production process may spot ways to cut costs by reorganizing an assembly line or by replacing labor-intensive operations with automated equipment requiring a capital outlay.

In corporations with incentive systems that encourage managers and other employees to think about opportunities for profitable growth and operating improvements, there is generally a regular flow of proposals for investment projects. The rest of this chapter discusses techniques for evaluating projects and deciding which ones are likely to enhance shareholder value.

Quick Check 6-1
Where do you think new project ideas come from in the movie business?

6.3 THE NET PRESENT VALUE INVESTMENT RULE

Chapter 4 developed the investment criterion that is most obviously related to the goal of maximizing shareholder wealth—the *net present value rule.* A project's **net present value** (*NPV*) is the amount by which it is expected to increase the wealth of the firm's current shareholders. Stated as an investment criterion for the firm's managers, the *NPV* rule is: *Invest if the proposed project's NPV is positive.*

To illustrate how to calculate a project's *NPV* we present the following example. Generic Jeans Company, a manufacturer of casual clothing, is considering whether to produce a new line of jeans called Protojeans. It requires an initial outlay of $100,000 for new specialized equipment, and the firm's marketing department forecasts that given the nature of consumer preferences for jeans the product will have an economic life of three years. The cash flow forecasts for the Protojean project are shown in Figure 6.1.

A negative sign in front of a cash flow forecast for a particular year means a cash outflow. In the case of the Protojean project, there is only one negative cash flow, and that is at the start of the project (time zero). Subsequent cash flows are all positive: $50,000 at the end of the first year, $40,000 at the end of year 2, and $30,000 at the end of year 3.

To calculate the project's *NPV* we need to specify the capitalization rate (*k*) to use to discount the cash flows. This is called the project's **cost of capital.**

Table 6.1 shows the calculation of the net present value of the Protojean project. Each year's cash flow is discounted at a rate of 8% per year, and the resulting present value is shown in column 3. Thus, the present value of the $50,000 to be received at the end of the first year is $46,296.30, and so on. Column 4 shows the cumulative sum of the present values of all of the cash flows.

The project's *NPV* is the last entry in column 4 of Table 6.1. To the nearest penny it is $4,404.82. This means that by going forward with the Protojean project, management expects to increase the wealth of the shareholders of the Generic Jeans Company by $4,404.82.

FIGURE 6.1   Cash Flow Forecasts for the Protojean Project

Year	*Cash Flows (in thousands of dollars)*
0	−$100
1	$50
2	$40
3	$30

Year	0	1	2	3
Net cash flow	−100	50	40	30

TABLE 6.1   Calculation of *NPV* of the Protojean Project

Year (1)	Cash Flows (thousands of dollars) (2)	Present Value of Cash Flow at 8% per Year (3)	Cumulative Present Value (4)
0	–100	–100.00000	–100.00000
1	50	46.29630	–53.70370
2	40	34.29355	–19.41015
3	30	23.81497	4.40482

Quick Check 6-2

Suppose that the Protojean project is expected to have a third-year cash flow of only $10,000 instead of $30,000. If all other cash flows are the same and the discount rate is still 8% per year, what is its *NPV*?

6.4 ESTIMATING A PROJECT'S CASH FLOWS

E-BOOK

6.4

Calculating a project's *NPV* once one has the cash flow forecasts is the easy part of capital budgeting. Much more difficult is estimating a project's expected cash flows. Project cash flow forecasts are built up from estimates of the incremental revenues and costs associated with the project. Let us illustrate how cash flow estimates can be derived from estimates of a project's sales volume, selling price, and fixed and variable costs.

Suppose you are a manager in the personal computer division of Compusell Corporation, a large firm that manufactures many different types of computers. You come up with an idea for a new type of personal computer, which you call the PC1000. You may be able to develop a prototype of the PC1000 and even test market it for relatively little money and, therefore, you do not bother doing a full-fledged discounted cash flow analysis in the early phases of the project.

If your project idea gets to the point at which a large sum of cash must be expended, then you must prepare a capital appropriation request that details the amount of capital required and the projected benefits to the corporation from undertaking the project. Table 6.2 shows the estimated annual sales revenue, operating costs, and profit for the PC1000. It also shows the estimated capital outlay required.

Your estimates assume that sales will be 4,000 units per year at a price of $5,000 per unit. A new production facility will be leased for $1.5 million per year and production equipment will have to be purchased at a cost of about $2.8 million. The equipment will be depreciated over seven years using the straight-line method. In addition, you estimate a need for $2.2 million for working capital—primarily to finance inventories—thus bringing the total initial outlay required to $5 million.

Now consider the project's expected cash flows in the future. First, over how long a period will the project generate cash flows? The natural planning horizon to use in the analysis is the seven-year life of the equipment because at that time presumably a new decision would have to be made about whether to renew the investment.

TABLE 6.2 Forecasting Cash Flows for the PC1000 Project

Sales:

4,000 units at a price of $5,000	$20,000,000 per year

Fixed Costs:

Lease payments	$1,500,000 per year
Property taxes	200,000
Administration	600,000
Advertising	500,000
Depreciation	400,000
Other	300,000
Total Fixed Costs	$3,500,000 per year

Variable Costs:

Direct labor	$2,000 per unit
Materials	1,000
Selling expenses	500
Other	250
Variable Cost Per Unit	$3,750 per unit
Total Variable Costs for 4,000 Units	$15,000,000 per year
Total Annual Operating Costs	$18,500,000 per year
Annual Operating Profit	$1,500,000 per year
Corporate Income Taxes at 40%	$600,000 per year
After-Tax Operating Profit	$900,000 per year

Forecast of Initial Capital Outlay for PC1000

Purchase of Equipment	$2,800,000
Working Capital	$2,200,000
Total Capital Outlay	$5,000,000

In years 1 through 7 the net cash inflow from operations can be computed in two equivalent ways:

(1) $$\text{Cash Flow} = \text{Revenue} - \text{Cash Expenses} - \text{Taxes}$$

(2) $$\text{Cash Flow} = \text{Revenue} - \text{Total Expenses} - \text{Taxes} + \text{Noncash Expenses}$$
$$= \text{Net Income} + \text{Noncash Expenses}$$

The two approaches (if done properly) will always result in precisely the same estimates of net cash flow from operations.

The only noncash operating expense in the case of the PC1000 is depreciation, and the relevant numbers are (in $ millions):

Revenue	Cash Expenses	Depreciation	Total Expenses	Taxes	Net Income	Cash Flow
$20	$18.1	$0.4	$18.5	$0.6	$0.9	$1.3

Using approach 1, we get:

(1)   Cash Flow = $20 − $18.1 − $0.6 = $1.3 million

Using approach 2, we get:

(2)   Cash Flow = $0.9 + $0.4 = $1.3 million

To complete the estimation of project cash flows we need to estimate the cash flow in the final year (year 7) of the planning horizon. The natural assumption to make in this case is that the equipment will have no residual value at the end of the seven years, but that the working capital will still be intact and, therefore, be worth $2.2 million. This does not mean that the project will be liquidated at the end of seven years. It only means that were Compusell to liquidate it, it could probably get back the full $2.2 million in working capital it had to invest initially.

To summarize the project's cash flows, there is an initial outlay of $5 million, cash inflows of $1.3 million at the end of years 1 through 7, and an additional $2.2 million cash inflow at the end of the project's life in year 7. The cash flow diagram for the investment, therefore, looks as follows:

Year	0	1	2	3	4	5	6	7
Cash flow	-5	1.3	1.3	1.3	1.3	1.3	1.3	1.3
								2.2

Notice that the cash flow pattern from this project looks like a seven-year coupon bond with an annual coupon payment of $1.3 million, a face value of $2.2 million, and a price of $5 million. This similarity makes the calculation of the project's *NPV* and *IRR* very simple using the standard time-value-of-money keys on a financial calculator.

The next step is to figure out what rate (k) to use to discount these cash flows and compute the project's net present value (*NPV*). Suppose that k is 15%. Then using the financial calculator to compute *NPV* we find:

n	*i*	*PV*	*FV*	*PMT*	*Result*
7	15	?	2.2	1.3	*PV* = $6.236 million

$$NPV = \$6.236 \text{ million} - \$5 \text{ million}$$
$$= \$1.236 \text{ million}$$

Quick Check 6-3

What would be the *NPV* of the PC1000 project if the variable costs are $4,000 per unit instead of $3,750?

6.5 COST OF CAPITAL

Cost of capital is the risk-adjusted discount rate (k) to use in computing a project's net present value. The standard way of dealing with uncertainty about future cash flows is to use a larger discount rate. We develop the ways for determining what risk premium to use in chapter 16. There are however three important points to keep in mind when figuring out a project's cost of capital:

- The risk of a particular project may be different from the risk of the firm's existing assets.
- The cost of capital should reflect only the market-related risk of the project (its beta as defined in chapter 13).
- The risk that is relevant in computing a project's cost of capital is the risk of the project's cash flows and not the risk of the financing instruments (stocks, bonds, etc.) the firm issues to finance the project.

Let us explain each of these three points.

The first point to keep in mind is that the discount rate relevant to a particular project may be different from the rate that is relevant to the firm's existing assets. Consider a firm whose *average* cost of capital for its existing assets is 16% per year. In evaluating a project, does this mean that the firm should use a 16% discount rate? If the project happens to be a "mini-replica" of the assets currently held by the firm, then the answer is yes. However, in general, using the firm's average cost of capital to evaluate specific new projects will not be correct.

To see why, take an extreme example. Assume the project under consideration is nothing more than the purchase of riskless U.S. government securities in which the firm has the opportunity to buy these securities at below-market prices. That is, suppose that 25-year U.S. Treasury bonds paying $100 per year are selling in the market at $1,000, but the firm has the opportunity to buy $1 million worth of these bonds for $950 each. If these cash flows are discounted at the firm's cost of capital (16% per year), the present value of each bond is $634 and, hence, the *NPV* of the project appears to be −$315,830!

Common sense tells us if the firm can buy for $950 something that can be immediately sold for $1,000, then the firm should do so. The problem is not the *NPV* method itself, but its improper use. The risk class of this project is not the same as that of the overall firm. The proper discount rate for this project is 10% not 16%, and when the *NPV* is computed using this proper rate, we find that the *NPV* = $50,000.

Having made the point in the extreme, consider a more practical example of an all-equity-financed firm with three divisions: (1) an electronics division, which is 30% of the market value of the firm's assets and has a cost of capital of 22%; (2) a chemical division, which is 40% of the market value of the firm with a cost of capital of 17%; and (3) a natural gas transmission division, which is 30% of the firm's value and has a cost of capital of 14%. The cost of capital for the firm is the weighted average of the costs of capital of each of its divisions or $0.3 \times 22\% + 0.4 \times 17\% + 0.3 \times 14\% = 17.6\%$.

If the firm adopts the capital budgeting rule of using 17.6% as the cost of capital for all projects, then it is likely to accept projects in the electronics division that have significantly negative *NPV* and to pass up profitable natural gas transmission projects with positive *NPV*. The fact that 17.6% is close to the correct discount rate for chemical projects is simply lucky. In this case, the firm should adopt a policy of using different costs of capital, at least at the divisional level.

Sometimes it may be necessary to use a cost of capital that is totally unrelated to the cost of capital of the firm's current operations. For example, imagine an all-equity-financed steel company that is considering the acquisition of an integrated oil company that is 60% crude oil reserves and 40% refining. Suppose that the market capitalization rate on crude oil investments is 18.6% and on refining projects is 17.6%. The market capitalization rate on the oil company shares is, therefore, $0.6 \times 18.6\% + 0.4 \times 17.6\% = 18.2\%$.

Suppose further that the market price of the oil company's shares is "fair" in the sense that at the current price of $100 per share, the expected return on the shares is 18.2%. Suppose that the market capitalization rate for steel projects is 15.3%. An analysis of the expected cash flows of the oil company shows that the present value computed using the *steel company's cost of capital* of 15.3% is $119.

An investment banker further reports that all the shares could be acquired for a tender offer bid of $110 per share. It would appear, therefore, that to undertake this acquisition will provide a positive *NPV* of -110 + $119 = $9 per share. In fact, the correct *NPV* is -110 + $100 = -$10 per share! If undertaken, we would expect to observe the oil company's shares rise and the steel company's shares fall in value to reflect this negative *NPV* decision.

To return to the PC1000 project, it should now be clear that the relevant discount rate to use in calculating the project's *NPV* must reflect the risk of the PC business and not Compusell's existing mix of businesses.

The second point to keep in mind is that *the risk that is relevant in computing a project's cost of capital is the risk of the project's cash flows and not the risk of the financing instruments used to fund the project.*

For example, suppose that Compusell Corporation is planning to finance the $5 million outlay required to undertake the PC1000 project by issuing bonds. Suppose Compusell has a high credit rating because it has almost no debt outstanding and, therefore, can issue $5 million worth of bonds at an interest rate of 6% per year.

It would be a mistake to use 6% per year as the cost of capital in computing the *NPV* of the PC1000 project. As we will see in chapter 16, the way a project is financed can have an effect on its *NPV*, but that effect is not measured correctly by discounting the project's expected future cash flows using the interest rate on the debt that is issued to finance the project.

The third point to make about the project's cost of capital is that it should reflect only the systematic or market-related risk of the project, not the project's unsystematic risk. We will discuss this point at length in chapter 13.

> **Quick Check 6-4**
> Suppose that the average cost of capital for Compusell's existing mix of businesses is 12% per year. Why might this not be the right discount rate to use in computing the *NPV* of the PC1000 project?

6.6 SENSITIVITY ANALYSIS USING SPREADSHEETS

Sensitivity analysis in capital budgeting consists of testing whether the project will still be worthwhile even if some of the underlying variables turn out to be different from our assumptions. A convenient and ubiquitous tool for doing sensitivity analysis is a computerized spreadsheet program such as Excel, Lotus 123, or Quattro Pro, which is illustrated in Table 6.3.

Table 6.3 lays out the estimation of the net cash flows for the PC1000 project in a spreadsheet format similar to the ones explored in chapter 3. Rows 1 through 5 state the input assumptions behind the forecast values in the spreadsheet. The formulas in each of the cells are written in terms of the variables in cells B2 through B5, so that when these inputs are changed, the entire table is recalculated. Thus, the input in cell B3 is unit sales. Initially this is set at 4,000 units.

Rows 8 through 15 are forecasts of the project's income statements over the next seven years. Row 16 contains the forecasts of operating cash flows in each year, calculated by adding together the contents of row 15 (net profit) and row 12 (depreciation). Rows 17 through 20 show the calculation of the investment cash flows—investment in working capital and plant and equipment. Row 17 contains

TABLE 6.3 Spreadsheet Analysis of the PC1000 Project

	A	B	C	D	E	F	G	H	I
1	*Assumptions:*								
2	Cost of capital	15%							
3	Unit sales in year 1	4,000							
4	Sales growth rate	0%							
5	Price	$5,000							
6	**Cash Flow Forecasts**		YEAR						
7		0	1	2	3	4	5	6	7
8	Sales revenue		$20,000,000	$20,000,000	$20,000,000	$20,000,000	$20,000,000	$20,000,000	$20,000,000
9	Expenses								
10	Cash fixed costs		$ 3,100,000	$ 3,100,000	$ 3,100,000	$ 3,100,000	$ 3,100,000	$ 3,100,000	$ 3,100,000
11	Variable costs		$15,000,000	$15,000,000	$15,000,000	$15,000,000	$15,000,000	$15,000,000	$15,000,000
12	Depreciation		$ 400,000	$ 400,000	$ 400,000	$ 400,000	$ 400,000	$ 400,000	$ 400,000
13	Operating profit		$ 1,500,000	$ 1,500,000	$ 1,500,000	$ 1,500,000	$ 1,500,000	$ 1,500,000	$ 1,500,000
14	Taxes		$ 600,000	$ 600,000	$ 600,000	$ 600,000	$ 600,000	$ 600,000	$ 600,000
15	Net profit		$ 900,000	$ 900,000	$ 900,000	$ 900,000	$ 900,000	$ 900,000	$ 900,000
16	**Operating Cash Flow**		$ 1,300,000	$ 1,300,000	$ 1,300,000	$ 1,300,000	$ 1,300,000	$ 1,300,000	$ 1,300,000
17	Working capital	$ 2,200,000	$ 2,200,000	$ 2,200,000	$ 2,200,000	$ 2,200,000	$ 2,200,000	$ 2,200,000	$ —
18	Change in working capital	$ 2,200,000	$ —	$ —	$ —	$ —	$ —	$ —	$(2,200,000)
19	Investment in plant and equipment	$ 2,800,000	$ —	$ —	$ —	$ —	$ —	$ —	$ —
20	**Investment Cash Flows**	$(5,000,000.00)							$ 2,200,000
21	**Net cash flow**	$(5,000,000.00)	$ 1,300,000	$ 1,300,000	$ 1,300,000	$ 1,300,000	$ 1,300,000	$ 1,300,000	$ 3,500,000
22	*NPV*	$ 1,235,607							

TABLE 6.4   Sensitivity of the PC1000's *NPV* to Sales Volume

Sales Volume (units per year)	Net Cash Flow from Operations	Net Present Value of Project
2,000	–$200,000	–$5,005,022
3,000	$550,000	–$1,884,708
3,604*	$1,003,009	0
4,000	$1,300,000	$1,235,607
5,000	$2,050,000	$4,355,922
6,000	$2,800,000	$7,476,237

*NPV break-even point

Assumptions: The investment in working capital is fixed at $2,200,000 for all levels of sales and is received back as a cash inflow in year 7.

the forecast of the working capital required each year, and row 18 calculates the change in this amount from year to year, (i.e., the additional cash invested in working capital during that year). Note that the only nonzero entries in row 18 are a cash inflow of $2,200,000 in cell B18 and a cash outflow of $2,200,000 in year 7. Row 19 contains the forecasts of new investment in plant and equipment in each year. Row 20 is the total investment cash flow in each year, the sum of rows 18 and 19. Finally, row 21 shows the net cash flow in each year, which is the sum of the operating cash flow (row 16) and the investment cash flow (row 20). The *NPV* is computed in cell B22.

Table 6.4 and Figure 6.2 show the sensitivity of the project's *NPV* to this assumed value for unit sales. It was produced by changing the entry in cell B3 of Table 6.3 and tracing the corresponding changes in net cash flow from operations and in *NPV*.

FIGURE 6.2   Sensitivity of the PC1000's *NPV* to Sales Volume

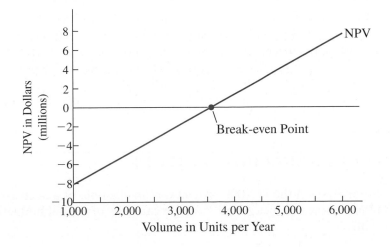

6.6.1 Break-Even Point

A particularly interesting question to ask is at what sales volume the *NPV* of the project would be zero. This is the project's **break-even point,** which means the point of indifference between accepting and rejecting the project.

From Figure 6.2 we can see that the break-even point is approximately 3,600 units per year. A little algebra shows that its exact value is 3,604 units per year. Thus, as long as the sales volume exceeds 3,604 units per year over the seven-year life of the equipment, the project shows a positive *NPV*.

The algebraic solution for the break-even volume is as follows. In order for the *NPV* to be 0, cash flow from operations must be $1,003,009. To find this break-even value for the cash flow from operations we do the following calculation:

n	*i*	*PV*	*FV*	*PMT*	*Result*
7	15	−5	2.2	?	*PMT* = 1,003,009

Now we must find the number of units per year (Q) that corresponds to an operating cash flow of this amount. A little algebra reveals that the break-even level of Q is 3,604 units per year:

$$\text{Cash Flow} = \text{Net Profit} + \text{Depreciation}$$
$$= 0.6(1,250Q - 3,500,000) + 400,000 = 1,003,009$$
$$Q = \frac{4,505,015}{1,250} = 3,604 \text{ units per year}$$

Quick Check 6-5

What would be the break-even volume for the PC1000 project if the cost of capital is 25% per year instead of 15% per year?

6.6.2 Sensitivity of *NPV* to Sales Growth

What happens if we change the assumed sales growth rate from zero to 5% per year? The answer is found in Table 6.5. Operating cash flow (row 16) grows by more than 5% per year because many of the production costs are fixed. Working capital (row 17), which is a fixed proportion of sales, grows at 5% per year. The increase in working capital (row 18) is a cash outflow each year and is recouped as a cash inflow in year 7. The net result is that the *NPV* of the project increases from $1,235,607 to $2,703,489.

6.7 ANALYZING COST-REDUCING PROJECTS

E-BOOK

6.7

Our analysis of the PC1000 project was an example of a decision about whether to launch a new product. Another major category of capital budgeting projects is cost saving.

TABLE 6.5 PC1000 Project with 5% Growth

	A	B	C	D	E	F	G	H	I
1	*Assumptions:*								
2	*Cost of capital*	15%							
3	*Unit sales in year 1*	4000							
4	*Sales growth rate*	5%							
5	*Price*	$5,000							
6	*Cash Flow Forecasts*					YEAR			
7		0	1	2	3	4	5	6	7
8	Sales		$20,000,000	$21,000,000	$22,050,000	$23,152,500	$24,310,125	$25,525,631	$26,801,913
9	Expenses								
10	Cash fixed costs		$ 3,100,000	$ 3,100,000	$ 3,100,000	$ 3,100,000	$ 3,100,000	$ 3,100,000	$ 3,100,000
11	Variable costs		$15,000,000	$15,750,000	$16,537,500	$17,364,375	$18,232,594	$19,144,223	$20,101,435
12	Depreciation		$ 400,000	$ 400,000	$ 400,000	$ 400,000	$ 400,000	$ 400,000	$ 400,000
13	Operating profit		$ 1,500,000	$ 1,750,000	$ 2,012,500	$ 2,288,125	$ 2,577,531	$ 2,881,408	$ 3,200,478
14	Taxes		$ 600,000	$ 700,000	$ 805,000	$ 915,250	$ 1,031,013	$ 1,152,563	$ 1,280,191
15	Net profit		$ 900,000	$ 1,050,000	$ 1,207,500	$ 1,372,875	$ 1,546,519	$ 1,728,845	$ 1,920,287
16	**Operating Cash Flow**		$ 1,300,000	$ 1,450,000	$ 1,607,500	$ 1,772,875	$ 1,946,519	$ 2,128,845	$ 2,320,287
17	Working capital	$ 2,200,000	$ 2,310,000	$ 2,425,500	$ 2,546,775	$ 2,674,114	$ 2,807,819	$ 2,948,210	$ —
18	Change in working capital	$ 2,200,000	$ 110,000	$ 115,500	$ 121,275	$ 127,339	$ 133,706	$ 140,391	$(2,948,210)
19	Investment in plant and equipment	$ 2,800,000	—	—	—	—	—	—	—
20	**Investment Cash Flow**	$ (5,000,000)	$ (110,000)	$ (115,500)	$ (121,275)	$ (127,339)	$ (133,706)	$ (140,391)	$ 2,948,210
21	**Net Cash Flow**	$ (5,000,000)	$ 1,190,000	$ 1,334,500	$ 1,486,225	$ 1,645,536	$ 1,812,813	$ 1,988,454	$ 5,268,497
22	*NPV*	$ 2,703,489							

For example, suppose a firm is considering an investment proposal to automate its production process to save on labor costs. It can invest $2 million now in equipment and thereby save $700,000 per year in pretax labor costs. If the equipment has an expected life of five years and if the firm pays income tax at the rate of $33\frac{1}{3}\%$, is this a worthwhile investment?

To answer this question we must compute the *incremental* cash flows due to the investment. Table 6.6 shows the cash inflows and outflows associated with this project. Column 1 shows the firm's revenues, costs, and cash flow *without* the investment; column 2 shows them *with* the investment. Column 3, the difference between columns 1 and 2, is the increment due to the investment.

There is an initial cash outflow of $2 million to purchase the equipment. In each of the five subsequent years, there is a cash inflow of $600,000, which is the increased net profit of $200,000 plus the $400,000 in annual depreciation charges. The

	Without Investment (1)	With Investment (2)	Difference Due to Investment (3)
Revenue	$5,000,000	$5,000,000	0
Labor costs	1,000,000	300,000	−$700,000
Other cash expenses	2,000,000	2,000,000	0
Depreciation	1,000,000	1,400,000	$400,000
Pretax profit	1,000,000	1,300,000	$300,000
Income taxes (at $33\frac{1}{3}\%$)	333,333	433,333	$100,000
After-tax profit	666,667	866,667	$200,000
Net cash flow (after-tax profit + depreciation)	$1,666,667	$2,266,667	$600,000

TABLE 6.6   Cash Flows With and Without Investment in Labor Saving Equipment

depreciation charges, although an expense for accounting purposes, are not a cash outflow. The cash flow diagram for this project is:

Year	0	1	2	3	4	5
Cash flow (in $ millions)	−2	.6	.6	.6	.6	.6

Now let us consider the impact of the project on the firm's value. How much will the firm be worth if it undertakes the project as compared to not undertaking it?

The firm must give up $2 million now, but in return it will receive an incremental after-tax cash flow of $600,000 at the end of each of the next five years. To compute the *NPV* of the project, we need to know the project's cost of capital, k. Let us assume that it is 10% per year.

Discounting the $600,000 per year for five years at 10% per year, we find that the present value of the after-tax cash flows is $2,274,472.

n	i	PV	FV	PMT	Result
5	10	?	0	600,000	PV = $2,274,472

$$NPV = \$2,274,472 - \$2,000,000 = \$274,472$$

Thus, the labor cost savings are worth $274,472 more than the $2 million cost of acquiring them by undertaking the project. The wealth of current shareholders of the firm is expected to increase by this amount if the project is undertaken.

Quick Check 6-6

Suppose that investing in the equipment would reduce labor costs by $650,000 per year instead of $700,000. Would the investment still be worthwhile?

6.8 PROJECTS WITH DIFFERENT LIVES

Suppose in the previous example of labor-saving equipment that there are two different types of equipment with different economic lives. The longer-lived equipment requires twice the initial outlay but lasts twice as long. A difficulty that arises in this situation is how to make the two investments comparable given that they last for different periods of time.

One approach is to assume that the shorter-lived equipment will be replaced at the end of five years with the same type of equipment that will last for another five years. Both alternatives will then have the same expected life of 10 years, and their *NPV*s can be computed and compared.

An easier approach is to employ a concept called **annualized capital cost.** It is defined as the annual cash payment that has a present value equal to the initial outlay. The alternative with the lowest annualized capital cost is the preferred alternative.

In our example, when we convert the $2 million initial capital outlay into an equivalent five-year annuity at a discount rate of 10% per year, we find that the *PMT* is $527,595:

n	i	PV	FV	PMT	Result
5	10	-2,000,000	0	?	PMT = $527,595

The longer-lived machine will last for 10 years but costs $4 million What is its annualized capital cost?

n	i	PV	FV	PMT	Result
10	10	-4,000,000	0	?	PMT = $650,982

So the machine that lasts for only five years and costs $2 million is the preferred alternative because it has the lower annualized capital cost.

Quick Check 6-7
What would have to be the economic life of the machine that costs $4 million for it to be preferred over the machine that costs $2 million?

6.9 RANKING MUTUALLY EXCLUSIVE PROJECTS

Sometimes two or more projects are mutually exclusive, meaning that the firm will take at most only one of them. An example is a project that requires exclusive use of the same unique resource such as a particular parcel of land. In all such cases, a firm should choose the project with the highest *NPV*. Some firms, however, rank projects according to their *IRR,* and this ranking system may be inconsistent with the objective of maximizing shareholder value.

For example, suppose that you own a parcel of land and have two alternatives for developing it. You can construct an office building on it, requiring an initial outlay of $20 million, or you can make a parking lot out of it, requiring an initial outlay of $10,000. If you build an office building, you estimate that you will be able to sell it in one year for $24 million and your *IRR* is, therefore, 20% ($24 million minus $20 million divided by $20 million). If you make it into a parking lot, you estimate that you will have a cash inflow of $10,000 per year forever. Your *IRR* on the parking lot is, therefore, 100% per year. Which project should you choose?

The parking lot has the higher *IRR,* but you would not necessarily want to choose it because at any cost of capital below 20% per year, the *NPV* of the office building is greater. For example, at a cost of capital of 15%, the *NPV* of the office building is $869,565 whereas the *NPV* of the parking lot is $56,667. Therefore, at a cost of capital of 15%, the shareholders of the corporation are better off if the office building project is taken.

Figure 6.3 shows the *NPV* on both projects as a function of the cost of capital. The discount rate used to compute the project's *NPV* (the project's cost of capital) is measured along the horizontal axis and the *NPV* is measured along the vertical axis. The figure shows clearly that a discount rate of 20% per year is the critical "switch-over point" for the two mutually exclusive projects. At any discount rate above 20% per year the parking lot has a higher *NPV,* and at rates below 20% the office building has a higher *NPV.*

To understand better why *IRR* is not a good measure for ranking mutually exclusive projects, note that a project's *IRR* is independent of its *scale.* In our example, the parking lot has a very high *IRR,* but its scale is small compared to the office building. If the parking lot were on a larger scale, it might offer a higher *NPV* than the office building.

Thus, suppose that the parking lot project requires an initial outlay of $200,000 to build a multistory facility and that the annual net cash flow will then be $200,000 per year forever. The *NPV* of the parking lot project would now be 20 times greater than before.

Quick Check 6-8
At what scale would the *NPV* of the parking lot project be equal to that of the office building project?

FIGURE 6.3   *NPV* as a Function of the Discount Rate

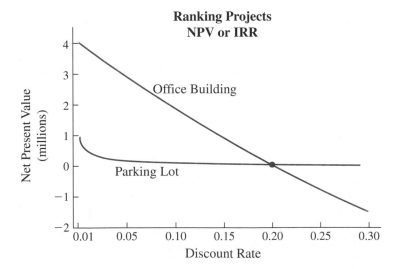

6.10 INFLATION AND CAPITAL BUDGETING

Now let us consider how to take account of inflation in evaluating capital projects. Consider an investment that requires an initial outlay of $2 million. In the absence of inflation it is expected to produce an annual after-tax cash flow of $600,000 for five years and the cost of capital is 10% per year. Under these assumptions we find that the project has an *NPV* of $274,472.

n	*i*	*PV*	*FV*	*PMT*	*Result*
5	10	?	0	600,000	$PV = \$2,274,472$

$$NPV = \$2,274,472 - \$2,000,000 = \$274,472$$

Now let us assume an inflation rate of 6% per year. The expected cash flows are presented in Table 6.7.

The *nominal* cash flow projections are inflated at the rate of 6% per year to reflect our expectations in terms of "then-year dollars." The *real* cash flow projections are in terms of "today's dollars."

Just as we distinguish between real and nominal cash flow projections, so too we distinguish between the real and nominal cost of capital. The real rate is the rate that would prevail in a zero-inflation scenario. The nominal rate is the rate that we actually observe.

Even if a firm does not explicitly set its cost of capital in real terms, setting one in nominal terms implies a certain real rate. For example, if the nominal cost of capital is 14% per year, and the expected rate of inflation is 6% per year, then the implied real cost of capital is approximately 8% per year.

RULE: There are two correct ways of computing *NPV:*

1. Use the nominal cost of capital to discount nominal cash flows.

2. Use the real cost of capital to discount real cash flows.

Let us illustrate the correct way of adjusting for inflation in our numerical example. We have already computed the *NPV* and *IRR* using the second approach that uses real cash flow estimates and a real cost of capital of 10% per year:

$$NPV = \$274,472$$

Because the *NPV* is positive, this project is worthwhile.

Now let us take the nominal approach. Before doing so, we must make a slight modification in the way we calculate the nominal rate. For most purposes it would

TABLE 6.7 Investment under 6% Inflation		
Year	*Real Cash Flow*	*Nominal Cash Flow (6% inflation)*
1	600,000	636,000
2	600,000	674,160
3	600,000	714,610
4	600,000	757,486
5	600,000	802,935

be perfectly adequate to approximate the nominal rate as 16%—the real rate of 10% plus the 6% expected rate of inflation. But in this case we want to be exact in order to demonstrate the exact equivalence of using the real and nominal approaches to capital budgeting, so we must present the exact relation between nominal and real rates.

The exact relation between the nominal and real rates is:

$$\text{Nominal Rate} = (1 + \text{Real Rate})(1 + \text{Expected Inflation}) - 1$$

Therefore, in our example the nominal rate would be 16.6% rather than 16% per year:

$$\text{Nominal Rate} = 1.1 \times 1.06 - 1 = 0.166 \text{ or } 16.6\%$$

Using this 16.6% rate to compute the *NPV* of the nominal cash flow estimates in Table 6.7 will produce an *NPV* of $274,472, exactly the same result as we obtain using the real approach. This is logical because the increase in the current wealth of shareholders from undertaking the project should not be affected by the unit of account chosen to compute the project's *NPV*, (i.e., whether we use inflated dollars or dollars of constant purchasing power).

Beware: Never compare the *IRR* computed using real cash flow estimates to a nominal cost of capital.

Quick Check 6-9
Analyze the same project assuming an expected rate of inflation of 8% per year instead of 6%.

Summary

- The unit of analysis in capital budgeting is the investment project. From a finance perspective, investment projects are best thought of as consisting of a series of contingent cash flows over time, whose amount and timing are partially under the control of management.

- The objective of capital budgeting procedures is to assure that only projects that increase shareholder value (or at least do not reduce it) are undertaken.

- Most investment projects requiring capital expenditures fall into three categories: new products, cost reduction, and replacement. Ideas for investment projects can come from customers and competitors, or from within the firm's own R&D or production departments.

- Projects are often evaluated using a discounted cash flow procedure wherein the incremental cash flows associated with the project are estimated and their *NPV* is calculated using a risk-adjusted discount rate, which should reflect the risk of the project.

- If the project happens to be a "mini-replica" of the assets currently held by the firm, then management should use the firm's cost of capital in computing the project's net present value. However, sometimes it may be necessary to use a discount rate that is totally unrelated to the cost of capital of the firm's current operations. The correct cost of capital is the one applicable to firms in the same industry as the new project.

- It is always important to check whether cash flow forecasts have been properly adjusted to take account of inflation over a project's life. There are two correct ways to make the adjustment: (1) Use the nominal cost of capital to discount nominal cash flows, and (2) use the real cost of capital to discount real cash flows.

Key Terms

- net present value   168
- cost of capital   168
- sensitivity analysis   173

- break-even point   176
- annualized capital cost   179

Answers to Quick Check Questions

Quick Check 6-1   *Where do you think new project ideas come from in the movie business?*

ANSWER: Sources of new project ideas in the movie business are:
- sequels to successful movies (e.g., *The Godfather II, III, IV,* etc.).
- best-selling novels.

Quick Check 6-2   *Suppose that the Protojean project is expected to have a third-year cash flow of only $10,000 instead of $30,000. If all other cash flows are the same and the discount rate is still 8% per year, what is its NPV?*

ANSWER: The new cash flow diagram for the Protojean project is:

Year	0	1	2	3
Net cash flow	−100	50	40	10

   NPV @ 8% per year = −$11,471.83

Quick Check 6-3   *What would be the NPV of the PC1000 project if the variable costs are $4,000 per unit instead of $3,750?*

ANSWER: If the variable costs for the PC1000 were $4,000 per unit instead of $3,750 we would have the following profit and cash flow projections:

Sales Revenue	
(4,000 units at a price of $5,000)	$20,000,000 per year
Total Fixed Costs	$3,500,000 per year
Total Variable Costs	
(4,000 units at $4,000 per unit)	$16,000,000 per year
Total Annual Operating Costs	$19,500,000 per year
Annual Operating Profit	$500,000 per year
Corporate Income Taxes at 40%	$200,000 per year
After-Tax Operating Profit	$300,000 per year
Net Cash Flow from Operations	$700,000 per year

   In other words, the net cash flow from operations in years 1 through 7 would fall by $600,000. This is because before-tax costs are higher by $1 million per year (4,000 units × $250 per unit). Because the tax rate is 0.4, after-tax profits and cash flow are lower by 0.6 × $1 million or $600,000.

Using a financial calculator to find the new *NPV*, we find:

n	i	PV	FV	PMT
7	15	?	2.2	0.7

$NPV = PV - \$5$ million

$\quad\quad = \$3.739355$ million $- \$5$ million

$\quad\quad = -\$1.260645$ million

So the project would not be worthwhile if the variable costs were \$4,000 per unit.

Quick Check 6-4 *Suppose that the average cost of capital for Compusell's existing mix of businesses is 12% per year. Why might this not be the right discount rate to use in computing the* NPV *of the PC1000 project?*

ANSWER: Compusell's existing lines of business may have a different risk than the risk of the PC business.

Quick Check 6-5 *What would be the break-even volume for the PC1000 project if the cost of capital is 25% per year instead of 15% per year?*

ANSWER: In order for the *NPV* to be 0 when the cost of capital is 25% per year, cash flow from operations must be \$1,435,757. To find this break-even value for the cash flow from operations we do the following calculation:

n	i	PV	FV	PMT
7	25	−5	2.2	?

$PMT = \$1,435,757$

Now we must find the number of units per year (Q) that corresponds to an operating cash flow of this amount. A little algebra reveals that the break-even level of Q is 4,181 units per year:

$$\text{Cash Flow} = \text{Net Profit} + \text{Depreciation}$$

$$= 0.6(1,250Q - 3,500,000) + 400,000 = 1,435,757$$

$$Q = \frac{5,226,262}{1,250} = 4,181 \text{ units per year}$$

Quick Check 6-6 *Suppose that investing in the equipment would reduce labor costs by \$650,000 per year instead of \$700,000. Would the investment still be worthwhile?*

ANSWER: Let us first show what the incremental after-tax cash flow is:

	Without Investment	With Investment	Difference Due to Investment
Revenue	\$5,000,000	\$5,000,000	0
Labor costs	1,000,000	350,000	−\$650,000
Other cash expenses	2,000,000	2,000,000	0
Depreciation	1,000,000	1,400,000	\$400,000
Pretax profit	1,000,000	1,250,000	\$250,000
Income taxes (at $33\frac{1}{3}\%$)	333,333	416,667	\$83,334
After-tax profit	666,667	833,333	\$166,666
Net cash flow (after-tax profit + depreciation)	\$1,666,667	\$2,233,333	\$566,666

Thus, if the labor cost saving is only $650,000 per year, the incremental net cash flow in years 1–5 is only $566,666 instead of $600,000. In other words, the incremental net cash flow falls by $33,333, which is $(1 - \text{tax rate}) \times$ the change in before-tax labor cost savings. The project's *NPV* falls but still remains positive.

n	i	PV	FV	PMT	Result
5	10	?	0	566,666	$PV = \$2,148,110$

$$NPV = \$2,148,110 - \$2,000,000 = \$148,110$$

Quick Check 6-7 *What would have to be the economic life of the machine that costs $4 million for it to be preferred over the machine that costs $2 million?*

ANSWER: To match the annualized capital cost of $527,595 per year for the first machine, the second machine would have to last 14.89 years. We find this number using a financial calculator as follows:

n	i	PV	FV	PMT	Result
?	10	−4,000,000	0	527,595	$n = 14.89$ years

Therefore, to be preferred to the first machine, the second machine would have to have an economic life longer than 14.89 years. Rounding to the nearest year, we get 15 years.

Quick Check 6-8 *At what scale would the* NPV *of the parking lot project be equal to that of the office building project?*

ANSWER: The parking facility project has an *NPV* of $56,667 for an investment of $10,000, and the *NPV* of the office building project has an *NPV* of $869,565. To find the scale at which the parking facility has an *NPV* of $869,565 we solve:

$$\text{Scale} = \$869,565/\$56,667 = 15.345$$

Thus, at a cost of capital of 15% per year, the scale of the parking facility project has to increase by a factor exceeding 15 to make its *NPV* greater than that of the office building project.

Quick Check 6-9 *Analyze the same project assuming an expected rate of inflation of 8% per year instead of 6%.*

ANSWER:

Year	Real Cash Flow	Nominal Cash Flow (8% inflation)
1	600,000	648,000
2	600,000	699,840
3	600,000	755,827
4	600,000	816,293
5	600,000	881,597

$$NPV = \$2,274,472 - \$2,000,000 = \$274,472$$

Nominal cost of capital $= 1.1 \times 1.08 - 1 = 0.188$ or 18.8%

Questions and Problems

1. Your firm is considering two investment projects with the following patterns of expected future net after-tax cash flows:

Year	Project A	Project B
1	$1 million	$5 million
2	2 million	4 million
3	3 million	3 million
4	4 million	2 million
5	5 million	1 million

    The appropriate cost of capital for both projects is 10%. If both projects require an initial outlay of $10 million, what would you recommend and why?

Investing in Cost-Reducing Equipment

2. A firm is considering investing $10 million in equipment that is expected to have a useful life of four years and is expected to reduce the firm's labor costs by $4 million per year. Assume the firm pays a 40% tax rate on accounting profits and uses the straight-line depreciation method. What is the after-tax cash flow from the investment in years 1 through 4? If the firm's hurdle rate for this investment is 15% per year, is it worthwhile? What are the investment's *IRR* and *NPV*?

Investing in a New Product

3. Tax-Less Software Corporation is considering an investment of $400,000 in equipment for producing a new tax preparation software package. The equipment has an expected life of four years. Sales are expected to be 60,000 units per year at a price of $20 per unit. Fixed costs excluding depreciation of the equipment are $200,000 per year, and variable costs are $12 per unit. The equipment will be depreciated over four years using the straight-line method with a zero salvage value. Working capital requirements are assumed to be $\frac{1}{12}$ of annual sales. The market capitalization rate for the project is 15% per year, and the corporation pays income tax at the rate of 34%. What is the project's *NPV*? What is the break-even volume?

Investing in a New Product

4. Healthy Hopes Hospital Supply Corporation is considering an investment of $500,000 in a new plant for producing disposable diapers. The plant has an expected life of four years. Sales are expected to be 600,000 units per year at a price of $2 per unit. Fixed costs excluding depreciation of the plant are $200,000 per year, and variable costs are $1.20 per unit. The plant will be depreciated over four years using the straight-line method with a zero salvage value. The hurdle rate for the project is 15% per year, and the corporation pays income tax at the rate of 34%. Find:
    a. The level of sales that would give a zero accounting profit.
    b. The level of sales that would give a 15% after-tax accounting rate of return on the $500,000 investment.
    c. The *IRR, NPV,* and payback period (both conventional and discounted) if expected sales are 600,000 units per year.
    d. The level of sales that would give an *NPV* of zero.
    e. The schedule of discounted cash flow depreciation charges.

Replacement Decision

5. Pepe's Ski Shop is contemplating replacing its ski boot foam injection equipment with a new machine. The old machine has been completely depreciated but has a current market value of $2,000. The new machine will cost $25,000 and have a life of 10 years and have no value after this time. The new machine will be depreciated on a straight-line basis assuming no salvage value. The new machine will increase annual revenues by $10,000 and increase annual nondepreciation expenses by $3,000.

    a. What is the additional after-tax net cash flow realized by replacing the old machine with the new machine? Assume a 50% tax rate for *all* income (i.e., the capital gains tax rate on the sale of the old machine is also 50%). Draw a time line.

    b. What is the *IRR* of this project?

    c. At a cost of capital of 12%, what is the net present value of this cash flow stream?

    d. At a cost of capital of 12%, is this project worthwhile?

6. PCs Forever is a company that produces personal computers. It has been in operation for two-years and is at capacity. It is considering an investment project to expand its production capacity. The project requires an initial outlay of $1,000,000: $800,000 for new equipment with an expected life of four years and $200,000 for additional working capital. The selling price of its PCs is $1,800 per unit, and annual sales are expected to increase by 1,000 units as a result of the proposed expansion. Annual fixed costs (excluding depreciation of the new equipment) will increase by $100,000, and variable costs are $1,400 per unit. The new equipment will be depreciated over four years using the straight line method with a zero salvage value. The hurdle rate for the project is 12% per year, and the company pays income tax at the rate of 40%.

    a. What is the accounting break-even point for this project?

    b. What is the project's *NPV*?

    c. At what volume of sales would the *NPV* be zero?

Inflation and Capital Budgeting

7. Patriots Foundry (PF) is considering getting into a new line of business: producing souvenir statues of Paul Revere. This will require purchasing a machine for $40,000. The new machine will have a life of two years (both actual and for tax purposes) and will have no value after two years. PF will depreciate the machine on a straight-line basis. The firm thinks it will sell 3,000 statues per year at a price of $10 each, variable costs will be $1 per statue, and fixed expenses (not including depreciation) will be $2,000 per year. PF's cost of capital is 10%. *All of the foregoing figures assume that there will be no inflation.* The tax rate is 40%.

    a. What is the series of expected future cash flows?

    b. What is the expected net present value of this project? Is the project worth undertaking?

    c. What is the *NPV* break-even quantity?

Now assume instead that there will be inflation of 6% per year during each of the next two years and that both revenues and nondepreciation expenses increase at that rate. Assume that the *real* cost of capital remains at 10%.

    d. What is the series of expected *nominal* cash flows?

    e. What is the net present value of this project, and is this project worth undertaking now?

    f. Why does the *NPV* of the investment project go down when the inflation rate goes up?

Understanding incremental cash flows

8. Determine which of the following cash flows are incremental cash flows that should be incorporated into a *NPV* calculation.
   a. The sale of an old machine, when a company is replacing property, plant, and equipment for a new-product launch.
   b. The cost of research and development for a new-product concept that was conducted over the past year that is now being put into production.
   c. Potential rental income that was forgone from a previously unused warehouse owned by the company, which is now being used as part of a new-product launch.
   d. New equipment purchased for a project.
   e. The annual depreciation expense on new equipment purchased for a project.
   f. Net working capital expenditures of $10 million in year 0, $12 million in year 1, and $5 million in year 2.
   g. A dividend payment that was funded in part by a given project's contribution to the net income for that year.

9. You have taken a product management position within a major consumer goods firm after graduation. The contract is for four years and your compensation package is as follows:

   - $5,000 relocation expense

   - $55,000

   - $10,000 bonus if annual goals are met

   - $15,000 additional bonus at the end of four years if your team achieves a given market share

   You are confident in your abilities and assume there is a 65% chance in receiving each annual bonus and a 75% chance in receiving the fourth-year additional bonus. The effective annual interest rate is 8.5%. What is the net present value of your compensation package?

Investing in a new project

10. You are in the finance department of a firm and you are evaluating a project proposal. You have developed the following financial projections and you are calculating:
    a. The incremental cash flows of the project.
    b. The net present value of the project given a discount rate of 15%.

    The corporate tax rate is 34% and the financial projections are in thousands.

	Year 0	Year 1	Year 2	Year 3	Year 4	Year 5
Sales revenue		10,000	10,000	10,000	10,000	10,000
Operating costs		3,000	3,000	3,000	3,000	3,000
Investment	15,000					
Depreciation		3,500	3,500	3,500	3,500	3,500
Net working capital	300	350	400	300	200	0

11. Leather Goods Inc., wants to expand its product line into wallets. It is considering producing 50,000 units per year. The price will be $15 per wallet the first year and the price will increase 3% per year. The variable cost is expected to be $10 per wallet and will increase by 5% per year. The machine will cost $400,000, and will have an economic life of five years. It will be fully depreciated using the straight-line method. The discount rate is 15% and the corporate tax rate is 34%. What is the *NPV* of the investment?

12. Steiness Danish Ham, Inc., is contemplating buying a new machine that has an economic life of five years. The cost of the machine is 1,242,000 krone and will be fully depreciated using the straight line depreciation method over five years. At the end of five years it will have a market value of 138,000 krone. It is estimated that the new machine will save the company 345,000 krone per year due to reduced labor costs. Moreover, it will lead to a reduction in net working capital of 172,500 krone because of the higher yield from raw materials inventory. The net working capital will be recovered by the end of the five years. If the corporate tax rate is 34% and the discount rate is 12%, what is the *NPV* of the project?

13. Hu's Software Design, Inc., is considering the purchase of a computer that has an economic life of four years and it is expected to have no salvage value. It will cost $80,000 and it will be depreciated using the straight-line depreciation method. It will save the company $35,000 the first year and it is assumed that the savings after that will have a growth rate of −5%. It will also reduce net working capital requirements by $7,000. The corporate tax rate is 35% and the appropriate discount rate is 14%. What is the value that the purchase would add to the firm?

14. Suppose Hu's Software Design, Inc., from the previous problem has a choice between two computer systems. The first one will cost $80,000 and will have an economic life of four years. Annual maintenance costs would be $10,000. The other alternative would cost $135,000 and would have an economic life of six years. The annual maintenance would cost $13,000. Both alternatives would be fully depreciated using the straight-line method. Neither computer system will have a salvage value. The cost savings generated on an annual basis are assumed to be the same and the company expects to generate sufficient profits to realize the depreciation tax shield. The discount rate (DR) is 11% and the corporate tax rate is 35%. Which computer system should be chosen?

15. Vogel's Classic Autos is doing a booming business exporting rebuilt vintage American vehicles to Japan. Fortunately, it is an almost perfect world and, consequently, the owner is certain of all revenues and costs. The problem is the revenues are in yen and the costs are in dollars. Future exchange rates are uncertain. Therefore, the owner is uncertain as to the *NPV* of his cash flows. Because it is a relatively small business, he has hired you to determine the value of his business. The current spot rate is 100 yen to $1. The risk-free rate in Japan is 3% and the risk-free rate in the United States is 7%. The corporate tax rate in Japan is 40% and the corporate tax rate in the United States is 34%. Assume there is no tax effect when funds denominated in yen are repatriated back the United States. The business has contracts for delivery outstanding for the next four years, at which time the owner will retire and close the business. Using the following certain cash flows, determine the *NPV* of the business.

	Year 1	Year 2	Year 3	Year 4
Revenues in yen	50,000,000	60,000,000	40,000,000	20,000,000
Cost in dollars				
Parts	50,000	60,000	40,000	20,000
Labor	100,000	105,000	85,000	50,000
Shipping	75,000	90,000	60,000	30,000
Other	75,000	75,000	65,000	55,000

Inflation and Capital Budgeting

16. You are a financial analyst at Wigit, Inc., and you are considering two mutually exclusive projects. Unfortunately, the figures for project 1 are in nominal terms and

the figures for project 2 are in real terms. The nominal discount rate for both projects is 17%, and inflation is projected to be 3%.

a. Determine which project to choose.

b. You are troubled about the cash flows in real terms. You are concerned that there may be a problem in determining the total cash flows in real terms and the depreciation tax shield. What is it that has you concerned?

	Project 1	*Project 2*
0	(100,000)	(90,000)
1	30,000	25,000
2	60,000	55,000
3	75,000	80,000

17. Your next assignment at Wigit, Inc., also entails determining the *NPV* of a project, which is expected to last four years. There is an initial investment of $400,000, which will be depreciated at the straight-line method over four years. At the end of four years it is assumed that you will be able to sell some of the equipment that is part of the initial investment for $35,000 (a nominal figure.) Revenues for the first year are expected to be $225,000 in real terms. The costs involved in the project for the first year are as follows: (1) Parts will be $25,000 in real terms the first year; (2) labor will be $60,000 in real terms for the first year; and (3) other costs will be $30,000 in real terms for the first year. The growth rates of revenues and costs are as follows: (1) Revenue will have a real growth rate of 5%; (2) the cost of parts will have a 0% real growth rate; (3) cost of labor will have a 2% real growth rate; and (4) other costs will have a 1% real growth rate from year 2 to year 3 and a -1% growth rate the last two years. The real changes in net working capital for the year 0 to year 4 are as follows: (1) -$20,000; (2) -$30,000; (3) -$10,000; (4) $20,000; and (5) $40,000. The real discount rate is 9.5% and the inflation rate is 3%. The tax rate is 35%.

18. Finnerty's Brew Pub is considering buying more machinery that will allow the pub to increase its portfolio of beers on tap. The new machinery will cost $65,000 and will be depreciated on a 10-year basis. It is expected to have no value after 10 years. The improved selection is anticipated to increase sales by $30,000 for the first year and increase at the rate of inflation of 3% for each year after that. Production costs are expected to be $15,000 for the first year and are also expected to increase at the rate of inflation. The real discount rate is 12% and the nominal risk-free interest rate is 6%. The corporate tax rate is 34%. Should Mr. Finnerty buy the machinery?

19. A. Fung Fashion, Inc., anticipates real net cash flows to be $100,000 this year. The real discount rate is 15% per year.

a. What is the present value of these cash flows if they are expected to continue forever?

b. What is the present value of these cash flows if the real net cash flows are expected to grow at 5% per year forever?

c. What is the present value of these cash flows if the expected growth rate is -5% per year?

20. Mr. Salles is considering a business venture that would offer guided tours of the romantic Greek isles and the Italian countryside. After four years, Mr. Salles intends to retire. The initial investment would be $50,000 in a computer and phone system. This investment would be depreciated on the straight-line method and is expected to have no salvage value. The corporate tax rate is 35%. The price of each tour will be $5,000 per customer and the price will remain constant in real terms. Mr. Salles will pay himself $50 per hour and anticipates an annual increase in salary of 5% in real terms. The cost of each customer during the tours is $3,500, and this cost is ex-

pected to increase by 3% in real terms. Assume that all revenues and costs occur at year end. The inflation rate is 3.5%. The risk-free nominal rate is 6% and the real discount rate for costs and revenues is 9%. Using the additional following data, calculate the *NPV* of the project.

	Year 1	Year 2	Year 3	Year 4
Number of customers	100	115	130	140
Hours worked	2,080	2,080	2,080	2,080

21. Saunders' Sportswear, Inc., is planning on expanding its line of sweatshirts. This will require an initial investment of $8 million. This investment will be depreciated on a straight-line method over four years and will have no salvage value. The firm is in the 35% tax bracket. The price of the sweatshirts will be $30 the first year and will increase in price by 4% per year in nominal terms thereafter. The unit cost of production will be $5 the first year and will increase by 3% per year in nominal terms thereafter. Labor costs will be $10 per hour the first year and will increase by 3.5% in nominal terms each subsequent year. Revenues and costs are paid at year end. The nominal discount rate is 12%. Calculate the *NPV* of the project using the following additional data.

	Year 1	Year 2	Year 3	Year 4
Unit sales	50,000	100,000	125,000	100,000
Labor hours	20,800	20,800	20,800	20,800

22. Camile, the owner of the Germanos Tree farm, has contracted with the government of his native land to provide cypress tree saplings to aid in that government's efforts to reforest part of the country and return the cypress tree to its past glory. The project is expected to continue in perpetuity. At the end of the first year, the following nominal and incremental cash flows are expected:

Revenues	$125,000
Labor Costs	$65,000
Other Costs	$45,000

Camille has contracted with an air freight shipping company to transport the saplings. The contract is for a fixed payment of $35,000 in nominal terms per year. The first payment is due at the end of the first year. Revenues are expected to grow at 4% in real terms. Labor costs are expected to grow at 3% per year. Other costs are expected to decrease at 0.5% per year. The real discount rate for revenues and costs is 8% and inflation is expected to be 3.5%. There are no taxes and all cash flows occur at year end. What is the *NPV* of the contract?

23. Kitchen Supplies, Inc., must replace a machine in its manufacturing plant that will have no salvage value. It has a choice between two models. The first machine will last five years and will cost $300,000. It will generate an annual cost savings of $50,000. Annual maintenance costs will be $20,000. The machine will be fully depreciated using the straight-line depreciation method and will have no salvage value. The second machine will last seven years and will cost $600,000. It will generate an annual cost savings of $70,000. The annual maintenance costs will be $20,000. This machine will also be fully depreciated using the straight-line depreciation method, but is expected to have a salvage value of $60,000 at the end of the seventh year. The annual maintenance cost is $15,000. Revenues in each case are expected to be the same. The annual tax rate is 35% and the cost of capital is 10%. Which machine should the company purchase?

24. Electricity, Inc., is choosing between two pieces of equipment. The first choice costs $500,000 and will last five years. It will be depreciated using the straight-line depreciation method and will have no salvage value. It will have an annual maintenance cost of $50,000. The second choice will cost $600,000 and will last eight years. It will also be depreciated using the straight-line depreciation method and will have no salvage value. It will have an annual maintenance cost of $55,000. The discount rate is 11% and the tax rate is 35%. Which machine should be chosen and what assumptions underlie that choice?

25. Refer to problem 24. Electricity, Inc., is faced with the same choices; however, now it expects that a new technology will be introduced into the industry in year 9. This will force the company to replace the choice made today at the end of year 9, because the new technology will be so cost-effective. All the other necessary information is the same as explained in problem 24. Which choice should be made?

26. Real Estate, Inc., has purchased a building for $1 million. The economic life of the building is 30 years and it will be fully depreciated over the 30 years using the straight-line depreciation method. The discount rate is 14% and the corporate tax rate is 35%. Assume there is no inflation. What is the minimum lease payment the company should ask for? Assume that the lease payment is due immediately.

CHAPTER 7

Principles of Asset Valuation

OBJECTIVES

- Understand why asset valuation is important in finance.
- Explain the *Law of One Price* as the principle underlying all asset-valuation procedures.
- Explain the meaning and role of valuation models.
- Explain how information gets reflected in security prices.

CONTENTS

Many financial decisions boil down to figuring out how much assets are worth. For example, in deciding whether to invest in a security such as a stock or a bond or in a business opportunity, you have to determine whether the price being asked is high or low relative to other investment opportunities. In addition to investment decisions, there are many other situations in which one needs to determine the value of an asset. For example, suppose that the tax assessor in your town has assessed your house at $500,000 for property tax purposes.

Is this value too high or too low? Or suppose you and your siblings inherit some property, and you decide to share it equally among yourselves. How do you decide how much it is worth?

Asset valuation is the process of estimating how much an asset is worth, and it is the second of the three analytical pillars of finance (the other two being time value of money and risk management). Asset valuation is at the heart of much of financial decision making. For firms, value maximization (maximizing the wealth of shareholders) is assumed to be the main objective of management. For households, too, many financial decisions can be made by selecting the alternative that maximizes value. This chapter explains the principles of asset valuation, and the following two chapters develop the quantitative techniques used in applying these principles.

The key idea underlying all valuation procedures is that to estimate how much an asset is worth, you must use information about one or more comparable assets whose market prices you know. By the Law of One Price, the prices of all equivalent assets must be the same. Chapter 8 shows how the Law of One Price can be used to deduce the value of assets with known cash flows from the observed market prices of bonds and other fixed-income securities. Chapter 9 examines the valuation of stocks using the discounted cash flow approach.

7.1 THE RELATION BETWEEN AN ASSET'S VALUE AND ITS PRICE

In this chapter, we define an asset's **fundamental value** as the price well-informed investors must pay for it in a free and competitive market.

There can be a temporary difference between the market price of an asset and its fundamental value. Security analysts make their living by researching the prospects of various firms and recommending which stocks to buy because their price appears low relative to fundamental value and which to sell because their price seems high relative to fundamental value.

However, in making most financial decisions, it is good practice to start by assuming that for assets that are bought and sold in competitive markets, price is an accurate reflection of value. As we will see, this assumption is generally warranted precisely because there are many well-informed professionals looking for mispriced assets who profit by eliminating discrepancies between the market prices and the fundamental values of assets.

7.2 VALUE MAXIMIZATION AND FINANCIAL DECISIONS

In many instances personal financial decisions can be made by selecting the alternative that maximizes value without even considering the individual's consumption or risk preferences. To give a simple example, consider the choice between alternative A—you get $100 today—and alternative B—you get $95 today.

Suppose you had to guess how a stranger, about whose preferences and future expectations you knew nothing at all, would choose. If the two alternatives are equivalent in every other respect, surely you would guess A on the grounds that more wealth is better than less.

Few financial decisions are this simple and straightforward. Suppose, now, that the choice is between a share of very risky stock and a completely safe bond. The stranger hates taking risks and is pessimistic about the price of the stock in the future. However, the current market price of the stock is $100, and the market price of the bond is $95.

Because the stranger hates taking risks and is pessimistic about the price of the stock in the future, you might predict that he would choose the bond. However, even if he ultimately wants to invest his money in safe bonds, the stranger should choose the stock.

Why?

The answer is that the stranger can sell the stock for $100 and buy the bond for $95. As long as the broker fees and other transaction costs of buying and selling the securities are less than the $5 difference in price, the stranger will come out ahead by choosing the stock. This simple example makes two important points:

1. The financial decision can rationally be made purely on the basis of value maximization, regardless of the stranger's risk preferences or expectations about the future.

2. The markets for financial assets provide the information needed to value the alternatives.

Just as households make financial decisions based on the criterion of value maximization, so too do firms. Managers of publicly held corporations are faced with the question of how to make capital budgeting, financing, and risk-management decisions. Because they are hired by the shareholders, their job is to make decisions that are in the best interests of shareholders. But a large corporation's managers do not even know the identities of many of their shareholders.[1]

Managers of corporations, therefore, look for a rule that will lead to the same decisions that each of the individual shareholders would have made had they made the decisions themselves. Both economic theory and common sense suggest the following rule for corporate financial decision-making: *Choose investment to maximize current shareholders' wealth.* Virtually every shareholder would agree with it, and so it can be made without any other information about shareholder preferences.

How can decision makers estimate the values of the assets and investment opportunities that are available to them? In some cases, they can look up the market price of the asset in the newspaper or on a computer screen. But some assets are not traded in any market and, therefore, we do not know their prices. To compare alternatives in such a case, we need to figure out what their market value would be if they were traded.

The essence of asset valuation in these cases is to estimate how much an asset is worth using information about one or more comparable assets whose current market prices we know. The method used to accomplish this estimation depends on the richness of the information set available. If we know the prices of assets that are virtually identical to the asset whose value we want to estimate, then we can apply the Law of One Price.

Quick Check 7-1

You win a contest, and the prize is a choice between a ticket to the opera and a ticket to the ball game. The opera ticket has a price of $100 and the ticket to the ball game has a price of $25. Assuming you prefer ball games to opera, which ticket should you choose?

---

[1]Because the shares of many firms change hands every day, even if CEOs tried, it is virtually impossible for them to know the identities of all their shareholders.

7.3 THE LAW OF ONE PRICE AND ARBITRAGE

The **Law of One Price** states that *in a competitive market, if two assets are equivalent, they will tend to have the same market price.* The Law of One Price is enforced by a process called **arbitrage,** the purchase and immediate sale of equivalent assets in order to earn a sure profit from a difference in their prices.

We illustrate how arbitrage works using gold. For thousands of years, gold has been widely used as a store of value and as a means of settling payments. It is a well-defined commodity whose quality can be precisely determined. When we talk about the price of gold, we mean the price of an ounce of gold of standard quality.

Consider the following question: If the price of gold in New York City is $300 per ounce, what is its price in Los Angeles?

The answer should be approximately $300 per ounce. To see why, let us consider what the economic consequences would be if the L.A. price were very different from $300 per ounce.

Suppose, for example, that the price of gold in Los Angeles was only $250. Consider how much it would cost to buy gold in Los Angeles and sell it in New York. There are the costs of shipping, handling, insuring, and broker fees. We call the totality of such costs **transaction costs.** If total transaction costs were less than $50 per ounce, it would pay for you to buy gold in Los Angeles and sell it in New York for $300 per ounce.

Say the transaction costs are $2 per ounce, and it takes a day to ship the gold by air. Then your profit would be $48 per ounce, and you would buy gold where it is cheap and sell it where it is dear. To eliminate the risk that the price in New York might fall while the gold was on its way from Los Angeles to New York, you would try to lock in the selling price of $300 at the same time that you buy the gold for $250. Moreover, if you can delay paying for the gold you purchase until you receive payment from selling it, then you will not have to use any of your own money in the transaction. If you can achieve both of these goals, then you will have engaged in a "pure," riskless arbitrage transaction.

If such a price discrepancy in the price of gold between New York and Los Angeles ever developed, it is unlikely that you would be the first or only person to find out about it. It is much more likely that gold dealers, who are in the business of buying and selling gold on a daily basis, would discover the discrepancy first. The first dealer to discover it would seek to buy as large a quantity as possible in Los Angeles at that price.

In addition to gold dealers, there is another group of market participants, called **arbitrageurs,** who watch the price of gold in different regions looking for large enough price discrepancies. Arbitrageurs engage in arbitrage for a living. (Arbitrageurs are active participants in many asset markets, not just the one for gold.)

Regardless of who or what group is doing the buying and selling, the acts of buying a lot of gold in Los Angeles and simultaneously selling it in New York would drive the price up in Los Angeles and down in New York. The arbitrage would stop only when the price in Los Angeles was within $2 per ounce of the price in New York. If the price in Los Angeles were *higher* than in New York (say the price of gold in New York is again $300 per ounce, but in Los Angeles it is $350), the force of arbitrage would work in the opposite direction. Gold dealers and arbitrageurs would buy gold in New York and ship it to Los Angeles until the price differential fell to $2 per ounce.

Thus, the force of arbitrage maintains a relatively narrow band around the price difference between the gold market in Los Angeles and the one in New York. The lower the transaction costs, the narrower the band.

Quick Check 7-2

If the price of silver is $10 per ounce in Chicago and the total transaction costs of shipping silver to New York is $1 per ounce, what can we say about the price of silver in New York?

7.4 ARBITRAGE AND THE PRICES OF FINANCIAL ASSETS

Now let us consider how the Law of One Price operates in the market for financial assets such as shares of stock, in which the transaction costs are much lower than those for gold. Shares of General Motors (GM) are traded on both the New York Stock Exchange (NYSE) and on the London Stock Exchange. If shares of General Motors stock were selling for $54 a share on the New York Stock Exchange at the same time they were selling for $56 on the London Stock Exchange, what would happen?

If the transaction costs were negligible, investors would sell their shares in London and would buy in New York. This activity would tend to drive down the price in London and drive up the price in New York.

Arbitrageurs could earn sure profits without investing a penny of their own money by buying 100,000 shares of GM on the NYSE for a total of $5,400,000 and then immediately (with a few strokes on the computer keyboard) selling them on the London Stock Exchange for a total of $5,600,000. Because they pay only $5,400,000 for the shares bought in New York but receive $5,600,000 for the shares sold in London, they are left with $200,000 in profits.

Notice that even though this set of transactions requires no cash outlays by the arbitrageurs at any time,[2] the arbitrageurs immediately increase their wealth by $200,000 as a result of these transactions. Indeed, as long as the prices for GM stock on the two exchanges are different, arbitrageurs can continue to increase their wealth by making these transactions and can continue to get something for nothing.

This process would be like the mythical goose that laid golden eggs except for an important fact: Such arbitrage opportunities do not persist for very long. The large profits earned by the arbitrageurs will attract attention to the price discrepancy. Other arbitrageurs will compete for the same arbitrage profits, and as a result, the stock prices in the two locations will converge.

As this simple example illustrates, the Law of One Price is a statement about the price of one asset *relative* to the price of another; it tells us that if we want to know the current price of GM stock, it is enough to know its price on the NYSE. If that price is $54, we can be reasonably sure that its price in London is the same.

---

[2]However, it does require that their credit standing be good enough to enable them to purchase the shares in New York without paying for them in advance.

The Law of One Price is the most fundamental valuation principle in finance. Indeed, if observed prices appeared to violate the law, so that seemingly identical assets were selling at different prices, our first suspicion would not be an exception to the Law of One Price but instead we would suspect that (1) something was interfering with the normal operation of the competitive market or (2) there was some (perhaps undetected) economic difference between the two assets.

To see this point, consider the following example. Normally a dollar bill is worth four quarters. We know that because we could take a dollar and exchange it costlessly for four quarters at a bank, a retail store, or with a person we meet on the street.

Yet we can describe a situation in which a dollar bill will be worth *less* than four quarters. Suppose you are desperate to do your laundry now. You need two quarters for the washer and one quarter for the dryer. You have no change, but you do have a dollar bill. If you are in a big hurry and the only other person at the laundromat has three quarters, you would likely agree to part with your dollar for three quarters.

When would a dollar be worth *more* than four quarters? Perhaps you are at a bus stop and are very thirsty. You find a beverage vending machine that will only accept dollar bills and not change. Under those circumstances you may be willing to pay someone more than four quarters in exchange for a dollar.

These situations do not violate the Law of One Price because in each instance the dollar bill is not really equivalent to the four quarters in all respects that have a bearing on their value. At the laundromat, a dollar bill is useless because it will not start the washer or dryer. At the bus stop, quarters are useless because they will not operate the vending machine. And in both situations you do not have costless access to a party who will exchange the two in the normal ratio.

Tautologically, no two distinct assets are identical in *all* respects. For example, even two different shares of stock in the same company differ in their serial numbers. Nevertheless, we would expect the shares to have the same price because they are the same in all respects that have a bearing on their value to investors (e.g., expected return, risk, voting rights, marketability, and so on).

Quick Check 7-3
Under what circumstances might two 25-cent coins have different values?

7.5 INTEREST RATES AND THE LAW OF ONE PRICE

Competition in financial markets ensures that not only the *prices* of equivalent assets are the same but also that *interest rates* on equivalent assets are the same. Suppose, for instance, that the interest rate the U.S. Treasury currently pays on its one year T-bills is 4% per year. What interest rate would you expect a major institution such as the World Bank to pay on its one-year, dollar-denominated debt securities (assuming them to be virtually free of default risk)?

Your answer should be approximately 4% per year.

To see why, suppose that the World Bank offered significantly *less* than 4% per year. Well-informed investors would not buy the bonds issued by the World Bank; instead they would invest in one-year T-bills. Thus, if the World Bank expects to sell its bonds, it must offer at least as high a rate as the U.S. Treasury.

Would the World Bank offer significantly *more* than 4% per year? Assuming that it wants to minimize its borrowing costs, it would offer no more than is necessary to attract investors. Thus, interest rates on *any* default-free borrowing and lending denominated in dollars with a maturity of one year will tend to be the same as the 4% per year interest rate on one-year U.S. T-bills.

If there are entities that have the ability to borrow and lend on the same terms (e.g., maturity, default risk) at different interest rates, then they can carry out *interest-rate arbitrage:* borrowing at the lower rate and lending at the higher rate. Their attempts to expand their activity will bring about an equalization of interest rates.

Quick Check 7-4

Suppose you have $10,000 in a bank account earning an interest rate of 3% per year. At the same time you have an unpaid balance on your credit card of $5,000 on which you are paying an interest rate of 17% per year. What is the arbitrage opportunity you face?

7.6 EXCHANGE RATES AND TRIANGULAR ARBITRAGE

The Law of One Price applies to the foreign exchange market as well as to other financial markets. Arbitrage ensures that for any three currencies that are freely convertible in competitive markets, it is enough to know the exchange rates between any two in order to determine the third. Thus, as we show, if you know that the yen price of the U.S. dollar is ¥100 and the yen price of the U.K. pound is ¥200, it follows by the Law of One Price that the dollar price of the pound is $2.

To understand how arbitrage works in the foreign exchange market, it is helpful to start by considering the price of gold in different currencies. Suppose you know that the current dollar price of gold is $100 per ounce and its price in yen is ¥10,000 per ounce. What would you expect the exchange rate to be between the dollar and the yen?

The Law of One Price implies that it should not matter which currency you use to pay for gold. Thus, the ¥10,000 price should be equivalent to $100, which implies that the dollar price of the yen must be $0.01 or 1 cent per yen.

Suppose that the Law of One Price is violated, and the dollar price of the yen is $0.009 rather than $0.01. Suppose you currently have $10,000 in cash sitting in the bank. Because, by assumption, you can buy or sell gold either for ¥10,000 per ounce or for $100 per ounce, you would convert your $10,000 into $10,000/$0.009 = ¥1,111,111.11. You would use the yen to buy 111.1111 ounces of gold (¥1,111,111.11/ ¥10,000 per ounce) and sell the gold for dollars to receive $11,111.11 (111.1111 ounces × $100 per ounce). You would now have $11,111.11 less the transaction costs of buying and selling the gold and the yen. As long as these transaction costs are less than $1,111.11, it would pay you to engage in the arbitrage.

> Note that to carry out this risk-free arbitrage transaction, you did not require any special knowledge, did not have to make any forecasts of future prices, and did not have to bear any risk.

This type of transaction is called **triangular arbitrage** because it involves three assets: gold, dollars, and yen.

Quick Check 7-5

Suppose that the exchange rate is $0.011 to the yen. How could you make arbitrage profits with your $10,000 if the dollar price of gold is $100 per ounce and the yen price is 10,000 yen per ounce?

Now let's look at the relations among the prices of three different currencies: yen, dollars, and pounds. Suppose the U.S. dollar price of the yen is $0.01 per yen (or equivalently 100¥ to the dollar), and the price of the yen in terms of British pounds is a half pence (£0.005) to the yen (or equivalently, ¥200 to the pound). From these two exchange rates, we can determine that the U.S. dollar price of the pound is $2.

Although it may not be immediately obvious, there are two ways to buy pounds for dollars. One way is *indirectly* through the yen market—by first buying yen for dollars and then using the yen to buy pounds. Because, by assumption, one pound costs ¥200, and ¥200 costs $2.00, this indirect way costs $2.00 per pound. Another way to buy pounds for dollars is to just do it *directly*.

The direct purchase of pounds for dollars must cost the same as the indirect purchase of pounds for dollars because of the Law of One Price. If it is violated, there will be an arbitrage opportunity that cannot persist for very long.

To see how the force of arbitrage works to uphold the Law of One Price in this example, let's look at what would happen if the price of the pound were $2.10 rather then $2. Suppose you walk into a bank in New York City, and you observe the following three exchange rates—$0.01 per yen, ¥200 per pound, and $2.10 per pound. Suppose that there is one window for exchanging dollars and yen, another for exchanging yen and pounds, and a third window for exchanging dollars and pounds.

Here is how you can make an instantaneous $10 profit without leaving the bank:

1. At the dollar/yen window, convert $200 into ¥20,000;
2. At the yen/pound window, convert the ¥20,000 into £100; and then
3. At the dollar/pound window, convert the ¥100 into $210.

Congratulations, you have just converted $200 into $210!

But why limit the scale of this arbitrage to a mere $200? If you did it with $2,000, your profit would be $100; and if you did it with $20 million, your arbitrage profit would be $1 million. If you could find an arbitrage opportunity like this, it would be the equivalent of alchemy—changing base metals into gold!

In the real world, you or I would not be able to find such an arbitrage opportunity. Not only would we not be able to make a profit through such transactions, but we would probably lose money because banks charge fees for exchanging foreign currencies.[3] As retail customers, therefore, the transactions costs we would face would eliminate any arbitrage profits.

Although retail customers like us would not be able to find or exploit arbitrage opportunities in foreign currencies, banks and other dealers in foreign exchange might be able to. Some banks and other financial service firms employ professional arbitrageurs who carry out purchases and sales of currencies from their trading desks using desktop computers. Rather than walking from one bank window to the next, they can execute arbitrage transactions at "windows" on their computer screens via an electronic hookup to other banks located almost anywhere in the world.

If professional arbitrageurs were faced with the three exchange rates in our example—$0.01 per yen, ¥200 per pound, and $2.10 per pound, they might seek to make an instantaneous profit of $1 billion by converting $20 billion into £10 billion via the yen market while selling the £10 billion for $21 billion in the market for pounds. The attempt to carry out such large transactions would immediately attract attention, and subsequent transactions would eliminate the price discrepancies. Thus, given the prices of the yen in dollars ($0.01 per yen) and in pounds (£0.005 per yen), arbitrage ensures that the dollar price of the pound will obey the Law of One Price and equal $2.00 per pound.

The general principle at work here is:

> For any three currencies that are freely convertible in competitive markets, it is enough to know the exchange rates between any two in order to know the third.

In our example, the dollar/yen rate was $0.01 per yen, and the pound/yen rate was £0.005 per yen. The dollar/pound exchange rate is the ratio of the two:

$$\$0.01 \text{ per Yen}/£0.005 \text{ per Yen} = \$2.00 \text{ per Pound}$$

The Law of One Price is a great convenience for anyone who needs to keep track of many different exchange rates. For example, suppose that as part of your job, you always need to know the exchange rates between four different currencies: the dollar, the yen, the pound, and the mark. There is a total of six possible exchange rates: dollar/yen, dollar/pound, dollar/mark, yen/pound, yen/mark, and pound/mark.

To know all six, however, you only need to know the three dollar-denominated exchange rates. Each of the other three can easily be computed as the ratio of two dollar-denominated exchange rates. The activities of professional, "high-technology" arbitrageurs, who carry out their trades quickly at very low cost, ensure that the direct exchange rates will conform closely with the computed indirect or "cross" rates.

Quick Check 7-6
You observe that the dollar prices of the peso and the shekel are $0.20 per peso and $0.30 per shekel. What must be the exchange rate between pesos and shekels?

---

[3]There are two types of charges: explicit fees and the difference between the prices at which the bank buys and sells various currencies.

7.7 VALUATION USING COMPARABLES

As stated previously, no two distinct assets are identical in all respects. The process of valuation requires that we find assets comparable to the one whose value we want to estimate and make judgments about which differences have a bearing on their value to investors.

For example, consider valuing a house using the observed prices of comparable houses. Suppose that you own a house and that each year you pay real estate taxes on it to the local town government that are computed as a proportion of the house's estimated market value. You have just received a notice from the town's real estate assessor notifying you that the estimated market value of your house this year is $500,000.

Suppose that your next-door neighbors just sold a house identical to yours for $300,000. You could justifiably appeal the town's assessment of $500,000 for the value of your house as being too high on the grounds that a house virtually identical to yours just sold for a price $200,000 less than your assessed value.

You are applying the Law of One Price in your valuation of your house. You are implying that if you were to put the house up for sale, your expectation is that it would fetch a price of $300,000 because a comparable house just sold for that amount.

Of course, the house next door is not *exactly* identical to yours because it is not located on your lot but on the one next to it. And you probably cannot *prove* that if you actually put your house up for sale it would fetch only $300,000 rather than the $500,000 that the town's assessor says it is worth. Nonetheless, unless the town's assessor can point to some economically relevant feature of your house that would make it worth $200,000 more than your neighbor's house (such as more land or floor space), you would have a strong logical case (and probably a strong legal case, too) for appealing the town's assessment.

The point is that even when the force of arbitrage cannot be relied on to enforce the Law of One Price, we still rely on its logic to value assets.

> **Quick Check 7-7**
> Suppose the town's assessor says that he arrived at his assessment of $500,000 for the value of your house by computing how much it would cost to rebuild your house from scratch using the current cost of building materials. What would be your response?

7.8 VALUATION MODELS

Valuation is fairly simple when you can apply the Law of One Price directly. However, because you almost never know the prices of assets that are exactly equivalent to the one being evaluated, you must employ some other method for estimating value from the known prices of other assets that are comparable but not quite the same. The quantitative method used to infer an asset's value from information about the prices of other comparable assets and market interest rates is called a **valuation model.**

The type of model that is best to use depends on its specific purpose. If you want to estimate the value of an asset over which you have no control, you might use a different model than if you can influence the asset's value through your actions. Thus, if you are an individual estimating a firm's stock as a personal investment, you will probably use a different model from the one used by a corporation contemplating taking over the firm and reorganizing it.

7.8.1 Valuing Real Estate

For example, consider the valuation problem faced by the town assessor discussed previously. He has to estimate the values of all houses in the town once a year. Because homeowners will have to pay taxes based on his assessments, the assessor must choose a valuation method that is perceived as fair and accurate. Valuation models used in real estate assessment vary significantly in their level of complexity and mathematical sophistication. Because the town's taxpayers will have to pay for the cost of the annual assessment, they will want the method chosen to be implementable at low cost.

Consider one simple model the assessor might use. He can collect all available data on prices of houses in the town that were sold during the past year (since the last revaluation of houses), average them, and use that average as his assessed value for all houses. This model is certainly inexpensive to construct and implement, but it almost surely would not be perceived as fair by those homeowners with houses that are worth less than the average.

Another simple method would be to take the original purchase price of each house and adjust it by a factor reflecting the general change in house prices in the town from the date of purchase to the current date. Thus, suppose that house prices in the town have increased at an average rate of 4% per year for the past 50 years. A house bought 50 years ago for a price of $30,000 would then have a current assessed value of $30,000 \times 1.04^{50}$ or $213,200.

But some homeowners are sure to object that this method ignores changes that have occurred over time in the house itself. Some houses will have undergone major improvements and others will have deteriorated. Moreover, the relative desirability of various locations in the town will have changed.

The assessor faces a difficult problem in choosing among valuation methods and may wind up using more than one.

Quick Check 7-8

Can you offer the assessor a way to alter his valuation model so as to take account of the specific neighborhood the house is located in?

7.8.2 Valuing Shares of Stock

A relatively simple model widely used in estimating the value of a share of a firm's stock is to take its most recent earnings per share (*EPS*) and multiply it by a price/earnings multiple derived from comparable firms. A firm's **price/earnings multiple** is the ratio of its stock price to its earnings per share.

Thus, suppose that you want to estimate the value of a share of XYZ stock and XYZ's earnings per share are $2. Suppose further comparable firms in the same line of business have an average price/earnings multiple of 10. Using this model, we would estimate the value of a share of XYZ stock to be $20:

$$\text{Estimated Value of a Share of XYZ Stock} = \text{XYZ Earnings per Share} \times$$
$$\text{Industry Average Price/Earnings Multiple} = \$2 \times 10 = \$20$$

In applying the price/earnings-multiple model, one must use great care to make sure that what is being measured is truly comparable. For example, shares of stock issued by two firms with identical assets but different debt/equity ratios are not really comparable. Moreover, firms classified as being in the same industry may have very different opportunities for profitable growth in the future and, therefore, differ in their price/earnings multiples.

Quick Check 7-9

A firm's earnings per share are $5, and the industry average price/earnings multiple is 10. What would be an estimate of the value of a share of the firm's stock?

In chapters 8 and 9, we explore specific types of valuation models that are used in finance to value different kinds of assets for different purposes. But first we digress to say a few words about *book values,* which are measures of value as they appear on accounting statements.

7.9 ACCOUNTING MEASURES OF VALUE

The value of an asset or a liability as reported on a balance sheet or other financial statement often differs from the asset's current market value because accountants usually measure assets by their original cost and then depreciate or "write them down" over time according to rules that ignore market values. The value of the asset as it appears in the financial statement is called the asset's **book value.**

An example will help to clarify. You buy a house for $100,000 on January 1, 20x0 and rent it out to make a profit. You finance the purchase with $20,000 of your own money (equity financing) and an $80,000 mortgage loan from the bank (debt financing). You set up a small real estate company to operate this rental business. Table 7.1 shows your company's starting balance sheet.

The $100,000 you paid for the property is allocated between the value of the land and the value of the building. Initially, all assets and liabilities are recorded at market prices. However, from that point on, book and market values will probably diverge. Accountants depreciate (i.e., mark down) the value of the building even if its market value goes up. The book value of the land remains fixed.

For example, suppose that on January 2 someone makes you a bona fide offer of $150,000 for the property. On the company's balance sheet it is still $100,000 (less one day's depreciation). This is its *book* value. What you could get for it if you sold it, however, is $150,000. This is its *market* value.

TABLE 7.1 ABC Realty Balance Sheet	
January 1, 20X0	
Assets	
Land	$25,000
Building	75,000
Liabilities	
Mortgage Loan	80,000
Owner's Equity (Net Worth)	20,000

Table 7.2 shows ABC Realty's market-value balance sheet on January 2 assuming that the market value of the property is $150,000 and the value of the mortgage loan has remained unchanged from the previous day.

If someone asks you on January 2 how wealthy you are, which measure of the business's value do you use to compute your net worth?[4] If you use the book value of owner's equity, the answer is $20,000, the amount that you invested in the business on January 1. But if you use the market value, your net worth is $70,000.

The point is that the user of financial statements must be careful not to interpret the values of assets that appear there as estimates of market values *unless they are specifically revalued to reflect their current market values.*

Quick Check 7-10

Suppose that on January 3 the market value of ABC Realty's property falls to $80,000. What is the market value of your net worth? What is its book value?

TABLE 7.2 ABC Realty Market Value Balance Sheet	
January 2, 20X0	
Assets	
Land and Building	$150,000
Liabilities	
Mortgage Loan	80,000
Owner's Equity (Net Worth)	70,000

---

[4]Recall from chapter 1 that the net worth (or owner's equity) is the difference between the assets and the liabilities.

7.10 HOW INFORMATION IS REFLECTED IN SECURITY PRICES

At the outset of this chapter we stated that the market price of an asset is a good measure of its fundamental value. In this section we develop more fully the reasoning behind this statement.

Sometimes a corporation's stock price "jumps" in response to a public announcement conveying news about the company's future prospects. For example, suppose that QRS Pharmaceuticals Corporation announces that its research scientists have just discovered a drug that will cure the common cold. The stock price will probably rise dramatically on this news. On the other hand, if it is announced that a judge has just ruled against QRS Pharmaceuticals in a lawsuit involving the payment of millions of dollars in compensation to customers who bought one of its products, QRS's stock price will probably fall.

In such situations, people say that the stock market is "reacting" to the information contained in these announcements. Implicit in this statement is the view that at least some of the investors who buy or sell QRS stock (or the stock analysts advising them) are paying attention to the fundamental factors that determine the stock's value. When those fundamentals change, so does the stock price. Indeed, if the stock price does not move when an important news item is officially made public, many observers of the stock market would say that the news was already reflected in the stock price. It is this idea that is behind the **efficient markets hypothesis.**

7.11 THE EFFICIENT MARKETS HYPOTHESIS

The *efficient markets hypothesis (EMH)* is the proposition that an asset's current price fully reflects all publicly available information about future economic fundamentals affecting the asset's value.[5]

The reasoning behind the EMH can be explained by considering the following somewhat simplified description of a typical analyst-investor's actions in making a decision about a particular company's stock.

First, the analyst collects the information or "facts" about the company and related matters that may affect the company. Second, she analyzes this information in such a way so as to determine her best estimate (as of today, time 0) of the stock price at a future date (time 1). This best estimate is the expected stock price at time 1, which we denote by $\overline{P}(1)$.

From looking at the current stock price, $P(0)$, she can estimate an *expected* return on the stock, $\overline{r}$, which is

$$\overline{r} = \frac{\overline{P}(1)}{P(0)} - 1$$

However, the analyst's job is not finished. Because she recognizes that her information is not perfect (e.g., subject to error or unforeseen events that may occur), she must also give consideration to the range of possible future prices.

In particular, she must estimate how disperse this range is about her best estimate and how likely is a deviation of a certain size from this estimate. This analysis then gives her an estimate of the deviations of the rate of return from the expected rate and the likelihood of such deviations. Obviously, the more accurate her information, the smaller will be the dispersion around her estimate and the less risky the investment.

---

[5]Stock market prices often reflect private information as well. See L. K. Meulbroek, "An Empirical Analysis of Illegal Insider Trading," *Journal of Finance*, December 1992, and L. K. Meulbroek and C. Hart, "The Effect of Illegal Insider Trading on Takeover Premia," *European Finance Review*, 1, 1997.

Third, armed with her estimates of the expected rate of return and the dispersion, she makes an investment decision or recommendation of how much of the stock to buy or sell. How much will depend on how good the risk-return trade-off on this stock is in comparison with alternative investments available and on how much money she has to invest (either personally or as an agent for others). The higher the expected return and the more money she has (or controls), the more of the stock she will want to buy or sell. The larger the dispersion (i.e., the less accurate the information that she has), the smaller the position she will take in the stock.

To see how the current market price of the stock is determined, we look at the aggregation of all analysts' estimates, and assume that on the average the market is in equilibrium [i.e., on average, the price will be such that total (desired) demand equals total supply]. Analysts' estimates may differ for two reasons:

1. They could have access to different amounts of information (although presumably public information is available to all); or

2. They could analyze the information differently with regard to its impact on future stock prices.

Nonetheless, each analyst comes to a decision as to how much to buy or sell at a given market price, $P(0)$. The aggregation of these decisions gives us the total demand for shares of the company at the price, $P(0)$.

Suppose that the price were such that there were more shares demanded than supplied (i.e., it is too low); then one would expect the price to rise, and vice versa, if there were more shares available at a given price than were demanded. Hence, the market price of the stock will reflect a *weighted average* of the opinions of all analysts.

The key question is what is the nature of this weighting? Because "votes" in the marketplace are cast with dollars, the analysts with the biggest impact will be the ones who control the larger amounts of money, and among these, the ones who have the strongest opinions about the stock will be the most important.

Note that the analysts with the strongest opinions have them because they believe that they have better information (resulting in a smaller dispersion around their best estimate). Furthermore, because an analyst who consistently overestimates the accuracy of his estimates will eventually lose his customers, one would expect that among the analysts who control large sums, the ones that believe that they have better information, on average, probably do.

From all this, we conclude that the market price of the stock will reflect the weighted average of analysts' opinions with heavier weights on the opinions of those analysts with control of more than the average amount of money and with better than average amounts of information. Hence, the estimate of "fair" or "intrinsic" value provided by the market price will be more accurate than the estimate obtained from an average analyst.

Now, suppose that you are an analyst and you find a stock whose market price is low enough that you consider it a "bargain" (if you never find this situation, then there is no point to being in the analyst business). From the previous discussion, there are two possibilities:

1. You *do* have a bargain—your estimate is more accurate than the market's (i.e., you have either better than average information about future events that may affect stock price and/or you do a better than average job of analyzing information) or

2. Others have better information than you do or process available information better, and your "bargain" is not a true bargain.

One's assessment of which it is depends on how good the other analysts are relative to oneself. There are important reasons why one would expect the quality of analysts to be high:

- The enormous rewards to anyone who can consistently beat the average attract large numbers of intelligent and hardworking people to the business;
- The relative ease of entry into the (analyst) business implies that competition will force the analysts to find better information and develop better techniques for processing this information just to survive; and
- The stock market has been around long enough for these competitive forces to take effect.

Precisely because professional analysts compete with each other, the market price becomes a better and better estimate of "fair value," and it becomes more difficult to find profit opportunities.

Quick Check 7-11
The DEF Corporation announces that over the next few years it will spend several billion dollars on developing a new product. The firm's stock price falls dramatically after the announcement. According to the efficient markets hypothesis, what is the reason for the drop in price? If you were the president of DEF Corporation, what conclusions would you draw from the decline in your firm's stock price?

Summary

In finance, the measure of an asset's value is the price it would fetch if it were sold in a competitive market. The ability to value assets accurately is at the heart of the discipline of finance because many personal and corporate financial decisions can be made by selecting the alternative that maximizes value.

The Law of One Price states that in a competitive market, if two assets are equivalent they will tend to have the same price. The law is enforced by a process called *arbitrage,* the purchase and immediate sale of equivalent assets in order to earn a sure profit from a difference in their prices.

Even if arbitrage cannot be carried out in practice to enforce the Law of One Price, unknown asset values can still be inferred from the prices of comparable assets whose prices are known.

The quantitative method used to infer an asset's value from information about the prices of comparable assets is called a *valuation model.* The best valuation model to employ varies with the information available and the intended use of the estimated value.

The *book value* of an asset or a liability as reported in a firm's financial statements often differs from its current market value.

In making most financial decisions, it is a good idea to start by assuming that for assets that are bought and sold in competitive markets, price is a pretty accurate reflection of fundamental value. This assumption is generally warranted precisely because there are many well-informed professionals looking for mispriced assets who profit by eliminating discrepancies between the market prices and the fundamental values of assets. The proposition that an asset's current price fully reflects all publicly available (and some private) information about future economic fundamentals affecting the asset's value is known as the *efficient markets hypothesis.*

The prices of traded assets reflect information about the fundamental economic determinants of their value. Analysts are constantly searching for assets whose prices are different from their fundamental value in order to buy/sell these "bargains." In deciding the best strategy for the purchase/sale of a "bargain," the analyst has to evaluate the accuracy of her information. The market price of an asset reflects the weighted average of all analysts' opinions with heavier weights on analysts who control large amounts of money and on those analysts who have better than average information.

Key Terms

- fundamental value   194
- Law of One Price   196
- arbitrage   196
- transaction costs   196
- arbitrageurs   196
- triangular arbitrage   200

- valuation model   202
- price/earnings multiple   203
- book value   204
- efficient markets hypothesis   206
- purchasing power parity   213
- real interest-rate parity   214

Answers to Quick Check Questions

Quick Check 7-1   *You win a contest, and the prize is a choice between a ticket to the opera and a ticket to the ball game. The opera ticket has a price of $100 and the ticket to the ball game has a price of $25. Assuming you prefer ball games to opera, which ticket should you choose?*

ANSWER: Provided the cost to you of taking the time and trouble to exchange the tickets does not exceed the $75 difference in the price of the tickets, you should take the opera ticket. Even if you prefer the ball game to the opera, you can exchange it for $100, buy a ticket to the ball game for $25, and pocket the $75 difference.

Quick Check 7-2   *If the price of silver is $10 per ounce in Chicago and the total transaction costs of shipping silver to New York is $1 per ounce, what can we say about the price of silver in New York?*

ANSWER: The price of silver in New York must be within $1 per ounce of its price in Chicago. Thus, the price of silver in New York must be between $9 and $11 per ounce.

Quick Check 7-3   *Under what circumstances might two 25-cent coins have different values?*

ANSWER: One of them might be a rare coin that is especially valuable to collectors. Alternatively, one of them might be slightly worn, so that a soda machine will reject it. To a thirsty person, the nonworn coin is more valuable.

Quick Check 7-4   *Suppose you have $10,000 in a bank account earning an interest rate of 3% per year. At the same time you have an unpaid balance on your credit card of $5,000* *on which you are paying an interest rate of 17% per year. What is the arbitrage opportunity you face?*

ANSWER: You could take $5,000 out of your bank account and pay down your credit card balance. You would give up 3% per year in interest earnings ($150 per year) but you would save 17% per year in interest expenses ($850 per year). So the arbitrage opportunity is worth $700 per year.

Quick Check 7-5   *Suppose that the exchange rate is $0.011 to the yen. How could you make arbitrage profits with your $10,000 if the dollar price of gold is $100 per ounce and the yen price is 10,000 yen per ounce?*

ANSWER:
a. Take $10,000, buy 100 ounces of gold for $100 per ounce.
b. Sell 100 ounces of gold in Japan for 1,000,000 yen (10,000 yen per ounce).
c. Take 1,000,000 yen and exchange it into dollars worth $11,000.

You make an arbitrage profit of $1,000.

Quick Check 7-6   *You observe that the dollar prices of the peso and the shekel are $0.20 per peso and $0.30 per shekel. What must be the exchange rate between pesos and shekels?*

ANSWER: Divide $0.20 per peso into $0.30 per shekel to get 1.5 pesos per shekel.

Quick Check 7-7   *Suppose the town's assessor says that he arrived at his assessment of $500,000 for the value of your house by computing how much it would cost to rebuild your house from scratch using the current cost of building materials. What would be your response?*

ANSWER: The cost to rebuild your house is not a measure of its market value. To estimate market value one should look at the actual prices of comparable houses—such as the one your neighbor just sold for $300,000.

Quick Check 7-8   *Can you offer the assessor a way to alter his valuation model so as to take account of the specific neighborhood the house is located in?*

ANSWER: One way to take account of the neighborhood effect in the valuation model would be to calculate average price changes *by neighborhood*. Then the assessor could apply a neighborhood price index in estimating price changes for individual houses.

Quick Check 7-9   *A firm's earnings per share are $5, and the industry average price/earnings multiple is 10. What would be an estimate of the value of a share of the firm's stock?*

ANSWER: An estimate of the value is $50 (*EPS* of $5 × *P/E* ratio of 10).

Quick Check 7-10   *Suppose that on January 3 the market value of ABC Realty's property falls to $80,000. What is the market value of your net worth? What is its book value?*

ANSWER: If the property value falls to $80,000, your net worth is 0. Its book value, however, is $20,000.

Quick Check 7-11   *The DEF Corporation announces that over the next few years it will spend several billion dollars on developing a new product. The firm's stock price falls dramatically after the announcement. According to the efficient markets hypothesis, what is the reason for the drop in price? If you were the president of DEF Corporation, what conclusions would you draw from the decline in your firm's stock price?*

ANSWER: According to the EMH, the price drop reflects a predominant view in the marketplace that DEF Corporation's proposed new product is not worth developing. If you were CEO and believed that the market analysts had as much information as you did, you might reconsider the desirability of developing the new product. However, if you had superior information about the new product that the market analysts were not aware of, then you might go ahead with the product development despite market opinion. Alternatively, you might make the information you have public in order to gauge the reaction of the market to this new piece of information.

Quick Check 7-12 (See appendix at the end of this chapter.) *Suppose the expected rate of inflation in the French franc is 10% per year. What should be the nominal interest rate in francs according to real interest rate parity?*

ANSWER: Franc Interest Rate = $1.03 \times 1.1 - 1 = 13.3\%$ per Year

Questions and Problems

Laws of One Price and Arbitrage

1. IBX stock is trading for $35 on the NYSE and $33 on the Tokyo Stock Exchange. Assume that the costs of buying and selling the stock are negligible.
   a. How could you make an arbitrage profit?
   b. Over time what would you expect to happen to the stock prices in New York and Tokyo?
   c. Now assume that the cost of buying or selling shares of IBX is 1% per transaction. How does this affect your answer?

2. Suppose you live in the state of Taxachusetts, which has a 16% sales tax on liquor. A neighboring state called Taxfree has no tax on liquor. The price of a case of beer is $25 in Taxfree and it is $29 in Taxachusetts.
   a. Is this a violation of the Law of One Price?
   b. Are liquor stores in Taxachusetts near the border with Taxfree going to prosper?

Triangular Arbitrage

3. Suppose the price of gold is 155 marks.
   a. If the dollar price of gold is $100 per ounce, what should you expect the dollar price of a mark to be?
   b. If it actually only costs $0.60 to purchase one mark, how could one make arbitrage profits?

4. You observe that the dollar price of the Italian lira is $0.0006 and the dollar price of the yen is $0.01. What must be the exchange rate between lira and yen for there to be no arbitrage opportunity?

5. Fill in the missing exchange rates in the following table:

	U.S. Dollar	British Pound	German Mark	Yen
U.S. dollar	$1	$1.50	$0.5	$0.01
British pound	£0.67			
German mark	DM2.0			
Japanese yen	¥100			

Valuation Using Comparables

6. Suppose you own a home that you purchased four years ago for $475,000. The tax assessor's office has just informed you that they are increasing the taxable value of your home to $525,000.
   a. How might you gather information to help you appeal the new assessment?
   b. Suppose the house next door is comparable to yours except that it has one fewer bedroom. It just sold for $490,000. How might you use that information to argue your case? What inference must you make about the value of an additional bedroom?

7. The *P/E* ratio of ITT Corporation is currently 6 while the *P/E* ratio of the S&P 500 is 10. What might account for the difference?

8. Suppose you are chief financial officer of a private toy company. The chief executive officer has asked you to come up with an estimate for the company's price per share. Your company's earnings per share were $2.00 in the year just ended. You know that you should look at public company comparables, however, they seem to fall into two camps: those with *P/E* ratios of 8× earnings and those with *P/E* ratios of 14× earnings. You are perplexed at the difference until you notice that on average, the lower *P/E* companies have higher leverage than the higher *P/E* group. The 8× *P/E* group has a debt/equity ratio of 2:1. The 14× *P/E* group has a debt/equity ratio of 1:1. If your toy company has a debt/equity ratio of 1.5:1, what might you tell the CEO about your company's equity value per share?

9. Assume that you have operated your business for 15 years. Sales for the most recent fiscal year were $12,000,000. Net income for the most recent fiscal year was $1,000,000. Your book value is $10,500,000. A similar company recently sold for the following statistics:

Multiple of Sales	0.8×
Multiple of Net Income	12×
Multiple of Book Value	0.9×

   a. What is an appropriate range of value for your company?
   b. If you know that your company has future investment opportunities that are far more profitable than the preceding company, what does that say about your company's likely valuation?

Efficient Markets Hypothesis

10. The price of Fuddy Co. stock recently jumped when the sudden unexpected death of its CEO was announced. What might account for such a market reaction?

11. Your analysis leads you to believe that the price of Outel's stock should be $25 per share. Its current market price is $30.
    a. If you do not believe that you have access to special information about the company, what do you do?
    b. If you are an analyst with much better than average information, what do you do?

Real Interest Rate Parity

12. Assume that the worldwide risk-free real rate of interest is 3% per year. Inflation in Switzerland is 2% per year and in the United States it is 5% per year. Assuming there is no uncertainty about inflation, what are the implied nominal interest rates denominated in Swiss francs and in U.S. dollars?

Integrative Problem

13. Suppose an aunt has passed away and bequeathed to you and your siblings (one brother, one sister) a variety of assets. The original cost of these assets follows.

Item	Cost	When Purchased
Jewelry	$500	by grandmother 75 years ago
House	1,200,000	10 years ago
Stocks and Bonds	1,000,000	3 years ago
Vintage (used) Car	200,000	2 months ago
Furniture	15,000	various dates during last 40 years

Because you are taking a course in finance, your siblings put you in charge of dividing the assets fairly among the three of you. Before you start, your brother approaches you and says:

"I'd really like the car for myself, so when you divide up the assets, just give me the car and deduct the $200,000 from my share."

Hearing that, your sister says:

"That sounds fair, because I really like the jewelry and you can assign that to me and deduct the $500 from my share."

You have always loved your aunt's house and its furnishings, so you would like to keep the house and the furniture.

a. How do you respond to your brother and sister's requests? Justify your responses.

b. How would you go about determining appropriate values for each asset?

APPENDIX

Purchasing Power and Real Interest Rate Parity

The Law of One Price is the basis for a theory of exchange rate determination known as **purchasing power parity** (PPP). The essence of the theory is that exchange rates adjust so as to maintain the same "real" price of a "representative" basket of goods and services around the world. In other words, the theory says that although some goods may cost different amounts in different countries, the general cost of living should be about the same.

To illustrate the reasoning behind PPP, assume that there are only two different countries—Japan and the United States—with their own currencies—the dollar and the yen. There is, therefore, only one exchange rate to be determined—the dollar price of the yen. There is a single good produced and consumed in both countries—wheat.

Suppose that the price of wheat is $1 per bushel in the United States and ¥100 per bushel in Japan. The equilibrium exchange rate is $0.01 per yen.

Consider what would happen at an exchange rate of $0.009 per yen. There would be an arbitrage opportunity. An arbitrageur could buy wheat in Japan and sell it to consumers in the United States. A bushel of imported Japanese wheat would cost $0.90 ($0.009 per yen × ¥100 per bushel) and sell for $1.00 in the United States market. To do this, arbitrageurs need to convert more dollars into yen than they would at the equilibrium exchange rate of $0.01 per yen. Japan would experience a trade surplus (i.e., it would be an exporter of wheat to the United States), and there would be excess demand for yen. This excess demand for yen would drive up the dollar price of the yen.

At an exchange rate that is higher than the equilibrium rate, the situation is reversed. The "undervalued" dollar makes United States wheat cheaper to Japanese consumers than Japanese wheat. Japan imports wheat from the U.S. instead of exporting it to the United States. There is an excess supply of yen, which drives its dollar price down toward the equilibrium level.

In reality, our simple example illustrating PPP has to be modified for several reasons. We assume that the same good is consumed in both countries and that it is transportable at low cost. In reality, although some are the same, many of the goods produced and consumed in each country are different. Moreover, many of them are too costly to transport across national borders. In many cases, governments restrict the flow of imports and exports through tariffs and quotas.

For all of these reasons, PPP, if it holds at all, holds only approximately and only in the long run.

Just as we have the theory of PPP to explain the relations among exchange rates, there is an analogous theory to explain the relations among interest rates denominated in different currencies. We call it the theory of **real interest-rate parity.** This theory states that the expected real interest rate on risk-free loans is the same all over the world. Given a value for this real interest rate, *the nominal interest rate for a loan denominated in any currency is determined by the expected rate of inflation in that currency.*

In chapter 5 we distinguish between real interest rates and nominal interest rates. We show that the realized real rate of interest on a loan is related to the nominal interest rate as follows:

$$1 + \text{Nominal Interest Rate} = (1 + \text{Real Interest Rate}) \times (1 + \text{Rate of Inflation})$$

Under the real interest-rate parity theory, this relation holds with respect to expected inflation.

To illustrate the implications of the theory of real interest-rate parity, let us assume that the worldwide risk-free real interest rate is currently 3% per year. Let us assume that the expected rate of inflation in Japan is 1% per year and in the United States it is 4% per year. The nominal interest rates in yen and dollars implied by real interest rate parity are

$$\text{Yen Interest Rate} = 1.03 \times 1.01 - 1 = 4.03\% \text{ per Year}$$
$$\text{Dollar Interest Rate} = 1.03 \times 1.04 - 1 = 7.12\% \text{ per Year}$$

Quick Check 7-12

Suppose the expected rate of inflation in the French franc is 10% per year. What should be the nominal interest rate in francs according to real interest-rate parity?

CHAPTER

8

Valuation of Known Cash Flows: Bonds

OBJECTIVES

- ■ To show how to value contracts and securities that promise a stream of cash flows that is known with certainty.
- ■ To understand how bond prices and yields change over time.

CONTENTS

Chapter 7 shows that the essence of the valuation process is to estimate an asset's market value using information about the prices of comparable assets, making adjustments for differences. A *valuation model* is a quantitative method used to infer an asset's value (the output of the model) from market information about the prices of other assets and market interest rates (the inputs to the model).

In this chapter, we examine the valuation of fixed-income securities and other contracts promising a stream of known future cash payments. Examples are fixed-income securities like bonds and contracts such as mortgages and pension annuities. These securities and contracts are important to households because they represent major sources of income and sources of financing for housing and other consumer durables. They are also important to firms and governments, primarily as sources of financing.

Having a method to value such contracts is important for at least two reasons. First, the parties to the contracts need to have an agreed-upon valuation procedure

215

in setting the terms of the contracts at the outset. Second, fixed-income securities are often sold before they mature. Because the market factors determining their value—namely, interest rates—change over time, both buyers and sellers have to reevaluate them each time they are traded.

Section 8.1 presents a basic valuation model that uses a discounted cash flow formula with a single discount rate to estimate the value of a stream of promised future cash flows. Section 8.2 shows how to modify such a model to take account of the fact that generally the yield curve is not flat (i.e., that interest rates vary with maturity). Sections 8.3–8.5 explain the main features of bonds in the real world and discuss how these features affect the prices and yields of bonds. Section 8.6 explores how changes in interest rates over time affect the market prices of bonds.

8.1 USING PRESENT VALUE FORMULAS TO VALUE KNOWN CASH FLOWS

Chapter 4 shows that in a world with a single risk-free interest rate, computing the present value of any stream of future cash flows is relatively uncomplicated. It involves applying a discounted cash flow formula using the risk-free interest rate as the discount rate.

For example, suppose you buy a fixed-income security that promises to pay $100 each year for the next three years. How much is this three-year annuity worth if you know that the appropriate discount rate is 6% per year? As shown in chapter 4, the answer—$267.30—can be found easily using a financial calculator, a table of present value factors, or by applying the algebraic formula for the present value of an annuity.

Recall that the formula for the present value of an ordinary annuity of $1 per period for n periods at an interest rate of i is:

$$PV = \frac{1 - (1 + i)^{-n}}{i}$$

On a financial calculator, we would enter the values for $n, i,$ and $PMT,$ and compute the PV:

n	i	PV	FV	PMT	Result
3	6	?	0	100	$PV = 267.30$

Now suppose that an hour after you buy the security, the risk-free interest rate rises from 6% to 7% per year, and you want to sell. How much can you get for it?

The level of market interest rates has changed, but the promised future cash flows from your security have not. In order for an investor to earn 7% per year on your security, its price has to drop. How much? The answer is that it must fall to the point at which its price equals the present value of the promised cash flows discounted at 7% per year:

n	i	PV	FV	PMT	Result
3	7	?	0	100	$PV = 262.43$

At a price of $262.43, a fixed-income security that promises to pay $100 each year for the next three years offers its purchaser a rate of return of 7% per year. Thus, the price of any existing fixed-income security falls when market interest rates rise because investors will only be willing to buy them if they offer a competitive yield.

Thus, a *rise* of 1% in the interest rate causes a *drop* of $4.87 in the market value of your security. Similarly, a fall in interest rates causes a rise in its market value.

This illustrates a basic principle in valuing known cash flows:

> A change in market interest rates causes a change in the *opposite direction* in the market values of all existing contracts promising fixed payments in the future.

Because interest rate changes are not predictable, it follows that the prices of fixed-income securities are uncertain up to the time they mature.

Quick Check 8-1
What happens to the value of a three-year fixed-income security promising $100 per year if the market interest rate falls from 6% to 5% per year?

In practice, valuation of known cash flows is not as simple as we just described because in practice *you do not usually know which discount rate to use in the present value formula.* As shown in chapter 2, market interest rates are not the same for all maturities. We reproduce as Figure 8.1 the graph showing the yield curve for U.S. Treasury bonds.

It is tempting to think that the interest rate corresponding to a three-year maturity can be applied as the correct discount rate to use in valuing the three-year annuity in our example. But that would not be correct. The correct procedure for using the information contained in the yield curve to value other streams of known cash payments is more complicated; that is the subject of the next few sections.

FIGURE 8.1   U.S. Treasury Yield Curve

Source: The Wall Street Journal, April 3, 1995, p. C21.

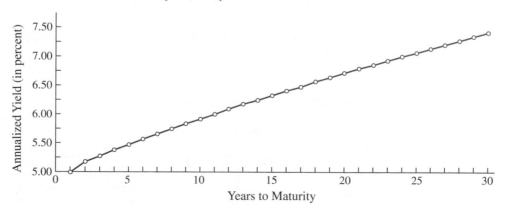

8.2 THE BASIC BUILDING BLOCKS: PURE DISCOUNT BONDS

In valuing contracts promising a stream of known cash flows, the place to start is a listing of the market prices of **pure discount bonds** (also called *zero-coupon bonds*). These are bonds that promise a single payment of cash at some date in the future, called the maturity date.

Pure discount bonds are the basic building blocks for valuing all contracts promising streams of known cash flows. This is because we can always decompose any contract—no matter how complicated its pattern of certain future cash flows—into its component cash flows, value each one separately, and then add them up.

The promised cash payment on a pure discount bond is called its **face value** or *par value*. The interest earned by investors on pure discount bonds is the difference between the price paid for the bond and the face value received at the maturity date. Thus, for a pure discount bond with a face value of $1,000 maturing in one year and a purchase price of $950, the interest earned is the $50 difference between the $1,000 face value and the $950 purchase price.

The *yield* (interest rate) on a pure discount bond is the annualized rate of return to investors who buy it and hold it until it matures. For a pure discount bond with a one-year maturity such as the one in our example, we get

$$\text{Yield on 1-Year Pure Discount Bond} = \frac{\text{Face Value} - \text{Price}}{\text{Price}}$$

$$= \frac{\$1000 - \$950}{\$950} = 0.0526 \text{ or } 5.26\%$$

If, however, the bond has a maturity different from one year, we would use the present value formula to find its annualized yield. Thus, suppose that we observe a two-year pure discount bond with a face value of $1,000 and a price of $880. We would compute the annualized yield on this bond as the discount rate that makes its face value equal to its price. On a financial calculator, we would enter the values for *n, PV, FV,* and compute *i*.

n	i	PV	FV	PMT	Result
2	?	-880	1,000	0	i = 6.60%

Return to the valuation of the security of section 8.1 that promises to pay $100 each year for the next three years. Suppose that we observe the set of pure discount bond prices in Table 8.1. Following standard practice, the bond prices are quoted as a fraction of their face value.

TABLE 8.1   Prices of Pure Discount Bonds and Yields

Maturity	Price per $1 of Face Value	Yield (per year)
1 year	0.95	5.26%
2 years	0.88	6.60%
3 years	0.80	7.72%

There are two alternative procedures that we can use to arrive at a correct value for the security. The first procedure uses the prices in the second column of Table 8.1, and the second procedure uses the yields in the last column. Procedure 1 multiplies each of the three promised cash payments by its corresponding per-dollar price and then adds them up:

Present Value of First Year's Cash Flow = $\$100 \times 0.95 = \$95.00$

Present Value of Second Year's Cash Flow = $\$100 \times 0.88 = \$88.00$

Present Value of Third Year's Cash Flow = $\$100 \times 0.80 = \$80.00$

Total Present Value = $263

The resulting estimate of the security's value is $263.

Procedure 2 gets the same result by discounting each year's promised cash payment at the yield corresponding to that maturity:

Present Value of First Year's Cash Flow = $\$100/1.0526 = \$95.00$

Present Value of Second Year's Cash Flow = $\$100/1.0660^2 = \$88.00$

Present Value of Third Year's Cash Flow = $\$100/1.0772^3 = \$80.00$

Total Present Value = $263

Note, however, that it would be a mistake to discount all three cash flows using the same three-year yield of 7.72% per year listed in the last row of Table 8.1. If we do so, we get a value of $259, which is $4 too low:

n	i	PV	FV	PMT	Result
3	7.72%	?	0	100	PV = $259

Is there a single discount rate that we can use to discount all three of the payments the way we did in section 8.1 to get a value of $263 for the security? The answer is yes: That single discount rate is 6.88% per year. To verify this, substitute 6.88% for *i* in the formula for the present value of an annuity or in the calculator:

n	i	PV	FV	PMT	Result
3	6.88%	?	0	100	PV = $263

The problem is that the 6.88% per-year discount rate appropriate for valuing the three-year annuity is not one of the rates listed anywhere in Table 8.1. We derived it from our knowledge that the value of the security has to be $263. In other words, we solved the present value equation to find *i:*

n	i	PV	FV	PMT	Result
3	?	−263	0	100	i = 6.88%

But it was that value (i.e., $263) that we were trying to estimate in the first place. Therefore, we have no direct way to find the value of the three-year annuity using a single discount rate with the bond price information available to us in Table 8.1.

We can summarize the main conclusion from this section as follows: When the yield curve is not flat (i.e., when observed yields are not the same for all maturities), the correct procedure for valuing a contract or a security promising a stream of known cash payments is to discount each of the payments at the rate corresponding to a pure discount bond of its maturity and then add the resulting individual payment values.

Quick Check 8-2

Suppose the observed yield on two-year pure discount bonds falls to 6% per year, but the other rates reported in Table 8.1 remain unchanged. What is your estimate of the value of the three-year annuity paying $100 per year? What single discount rate applied to the present value formula for annuities would give this same value?

8.3 COUPON BONDS, CURRENT YIELD, AND YIELD TO MATURITY

A **coupon bond** obligates the issuer to make periodic payments of interest—called *coupon payments*—to the bondholder for the life of the bond, and then to pay the face value of the bond when the bond matures (i.e., when the last payment comes due). The periodic payments of interest are called *coupons* because at one time most bonds had coupons attached to them that investors would tear off and present to the bond issuer for payment.

The **coupon rate** of the bond is the interest rate applied to the face value to compute the coupon payment. Thus, a bond with a face value of $1,000 that makes annual coupon payments at a coupon rate of 10% obligates the issuer to pay $0.10 \times \$1,000 = \$100$ every year. If the bond's maturity is six years, then at the end of six years, the issuer pays the last coupon of $100 *and* the face value of $1,000.[1]

The cash flows from this coupon bond are displayed in Figure 8.2. We see that the stream of promised cash flows has an annuity component (a fixed per period amount) of $100 per year and a "balloon" or "bullet" payment of $1,000 at maturity.

The $100 annual coupon payment is fixed at the time the bond is issued and remains constant until the bond's maturity date. On the date the bond is issued, it usually has a price (equal to its face value) of $1,000.

Year	0	1	2	3	4	5	6
Coupon		100	100	100	100	100	100
Face value							1,000

FIGURE 8.2   Cash Flows for 10% $1,000 Coupon Bond

---

[1]In the United States, coupon payments on bonds are usually made semiannually. Thus, a bond with a coupon rate of 10% per year actually pays a coupon of $50 every six months. To keep the calculations in the chapter simple, we will ignore this fact.

The relation between prices and yields on coupon bonds is more complicated than for pure discount bonds. As we will see, when the prices of coupon bonds are different from their face value, the meaning of the term *yield* is itself ambiguous.

Coupon bonds with a market price equal to their face value are called **par bonds.** When a coupon bond's market price equals its face value, its yield is the same as its coupon rate. For example, consider a bond maturing in one year that pays an annual coupon at a rate of 10% of its $1,000 face value. This bond will pay its holder $1,100 a year from now—a coupon payment of $100 and the face value of $1,000. Thus, if the current price of our 10% coupon bond is $1,000, its yield is 10%.

Bond Pricing Principle 1: Par Bonds

If a bond's price equals its face value, then its yield equals its coupon rate.

Often the price of a coupon bond and its face value are not the same. This situation would occur, for instance, if the level of interest rates in the economy falls after the bond is issued. So, for example, suppose that our one-year 10% coupon bond was originally issued as a 20-year-maturity bond 19 years ago. At that time, the yield curve was flat at 10% per year. Now the bond has one year remaining before it matures, and the interest rate on one-year bonds is 5% per year.

Although the 10% coupon bond was issued at par ($1,000), its market price will now be $1,047.62. Because the bond's price is now higher than its face value, it is called a **premium bond.**

What is its yield?

There are two different yields that we can compute. The first is called the **current yield,** the annual coupon divided by the bond's price:

$$\text{Current Yield} = \frac{\text{Coupon}}{\text{Price}} = \frac{\$100}{\$1,047.62} = 9.55\%$$

The current yield overstates the true yield on the premium bond because it ignores the fact that at maturity you will receive only $1,000—$47.62 less than you paid for the bond.

To take account of the fact that a bond's face value and its price may differ, we compute a different yield called the **yield to maturity.** The yield to maturity is defined as the discount rate that makes the present value of the bond's stream of promised cash payments equal to its price.

The yield to maturity takes account of all of the cash payments you will receive from purchasing the bond, including the face value of $1,000 at maturity. In our example, because the bond is maturing in one year, it is easy to compute the yield to maturity.

$$\text{Yield to Maturity} = \frac{\text{Coupon} + \text{Face value} - \text{Price}}{\text{Price}}$$

$$\text{Yield to Maturity} = \frac{\$100 + \$1,000 - \$1,047.62}{\$1,047.62} = 5\%$$

Thus, we see that if you used the current yield of 9.55% as a guide to what you would be earning if you bought the bond, you would be seriously misled.

When the maturity of a coupon bond is greater than a year, the calculation of its yield to maturity is more complicated than just shown. For example, suppose that you are considering buying a two-year 10% coupon bond with a face value of $1,000 and a current price of $1,100. What is its yield?

Its current yield is 9.09%:

$$\text{Current Yield} = \frac{\text{Coupon}}{\text{Price}} = \frac{\$100}{\$1,100} = 9.09\%$$

But as in the case of the one-year premium bond, the current yield ignores the fact that at maturity, you will receive less than the $1,100 that you paid. The yield to maturity when bond maturity is greater than one year is the discount rate that makes the present value of the stream of cash payments equal to the bond's price:

$$PV = \sum_{i=1}^{n} \frac{PMT}{(1+i)^t} + \frac{FV}{(1+i)^n} \qquad (8.1)$$

where n is the number of annual payment periods until the bond's maturity, i is the annual yield to maturity, PMT is the coupon payment, and FV is the face value of the bond received at maturity.

The yield to maturity on a multiperiod coupon bond can be computed easily on most financial calculators by entering the bond's maturity as n, its price as PV (with a negative sign), its face value as FV, its coupon as PMT, and computing i.

n	i	PV	FV	PMT	Result
2	?	−1,100	1,000	100	$i = 4.65\%$

Thus, the yield to maturity on this two-year premium bond is considerably less than its current yield.

These examples illustrate a general principle about the relation between bond prices and yields:

Bond Pricing Principle 2: Premium Bonds

If a coupon bond has a price higher than its face value, its yield to maturity is less than its current yield, which is in turn less than its coupon rate.

For a premium bond:

Yield to Maturity < Current Yield < Coupon Rate

Now let us consider a bond with a 4% coupon rate maturing in two years. Suppose that its price is $950. Because the price is below the face value of the bond, we call it a *discount bond*. (Note it is not a *pure* discount bond because it does pay a coupon.)

What is its yield? As in the previous case of a premium bond, we can compute two different yields—the current yield and the yield to maturity.

$$\text{Current Yield} = \frac{\text{Coupon}}{\text{Price}} = \frac{\$40}{\$950} = 4.21\%$$

The current yield understates the true yield in the case of the discount bond because it ignores the fact that at maturity you will receive more than you paid for the bond. When the discount bond matures, you receive the $1,000 face value, not the $950 price that you paid for it.

The yield to maturity takes account of all of the cash payments you will receive from purchasing the bond, including the face value of $1,000 at maturity. Using the financial calculator to compute the bond's yield to maturity, we find:

n	i	PV	FV	PMT	Result
2	?	-950	1,000	40	$i = 6.76\%$

Thus, the yield to maturity on this discount bond is greater than its current yield.

Bond Pricing Principle 3: Discount Bonds

If a coupon bond has a price lower than its face value, its yield to maturity is greater than its current yield, which is in turn greater than its coupon rate.

For discount bonds:

Yield to Maturity > Current Yield > Coupon Rate

8.3.1 Beware of "High-Yield" U.S. Treasury Bond Funds

In the past, some investment companies that invest exclusively in U.S. Treasury bonds have advertised yields that appear much higher than the interest rates on other known investments of the same maturity. The yields that they are advertising are *current* yields, and the bonds that they are investing in are premium bonds that have relatively high coupon rates. Thus, according to Bond Pricing Principle 2, the actual return you will earn is expected to be considerably less than the advertised current yield.

Suppose that you have $10,000 to invest for one year. You are deciding between putting your money in a one-year, government-insured, bank CD offering an interest rate of 5% and investing in the shares of a U.S. Treasury bond fund that holds one-year bonds with a coupon rate of 8%. The bonds held by the fund are selling at a premium over their face value: For every $10,000 of face value that you will receive at maturity a year from now, you must pay $10,285.71 now. The current yield on the fund is $800/$10,285.71 or 7.78%, and this is the yield that the fund is advertising. If the fund charges a 1% annual fee for its services, what rate of return will you actually earn?

If there were no fees at all for investing in the fund, your rate of return for the year would be 5%, precisely the same rate of return as on the bank CD. This is because investing your $10,000 in the fund will achieve the same return as buying an 8% coupon bond with a face value of $10,000 for a price of $10,285.71:

$$\text{Rate of Return} = \frac{\text{Coupon} + \text{Face Value} - \text{Price}}{\text{Price}}$$

$$= \frac{\$800 + \$10,000 - \$10,285.71}{\$10,286} = 5\%$$

Because you have to pay the fund a fee equal to 1% of your $10,000, your rate of return will be only 4% rather than the 5% you can earn on the bank CD.

Quick Check 8-3
What are the current yield and yield to maturity on a three-year bond with a coupon rate of 6% per year and a price of $900?

8.4 READING BOND LISTINGS

E-BOOK

8.4

The prices of bonds are published in a variety of places. For investors and analysts who need the most up-to-the-minute price data, the best sources are on-line information services that feed the information electronically to computer terminals. For those who do not need data that are quite so up-to-date, the daily financial press provides bond listings.

Table 8.2 is a partial listing of the prices of U.S. Treasury strips on August 23, 1998 taken from *The Wall Street Journal.* U.S. Treasury strips are pure discount bonds that are created from U.S. Treasury coupon bonds by firms that buy the coupon bonds and then resell each of the coupon payments and the repayment of the principal as separate securities. (This activity is called *stripping* the coupon bonds.)

To interpret the prices, we must understand several conventions:

1. *Type* in the second column tells the original source of the strip: *ci* is coupon interest, *bp* is principal from a Treasury bond, and *np* is principal from a Treasury note. Bonds have original maturities of more than 10 years; notes have original maturities of 10 years or less.

2. The *ask price* is the price at which dealers in Treasury bonds are willing to sell, and the *bid price* is the price at which they are willing to buy. Therefore, the asked price always exceeds the bid price. The difference is, in effect, the dealer's commission. *Ask Yld.* in the last column is the yield to maturity computed using the asked price. It assumes semiannual compounding.

TABLE 8.2   Listing of Prices of U.S. Treasury Strips

Maturity	Type	Bid	Asked	Chg	Ask Yld.
May 00	np	89:19	89:19	+1	5.60
May 05	bp	66:30	67:03	+1	5.74
May 27	ci	17:26	17:31	—	6.01

Notes: U.S. Treasury strips as of 3 P.M. Eastern time, based on transactions of $1 million or more. Colons in bid-and-asked quotes represent 32nds; 101:01 means $101\frac{1}{32}$. Net changes are in 32nds. Yields are calculated on the asked quotation.

ci—stripped coupon interest.
bp—Treasury bond, stripped principal.
np—Treasury note, stripped principal.

Source: Bear, Stearns & Co. via Street Software Technology Inc.

TABLE 8.3	Listing or Prices of U.S. Treasury Bonds				

Rate	Maturity Mo./Yr.	Bid	Asked	Chg.	Ask Yld.
9	May 98n	102:26	102:28	−1	5.95
6	May 98n	99:31	100:01	—	5.97
$13\frac{1}{8}$	May 01	122:23	122:29	−2	6.51
$6\frac{1}{2}$	May 01n	99:27	99:29	−1	6.53
$8\frac{3}{4}$	May 20	119:15	119:16	−5	7.02

Notes: Representative and indicative. Over-the-counter quotations based on million or more. Treasury bond, note, and bill quotes are as of afternoon.

3. The price quotations are cents per $1 of face value.

4. The numbers after the colon mean 32nds and not 100ths of a cent. Thus, 97:11 means 97 and $\frac{11}{32}$ (or $0.9734375), not $0.9711.

Table 8.2 shows that the ask price for a Treasury strip maturing in February 1996 was 97 and $\frac{11}{32}$ (97.34375) cents per dollar of face value and for one maturing in February 2004, 57 and $\frac{5}{32}$ (or 57.15625 cents per dollar of face value).

Table 8.3 is a partial listing of the prices of U.S. Treasury Bonds taken from *The Wall Street Journal*. It differs from the previous listing in that it displays each bond's coupon rate in the first column. The letter *n* that appears after the maturity date indicates that the bond is a U.S. Treasury note, meaning that it had an original maturity of less than 10 years.

8.5 WHY YIELDS FOR THE SAME MATURITY MAY DIFFER

Often we observe that two U.S. Treasury bonds with the same maturity have different yields to maturity. Is this a violation of the Law of One Price? The answer is no. In fact, for bonds with different coupon rates, the Law of One Price implies that, unless the yield curve is flat, bonds of the same maturity *will* have different yields to maturity.

8.5.1 The Effect of the Coupon Rate

For example, consider two different two-year coupon bonds—one with a coupon rate of 5% and the other with a coupon rate of 10%. Suppose the current market prices and yields of one- and two-year pure discount bonds are as follows:

Maturity	Price per $1 of Face Value	Yield (per year)
1 year	$0.961538	4%
2 years	$0.889996	6%

According to the Law of One Price, the first-year cash flows from each coupon bond must have a per-dollar price of $0.961538, and the second-year cash flows must have a per-dollar price of $0.889996. Therefore, the market prices of the two different coupon bonds should be:

For the 5% coupon bond:

$$0.961538 \times \$50 + 0.889996 \times \$1,050 = \$982.57$$

For the 10% coupon bond:

$$0.961538 \times \$100 + 0.889996 \times \$1,100 = \$1,075.15$$

Now let us compute the yields to maturity on each of the coupon bonds that correspond to these market prices. Using the financial calculator we find:

For the 5% coupon bond:

n	i	PV	FV	PMT	Result
2	?	−982.57	1,000	50	$i = 5.9500\%$

For the 10% coupon bond:

n	i	PV	FV	PMT	Result
2	?	−1075.15	1,000	100	$i = 5.9064\%$

Thus, we see that in order to obey the Law of One Price, the two bonds must have different yields to maturity. As a general principle:

> When the yield curve is not flat, bonds of the same maturity with different coupon rates have different yields to maturity.

Quick Check 8-4

Using the same prices for pure discount bonds as in the previous example, what would be the price and yield to maturity on a two-year coupon bond with a coupon rate of 4% per year?

8.5.2 The Effect of Default Risk and Taxes

At times, one will encounter examples of bonds with the same coupon rate and maturity selling at different prices. These differences occur because of the other ways *seemingly* identical securities differ.

Bonds offering the same future stream of promised payments can differ in a number of ways, but the two most important are default risk and taxability. To illustrate, consider a bond promising to pay $1,000 a year from now. Suppose that the one-year U.S. Treasury rate is 6% per year. If the bond is completely free of default risk, its price would, therefore, be $1,000/1.06 = $943.40. But if it is subject to some default risk (i.e., that what is promised may not be paid), no matter how slight, its price will be less than $943.40, and its yield will be higher than 6% per year.

The taxability of bonds can vary according to the issuer or type of bond, and this fact will certainly influence their price. For example, interest earned on bonds issued by state and local governments in the United States is exempt from federal income taxes. Other things equal, this feature makes them more attractive to tax-paying investors and will cause their prices to be higher (and their yields lower) than otherwise comparable bonds.

8.5.3 Other Effects on Bond Yields

There are many other features that may differentiate seemingly identical fixed-income securities and, therefore, cause their prices to differ. Check your intuition about the effect of the following two bond features. In each case consider whether the inclusion of the feature should increase or decrease the price of an otherwise identical bond (i.e., one which offers the same stream of promised cash flows) that does not have the feature:

1. *Callability*. This feature gives the issuer of the bond the right to redeem it before the final maturity date. A bond that has this feature is a **callable bond.**

2. *Convertibility*. This feature gives the holder of a bond issued by a corporation the right to convert the bond into a prespecified number of shares of common stock. A bond that has this feature is a **convertible bond.**

Your intuition should tell you that any feature that makes the bond more attractive to the issuer will lower its price, and any feature that makes it more attractive to the bondholders will raise its price. Thus, callability will cause a bond to have a lower price (and a higher yield to maturity). On the other hand, convertibility will cause a bond to have a higher price and a lower yield to maturity.

8.6 THE BEHAVIOR OF BOND PRICES OVER TIME

In this section we examine how bond prices change over time as a result of the passage of time and changes in interest rates.

8.6.1 The Effect of the Passage of Time

If the yield curve were flat and interest rates did not change, any default-free discount bond's price would rise with the passage of time, and any premium bond's price would fall. This is because eventually bonds mature, and their price must equal their face value at maturity. We should, therefore, expect the prices of discount bonds and premium bonds to move toward their face value as they approach maturity. This implied price pattern is illustrated for the case of 20-year pure discount bonds in Figure 8.3.

Let us illustrate the calculation assuming the face value of the bond is $1,000 and the yield remains constant at 6% per year. Initially the bond has a maturity of 20 years and its price is:

n	i	PV	FV	PMT	Result
20	6%	?	1,000	0	PV = $311.80

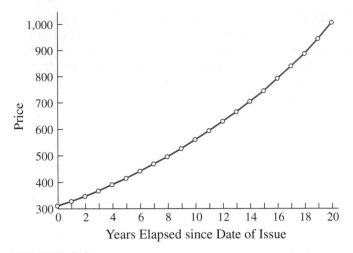

FIGURE 8.3   Movement of a Pure Discount Bond's Price over Time

Note: In the absence of changes in interest rates and with a flat term structure, the price of a zero-coupon bond might be expected to rise over time at a rate equal to its yield to maturity. In the figure, we assume a face value of $1,000 and a yield of 6% per year.

After one year goes by, the bond has a remaining maturity of 19 years and its price is:

n	i	PV	FV	PMT	Result
19	6%	?	1,000	0	PV = $330.51

The proportional change in price is, therefore, exactly equal to the 6% per year yield on the bond:

$$\text{Proportional Change in Price} = \frac{\$330.51 - \$311.80}{\$311.80} = 6\%$$

Quick Check 8-5
What will the pure discount bond's price be after two years, assuming the yield stays at 6% per year? Verify that the proportional change in price during the second year is 6%.

8.6.2 Interest-Rate Risk

Normally, we think of buying U.S. Treasury bonds as a conservative investment policy because there is no risk of default involved. However, an economic environment of changing interest rates can produce big gains or losses for investors in long-term bonds.

Figure 8.4 illustrates the sensitivity of long-term bond prices to interest rates. It shows the magnitude of the changes that would occur in the prices of 30-year pure

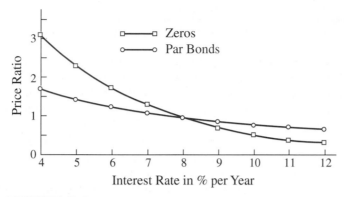

FIGURE 8.4   Sensitivity of Bond Price to Interest Rates

discount bonds and 30-year 8% coupon par bonds if the level of interest rates moved to a value different from 8% immediately after the bonds are purchased. Each curve in Figure 8.4 corresponds to a different bond. Along the ordinate we measure the ratio of the bond's price computed using the indicated interest rate to its price computed at a discount rate of 8%.

For example, at an interest rate of 8% per year, the price of a 30-year 8% coupon bond with a face value of $1,000 would be $1,000, whereas at an interest rate of 9% per year its price is $897.26. The ratio of its price at a 9% interest rate to its price at an 8% interest rate is, therefore, $897.26/1,000 = 0.89726$. We can, therefore, say that if the level of interest rates were to rise from 8% to 9%, the price of the par bond would fall by roughly 10%.

The figure shows the magnitude of the changes that would occur in the prices of 30-year pure discount bonds and 30-year 8% coupon par bonds if the level of interest rates moved to a value different from 8% immediately after the bonds are purchased. The ordinate measures the ratio of the bond's price computed at the indicated interest rate to its price computed at a discount rate of 8%. Thus, at an interest rate of 8%, the price ratios for both bonds are 1.

On the other hand, the price of a 30-year pure discount bond with a face value of $1,000 is $99.38 at an interest rate of 8% per year and $75.37 at an interest rate of 9%. The ratio of its price at a 9% interest rate to its price at an 8% interest rate is, therefore, $75.37/99.38 = 0.7684$. We can, therefore, say that if the level of interest rates were to rise from 8% to 9%, the price of the pure discount bond would fall by roughly 23%.

Note in Figure 8.4 that the curve corresponding to the pure discount bond is steeper than the par bond's curve. This greater steepness reflects its greater interest-rate sensitivity.

Quick Check 8-6

Suppose you buy a 30-year pure discount bond with a face value of $1,000 and a yield of 6% per year. A day later market interest rates rise to 7% and so does the yield on your bond. What is the proportional change in the price of your bond?

Summary

A change in market interest rates causes a change in the opposite direction in the market values of all existing contracts promising fixed payments in the future.

The market prices of $1 to be received at every possible date in the future are the basic building blocks for valuing all other streams of known cash flows. These prices are inferred from the observed market prices of traded bonds and then applied to other streams of known cash flows to value them.

An equivalent valuation can be carried out by applying a discounted cash flow formula with a different discount rate for each future time period.

Differences in the prices of fixed-income securities of a given maturity arise from differences in coupon rates, default risk, tax treatment, callability, convertibility, and other features.

Over time the prices of bonds converge toward their face value. Before maturity, however, bond prices can fluctuate a great deal as a result of changes in market interest rates.

Key Terms

- pure discount bonds   218
- face value   218
- coupon bond   220
- coupon rate   220
- par bonds   221

- premium bond   221
- current yield   221
- yield to maturity   221
- callable bond   227
- convertible bond   227

Answers to Quick Check Questions

Quick Check 8-1   *What happens to the value of the three-year fixed-income security promising $100 per year if the market interest rate falls from 6% to 5% per year?*

ANSWER: If the interest rate falls to 5% per year, the value of the fixed-income security rises to $272.32.

Quick Check 8-2   *Suppose the observed yield on two-year pure discount bonds falls to 6% per year, but the other rates reported in Table 8.1 remain unchanged. What is your estimate of the value of the three-year annuity paying $100 per year? What single discount rate applied to the present value formula for annuities would give this same value?*

ANSWER: The value of the three-year annuity would be:

Present Value of First Year's Cash Flow $= \$100/1.0526 = \$95.00$
Present Value of Second Year's Cash Flow $= \$100/1.06^2 = \$89.00$
Present Value of Third Year's Cash Flow $= \$100/1.0772^3 = \$80.00$
Total Present Value $= \$264$

So the value of the annuity increases by $1.
To find the single discount rate that makes the present value of the three promised payments equal to $264, we solve:

n	i	PV	FV	PMT	Result
3	?	−264	0	100	$i = 6.6745\%$

Quick Check 8-3   *What are the current yield and yield to maturity on a three-year bond with a coupon rate of 6% per year and a price of $900?*

ANSWER: The current yield is $\frac{60}{900} = 0.0667 = 6.67\%$
We find the yield-to-maturity as follows:

n	i	PV	FV	PMT	Result
3	?	−900	1,000	60	$i = 10.02\%$

Quick Check 8-4   *Using the same prices for pure discount bonds as in the previous example, what would be the price and yield to maturity on a two-year coupon bond with a coupon rate of 4% per year?*

ANSWER: For the 4% coupon bond the price would be:

$$0.961538 \times \$40 + 0.889996 \times \$1,040 = \$964.05736$$

and the yield to maturity:

n	i	PV	FV	PMT	Result
2	?	−964.057	1,000	50	$i = 5.9593\%$

Quick Check 8-5   *What will the pure discount bond's price be after two years, assuming the yield stays at 6% per year? Verify that the proportional change in price during the second year is 6%.*

ANSWER: After two years the bond has a remaining maturity of 18 years and its price is:

n	i	PV	FV	PMT	Result
18	6%	?	1,000	0	$PV = \$350.34$

The proportional change in price is, therefore, exactly equal to the 6% per year yield on the bond:

$$\text{Proportional Change in Price} = \frac{\$350.34 - \$330.51}{\$330.51} = 6\%$$

Quick Check 8-6   *Suppose you buy a 30-year pure discount bond with a face value of $1,000 and a yield of 6% per year. A day later market interest rates rise to 7% and so does the yield on your bond. What is the proportional change in the price of your bond?*

ANSWER: The 30-year pure discount bond's initial price is:

n	i	PV	FV	PMT	Result
30	6%	?	1,000	0	$PV = \$174.11$

A day later its price is:

n	i	PV	FV	PMT	Result
30	7%	?	1,000	0	$PV = \$131.37$

The proportional decline in price is 24.55%.

Questions and Problems

TEMPLATE

8.1–8.3

Bond Valuation with a Flat Term Structure

1. Suppose you want to know the price of a 10-year 7% coupon Treasury bond that pays interest *annually.*
   a. You have been told that the yield to maturity is 8%. What is the price?
   b. What is the price if coupons are paid *semiannually,* and the yield to maturity is 8% per year?
   c. Now you have been told that the yield to maturity is 7% per year. What is the price? Could you have guessed the answer without calculating it? What if coupons are paid semiannually?

2. Assume six months ago the U.S. Treasury yield curve was *flat* at a rate of 4% per year (with annual compounding) and you bought a 30-year U.S. Treasury bond. Today it is flat at a rate of 5% per year. What rate of return did you earn on your initial investment:
   a. If the bond was a 4% coupon bond?
   b. If the bond was a zero coupon bond?
   c. How do your answers change if compounding is semiannual?

Bond Valuation with a Non-Flat Term Structure

3. Suppose you observe the following prices for zero-coupon bonds (pure discount bonds) that have no risk of default:

Maturity	Price per $1 of Face Value	Yield to Maturity
1 year	0.97	3.093%
2 years	0.90	

   a. What should be the price of a two-year coupon bond that pays a 6% coupon rate, assuming coupon payments are made once a year starting one year from now?
   b. Find the missing entry in the table.
   c. What should be the yield to maturity of the two-year coupon bond in part a?
   d. Why are your answers to parts b and c of this question different?

Coupon Stripping

4. You would like to create a two-year synthetic zero-coupon bond. Assume you are aware of the following information: One-year zero-coupon bonds are trading for $0.93 per dollar of face value and two-year 7% coupon bonds (annual payments) are selling at $985.30 (face = $1,000).
   a. What are the two cash flows from the two-year coupon bond?
   b. Assume you can purchase the two-year coupon bond and unbundle the two cash flows and sell them.
      i. How much will you receive from the sale of the first payment?
      ii. How much do you need to receive from the sale of the two-year Treasury strip to break even?

The Law of One Price and Bond Pricing

5. Assume that all of the bonds listed in the following table are the same except for their pattern of promised cash flows over time. Prices are quoted per $1 of face value. Use the information in the table and the Law of One Price to infer the values of the missing entries. Assume that coupon payments are annual.

Coupon Rate	Maturity	Price	Yield to maturity
6%	2 years		5.5%
0	2 years		
7%	2 years		
0	1 year	$.95	

Bond Features and Bond Valuation

6. What effect would adding the following features have on the market price of a similar bond that does not have this feature?

a. 10-year bond is *callable* by the company after five years (compare to a 10-year *noncallable* bond);

b. bond is *convertible* into 10 shares of common stock at any time (compare to a *noncovertible* bond);

c. 10-year bond can be "put back" (i.e., sold back) to the company after three years at par (compare to a 10-year *nonputtable bond)*;

d. 25-year bond has tax-exempt coupon payments.

Inferring the Value of a Bond Guarantee

7. Suppose that the yield curve on dollar bonds that are free of the risk of default is flat at 6% per year. A two-year 10% coupon bond (with annual coupons and $1,000 face value) issued by Dafalto Corporation is rated B, and it is currently trading at a market price of $918. Aside from its risk of default, the Dafalto bond has no other financially significant features. How much should an investor be willing to pay for a guarantee against Dafalto's defaulting on this bond?

The Implied Value of a Call Provision and Convertibility

8. Suppose that the yield curve on bonds that are free of the risk of default is flat at 5% per year. A 20-year default-free coupon bond (with annual coupons and $1,000 face value) that becomes callable after 10 years is trading at par and has a coupon rate of 5.5%

a. What is the implied value of the call provision?

b. A Safeco Corporation bond, which is otherwise identical to the callable 5.5% coupon bond just described, is also convertible into 10 shares of Safeco stock at any time up to the bond's maturity. If its yield to maturity is currently 3.5% per year, what is the implied value of the conversion feature?

Changes in Interest Rates and Bond Prices

9. All else being equal, if interest rates rise along the entire yield curve, you should expect that:

i. Bond prices will fall.

ii. Bond prices will rise.

iii. Prices on long-term bonds will fall more than prices on short-term bonds.

iv. Prices on long-term bonds will rise more than prices on short-term bonds.

a. ii and iv are correct.

b. We can't be certain that prices will change.

c. Only i is correct.

d. Only ii is correct.

e. i and iii are correct.

CHAPTER

9

Valuation of Common Stocks

OBJECTIVES

- To explain the theory and application of the discounted cash flow valuation method as applied to the equity of a firm.
- To explain how a firm's dividend policy can affect shareholder wealth.

CONTENTS

Chapter 8 shows how the Law of One Price can be used to deduce the value of known cash flows from the observed market prices of bonds. In this chapter we consider the valuation of uncertain cash flows using a *discounted cash flow (DCF)* approach. The method is applied to the valuation of common stock.

9.1 READING STOCK LISTINGS

Table 9.1 shows the newspaper listing for IBM stock, which is traded on the New York Stock Exchange.

The first two columns in the listing provide the highest and lowest prices at which the stock has traded in the last 52 weeks. The next two columns give the name of the stock and its symbol. The next figure is the dividend payout. The 4.84 means that the firm paid shareholders an annualized cash dividend in the last quarter of $4.84 per share (i.e., the actual quarterly dividend was $1.21).

TABLE 9.1 New York Stock Exchange Listing

52 Weeks											
Hi	Lo	Stock	Sym	Div	Yld%	PE	Vol 100s	Hi	Lo	Close	Net Chg
$123\frac{1}{8}$	$93\frac{3}{8}$	IBM	IBM	4.84	4.2	16	14591	115	113	$114\frac{3}{4}$	$+1\frac{3}{8}$

Next is the **dividend yield,** defined as the annualized dollar dividend divided by the stock's price, expressed as a percentage. Next is the **price/earnings ratio,** the ratio of the current stock price to earnings during the most recent four quarters.

The volume column shows how many shares were traded on the exchange on that trading day. Shares are usually traded in *round lots* of 100 shares. Investors who want to trade in smaller quantities called *odd lots* generally must pay higher commissions to their stockbrokers. The last four columns of Table 9.1 show the day's high, low, and closing stock prices and the change from the previous closing price.

9.2 THE DISCOUNTED DIVIDEND MODEL

E-BOOK

9.2

The *DCF* approach to determining the value of a stock discounts the expected cash flows—either dividends paid to shareholders or net cash flows from operations of the firm. A **discounted-dividend model** (*DDM*) is defined as any model that computes the value of a share of stock as the present value of its expected future cash dividends.

Any *DDM* starts from the observation that an investor in common stock expects a return consisting of cash dividends and the change in price. For example, assume a one-year holding period, and suppose that ABC stock has an expected dividend per share, D_1, of \$5, and the expected *ex-dividend* price at the end of the year, P_1, is \$110.[1]

The **risk-adjusted discount rate** or **market capitalization rate** is the expected rate of return that investors require in order to be willing to invest in the stock. How this rate is determined is explained in chapter 13. In this chapter we take it as given and denote it by k. In the current example, suppose that it is 15% per year.

The rate of return that investors *expect*, $E(r_1)$, is D_1 plus the expected price appreciation, $P_1 - P_0$, all divided by the current price P_0. Setting this expected rate of return equal to the 15% required rate of return, we get

$$E(r_1) = \frac{D_1 + P_1 - P_0}{P_0} = k$$

$$0.15 = \frac{5 + 110 - P_0}{P_0}$$

(9.1)

Equation 9.1 embodies the most important feature of the *DDM:* that the expected rate of return during *any* period equals the market capitalization rate, k. From this equation, we can derive the formula for the current stock price in terms of the expected end-of-year price:

$$P_0 = \frac{D_1 + P_1}{1 + k}$$

(9.2)

---

[1]The *ex-dividend* price is the price of the stock without the right to receive a recently declared dividend.

In other words, the price is the present value of the expected end-of-year dividend plus the expected ex-dividend price discounted at the required rate of return. In the case of ABC, we find:

$$P_0 = \frac{\$5 + \$110}{1.15} = \$100$$

The model to this point relies on an estimate of the end-of-year price, P_1. But how can investors forecast this price? Using the same logic employed to derive P_0, the expected price of ABC stock at the beginning of the second year is:

$$P_1 = \frac{D_2 + P_2}{1 + k} \tag{9.3}$$

By substitution, we can express P_0 in terms of D_1, D_2, and P_2:

$$P_0 = \frac{D_1 + P_1}{1 + k} = \frac{D_1 + \dfrac{D_2 + P_2}{(1 + k)}}{1 + k}$$
$$P_0 = \frac{D_1}{1 + k} + \frac{D_2 P_2}{(1 + k)^2} \tag{9.4}$$

By repeating this chain of substitutions, we get the general formula of the *DDM:*

$$P_0 = \frac{D_1}{(1 + k)} + \frac{D_2}{(1 + k)^2} + \cdots = \sum_{t=1}^{\infty} \frac{D_t}{(1 + k)^t} \tag{9.5}$$

In other words, the price of a share of stock is the present value of all expected future dividends per share, discounted at the market capitalization rate.

Note that despite what seems like its exclusive focus on dividends, the discounted dividend model is not in conflict with the notion that investors look at both dividends and expected future prices when they evaluate a stock. On the contrary, we have just seen that the *DDM* is derived from that assumption.

9.2.1 The Constant-Growth-Rate, Discounted Dividend Model

Because in the general form expressed by equation 9.5 the *DDM* requires forecasts of an *infinite* number of future dividends, it is not very practical. But by making some simplifying assumptions about future dividends, the *DDM* can be made into a practical tool.

The most basic assumption is that dividends will grow at a constant rate g. For example, suppose that Steadygrowth Corporation's dividends per share are expected to grow at a constant rate of 10% per year.

The expected stream of future dividends is:

D_1	D_2	D_3	etc.
$5	$5.50	$6.05	etc.

Substituting the dividend growth forecasts, $D_t = D_1(1 + g)^{t-1}$, into equation 9.5 and simplifying, we find that the present value of a perpetual stream of dividends growing at a constant rate, g, is

$$P_0 = \frac{D_1}{k - g} \tag{9.6}$$

With Steadygrowth's data, this formula implies that the price of the stock is:

$$P_0 = \frac{5}{0.15 - 0.10} = \frac{5}{0.05} = \$100$$

Let us explore some implications of the constant-growth-rate *DDM*. First, note that if the expected growth rate is zero, then the valuation formula reduces to the formula for the present value of a level perpetuity: $P_0 = D_1/k$.

Holding constant D_1 and k, the higher the value of g, the higher the price of the stock. But as g approaches k in value, the model starts to "explode"; that is, the price of the stock tends to infinity. Thus, the model is valid only if the expected growth rate of dividends is less than the market capitalization rate, k. In section 9.3 we consider how analysts adjust the discounted-dividend valuation model to deal with firms that have growth rates that are greater than k.

Note that another implication of the constant growth rate *DDM* is that the stock price is expected to grow at the same rate as dividends. For example, consider Table 9.2, which shows the expected dividends and expected future prices for Steadygrowth over the next three years.

To see why this is so, let us write down the formula for next year's price:

$$P_1 = \frac{D_2}{k - g}$$

Because $D_2 = D_1(1 + g)$, we get by substitution:

$$P_1 = \frac{D_1(1 + g)}{k - g} = P_0(1 + g)$$

and the expected proportional change in price is:

$$\frac{P_1 - P_0}{P_0} = \frac{P_0(1 + g) - P_0}{P_0} = g$$

TABLE 9.2   Steadygrowth's Future Dividends and Price

Year	Price at Beginning of Year	Expected Dividend	Expected Dividend Yield	Expected Rate of Price Increase
1	$100	$5.00	5%	10%
2	$110	$5.50	5%	10%
3	$121	$6.05	5%	10%

Therefore, *the DDM implies that in the case of constant growth of dividends, the rate of price appreciation in any year will equal the constant growth rate, g.* In the case of Steadygrowth, the expected rate of return of 15% per year, therefore, consists of an expected dividend yield of 5% per year and a rate of price appreciation of 10% per year.

Quick Check 9-1
XYZ stock is expected to pay a dividend of $2 per share a year from now, and its dividends are expected to grow by 6% per year thereafter. If its price is now $20 per share, what must be the market capitalization rate?

9.3 EARNINGS AND INVESTMENT OPPORTUNITIES

A second approach to *DCF* valuation focuses on future earnings and investment opportunities. Focusing on earnings and investment opportunities rather than dividends helps to concentrate the analyst's attention on the core business determinants of value. A firm's dividend policy is not such a core determinant. To see this, consider an investor planning to take over the firm. Takeover investors are not concerned with the pattern of future dividends because they can choose any pattern they wish.

Assuming that no new shares of stock are issued, the relation between earnings and dividends in any period is:[2]

$$\text{Dividends}_t = \text{Earnings}_t - \text{Net New Investment}_t$$

Therefore, we get as a formula for the value of the stock:

$$P_0 = \sum_{t=1}^{\infty} \frac{D_t}{(1+k)^t} = \sum_{t=1}^{\infty} \frac{E_t}{(1+k)^t} - \sum_{t=1}^{\infty} \frac{I_t}{(1+k)^t} \qquad (9.7)$$

where E_t is earnings in year t and I_t is net investment in year t.

An important point to recognize from this equation is that the value of a firm is not equal to the present value of its expected future earnings. Instead, the firm's value equals the present value of expected future earnings *less* the present value of the earnings reinvested in the firm. Note that computing the value of the firm as the present value of expected future earnings may either overstate or understate the correct market value because net new investment can be either negative or positive.

In a *declining* industry, one might expect to find that gross investment may not be as large as required for full replacement of current capital: net investment is negative and, hence, capacity would decline over time. In a *stable* or stagnant industry, gross investment typically just matches replacement requirements: Net investment is zero, and capacity remains about constant over time. In an *expanding* industry, gross investment would probably exceed replacement requirements, net investment is positive, and capacity increases over time.

---

[2]The issuance of new shares complicates the analysis but does not change the basic result.

A useful way to estimate a firm's value based on earnings and investment opportunities is to partition the firm's value into two parts: (1) the present value of the current level of earnings projected into the future as a perpetuity, and (2) the net present value of any future investment opportunities (i.e., new earnings generated less the new investments necessary to generate them). We can express this as:

$$P_0 = \frac{E_1}{k} + \text{Net Present Value of Future Investment Opportunities}$$

For example, consider a firm called Nogrowth Corporation, whose earnings per share are \$15. The firm invests an amount each year that is just sufficient to replace the production capacity that is wearing out, and so its net investment each year is zero. Thus, it pays all of its earnings out as dividends, and there is no growth.

Assuming that the capitalization rate is 15% per year, Nogrowth's stock price would be \$100:

$$P_0 = \$15/0.15 = \$100$$

Now consider Growthstock Corporation. Growthstock initially has the same earnings as Nogrowth, but it reinvests 60% of its earnings each year into new investments that yield a rate of return of 20% per year (i.e., 5% per year higher than the market capitalization rate of 15% per year). As a consequence, Growthstock's dividends per share are initially lower than Nogrowth's. Instead of paying out \$15 per share in dividends like Nogrowth, Growthstock will pay out only 40% of \$15, or \$6 per share. The other \$9 per share are reinvested in the firm to earn a rate of return of 20% per year.

Although Growthstock's dividend per share is initially lower than Nogrowth's, Growthstock's dividends will grow over time. Growthstock's share price is higher than Nogrowth's. To see why, let us compute what its growth rate of dividends will be and then apply the discounted dividend model.

The formula for the growth rate of dividends and earnings per share is:[3]

$$g = \text{Earnings Retention Rate} \times \text{Rate of Return on New Investments}$$

For Growthstock we get:

$$g = 0.6 \times 0.2 = 0.12, \text{ or } 12\% \text{ per Year}$$

Using the constant growth formula to estimate Growthstock's stock price, we have:

$$P_0 = \frac{6}{0.15 - 0.12} = \frac{6}{0.03} = \$200$$

---

[3]Proof: By definition, the expected growth rate of earnings is equal to the change in earnings divided by current earnings:

$$g = \frac{\Delta E}{E}$$

By multiplying both numerator and denominator by net investment (I), we find:

$$g = \frac{I}{E} \times \frac{\Delta E}{I}$$

Now note that the first term on the right-hand side is the earnings retention rate and that the second is the rate of return on net new investment.

The net present value of Growthstock's future investments is the $100 difference in price between its shares and Nogrowth's shares:

$$NPV \text{ of Future Investments} = \$200 - \$100 = \$100$$

It is important to realize that the reason that Growthstock has a higher share price than Nogrowth is not growth per se, but rather the fact that its reinvested earnings yield a rate of return in excess of the market capitalization rate—20% per year versus 15% per year. To emphasize this point, let us consider what would happen if the rate of return on future investments were only 15% per year instead of 20% per year. To distinguish this case from the case of Growthstock, we will call the firm with the lower rate of return Normalprofit.

Normalprofit's rate of return on future investments is 15% per year and it reinvests 60% of its earnings each year. Its growth rate of earnings and dividends is, therefore, 9% per year:

$$g = \text{Earnings Retention Rate} \times \text{Rate of Return on New Investments}$$
$$g = 0.6 \times 0.15 = 0.09, \text{ or 9\% per Year}$$

Applying the constant-growth *DDM* formula, we find Normalprofit's share price to be:

$$P_0 = \frac{6}{0.15 - 0.09} = \frac{6}{0.06} = \$100$$

Normalprofit has the same current share price as Nogrowth, even though Normalprofit's dividend per share is expected to grow at 9% per year. This is because Normalprofit's higher growth rate exactly offsets its lower initial dividend. Table 9.3

TABLE 9.3 Comparison of Nogrowth and Normalprofit

a. Nogrowth

Year	Price at Beginning of Year	Expected Earnings	Expected Dividend	Expected Dividend Yield	Expected Rate of Price Increase
1	$100.00	$15.00	$15.00	15%	0%
2	$100.00	$15.00	$15.00	15%	0%
3	$100.00	$15.00	$15.00	15%	0%

b. Normalprofit

Year	Price at Beginning of Year	Expected Earnings	Expected Dividend	Expected Dividend Yield	Expected Rate of Price Increase
1	$100.00	$15.00	$6.00	6%	9%
2	$109.00	$16.35	$6.54	6%	9%
3	$118.81	$17.82	$7.13	6%	9%

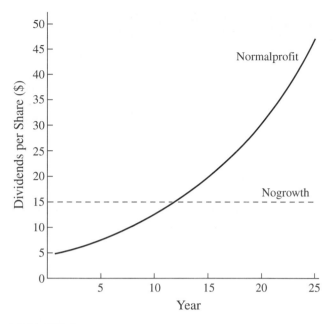

FIGURE 9.1   Dividend Growth for Two Different Earnings Reinvestment Policies

and Figure 9.1 compare the expected earnings and dividends for Nogrowth and Normalprofit for the next few years.

Nogrowth and Normalprofit have the same current stock price, which is equal to the present value of expected earnings per share in the next year:

$$P_0 = E_1/k = \$15/0.15 = \$100.$$

Thus, even though the earnings per share, dividends per share, and the price of Normalprofit stock are expected to grow at 9% per year, this growth does not add any value to the firm's current stock price beyond what it would be if all of its earnings are paid as dividends. The reason is that the rate of return on Normalprofit's reinvested earnings is equal to the market capitalization rate.

To summarize the main point of this section: Growth per se does not add value. What adds value is the opportunity to invest in projects that can earn rates of return in excess of the required rate, k. When a firm's future investment opportunities yield a rate of return equal to k, the stock's value can be estimated using the formula $P_0 = E_1/k$.

Quick Check 9-2

An analyst uses the constant growth *DDM* to evaluate QRS stock. She assumes expected earnings of $10 per share, an earnings retention rate of 75%, an expected rate of return on future investments of 18% per year, and a market capitalization rate of 15% per year. What is her estimate of QRS's price? What is the implied net present value of future investments?

9.4 A RECONSIDERATION OF THE PRICE/EARNINGS MULTIPLE APPROACH

In chapter 7, we briefly discussed the price/earnings multiple approach to valuing a firm's stock. We said that a widely used approach for quickly estimating the value of a share of a firm's stock is to take its projected earnings per share and to multiply it by an appropriate price/earnings (*P/E*) multiple derived from other comparable firms. We can now gain some further insight into that approach by using the discounted cash flow model discussed in the previous section.

As we have seen, one can write the formula for a firm's stock price as:

$$P_0 = E_1/k + \ NPV \text{ of Future Investments}$$

Firms with consistently high *P/E* multiples are, therefore, interpreted to have either relatively low market capitalization rates or relatively high present value of value-added investments, that is, opportunities to earn rates of return on future investments that exceed their market capitalization rates.

Stocks that have relatively high *P/E* ratios because their future investments are expected to earn rates of return in excess of the market capitalization rate are called **growth stocks.**

Some observers of the stock market say that the reason growth stocks have high *P/E* ratios is that their earnings per share are expected to grow. But that is a misleading statement. As we saw in section 9.3, Normalprofit had an expected growth rate of 9% per year, yet it is priced with the same *P/E* ratio as Nogrowth, which was not expected to grow at all. It is not growth per se that produces a high *P/E* ratio, but rather the presence of future investment opportunities that are expected to yield a rate of return greater than the market's required risk-adjusted rate, *k*.

For example, suppose that you are trying to value the common stock of Digital Biomed Corporation, a hypothetical firm in the pharmaceutical industry that applies biotechnology to the discovery of new drugs. The average price/earnings multiple in the pharmaceutical industry is 15. Digital Biomed's expected earnings per share are $2. If you apply the industry average multiple, the resultant value for Digital Biomed stock is $30. However, suppose that the actual price at which Digital Biomed stock is trading in the stock market is $100 per share. How can you account for the difference?

The $70 difference ($100 − $30) may reflect the beliefs of investors that Digital Biomed will have much better future investment opportunities than the average for the pharmaceutical industry.

P/E ratios tend to vary over time. As new information arrives in the market, investor expectations of earnings change. Relatively small changes in expected growth rates of earnings or capitalization rates can result in large changes in *P/E* ratios. This is true for individual stocks and for the stock market as a whole.

9.5 DOES DIVIDEND POLICY AFFECT SHAREHOLDER WEALTH?

Dividend policy means a corporation's policy regarding paying out cash to its shareholders *holding constant its investment and borrowing decisions.* In a "frictionless" financial environment, in which there are no taxes and no transaction costs, the wealth of shareholders is the same no matter what dividend policy the firm adopts. In the real world, there are a number of frictions that can cause dividend policy to have an effect on the wealth of shareholders. These include taxes, regulations, the costs of external finance, and the informational or "signaling" content of dividends.

9.5.1 Cash Dividends and Share Repurchases

There are two ways a corporation can distribute cash to its shareholders: by paying a **cash dividend** or by repurchasing the company's shares in the stock market. When a company pays a cash dividend, all shareholders receive cash in amounts proportional to the number of shares they own. Let us assume that when cash is distributed through a cash dividend, all else the same, the share price declines immediately after payment by the amount of the dividend.

In a **share repurchase,** the company pays cash to buy shares of its stock in the stock market, thereby reducing the number of shares outstanding.[4] Therefore, only those shareholders who *choose* to sell some of their shares will receive cash. Let us assume that when cash is distributed through a share repurchase, *all else the same,* the share price remains unchanged.

For example, Cashrich Corporation has total assets with a market value of $12 million: $2 million in cash, and $10 million in other assets. The market value of its debt is $2 million and of its equity $10 million. There are 500,000 shares of Cashrich common stock outstanding, each with a market price of $20.

Table 9.4 illustrates the different effects of Cashrich Corporation's paying out cash to its shareholders through a cash dividend and a share repurchase. If Cashrich distributes a cash dividend of $2 per share, the market value of its assets declines by $1 million, and its equity declines by $1 million to $9 million.

Because there are still 500,000 shares outstanding, the market price of each share declines by $2. If, instead, Cashrich repurchases shares worth $1 million, it will retire 50,000 shares, leaving 450,000 shares with a price per share of $20.

Under the assumptions used in constructing Table 9.4, the wealth of shareholders is unaffected by the choice of method Cashrich uses to pay out the $1 million. In the case of a cash dividend of $2 per share, all shareholders receive cash in proportion to the number of shares they own, and the market value of their shares declines by $2 per share, ex-dividend. In the case of a share repurchase, only those shareholders who choose to sell shares receive cash, and the others experience no change in the market value of their shares.

> **Quick Check 9-3**
> Compare the effects of Cashrich's paying $1.5 million in cash dividends versus repurchasing shares for $1.5 million.

---

[4]The corporation keeps the shares that it has repurchased as treasury stock and can decide to resell them to raise cash at a future date.

TABLE 9.4   Cash Dividends and Share Repurchase for Cashrich, Inc.

a. Original Balance Sheet

	Assets		Liabilities and Shareholders' Equity
Cash	$ 2 million	Debt	$ 2 million
Other assets	$10 million	Equity	$10 million
Total	$12 million	Total	$12 million

Number of shares outstanding = 500,000

Price per share = $20

b. Balance Sheet after Payment of Cash Dividend

	Assets		Liabilities and Shareholders' Equity
Cash	$ 1 million	Debt	$ 2 million
Other assets	$10 million	Equity	$ 9 million
Total	$11 million	Total	$11 million

Number of shares outstanding = 500,000

Price per share = $18

c. Balance Sheet after Share Repurchase

	Assets		Liabilities and Shareholders' Equity
Cash	$ 1 million	Debt	$ 2 million
Other assets	$10 million	Equity	$ 9 million
Total	$11 million	Total	$11 million

Number of shares outstanding = 450,000

Price per share = $20

9.5.2 Stock Dividends

Corporations sometimes declare *stock splits* and distribute *stock dividends*. These activities do not distribute cash to shareholders; they increase the number of shares of stock outstanding.

For example, suppose that Cashrich's management declares a two-for-one stock split. This means that each old share will now be counted as two shares. The total number of Cashrich shares outstanding will increase from 500,000 to 1 million. Under the assumption that shareholder wealth is unaffected by this management action, the market price of a share will immediately drop from $20 to $10.

In the case of a stock dividend, the corporation distributes additional shares of stock to each stockholder. Payment of a stock dividend can be seen as distributing a cash dividend to existing shareholders, and then requiring them to immediately use the cash to buy additional shares of the company's stock. The company does not pay out any cash to shareholders, and there are no tax effects.

Let us return to the example of Cashrich Corporation to clarify the different effects of paying a cash dividend and a stock dividend. Suppose that Cashrich normally would pay out a cash dividend of $2 per share, but management thinks the company has extraordinary investment opportunities and decides to keep the $1 million in cash that it would otherwise pay out in cash dividends. Instead of the cash dividend, management, therefore, decides to pay a 10% stock dividend. This means that shareholders will receive one new share for every 10 old shares they own, and the company keeps the $1 million in cash that would have been paid in cash dividends.

Table 9.5 illustrates and compares the effects of the payment of cash dividends and stock dividends on the assumption that shareholder wealth is unaffected by either. First compare Panel A with Panel C. Panel C of Table 9.5 shows Cashrich's market value balance sheet after the stock dividend is paid. The totals for assets, liabilities, and shareholders' equity are identical to Panel A, which shows Cashrich's market value balance sheet before the stock dividend is paid. The only difference between the two is that in Panel C, the number of shares has increased to 550,000 and, therefore, the price per share drops to $18.18.

TABLE 9.5   Cash Dividends versus Stock Dividends for Cashrich, Inc.

a. Original Balance Sheet

Assets		Liabilities and Shareholders' Equity	
Cash	$ 2 million	Debt	$ 2 million
Other assets	$10 million	Equity	$10 million
Total	$12 million	Total	$12 million

Number of shares outstanding = 500,000

Price per share = $20

b. Balance Sheet after Payment of Cash Dividend

Assets		Liabilities and Shareholders' Equity	
Cash	$ 1 million	Debt	$ 2 million
Other assets	$10 million	Equity	$ 9 million
Total	$11 million	Total	$11 million

Number of shares outstanding = 500,000

Price per share = $18

c. Balance Sheet after Stock Dividend

Assets		Liabilities and Shareholders' Equity	
Cash	$ 2 million	Debt	$ 2 million
Other assets	$10 million	Equity	$10 million
Total	$12 million	Total	$12 million

Number of shares outstanding = 550,000

Price per share = $18.18

> **Quick Check 9-4**
> What would be the effect of Cashrich's paying a 20% stock dividend?

9.5.3 Dividend Policy in a Frictionless Environment

We have assumed that the payment of cash to shareholders by means of a cash dividend or a share repurchase has no effect on the wealth of shareholders. Is this a valid assumption? Or is there possibly a way for a corporation to use dividend policy to increase shareholder wealth?

In 1961, Modigliani and Miller (M&M) presented an argument to prove that in a "frictionless" financial environment, in which there are no taxes and no costs of issuing new shares of stock or repurchasing existing shares, a firm's dividend policy can have no effect on the wealth of its current shareholders.[5] The essence of the M&M argument is that shareholders can achieve the effect of any corporate dividend policy by costlessly reinvesting dividends or selling shares of stock on their own.

Let us illustrate the M&M argument for the case of Cashrich Corporation. First, suppose that Cashrich's managers decide *not* to pay out the $2 million in cash, but rather to invest it in a project that leaves the total market value of the firm unchanged. Suppose a shareholder who owns 100 shares of Cashrich stock would have preferred a cash dividend of $2 per share. The shareholder can simply sell 10 shares of stock at the current market price of $20. He winds up with Cashrich stock worth $1,800 and cash of $200—exactly the same result as if the company had paid a dividend of $2 per share.

But the reverse situation is also possible. Suppose Cashrich pays out a cash dividend of $2 per share, and a shareholder who owns 100 shares of Cashrich stock does not want the cash. After the payment of the dividend, she has $200 in cash and $1,800 in stock. She can easily reestablish her original position by using the $200 in cash she received to buy more shares of the stock at the new price of $18 per share.

What about the case where the firm has to raise cash to finance a new investment project that has a positive *NPV*? Surely in that case one might think that the firm's managers can increase shareholder wealth by cutting the cash dividend and reinvesting the money in the firm. But M&M argue that in a frictionless financial environment, the price of the stock will reflect the *NPV* of the project. Therefore, it will not make any difference to the wealth of the firm's existing shareholders whether the firm finances the new investment project by cutting dividends (internal equity financing) or by issuing new stock (external equity financing).

To understand the M&M argument, let us consider a specific example. Consider Cashpoor Corporation, which currently has assets consisting of cash of $0.5 million, plant and equipment worth $1 million, and debt with a market value of $1 million. Suppose that Cashpoor has an investment opportunity requiring an immediate outlay of $0.5 million on additional plant and equipment, and the project's *NPV* is $1.5 million. There are 1 million shares of Cashpoor common stock outstanding. The market price per share is $2, and it reflects the information that Cash-

---

[5]Franco Modigliani and Merton Miller, "Dividend Policy, Growth and the Valuation of Shares," *Journal of Business* (October 1961), pp. 411–33.

TABLE 9.6 Cashpoor Corporation Market Value Balance Sheet

Assets		Liabilities and Shareholders' Equity	
Cash	$0.5 million	Debt	$1 million
Plant and equipment	$1.0 million		
NPV of new investment project	$1.5 million	Equity	$2 million
Total	$3.0 million	Total	$3 million

Number of shares outstanding = 1 million

Price per share = $2

poor has an investment opportunity with an *NPV* of $1.5 million. Table 9.6 shows Cashpoor's market value balance sheet before making the investment.

Cashpoor could use its $0.5 million in cash to finance the new project internally, or it could pay out the $0.5 million as a cash dividend to shareholders and finance the new investment by issuing new shares. In a frictionless financial environment, the same information is costlessly available to all investors, and the cost of issuing new shares is negligible. Therefore, in such an idealized world, the wealth of existing shareholders will be unaffected by the dividend policy decision.

If Cashpoor uses its $0.5 million in cash to finance the investment, then the balance sheet will reflect this by a $0.5 million reduction in the firm's cash account and an increase of $0.5 million in plant and equipment. There will be 1 million shares outstanding, each with a price of $2.

What happens if Cashpoor pays the $0.5 million in cash to shareholders as a cash dividend ($0.50 per share) and issues new stock to finance the purchase of plant and equipment? According to M&M, the price of a share will decline by the amount of the cash dividend paid (i.e., from $2 to $1.50 per share). The wealth of old shareholders is still $2 million—the $0.5 million they receive in cash dividends and the $1.5 million in the market value of their shares. Cashpoor will have to issue 333,333 new shares ($500,000/$1.50 per share = 333,333 shares) to raise the $0.5 million needed for the new plant and equipment.

Quick Check 9-5
What would happen under the M&M assumptions if a cash dividend of $0.25 million is paid to Cashpoor's current shareholders, and the remaining $0.25 million for the new investment is raised by issuing new stock?

9.5.4 Dividend Policy in the Real World

We have seen that in a hypothetical, frictionless financial environment, dividend policy does not matter from a shareholder-wealth perspective. In the real world, however, there are a number of frictions that can cause dividend policy to have an effect on the wealth of shareholders. In this section we consider the most important ones: taxes, regulations, the costs of external finance, and the informational content of dividends.

In the United States and many other countries, the tax authorities require shareholders to pay personal income taxes on cash dividends. Thus, if a corporation distributes cash by paying dividends, it forces all of its shareholders to pay taxes. If instead the firm distributes the cash by repurchasing shares, it does not create a tax liability for all of its shareholders. From a shareholder tax perspective it is, therefore, always better for the corporation to pay out cash by repurchasing shares.

However, in the United States, there are laws that prevent corporations from using share repurchase as an alternative to dividends as a regular mechanism for paying cash to shareholders. The authorities take the view that taxes ought to be paid on these distributions of cash. Indeed, there are also laws that prevent corporations from retaining cash in the business that is not needed to run the business. The tax authorities view such retentions as ways of avoiding the payment of personal taxes on dividends.

Another factor favoring the nonpayment of cash to shareholders, either in the form of dividends or repurchase of shares, is the cost of raising funds externally. The investment bankers who intermediate the sale of new shares to outside investors have to be paid, and it is the firm's current shareholders who bear that cost.

Another cost arises from differences in information that is available to the firm's management (insiders) and the potential buyers of new stock issued by the firm (outsiders). The outsiders may be skeptical about the reasons for issuing new stock and worry that the insiders know something negative about the firm. They will, therefore, have to be offered a bargain price to induce them to buy new shares. Thus, internal equity financing is likely to be more wealth enhancing for the firm's existing shareholders than issuing new shares to outsiders.

Another potentially important real-world factor influencing a firm's dividend policy is the informational content of dividends. Outside investors may interpret an increase in a corporation's cash dividend as a positive sign and, therefore, a dividend increase might cause a rise in the stock's price. Conversely, a decrease in the cash dividend might be interpreted as a bad sign and cause a decline in the stock price. Because of this informational impact, corporate management is cautious about making changes in dividend payouts and usually offers an explanation to the investing public whenever such changes are made.

Quick Check 9-6

Why do tax considerations and the cost of issuing new stock favor the nonpayment of cash dividends?

Summary

The discounted cash flow (*DCF*) method of valuing assets consists of discounting expected future cash flows at a risk-adjusted discount rate.

The discounted dividend model (*DDM*) for valuing shares of stock starts from the observation that an investor in common stock expects a rate of return (consisting of cash dividends and price appreciation) that is equal to the market capitalization rate. The resulting formula shows that the current price of a share is the present value of all expected future dividends.

In the constant growth rate *DDM,* the growth rate of dividends is also the expected rate of price appreciation.

Growth per se does not add value to a share's current price. What adds value is the opportunity to invest in projects that yield a rate of return in excess of the market capitalization rate.

In a frictionless financial environment, in which there are no taxes and no transaction costs, the wealth of shareholders is the same no matter what dividend policy the firm adopts.

In the real world there are a number of frictions that can cause dividend policy to have an effect on the wealth of shareholders. These include taxes, regulations, the costs of external finance, and the informational content of dividends.

Summary of Formulas

The price of a share of stock is the present value of all expected future dividends discounted at the market capitalization rate:

$$P_0 = \frac{D_1}{(1+k)} + \frac{D_2}{(1+k)^2} + \cdots = \sum_{t=1}^{\infty} \frac{D_t}{(1+k)^t}$$

The price of a share of stock in terms of earnings and investments is:

$$P_0 = \sum_{t=1}^{\infty} \frac{D_t}{(1+k)^t} = \sum_{t=1}^{\infty} \frac{E_t}{(1+k)^t} - \sum_{t=1}^{\infty} \frac{I_t}{(1+k)^t}$$

where E_t is earnings in year t and I_t is net investment in year t.

The present value of a perpetual stream of dividends growing at a constant rate, g, is:

$$P_0 = \frac{D_1}{k - g}$$

The formula for the growth rate of dividends and earnings per share is:

$$g = \text{Earnings Retention Rate} \times \text{Rate of Return on New Investments}$$

We can express the value of a share of stock as:

$$P_0 = E_1/k + \text{Net Present Value of Future Investments}$$

Key Terms

- dividend yield   235
- price/earnings ratio   235
- discounted dividend model   235
- risk-adjusted discount rate   235
- market capitalization rate   235

- growth stocks   242
- dividend policy   242
- cash dividend   243
- share repurchase   243

Answers to Quick Check Questions

Quick Check 9-1   *XYZ stock is expected to pay a dividend of $2 per share a year from now, and its dividends are expected to grow by 6% per year thereafter. If its price is now $20 per share, what must be the market capitalization rate?*

ANSWER: Use the constant growth formula $P_0 = D_1/(k - g)$ to solve for k.

$$k = D_1/P_0 + g = 2/20 + 0.06 = 0.16 \text{ or } 16\%$$

Quick Check 9-2   *An analyst uses the constant-growth DDM to evaluate QRS stock. She assumes expected earnings of $10 per share, an earnings retention rate of 75%, an expected rate of return on future investments of 18% per year, and a market capitalization rate of 15% per year. What is her estimate of QRS's price? What is the implied net present value of future investments?*

ANSWER: Use the constant-growth formula $P_0 = D_1/(k - g)$.

$$P_0 = \$2.50/(0.15 - 0.135) = \$166.67$$

Next apply the formula $P_0 = E_1/k = \$10/0.15 = \$66.67$.
   The *NPV* of future investments is the difference between the two values:

$$\$166.67 - \$66.67 = \$100.00$$

Quick Check 9-3   *Compare the effects of Cashrich's paying $1.5 million in cash dividends versus repurchasing shares for $1.5 million.*

ANSWER: In the case of a cash dividend the share price will decline by the amount of the $3 dividend per share—from $20 to $17. In the case of the share repurchase, the price of a share will remain $20 but the number of shares outstanding will fall by 75,000 to 425,000.

Quick Check 9-4   *What would be the effect of Cashrich's paying a 20% stock dividend?*

ANSWER: The number of shares outstanding would increase to 600,000, and the price per share would fall to $16.67.

Quick Check 9-5   *What would happen under the M&M assumptions if a cash dividend of $0.25 million is paid to Cashpoor's current shareholders, and the remaining $0.25 million for the new investment is raised by issuing new stock?*

ANSWER: The stock price will fall by $0.25 per share to $1.75, and the number of new shares issued would be 142,857 ($250,000/$1.75 per share). The wealth of current shareholders is not affected.

Quick Check 9-6   *Why do tax considerations and the cost of issuing new stock favor the nonpayment of cash dividends?*

ANSWER: Payment of cash dividends may cause some shareholders to have to pay income taxes that they could avoid if cash dividends are not paid. Raising cash by issuing new stock is more costly to the corporation than raising cash by forgoing the payment of dividends. Existing shareholders bear these costs.

Questions and Problems

1. The DDM Corporation has just paid a cash dividend (D_0) of $2 per share. It has consistently increased its cash dividends in the past by 5% per year, and you expect it to continue to do so. You estimate that the market capitalization rate for this stock should be 13% per year.
   a. What is your estimate of the intrinsic value of a share (derived using the DDM model)?
   b. Suppose that the actual price of a share is $20. By how much would you have to adjust each of the following model parameters to justify this observed price:
      i. The growth rate of dividends.
      ii. The market capitalization rate.

2. The Rusty Clipper Fishing Corporation is expected to pay a cash dividend of $5 per share this year. You estimate that the market capitalization rate for this stock should be 10% per year. If its current price is $25 per share, what can you infer about its expected growth rate of dividends?

3. The Constant Growth Corporation (CGC) has expected earnings per share (E_1) of $5. It has a history of paying cash dividends equal to 20% of earnings. The market capitalization rate for CGC's stock is 15% per year, and the expected *ROE* on the firm's future investments is 17% per year. Using the constant growth rate discounted dividend model,
   a. What is the expected growth rate of dividends?
   b. What is the model's estimate of the present value of the stock?
   c. If the model is right, what is the expected price of a share a year from now?
   d. Suppose that the current price of a share is $50. By how much would you have to adjust each of the following model parameters to justify this observed price:
      i. The expected *ROE* on the firm's future investments.
      ii. The market capitalization rate.
      iii. The dividend payout ratio.

4. The stock of Slogro Corporation is currently selling for $10 per share. Earnings per share in the coming year are expected to be $2 per share. The company has a policy of paying out 60% of its earnings each year in dividends. The rest is retained and invested in projects that earn a 20% rate of return per year. This situation is expected to continue forever.
   a. Assuming the current market price of the stock reflects its intrinsic value as computed using the constant growth rate *DDM,* what rate of return do Slogro's investors require?
   b. By how much does its value exceed what it would be if all earnings were paid as dividends and nothing were reinvested?
   c. If Slogro were to cut its dividend payout ratio to 25%, what would happen to its stock price? What if Slogro eliminated the dividend altogether?
   d. Suppose that Slogro wishes to maintain its current 60% dividend payout policy but that it also wishes to invest an amount each year equal to that year's total earnings. All the money would be invested in projects earning 20% per year. One way that Slogro could do so would be to issue an amount of new stock each year equal to one-half that year's earnings. What do you think would be the effect of this policy on the current stock price?

5. The Amazing.com Corporation currently pays no cash dividends, and it is not expected to for the next 5 years. Its sales have been growing at 25% per year.
   a. Can you apply the constant growth rate *DDM* to estimate its intrinsic value? Explain.

b. It is expected to pay its first cash dividend—$1 per share—5 years from now. If its market capitalization rate is 20% and its dividends are expected to grow by 10% per year, what would you estimate its intrinsic value to be?

c. If its current market price is $100 per share, what would you infer the expected growth rate of its future dividends to be?

6. The Digital Growth Corp. pays no cash dividends currently and is not expected to for the next 5 years. Its latest *EPS* was $10, all of which was reinvested in the company. The firm's expected *ROE* for the next 5 years is 20% per year, and during this time it is expected to continue to reinvest all of its earnings. Afterward, the firm's *ROE* on new investments is expected to fall to 15%, and the company is expected to start paying out 40% of its earnings in cash dividends, which it will continue to do forever after. DG's market capitalization rate is 15% per year.

   a. What is your estimate of DG's intrinsic value per share?

   b. Assuming its current market price is equal to its intrinsic value, what do you expect to happen to its price over the next year? The year after?

   c. What effect would it have on your estimate of DG's intrinsic value if you expected DG to pay out only 20% of earnings?

7. The 2Stage Co. just paid a dividend of $1 per share. The dividend is expected to grow at a rate of 25% per year for the next three years and then to level off to 5% per year forever. You think the appropriate market capitalization rate is 20% per year.

   a. What is your estimate of the intrinsic value of a share of the stock?

   b. If the market price of a share is equal to this intrinsic value, what is the expected dividend yield?

   c. What do you expect its price to be one year from now? Is the implied capital gain consistent with your estimate of the dividend yield and the market capitalization rate?

8. *The Simp Stock Guide* offers the following method for selecting stocks: Compute a stock's *PEG* ratio by dividing its *P/E* multiple by its growth rate of earnings. Select only those stocks whose *PEG* ratio is in the lowest quartile.

   a. If a stock is fairly priced according to the constant-growth-rate *DDM*, what should be its *PEG* ratio as a function of the following three variables: the stock's market capitalization rate (k), the expected profitability of its future investments (*ROE*), and its plowback ratio (b)? (Assume the *P/E* ratio used in computing *PEG* is the ratio of the stock's current price to its expected earnings per share, P_0/E_1.)

   b. Assume the *CAPM* and the *DDM* are valid. The risk-free rate is 0.04, and the risk premium on the market portfolio is 0.06. What should be the relationship between the *PEG* for a stock whose *ROE* is 0.10 and a stock whose *ROE* is 0.15, assuming the two stocks have the same beta (equal to 1) and plowback ratio (equal to 0.6)?

   c. What do you think of the Simp method?

9. ***Using the Internet for Stock Picking***
   Pick a company whose stock is traded on the NYSE. Use one of the stock valuation models discussed in this chapter together with information that you can find by searching the Internet to compute an intrinsic value for the stock. Compare your estimate of intrinsic value with the stock's actual price. Would you be willing to make an investment decision on the basis of your research? Why or why not?

10. ***Dividend Policy***
    Divido Corporation is an all-equity financed firm with a total market value of $100 million. The company holds $10 million in cash equivalents and has $90 million in other assets. There are 1,000,000 shares of Divido common stock outstanding, each with a market price of $100. What would be the impact on Divido's stock price and

on the wealth of its shareholders of each of the following decisions? Consider each decision separately.
   a. The company pays a cash dividend of $10 per share.
   b. The company repurchases 100,000 shares.
   c. The company pays a 10% stock dividend.
   d. The company has a 2-for-1 stock split.
   e. The company invests $10 million in an expansion that has an expected *IRR* equal to the firm's cost of capital.

11. It has been found empirically that on average the total market value of a firm's stock rises when it announces a stock split. What hypotheses might you offer to explain this phenomenon?

12. Suppose that a company has had an extraordinarily profitable year, and it announces that it will use most of its net cash inflow to buy back shares of its stock in the market. Would you expect the price of its stock to rise or fall when the announcement is made? Explain.

CHAPTER

10

An Overview of Risk Management

OBJECTIVES

- To explore how risk affects financial decision making.
- To provide a conceptual framework for the management of risk.
- To explain how the financial system facilitates the efficient allocation of risk bearing.

CONTENTS

In the preface, we said that there are three analytical "pillars" to finance as an intellectual discipline—the time value of money, valuation, and risk management. Part IV focuses on the third pillar, risk management.

We have already discussed some aspects of risk management in earlier chapters. Chapter 2 showed that the redistribution of risks is a fundamental function of the financial system and it described some of the institutional mechanisms that have developed for facilitating the redistribution of risk and reaping the benefits of diversification.

Part IV provides a more detailed treatment of these topics. This first of the three chapters in Part IV offers an overview of the basic principles of risk management. Section 10.1 clarifies the meaning of risk and risk aversion. Section 10.2 examines the ways in which risk influences the financial decisions of each of the major types of economic organizations—households, firms, and government. Section 10.3 explores the steps in the risk-management process: identifying and assessing risks, selecting techniques to manage risk, and implementing and revising risk-management decisions. Section 10.4 analyzes the methods available to transfer risk: *hedging, insuring,* and *diversifying.* Section 10.5 explores how the facility to transfer risks among people permits effective risk bearing and the efficient allocation of resources to risky projects. Section 10.6 considers the scope of institutional arrangements for the efficient management of risk and the factors that limit it. Section 10.7 discusses portfolio theory, which is the quantitative analysis of the optimal trade-off between the costs and benefits of risk management, and section 10.8 explains probability distributions of rates of return.

The other chapters in Part IV elaborate on the topics introduced here. Chapter 11 focuses on hedging, insuring, and diversifying; chapter 12 applies these concepts to personal investing.

10.1 WHAT IS RISK?

We begin by distinguishing between uncertainty and risk. *Uncertainty* exists whenever one does not know for sure what will occur in the future. *Risk* is uncertainty that "matters" because it affects people's welfare. Thus, uncertainty is a necessary but not a sufficient condition for risk. Every risky situation is uncertain, but there can be uncertainty without risk.

To illustrate, suppose that you plan to have a party, and you invite a dozen of your friends. Your best guess is that 10 of the 12 invitees will come, but there is uncertainty—all 12 might show up, or only 8. There is, however, risk only if the uncertainty affects your plans for the party. Would having a perfect forecast of the number of guests change your actions? If not, then there is uncertainty but no risk.

For example, in providing for your guests, you have to decide how much food to prepare. If you knew for sure that 10 people will show up, then you would prepare exactly enough for 10—no more and no less. If 12 actually show up, there will not be enough food, and you will be displeased with that outcome because some guests will be hungry and dissatisfied. If 8 actually show up, there will be too much food, and you will be displeased with that too because you will have wasted some of your limited resources on surplus food. Thus, the uncertainty matters and, therefore, there is risk in this situation.

On the other hand, suppose that you have told your guests that there will be a "pot-luck" dinner, and that each guest is to bring enough food for one person. Then it might not matter to you in planning the party whether more or fewer than 10 people come. In that case, there is uncertainty but no risk.[1]

In many risky situations, the possible outcomes can be classified either as losses or gains in a simple and direct way. For example, suppose that you invest in the stock market. If the value of your stock portfolio goes down, it is a loss, and if it

---

[1]A subtle point: If you chose to have a pot-luck dinner because of uncertainty about the number of guests, then there is risk. Having a pot-luck dinner is the action you took to manage that risk.

goes up, it is a gain. People normally consider the "downside" possibility of losses to be the risk, not the "upside" potential for a gain.

But there are situations in which there is no obvious downside or upside. Indeed, your planned party is an example. The uncertainty regarding the number of people who will attend your party creates risk whether more or fewer than the expected number of guests show up. Thus, in some situations, deviations from the expected value can be undesirable or costly no matter in which direction.

Risk aversion is a characteristic of an individual's preferences in risk-taking situations. It is a measure of willingness to pay to reduce one's exposure to risk. In evaluating trade-offs between the costs and benefits of reducing risk, risk-averse people prefer the lower-risk alternatives for the same cost. For example, if you are generally willing to accept a lower expected rate of return on an investment because it offers a more predictable rate of return, you are risk averse. When choosing among investment alternatives with the *same* expected rate of return, a risk-averse individual chooses the alternative with the lowest risk.

10.1.1 Risk Management

Let us assume that your party cannot possibly be a pot-luck affair and, therefore, the uncertainty does matter. Moreover, you prefer that there is just enough food for those guests who show up. There are several alternative courses of action open to you, each with a certain cost.

For instance, you could order enough for 12 together with an option to return any surplus to the caterer for a refund. Instead, you could order enough for only 8 together with an option to order more at the last minute if needed. You almost surely will have to pay extra for these options.

Thus, there is a trade-off between the benefit of eliminating the risk of having the wrong amount of food and the cost of that risk reduction. The process of formulating the benefit-cost trade-offs of risk reduction and deciding on the course of action to take (including the decision to take no action at all) is called **risk management.**

People at times express regret at having taken costly measures to reduce risk when the bad outcomes they feared do not subsequently materialize. If you sell a risky stock just before it triples in price, you will surely regret that decision. It is, however, important to remember that all decisions made with respect to uncertainty must be made *before* that uncertainty is resolved. What matters is that your decision is the best one you could make based on the information available to you at the time you made it. Everyone has "20/20 hindsight"; no one, however, has perfect foresight.

It is difficult in practice to distinguish between the skill and the luck of a decision maker. By definition, risk-management decisions are made under conditions of uncertainty and, therefore, multiple outcomes are possible. After the fact, only one of these outcomes will occur. Neither recriminations nor congratulations for a decision seem warranted when such are based on information not available at the time the decision was made. *The appropriateness of a risk-management decision should be judged in the light of the information available at the time the decision is made.*

For example, if you carry an umbrella with you to work because you think it might rain, and it does not, then you should not recriminate yourself for having made the wrong decision. On the other hand, suppose all the weather forecasters say rain is very likely, and you do not take your umbrella. If it does not rain, you should not congratulate yourself on your wisdom. You were just lucky.

Quick Check 10-1
To eliminate the risk of a decline in house prices over the next three months, Joe agrees to sell his house three months from now at a price of $100,000. After three months, by the time of the transfer of ownership and the conclusion of the sale, housing prices have gone up and it turns out that Joe could have gotten $150,000 for his house. Should Joe chastise himself for his decision to eliminate his price risk?

10.1.2 Risk Exposure

If you face a particular type of risk because of your job, the nature of your business, or your pattern of consumption, you are said to have a particular **risk exposure.** For example, if you are a temporary office worker, your exposure to the risk of a layoff is relatively high. If you are a tenured professor at a major university, your exposure to the risk of a layoff is relatively low. If you are a farmer, you are exposed both to the risk of a crop failure and to the risk of a decline in the price at which you can sell your crops. If your business significantly involves imports or exports of goods, you are exposed to the risk of an adverse change in currency exchange rates. If you own a house, you are exposed to the risks of fire, theft, storm damage, earthquake damage, as well as the risk of a decline in its market value.

Thus, *the riskiness of an asset or a transaction cannot be assessed in isolation or in the abstract.* In one context, the purchase or sale of a particular asset may add to your risk exposure; in another, the same transaction may be risk reducing. Thus, if I buy a one-year insurance policy on my life, it is risk reducing to my family because the benefit paid offsets their loss in income in the event that I die. If people unrelated to me buy the policy on my life they are not reducing risk; they are betting that I will die during the year. Or if a farmer with wheat ready to be harvested enters a contract to sell wheat at a fixed price in the future, the contract is risk reducing. But for someone who has no wheat to sell, entering into that same contract is to speculate that wheat prices will fall because they profit only if the market price at the contract delivery date is below the contractually fixed price.

Speculators are defined as investors who take positions that increase their exposure to certain risks in the hope of increasing their wealth. In contrast, **hedgers** take positions to reduce their exposures. The same person can be a speculator on some exposures and a hedger on others.

10.2 RISK AND ECONOMIC DECISIONS

Some financial decisions, such as how much insurance to buy against various risk exposures, relate exclusively to the management of risk. But many general resource allocation decisions, such as saving, investment, and financing decisions, are also significantly influenced by the presence of risk and, therefore, are partly risk-management decisions.

For example, some household saving is motivated by the desire for the increased security that comes from owning assets that can cover unanticipated expenses in the future. Economists call this **precautionary saving.** In chapter 5, we showed how households can use time value of money concepts to make optimal saving decisions over the life cycle. In that analysis, however, we ignored risk and precautionary saving. In the real world, households should not and do not ignore it.

In the sections to follow, we discuss the influence of risk on some of the major financial decisions of households, firms, and government. But first let us recall why we begin with households (i.e., people). The ultimate function of the financial system is to help implement optimal consumption and resource allocation of households. Economic organizations such as firms and governments exist primarily to facilitate the achievement of that ultimate function and, therefore, we cannot properly understand the optimal functioning of those organizations without first understanding the financial-economic behavior of people, including their response to risk.

10.2.1 Risks Facing Households

Although many possible risk classification schemes are possible, we distinguish among five major categories of risk exposures for households:

- *Sickness, disability, and death:* Unexpected sickness or accidental injuries can impose large costs on people because of the need for treatment and care and because of the loss of income caused by the inability to work.

- *Unemployment risk:* This is the risk of losing one's job.

- *Consumer-durable asset risk:* This is the risk of loss arising from ownership of a house, car, or other consumer-durable asset. Losses can occur due to hazards such as fire or theft, or due to obsolescence arising from technological change or changes in consumer tastes.

- *Liability risk:* This is the risk that others will have a financial claim against you because they suffer a loss for which you can be held responsible. For example, you cause a car accident through reckless driving and are required to cover the cost to others of personal injury and property damage.

- *Financial-asset risk:* This is the risk arising from holding different kinds of financial assets such as equities or fixed-income securities denominated in one or more currencies. The underlying sources of financial-asset risk are the uncertainties faced by the firms, governments, or other economic organizations that have issued these securities.

The risks faced by households influence virtually all of their economic decisions. Consider, for example, an individual's decision to invest in a graduate education. In chapter 5 we analyzed this decision using time value of money techniques and ignored risk. However, an important reason to invest in more education is to increase the *flexibility* of one's human capital. A person with a broader education is generally better equipped to deal with the risk of unemployment.

Quick Check 10-2
Think of an insurance policy that you or someone you know has recently purchased or canceled. List the steps that led to the decision.

10.2.2 Risks Facing Firms

Firms are organizations whose primary economic function is to produce goods and services. Virtually every activity of the firm entails exposures to risks. Taking risks is an essential and inseparable part of business enterprise.

Business risks of the firm are borne by its stakeholders: shareholders, creditors, customers, suppliers, employees, and government. The financial system can be used to transfer risks faced by firms to other parties. Specialized financial firms, such as insurance companies, perform the service of pooling and transferring risks. Ultimately, however, all risks faced by firms are borne by people.

Consider, for example, the risks associated with producing baked goods. Bakeries are the firms that carry on this activity. Bakeries, like firms in other industries, face several categories of risks:

- *Production risk:* This is the risk that machines (e.g., ovens, delivery trucks) will break down, that deliveries of raw materials (e.g., flour, eggs) will not arrive on time, that workers will not show up for work, or that a new technology will make the firm's existing equipment obsolete.

- *Price risk of outputs:* This is the risk that the demand for the baked goods produced by the bakery will unpredictably change because of an unanticipated shift in consumer preferences (e.g., celery becomes a popular substitute for bread at restaurants) and, therefore, the market price of baked goods might fall. Or competition can become more intense, and the bakery might be forced to lower its prices.

- *Price risk of inputs:* This is the risk that the prices of some of the inputs of the bakery will change unpredictably. Flour can become more expensive, or wage rates rise. If the bakery borrows money to finance its operations at a floating interest rate, it is exposed to the risk that interest rates might rise.

The bakery's owners are not the only people who bear the risks of the business. Its managers (if they are different from the owners) and its other employees bear some of them, too. If profitability is low or if the production technology changes, some of them may be forced to take a cut in pay or even lose their jobs altogether.

Expertise in managing risks is part of the skill recipe for effective management of a bakery. The firm's management team can manage these risks using several techniques: It can keep extra flour in inventory to protect itself against delays in delivery; it can maintain spare parts for its machinery; and it can subscribe to services that forecast trends in the demand for its products. It can also buy insurance against some risks, such as accidental injury to its employees or theft of its equipment. It can also reduce some price risks by either engaging in fixed-price contracting with customers and suppliers directly or by transacting in the forward, futures, and options markets for commodities, foreign exchange, and interest rates. Making trade-offs among the costs and benefits of these risk-reducing measures is an essential part of managing a bakery.

The size and organizational form of the firm itself can also be affected by risk. Bakeries come in many different types and sizes. At one extreme are small production and retail operations owned and operated by a single individual or family. At the other extreme are large corporations such as Continental Baking Company, with a workforce of thousands of people and an even larger number of shareholder owners. One purpose (and usually not the only one) of organizing as a large corporation is to better manage the production, demand, or price risks of the business.

> **Quick Check 10-3**
> Think of a fast-food restaurant. What risks is such a business exposed to, and who bears them?

10.2.3 The Role of Government in Risk Management

Governments at all levels play an important role in managing risks either by preventing them or redistributing them. People often rely on government to provide protection and financial relief from natural disasters and various human-caused hazards, including war and pollution of the environment. An argument in favor of an activist role for government in economic development is that government can readily spread the risk of an investment in infrastructure among all of the taxpayers within its jurisdiction. Government managers often use the markets and other channels of the financial system to implement their own risk-management policies in much the same way that managers of firms and other nongovernmental economic organizations do.

As is the case with these other organizations, however, all risks are ultimately borne by the people. Whether government offers insurance against the risk of natural disasters or insurance against default on bank deposits, it is not free. The government either charges the insured parties a price sufficient to cover the costs of these insurance services, or taxpayers pay the claims.

> **Quick Check 10-4**
> If the government mandates that all automobile owners must buy accident insurance, who bears the risk of auto accidents?

10.3 THE RISK-MANAGEMENT PROCESS

The **risk-management process** is a systematic attempt to analyze and deal with risk. The process can be broken down into five steps:

- *Risk identification*
- *Risk assessment*
- *Selection of risk-management techniques*
- *Implementation*
- *Review*

10.3.1 Risk Identification

Risk identification consists of figuring out what the most important risk exposures are for the unit of analysis, be it a household, a firm, or some other entity. Households or firms are sometimes not aware of all of the risks to which they are exposed. For example, a person who has never missed a day of work because of illness or injury may give little thought to the risk of disability. Buying insurance against disability risk might make sense, but may not even be considered.

On the other hand, there may be some risks for which a person buys insurance coverage, but does not have an exposure. For example, many single people who have no dependents buy retirement saving instruments with survivors' benefits. Should they die before retirement, their designated beneficiaries receive the accumulated value in the account. But if they have no dependents, they do not need this protection (see Box 10.1).

Effective risk identification requires that one take the perspective of the entity as a whole and consider the totality of uncertainties affecting it. For example, consider a household's exposure to stock market risk. If you work as a stockbroker, then your future earnings depend critically on how well stocks perform. Your human capital is, therefore, exposed to the performance of the stock market, and you probably should not invest your other non–human-capital wealth in stocks as well. On the other hand, your friend, who is your age but works as a government administrator earning a salary equal to yours, may be well advised to invest a large fraction of her investment portfolio in stocks because her human capital is not as exposed to the risk of the stock market.

The principle that one should take the perspective of the entity as a whole when identifying risks applies to firms, too. For example, consider the impact of foreign-exchange uncertainty on a firm that sells products and buys inputs abroad in prices that are fixed in foreign currencies. It makes little sense for the firm's managers to consider the effect of exchange-rate uncertainty *only* on the firm's revenues or on its costs. What matters to all of the firm's stakeholders is the net effect of exchange-rate uncertainty on the firm's revenues less its costs. Even though its revenues and its costs might each be greatly affected by fluctuations in exchange rates, the firm's net exposure to exchange-rate uncertainty might be zero.

Or consider farmers whose revenues are subject to both price and quantity uncertainty. Suppose crop failures always cause prices to rise so that farm revenue (equal to price × quantity) is constant. Although at first it might appear that the farmer is exposed to *both* price risk *and* quantity risk (the risk of crop failure), there may be no risk at the level of analysis of total farm revenue. Taking steps to reduce

---

BOX 10.1

Who Needs Life Insurance?

1. *You're single with no dependents.* Forget life insurance. Buy disability coverage, and add to your investments instead.
2. *You're single with dependents.* What happens to those dependents if you die? If you're divorced and the other spouse can afford to take care of the kids, then you don't need life insurance.
3. *You're a DINK—a double-income couple with no kids.* If each spouse is self-supporting, you don't need life insurance.
4. *You're an OINK—a one-income couple with no kids.* The working spouse probably needs life

insurance, if you want to preserve the standard of living of the other spouse.

5. *You're married with young children.* You need a lot of life insurance. Those kids have to be raised and educated, and it's not cheap. But you probably need the coverage only until they're on their own.

Source: Adapted with permission of Simon & Schuster, Inc., from *Making the Most of Your Money* by Jane Bryant Quinn. Copyright © 1991 by Berrybrook Publishing Inc.

the farmer's exposure to the volatility of farm prices might have the "perverse" effect of increasing the uncertainty of the farmer's total revenue.

To help in identifying risk exposures, it is a good idea to have a checklist that enumerates all of the entity's potential exposures and the relations among them. In the case of a firm, this may require a good deal of detailed knowledge about the economics of the industry in which the firm competes, the technology of the firm, and its sources of supply.

10.3.2 Risk Assessment

Risk assessment is the quantification of the costs associated with the risks that have been identified in the first step of risk management. For example, consider a single woman who has just graduated from college and started a job. When she was in college, she was covered by her parents' health insurance policy, but now she has no health insurance coverage. She, therefore, identifies illness as a major risk exposure. To assess her exposure, information is needed. How likely is it that someone of her age and health status will get sick? What is the cost of treatment?

Clearly, she needs information, and information may be costly to gather. One of the main functions of insurance companies is to provide this kind of information. They employ **actuaries,** who are professionals specially trained in mathematics and statistics, to gather and analyze data and estimate the probabilities of illness, accidents, and other such risks.

In the realm of financial-asset risks, households and firms often need expert advice in assessing their exposures and in quantifying the trade-offs between the risks and rewards of investing in various categories of assets, such as stocks and bonds. They typically turn to professional investment advisors, mutual funds, or other financial intermediaries and service firms that help them make those assessments.

10.3.3 Selection of Risk-Management Techniques

There are four basic techniques available for reducing risk:

- *Risk avoidance*
- *Loss prevention and control*
- *Risk retention*
- *Risk transfer*

Let us briefly explain each technique.

- *Risk avoidance:* A conscious decision not to be exposed to a particular risk. People may decide to avoid the risks of going into certain professions and firms may avoid certain lines of business because they are considered too risky. But it is not always feasible to avoid risks. For example, all people are inevitably exposed to the risk of illness by virtue of being human. They cannot avoid it.

- *Loss prevention and control:* Actions taken to reduce the likelihood or the severity of losses. Such actions can be taken prior to, concurrent with, or after a loss occurs. For example, you can reduce your exposure to the risk of illness by eating well, getting plenty of sleep, not smoking, and keeping your distance from people known to have fresh colds. If you catch a cold, you can stay in bed and reduce the possibility of having it turn into pneumonia.

- *Risk retention:* Absorbing the risk and covering losses out of one's own resources. This sometimes happens by default, as for example, when one is unaware that there was any risk or one chooses to ignore it. But one may make a conscious decision to absorb certain risks. For example, some people may decide to absorb the costs of treating illnesses from their own accumulated wealth and do not buy health insurance. Household precautionary saving is to facilitate risk retention.

- *Risk transfer:* Transferring the risk to others. Selling a risky asset to someone else and buying insurance are examples of this technique of risk management. Taking no action to reduce risk and relying on others to cover your losses is another example.

There are three basic methods of accomplishing the transfer of risk: hedging, insuring, and diversifying. They are explained in section 10.4 of this chapter and elaborated on in chapter 11.

10.3.4 Implementation

Following a decision about how to handle the risks identified, one must implement the techniques selected. The underlying principle in this step of the risk-management process is to minimize the costs of implementation. Thus, if you decide to buy health insurance of a certain kind, you should shop around for the lowest-cost provider. If you have decided to invest in the stock market, you should compare the costs of doing so through mutual funds or buying stocks through a broker.

10.3.5 Review

Risk management is a dynamic feedback process in which decisions are periodically reviewed and revised. As time passes and circumstances change, new exposures may arise, information about the likelihood and severity of risks may become more readily available, and techniques for managing them may become less costly. Thus, you will probably decide not to purchase life insurance if you are single, but reverse that decision if you get married and have children. Or you may decide to change the proportion of your asset portfolio invested in stocks.

> **Quick Check 10-5**
> Identify a major risk in your life and describe the steps you take to manage it.

10.4 THE THREE DIMENSIONS OF RISK TRANSFER

Among the four techniques of risk management listed in section 10.3.3, transferring some or all of the risk to others is where the financial system plays the greatest role. The most basic method of transferring risk is to simply sell the asset that is the source of the risk. For example, an owner of a house is subject to at least three risk exposures: fire, storm damage, and the risk that the market value of the house will decline. By selling the house, the owner gets rid of all three of those exposures.

However, suppose that one either cannot or does not choose to sell the asset that is the source of the risk. It is nevertheless possible to manage some of the risks of ownership in other ways. For example, one can buy insurance against fire and storm damage, and thereby retain only the market-value risk of the house.

We distinguish among three methods for transferring risks, called the three dimensions of risk transfer: **hedging, insuring,** and **diversifying.** We explain and illustrate each method in the sections to follow.

10.4.1 Hedging

One is said to *hedge* a risk when the action taken to reduce one's exposure to a loss also causes one to give up of the possibility of a gain. For example, farmers who sell their future crops before the harvest at a fixed price to eliminate the risk of a low price at harvest time also give up the possibility of profiting from high prices at harvest time. They are hedging their exposure to the price risk of their crops. If you subscribe to a magazine for three years instead of subscribing one year at a time, you are hedging against the risk of a rise in the price of the magazine. You eliminate the potential loss due to an increase in the price of a subscription, but you give up the gain from a potential drop in subscription prices.

10.4.2 Insuring

Insuring means paying a *premium* (the price paid for the insurance) to avoid losses. By buying insurance, you substitute a sure loss (the premium you pay for the policy) for the possibility of a larger loss if you do not insure. For example, if you own a car, you almost surely have bought some insurance against the risks of damage, theft, and injury to yourself and others. The premium may be $1,000 today to insure your car for the next year against the potential losses stemming from these contingencies. The sure loss of $1,000 is substituted for the possibility of losses that can run to hundreds of thousands of dollars.

There is a fundamental difference between insuring and hedging. When you hedge, you eliminate the risk of loss by giving up the potential for gain. When you insure, you pay a premium to eliminate the risk of loss and *retain* the potential for gain.

For example, suppose you live in the United States and own an import/export business. A month from now you know that you will receive 100,000 German marks. The dollar price of a German mark is $1.50 per mark now, but you do not know what it will be a month from now. You are, therefore, exposed to exchange-rate risk.

You can manage this risk either by hedging or by insuring. Hedging involves entering into a contract now to sell your 100,000 marks at the end of the month at a fixed dollar price of, say, $1.50 per mark. The contract that protects you against a decline in the dollar price of the mark costs you nothing, but by hedging you have also given up the potential gain from a rise in the dollar price of the mark over the next month.

Alternatively, you could insure against a decline in the dollar price of the mark by paying a premium now for a put option that gives you the right (but not the obligation) to sell your 100,000 marks a month from now at a price of $1.50 per mark.[2] If the dollar price of the mark falls below $1.50, you are protected because you can exercise your option a month from now and sell your marks at $1.50 per mark. But, if the dollar price of the mark rises, you get the benefit of the increased dollar value of your 100,000 marks.

---

[2]A put option is a security that gives its holder the right to sell some asset at a specified price, called the *exercise* or *strike price,* on or before some specified expiration date. The pricing of put options is discussed in chapter 15.

Quick Check 10-6

Suppose you are a U.S. citizen studying in Germany. A month from now you know that you will receive $100,000 from the United States as a scholarship grant. How can you hedge your foreign-exchange risk? How can you insure against it?

10.4.3 Diversifying

Diversifying means holding similar amounts of many risky assets instead of concentrating all of your investment in only one. Diversification thereby limits your exposure to the risk of any single asset.

For example, consider the diversification of business risks. Suppose that you are thinking about investing $100,000 in the biotechnology business because you believe that the discovery of new genetically engineered drugs offers great profit potential over the next several years. You could invest all $100,000 in a single firm that is developing a single new drug. In that case, your biotech investment would be concentrated, not diversified.

Diversification can be carried out by the individual investor directly in the market, or by the firm, or by a financial intermediary. Thus, you can diversify your investment in the biotechnology business by:

- Investing in several firms, each of which is developing a new drug.
- Investing in a single firm that is developing many drugs.
- Investing in a mutual fund that holds shares in many firms that are developing new drugs.

To illustrate how diversification reduces your exposure to risk, compare your situation if you have all $100,000 invested in the development of a single new drug with the situation if you have $50,000 invested in each of two different drugs. Suppose that for each drug, success means that you will quadruple your investment, but failure means a loss of your entire investment. Thus, if you invest $100,000 in a single drug, either you wind up with $400,000 or nothing.

If you diversify by investing $50,000 in each of two drugs, there is still a chance of winding up with either $400,000 (if both drugs succeed) or nothing (if both drugs fail). However, there is also the intermediate possibility that one drug succeeds and the other fails. In that event, you will wind up with $200,000 (four times your investment of $50,000 in the drug that succeeds and zero from the drug that fails).

Diversification does not reduce your risk exposure if the individual drugs you invest in always either succeed or fail together. That is, in the two-drug example, if there is *no* chance that one drug succeeds and the other fails, it would make no difference to your risk whether you invested all $100,000 in a single drug or split your investment among the two. Either way, there are only two possible outcomes—either you wind up with $400,000 (from success on all drugs) or you lose your entire investment (from the failure of all drugs). In such a case, the risks of commercial success for each separate drug are said to be *perfectly correlated* with each other. In order for diversification to reduce your risk exposure, the risks must be less than perfectly correlated with each other.[3]

Diversification can improve households' welfare by reducing the exposure to any particular risky venture borne by each household. However, diversification by itself does not reduce uncertainty in the aggregate. Thus, if 1,000 new drugs are discovered each year, the aggregate uncertainty about the number that will be commercially successful does not depend on how widely the uncertainty is spread among investors in drug company stocks. However, the adverse impact of that uncertainty on households' welfare is reduced through diversification.

When comparing the ex post performance of diversified investors with those who do not diversify, the more spectacular winners are most likely to come from among undiversified investors. But this is also the group that produces the more spectacular losers. By diversifying your portfolio, you reduce your chances of ending up at either extreme.

To underscore this point, let us return to the previous example of investing in the development of new drugs. For each drug that succeeds you quadruple your investment, but for each that fails, you lose your entire investment. Thus, if you concentrate your investment of $100,000 in a single drug, either you wind up with $400,000 or nothing.

Consider two investors, each of whom invests $100,000 in a single new drug. Investor 1 invests in drug A, and investor 2 invests in drug B. Now add a third investor. Investor 3 invests half his money in drug A and the other half in drug B.

Suppose drug A succeeds and B fails. Then investor 1 makes $400,000. She may find herself labeled an investment "genius" for quadrupling her money. Investor 2, however, is correspondingly labeled a "dunce" for the colossal failure of losing his entire investment. Suppose, however, that drug A fails and B succeeds. Then the labels attached to investors 1 and 2 are reversed. The diversified investor, investor 3, makes "only" $200,000 in either scenario and, thus, is the "middle" or "average" performer.

Of course, one always prefers to be a big winner and called a genius. But if that can only be accomplished by a decision ex ante that results in either being a big winner or a big loser ex post, then perhaps it is preferable to choose an alternative that leaves you in the middle.

As obvious as this point may seem, people often lose sight of it. Good luck is often interpreted as skill. Thus, it is not uncommon to find press reports about the spectacular successes of particular stock market investors who do not diversify their portfolios at all but concentrate instead in a single stock. Although such investors may indeed be investment geniuses, it is more likely that they are simply lucky.

It is also not uncommon to find stories about big losers who are portrayed as "sinful" or stupid for not choosing the stocks that had big payoffs. A more valid criticism might be that they were undiversified.

Quick Check 10-7

How might farmers reduce their exposure to risks of crop failure through diversification?

---

[3]A precise statistical definition of *correlation* is given in chapter 11.

10.5 RISK TRANSFER AND ECONOMIC EFFICIENCY

Institutional arrangements for the transfer of risk contribute to economic efficiency in two fundamental ways—they reallocate existing risks to those most willing to bear them, and they cause a reallocation of resources to production and consumption in accordance with the new distribution of risk bearing. By allowing people to reduce their exposure to the risk of undertaking certain business ventures, they may encourage entrepreneurial behavior that can have a benefit to society. We now explore each of these in greater detail.

10.5.1 Efficient Bearing of Existing Risks

We first investigate how the facility to reallocate risks among people can make everyone better off. Consider the hypothetical case of two investors in very different economic circumstances. The first is a retired widow who has an accumulated "nest egg" of $100,000, which is her sole source of income. The second is a college student who has $100,000 and who anticipates a good stream of earnings in the future after graduating from college.

Typically, the widow is assumed to be a more conservative investor and the student more aggressive. That is, we would expect the widow to be concerned primarily with the safety of her stream of investment income, whereas we might expect the student to be willing to bear more risk in exchange for a higher expected return.

Suppose the widow currently holds all of her wealth in the form of a portfolio of stocks left to her by her recently deceased husband, and suppose the college student has all of her wealth in a bank certificate of deposit (CD) that her parents started for her years before. Both would be better off if they could somehow swap their assets so that the widow winds up holding the CD and the student the stock portfolio.

One of the most important functions of the financial system is to facilitate such transfers of risk. One way for this transfer of risk to take place is for the widow to simply sell her stocks and for the student to buy them. Typically, several financial intermediaries would be involved in the process. For example, the widow might have her stocks in an account at a brokerage firm. She gives the broker an order to sell them and to invest the proceeds of the sale in a bank CD. The student, on the other hand, cashes in her CD at the bank and buys the stocks through her broker.

In this set of transactions no immediate change occurs in the wealth of either party except that each must pay the cost of carrying out the transactions (i.e., broker fees and bank charges). The student and the widow each had $100,000 of assets before, and immediately afterwards they each have $100,000 (less the broker fees and bank charges). The sole purpose and result of the transactions is to allow each party to hold the portfolio of assets offering them the combination of risk and expected return most attractive for their circumstances.

10.5.2 Risk and Resource Allocation

Now let us consider how the ability to reallocate risks facilitates the undertaking of valuable projects that might not otherwise be undertaken because they are too risky. The ability to pool and share risks can lead to an increase in inventive activity and the development of new products.

For example, consider the case of creating new pharmaceuticals. The research and development effort that goes into the discovery, testing, and production of new drugs requires enormous amounts of investment extended over a considerable period of time.[4] The return on that investment is highly uncertain. Even if an individual investor had the wealth necessary to finance the development of a new drug, risk aversion might deter him from doing so on his own.

To be more specific, suppose that a scientist discovers a new drug designed to treat the common cold. She requires $1 million to develop, test, and produce it. At this stage, the drug has a small probability of commercial success. Even if the scientist has $1 million in her bank account, she might not be willing to risk it all on the drug. She might instead set up a firm to develop the drug, and bring in other investors to share both the risks and the potential rewards of her discovery.

In addition to risk pooling and sharing, *specialization* in the bearing of risks can also facilitate undertaking risky investments. Potential investors may be willing to accept some of the exposures associated with a business enterprise, but not others.

For example, suppose a real estate developer is planning to construct a new shopping mall in a downtown location. A consortium of banks and other lending institutions agrees to finance the project but only on the condition that it is insured against fire. That is, the lenders accept the risk that the mall might not be a commercial success, but they do not accept the exposure of their investment to the risk of a fire. The existence of specialized insurance companies that accept the risk of fire makes possible the financing of the new shopping mall.

Quick Check 10-8
Give an example of an investment project or a new business that would not be feasible if the risks associated with it could not be shared or transferred through the financial system.

10.6 INSTITUTIONS FOR RISK MANAGEMENT

Imagine a hypothetical world in which there exists such a wide range of institutional mechanisms (such as securities markets and insurance contracts) that people can pick and choose exactly those risks they wish to bear and those they want to shed. In such a hypothetical world, we would all be able (for a price) to shed the risks associated with job loss or a decline in the market value of our house. This world would represent the theoretical limiting case of what the financial system can provide in the way of efficient risk allocation for society (see Box 10.2).

Over the centuries, various economic organizations and contractual arrangements have evolved to facilitate a more efficient allocation of risk bearing both by expanding the scope of diversification and by permitting greater specialization in the management of risk. Insurance companies and futures markets are examples of institutions whose primary economic function is to further these ends.

The allocation of risks is also an important consideration in the design of securities. Debt and equity securities issued by firms are intentionally designed to differ in the risks of the business that they carry. By choosing to invest in either the debt or the equity securities of a firm or some combination of them, people can thus select the kinds of risk they wish to bear.

---

[4]According to Judy Lewent, the chief financial officer of Merck, Inc. (*Harvard Business Review,* January/February 1994), it costs $359 million and takes ten years to bring a new drug to market. Once there, only three out of ten drugs succeed.

BOX 10.2

Arrow on Complete Markets for Risk

Suppose that we could introduce into the economic system any institutions we wish for shifting risks instead of being confined to those developed historically. . . . It is not hard to see what an ideal arrangement would consist of. We would want to find a market in which we can insure freely against any economically relevant event. That is, an individual should be able to bet, at fixed odds, any amount he wishes on the occurrence of any event which will affect his welfare in any way. The odds,

or, in a different and more respectable language, the premium on the insurance, should be determined, as any other price, so that supply and demand are equal.

Under such a system, productive activity and risk bearing can be divorced, each being carried out by the one or ones best qualified.

Source: adapted from Kenneth Arrow, *Aspects of the Theory of Risk Bearing* (Helsinki: Yejö Johannsonin Säätio, 1965).

In the last few decades, the rate of introduction of innovations that facilitate risk management has greatly accelerated because of changes on both the supply side and the demand side of the markets for risk bearing. New discoveries in telecommunications, information processing, and finance theory have significantly lowered the costs of achieving greater global diversification and specialization in the bearing of risks. At the same time, increased volatility of exchange rates, interest rates, and commodity prices has increased the demand for ways to manage risk. Thus, the rapid and widespread development of futures, options, and swap contracts starting in the 1970s and 1980s can largely be explained as market responses to these cost and demand factors.

But the theoretical ideal of complete markets for allocating risks can never be fully achieved because in the real world there are a number of limiting factors that can never be overcome entirely. Two key categories of factors limiting the efficient allocation of risks are *transactions costs* and *incentive problems*.

Transactions costs include the costs of establishing and running institutions such as insurance companies or securities exchanges and the costs of writing and enforcing contracts. These institutions will not come into existence unless the pecuniary benefits from their creation exceed the costs.

The primary incentive problems standing in the way of the development of institutions for efficient risk sharing are moral hazard and adverse selection. The **moral hazard** problem exists when having insurance against some risk causes the insured party to take greater risk or to take less care in preventing the event that gives rise to the loss. Moral hazard can lead to unwillingness on the part of insurance companies to insure against certain types of risk.

For example, if a warehouse owner buys fire insurance, the existence of the insurance reduces his incentive to spend money to prevent a fire. Failure to take the same precautions makes a warehouse fire a more likely occurrence. In an extreme case, the owner may be tempted to actually start a fire in order to collect the insurance money if the coverage exceeds the market value of the warehouse. Because of this potential moral hazard, insurance companies may limit the amount they will insure or simply refuse to sell fire insurance under certain circumstances.

Another class of incentive problems is **adverse selection**—those who purchase insurance against risk are more likely than the general population to be at risk. For example, consider **life annuities,** which are contracts that pay a fixed amount of money each month for as long as the purchaser lives. A firm selling such annuities cannot assume that the people who buy them will have the same expected length of life as the general population.

For example, suppose that a firm sells life annuities to people retiring at age 65. There are equal numbers of three types of people in the general population: type A live for 10 years, type B for 15 years, and type C for 20 years. On average, people aged 65 live for 15 years. If the firm charges a price that reflects a 15-year life expectancy, however, it will find that the people who buy the annuities are disproportionately of types B and C. Type A people will think that your annuities are not a good deal for them, and will not purchase them.

If the annuity firm knew the type of each potential customer—A, B, or C—and could charge a price that reflected the true life expectancy for that type, then there would be no adverse selection problem. But the annuity firm cannot get enough information about each potential customer to know as much about their true life expectancies as they themselves do. Unless the insurer can charge a price that accurately reflects each person's true life expectancy, a disproportionately large number of the annuities sold will be bought by healthy people who expect to live a long time. In our example, the average life expectancy of buyers of annuities might be 17.5 years, which is 2½ years longer than in the general population.

Therefore, if annuity firms used life expectancies of the general population to price their annuities without adding more to adjust for the adverse selection problem, they would all lose money. As a result, firms in this market charge a price for annuities that is relatively unattractive to people with an average life expectancy, and the market is much smaller than it would be if there were no problem of adverse selection.

To examine the real-world limitations to efficient risk allocation and to illustrate how they are addressed, let us consider the risk of ownership of consumer-durable assets such as automobiles. People reduce some of the risks of car ownership by buying insurance. Insurance contracts against theft and accidental damage are generally available. But insurance against the risk of technological obsolescence is rarely available as a direct contractual arrangement.

Instead, institutional arrangements for dealing with the risk of obsolescence include *renting* or *leasing.* Rental contracts run for periods up to a year. Lease contracts are rental contracts for periods exceeding a year. Rental and leasing firms allow people to have the use of a car without exposure to the risk of obsolescence.

There is a cost to providing the facilities for car rentals and, therefore, they are not available everywhere. Specially equipped garages have to be built, and the cars must be serviced. Rentals are more readily available in tourist and vacation areas, where the demand for short-term rentals is relatively high.

There is a problem of adverse selection in the auto rental and leasing businesses. People who drive a lot and who do not want to service their cars will tend to rent rather than buy. Rental companies have few ways to detect in advance what kind of a driver a customer is. When firms set rental and lease rates, they therefore must presume that their customers will have a tendency to drive more than the average automobile owner.

There is also a moral hazard problem in the auto-rental business. People who rent rather than buy have a reduced incentive to maintain the cars in good condition and they are, therefore, more likely to abuse rented cars than their own.

To deal with problems of adverse selection and moral hazard, rental companies often charge extra for extra miles over a specified limit and for excessive wear and tear to the rented vehicle. But in the absence of a low-cost way to screen out the more costly customers, rental companies will have to charge higher prices for all renters. For people who take good care of cars, it will in general pay to own rather than rent.

10.7 PORTFOLIO THEORY: QUANTITATIVE ANALYSIS FOR OPTIMAL RISK MANAGEMENT

Portfolio theory is defined as quantitative analysis for optimal risk management. Whether the unit of analysis is a household, a firm, or some other economic organization, applying portfolio theory consists of formulating and evaluating the trade-offs between the benefits and costs of risk reduction in order to find an optimal course of action.

For households, consumption and risk preferences are taken as given. Preferences do change over time, but the mechanisms and reasons for those changes are not addressed by the theory. Instead, portfolio theory addresses the problem of how to choose among financial alternatives so as to maximize their given preferences. In general, the optimal choice involves evaluating the trade-off between receiving a higher expected return and taking greater risk.

However, not every decision to reduce one's risk exposure involves incurring a cost of either lower expected return or greater risk. There are circumstances in which both parties to a risk-transfer contract can reduce their risks at no cost other than the expense of drawing up the contract. For example, a buyer and a seller of a house can contractually settle on a transaction price for the house now even though the transfer of ownership will not take place until three months from now. Such an agreement is an example of a *forward contract.* By agreeing to enter into this forward contract, both parties eliminate the uncertainty associated with price volatility in the housing market during the next three months.

> Thus, when different parties perceive the same event from opposite risk perspectives, both can be made better off with a contractual transfer of risks without either party incurring significant costs.

Quick Check 10-9

Describe an uncertain event that two parties perceive from opposite risk perspectives. How might they achieve a mutual reduction in risk?

Risk-management decisions in which there are no costs borne by either party are the exception rather than the norm. In general, there is a trade-off between the costs and benefits of risk reduction. This trade-off is perhaps most apparent in household decisions about how to allocate their wealth among asset categories, such as equities, fixed-income securities, and residential real estate.

The early formal models in portfolio theory were developed to deal with this class of risk-management decision.[5] These models use **probability distributions** to

---

[5]This model is associated with the name of the man who pioneered it, Harry Markowitz. Markowitz's seminal article, "Portfolio Selection," appeared in the *Journal of Finance* in 1952.

quantify the trade-off between risk and expected return. An asset portfolio's expected return is identified with the **mean** of the distribution, and its risk with the **standard deviation.**

These concepts are developed more fully in the next section.

10.8 PROBABILITY DISTRIBUTIONS OF RETURNS

Consider the case of Genco stock. Suppose you buy shares of Genco Corporation at a price of $100 per share and intend to hold it for a year. As shown in chapter 2, the *total* rate of return can be decomposed into the sum of a dividend-income component and a price-change component:

$$r = \frac{\text{Cash Dividend}}{\text{Beginning Price}} + \frac{\text{Ending Price of a Share} - \text{Beginning Price}}{\text{Beginning Price}}$$

$$r = \text{Dividend-Income Component} + \text{Price-Change Component}$$

In Genco's case, suppose that you expect the dividend component to be 3%, and the price-change component to be 7% so that the *expected* rate of return is 10%:

$$r = 3\% + 7\% = 10\%$$

A commonly used measure of the riskiness of an asset such as Genco stock is **volatility.**[6] Volatility is related to the range of possible rates of return from holding the stock and to their likelihood of occurring. *A stock's volatility is larger, the wider the range of possible outcomes and the larger the probabilities of those returns at the extremes of the range.*

For example, if asked to give a best "point estimate" of next year's rate of return on Genco stock, your answer would be 10%. You would not be surprised, however, if the actual return turned out to be different from 10%. It might turn out to be as low as –50% or as high as +80%. The wider the range of possible outcomes, the greater is the volatility.

To derive a further understanding of volatility, let us consider the entire probability distribution of rates of return on Genco stock. All possible returns are assigned probabilities ranging from zero (no possibility of occurring) to one (absolutely certain to occur).

Perfect certainty is the "degenerate" case of a probability distribution. Suppose it is absolutely certain that the return will be 10% over the next year. In that case there is only one possible rate of return, and its probability of occurrence is 1.0.

Now suppose that several different rates of return on Genco are possible, depending on the state of the economy. If the economy is strong over the coming year, Genco's sales and profits will tend to be high, and the rate of return on its stock will be 30%. If the economy is weak, the rate of return will be –10%, a loss. If the economy is just normal, the realized return will be 10%. The estimated probabilities for each of these states in this hypothetical example are shown in Table 10.1 and illustrated in Figure 10.1.

---

[6]As we will see in chapter 11, the cost of insuring against a risk depends directly on volatility. So using volatility as a measure of risk is similar to using the cost of insuring against it.

TABLE 10.1 Probability Distribution of Rate of Return on Genco

State of the Economy	Rate of Return on Genco	Probability
Strong	30%	.20
Normal	10%	.60
Weak	−10%	.20

The probability distribution in Table 10.1 implies that if you invest in Genco stock, 10% is the most likely return that you will receive. It is three times more likely than either of the other two possible returns, -10% or 30%.

The **expected rate of return** (the mean) is defined as the sum over all possible outcomes of each possible rate of return multiplied by the respective probability of its happening:

Expected Return = Sum of (Probability of Return) × Possible Return

$$E(r) = P_1 r_1 + P_2 r_2 + \cdots + P_n r_n$$

$$E(r) = \sum_{i=1}^{n} P_i r_i$$

(10.1)

Applying this formula to the case at hand, we find that the expected rate of return on Genco is:

$$E(r) = .2 \times 30\% + .6 \times 10\% + .2 \times (-)10\% = 10\%$$

← Typo

You are obviously more uncertain about the rate of return in this case than in the special case of complete certainty. But now consider another stock, Risco, that has a wider range of possible rates of return than Genco. The probability distribution of Risco is compared to that of Genco in Table 10.2 and in Figure 10.2.

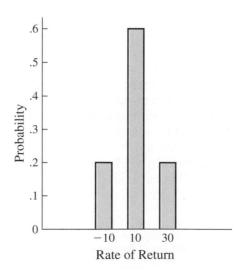

FIGURE 10.1 Probability Distribution of Returns for Genco

TABLE 10.2 Probability Distributions of Rate of Return on Risco and Genco

State of the Economy	Rate of Return on Risco	Rate of Return on Genco	Probability
Strong	50%	30%	.20
Normal	10%	10%	.60
Weak	–30%	–10%	.20

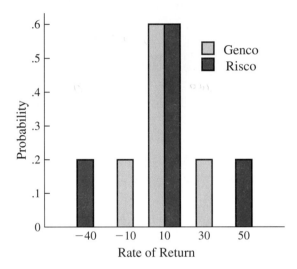

FIGURE 10.2 Probability Distribution of Returns for Genco and Risco

Note that the event probabilities are the same for both stocks, but Risco has a wider range of possible returns. If the economy is strong, Risco will produce a return of 50% compared to Genco's 30%. But if the economy is weak, Risco will produce a return of –30% compared to Genco's –10%. Risco is, therefore, more volatile.

10.9 STANDARD DEVIATION AS A MEASURE OF RISK

The volatility of a stock's return was shown to depend on the range of possible outcomes and on the probabilities of extreme values occurring. The statistic that is used most widely in finance to quantify and measure the volatility of a stock's probability distribution of returns is *standard deviation,* which is computed as follows:

Standard Deviation (σ) = Square Root of the Sum of (Probability)(Possible Return − Expected Return)^2

σ = Square Root of $[P_1(r_1 - E(r))^2 + P_2(r_2 - E(r))^2 + \cdots + P_n(r_n - E(r))^2]$

$$\sigma = \sqrt{\sum_{i=1}^{n} P_i(r_i - E(r))^2} \qquad (10.2)$$

The larger is the standard deviation, the greater is the volatility of the stock. The standard deviation for the riskless investment that pays 10% with certainty would be zero:

$$\sigma = \text{Square Root of } 1.0(10\% - 10\%)^2 = 1.0(0.0) = 0$$

The standard deviation for Genco stock is

$$\sigma = \text{Square Root of } [(.2)(30\% - 10\%)^2 + (.6)(10\% - 10\%)^2 + (.2)(-10\% - 10\%)]$$

$$\sigma = 12.65\%$$

(handwritten annotations: .008, 0, -.04, √-.032, -0.03)

The standard deviation for Risco stock is

$$\sigma = \text{Square Root of } [(.2)(50\% - 10\%)^2 + (.6)(10\% - 10\%)^2 + (.2)(-30\% - 10\%)]$$

$$\sigma = 25.30\%$$

(handwritten annotations: 320, 0, 320, ←√640)

Risco's standard deviation is twice that of Genco because the possible deviations from its expected value are twice those of Genco.

> **Quick Check 10-10**
> Suppose that XYZ stock's rate of return can take three possible values: -50%, 50%, and 100%, each with equal probability. What is XYZ's expected rate of return and its standard deviation?

In the real world, the range of stock returns is not limited to a few numerical values as in our previous examples. Instead, the rate of return can be virtually any number. We, therefore, say that the distribution of stock returns is a **continuous probability distribution.** The most widely used distribution of that sort is the **normal distribution** with its familiar bell-shaped curve, shown in Figure 10.3.

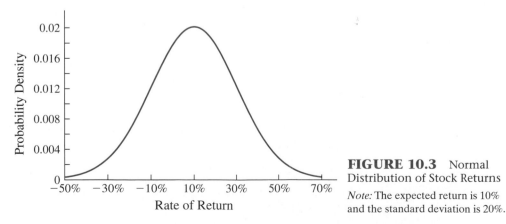

FIGURE 10.3   Normal Distribution of Stock Returns

Note: The expected return is 10% and the standard deviation is 20%.

For the normal distribution and other symmetric distributions similar to it, standard deviation is a natural measure of volatility. (Its symbol, σ, is pronounced "sigma.") The terms *volatility* and *sigma* are often used interchangeably.

The normal distribution encompasses an unbounded range of rates of return, from minus infinity to plus infinity. To interpret different values of the standard deviation, one usually employs **confidence intervals**—a certain range of values ("an interval") within which the actual return on the stock in the next period will fall with a specified probability. Thus, with a normal distribution, a return on the stock that falls within a confidence interval that encompasses all rates of return that are within one standard deviation on either side of the mean has a probability of about .68. A corresponding two-standard-deviation confidence interval has a probability of about .95, and a three-standard-deviation confidence interval encompasses a probability of about .99.

For example, consider a stock with an expected return of 10% and a standard deviation of 20%. If it is normally distributed, then there is a probability of about .95 that the actual return will turn out to fall in the interval between the expected return plus two standard deviations (10% + 2 × 20% = 50%) and the expected return minus two standard deviations (10% − 2 × 20% = −30%). The range of rates of return that is bounded on the low end by −30% and on the upper end by 50% is a .95 confidence interval for this stock's rate of return.

Quick Check 10-11
What are the bounds of a .99 confidence interval for this stock's rate of return?

Summary

Risk is defined as uncertainty that matters to people. *Risk management* is the process of formulating the benefit-cost trade-offs of risk reduction and deciding on a course of action to take. *Portfolio theory* is the quantitative analysis of those trade-offs to find an optimal course of action.

All risks are ultimately borne by people in their capacity as consumers, stakeholders of firms and other economic organizations, or taxpayers.

The riskiness of an asset or a transaction cannot be assessed in isolation or in the abstract; it depends on the specific frame of reference. In one context, the purchase or sale of a particular asset may add to one's risk exposure; in another, the same transaction may be risk reducing.

Speculators are investors who take positions that increase their exposure to certain risks in the hope of increasing their wealth. In contrast, hedgers take positions to reduce their exposures. The same person can be a speculator on some exposures and a hedger on others.

Many resource allocation decisions, such as saving, investment, and financing decisions, are significantly influenced by the presence of risk and, therefore, are partly risk-management decisions.

We distinguish among five major categories of risk exposures for households: sickness, disability, and death; job loss; consumer-durable asset risk; liability risk; and financial asset risk.

Firms face several categories of risks: production risk, price risk of outputs, and price risk of inputs.

There are five steps in the risk-management process:

- Risk identification
- Risk assessment
- Selection of risk-management techniques
- Implementation
- Review

There are four techniques of risk management:

- Risk avoidance
- Loss prevention and control
- Risk retention
- Risk transfer

There are three dimensions of risk transfer: hedging, insuring, and diversifying.

Diversification improves welfare by spreading risks among many people, so that the existing uncertainty matters less.

From society's perspective, risk-management institutions contribute to economic efficiency in two important ways. First, they shift risk away from those who are least willing or able to bear it to those who are most willing to bear it. Second, they cause a reallocation of resources to production and consumption in accordance with the new distribution of risk bearing. By allowing people to reduce their exposure to the risk of undertaking certain business ventures, they may encourage entrepreneurial behavior that can have a benefit to society.

Over the centuries, various economic organizations and contractual arrangements have evolved to facilitate a more efficient allocation of risk bearing by expanding the scope of diversification and the types of risk that are shifted.

Among the factors limiting the efficient allocation of risks are transactions costs and problems of adverse selection and moral hazard.

Key Terms

- risk aversion   257
- risk management   257
- risk exposure   258
- speculators   258
- hedgers   258
- precautionary saving   258
- risk-management process   261
- actuaries   263
- hedging   265
- insuring   265
- diversifying   265
- moral hazard   270

- adverse selection   270
- life annuities   270
- portfolio theory   272
- probability distributions   272
- mean   273
- standard deviation   273
- volatility   273
- expected rate of return   274
- continuous probability distribution   276
- normal distribution   276
- confidence intervals   277

Answers to Quick Check Questions

Quick Check 10-1 *To eliminate the risk of a decline in house prices over the next three months, Joe agrees to sell his house three months from now at a price of $100,000. After three months, by the time of the transfer of ownership and the conclusion of the sale, housing prices have gone up and it turns out that Joe could have gotten $150,000 for his house. Should Joe chastise himself for his decision to eliminate his price risk?*

ANSWER: No. Based on the information Joe had at the time and his preference to eliminate risk, Joe made the right decision.

Quick Check 10-2 *Think of an insurance policy that you or someone you know has recently purchased or canceled. List the steps that led to the decision.*

ANSWER: Answers will vary with each student's specific situation.

Quick Check 10-3 *Think of a fast-food restaurant. What risks is such a business exposed to, and who bears them?*

ANSWER: *Major Risks*

- Risk that ovens will break down.
- Risk that raw materials will not arrive on time.
- Risk that employees will be late or absent.
- Risk of new competition in the area.
- Risk that raw material prices will increase unpredictably.

Who Bears the Risk

Shareholders in the business bear the bulk of the risks as they impact the value of the business.

Quick Check 10-4 *If the government mandates that all automobile owners must buy accident insurance, who bears the risk of auto accidents?*

ANSWER: If all automobile owners are required to purchase accident insurance, then all automobile owners ultimately are the ones who bear the risk of auto accidents through the payment of higher insurance premiums.

Quick Check 10-5 *Identify a major risk in your life and describe the steps you take to manage it.*

ANSWER: Sample Answer:

Major Risks

Sickness (hospitalization)

Unemployment (difficulty finding a job)

Liability risk (car accident)

Typical Management Techniques

Purchase health insurance.

Invest in higher education to increase likelihood of getting a job.

Purchase liability insurance (usually with auto insurance policy).

Quick Check 10-6   *Suppose you are a U.S. citizen studying in Germany. A month from now you know that you will receive $100,000 from the United States as a scholarship grant. How can you hedge your foreign-exchange risk? How can you insure against it?*

ANSWER: In order to hedge your risk, you would enter into a contract now to sell your $100,000 at a fixed price per German mark. If you wanted to insure against a decline in the German mark price of the dollar, you could pay a premium now for a put option that would give you the right to sell your $100,000 a month from now at a fixed mark price per dollar.

Quick Check 10-7   *How might farmers reduce their exposure to risks of crop failure through diversification?*

ANSWER: Farmers could plant several different types of plants instead of just one. In addition, they could own plots of land in several locations rather than own the same amount of land in just one location.

Quick Check 10-8   *Give an example of an investment project or a new business that would not be feasible if the risks associated with it could not be shared or transferred through the financial system.*

ANSWER: Examples:

      Chemical company

      Child safety products company

      Airline

      Bank

      Hospital

      Environmental consulting

      Hazardous waste disposal

Quick Check 10-9   *Describe an uncertain event that two parties perceive from opposite risk perspectives. How might they achieve a mutual reduction in risk?*

ANSWER: Suppose a college with large oil heating bills is concerned about rising oil prices. A reseller of heating oil is concerned about falling prices. These two parties could contractually agree on a price per gallon that would eliminate price risk for both parties.

Quick Check 10-10   *Suppose that XYZ stock's rate of return can take three possible values: −50%, 50%, and 100%, each with equal probability. What is XYZ's expected rate of return and its standard deviation?*

ANSWER: Expected Return = $(\frac{1}{3})(-50\%) + (\frac{1}{3})(50\%) + (\frac{1}{3})(100\%)$ = 33.33% Standard Deviation = Square Root of $(\frac{1}{3})(33.33 + 50)^2 + (\frac{1}{3})(33.33 - 50)^2 + (\frac{1}{3})(33.33 - 100)^2$ = 62.36%

Quick Check 10-11   *What are the bounds of a .99 confidence interval for this stock's rate of return?*

ANSWER: The bounds are three standard deviations on either side of the expected return.

Questions and Problems

1. Suppose that you and a friend have decided to go to a movie together next Saturday. You will select any movie for which tickets are available when you get to the theater. Is this a risky situation for you? Explain.

    Now suppose that your friend has already purchased a ticket for a movie that is going to be released this Saturday. Why is this a risky situation? How would you deal with the risk?

2. Suppose you are aware of the following investment opportunity: You could open a coffee shop around the corner from your home for $25,000. If business is strong, you could net $15,000 in after-tax cash flows each year over the next five years.
   a. If you knew for certain the business would be a success, would this be a risky investment?
   b. Now assume this is a risky venture and that there is a 50% chance it is a success and a 50% chance you go bankrupt within two years. You decide to go ahead and invest. If the business subsequently goes bankrupt, did you make the wrong decision based on the information you had at the time? Why or why not?

3. Suppose you are a pension fund manager and you know today that you need to make a $100,000 payment in three months.
   a. What would be a risk-free investment for you?
   b. If you had to make that payment in 20 years instead, what would be a risk-free investment?
   c. What do you conclude from your answers to parts a and b of this question?

4. Is it riskier to make a loan denominated in dollars or in yen?

5. Which risk-management technique has been chosen in each of the following situations?

   • Installing a smoke detector in your home
   • Investing savings in T-bills rather than in stocks
   • Deciding not to purchase collision insurance on your car
   • Purchasing a life insurance policy for yourself

6. You are considering a choice between investing $1,000 in a conventional one-year T-bill offering an interest rate of 8% and a one-year index-linked inflation plus T-bill offering 3% plus the rate of inflation.
   a. Which is the safer investment?
   b. Which offers the higher expected return?
   c. What is the real return on the index-linked bond?

7. *Hedging and Insurance*
   Suppose you are interested in financing your new home purchase. You have your choice of many financing options. You could enter into any one of the following agreements: 8% fixed rate for 7 years, 8.5% fixed rate for 15 years, 9% fixed for 30 years. In addition, you could finance with a 30-year variable rate that begins at 5% and increases and decreases with the prime rate, or you could finance with a 30-year variable rate that begins at 6% with ceilings of 2% per year to a maximum of 12% and no minimum.
   a. Suppose you believe that interest rates are on the rise. If you want to completely eliminate your risk of rising interest rates for the longest period of time, which option should you choose?
   b. Would you consider that hedging or insuring? Why?
   c. What does your risk-management decision "cost" you in terms of quoted interest rates during the first year?

8. Referring to the information in problem 7, answer the following:
   a. If you believe interest rates are going to fall, which option should you choose?
   b. What risk do you face in that transaction?
   c. How might you insure against that risk? What does that cost you in terms of quoted interest rates?

9. Suppose you are thinking of investing in real estate. How might you achieve a diversified real estate investment?

10. Suppose the following represents the historical returns for Microsoft and Lotus Development Corporation:

Historical Returns

Year	MSFT	LOTS
1	10%	9%
2	15%	12%
3	–12%	–7%
4	20%	18%
5	7%	5%

a. What is the mean return for Microsoft? For Lotus?
b. What is the standard deviation of returns for Microsoft? For Lotus?
c. Suppose the returns for Microsoft and Lotus have normally distributed returns with means and standard deviations calculated as shown. For each stock, determine the range of returns within one expected standard deviation of the mean and within two standard deviations of the mean.

APPENDIX

Leasing, A Cost-Benefit Analysis of Eliminating the Risk of Obsolescence

Leases were analyzed in chapter 4, in which the concept of present value is used to evaluate whether it costs less to buy or lease an asset. The analysis concluded that you would lease the asset if the present value of the after-tax lease payments is less than the present value of the after-tax cash outflows associated with buying it. That analysis considered only the role of interest rates and taxes and ignored the effect of uncertainty about the asset's future price. However, price uncertainty is an important consideration in the analysis of leasing.

For example, suppose that you are in the habit of buying a new car every three years. Your present car is almost three years old, and you are considering whether to buy a new one or lease it. The new model has a purchase price of $20,000. You can either buy the car or you can lease it from the dealer for 36 months at a rate of $402.84 per month. If you buy it, the dealer can arrange for you to borrow the full purchase price of $20,000 at an interest rate of 8% per year (APR), so that you make monthly payments on the car loan that will match the $402.84 per month lease payments.[7] The loan is fully amortized over a five-year period, so the balance of the loan at the end of 36 months will be $8,907.06. The maintenance expenses, taxes, and insurance will be the same whether you lease or buy.

Under these conditions, what is the difference between leasing the car and buying it on credit? Table 10A.1 summarizes the cash flows.

Under both arrangements, you have the use of the car for 36 months in return for a monthly payment of $402.84. The difference is that if you purchase the car now, then three years from now you will sell it at an uncertain market price and pay off the $8,907.06 balance of your loan. Your net cash flow will be the difference be-

---

[7]APR stands for *annual percentage rate* and was explained in chapter 4. When payments are monthly, an APR of 8% is equivalent to a monthly interest rate of $\frac{2}{3}$%.

TABLE 10A.1	Comparison of Leasing a Car or Buying It on Credit	
Alternative	*Monthly Payment*	*Final Cash Flow*
Lease for three years	$402.84	0
Buy on credit and sell at end of three years	$402.84	Resale price minus $8,907.06
Difference	0	Resale price minus $8,907.06

tween the price of the car on the used-car market three years in the future and $8,907.06.

If you lease the car, however, at the end of three years you neither own it nor owe any money on it. In effect, it is as if you had sold the car in advance for $8,907.06—the balance of your loan. Thus, under the lease arrangement, the dealer effectively agrees in advance to repurchase the car from you three years from now at a price equal to the remaining balance of the loan.[8]

If you were absolutely sure that the car's residual value after three years was going to be $11,000, then clearly it would pay to purchase the car now rather than lease it. This is because you could resell it in three years, pay off the $8,907 balance of the loan, and pocket the $2,093 difference.

But you do not know the resale value with certainty. Even if you take very good care of it, the resale value of the car three years from now will be determined by a variety of factors (such as consumer tastes, cost of gasoline, level of economic activity) that can only be estimated now.

---

[8]Real-world leases contain certain provisions designed to deter customers who wear cars out quickly and to discourage abuse of the car. Thus, customers who exceed a certain mileage limitation must pay extra and must pay for any damage done to the car. Many leases also give you the right, but not the obligation, to purchase the car at a prespecified price at the lease's end. This right has value and is similar to a call option. The valuation of options is covered in chapter 15.

C H A P T E R

11

Hedging, Insuring, and Diversifying

OBJECTIVES

■ To explain the various methods and institutional mechanisms for the transfer of risk through the financial system by hedging, insuring, and diversifying.

■ To explain how diversification can reduce the cost of insurance.

CONTENTS

In the previous chapter we said that there are three ways of transferring risk to others: hedging, insuring, and diversifying. The purpose of this chapter is to give you a more detailed and concrete understanding of all three methods and how they are used in practice.

One is said to hedge a risk when reducing one's exposure to a loss entails giving up the possibility of a gain. Thus, farmers who sell their future crops at a fixed price in order to eliminate the risk of a low price at harvest time give up the possibility of profiting from higher prices at harvest time. Financial markets offer a variety of mechanisms for hedging against the risks of uncertain commodity prices, stock prices, interest rates, and exchange rates. In this chapter we explore the use of derivatives and the matching of assets to liabilities in order to hedge market risks.

Insuring means paying a *premium* (the price paid for the insurance) to avoid losses. By buying insurance, you substitute a *sure* loss (the premium you pay for the policy) for the *possibility* of a larger loss if you do not insure.

In addition to insurance policies, there are other types of contracts and securities not usually called insurance that serve the same economic function of providing compensation for losses. A common example is a *credit guarantee,* which insures creditors against losses stemming from a debtor's failure to make promised payments. *Option contracts* are another means for insuring against losses. This chapter explores these different contractual mechanisms for insuring against risk.

Finally, diversifying is the pooling and sharing of risks. Diversifying your portfolio of stocks means splitting your investment among several stocks rather than concentrating it all in just a single stock. The volatility of a diversified portfolio is generally less than the volatilities of each of its individual components. In this chapter we will explore the way diversification works to reduce volatility and the cost of insurance.

11.1 USING FORWARD AND FUTURES CONTRACTS TO HEDGE RISK

Anytime two parties agree to exchange some item in the future at a prearranged price they are entering into a **forward contract.** Often people enter into forward contracts without knowing that is what they are called.

For example, you may be planning a trip from Boston to Tokyo a year from now. You make your flight reservations now, and the airline reservation clerk tells you that you can either lock in a price of $1,000 now or you can pay whatever the price may be on the day of your flight. In either case payment will not take place until the day of your flight. If you decide to lock in the $1,000 price, you have entered into a forward contract with the airline.

In entering the forward contract you eliminate the risk of the cost of your airfare going above $1,000. If the price of a ticket turns out to be $1,500 a year from now, you will be happy that you had the good sense to lock in a forward price of $1,000. On the other hand, if the price turns out to be $500 on the day of your flight, you will still have to pay the $1,000 forward price to which you agreed. In that case, you will regret your decision.

The main features of forward contracts and the terms used to describe them are as follows:

- Two parties agree to exchange some item in the future at a price specified now—the **forward price.**[1]
- The price for *immediate* delivery of the item is called the **spot price.**
- No money is paid in the present by either party to the other.
- The **face value** of the contract is the quantity of the item specified in the contract times the forward price.
- The party who agrees to *buy* the specified item is said to take a **long position,** and the party who agrees to *sell* the item is said to take a **short position.**

---

[1]More precisely, the *forward price* is that delivery price that makes the value of the forward contract equal to zero at the time the contract is made.

A **futures contract** is essentially a *standardized* forward contract that is traded on some organized exchange. The exchange interposes itself between the buyer and the seller, so that each has a separate contract with the exchange. Standardization means that the terms of the futures contract (e.g., quantity and quality of the item to be delivered, etc.) are the same for all contracts.

A forward contract can often reduce the risks faced by both the buyer and the seller. Let us illustrate how with a detailed example.

Suppose a farmer has planted her fields with wheat. It is now a month before harvest time, and the size of the farmer's crop is reasonably certain. Because a large fraction of the farmer's wealth is tied up in her wheat crop, she may want to eliminate the risk associated with uncertainty about its future price by selling it now at a fixed price for future delivery.

Let's also suppose that there is a baker who knows that he will need wheat a month from now to produce bread. The baker has a large fraction of his wealth tied up in his bakery business. Like the farmer, the baker is also faced with uncertainty about the future price of wheat, but the way for him to reduce the price risk is to *buy* wheat now for future delivery. Thus, the baker is a natural match for the farmer, who would like to reduce her risk by selling wheat now for future delivery.

The farmer and the baker, therefore, agree to a certain *forward* price that the baker will pay the farmer at the time of delivery.

The forward contract stipulates that the farmer will deliver a specified quantity of wheat to the baker at the forward price *regardless of what the spot price turns out to be at the delivery date.*

Let's put some actual quantities and prices into our example to see how forward contracts work. Suppose that the size of the farmer's wheat crop is 100,000 bushels and that the forward price for delivery a month from now is $2 per bushel. The farmer agrees to sell her entire crop to the baker with delivery a month from now at $2 per bushel. At that time, the farmer will deliver 100,000 bushels of wheat to the baker and receive $200,000 in return. With an agreement such as this, both parties eliminate the risk associated with the uncertainty about the spot price of wheat at the delivery date. They are both hedging their exposures.

Now let us consider why it is convenient to have standardized *futures* contracts for wheat that are traded on exchanges instead of forward contracts. The forward contract in our example calls for the farmer to deliver wheat to the baker on the contract delivery date. However, it can be difficult for a farmer to find a baker who wants to buy wheat at the time and place that are most convenient to the farmer. Similarly, it may be difficult for the baker to find a farmer who wants to sell wheat at the time and place that are most convenient to the baker.

For example, suppose that the farmer and the baker are separated by a great distance, for example, the farmer might be located in Kansas and the baker in New York. The baker usually buys wheat from a local supplier in New York and the farmer usually sells her wheat to a local distributor in Kansas. By using wheat futures contracts, the farmer and the baker can retain the risk-reducing benefits of the forward contract (and save paying costs to transport wheat) without having to change their usual supplier and distributor relationships.

The futures exchange operates as an intermediary matching buyers and sellers. Indeed, the buyer of a wheat futures contract never knows the identity of the seller because the contract is officially between the buyer and the futures exchange. Similarly, the seller never knows the identity of the buyer. Only a small fraction of the wheat futures contracts traded on the exchange result in actual delivery of wheat. Most of them are settled in cash.

Let us illustrate how this works in the case of the farmer and the baker. Instead of entering a forward contract calling for the farmer in Kansas to deliver her wheat to the baker in New York at a delivery price of $2 per bushel, there are two separate transactions. The farmer and baker each enter a wheat futures contract with the futures exchange at a futures price of $2 per bushel. The farmer takes a short position; the baker takes a long position, and the exchange matches them. In a month's time, the farmer sells her wheat to her normal distributor in Kansas, and the baker buys his wheat from his normal supplier in New York at the spot price. They settle their futures contract by paying to (or receiving from) the futures exchange the *difference* between the $2 per bushel futures price and the spot price multiplied by the quantity specified in the contract (100,000 bushels). The futures exchange transfers the payment from one party to the other.[2]

Let us further illustrate how this all works step by step with the help of Table 11.1. Consider first the farmer, whose situation is shown in the top panel. To hedge her exposure to the price risk, she takes a short position in a one-month wheat futures contract for 100,000 bushels at a futures price of $2 per bushel.

Table 11.1 illustrates what happens at three different spot prices on the delivery date: $1.50, $2.00, and $2.50 per bushel. If the spot price of wheat turns out to be $1.50 per bushel a month from now (column 1), the farmer's proceeds from the sale of wheat to the distributor in Kansas are $150,000. However, she gains $50,000 from her futures contract. Thus, her total receipts are $200,000.

If the spot price turns out to be $2.00 per bushel (column 2), the farmer's proceeds from the sale of her wheat to the distributor in Kansas are $200,000, and there

TABLE 11.1   Hedging Price Risk with Futures Contracts

Farmer's Transaction	Spot Price of Wheat on Delivery Date		
	$1.50 per bu. (1)	$2.00 per bu. (2)	$2.50 per bu. (3)
Proceeds from sale of wheat to distributor	$150,000	$200,000	$250,000
Cash flow from the futures contract	$50,000 paid to farmer	0	$50,000 paid by farmer
Total receipts	$200,000	$200,000	$200,000

Baker's Transaction	Spot Price of Wheat on Delivery Date		
	$1.50 per bu. (1)	$2.00 per bu. (2)	$2.50 per bu. (3)
Cost of wheat bought from supplier	$150,000	$200,000	$250,000
Cash flow from the futures contract	$50,000 paid by baker	0	$50,000 paid to baker
Total outlays	$200,000	$200,000	$200,000

The futures price is $2.00 per bushel, and the quantity is 100,000 bushels.

---

[2]Rather than wait until the contract maturity date, the cash value of futures contracts are usually settled on a daily basis; this reduces the risk to the exchange of either party defaulting on their contracts.

is no gain or loss on the futures contract. If the spot price turns out to be $2.50 per bushel, the farmer receives $250,000 from the sale of her wheat to the distributor in Kansas but loses $50,000 on the futures contract. Her total receipts are then $200,000.

Thus, no matter what the spot price of wheat turns out to be, the farmer winds up with total receipts of $200,000 from the combination of selling her wheat to the distributor in Kansas and her short position in the wheat futures contract.

The bottom panel of Table 11.1 shows the situation of the baker. A month from now the baker buys wheat from his supplier in New York at the spot price. If the spot price is $1.50 per bushel (column 1), the baker pays only $150,000 to the supplier for the wheat but also loses $50,000 on his wheat futures contract. His total outlay is, therefore, $200,000. If the spot price is $2.00 per bushel (column 2), the baker pays the supplier $200,000, and there is no gain or loss on the futures contract. If the spot price is $2.50 per bushel (column 3), the baker pays the supplier $250,000 for wheat but gains $50,000 on his futures contract, thus making his total outlay $200,000.

To better understand Table 11.1 consider what would happen *without* the futures contract. If the spot price of wheat turns out to be $1.50 per bushel, then the farmer receives and the baker pays $150,000. If the spot price turns out to be $2.50, then the farmer receives and the baker pays $250,000. But *with* the futures contract, no matter what the spot price turns out to be, the farmer receives and the baker pays a *total* of $200,000. Because both parties know for certain what they will get and what they will pay out, the futures contract has eliminated the risk posed by price uncertainty.

Figure 11.1 displays the same information that is contained in the top panel of Table 11.1. It shows the *total* cash flows to the farmer from selling her wheat *and* the futures contract combined for *any* spot price on the delivery date.

Figure 11.1 illustrates that no matter what the spot price of wheat turns out to be on the delivery date, the farmer will wind up with $200,000.

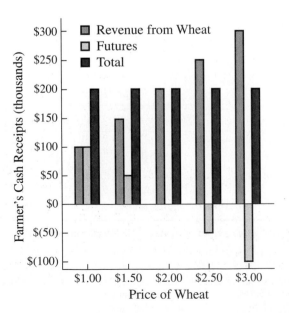

FIGURE 11.1 Farmer's Total Cash Flows from Hedging with Futures

Notes: The farmer's wheat crop is 100,000 bushels, and the futures price of wheat that she has agreed to in her futures contract is $2 per bushel. Gains or losses on the futures contract serve to keep her total receipts at $200,000 regardless of the spot price of wheat on the delivery date.

To summarize, the farmer is able to eliminate the price risk she faces from owning the wheat by taking a *short* position in a futures contract, effectively *selling* the wheat for future delivery at the futures price. The baker too is able to eliminate the price risk he faces by taking a *long* position in the futures market for wheat, effectively *buying* wheat for future delivery at a fixed price. Futures contracts make it possible for both the farmer and the baker to hedge their exposure to price risk while continuing their normal relationships with distributors and suppliers.

Quick Check 11-1
Show what happens to the farmer and the baker if the spot price on the delivery date is:
a. $1.00 per bushel.
b. $3.00 per bushel.

The example of the farmer and the baker illustrates three important points about risk and risk transfer:

- *Whether a transaction is risk reducing or risk increasing depends on the particular context in which it is undertaken.*

Transactions in futures markets are sometimes characterized as being very risky. But for the farmer, whose wealth is tied up in the business of growing wheat, taking a short position in a wheat futures contract is risk reducing. For the baker, whose wealth is tied up in the business of baking bread, taking a long position in a wheat futures contract is risk reducing.

Of course, for someone who is not in the business of either growing wheat or producing products that require wheat as an input, taking a position in wheat futures might be risky.[3] Thus, the transaction of buying or selling wheat futures should not be characterized as risky in the abstract. It may be risk reducing or risk increasing depending on the context.

- *Both parties to a risk-reducing transaction can benefit by it even though in retrospect it may seem as if one of the parties has gained at the expense of the other.*

When entering the futures contract, neither the farmer nor the baker knows whether the price of wheat will turn out to be greater or less than $2.00 per bushel. By entering the futures contract, they *both* achieve a reduction in risk and are thereby *both* made better off. In a month's time, if the spot price of wheat is different from $2.00, one of them will gain and the other will lose on the futures contract. But that does not alter the fact that they were both made better off by entering the contract when they did.

- *Even with no change in total output or total risk, redistributing the way the risk is borne can improve the welfare of the individuals involved.*

This last point is related to the second. From a social perspective, the total quantity of wheat produced in the economy is not directly affected by the existence of the futures contract between the farmer and the baker. It might, therefore, appear as though there is no gain in social welfare from the existence of futures contracts.

---

[3]As stated in chapter 10, such parties are known as *speculators.*

However, as we have seen, by allowing both the farmer and the baker to lower their exposure to price risk, the futures contract improves their welfare.

Using futures contracts to hedge commodity price risk has a long history. The earliest known futures markets came into existence in the Middle Ages to meet the needs of farmers and merchants. Today many organized futures exchanges exist around the world not only for commodities (such as grains, oilseeds, livestock, meat, metals, and petroleum products) but also for a variety of financial instruments (such as currencies, bonds, and stock market indexes). The futures contracts traded on these exchanges allow businesses to hedge against commodity-price risk, foreign-exchange risk, stock market risk, and interest-rate risk and the list is constantly expanding to include other sources of risk.

11.2 HEDGING FOREIGN-EXCHANGE RISK WITH SWAP CONTRACTS

A swap is another type of contract that facilitates the hedging of risks. A **swap contract** consists of two parties exchanging (or "swapping") a series of cash flows at specified intervals over a specified period of time. The swap payments are based on an agreed principal amount (the *notional* amount). There is no immediate payment of money and, hence, the swap agreement itself provides no new funds to either party.

In principle, a swap contract could call for the exchange of anything. In current practice, however, most swap contracts involve the exchange of returns on commodities, currencies, or securities.

Let's look at how a currency swap works and how it can be used to hedge risk. Suppose that you have a computer software business in the United States, and a German company wants to acquire the right to produce and market your software in Germany. The German company agrees to pay you 100,000 marks (DM100,000) each year for the next 10 years for these rights.

If you want to hedge the risk of fluctuations in the dollar value of your expected stream of revenues (due to fluctuations in the dollar/mark exchange rate), you can enter a currency swap now to exchange your future stream of marks for a future stream of dollars at a set of forward exchange rates specified now.

The swap contract is, therefore, equivalent to a series of forward contracts. The notional amount in the swap contract corresponds to the face value of the implied forward contracts.

To illustrate with numbers, suppose the dollar/mark exchange rate is currently $0.50 per mark and that that exchange rate also applies to all forward contracts covering the next 10 years. The notional amount in your swap contract is 100,000 marks per year. By entering the swap contract, you lock in a dollar revenue of $50,000 per year (DM100,000 × $0.50 per DM). Each year on the settlement date you will receive (or pay) an amount of cash equal to 100,000 marks times the difference between the forward rate and the actual spot rate at that time.

Thus, suppose that one year from now on the settlement date, the spot rate of exchange is $0.40 per mark. The party on the other side of your swap contract, called the **counterparty** (the German company in our example), is obliged to pay you 100,000 times the difference between the $0.50 per mark forward rate and the $0.40 per mark spot rate (i.e., $10,000).

Without the swap contract, your cash revenues from the software license agreement would be $40,000 (100,000 times the spot rate of $0.40 per mark). But *with* the swap contract, your total revenues will be $50,000: You receive DM100,000 from the German company, which you sell to get $40,000, *and* you receive another $10,000 from the counterparty to your swap contract.

Now suppose that in the second year on the settlement date, the spot rate of exchange is $0.70 per mark. You will be obliged to pay the counterparty to your swap agreement 100,000 times the difference between the $0.70 per mark spot rate and the $0.50 per mark forward rate, i.e., $20,000. *Without* the swap contract your cash revenues from the software license agreement would be $70,000 (100,000 times the spot rate of $0.70 per mark). But *with* the swap contract, your total revenues will be $50,000. Thus, in the second year, you will probably wish that you did not have the swap contract. (But the possibility of giving up potential gains in order to eliminate potential losses is the essence of hedging.)

Quick Check 11-2

Suppose that in the third year on the settlement date, the spot rate of exchange is $0.50 per mark. How much money is transferred between the counterparties to the swap contract?

The international swap market began in the early 1980s and has grown rapidly. In addition to currency and interest-rate swaps, many other items can be and are exchanged through swap agreements, for example, returns on different stock indexes, and even bushels of wheat for barrels of oil.

11.3 HEDGING SHORTFALL RISK BY MATCHING ASSETS TO LIABILITIES

As we saw in chapter 2, insurance companies and other financial intermediaries that sell insured savings plans and other insurance contracts need to assure their customers that the product they are buying is free of default risk. One way to assure customers about the risk of contract default is for insurance companies to hedge their liabilities in the financial markets by investing in assets that match the characteristics of their liabilities.

For example, suppose that an insurance company sells a customer a guaranteed investment contract that promises to pay $1,000 five years from now for a one-time premium today of $783.53. (This implies that the customer is earning an interest rate of 5% per year.) The insurance company can *hedge* this customer liability by buying a default-free zero-coupon bond with a face value of $1,000 issued by the government.

The insurance company is *matching assets to liabilities.* In order to earn a profit on this set of transactions, the insurance company has to be able to buy the five-year government bond for less than $783.53. (In other words, the interest rate on the five-year government bond must be greater than 5% per year.) If instead of hedging its liability by buying a bond, the insurance company invests the premium in a portfolio of stocks, then there will be a risk of a shortfall—the value of the stocks in five years may turn out to be less than the $1,000 promised to the customer.

Many financial intermediaries pursue hedging strategies that involve matching their assets to their liabilities. In each case, the objective is to reduce the risk of a shortfall. The nature of the hedging instrument varies with the type of customer liability.

Thus, if a savings bank has customer liabilities that are short-term deposits earning an interest rate that floats, the appropriate hedging instrument is a floating-rate bond, or a strategy of "rolling over" short-term bonds. Another way the bank might hedge its floating-rate deposit liabilities is to invest in long-term fixed-rate bonds and enter into a swap contract to swap the fixed rate it receives on its bonds for a floating rate.

11.4 MINIMIZING THE COST OF HEDGING

As just noted, there is often more than one mechanism for hedging risk available to a decision maker. When there is more than one way to hedge risk, a rational manager will choose the one that costs the least.

For example, suppose that you live in Boston and are planning to move to Tokyo a year from now for an extended visit. You have found a wonderful apartment there and have agreed to buy it for 10.3 million yen, which you will pay to the apartment's current owner at the time you move in. You have just sold your condominium in Boston for $100,000, and plan to use that money to pay for the apartment in Tokyo. You have invested the money in one-year U.S. Treasury bills at an interest rate of 3%, so you know that you will have $103,000 a year from now.

The dollar/yen exchange rate is currently $0.01 per yen (or 100 yen per dollar). If it remains unchanged for a year, you will have exactly the 10.3 million yen you need to pay for the Tokyo apartment a year from now. But you discover that in the past year the dollar/yen exchange rate has fluctuated quite a bit. It was as low as $0.008 per yen and as high as $0.011. You are, therefore, concerned that, one year from now, your $103,000 may not buy enough yen to pay for the Tokyo apartment.

If the exchange rate is $0.008 per yen in a year, you will receive 12.875 million yen for your $103,000 ($103,000/$0.008 per yen)—enough to buy the apartment and some nice furnishings. If, however, the exchange rate is $0.012 per yen a year from now, then you will get only 8.583 million yen ($103,000/$0.012 per yen), and you will be 1.717 million yen short of the purchase price you agreed to a year earlier.

Suppose that there are two ways you can eliminate your exposure to the risk of a rise in the dollar price of the yen. One way is to get the owner of the Tokyo apartment to sell it to you for a price fixed in U.S. dollars. The other way is by entering a forward contract for yen with a bank.

Let us compare the costs to you of the two methods of hedging the foreign-exchange risk. Suppose that in our example the bank's forward price is $0.01 per yen. Then by entering into a forward contract with the bank to exchange your $103,000 in a year at $0.01 per yen, you can completely eliminate your risk. No matter what happens to the dollar/yen exchange rate over the next year, you will have the 10.3 million yen you need to buy your apartment in Tokyo one year from now.

Now consider the other alternative of negotiating a fixed price in U.S. dollars with the owner of the apartment. If the owner of the Tokyo apartment is willing to sell you the apartment for a dollar price less than $103,000, then that is a better deal than entering into a forward contract with the bank.

On the other hand, if the owner of the Tokyo apartment demands a dollar price higher than $103,000, then you are better off setting the price in yen (10.3 million yen) and entering into a forward contract with the bank to exchange the yen for dollars at the forward price of $0.01 per yen. You also have to consider the transaction costs (broker fees, the amount of time and effort involved, etc.) associated with each method of hedging the risk.

The important point to recognize in this example is that *the mechanism chosen to implement the hedge should be the one that minimizes the cost of achieving the desired reduction of risk.*

11.5 INSURING VERSUS HEDGING

There is a fundamental difference between insuring and hedging. When you hedge, you eliminate the risk of loss by giving up the potential for gain. When you insure, you pay a premium to eliminate the risk of loss and *retain* the potential for gain.

Let us return to an earlier example to clarify the difference between insuring and hedging. You are planning a trip from Boston to Tokyo a year from now. You make your flight reservations now, and the airline reservation clerk tells you that you can either lock in a price of $1,000 now, or you can pay whatever the price turns out be on the day of your flight. If you decide to lock in the $1,000 price, you have *hedged* against the risk of loss. It costs you nothing to do so, but you have given up the possibility of paying less than $1,000 for your flight a year from now.

Alternatively, the airline may offer you the possibility of paying $20 now for the *right* to purchase your ticket a year from now at a price of $1,000. By buying this right you have insured that you will pay no more than $1,000 to fly to Tokyo. If the price should turn out to be more than $1,000 a year from now, you will exercise this right; otherwise you will let it expire. By paying $20 you have purchased insurance against the risk that you will have to pay more than $1,000 for the ticket and, thus, you have insured that the total cost to you will not exceed $1,020 ($1,000 for the ticket plus $20 for the insurance).

Earlier we discussed a farmer who has wheat to sell in another month. The size of the farmer's wheat crop is 100,000 bushels, and the forward price for delivery a month from now is $2 per bushel. If the farmer hedges with a short position in a forward contract for 100,000 bushels, she will receive $200,000 a month from now regardless of what the price of wheat turns out to be on the delivery date.

Instead of taking a short position in the forward market, however, she can buy insurance that guarantees a *minimum* price of $2 per bushel.[4] Say the insurance costs $20,000. Then, should the price of wheat turn out to be higher than $2.00 per bushel, the farmer will simply not need to use the insurance, and the policy will expire. If, however, the price should turn out to be less than $2.00 per bushel, the farmer will collect on her insurance and wind up with $200,000 less the cost of the insurance or $180,000.

Figure 11.2 illustrates the difference between the farmer's revenues a month from now under three different alternative courses of action: (1) taking no measures to reduce her exposure to price risk, (2) hedging with a forward contract, and (3) insuring.

The horizontal axis measures the price of wheat a month from now, and the vertical axis measures the farmer's revenue. In the case of insuring (alternative 3), the revenue is net of the premium paid for the insurance.

---

[4]As we will see later in this chapter, this is done by buying a put option.

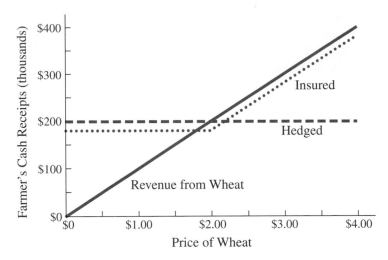

FIGURE 11.2   Hedging versus Insuring against Price Risk:
The Farmer

Note that by insuring, the farmer retains much of the economic benefit of an increase in the price of wheat while eliminating the downside risk. This benefit comes at the cost of paying a premium for the insurance.

Note that none of the three alternatives depicted in Figure 11.2 is superior to the others under *all* circumstances. Of course, it would never pay to buy the insurance if the future price were known with certainty.

Thus, if the farmer knew for sure that the price was going to be higher than $2.00 per bushel, she would choose not to reduce her risk exposure at all (alternative 1). If she knew the price was going to be lower than $2.00 per bushel, she would *sell forward* at $2.00 (alternative 2). But the essence of the farmer's risk-management problem is that she does *not* know in advance what the price will be.

Quick Check 11-3
Look at this question from the point of view of a baker, who is concerned about the price of wheat *rising* rather than falling. How can the baker insure against his risk exposure?

11.6 BASIC FEATURES OF INSURANCE CONTRACTS

In discussing insurance contracts and understanding how to use them to manage risk, it is important to understand some basic terms and features. Four of the most important features of insurance contracts are **exclusions, caps, deductibles,** and **co-payments.** Let us briefly explain each.

11.6.1 Exclusions and Caps

Exclusions are losses that might *seem* to meet the conditions for coverage under the insurance contract but are specifically excluded. For example, life insurance policies pay benefits if the insured party dies, but such policies typically exclude payment of death benefits if the insured person takes his own life. Health insurance policies may exclude from coverage certain illnesses the insured party had *before* the policy was purchased. Thus, a health insurance policy may state that it excludes coverage for preexisting medical conditions.

    Caps are limits placed on compensation for particular losses covered under an insurance contract. Thus, if a health insurance policy is capped at $1 million, it means the insurance company will pay no more than this amount for the treatment of an illness.

11.6.2 Deductibles

A *deductible* is an amount of money that the insured party must pay out of his or her own resources before receiving any compensation from the insurer. Thus, if your automobile insurance policy has a $1,000 deductible for damage due to accidents, you must pay the first $1,000 in repair costs and the insurer will only pay for the amount in excess of $1,000.

    Deductibles create incentives for insured parties to control their losses. People with automobile insurance who have to pay the first $500 of repair costs out of their own pockets tend to drive more carefully than drivers with no deductibles. However, this incentive to control losses disappears once the loss exceeds the deductible amount.

11.6.3 Copayments

A *copayment* feature means that the insured party must cover a fraction of the loss. For example, an insurance policy might stipulate that the copayment is 20% of any loss, and the insurance company pays the other 80%.

    Copayments are similar to deductibles in that the insured party winds up paying part of the losses. The difference is in the way the partial payment is computed and in the incentives created for the insured party to control losses.

    Take the case of a health insurance policy that covers visits to the physician. With a copayment feature, the patient must pay part of the fee for each visit. If the policy had a $1,000 deductible instead of a copayment feature, the patient would pay the entire cost of all visits until the $1,000 deductible was met and then nothing for additional visits. Thus, the deductible feature does not create any incentive for patients to forgo additional visits once the $1,000 deductible is met; a copayment feature does. Insurance policies can contain both deductibles and copayments.

11.7 FINANCIAL GUARANTEES

Financial guarantees are insurance against **credit risk,** which is the risk that the other party to a contract into which you have entered will default. A *loan guarantee* is a contract that obliges the guarantor to make the promised payment on a loan if the borrower fails to do so. Loan guarantees are pervasive in the economy, playing a critical role in facilitating trade.

For example, consider credit cards, which in today's world have become a principal means of payment by consumers. Banks and other issuers of credit cards guarantee to merchants that they will stand behind all customer purchases made with their credit cards. Credit card issuers thus provide merchants with insurance against credit risk.

Banks, insurance companies, and on occasion, governments offer guarantees on a broad spectrum of financial instruments ranging from credit cards to interest-rate and currency swaps. Parent corporations routinely guarantee the debt obligations of their subsidiaries. Governments guarantee residential mortgages, farm and student loans, loans to small and large business firms, and loans to other governments. Governments sometimes serve as the guarantor of last resort, guaranteeing the promises made by guarantors in the private sector such as banks and pension funds. However, in cases in which the credit standing of a governmental organization is in doubt, private sector organizations have been called upon to guarantee the government's debts.

11.8 CAPS AND FLOORS ON INTEREST RATES

Interest-rate risk depends on one's perspective—whether you are a borrower or a lender. For example, suppose you have $5,000 on deposit in a bank money market account in which the interest rate you earn is adjusted on a daily basis to reflect current market conditions. From your perspective as a depositor (i.e., a lender), interest-rate risk is the risk that the interest rate will *fall*. An interest-rate insurance policy for you would take the form of an **interest-rate floor,** which means a guarantee of a *minimum* interest rate.

But suppose that you are a borrower. For example, suppose that you just bought a house and took a $100,000 adjustable-rate mortgage loan from a bank. Suppose the mortgage interest rate you pay is tied to the one-year U.S. Treasury bill rate. Then from your perspective, interest-rate risk is the risk that the interest rate will *rise*. An interest-rate insurance policy for you would take the form of an **interest-rate cap,** which means a guarantee of a *maximum* interest rate.

Most adjustable-rate mortgage loans (ARMs) made in the United States during the 1980s and 1990s contain interest-rate caps. Often the cap takes the form of a maximum amount that the mortgage interest rate can rise in any one-year period and then there may also be a *global* cap on the interest rate for the life of the mortgage loan.

11.9 OPTIONS AS INSURANCE

Options are another ubiquitous form of insurance contract. An **option** is the right to either purchase or sell something at a fixed price in the future. As we saw before in the case of the airline ticket, the purchase of an option to reduce risk is *insuring* against loss. An option contract is to be distinguished from a forward contract, which is the *obligation* to buy or sell something at a fixed price in the future.

Any contract that gives one of the contracting parties the right to buy or sell something at a prespecified exercise price is an option. There are as many different kinds of option contracts as there are items to buy or sell: commodity options, stock options, interest rate options, foreign-exchange options, and so on. Some kinds of option contracts have standardized terms and are traded on organized exchanges such as the Chicago Board Options Exchange in the United States or the Osaka Options and Futures Exchange in Japan.

There is a special set of terms associated with option contracts:

- An option to *buy* the specified item at a fixed price is a **call;** an option to *sell* is a **put.**
- The fixed price specified in an option contract is called the option's **strike price** or **exercise price.**
- The date after which an option can no longer be exercised is called its **expiration date** or *maturity* date.

If an option can only be exercised on the expiration date only, it is called a *European-type* option. If it can be exercised at any time up to and including the expiration date it is called an *American-type* option.

11.9.1 Put Options on Stocks

Put options on stocks protect against losses from a decline in stock prices. For example, consider Lucy, a manager working for XYZ Corporation. Suppose that she has received shares of XYZ stock as compensation in the past and now owns 1,000 shares. The current market price of XYZ is $100 per share. Let us consider how she can insure against the risk associated with her shares of XYZ stock by buying XYZ put options.

An XYZ put option gives her the right to sell a share of XYZ stock at a fixed exercise price, thus insuring her that she will receive at least the exercise price at the option's expiration date. For example, she can buy XYZ puts at an exercise price of $100 per share expiring in 1 year. Say the current price of a one-year European-style put on a single share of XYZ with a $100 exercise price is $10. Then the premium she must pay to insure her 1,000 shares of XYZ (currently worth $100,000) for the year is $10,000.

Buying put options on a stock portfolio is similar in many respects to buying term insurance on an asset such as a house or a car. For example, suppose that in addition to her shares of XYZ, Lucy owns an apartment in a condominium complex. The apartment's market value is $100,000. Although she cannot buy a put option on her apartment to protect her against a decline in its market value, she can buy insurance against losses of certain types. Suppose she buys a one-year fire insurance policy with a $100,000 cap for $500.

Table 11.2 summarizes the analogy between a put option and a term insurance policy. The insurance policy provides Lucy with protection against losses in the value of her apartment that stem from fire for a period of one year. The put option provides her with protection against losses in the value of her XYZ stocks that stem from a decline in their market price for a period of one year.

TABLE 11.2   Similarity between a Term Insurance Policy and a Put Option

	Insurance Policy	*Put Option*
Asset insured	Condominium	1,000 shares of XYZ stock
Asset's current value	$100,000	$100,000
Term of policy	1 year	1 year
Insurance premium	$500	$10,000

Lucy can lower the cost of her fire insurance by having a deductible. For example, if Lucy's fire insurance policy has a deductible of $5,000, then she has to pay the first $5,000 of any losses, and the insurance company compensates her only for losses in excess of $5,000. Analogously, Lucy can lower the cost of the insurance on her XYZ stock by choosing puts with a lower exercise price. If the current stock price is $100, and Lucy buys puts with an exercise price of $95, then she must absorb the first $5 per share of any loss resulting from a stock price decline. By choosing a put with a lower exercise price, she increases the deductible and lowers the cost of the insurance.

Quick Check 11-4
Suppose Lucy wanted market value insurance on her 1,000 shares of XYZ stock with a deductible of $10 per share and a copayment of 20%. How could she achieve this with XYZ put options?

11.9.2 Put Options on Bonds

As we saw in chapter 8, even when bonds are free of default risk, their prices can fluctuate substantially as a result of changes in interest rates. When bonds are subject to default risk, then their prices can change either because of changes in the level of risk-free interest rates or changes in the possible losses to bondholders from default. A put option on a bond, therefore, provides insurance against losses stemming from *either* source of risk.

For example, consider hypothetical 20-year zero-coupon bonds issued by Risky Realty Corporation. The bonds are secured by the fictitious firm's assets, which consist of apartment houses in various cities in the northeastern part of the United States. The firm has no other debt. The face value of the bonds is $10 million and the value of the firm's real estate holdings is currently $15 million.

The market price of the bonds reflects both the current level of risk-free interest rates, say 6% per year, and the market value of the real estate securing the bonds. Suppose that the yield to maturity on the bonds is 15% per year. Then the current market price of the bonds is $611,003.[5]

Suppose that you buy a one-year put option on the bonds with an exercise price of $600,000. Then if the bond's price falls either because the level of risk-free interest rates rises during the year (say from 6% per year to 8% per year) or because the value of the apartment houses securing the bonds falls (say from $15 million to $8 million), you are guaranteed a minimum price of $600,000 for the bonds.

11.10 THE DIVERSIFICATION PRINCIPLE

Diversifying means splitting an investment among many risky assets instead of concentrating it all in only one. Its meaning is captured by the familiar saying: "Don't put all your eggs in one basket." The **diversification principle** states that by diversifying across risky assets people can sometimes achieve a reduction in their overall risk exposure with no reduction in their expected return.

---

[5]$10 million$/1.15^{20} = $611,003.

11.10.1 Diversification with Uncorrelated Risks

To clarify how portfolio diversification can reduce your total risk exposure, let us return to an example introduced in chapter 10, in which risks were uncorrelated with each other.[6] You are thinking about investing $100,000 in the biotechnology business because you believe that the discovery of new genetically engineered drugs offers great profit potential over the next several years. For each drug you invest in, success means that you will quadruple your investment, but failure means a loss of your entire investment. Thus, if you invest $100,000 in a single drug, either you wind up with $400,000 or nothing.

Assume there is a .5 probability of success for each drug and a .5 probability of failure. Table 11.3 shows the probability distribution of final payoffs and rates of return on an investment in a single drug.

If you diversify by investing $50,000 in each of two drugs, there is still a chance of winding up with either $400,000 (if both drugs succeed) or nothing (if both drugs fail). However, there is also the intermediate possibility that one drug succeeds and the other fails. In that event, you will wind up with $200,000 (four times your investment of $50,000 in the drug that succeeds and zero from the drug that fails).

Thus, there are now four possible outcomes and three possible payoffs:

1. Both drugs succeed, and you receive $400,000.
2. Drug 1 succeeds and drug 2 doesn't, so you receive $200,000.
3. Drug 2 succeeds and drug 1 doesn't, so you receive $200,000.
4. Both drugs fail, and you receive nothing.

Thus, by diversifying and holding a portfolio of two drugs you reduce the probability of losing your entire investment to only one-half of what it would be without diversification. On the other hand, the probability of winding up with $400,000 has fallen from .5 to .25. The other two possible outcomes result in your receiving $200,000. The probability of this happening is .5 (computed as $2 \times .5 \times .5$). Table 11.4 summarizes the probability distribution of payoffs facing you if you split your investment between two drugs.

Now let us look at this probability distribution of payoffs in terms of expected payoffs and standard deviations. The formula for the expected payoff is:

$$E(X) = \sum_{i=1}^{n} p_i X_i$$

Expected Payoff = Sum of (Probability of Payoff) × (Possible Payoff)

TABLE 11.3 Probability Distribution for Investment in a Single Drug

Outcome	Probability	Payoff	Rate of Return
Drug does not succeed	.5	0	−100%
Drug succeeds	.5	$400,000	300%

Note: The cost of developing a drug is $100,000. The rate of return is the payoff minus the cost divided by the cost.

[6]The precise statistical meaning and measurement of correlation is discussed in the appendix to this chapter.

TABLE 11.4	Diversification with Two Drugs		
Outcome	*Probability*	*Payoff*	*Rate of Return*
No drugs succeed	.25	0	−100%
One drug succeeds	.50	$200,000	100%
Both drugs succeed	.25	$400,000	300%

Applying this formula to the case of a single drug, we find:

$$\text{Expected Payoff} = .5 \times 0 + .5 \times \$400,000 = \$200,000$$

The formula for standard deviation is:

$$\text{Standard Deviation } (\sigma) = \text{Square Root of the Sum}$$
$$\text{of (Probability)(Possible Payoff} - \text{Expected Payoff)}^2$$

Applying this formula to the case of a single drug, we find:

$$\sigma = \text{Square Root of } [(.5)(0 - \$200,000)^2 + (.5)(\$400,000 - \$200,000)^2]$$
$$\sigma = \$200,000$$

For the case of a portfolio of two uncorrelated drugs, we find:

$$\text{Expected Payoff} = .25 \times 0 + .5 \times \$200,000 + .25 \times \$400,000$$
$$\text{Expected Payoff} = \$200,000$$
$$\sigma = \text{Square Root of } [(.25)(0 - \$200,000)^2$$
$$+ (.5)(\$200,000 - \$200,000)^2 + (.25)(\$400,000 - \$200,000)^2]$$
$$\sigma = \$200,000/\sqrt{2} = \$141,421$$

Thus, when we diversify between two uncorrelated drugs the expected payoff remains $200,000, but the standard deviation falls by a factor of $1/\sqrt{2}$ from $200,000 to $141,421. The standard deviation of the rate of return falls from 200% to 141.4%.

Now consider what happens to the expected payoff and the standard deviation as the number of drugs in the portfolio increases even further (under the assumption that the success of each drug is uncorrelated with the success of the others).[7] The expected payoff stays the same, but the standard deviation declines in proportion to the square root of the number of drugs:

$$\sigma_{\text{portfolio}} = \$200,000/\sqrt{N}$$

Quick Check 11-5
How many uncorrelated drugs have to be in the portfolio for the standard deviation to be $100?

---

[7]The probability distribution of the portfolio rate of return in the case of one drug is the *binomial distribution.* As the number of drugs in the portfolio becomes large, the distribution can be closely approximated by a *normal distribution.*

11.10.2 Nondiversifiable Risk

In our example of diversification in the previous section, we assumed that the risks were uncorrelated with each other. In practice, many important risks are positively correlated with each other.[8] This is because they are affected by common underlying economic factors.

For example, the returns to investors who buy shares in stocks are all related to the health of the economy. An economic downturn will tend to have an adverse impact on the profits of almost all firms resulting in poor stockholder returns for almost all stocks. Consequently, one's ability to reduce one's exposure to stock market risk by buying many different stocks is limited.

Suppose that you buy a portfolio of stocks traded on the New York Stock Exchange. To achieve diversification you choose stocks by pasting the stock listings on a wall, blindfolding yourself, and throwing darts at them. You select those stocks that your darts land on. This results in a *randomly selected* portfolio.

Table 11.5 and the colored curve in Figure 11.3 show the effect of increasing the number of stocks in your randomly selected portfolio on the standard deviation of the portfolio's rate of return.[9] In column 2 of Table 11.5, we see that the average volatility for a single randomly selected stock traded on the New York Stock Exchange is

TABLE 11.5	Effect of Increasing the Number of Stocks in the Portfolio on Volatility of Return	
Number of Stocks in Portfolio *(1)*	*Average Volatility of Annual Portfolio Returns* *(2)*	*Ratio of Portfolio Volatility to Volatility of a Single Stock* *(3)*
1	49.24%	1.00
2	37.36	0.76
4	29.69	0.60
6	26.64	0.54
8	24.98	0.51
10	23.93	0.49
20	21.68	0.44
30	20.87	0.42
40	20.46	0.42
50	20.20	0.41
100	19.69	0.40
200	19.42	0.39
300	19.34	0.39
400	19.29	0.39
500	19.27	0.39
1,000	19.21	0.39

Source: Meir Statman, "How Many Stocks Make a Diversified Portfolio?" *Journal of Financial and Quantitative Analysis* 22 (September 1987), pp. 353–64.

[8]The precise statistical meaning of correlation is discussed in the appendix to this chapter.

[9]These numbers are taken from Meir Statman, "How Many Stocks Make a Diversified Portfolio" *Journal of Financial and Quantitative Analysis* 22 (September 1987) pp. 353–64.

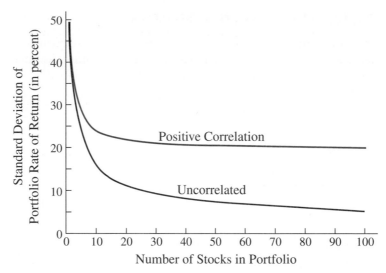

FIGURE 11.3   Effect of Increasing the Number of Stocks in the Portfolio on Volatility of Return

about 49.24% per year. If you selected an equally weighted portfolio of two stocks by such a random procedure, the average volatility would be about 37.36%. A three-stock portfolio would have a volatility of 29.69%, and so on.

The black curve in Figure 11.3 shows what the portfolio's volatility would be if there were zero correlation among all the stocks. Note that both the colored and black curves show that the reduction in standard deviation that comes from adding more stocks to the portfolio seems less and less significant as the number in the portfolio grows. After about 30 stocks, further reductions in the portfolio's volatility are barely noticeable.

For the colored curve, the standard deviation will go no lower than about 19.2% no matter how many more stocks are added. This is the risk that cannot be "diversified away" in an equally weighted portfolio of stocks. The part of the portfolio volatility that *can* be eliminated by adding more stocks is the **diversifiable risk,** and the part that remains no matter how many stocks are added is the **nondiversifiable risk.**

What accounts for nondiversifiable risk?

Stock prices fluctuate for many reasons, some of which are common to many stocks and some of which are relevant to a single firm or at most a small group of firms. Stock prices respond to random events that affect the current and expected future profits of firms. If an event occurs that affects many firms, such as an unanticipated downturn in general economic conditions, then many stocks will be affected. The risk of loss stemming from such events is sometimes called *market risk.*

On the other hand, random events that affect the prospects of only one firm, such as a lawsuit, a strike, or a new-product failure, give rise to random losses that are uncorrelated across stocks and can, therefore, be diversified away. The risk of loss stemming from this kind of event is called *firm-specific risk.*

These concepts of diversifiable and nondiversifiable risk apply to international diversification. By combining stocks of firms located in different countries it is possible to reduce the risk of one's stock portfolio, but there is a limit to this risk reduction. There are still common factors that affect nearly all firms no matter where in the world they are located. Thus, although international diversification can improve the prospects for risk reduction for people around the world, a significant amount of risk remains for even the best-diversified global stock portfolio.

Quick Check 11-6

Suppose you invest in a firm that produces software for personal computers. What would be some firm-specific risks affecting the rate of return on this investment?

11.11 DIVERSIFICATION AND THE COST OF INSURANCE

The cost of insuring a diversified portfolio of risks against a loss is almost always less than the cost of insuring against each risk separately. To see why, let us return to the biotechnology example of section 11.10.1. You are investing $100,000 in drug stocks. The success or failure of each drug is independent of the others.

Let us assume that you have decided to invest $50,000 in each of two drug stocks and, therefore, face the probability distribution in Table 11.4. For each separate drug stock there is a probability of .5 that you will lose 100% of your investment in that drug. But for the portfolio as a whole there is a probability of .25 that you will lose 100% of your $100,000 investment.

If you insure *each* $50,000 stock investment against a loss, it will cost more than insuring the $100,000 portfolio of *both* stocks against a loss. To see this, suppose that the cost of insurance equals the expected amount that the insurance company will pay you. Then the cost of an insurance policy on the total portfolio would be the probability of a loss times the magnitude of the loss:

$$.25 \times \$100,000 = \$25,000$$

The cost of insuring each of the two separate investments would be the probability of both stocks losing (.25) times $100,000 plus the probability of only one losing (.5) times $50,000:

$$.25 \times \$100,000 + .5 \times \$50,000 = \$50,000$$

So insuring each stock separately would cost *twice* as much as insuring the portfolio of two stocks. To protect against loss of wealth, you do not need separate insurance on each stock. If only one of the two drugs fails, then the profit from the successful drug will more than offset the loss from the failed one, so that your total wealth will be $200,000. You only need insurance against the risk that *both* drugs will fail (see Box 11.1). This example suggests the following general proposition:

> The more diversified are the risks in a portfolio of a given size, the less it will cost to insure the portfolio's total value against a loss.

Quick Check 11-7

How much should it cost to insure a portfolio of stocks, if it consists of $25,000 invested in each of four drug stocks whose chances of success are each .5 and are independent of each other?

The Advantages of Integrated Risk Management

Big changes are occurring in the way both the insurance industry and its corporate clients are approaching the management of risk. The new trend is called *integrated risk management*, and its goal is to lower the costs of managing the whole collection of risks faced by a firm.

In the past, corporations tended to compartmentalize the management of risks: currency, interest-rate, and credit risk exposures were handled by treasury, safety issues by human resources, environmental liability and asset protection by engineering, and property/casualty exposures by risk management. Now some firms are integrating these separate exposures and purchasing insurance against aggregate losses in excess of some level deemed to be acceptable.

A steel manufacturing company, for example, bought a combined workers' compensation and nonoccupational disability policy from an insurance company and estimates that the policy was about a third cheaper than what it previously paid for two separate policies. As another example, AIG has sold Honeywell a multirisk policy that includes foreign-exchange protection along with property and liability coverage. Honeywell retains a deductible of slightly more than its expected aggregate combined losses.

Summary

- Market mechanisms for *hedging* risk exposures are forward and futures contracts, swaps, and matching assets to liabilities.

- A forward contract is the obligation to deliver a specified asset at a specified future delivery date at a specified price. Futures contracts are standardized forward contracts that are traded on exchanges.

- A swap contract consists of two parties exchanging a series of payments at specified intervals over a specified period of time. A swap contract could call for the exchange of almost anything. In current practice, however, most swap contracts involve the exchange of commodities, currencies, or securities.

- Financial intermediaries such as insurance companies often hedge their customer liabilities by matching their assets to their liabilities. This is done to reduce the risk of a shortfall.

- When there is more than one way to hedge a given risk exposure, the mechanism chosen should be the one that minimizes the cost of achieving the desired reduction of risk.

- There is a fundamental difference between insuring and hedging. When you hedge, you eliminate the risk of loss by giving up the potential for gain. When you insure, you pay a premium to eliminate the risk of loss and *retain* the potential for gain.

- Put options on stocks protect against losses from a decline in stock prices.

- Financial guarantees act as insurance against credit risk. Interest-rate floors and caps offer insurance against interest-rate risk to lenders and borrowers, respectively. A put option on a bond offers the bondholder insurance against *both* default risk and interest-rate risk.

- The more diversified are the risks in a portfolio of a given size, the less it will cost to insure the portfolio against a loss.

Key Terms

- forward contract   285
- forward price   285
- spot price   285
- face value   285
- long position   285
- short position   285
- futures contract   286
- swap contract   290
- counterparty   290
- exclusions   294
- caps   294
- deductibles   294
- copayments   294
- financial guarantees   295

- credit risk   295
- interest-rate floor   296
- interest-rate cap   296
- option   296
- call   297
- put   297
- strike price   297
- exercise price   297
- expiration date   297
- diversification principle   298
- diversifiable risk   302
- nondiversifiable risk   302
- correlation   314

Answers to Quick Check Questions

Quick Check 11-1   *Show what happens to the farmer and the baker if the spot price on the delivery date is:*
a. $1.00 per bushel.
b. $3.00 per bushel.

ANSWER:

Farmer's Transaction	*$1.00/Bushel*	*$3.00/Bushel*
Proceeds from sale of wheat	$100,000	$300,000
Cash flow from futures contract	$100,000 paid to farmer	$100,000 paid by farmer
Total receipts	$200,000	$200,000

Baker's Transaction	*$1.00/Bushel*	*$3.00/Bushel*
Cost of wheat from supplier	$100,000	$300,000
Cash flow from futures contract	$100,000 paid by baker	$100,000 paid to baker
Total outlays	$200,000	$200,000

Quick Check 11-2   *Suppose that in the third year on the settlement date, the spot rate of exchange is $0.50 per mark. How much money is transferred between the counterparties to the swap contract?*

ANSWER: Because the spot price is the same as the forward price on the settlement date, no money changes hands.

Quick Check 11-3   *Look at this question from the point of view of the baker, who is concerned about the price of wheat rising rather than falling. How can the baker insure against his risk exposure?*

ANSWER: The baker needs to buy 100,000 bushels of wheat in another month. The baker is concerned about rising wheat prices. The baker could take a long position in the forward market, committing to buy 100,000 bushels of wheat at $2.00 per bushel. However, the baker is locked in at that price and will not benefit at all if prices fall. By purchasing an option to purchase wheat at $2.00 a bushel; the baker now knows he will pay a maximum of $2.00 a bushel; but if prices fall, he will not exercise the option and buy wheat at the market or spot price. This option will cost him something, however. Assume that it will cost $20,000 as the illustrated put option did.

Quick Check 11-4   *Suppose Lucy wanted market value insurance on her 1,000 shares of XYZ stock with a deductible of $10 per share and a copayment of 20%. How could she achieve this with XYZ put options?*

ANSWER: Deductible of $10 means the strike price must be $90 ($100 − $10). A copayment of 20% means that she will only buy puts on 800 shares rather than the full 1,000.

Quick Check 11-5   *How many uncorrelated drugs have to be in a portfolio for the standard deviation to be $100?*

ANSWER: 4,000,000 uncorrelated drugs.

Quick Check 11-6   *Suppose you invest in a firm that produces software for personal computers. What would be some firm-specific risks affecting the rate of return on this investment?*

ANSWER: The risks would be failure of the personal computing software because of defects in the programming, or other technical difficulties; competition from other software manufacturers; pending lawsuit on the firm's practices; loss of the major software developers to other companies, and so on.

Quick Check 11-7   *How much should it cost to insure a portfolio of stocks, if it consists of $25,000 invested in each of four drug stocks whose chances of success are each .5 and are independent of each other?*

ANSWER: There is now a different probability distribution of loss on the portfolio. The only possibility of a loss is if all four drugs fail. (If three drugs fail and the fourth succeeds, then the portfolio will be worth $4 \times \$25,000 = \$100,000$.) The probability of this happening is $.5^4 = .0625$. Therefore, the cost of the insurance will be the expected value of the payout or $.0625 \times \$100,000 = \$6,250$.

Quick Check 11-8   *Compute the correlation coefficient between the rate of return on Posicorr and on Genco stocks.*

ANSWER: Expected return on Posicorr stock is .16 and the standard deviation is .245 whereas for Genco it is .14 and .2, respectively. The covariance between the two stocks is .049 and the correlation coefficient $= (.049)/(.245 \times .2) = 1$. The two are perfectly positively correlated.

Questions and Problems

1. *Hedging Price Risk with Futures Contracts*
   Suppose you own a grove of orange trees. The harvest is still two months away but you are concerned about price risk. You want to guarantee that you will receive $1.00 per pound in two months regardless of what the spot price is at that time. You are selling 250,000 pounds.
   a. Show the economics of a short transaction in the forward market if the spot price on delivery date is $0.75 per pound, $1.00 per pound, or $1.25 per pound.
   b. What would have happened to you if you had not entered the hedge and each scenario is equally likely?
   c. What is the variability of your receipts after the hedge is in place?

2. *Mutual Benefits of Hedge Transaction*

Suppose in six months' time the cost of a gallon of heating oil will either be $0.90 or $1.10. The current price is $1.00 per gallon.

   a. What are the risks faced by a reseller of heating oil that has a large inventory on hand? What are the risks faced by a large user of heating oil with a very small inventory?

   b. How can these two parties use the heating oil futures market to reduce their risks and lock in a price of $1.00 per gallon? Assume each contract is for 50,000 gallons and they each need to hedge 100,000 gallons.

   c. Can you say that each party has been made better off? Why or why not?

3. *Hedging Price Risk with Futures Contracts*

Suppose you are chief financial officer of Hotels International and you purchase a large quantity of coffee each month. You are concerned about the price of coffee one month from now. You want to guarantee that you will not pay more than $1.50 per pound for 35,000 pounds. You do not want to pay for insurance but you do want to lock in a price of $1.50 per pound for 35,000 pounds.

   a. Show the economics of a futures transaction if the spot price on the delivery date is $1.25, $1.50, or $1.75.

   b. What is the variability of Hotels International's total outlays under the futures contract?

   c. If at the time of delivery coffee is $1.25 per pound, should you have forgone entering into the futures contract? Why or why not?

4. *Risk Reduction versus Speculation*

Suppose you are treasurer of a large municipality in Michigan and you are investing in cattle futures. You purchase futures contracts worth 400,000 pounds of cattle with an exercise price of $0.60 per pound and an expiration date in one month.

   a. Show the economics of a futures transaction if the price of cattle at delivery date is $0.40 per pound, $0.60 per pound, or $0.80 per pound.

   b. Is this a risk-reducing transaction?

   c. Would your answer be different if the treasurer were investing in oil futures? What about interest-rate futures?

5. *Risk Reduction versus Speculation*

Your cousin is a hog farmer and he invests in pork belly futures and options contracts. He has told you that he believes pork belly prices are on the rise. You decide to purchase a call option on pork bellies with a strike price of $0.50 per pound. That way, if pork belly prices go up, you can exercise the call, buy the pork bellies, and sell them for the higher spot price. Assume the price of an option on 40,000 pounds is $1,000 and you purchase five options for $5,000 on 200,000 pounds.

   a. Would this be a risk-reducing or speculative transaction for you?

   b. What is your downside risk in dollars and percentage terms?

   c. If the price per pound increases to $0.55 per pound, how much would you net after paying for the options?

6. *Hedging Price and Availability Risk with Forward Contracts*

Suppose you are expecting your fourth child in six months and you need a bigger car. You have your eye on a used, three-year old Minivan, which currently costs approximately $10,000. You are concerned about the pricing and availability of this specific car in six months' time, but you won't have enough money to purchase the car until six months from today.

   a. How could you advertise in the newspaper for a forward contract with a counterparty that would eliminate your risk?

   b. Who would be willing to take the short position on your forward contract? (Who is the likely counterparty?)

7. *Hedging Price Risk with Forward Contracts*

Suppose you are interested in taking a safari to Kenya, Africa, next summer but are worried about the price of the trip, which has ranged from $2,500 to $3,500 over the past five years. The current price is $3,000.

   a. How could you enter into a forward contract with a safari sponsor to eliminate your price risk?

   b. Why would the safari sponsor be interested in accepting your forward contract?

8. *Hedging Foreign-Exchange Risk with Swap Contracts*

Suppose you are treasurer of Photo Processing, Inc. Approximately 50% of your sales are in the United States (headquarters) whereas 40% are in Japan and 10% are in the rest of the world. You are concerned about the dollar value of your Japanese sales over the next five years. Japanese sales are expected to be 2,700,000,000 yen each year over the next five years. The current dollar/yen exchange rate is 90 yen to the U.S. dollar and you would be happy if this would remain so during all five years.

   a. How could you use swap contracts to eliminate the risk that the dollar depreciates against the yen?

   b. What is the notional amount of your swap contract per year?

   c. Who might take the opposite side of this swap contract (who is a logical counterparty)?

9. Suppose you are a consultant living in the United States and have been engaged by a French company to perform a market study, which should take 18 months to complete. They are planning to pay you 100,000 francs monthly. The current exchange rate is $0.20 per franc. You are concerned that the French franc will strengthen versus the dollar and that you will receive fewer U.S. dollars each month. The French company does not want to have to come up with dollars to pay you each month and is not willing to agree to a fixed exchange rate of $0.20 per franc.

   a. How could you use swap contracts and a financial intermediary to eliminate your risk?

   b. Suppose that in the sixth month, the spot price of the franc is $0.18. Without the swap contract, what would be your cash revenues in dollars? With the swap contract what will they be?

   c. Suppose that in the tenth month, the spot price of the franc is $0.25. Without the swap contract, what would be your cash revenues in dollars? With the swap contract what will they be?

10. *Matching Assets and Liabilities*

At Montgomery Bank and Trust most of its liabilities are customer deposits, which earn a variable interest rate tied to the three-month Treasury bill rate. On the other hand, most of its assets are fixed-rate loans and mortgages. Montgomery Bank and Trust does not want to stop selling fixed-rate loans and mortgages, but it is worried about rising interest rates, which would cut into their profits. How could Montgomery Bank and Trust develop a hedge against interest-rate risk without selling the loans? Assume that its exposure is $100 million at an average fixed rate of 9% while paying out T-bills + 75 basis points.

11. *Choosing among Hedging Options*

Suppose you are chief financial officer of an oil company. You are constantly presented with ways to hedge your exposure to falling oil prices by several different investment banks. You probably receive 10 different proposals each month. If each proposal hedges your risk exposure equally, how should you decide among the different proposals?

12. *Hedging versus Insuring*

Note whether the following are ways to avoid losses through hedging or insuring:

Lock in a $979.00 fare home for the holidays.

Purchase a put option on a stock you do own.

Agree to purchase a house in one year for a fixed price of $200,000.

Lease a car with an option to purchase it in three years.

Enter into a swap contract to exchange fixed interest payments for floating-rate payments because you have floating-rate assets.

As a wheat grower, enter into a forward contract to sell your wheat in two months at a fixed price set today.

Pay a premium for catastrophic health care coverage.

Pay for a credit guarantee on a loan you are worried about collecting.

13. *Insuring Price and Availability Risk with Call Options*

Suppose you are expecting your fourth child in six months and you need a bigger car. You have your eye on a used, three-year-old minivan that currently costs approximately $10,000. You are concerned about the pricing and availability of this specific car in six months' time, but you won't have enough money to purchase the car until six months from today.

a. How could you structure a transaction whereby you would pay a maximum of $10,000 but would still benefit if prices declined?

b. Would anyone give you that option for free? What is the maximum amount you would be willing to pay for that option?

14. *Insuring and Credit Risk*

Suppose you own a small company in the import/export business. You have ordered some doll clothing, which is being sewn in China. The company in China has asked for the money up front to do this work because it is nervous about your company as a credit risk. If you are unwilling to live by these terms, how might you go about purchasing insurance that would make the company in China satisfied that it will receive the money owed? Would you be able to obtain this insurance for free? How might you pay for it?

15. *Insuring against Price Risk with Options*

Suppose you are interested in taking a safari to Kenya, Africa, next summer but are worried about the price of the trip, which has ranged from $2,500 to $3,500 over the past five years. The current price is $3,000. Suppose you wanted to maintain the possibility of a lower price.

a. How could you eliminate the possibility of rising prices but still maintain the possible gain from lower prices?

b. How might you pay for this option?

16. *Insuring and Credit Guarantees*

Suppose you are a local dry cleaners. Historically you have accepted cash and checks as payments for services rendered. However, over the years you realize you have lost a lot of money on "bad checks." How could you obtain insurance against credit risk without moving to a policy of "cash only"? How would you pay for this insurance?

17. *Hedging and Interest-Rate Exposure*

Suppose you just signed a purchase and sale agreement on a new home and you have six weeks to obtain a mortgage. Interest rates have been falling, so fixed-rate loans are now very attractive. You could lock in a fixed rate of 7% (annual percentage rate) for 30 years. On the other hand, rates are falling, so you are thinking about a 30-year, variable-rate loan, which is currently at 4.5% and which is tied to the six-month Treasury bill rate. A final mortgage option is a variable-rate loan that begins at 5%, cannot fall below 3%, but which can increase by only as much as 2% per year up to a maximum of 11%.

a. If you wanted to hedge all risk of interest-rate exposure, which financing plan would you choose?

b. What would be your monthly payment on a $100,000, 30-year, fixed-rate mortgage?

c. If you took out a fixed-rate mortgage, what would happen to your monthly payment if interest rates increased to 10%?

18. ***Caps and Floors on Interest Rates***
Refer to the information presented in question 6.

a. If you wanted to take advantage of a possible fall in rates but not assume the risk that rates would increase dramatically, which financing plan would you choose?

b. What is the interest-rate cap in this example?

c. What is the interest-rate floor in this example?

d. How is an interest-rate cap like buying insurance? How are you paying for this insurance?

19. ***Insuring against Adverse Price Changes with Put Options***
Suppose you own a grove of orange trees. The harvest is still two months away but you are concerned about price risk. You want to guarantee that you will receive $1.00 per pound in two months regardless of what the spot price is at that time. You are selling 250,000 pounds. Now suppose instead of taking a short position in the futures market, you purchase insurance (in the form of a put option on 250,000 pounds) that guarantees you a minimum price of $1.00 per pound. Assume the option cost you $25,000.

a. Show the economics of this transaction if the spot price on the delivery date is $0.75, $1.00, or $1.25 per pound. Under what circumstances would you exercise your option?

b. How does your potential for gain differ between the hedge transaction and the insurance transaction?

20. ***Insuring against Price Risk with Call Options***
Suppose you are chief financial officer of Hotels International and you purchase a large quantity of coffee each month. You are concerned about the price of coffee one month from now. You want to guarantee that you will not pay more than $1.50 per pound for 35,000 pounds. You decide to purchase a call option on 35,000 pounds with a strike price of $1.50.

a. Show the economics of purchasing a call option for $2,000 if the spot price on the delivery date is $1.25, $1.50, or $1.75.

b. If at the time of delivery coffee is $1.25 per pound, should you have forgone purchasing the call option? Why or why not?

21. ***Leasing and Price Insurance***
Suppose you are in the habit of changing cars every three years. You face the risk that new car prices will go up when it comes time to buy a replacement. Show that if you have a three-year lease that gives you the right to buy your current car at a fixed price, say $9,000, then this is like having insurance.

22. *Put Options on Stocks*

Suppose you own a stock that is currently trading for $65. You purchased it for $60. You would like to wait a while before you sell it because you think there is a good chance the stock will increase further.

a. How can you structure a transaction that will insure that you can sell the stock for $65, even if it falls below that price, say, to $60 or $55.

b. If that option costs you $5 and the stock reaches $75 at which time you sell it, what was your dollar profit? Did you exercise the option? Why or why not? Was buying the option a waste of money?

c. If the price of the stock falls to $57, what is your dollar profit or loss?

Challenge Problems

23. *Interest-Rate Swaps*

Suppose that Yankee Savings Bank pays its depositors an interest rate on six-month CDs that is 25 basis points (.25%) higher than the 6-month Treasury bill rate. Because its assets are long-term fixed-rate mortgages, Yankee would prefer to be borrowing at a 10-year, fixed interest rate. If it borrowed on its own, Yankee would have to pay 12% per year. On the other hand, suppose Global Products, Inc. has good access to fixed-rate borrowing overseas. It can borrow for 10 years at a fixed rate of 11%. However, it would prefer to borrow on floating-rate terms. If it did so, it would have to pay 50 basis points over the 6-month Treasury bill. Show how both companies could improve their situations through an interest-rate swap.

24. *Risk Avoidance and Risk Retention*

Suppose that SoftCola, a multinational soft-drink company, is thinking about opening a plant in a developing country. The exchange rate in that country is pegged to the dollar, but due to economic and political problems in that country, there are restrictions on the convertibility and repatriation of profits to the United States. Also, the level of these restrictions is liable to change with the whims of those in power. The CEO of SoftCola calls you in to evaluate the risks involved in such a venture.

a. Would SoftCola face exchange-rate risks if it decided to open a plant in this developing country? What risk would it face and how could it avoid this risk?

b. If the CEO decides to go ahead and open a plant in the developing country, what in effect has been SoftCola's risk-management strategy?

25. *Exchange-Rate Risk Management*

You are a bright new hire in the risk-management division at SoftCola, a multinational cola company, and have recently been put in charge of managing the franc/dollar exchange-rate risks that SoftCola faces. Consider SoftCola's operations in France and the United States.

a. Suppose monthly revenues in France average Ffr. 100 million and monthly production and distribution costs average Ffr. 80 million. If the resulting profits are repatriated to the production unit in the United States monthly, what risk does this production unit face? How might it hedge this risk?

b. SoftCola's worldwide retirement benefits unit is located in the United States and has an obligation to pay its retired French employees Ffr. 20 million monthly. What risk does this unit face and how could it hedge the risk?

c. Given the transactions of the production and retirement units as given previously, what do you conclude are the exchange-rate risks faced by SoftCola as a whole in France? Does SoftCola need to enter into forward contracts?

26. *Matching Assets to Liabilities: The FDIC*

Federal deposit insurance originated in 1933 in part to protect the small investor and in part to safeguard the financial system. By insuring the savings of hundreds of thousands of individuals, the government has increased public confidence in the banking system and has reduced the number of speculative runs on banks and savings institutions. Banks and savings and loan associations (S&Ls) covered by this insurance pay the Federal Deposit Insurance Corporation (FDIC) a premium. You work at the FDIC and it is your job to evaluate the portfolios of the institutions that the agency covers. Consider the assets and liabilities of one S&L, Mismatch Ltd. It has liabilities of $100 million in checking, NOW, and short-term deposits for which it pays current market interest rates. Its assets are in the form of long-term consumer mortgages and other business loans made at fixed rates.

a. What do you conclude are the risks faced by Mismatch?

b. What steps could you recommend that Mismatch take in order to reduce or eliminate its risks?

You are asked by your employers to think next about banks: The insured liabilities are predominantly in the form of liquid checking and savings accounts, whereas the assets tend to be more opaque and illiquid loans to firms and businesses. One of the risks involved in banking is the risk of default by borrowers. Banks as intermediaries can diversify this risk by making loans to several different borrowers. However, they cannot get rid of the risk entirely and in the absence of deposit insurance, this risk would have to be borne by the customers of the bank, the depositors.

c. What risk-free and liquid assets could banks hold to cover their liabilities? If banks in fact held these assets, would we continue to require deposit insurance?

d. How might banks obtain funds to make loans? Who would bear the risks of default in this case? Would government insurance be required to protect them?

27. *Inflation Insurance*

You expect to receive $10,000 one year from now and want to insure it against inflation in excess of 6% per year. Structure a call option on the consumer price index that offers the desired insurance.

28. *Insurance versus Prepaid Expenses*

Suppose that you are a healthy person and you buy a one-year insurance policy against becoming ill. You pay the fair expected value of this policy up front, which is a 1% chance that your expenses will be $100,000, so the premium you would pay is $1,000.

a. How would you characterize this transaction?

b. Now suppose another person has AIDS and knows that his expenses next year will be $100,000 for his treatment. From an insurance company's point of view, what would be the fair premium for this individual?

c. Suppose an insurance company offers him the ability to pay $100,000 up front to administer and pay all of his medical expenses for the next year. How would you characterize this transaction?

29. *Insurance versus Welfare or Hidden Subsidies*

Suppose the midwestern part of the country is flooded and many farmers lose all their crops. If the government sets up a flood relief plan that reimburses those farmers who did not have private insurance, is that an insurance plan? Who pays for this "insurance" program?

Personal Integrative Problem

30. Suppose you are French and are considering graduate study in the United States. It is April and you have been admitted into a two-year master's program at a good school. Your tuition per semester will be $5,000 and living expenses will amount to $1,000 per month. (You, therefore, estimate needing a total of $22,000 per year.) You are assured by the college that you will be able to find on-campus work to pay for your living expenses. You, therefore, need only worry about paying tuition. It is now July. You applied for and just received a tuition scholarship from the French government for the amount of Ffr 60,000 per annum for two years. The current exchange rate between the dollar and the Franc is 6 Ffr/$. You are obviously ecstatic about having won the award. You are told that you will get the money for the first year in September.

a. What risks do you face?

b. Upon inquiry at your bank, you find that the forward price for a September contract to buy dollars is 6 Ffr/$. How might you hedge your exchange-rate risk for the first year?

c. If in September the market rate for the dollar turns out to be 5.5 Ffr/$, would you gain or lose on the forward contract? Does this mean that because you are worse off you shouldn't have entered the contract in the first place?

It is still July. The representative at the French government award office is offering you a set of choices for how you can be paid your award: (1) You could get Ffr 60,000 this coming September and the same amount the following September, or (2) you could avoid the exchange-rate risk this coming year by being paid $5,000 per semester for the coming year (get paid in September and February) and then you would have the option to decide next July how you wish to be paid for the following year.

In addition, you know the following: (1) The forward price of the dollar for a September contract is 6 Ffr/$, and (2) the U.S. risk-free interest rate is 5% per annum.

d. Which payment option would you choose and why?

e. If instead of hedging you chose to insure yourself against a rise in the price of the dollar, how might you do this? What is the difference between hedging and insuring in this case?

Suppose that instead of promising you Ffr 60,000 for your second year in college, the French government made the second-year grant conditional on your grades and progress in your first year.

f. What is the French government hoping to achieve by doing this?

It is now July after your first year. Tuition at your college is unchanged. You worked hard in your first year and your funding has been approved for another year. You have to decide, as you did last year, how you wish to get the funds for your coming year of schooling. This year (1) the forward price of the dollar for a September contract is 6.1 Ffr/$, and (2) the dollar risk-free rate has gone up to 7% per annum.

g. Would you choose to get Ffr 60,000 in September or $5,000 per semester?

31. In the drug example in section 11.3.1, it was illustrated that diversifying investment from a single drug company to two drug companies lowered the probability of ending up with nothing from .5 to .25. Suppose that there are four medical supply companies all racing to develop products and gain FDA approval for their products. Market forecasts suggest that large profits will be enjoyed by any company which gains FDA approval and takes its product to market. Investors in such a company stand to gain $100,000 on a $20,000 investment.

Assume that the probability for success for each company is .5; i.e., a company will either gain FDA approval, or not, and that the FDA's decision for a company is independent of its decision on the other companies.

a. If you invest 25% of your money in each company, what are all of the possible outcomes, along with their probabilities?

b. What is the payoff of each outcome?

    c. What is the expected return of the strategy?

    d. What is the probability of ending up with nothing? How does this compare to the results in section 12.3.1?

    e. What is the probability of earning more than the $20,000 original investment?

    f. Your strategy of investing 25% of your money in each of the 4 companies is an attempt to reduce what type of risk? For each company, what is that specific risk in this example?

A P P E N D I X

Correlation

When mixing two risky assets, the **correlation** between the two rates of return plays an important part in determining the standard deviation of the resulting portfolio. Intuitively, correlation means the degree to which the rates of return on the assets tend to "move together."

    The significance of the degree of correlation between the returns on two different risky assets and its implication for risk reduction through diversification are best illustrated with an example involving two stocks. Our first stock is Genco, which has the probability distribution shown in column 3 of Table 11A.1. Genco's stock returns are *procyclical;* that is, the stock does well when the economy is strong and does poorly when the economy is weak. The second stock is Negacorr, which is *countercyclical,* it performs poorly when the economy is strong and performs well when the economy is weak. The third column of Table 11A.1 shows the probability distribution of rates of return on Negacorr stock.

    Table 11A.2 shows the calculation of the expected rate of return and the standard deviation for the two stocks. Because each state of the economy is equally likely and because the probability distributions are symmetric, the computation is fairly simple. The expected rate of return on Genco is equal to its rate of return in a normal state of the economy: .14 per year. Similarly, the expected rate of return on Negacorr is equal to its rate of return in a normal state of the economy: .02 per year. The standard deviation (the square root of the variance) is the same for both stocks: .20.

    Now consider an equally weighted portfolio consisting of 50% Genco stock and 50% Negacorr stock. What is its expected return and standard deviation?

    Table 11A.3 shows us. It assumes a total investment of $100,000, with $50,000 invested in each of the two stocks.

TABLE 11A.1	Rate of Return Assumptions for Genco and Negacorr		
State of the Economy (1)	*Probability (2)*	*Rate of Return on Genco (3)*	*Rate of Return on Negacorr (4)*
Strong	1/3	.385	−.225
Normal	1/3	.140	.020
Weak	1/3	−.105	.265

TABLE 11A.2   Computation of Expected Rate of Return and Volatility

State of the Economy	Genco			Negacorr		
	Rate of Return	Deviation from Expected Return	Squared Deviation	Rate of Return	Deviation from Expected Return	Squared Deviation
Strong	.385	.245	.0600	−.225	−.245	.0600
Normal	.140	0	0	.020	0	0
Weak	−.105	−.245	.0600	.265	.245	.0600
Expected return	$1/3(.385 + .14 − .105) = .14$			$1/3(−.225 + .02 + .265) = .02$		
Variance	$1/3(.0600 + 0 + .0600) = .04$			$1/3(.0600 + 0 + .0600) = .04$		
Standard deviation	.20			.20		

First, look at the row corresponding to the strong state of the economy. The $50,000 invested in Genco will grow to $69,250 ($50,000 × 1.385), and the $50,000 invested in Negacorr stock will decline to $38,750. The portfolio will have a total value of $69,250 + $38,750 = $108,000. The rate of return in the strong state of the economy is therefore .08.

Now consider what happens if the state of the economy turns out to be weak. The $50,000 invested in Genco will decline to $44,750 ($50,000 × .895), and the $50,000 invested in Negacorr stock will grow to $63,250. Again, you will have a portfolio with a total value of $108,000. The portfolio rate of return in the weak state of the economy is therefore also .08.

The second row of Table 11A.3 reveals that the same .08 rate of return occurs in the normal state of the economy. Regardless of the state of the economy the portfolio's rate of return is .08. Therefore, the volatility of the portfolio's rate of return is zero. *All* of the risk is eliminated.

The reason all of the risk could be eliminated in this example is because the two stocks are *perfectly negatively correlated*, which means that they vary in opposite

TABLE 11A.3   Rates of Return on a Portfolio of Perfectly Negatively Correlated Stocks

State of the Economy (1)	Rate of Return on Genco (2)	Rate of Return on Negacorr (3)	Dollar Payoff from $50,000 Investment in Genco (4)	Dollar Payoff from $50,000 Investment in Negacorr (5)	Total Dollar Payoff from $100,000 Portfolio (6) = (4) + (5)
Strong	.385	−.225	1.385 × $50,000 = $69,250	.775 × $50,000 = $38,750	$69,250 + $38,750 = $108,000
Normal	.140	.020	1.14 × $50,000 = $57,000	1.02 × $50,000 = $51,000	$57,000 + $51,000 = $108,000
Weak	−.105	.265	.895 × $50,000 = $44,750	1.265 × $50,000 = $63,250	$44,750 + $63,250 = $108,000
Expected return	.140	.020			
Standard deviation	.200	.200			

| TABLE 11A.4 | Covariance and Correlation Coefficient | | | | |

| State of the Economy | Genco | | Negacorr | | |
	Rate of Return	Deviation from Expected Return	Rate of Return	Deviation from Expected Return	Product of Deviations
Strong	.385	.245	−.225	−.245	−.0600
Normal	.140	0	.020	0	0
Weak	−.105	−.245	.265	.245	−.0600

Covariance = $1/3(-.0600 + 0 - .0600) = -.04$

Correlation Coefficient = $-.04/.04 = -1$

directions with respect to each other. The statistic used to measure the degree of co-variation between two rates of return is the *correlation coefficient*. To understand the correlation coefficient, however, we first define *covariance*.

Table 11A.4 shows how to calculate the covariance between the rates of return on Genco and Negacorr. For each state of the economy, we compute the deviation of each stock's rate of return from its expected value and multiply them together to find the product of the deviations. The products of the deviations are negative in our case because the rates of return move in opposite directions with the state of the economy. If they tended to move in the same direction, the products would tend to be positive.

The covariance is the average (the probability weighted sum) of these products of deviations over all states of the economy. It, therefore, gives us a measure of the average tendency of the returns to *vary* in the same (positive) direction or in opposite directions (negative), hence, the term *covariance*. The mathematical formula for the covariance between the rates of return on two risky assets is:

$$\sigma_{1,2} = \sum_{i=1}^{n} p_i(X_{1i} - E(X_1))(X_{2i} - E(X_2))$$

To standardize the covariance measure so that it is easier to interpret, we divide it by the product of the standard deviations of each stock. The resulting ratio is called the *correlation coefficient*. It is denoted by the Greek letter ρ (pronounced "rho"). Its formula is:

$$\rho = \frac{\sigma_{1,2}}{\sigma_1 \sigma_2}$$

Correlation coefficients can range from values of +1 (perfect positive correlation) to −1 (perfect negative correlation). If $\rho = 0$, the two stocks are said to be uncorrelated. In our example:

ρ = Covariance/(Product of Standard Deviations)

$= -.04/.04$

$= -1$

Quick Check 11-8

You are given the following assumptions for the rate of return on Posicorr stock:

State of the Economy (1)	Probability (2)	Rate of Return on Posicorr (4)
Strong	⅓	.46
Normal	⅓	.16
Weak	⅓	−.14

Compute the correlation coefficient between the rate of return on Posicorr and on Genco stocks.

CHAPTER

12

Choosing an Investment Portfolio

OBJECTIVES

- To understand the process of personal portfolio selection in theory and in practice.
- To build a quantitative model of the trade-off between risk and reward.

CONTENTS

This chapter is about how people should invest their wealth, a process called _portfolio selection._ A person's wealth portfolio includes all of his or her assets (stocks, bonds, shares in unincorporated businesses, houses or apartments, pension benefits, insurance policies, etc.) and all of his or her liabilities (student loans, auto loans, home mortgages, etc.).

There is no single portfolio selection strategy that is best for all people. There are, however, some general principles, such as the principle of diversification, that apply to all _risk-averse_ people. In chapter 11 we discussed diversification as a method of managing risk. This chapter extends that discussion and analyzes the quantitative trade-off between risk and expected return.

Section 12.1 examines the role of portfolio selection in the context of a person's life-cycle financial planning process and shows why there is no single strategy that is best for all people. It also examines how the investor's time horizon and risk tolerance affect portfolio selection. Section 12.2 analyzes the choice between a single risky asset and a riskless asset, and Section 12.3 examines optimal portfolio selection with many risky assets.

12.1 THE PROCESS OF PERSONAL PORTFOLIO SELECTION

Portfolio selection is the study of how people should invest their wealth. It is a process of trading off risk and expected return to find the best portfolio of assets and liabilities. A narrow definition of portfolio selection includes only decisions about how much to invest in stocks, bonds, and other securities. A broader definition includes decisions about whether to buy or rent one's house, what types and amounts of insurance to purchase, and how to manage one's liabilities. An even broader definition includes decisions about how much to invest in one's human capital (e.g., by furthering one's professional education). The common element in all of these decisions is the trade-off between risk and expected return.

This chapter is devoted to exploring the concepts and techniques you need to know to evaluate risk-reward trade-offs and to manage your wealth portfolio efficiently. A major theme is that although there are some general rules for portfolio selection that apply to virtually everyone, there is no single portfolio or portfolio strategy that is best for everyone. We begin by explaining why.

12.1.1 The Life Cycle

In portfolio selection the best strategy depends on an individual's personal circumstances (age, family status, occupation, income, wealth, etc.). For some people holding a particular asset may add to their total risk exposure, but for others the same asset may be risk reducing. An asset that is risk reducing at an early stage in the life cycle may not be at a later stage.

For a young couple starting a family it may be optimal to buy a house and take out a mortgage loan. For an older couple about to retire it may be optimal to sell their house and invest the proceeds in some asset that will provide a steady stream of income for as long as they live.

Consider the purchase of life insurance. The optimal insurance policy for Miriam, a parent with dependent children, will differ from the policy appropriate for Sanjiv, a single person with no dependents, even if the two people are the same in all other respects (age, income, occupation, wealth, etc.). Miriam would be concerned about protecting her family in the event of her death and would, therefore, want a policy that provides cash benefits payable to her children upon her death. Sanjiv, on the other hand, would not be concerned about benefits payable if he dies; therefore, the purchase of life insurance would not be risk reducing for him. At a later stage in her life, Miriam too may find that her children can provide for themselves and no longer need the protection afforded by life insurance.

Now consider the situation of Miriam and Sanjiv after they reach retirement age. Miriam has children and is happy to have them inherit any assets that are left after she dies. If she should live an extraordinarily long time and exhaust her own wealth, she is confident her children will provide financial support for her.

Sanjiv is a loner with no one to whom he cares to leave a bequest. He would like to consume all of his wealth during his own lifetime but is concerned that if he increases his spending he will exhaust his wealth if he happens to live an extraordinarily long time. For Sanjiv buying an insurance policy that guarantees him an income for as long as he lives would be risk reducing; for Miriam it would not be. Such an insurance policy is called a **life annuity.**

As these examples make clear, even people of the same age, with the same income and wealth, may have different perspectives on buying a house or buying insurance. The same is true of investing in stocks, bonds, and other securities. There is no single portfolio that is best for all people.

To see this, consider two different individuals of the same age and family status. Chang is 30 years old and works as a security analyst on Wall Street. His current and future earnings are very sensitive to the performance of the stock market. Obi is also 30 years old and teaches English in the public school system. Her current and future earnings are not very sensitive to the stock market. For Chang investing a significant proportion of his investment portfolio in stocks would be more risky than it would be for Obi.

Quick Check 12-1
How would the investment portfolio that is best for a young person with a secure job differ from the one that is best for a retired person whose only source of income is an investment portfolio?

12.1.2 Time Horizons

In formulating a plan for portfolio selection you begin by determining your goals and time horizons. The *planning horizon* is the total length of time for which one plans.

The longest time horizon would typically correspond to the retirement goal and would be the balance of one's lifetime.[1] Thus, for a 25-year-old who expects to live to age 85, the planning horizon would be 60 years. As one ages, the planning horizon typically gets shorter and shorter (see Box 12.1).

There are also shorter planning horizons that correspond to specific financial goals, such as paying for a child's education. For example, if you have a child who is three years old and plan to pay for her college education when she reaches age 18, the planning horizon for this goal is 15 years.

The *decision horizon* is the length of time between decisions to revise the portfolio. The length of the decision horizon is controlled by the individual within certain limits.

Some people review their portfolios at regular intervals, for example, once a month (when they pay their bills), or once a year (when they file income tax forms). People of modest means with most of their wealth invested in bank accounts might review their portfolios very infrequently and at irregular intervals determined by some triggering event such as getting married or divorced, having a child, or receiving a bequest. A sudden rise or fall in the price of an asset a person owns might also trigger a review of the portfolio.

People with substantial investments in stocks and bonds might review their portfolios every day or even more frequently. The shortest possible decision horizon is the *trading horizon,* defined as the *minimum* time interval over which investors can revise their portfolios.

The length of the trading horizon is not under the control of the individual. Whether the trading horizon is a week, a day, an hour, or a minute is determined by

---

[1]Some people plan not only for their own lifetimes but also for those of future generations. For them the planning horizon might be very long, perhaps infinite.

B O X   1 2 . 1

Computing Life Expectancy

Your life expectancy is the number of years that you are expected to live. It is computed using statistics on mortality (i.e., death) rates collected and analyzed by actuaries, who are professionals that specialize in the mathematical techniques relevant to computing insurance premiums.

To estimate the probability of death at a given age, actuaries use *mortality tables* such as the one that follows, which is for U.S. residents. For each age from 65 to 95 the table states the mortality rate in terms of deaths per 1,000 and the expectation of life (expected value of the number of years remaining before death). There are separate statistics given for males and females.

The second column of the table shows that a 60-year-old male has a .01608 probability of dying before reaching the age of 61 (16.08/1,000), a .01754 probability of dying before reaching the age of 62, and so on. The third column shows the life expectancy for a male at each age, computed using the death rates in the second column. Thus, a 60-year-old male has a life expectancy of another 17.51 years, a 61-year-old male has a life expectancy of another 16.79 years, and so on. A 95-year-old male faces a probability of .32996 of dying before reaching the age of 96 and has a life expectancy of another 1.87 years. Columns 4 and 5 show the comparable statistics for females.

| | Mortality Table, Ages 60–95 | | | |
| | Male | | Female | |
Age	Deaths per 1,000	Expectation of Life (years)	Deaths per 1,000	Expectation of Life (years)
60	16.08	17.51	9.47	21.25
61	17.54	16.79	10.13	20.44
65	25.42	14.04	14.59	17.32
70	39.51	10.96	22.11	13.67
75	64.19	8.31	38.24	10.32
80	98.84	6.18	65.99	7.48
85	152.95	4.46	116.10	5.18
90	221.77	3.18	190.75	3.45
95	329.96	1.87	317.32	1.91

Source: Commissioners Standard Ordinary (CSO) Mortality Table.

the structure of the markets in the economy (e.g., when the securities exchanges are open or whether organized off-exchange markets exist).

In today's global financial environment trading in many securities can be carried on somewhere on the globe around the clock. For these securities at least the trading horizon is very short.

Portfolio decisions you make today are influenced by what you think might happen tomorrow. A plan that takes account of *future* decisions in making *current* decisions is called a **strategy.**

How frequently investors can revise their portfolios by buying or selling securities is an important consideration in formulating investment strategies. If you know that you can adjust the composition of your portfolio frequently, you may invest differently than if you cannot adjust it.

For example, a person may adopt a strategy of investing "extra" wealth in stocks, meaning wealth in excess of the amount needed to insure a certain threshold standard of living. If the stock market goes up over time, a person will increase the proportion of his or her portfolio invested in stocks. However, if the stock market goes down, a person will reduce the proportion invested in stocks. If the stock market falls to the point at which the person's threshold standard of living is threatened, he or she will get out of stocks altogether. An investor pursuing this particular strategy is more likely to have a higher threshold if stocks can only be traded infrequently.

Quick Check 12-2

Do you have a decision horizon of fixed length? How long is it?

12.1.3 Risk Tolerance

A person's *tolerance* for bearing risk is a major determinant of portfolio choices.[2] We expect risk tolerance to be influenced by such characteristics as age, family status, job status, wealth, and other attributes that affect people's ability to maintain their standard of living in the face of adverse movements in the market value of their investment portfolio. One's attitude towards risk also plays a role in determining a person's tolerance for bearing risk. Even among people with the same apparent personal, family, and job characteristics, some may have a greater willingness to take risk than others.

When we refer to a person's risk tolerance in our analysis of optimal portfolio selection, we do not distinguish between capacity to bear risk and attitude toward risk. Thus, whether a person has a relatively high tolerance for risk because he is young or rich, because he handles stress well, or because he was brought up to believe that taking chances is the morally right path, all that matters in the analysis to follow is that he is more willing than the average person to take on additional risk to achieve a higher expected return.

Quick Check 12-3

Do you think that risk tolerance increases with a person's wealth? Why?

12.1.4 The Role of Professional Asset Managers

Most people have neither the knowledge nor the time to carry out portfolio optimization. Therefore they hire an investment advisor to do it for them or they buy a "finished product" from a financial intermediary. Such finished products include various investment accounts and mutual funds offered by banks, securities firms, investment companies, and insurance companies.

---

[2]In chapter 10 we used the term *risk aversion* instead of *risk tolerance*. One is the mirror image of the other. The more risk tolerant the person is, the less risk averse.

When financial intermediaries decide what asset choices to offer to households, they are in a position analogous to a restaurant deciding on its menu. There are many ingredients available (the basic stocks, bonds, and other securities issued by firms and governments) and an infinite number of possible ways to combine them, but only a limited number of items will be offered to customers. The portfolio theory developed in the rest of this chapter offers some guidance in finding the least number of items to offer that still cover the full array of customer demands.

12.2 THE TRADE-OFF BETWEEN EXPECTED RETURN AND RISK

The next two sections present the analytical framework used by professional portfolio managers for examining the quantitative trade-off between risk and expected return. The objective is to find the portfolio that offers investors the highest expected rate of return for any degree of risk they are willing to tolerate. Throughout the analysis we will refer to *risky* assets without specifically identifying them as bonds, stocks, options, insurance policies, and so on. This is because, as explained in the preceding sections of this chapter, the riskiness of a particular asset depends critically on the specific circumstances of the investor.

Portfolio optimization is often done as a two-step process: (1) Find the optimal combination of risky assets, and (2) mix this optimal risky-asset portfolio with the riskless asset. For simplicity, we start with the second step: mixing a single risky-asset portfolio and a riskless asset. (We discuss the identity of the riskless asset in the next section.) The single risky-asset portfolio is composed of many risky assets chosen in an optimal way. In section 12.3.4 we investigate how the optimal composition of this risky-asset portfolio is found.

12.2.1 What Is the Riskless Asset?

In chapter 4 we discussed interest rates and showed that there is a different riskless asset that corresponds to each possible unit of account (dollars, yen, etc.) and to each possible maturity. Thus, a 10-year, dollar-denominated, zero-coupon bond that offers a default-free yield-to-maturity of 6% per year is riskless only in terms of dollars and only if held to maturity. The dollar rate of return on that same bond is uncertain if it is sold before maturity because the price to be received is uncertain. And even if held to maturity, the bond's rate of return denominated in yen or in terms of consumer purchasing power is uncertain because future exchange rates and consumer prices are uncertain.

In the theory of portfolio selection the riskless asset is defined as a security that offers a perfectly predictable rate of return in terms of the unit of account selected for the analysis and the length of the investor's *decision horizon*. When no specific investor is identified, the riskless asset refers to an asset that offers a predictable rate of return over the *trading horizon* (i.e., the shortest possible decision horizon).

Thus, if the U.S. dollar is taken as the unit of account and the trading horizon is a day, the riskless rate is the interest rate on U.S. Treasury bills maturing the next day.

> **Quick Check 12-4**
> What is the riskless asset if the unit of account is the Swiss franc and the length of the decision horizon is a week?

12.2.2 Combining the Riskless Asset and a Single Risky Asset

Suppose that you have $100,000 to invest. You are choosing between a riskless asset with an interest rate of .06 per year and a risky asset with an expected rate of return of .14 per year and standard deviation of .20.[3] How much of your $100,000 should you invest in the risky asset?

We examine all of the risk-return combinations open to you with the aid of Table 12.1 and Figure 12.1. Start with the case in which you invest all of your money in the riskless asset. This corresponds to the point labeled *F* in Figure 12.1 and the first row in Table 12.1. Column 2 in Table 12.1 gives the proportion of the portfolio invested in the risky asset (0) and column 3 the proportion invested in the riskless asset (100%). The proportions always add to 100%. Columns 4 and 5 of Table 12.1 give the expected return and standard deviation that correspond to portfolio *F*: $E(r)$ of .06 per year and σ of 0.00.

The case in which you invest all of your money in the risky asset corresponds to the point labeled *S* in Figure 12.1 and the last row in Table 12.1. Its expected return is .14 and its standard deviation .20.

In Figure 12.1 the portfolio expected rate of return, $E(r)$, is measured along the vertical axis and the standard deviation, σ, along the horizontal axis. The portfolio proportions are not explicitly shown in Figure 12.1, however, we know what they are from Table 12.1.

Figure 12.1 graphically illustrates the trade-off between risk and reward. The line connecting points *F, G, H, J,* and *S* in Figure 12.1 represents the set of alternatives open to you by choosing different combinations (portfolios) of the risky asset and riskless asset. Each point on the line corresponds to the mix of these two assets given in columns 2 and 3 of Table 12.1.

At point *F*, which is on the vertical axis in Figure 12.1, with $E(r)$ of .06 per year and σ of zero, all of your money is invested in the riskless asset. You face no risk, and your expected return is .06 per year. As you shift money out of the riskless asset and into the risky asset, you move to the right along the trade-off line and face both a higher expected rate of return and a greater risk. If you invest all of your

TABLE 12.1 Portfolio Expected Rate of Return and Standard Deviation as a Function of the Proportion Invested in the Risky Asset

Portfolio (1)	Proportion Invested in the Risky Asset (2)	Proportion Invested in Riskless Asset (3)	Expected Rate of Return E(r) (4)	Standard Deviation σ (5)
F	0	100%	.06	.00
G	25%	75%	.08	.05
H	50%	50%	.10	.10
J	75%	25%	.12	.15
S	100%	0	.14	.20

[3]The definitions and formulas for the expected rate of return and its standard deviation are presented in sections 10.8 and 10.9. Note that in this chapter we write rates of return as decimal fractions rather than percentages.

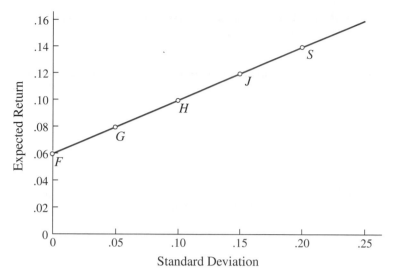

FIGURE 12.1   The Risk-Reward Trade-Off Line

Notes: At point *F,* the portfolio is 100% invested in riskless securities offering a rate of .06 per year. At point *S,* it is 100% invested in the risky asset, with an expected rate of return of .14 per year and σ of .20. At point *H,* the portfolio is half in the risky asset and half in the riskless asset.

money in the risky asset, you would be at point *S,* with expected return, $E(r)$, of .14 and standard deviation, σ, of .20.

Portfolio *H* (corresponding to the third row of Table 12.1) is half invested in the riskless asset and half in the risky asset. With $50,000 invested in the risky asset and $50,000 invested in the riskless asset, you would have an expected rate of return that is halfway between the expected return on the all-stock portfolio (.14) and the riskless rate of interest (.06). The expected rate of return of .10 is shown in column 4 and the standard deviation of .10 in column 5.

Quick Check 12-5

Locate the point corresponding to portfolio *J* in Figure 12.1. Consult Table 12.1 for the portfolio's composition, its expected rate of return, and standard deviation. How much of your $100,000 would be invested in the risky asset if you chose portfolio *J*?

Now let us show how we can find the portfolio composition for *any* point lying on the trade-off line in Figure 12.1, not only the points listed in Table 12.1. For example, suppose we want to identify the portfolio that has an expected rate of return of .09. We can tell from Figure 12.1 that the point corresponding to such a portfolio lies on the trade-off line between points *G* and *H*. But what is the portfolio's composition and what is its standard deviation? In answering this question we shall also derive the formula for the trade-off line connecting all of the points in Figure 12.1.

Step 1: Relate the portfolio's expected return to the proportion invested in the risky asset.

Let w denote the proportion of the $100,000 investment to be allocated to the risky asset. The remaining proportion, $1 - w$, is to be invested in the riskless asset. The expected rate of return on any portfolio, $E(r)$, is given by:

$$E(r) = wE(r_s) + (1 - w)r_f$$
$$= r_f + w[E(r_s) - r_f] \tag{12.1}$$

where $E(r_s)$ denotes the expected rate of return on the risky asset and r_f is the riskless rate. Substituting .06 for r_f and .14 for $E(r_s)$ we get:

$$E(r) = .06 + w(.14 - .06)$$
$$= .06 + .08w$$

Equation 12.1 is interpreted as follows. The base rate of return for any portfolio is the riskless rate (.06 in our example). In addition, the portfolio is expected to earn a risk premium which depends on (1) the risk premium on the risky asset, $E(r_s) - r_f$ (.08 in our example) and (2) the proportion of the portfolio invested in the risky asset, denoted by w.

To find the portfolio composition corresponding to an expected rate of return of .09, we substitute in equation 12.1 and solve for w:

$$.09 = .06 + .08w$$
$$w = \frac{.09 - .06}{.08} = .375$$

Thus, the portfolio mix is 37.5% risky asset and 62.5% riskless asset.

Step 2: Relate the portfolio standard deviation to the proportion invested in the risky asset.

When we combine a risky and a riskless asset in a portfolio, the standard deviation of that portfolio is the standard deviation of the risky asset times the weight of that asset in the portfolio. Denoting the standard deviation of the risky asset σ_s, we have an expression for the portfolio's standard deviation:

$$\sigma = \sigma_s w = .2w \tag{12.2}$$

To find the standard deviation corresponding to an expected rate of return of .09, we substitute .375 for w in equation 12.2 and solve for σ:

$$\sigma = \sigma_s w = .2 \times .375 = .075$$

Thus, the portfolio standard deviation is .075.

Finally, we can eliminate w to derive the formula directly relating the expected rate of return to standard deviation along the trade-off line.

Step 3:   Relate the portfolio expected rate of return to its standard deviation.

To derive the exact equation for the trade-off line in Figure 12.1, we rearrange equation 12.2 to find that $w = \sigma/\sigma_s$. By substituting for w in equation 12.1, we have that:

$$E(r) = r_f + \frac{E(r_s) - r_f}{\sigma_s}\sigma = .06 + .40\sigma \qquad (12.3)$$

In words, the portfolio's expected rate of return expressed as a function of its standard deviation is a straight line, with an intercept $r_f = .06$ and a slope:

$$\frac{E(r_s) - r_f}{\sigma_s} = \frac{.08}{.2} = .40$$

The slope of the trade-off line measures the extra expected return the market offers for each unit of extra risk an investor is willing to bear.

12.2.3 Achieving a Target Expected Return: 1

Find the portfolio corresponding to an expected rate of return of .11 per year. What is its standard deviation?

Solution:

To find the portfolio composition corresponding to an expected rate of return of 0.11, we substitute in equation 12.1 and solve for w:

$$.11 = .06 + .08w$$

$$w = \frac{.11 - .06}{.08} = .625$$

Thus, the portfolio mix is 62.5% risky asset and 37.5% riskless asset.

To find the standard deviation corresponding to an expected rate of return of .11, we substitute .625 for w in equation 12.2 and solve for σ.

$$\sigma = .2w = .2 \times .625 = .125$$

Thus, the portfolio standard deviation is .125.

> **Quick Check 12-6**
> What happens to the intercept and the slope of the trade-off line in Figure 12.1 if the risk-free rate changes to .03 per year and the expected rate of return on the risky asset to .10 per year?

12.2.4 Portfolio Efficiency

An **efficient portfolio** is defined as the portfolio that offers the investor the highest possible expected rate of return at a specified level of risk.

The significance of the concept of portfolio efficiency and how to achieve it are illustrated by adding a second risky asset to our previous example. Risky Asset 2 has an expected rate of return of .08 per year and a standard deviation of .15 and is represented by point *R* in Figure 12.2.

An investor requiring an expected rate of return of .08 per year could achieve this by investing all of his or her money in Risky Asset 2 and, thus, would be at point *R*. But point *R* is *inefficient* because the investor can get the *same* expected rate of return of .08 per year *and* a lower standard deviation at point *G*.

From Table 12.1 we know that at point *G* the standard deviation is only 0.05 and that this is achieved by holding 25% of the portfolio in Risky Asset 1 and 75% in the riskless asset. Indeed, we can see that a risk-averse investor would be better off at any point along the trade-off line connecting points *G* and *S* than at point *R*. All of these points are feasible and are achieved by mixing Risky Asset 1 with the riskless asset. For example, portfolio *J* has a standard deviation equal to that of Risky Asset 2 ($\sigma = .15$), but its expected return is .12 per year rather than .08. From Table 12.1 we know that its composition is 75% Risky Asset 1 and 25% riskless asset.

We can use equations 12.1 and 12.2 to find the composition of other efficient portfolios that lie between points *G* and *J* and, therefore, have both a higher expected rate of return and a lower standard deviation than Risky Asset 2. For example, consider a portfolio that consists of 62.5% Risky Asset 1 and 37.5% riskless asset. Its expected rate of return is .11 per year and its standard deviation is .125.

Quick Check 12-7

How can an investor achieve an expected rate of return of .105 per year with Risky Asset 1 and the riskless asset? What is the standard deviation of this portfolio? Compare it to the standard deviation of Risky Asset 2?

FIGURE 12.2 Portfolio Efficiency

Notes: At point *R*, the portfolio is 100% invested in Risky Asset 2 offering an expected return of .08 and a σ of .15. The investor can have both a higher expected rate of return and a lower standard deviation at any point on the line connecting points *G* and *J*.

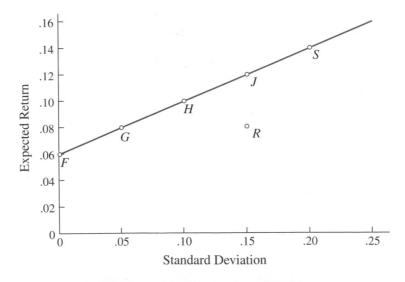

12.3 EFFICIENT DIVERSIFICATION WITH MANY RISKY ASSETS

E-BOOK

12.3

Although holding Risky Asset 2 by itself is inefficient, what about holding portfolios that mix the two risky assets? Or portfolios that mix the two risky assets with the riskless asset?

We will explore the ways to efficiently combine the three assets in two steps. The first step is to consider the risk and return combinations attainable by mixing only Risky Assets 1 and 2, and then in the second step we add the riskless asset.

12.3.1 Portfolios of Two Risky Assets

Combining two risky assets in a portfolio is similar to combining a risky asset with a riskless asset discussed in section 12.2. (Take a moment to review Table 12.1, Figure 12.1, and equations 12.1 and 12.2.) When one of the two assets is riskless, the standard deviation of its rate of return and its correlation with the other asset are zero. When both assets are risky, the analysis of the risk and return trade-off is somewhat more involved.

The formula for the mean rate of return of any portfolio consisting of a proportion w in Risky Asset 1 and a proportion $1 - w$ in Risky Asset 2 is:

$$E(r) = wE(r_1) + (1 - w)E(r_2) \tag{12.4}$$

and the formula for variance is:

$$\sigma^2 = \sigma_1^2 + (1 - w)^2\sigma_2^2 + 2w(1 - w)\rho\sigma_1\sigma_2 \tag{12.5}$$

These two equations should be compared to equations 12.1 and 12.2. Equation 12.4 is essentially the same as equation 12.1 with the expected return on Risky Asset 2, $E(r_2)$, substituted for the interest rate on the riskless asset, r_f. Equation 12.5 is a more general form of equation 12.2. When asset 2 is riskless, then $\sigma_2 = 0$, and equation 12.5 simplifies to equation 12.2.

Table 12.2 summarizes our assessments of the probability distribution of the rates of return on Risky Assets 1 and 2. Note that we assume the correlation coefficient is zero ($\rho = 0$).

Table 12.3 and Figure 12.3 show the combinations of mean and standard deviation of returns attainable by combining Risky Asset 1 and Risky Asset 2. Point S in Figure 12.3 corresponds to a portfolio consisting entirely of Risky Asset 1 and point R to a portfolio entirely of Risky Asset 2.

Let us demonstrate how the expected rates of return and standard deviations in Table 12.3 were computed using the formulas in equations 12.4 and 12.5. Consider portfolio C, which consists of 25% Risky Asset 1 and 75% Risky Asset 2.

TABLE 12.2   Distribution of Rates of Return on Risky Assets

	Risky Asset 1	Risky Asset 2
Mean	.14	.08
Standard deviation	.20	.15
Correlation	0	0

TABLE 12.3   The Risk-Reward Trade-Off for Portfolios of Two Risky Assets

Portfolio	Proportion Invested in Risky Asset 1	Proportion Invested in Risky Asset 2	Expected Rate of Return	Standard Deviation
R	0	100%	.0800	.1500
C	25%	75%	.0950	.1231
Minimum variance	36%	64%	.1016	.1200
D	50%	50%	.1100	.1250
S	100%	0	.1400	.2000

Substituting into equation 12.4, we find the expected rate of return at point C to be 0.095 per year:

$$E(r) = .25E(r_1) + .75E(r_2)$$
$$= .25 \times .14 + .75 \times .08$$
$$= .095$$

And substituting for w into equation 12.5, we find the standard deviation to be:

$$\sigma^2 = w^2\sigma_1^2 + (1-w)^2\sigma_2^2 + 2w(1-w)\rho\sigma_1\sigma_2$$
$$= .25^2 \times .2^2 + .75^2 \times .15^2 + 0$$
$$= .01515625$$
$$\sigma = \sqrt{.01515625} = .1231$$

FIGURE 12.3   The Risk-Reward Trade-Off Curve: Risky Assets Only

Notes: The assumptions are $E(r_1) = .14$, $\sigma_1 = .20$, $E(r_2) = .08$, $\sigma_2 = .15$, and $\rho = 0$.

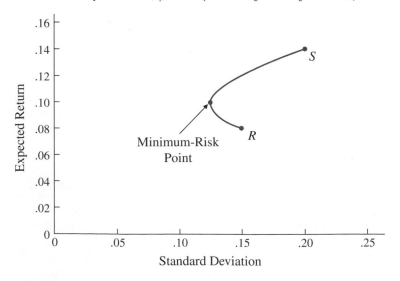

Let us follow the curve connecting points *R* and *S* in Figure 12.3 with the aid of Table 12.3. Start at point *R* and move some of our money from Risky Asset 2 to Risky Asset 1. Not only does the mean rate of return go up, but the standard deviation goes down. It keeps going down until we reach a portfolio that has 36% invested in Risky Asset 1 and 64% invested in Risky Asset 2.

This point is the **minimum-variance portfolio** of Risky Asset 1 and Risky Asset 2.[4] Increasing the proportion invested in Risky Asset 1 beyond 36% causes the standard deviation of the portfolio to increase.

Quick Check 12-8

What are the mean and standard deviation of a portfolio that is 60% Risky Asset 1 and 40% Risky Asset 2, if the correlation coefficient is .1?

12.3.2 The Optimal Combination of Risky Assets

Now let us consider the risk-reward combinations we can obtain by combining the riskless asset with Risky Asset 1 and Risky Asset 2. Figure 12.4 presents a graphical description of all possible risk-reward combinations and also illustrates how one locates the optimal combination of risky assets to mix with the riskless asset.

First consider the straight line connecting point *F* with point *S*. This should be familiar to you as the risk-reward trade-off line we looked at in Figure 12.1. It

FIGURE 12.4 The Optimal Combination of Risky Assets

Notes: The assumptions are $r_f = .06$, $E(r_1) = .14$, $\sigma_1 = .20$, $E(r_2) = .08$, $\sigma_2 = .15$, and $\rho = 0$.

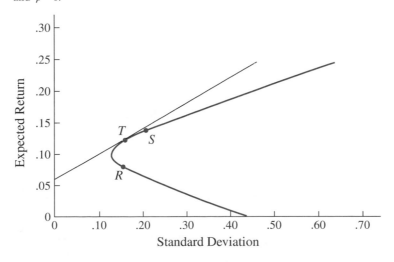

---

[4]The formula for the proportion of Risky Asset 1 that minimizes the variance of the portfolio is:

$$w_{min} = \frac{\sigma_2^2 - \rho\sigma_1\sigma_2}{\sigma_1^2 + \sigma_2^2 - 2\rho\sigma_1\sigma_2}$$

represents the risk-reward combinations that can be obtained by mixing the riskless asset with Risky Asset 1.

A straight line connecting point *F* to *any* point along the curve connecting points *R* and *S* represents a risk-reward trade-off line involving a particular mix of Risky Assets 1 and 2 and the riskless asset. The highest trade-off line we can get to is the one connecting points *F* and *T*. Point *T* is the *point of tangency* between a straight line from point *F* drawn to the curve connecting points *R* and *S*. We call this particular risky portfolio, which corresponds to the tangency point *T* in Figure 12.4, the **optimal combination of risky assets.** It is the portfolio of risky assets that is then mixed with the riskless asset to achieve the most efficient portfolios. The formula for finding the portfolio proportions at point *T* is:

$$w_1 = \frac{[E(r_1) - r_f]\sigma_2^2 - [E(r_2) - r_f]\rho\sigma_1\sigma_2}{[E(r_1) - r_f]\sigma_2^2 + [E(r_2) - r_f]\sigma_1^2 - [E(r_1) - r_f + E(r_2) - r_f]\rho\sigma_1\sigma_2}$$

$$w_2 = 1 - w_1$$

Substituting into equation 12.6, we find that the optimal combination of risky assets (the tangency portfolio) is composed of 69.23% Risky Asset 1 and 30.77% Risky Asset 2. Its mean rate of return, $E(r_T)$, and standard deviation, σ_T, are:

$$E(r_T) = .122$$

$$\sigma_T = .146$$

Thus, the new efficient trade-off line is given by the formula:

$$E(r) = r_f + w[E(r_T) - r_f]$$

$$= r_f + \frac{[E(r_T) - r_f]}{\sigma_T}\sigma$$

$$= .06 + \frac{.122 - .06}{.146}\sigma$$

$$= .06 + .42\sigma$$

where the slope, the reward-to-risk ratio, is .42.

Compare this to the formula for the old trade-off line connecting points *F* and *S*:

$$E(r) = .06 + .40\sigma$$

where the slope is .40. Clearly the investor is better off now because he or she can achieve a higher expected rate of return for any level of risk he or she is willing to tolerate.

12.3.3 Selecting the Preferred Portfolio

To complete the analysis, let us now consider the investor's choice of his or her preferred portfolio along the efficient trade-off line. Recall from our discussion in section 12.1 that a person's preferred portfolio will depend on his or her stage in the life cycle, planning horizon, and risk tolerance. Thus, an investor might choose to be at a point that is halfway between points *F* and *T.* Figure 12.5 shows this as point *E.* The portfolio that corresponds to point *E* consists of 50% invested in the tangency portfolio and 50% invested in the riskless asset. By transforming equations 12.1 and 12.2 to reflect the fact that the tangency portfolio is now the single risky asset to combine with the riskless asset, we find that the expected return and standard deviation of portfolio *E* are:

$$E(r_E) = r_f + .5 \times [E(r_T) - r_f]$$
$$= .06 + .5(.122 - .06) = .091$$
$$\sigma_E = .5 \times \sigma_T$$
$$= .5 \times .146 = .073$$

Noting that the tangency portfolio is itself composed of 69.2% Risky Asset 1 and 30.8% Risky Asset 2, the composition of portfolio *E* is found as follows:

Weight in riskless asset		50.0%
Weight in Risky Asset 1	.5 × 69.2% =	34.6%
Weight in Risky Asset 2	.5 × 30.8% =	15.4%
Total		100.0%

Thus, if you were investing $100,000 in portfolio *E,* you would invest $50,000 in the riskless asset, $34,600 in Risky Asset 1, and $15,400 in Risky Asset 2.

Let us now summarize what we have learned about creating efficient portfolios when the raw materials are two risky assets and a riskless asset. There is a single portfolio of the two risky assets that it is best to combine with the riskless asset. We call this particular risky portfolio, which corresponds to the tangency point *T* in Figure 12.4, the *optimal combination of risky assets.* The preferred portfolio is always some combination of this tangency portfolio and the riskless asset.

FIGURE 12.5   Selection of the Preferred Portfolio

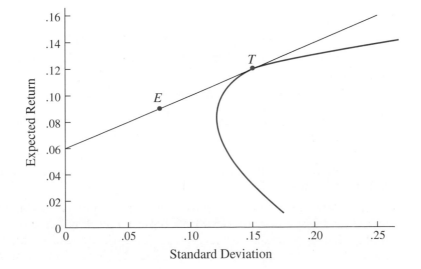

12.3.4 Achieving a Target Expected Return: 2

Suppose you have $100,000 to invest and want an expected rate of return of .10 per year. Compare the standard deviation you would have to tolerate under the old risk-reward trade-off line (connecting points *F* and *S*) with the standard deviation under the new trade-off line (connecting points *F* and *T*). What is the composition of each of the two portfolios you are comparing?

Solution:

First, let us write down the formula relating the expected return on the portfolio to the proportion invested in risky assets and solve it to find the proportion to invest in risky assets. For the new trade-off line using the optimal combination of two risky assets it is:

$$E(r) = E(r_T)w + r_f(1 - w)$$
$$E(r) = .122w + .06(1 - w)$$

Setting the expected rate of return on the portfolio equal to 0.10 and solving for *w* we find:

$$E(r) = .06 + .062w = .10$$
$$w = \frac{.10 - .06}{.062} = .65$$

Thus, 65% of the $100,000 must be invested in the optimal combination of risky assets and 35% in the riskless asset.

The standard deviation of this portfolio is given by:

$$\sigma = w\sigma_T$$
$$= .65 \times .146 = .095$$

Because the optimal combination of risky assets is itself composed of 69.2% Risky Asset 1 and 30.8% Risky Asset 2, the composition of the final desired portfolio with expected return of .10 per year is found as follows:

Weight in riskless asset		35%
Weight in Risky Asset 1	.65 × 69.2% =	45%
Weight in Risky Asset 2	.65 × 30.8% =	20%
Total		100%

For the old trade-off line with a single risky asset the formula relating the expected return and *w* was:

$$E(r) = E(r_s)w + r_f(1 - w)$$
$$E(r) = .14w + .06(1 - w)$$

Setting the expected rate of return on the portfolio equal to 0.10 and solving for w we find:

$$E(r) = .06 + .08w = .10$$

$$w = \frac{.10 - .06}{.08} = .50$$

Thus, 50% of the $100,000 must be invested in Risky Asset 1 and 50% in the riskless asset.

The standard deviation of this portfolio is given by:

$$\sigma = w\sigma_s$$

$$= .5 \times .2 = .10$$

Quick Check 12-9

Suppose an investor chooses a portfolio that is three-fourths of the way between points F and T in Figure 12.5. In other words, it has 75% invested in the tangency portfolio and 25% in the riskless asset. What is the expected rate of return and standard deviation of this portfolio? If the investor has $100,000, how much will he invest in each of the three assets?

It is important to note that in finding the *optimal combination of risky assets* we do *not* need to know anything about investor wealth or preferences. The composition of this portfolio depends only on the expected rate of returns and standard deviations of Risky Asset 1 and Risky Asset 2 and on the correlation between them. This implies that *all investors who agree on the probability distributions for rates of return will want to hold this same tangency portfolio in combination with the riskless asset.*

This is a general result that carries over to the case in which there are many risky assets in addition to Risky Asset 1 and Risky Asset 2:

> There is always a particular optimal portfolio of risky assets that all risk-averse investors who share the same forecasts of rates of return will combine with the riskless asset to reach their most preferred portfolio.

12.3.5 Portfolios of Many Risky Assets

When there are many risky assets we use a two-step method of portfolio construction similar to the one used in the previous section. In the first step, we consider portfolios constructed from the risky assets only, and in the second step we find the *tangency* portfolio of risky assets to combine with the riskless asset. Because the computation involves a lot of number crunching, it is best done using computers.

Figure 12.6 illustrates the inputs and outputs of an electronic spreadsheet used to carry out portfolio optimization.[5] The individual *basic assets* are Risky Asset 1, Risky Asset 2, and so on. They are represented as shaded points in the diagram on the left. The curved colored line lying to the northwest of these points is called the **efficient**

---

[5]Figure 12.6 was generated using the software provided with this textbook.

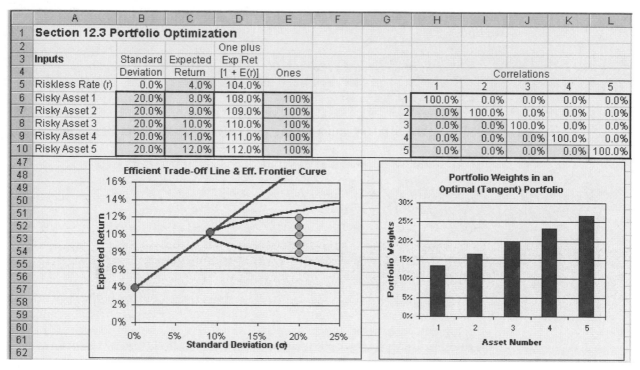

	A	B	C	D	E	F	G	H	I	J	K	L
1	**Section 12.3 Portfolio Optimization**											
2				One plus								
3	Inputs	Standard	Expected	Exp Ret								
4		Deviation	Return	[1 + E(r)]	Ones					Correlations		
5	Riskless Rate (r)	0.0%	4.0%	104.0%				1	2	3	4	5
6	Risky Asset 1	20.0%	8.0%	108.0%	100%		1	100.0%	0.0%	0.0%	0.0%	0.0%
7	Risky Asset 2	20.0%	9.0%	109.0%	100%		2	0.0%	100.0%	0.0%	0.0%	0.0%
8	Risky Asset 3	20.0%	10.0%	110.0%	100%		3	0.0%	0.0%	100.0%	0.0%	0.0%
9	Risky Asset 4	20.0%	11.0%	111.0%	100%		4	0.0%	0.0%	0.0%	100.0%	0.0%
10	Risky Asset 5	20.0%	12.0%	112.0%	100%		5	0.0%	0.0%	0.0%	0.0%	100.0%

FIGURE 12.6 Portfolio Optimization Spreadsheet

portfolio frontier of risky assets. It is defined as the set of *portfolios* of risky assets offering the highest possible expected rate of return for any given standard deviation.

The reason the individual basic assets lie *inside* the efficient frontier is that there is usually some combination of two or more basic securities that has a higher expected rate of return than the basic security for the same standard deviation.

The optimal combination of risky assets is then found as the point of tangency between a straight line from the point representing the riskless asset (on the vertical axis) and the efficient frontier of risky assets. The straight line connecting the riskless asset and the tangency point representing the *optimal combination of risky assets* is the best risk-reward trade-off line achievable.

We now return to the issue raised in Section 12.1. How can a financial intermediary, such as a firm offering mutual funds to the investing public, decide on the menu of asset choices to offer to its customers? We just showed that the composition of the optimal combination of risky assets depends only on the expected returns and standard deviations of the basic risky assets and on the correlations among them. It does *not* depend on investor preferences. Therefore, one does not need to know anything about investor preferences in order to create this portfolio.

If customers delegate the task of forecasting expected asset returns, standard deviations, and correlations to a financial intermediary that specializes in doing it and they delegate the task of combining the basic assets in the optimal proportions, then the only choice the customers need to make is the proportion to invest in the optimal risky portfolio.

The static mean-variance model thus leads to an elementary theory of mutual fund financial intermediation. Since the late 1960s, academic research on optimal portfolio selection has gone beyond that model to dynamic versions that integrate intertemporal optimization of the life-cycle consumption–saving decisions with the allocation of those savings among alternative investments. In these models, the demands for individual assets depend on more than just optimal diversification as presented here; they also come from the desire to *hedge* various risks not included in the original model. Some of the risks indentified as creating these hedging demands in portfolio decisions are mortality risk and stochastic changes in interest rates and in the trade-off between expected return and risk, in returns to human captial, and in relative consumption goods prices. These models provide a richer theory for the role of securities and financial intermediation than the static mean-variance model.[6]

The basic mean-variance approach to quantitative investment management is still the dominant one used in the practice of asset management. However, this is changing. The more complete models of portfolio selection provide design guidance for investment firms to offer a wider "family" of mutual funds beyond just the optimal combination of risky assets and the riskless asset. Those additional funds represent optimal hedging portfolios more tailored to the needs of different clienteles. The investment firm can create integrated products from its funds by putting various combinations of its member funds together in proportions that reflect the right mix for customers in various stages of their life cycle.

Summary

- There is no single portfolio selection strategy that is best for all people.
- Stage in the life cycle is an important determinant of the optimal composition of a person's optimal portfolio of assets and liabilities.
- Time horizons are important in portfolio selection. We distinguish among three time horizons: the planning horizon, the decision horizon, and the trading horizon.
- In making portfolio selection decisions, people can in general achieve a higher expected rate of return only by exposing themselves to greater risk.
- One can sometimes reduce risk without lowering expected return by diversifying more completely either within a given asset class or across asset classes.
- The power of diversification to reduce the riskiness of an investor's portfolio depends on the *correlations* among the assets that make up the portfolio. In practice, the vast majority of assets are *positively correlated* with each other because they are all affected by common economic factors. Consequently, one's ability to reduce risk through diversification among risky assets without lowering expected return is limited.
- Although in principle people have thousands of assets to choose from, in practice they make their choices from a menu of a few final products offered by financial intermediaries such as bank accounts, stock and bond mutual funds, and real estate. In designing and producing the menu of assets to offer to their customers these intermediaries make use of the latest advances in financial technology.

Key Terms

- portfolio selection 319
- life annuity 319
- strategy 321
- efficient portfolio 327

- minimum-variance portfolio 331
- optimal combination
  of risky assets 332
- efficient portfolio frontier 336

[6]See R. C. Merton, *Continuous-Time Finance,* Blackwell, 1992, chapters 4–6, 14, 15, and 21.

Answers to Quick Check Questions

Quick Check 12-1 *How would the investment portfolio that is best for a young person with a secure job differ from the one that is best for a retired person whose only source of income is his investment portfolio?*

ANSWER: The young person with a secure job can look forward to a long period of earning a salary that will probably increase with the rate of inflation. For her, investment in stocks would not be as risky as for the older person who needs to ensure a steady source of income for the rest of his life. The young person is somewhat protected against inflation but the older person is not and may have to try to find insurance against price increases.

Quick Check 12-2 *Do you have a decision horizon of fixed length? How long is it?*

ANSWER: Answer will vary by student.

Quick Check 12-3 *Do you think that risk tolerance increases with a person's wealth? Why?*

ANSWER: A wealthier individual may be willing to take more risks (than a poorer person) because his capacity to take bigger gambles and lose is higher. That is, he may still be quite wealthy after his losses.

Quick Check 12-4 *What is the riskless asset if the unit of account is the Swiss franc and the length of the decision horizon is a week?*

ANSWER: A Swiss-franc-denominated, one-week, zero-coupon bond.

Quick Check 12-5 *Locate the point corresponding to portfolio J in Figure 12.1. Consult Table 12.1 for the portfolio's composition, its expected rate of return and standard deviation. How much of your $100,000 would be invested in the risky asset if you chose portfolio J?*

ANSWER: $75,000 would be invested in the risky asset and $25,000 in the risk-free asset.

Quick Check 12-6 *What happens to the intercept and the slope of the trade-off line in Figure 12.1 if the risk-free rate changes to .03 per year and the expected rate of return on the risky asset to .10 per year?*

ANSWER: The y intercept falls to .03 and the slope of the line falls from .4 to .35.

Quick Check 12-7 *How can an investor achieve an expected rate of return of .105 per year with Risky Asset 1 and the riskless asset? What is the standard deviation of this portfolio? Compare it to the standard deviation of Risky Asset 2.*

ANSWER: Hold 56.25% in the risky asset and the rest in the risk-free asset to achieve an expected rate of return of .105. The standard deviation of the portfolio is .1125 compared to Risky Asset 2's standard deviation of .15.

Quick Check 12-8 *What are the mean and standard deviation of a portfolio that is 60% Risky Asset 1 and 40% Risky Asset 2, if the correlation coefficient is .1?*

ANSWER:

$$E(r) = .6 \times .4 + .4 \times .08 = .116$$
$$\sigma^2 = (.6)^2 \times (.2)^2 + (.4)^2 \times (.15)^2 + 2(.6)(.4)(.1)(.2)(.15) = .01944$$
$$\sigma = .1394$$

Quick Check 12-9 *Suppose an investor chooses a portfolio that is three-fourths of the way between points F and T in Figure 12.5. In other words it has 75% invested in the tangency portfolio and 25% in the riskless asset. What is the expected return and standard de-*

viation of this portfolio? If the investor has $100,000, how much will he invest in each of the three assets?

ANSWER:

$$E(r) = .12154 \times .75 + .06 \times .25 = .1062$$
$$= .75 \times .14595 = .1095$$

Invest 25% in the riskless asset, 51.9% (.75 × 69.2) in Risky Asset 1, and 23.1% (.75 × 30.8) in Risky Asset 2.

Questions and Problems

1. Suppose that your 58-year-old father works for the Ruffy Stuffed Toy Company and has contributed regularly to his company-matched savings plan for the past 15 years. Ruffy contributes $0.50 for every $1.00 your father puts into the savings plan, up to the first 6% of his salary. Participants in the savings plan can allocate their contributions among four different investment choices: a fixed-income bond fund; a "blend" option that invests in large companies, small companies, and the fixed-income bond fund; a growth-income mutual fund whose investments do not include other toy companies; and a fund whose sole investment is stock in the Ruffy Stuffed Toy Company. Over Thanksgiving vacation, Dad realizes that you have been majoring in finance and decides to reap some early returns on that tuition money he's been investing in your education. He shows you the most recent quarterly statement for his savings plan, and you see that 98% of its current value is in the fourth investment option, that of the Ruffy stock.

    Assume that your dad is a typically risk-averse person who is considering retirement in five years. When you ask him why he has made the allocation in this way, he responds that the company stock has continually performed quite well, except for a few declines that were caused by problems in a division that the company has long since sold off. In addition, he says, many of his friends at work have done the same. What advice would you give your dad about adjustments to his plan allocations? Why?

    If you consider the fact that your dad works for Ruffy in addition to his 98% allocation to the Ruffy stock fund, does this make his situation more risky, less risky, or does it make no difference? Why?

2. Refer to Table 12.1.
    a. Perform the calculations to verify that the expected returns of each of the portfolios (*F, G, H, J, S*) in the table (column 4) are correct.
    b. Do the same for the standard deviations in column 5 of the table.
    c. Assume that you have $1 million to invest. Allocate the money as indicated in the table for each of the five portfolios and calculate the expected dollar return of each of the portfolios.
    d. Which of the portfolios would someone who is extremely risk tolerant be most likely to select?

3. A mutual fund company offers a safe money market fund whose current rate is 4.50% (.045). The same company also offers an equity fund with an aggressive growth objective, which historically has exhibited an expected return of 20% (.20) and a standard deviation of .25.
    a. Derive the equation for the risk-reward trade-off line.
    b. How much extra expected return would be available to an investor for each unit of extra risk that she bears?
    c. What allocation should be placed in the money market fund if an investor desires an expected return of 15% (.15)?

4. If the risk-reward trade-off line for a riskless asset and a risky asset results in a negative slope, what does that imply about the risky asset vis-à-vis the riskless asset?

5. Suppose that you have the opportunity to buy stock in AT&T and Microsoft.

	AT&T	Microsoft
Mean	.10	.21
Standard deviation	.15	.25

   a. What is the minimum risk (variance) portfolio of AT&T and Microsoft if the correlation between the two stocks is 0? .5? 1? –1? What do you notice about the change in the allocations between AT&T and Microsoft as their correlation moves from –1 to 0 to .5 to +1? Why might this be?
   b. What is the variance of each of the minimum-variance portfolios in part a?
   c. What is the optimal combination of these two securities in a portfolio for each value of the correlation, assuming the existence of a money market fund that currently pays 4.5% (.045)? Do you notice any relation between these weights and the weights for the minimum-variance portfolios?
   d. What is the variance of each of the optimal portfolios?
   e. What is the expected return of each of the optimal portfolios?
   f. Derive the risk-reward trade-off line for the optimal portfolio when the correlation is .5. How much extra expected return can you anticipate if you take on an extra unit of risk?

6. Using the optimal portfolio of AT&T and Microsoft stock when the correlation of their price movements is .5, along with the results in part f of question 12-6, determine:
   a. The expected return and standard deviation of a portfolio that invests 100% in a money market fund returning a current rate of 4.5%. Where is this point on the risk-reward trade-off line?
   b. The expected return and standard deviation of a portfolio that invests 90% in the money market fund and 10% in the portfolio of AT&T and Microsoft stock.
   c. The expected return and standard deviation of a portfolio that invests 25% in the money market fund and 75% in the portfolio of AT&T and Microsoft stock.
   d. The expected return and standard deviation of a portfolio that invests 0% in the money market fund and 100% in the portfolio of AT&T and Microsoft stock. What point is this?

7. Again using the optimal portfolio of AT&T and Microsoft stock when the correlation of their price movements is .5, take $10,000 and determine the allocations among the riskless asset, AT&T stock, and Microsoft stock for:
   a. A portfolio that invests 75% in a money market fund and 25% in the portfolio of AT&T and Microsoft stock. What is this portfolio's expected return?
   b. A portfolio that invests 25% in a money market fund and 75% in the portfolio of AT&T and Microsoft stock. What is this portfolio's expected return?
   c. A portfolio that invests nothing in a money market fund and 100% in the portfolio of AT&T and Microsoft stock. What is this portfolio's expected return?

8. What strategy is implied by moving further out to the right on a risk-reward trade-off line beyond the tangency point between the line and the risky-asset risk-reward curve? What type of an investor would be most likely to embark on this strategy? Why?

9. Determine the correlation between price movements of stock A and B using the forecasts of their rates of return and the assessments of the possible states of the

world in the following table. The standard deviations for stock A and stock B are 0.065 and 0.1392, respectively. Before doing the calculation, form an expectation of whether that correlation will be closer to 1 or –1 by merely inspecting the numbers.

State of the Economy	Probability	Stock A: Rate of Return	Stock B: Rate of Return
Moderate recession	.05	–.02	–.20
Slight recession	.15	–.01	–.10
2% growth	.60	.15	.15
3% growth	.20	.15	.30

10. Analyze the "expert's" answers to the following question:
    a. **Question:** I have approximately one-third of my investments in stocks and the rest in a money market. What do you suggest as a somewhat safer place to invest another one-third. I like to keep one-third accessible for emergencies.
    Expert's answer: Well, you could try one- or two-year Treasury bonds. You'd get a little bit more yield with no risk.
    b. **Question:** Where would you invest if you were to start today?
    Expert's answer: That depends on your age and short-term goals. If you're very young—say, under 40—and don't need the money you're investing for a home or college tuition, I'd put it in a stock fund. Even if the market tanks, you have time to recoup. And, so far, nothing has beaten stocks over a period of 10 years or more. But if you're going to need money fairly soon, for a home or for your retirement, you need to play it safer.

Summary of Formulas

The expected rate of return on any portfolio, $E(r)$, is given by:

$$E(r) = wE(r_s) + (1 - w)r_f$$
$$= r_f + w[E(r_s) - r_f]$$

where w is the fraction of the portfolio invested in the risky asset, $E(r_s)$ is the expected rate of return on the risky asset, and r_f is the riskless rate. The standard deviation of the portfolio is given by:

$$\sigma = \sigma_s w$$

where σ_s is the standard deviation on the risky asset.
The formula for the trade-off line between risk and expected return is:

$$E(r) = r_f + w[E(r_s) - r_f]$$
$$= r_f + \frac{[E(r_s) - r_f]}{\sigma_s} \sigma$$

The formula for the variance of a portfolio of two risky assets is:

$$\sigma^2 = w^2 \sigma_1^2 + (1 - w)^2 \sigma_2^2 + 2w(1 - w)\rho\sigma_1\sigma_2$$

The formula for finding the proportions of the optimal combination of two risky assets is:

$$w_1 = \frac{[E(r_1) - r_f]\sigma_2^2 - [E(r_2) - r_f]\rho\sigma_1\sigma_2}{[E(r_1) - r_f]\sigma_2^2 + [E(r_2) - r_f]\sigma_1^2 - [E(r_1) - r_f + E(r_2) - r_f]\rho\sigma_1\sigma_2}$$

$$w_2 = 1 - w_1$$

A P P E N D I X

The Fallacy of Time Diversification

There is a widespread—but mistaken—belief that stocks are less risky in the long run than in the short run. Based on this belief, it is generally inferred that you should invest more of your money in stocks the longer your planned holding period.

Two propositions have been used to persuade skeptics that this so-called time diversification effect is valid:

- The longer the investor's holding period, the smaller the standard deviation of the annualized rate of return on stocks.

- The longer the investor's holding period, the lower the probability that stocks will earn a rate of return less than the corresponding risk-free interest rate on bonds.

Although they are true, these propositions do not validity support the claim that stocks are less risky in the long run than in the short run or that you should invest more in stocks because you have a longer planned holding period. Let us explain why.

First, the fact that the standard deviation of the *annualized* rate of return on an investment in stocks declines as the length of the holding period increases is merely an artifact of expressing investment performance in terms of the annualized rate of return. There is no genuine diversification in this situation. You care about the amount of wealth that you will have at the end of the holding period, and there is no decline in its standard deviation. For example, compare the results of investing all of your money in stocks versus risk-free bonds for one year and for 25 years. Even though the standard deviation of your annualized rate of return for the 25-year-period is approximately one-fifth of the one-year result, the standard deviation of your ending wealth for the 25-year holding period is five times *greater* than the one-year standard deviation.

Second, it is true that the longer the holding period, the lower the probability of a *shortfall*—defined as the stock portfolio's earning less than the risk-free inter-est rate over that same period. However, the risk of a shortfall depends on its *sever-ity* when it happens as well as its probability of happening. If we consider measures of risk that take account of *both* the severity and the probability of a shortfall, there is no decline in risk as the holding period lengthens. For example, consider as a mea-sure of risk the price of insuring a stock portfolio against a shortfall. It actually *in-creases* with the length of the holding period.[7]

---

[7]As shown in chapter 11, such an insurance policy is equivalent to a put option on the ending value of the stock portfolio. In chapter 15, we demonstrate that the price of this put must increase as the holding period lengthens.

CHAPTER

13

The Capital Asset Pricing Model

OBJECTIVES

- Explain the theory behind the capital asset pricing model (CAPM).
- Explain how to use the CAPM to establish benchmarks for measuring the performance of investment portfolios.
- Explain how to infer from the CAPM the correct risk-adjusted discount rate to use in discounted cash flow valuation models.
- Explain how the CAPM has been modified and supplemented by other theories to add greater realism.

CONTENTS

The capital asset pricing model (CAPM) is a theory about equilibrium prices in the markets for risky assets. It builds on the theory of portfolio selection developed in chapter 12 and derives the quantitative relations that must exist among expected rates of return on risky assets on the assumption that asset prices adjust to equate supply and demand.

The CAPM is important for two reasons. First, it provides a theoretical justification for the widespread practice of passive investing known as *indexing*. Indexing means holding a diversified portfolio in which securities are held in the same relative proportions as in a broad market index such as the Standard & Poor's 500 or the Morgan Stanley index of international stocks. Today many billions of dollars invested worldwide by pension funds, mutual funds, and other institutions are managed passively by indexing, and indexing provides a simple feasible benchmark against which the performance of active investment strategies are measured.

Second, the CAPM provides a way of estimating expected rates of return for use in a variety of financial applications. For example, chapter 9 shows that risk-adjusted expected rates of return are needed as inputs to discounted-cash-flow valuation models for stocks. Chapter 16 shows how corporate managers use these models in making capital-budgeting decisions. The CAPM is also used to establish "fair" rates of return on invested capital in regulated firms or in firms that do business on a cost-plus basis.

13.1 THE CAPITAL ASSET PRICING MODEL IN BRIEF

The **capital asset pricing model** is an equilibrium theory that is based on the theory of portfolio selection presented in chapter 12. The CAPM was developed in the early 1960s.[1] It was derived by posing the question: What would risk premiums on securities be in equilibrium if people had the same set of forecasts of expected returns and risks and all chose their portfolios optimally according to the principles of efficient diversification?

The fundamental idea behind the CAPM is that in equilibrium the market rewards people for bearing risk. Because people generally exhibit risk-averse behavior, the risk premium for the aggregate of all risky assets must be positive to induce people to willingly hold all of the risky assets that exist in the economy.

But the market does not reward people for holding inefficient portfolios—that is, for exposing themselves to risks that could be eliminated by optimal diversification behavior. The risk premium on any individual security is, therefore, not related to the security's "stand-alone" risk, but rather to its contribution to the risk of an efficiently diversified portfolio.

Chapter 12 showed that every efficient portfolio can be constructed by mixing just two particular assets: the riskless asset and the optimal combination of risky assets (i.e., the tangency portfolio). To derive the CAPM, we need two assumptions:

- *Assumption 1:* Investors agree in their forecasts of expected rates of return, standard deviations, and correlations of the risky securities, and they, therefore, optimally hold risky assets in the same relative proportions.

- *Assumption 2:* Investors generally behave optimally. In equilibrium, the prices of securities adjust so that when investors are holding their optimal portfolios, the aggregate demand for each security is equal to its supply.

From these two assumptions, because every investor's relative holdings of risky assets is the same, the only way the asset market can clear is if those optimal relative proportions are the proportions in which they are valued in the marketplace. A portfolio that holds all assets in proportion to their observed market values is called the **market portfolio.** The composition of the market portfolio reflects the supplies of existing assets evaluated at their current market prices.

Let us clarify what is meant by the market portfolio. In the market portfolio, the fraction allocated to security *i* equals the ratio of the market value of the *i*th security outstanding to the market value of all assets outstanding. Thus, for simplicity

---

[1]William F. Sharpe received the 1990 Nobel Prize in economics for his work on the CAPM published in 1964. Others who independently developed the CAPM at about the same time were John Lintner and Jan Mossin.

suppose that there are only three assets: GM stock, Toyota stock, and the risk-free asset. The total market values of each at current prices are $66 billion of GM, $22 billion of Toyota, and $12 billion of the risk-free asset. The total market value of all assets is $100 billion. The composition of the market portfolio is, therefore, 66% GM stock, 22% Toyota stock, and 12% risk-free asset.

The CAPM says that *in equilibrium any investor's relative holdings of risky assets will be the same as in the market portfolio.* Depending on their risk aversion, investors hold different mixes of risk-free and risky assets, but the relative holdings of risky assets are the same for all investors. Thus, in our simple example, all investors will hold GM and Toyota stock in the proportions of 3 to 1 (i.e., 66/22). Another way to state this is to say that the composition of the risky part of any investor's portfolio will be 75% GM stock and 25% Toyota stock.

Consider two investors, each with $100,000 to invest. Investor 1 has risk aversion equal to the average for all investors and, therefore, holds each asset in the same proportions as the market portfolio—$66,000 in GM, $22,000 in Toyota stock, and $12,000 in the risk-free asset. Investor 2 is more risk averse than the average and, therefore, chooses to invest $24,000 (twice as much as Investor 1) in the risk-free asset and $76,000 in risky assets. Investor 2's investment in GM stock will be .75 × $76,000 or $57,000, and the investment in Toyota stock will be .25 × $76,000 or $19,000. Thus, both investors will hold three times as much in GM stock as in Toyota stock.

Quick Check 13-1
Investor 3 has a $100,000 portfolio with nothing invested in the risk-free asset. How much is invested in GM and how much in Toyota?

This basic idea of the CAPM can also be explained with the help of Figure 13.1, which depicts the risk-reward trade-off line facing each investor. Because the tangency portfolio or optimal combination of risky assets has the same relative holdings of risky assets as the market portfolio, the market portfolio is located somewhere on the risk-return trade-off line. In the CAPM, the trade-off line is called the **capital market line** (CML). In Figure 13.1, point *M* represents the market portfolio, point *F* is the risk-free asset, and the CML is the straight line connecting these two points.

The CAPM says that in equilibrium, the CML represents the best risk-reward combinations available to all investors. Although everyone will strive to achieve points that are above the CML, the forces of competition will move asset prices so that everyone achieves points that are on the line.

The CML's formula is

$$E(r) = r_f + \frac{E(r_M) - r_f}{\sigma_M} \sigma \tag{13.1}$$

The slope of the CML is, thus, the risk premium on the market portfolio divided by its standard deviation:

$$\text{Slope of CML} = \frac{E(r_M) - r_f}{\sigma_M}$$

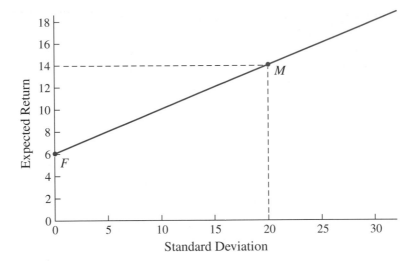

FIGURE 13.1 The Capital Market Line

Note: The CML is given by the formula:

$$E(r) = r_f + \frac{E(r_M) - r_f}{\sigma_M} \sigma$$
$$= .06 + .40\sigma$$

The CAPM implies that most investors would do just as well to passively combine the risk-free asset with an index fund holding risky assets in the same proportions as in the market portfolio as they would by actively researching securities and trying to "beat" the market. Especially diligent and competent investors do tend to earn rewards for their efforts, but over time the competition among them reduces those rewards to the minimum necessary to induce them to perform their work. The rest of us can then benefit from their work by investing passively.

Another implication of the CAPM is that the risk premium on any individual security is proportional only to its contribution to the risk of the market portfolio. The risk premium does not depend on the security's stand-alone risk. Thus, according to the CAPM, in equilibrium, investors get rewarded with a higher expected return only for bearing market risk. This is an *irreducible* or necessary risk that they must take to get their desired expected return.

The logic here is that because all efficient risk-reward combinations can be achieved simply by mixing the market portfolio and the risk-free asset, the only risk an investor need bear to achieve an efficient portfolio is market risk. Therefore, the market does not reward investors for bearing any nonmarket risk.

The market does not reward investors for choosing inefficient portfolios.

Sometimes this implication of the CAPM is emphasized by saying that only the market-related risk of a security "matters."

Quick Check 13-2
According to the CAPM, what is a simple way for investors to form their optimal portfolios?

13.2 DETERMINANTS OF THE RISK PREMIUM ON THE MARKET PORTFOLIO

According to the CAPM, the size of the risk premium of the market portfolio is determined by the aggregate risk aversion of investors and the volatility of the market return. To be induced to accept the risk of the market portfolio, investors must be offered an expected rate of return that exceeds the risk-free rate of interest. The greater the average degree of risk aversion of the population, the higher the risk premium required.

In the CAPM, the equilibrium risk premium on the market portfolio is equal to the variance of the market portfolio times a weighted average of the degree of risk aversion of the holders of wealth (A):

$$E(r_M) - r_f = A\sigma_M^2 \tag{13.2}$$

A should be thought of as an *index* of the degree of risk aversion in the economy.

Suppose that the standard deviation of the market portfolio is .20, and the average degree of risk aversion is 2. Then the risk premium on the market portfolio is .08:

$$E(r_M) - r_f = 2 \times .2^2 = 2 \times .04 = .08$$

Thus, according to the CAPM, the market risk premium can change over time either because the variance of the market changes, because the degree of risk aversion changes, or both.

Note that the CAPM explains the *difference* between the riskless interest rate and the expected rate of return on the market portfolio, but not their *absolute* levels. As discussed in chapter 4, the absolute level of the equilibrium expected rate of return on the market portfolio is determined by factors such as the expected productivity of the capital stock and household intertemporal preferences for consumption.

Given a particular level for the expected return on the market, the CAPM can be used to determine the riskless rate of interest. In our numerical example, if the expected return on the market portfolio is .14 per year, then the CAPM implies that the risk-free rate must be .06 per year.

Substituting these values into equation 13.1, the CML is given by the following formula:

$$E(r) = r_f + \frac{E(r_M) - r_f}{\sigma_M} \sigma$$

$$= .06 + .40\sigma$$

where the slope, the market *reward-to-risk ratio,* is .40.

Quick Check 13-3
What would the slope of the CML be if the average degree of risk aversion increased from 2 to 3?

13.3 BETA AND RISK PREMIUMS ON INDIVIDUAL SECURITIES

By definition, equilibrium asset prices and expected returns are such that knowledgeable investors willingly hold the assets they have in their optimal portfolios. With the idea that investors must be compensated in terms of expected return for bearing risk, we define the *risk of a security* by the size of its equilibrium expected return. Thus, the risk of security *A* is larger than the risk of security *B* if in equilibrium the expected return on *A* exceeds the expected return on *B*. By inspection of the CML in Figure 13.1, among optimal (*efficient*) portfolios, the larger the standard deviation of its return, the larger the equilibrium expected return $E(r)$, and, therefore, the larger the risk. Hence, the *risk of an efficient portfolio* is measured by σ. However, standard deviation of return *does not* measure generally the risk of securities in the CAPM. Instead, the general measure of a security's risk is its **beta** (the Greek letter β). Technically, beta describes the marginal contribution of that security's return to the standard deviation of the market portfolio's return. The formula for the beta of security *j* is given by

$$\beta_j \equiv \frac{\sigma_{jM}}{\sigma_M^2}$$

where σ_{jM} denotes the covariance between the return on security *j* and the return on the market portfolio.[2]

According to the CAPM, in equilibrium, the risk premium on any asset is equal to its beta times the risk premium on the market portfolio. The equation expressing this relation is

$$E(r_j) - r_f = \beta_j[E(r_M) - r_f] \tag{13.3}$$

This is called the **security market line** (SML) relation, and it is depicted in Figure 13.2. Note that in Figure 13.2, we plot the security's beta on the horizontal axis and its expected return on the vertical. The slope of the SML is the risk premium on the market portfolio. In our example, because the market risk premium is .08 or 8% per year, the SML relation is

$$E(r_j) - r_f = .08\beta_j$$

Beta also provides a proportional measure of the sensitivity of a security's realized return to the realized return on the market portfolio. Thus, if the realized return on the market portfolio is *Y*% greater (less) than was expected, then the realized return on security *j* will tend to be $\beta_j \times Y\%$ greater (less) than was expected. Thus, securities with high betas (greater than 1) are called "aggressive" because their returns tend to accentuate those of the overall market portfolio, going up more in up markets and down more in down markets. Similarly, securities with low betas (less than 1) are called "defensive." The market portfolio, by definition, has a beta of 1, and securities with a beta of 1 are said to have "average risk."

If any security had an expected return and beta combination that was not on the SML, it would be a contradiction of the CAPM. In particular, imagine a security with an expected return/beta combination represented by point *J* in Figure 13.2. Because it lies below the SML, its expected return is "too low" to support equilibrium. (Equivalently, we can say that its market price is too high.)

---

[2]Beta corresponds to what is called a *regression coefficient* in statistics, where the regression has the return on the market as the independent variable and the return on the security as the dependent one.

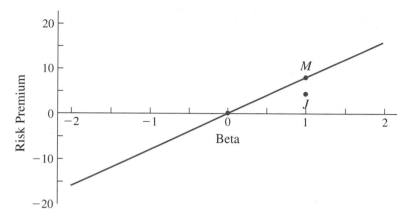

FIGURE 13.2 The Security Market Line

Note: All securities (not just efficient portfolios) plot on the SML, if they are correctly priced according to the CAPM.

The existence of such a situation contradicts the CAPM because it implies either that the market is not in equilibrium or that investors do not agree on the distribution of returns or that investors are not behaving as mean-variance optimizers. Under the assumptions of the CAPM, investors could improve their portfolios by investing less in security *J* and more in the other securities. Therefore, there is excess supply of security *J* and excess demand for the other securities.

Any portfolio that lies on the CML (i.e., any portfolio formed by mixing the market portfolio and the riskless asset) has a beta equal to the fraction of the portfolio invested in the market portfolio. For example, the beta of a portfolio that is 0.75 invested in the market portfolio and 0.25 invested in the risk-free asset is 0.75.

Quick Check 13-4

Suppose you are examining a stock that has a beta of 0.5. According to the CAPM, what should be its expected rate of return? Where should the stock be located in relation to the CML and the SML?

13.4 USING THE CAPM IN PORTFOLIO SELECTION

As we saw in section 13.3, the CAPM implies that the market portfolio of risky assets is an efficient portfolio. This means that an investor will do as well by simply following a passive portfolio selection strategy of combining a market index fund and the risk-free asset as by following an active strategy of trying to beat the market.

Whether or not the CAPM applies to real-world asset prices, it nevertheless provides a rationale for a simple passive portfolio strategy:

- Diversify your holdings of risky assets in the proportions of the market portfolio, and

- Mix this portfolio with the risk-free asset to achieve a desired risk-reward combination.

The same passive strategy can serve as a risk-adjusted benchmark for measuring the performance of active portfolio selection strategies.

Let us illustrate. Suppose that you have $1 million to invest. You are deciding how to allocate it among two risky asset classes: stocks and bonds and the risk-free asset. You know that in the economy as a whole, the net relative supplies of these three asset classes are 60% in stocks, 40% in bonds, and 0% in the risk-free asset. This, therefore, is the composition of the market portfolio.

If you have an average degree of risk aversion, then you will invest $600,000 in stocks, $400,000 in bonds, and nothing in the risk-free asset. If you are more risk averse than average, you will invest some of your $1 million in the risk-free asset and the rest in stocks and bonds. Whatever amount you invest in stocks and bonds will be allocated in the proportions 60% in stocks and 40% in bonds.

In assessing the performance of portfolio managers on a risk-adjusted basis, the CAPM suggests a simple benchmark based on the CML. It consists of comparing the rate of return earned on the managed portfolio to the rate of return attainable by simply mixing the market portfolio and risk-free asset in proportions that would have produced the same volatility.

The method requires one to compute the volatility of the managed portfolio over the relevant period in the past—for instance, the last 10 years—and then to figure out what the average rate of return would have been on a strategy of mixing the market portfolio and risk-free asset to produce a portfolio with that same volatility. Then compare the managed portfolio's average rate of return to this simple benchmark portfolio's average rate of return.

In practice, the market portfolio actually used in measuring the performance of portfolio managers is a well-diversified portfolio of stocks rather than the true market portfolio of all risky assets. It turns out that the simple benchmark strategy has been a difficult one to beat. Studies of the performance of managed equity mutual funds consistently find that the simple strategy outperforms around two-thirds of the funds. As a result, more households and pension funds have been adopting the passive investment strategy used as the performance benchmark. This type of strategy has come to be known as **indexing,** because the portfolio used as a proxy for the market portfolio often has the same weights as well-known stock market indexes such as the Standard & Poor's 500.

Whether or not the CAPM is a valid theory, indexing is an attractive investment strategy for at least two reasons. First, as an empirical matter, it has historically performed better than most actively managed portfolios. Second, it costs less to implement than an active portfolio strategy, because one does not incur the costs of research to look for mispriced securities, and the cost of transactions is typically much less.

As we have seen, the CML provides a convenient and challenging benchmark for measuring the performance of an investor's entire portfolio of assets. However, households and pension funds often use several different portfolio managers, each of whom manages only a part of the whole portfolio. For measuring performance of such managers, the CAPM suggests a different benchmark—the SML.

As we saw in section 13.3, the CAPM holds that every security has a risk premium equal to its beta times the risk premium on the market portfolio. The difference between the average rate of return on a security or a portfolio of securities and its SML relation is called **alpha** (the Greek letter α).

If a portfolio manager can consistently produce a positive alpha, then her performance is judged to be superior, even if the managed portfolio does not outperform the CML as a stand-alone investment.

To understand this puzzle, consider how a fund with a positive alpha can be used by an investor in combination with the market portfolio and the risk-free asset to create a total portfolio that outperforms the CML. Let us illustrate with an example.

Assume that the risk-free rate is 6% per year, the risk premium on the market portfolio is 8% per year, and the standard deviation on the market portfolio is 20% per year. Suppose the Alpha Fund is a managed mutual fund with a beta of 0.5, an alpha of 1% per year, and a standard deviation of 15%.

Figures 13.3 and 13.4 show the relation of Alpha Fund to the SML and the CML. In both figures, point *Alpha* represents the Alpha Fund. In Figure 13.3, *Alpha* lies above the SML. Alpha Fund's α is measured as the vertical distance between *Alpha* and the SML.

FIGURE 13.3   Alpha Fund and the Security Market Line

Note: The SML has a slope of 8% per year. Alpha Fund is a managed mutual fund with a β of 0.5 and an α of 1% per year.

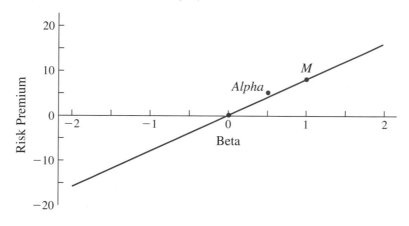

FIGURE 13.4   Alpha Fund and the Capital Market Line

Note: The risk-free rate is 6% per year, the risk-premium on the market portfolio is 8% per year, and the standard deviation on the market portfolio is 20% per year. The CML has a slope of .4. Alpha Fund is a managed mutual fund with an expected rate of return of 11% per year and a σ of 15%.

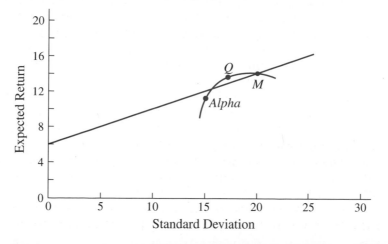

In Figure 13.4, *Alpha* lies below the CML and, therefore, is not efficient. Alpha Fund would never be held by any investor as a total portfolio because investors could achieve lower risk and/or a higher expected return by mixing the market portfolio and the risk-free asset. However, by combining Alpha Fund with the market portfolio in certain optimal proportions, investors can achieve points that lie above the CML.

Point Q in Figure 13.4 corresponds to the optimal combination of Alpha Fund and the market portfolio. By mixing this portfolio with the risk-free asset, investors can achieve risk-return combinations anywhere along the line connecting points F and Q, which lie above the CML. Thus, *if you can find a portfolio manager with a positive* α, *you can beat the market* (*indexing investment strategy*).

Quick Check 13-5

If the CAPM were empirically accurate, then what should be the alpha of all portfolios?

13.5 VALUATION AND REGULATING RATES OF RETURN

In addition to their use in portfolio selection, risk premiums derived from the CAPM are employed in discounted cash flow (DCF) valuation models and in capital-budgeting decisions of firms. They are also used to establish "fair" rates of return on invested capital in regulated firms or in firms that do business on a cost-plus basis. In this section, we offer brief examples of each of these applications.

13.5.1 Discounted Cash Flow Valuation Models

As we saw in chapter 7, some widely used methods of valuing a firm's stock view the price of a share as the present value of all expected future dividends discounted at the market capitalization rate.

$$P_0 \frac{D_1}{(1+k)} + \frac{D_2}{(1+k)^2} + \cdots = \sum_{t=1}^{\infty} \frac{D_t}{(1+k)^t}$$

where D_t is the expected dividend per share in period t and k is the risk-adjusted discount rate, which is the expected rate of return that investors require to invest in the stock. In applying this formula, analysts often employ the CAPM to compute k.

For example, Steadygrowth Corporation's dividends per share are expected to grow at a constant rate of 10% per year. The expected stream of future dividends is

D_1	D_2	D_3	etc.
$5	$5.50	$6.05	etc.

As we showed in chapter 9, the present value of a perpetual stream of dividends growing at a constant rate, g, is

$$P_0 = \frac{D_1}{k-g}$$

With Steadygrowth's data, this implies that the price of the stock is

$$P_0 = \frac{5}{k - .10}$$

One way to find k is to estimate Steadygrowth's beta and infer Steadygrowth's risk premium from the SML relation:

$$k_{steady} = r_f + \beta_{steady}[E(r_M) - r_f]$$

Thus, suppose that the risk-free rate is .03, $\beta_{steady} = 1.5$, and the risk premium on the market portfolio is .08. Then $k = .15$ per year. Substituting this value into the constant growth rate DDM, the estimated value of Steadygrowth stock is

$$P_0 = \frac{5}{k - .10} = \frac{5}{.15 - .10} = 100$$

Quick Check 13-6
What would be the estimated value of Steadygrowth stock if its beta were 2 instead of 1.5?

13.5.2 Cost of Capital

As we will see in chapter 16, corporate financial managers need to know their firm's cost of capital to make investment (capital-budgeting) decisions. The firm's cost of capital is a weighted average of its cost of equity capital and debt. Practitioners often use a CAPM-based method similar to the one we just demonstrated for Steadygrowth Corporation to estimate the cost of equity capital.

For example, suppose that you are the financial manager of ABC Corporation and you want to compute your firm's cost of equity capital. You compute the beta of ABC stock and find it to be 1.1. The current risk-free rate is .06 per year, and you assume that the market risk premium is .08 per year. Then according to the SML, the equilibrium expected rate of return on ABC stock is

$$E(r_{ABC}) = r_f + \beta_{ABC}[E(r_M) - r_f]$$
$$= .06 + 1.1 \times .08 = .148$$

Thus, .148 per year is ABC's cost of equity capital.

13.5.3 Regulation and Cost-Plus Pricing

Regulators use the CAPM to establish a "fair" rate of return on invested capital for public utilities and other firms subject to price regulation. For example, a commission regulating an electric power company may have to establish a price that the company is allowed to charge its customers for electricity. The commission will do so by computing the cost of producing the electricity, including an allowance for the cost of capital.

Similarly, in situations in which a price is negotiated by two parties based on production cost, there is often a need to decide on a fair allowance for the cost of capital. An example would be a noncompetitive (secret) contract to develop or produce military equipment for a government.

In computing the cost of capital, a regulatory commission must compensate the providers of capital for the risk they bear by investing in the electric utility. Because the investors are able to diversify their investment portfolios, the only risk the regulators need to compensate them for is market risk, as measured by beta.

13.6 MODIFICATIONS AND ALTERNATIVES TO THE CAPM

As early as the 1970s, researchers testing the empirical validity of the Security Market Line using the historical returns of common stocks in the United States found that it did not seem to fit the data well enough to explain fully the structure of expected returns on assets. Subsequent and currently ongoing research formulated and tested a variety of enriched CAPM and alternative models using data from a variety of asset markets around the world. A consensus has emerged that the original simple version of the CAPM needs to be modified.[3]

Potential explanations for the apparent deviations from the CAPM fall into three categories. One such is that the CAPM actually does hold, but the "market" portfolios used in the testing were incomplete and inadequate representations of the true market portfolio. Another focuses on market imperfections not contemplated in the CAPM, such as borrowing costs and constraints, shortsale restrictions and costs, different tax treatments for various assets, and the nontradability of some important assets such as human capital. These elements are likely to change over time with changes in technology, institutional structures, and regulations. A third approach has been to add greater realism to the modeling assumptions, while maintaining the CAPM's basic methodology. This means retaining the fundamental assumption of the CAPM that investors (or their agents) follow the principles of optimal portfolio selection, and deriving the equilibrium implications of such optimizing behavior in the presence of additional complicating factors. One such model is the multifactor Intertemporal Capital Asset Pricing Model (ICAPM), in which equilibrium risk premiums on securities in this dynamic model come from several dimensions of risks, reflected not only by their return sensitivities or beta on the market portfolio but also by their sensitivity to other systematic risks such as changes in interest rates and expected returns on assets and changes in consumption good prices. In this world, securities have a richer set of hedging roles in addition to their place in the market portfolio.

Another line of research has been to develop alternative theories. The most prominent is the Arbitrage Pricing Theory (APT). According to the APT a relation similar to the Security Market Line can exist even if investors are not mean-variance optimizers. If there are enough different securities to "diversify away" all but market risk, the APT shows that an expected-return-to-beta relation will exist as a consequence of there not being any arbitrage opportunities. Although the specific structure of asset risks in these models differs from the CAPM, the basic insights of the CAPM—that the risk premiums are related to broad systematic risk factors that matter to large segments of the population—still hold.

[3]See F. Black, M. Jensen, and M. Scholes, "The Capital Asset Pricing Model: Some Empirical Tests," in M. Jensen, ed., *Studies in the Theory of Capital Markets,* New York: Praeger, 1972; E. Fama and J. MacBeth, "Risk, Return and Equilibrium: Some Empirical Tests," *Journal of Political Economy,* 8, 1973; E. Fama and K. French, "Multifactor Explanations of Asset Pricing Anomalies," *Journal of Finance,* 51, 1996.

Summary

The CAPM has three main implications:

- In equilibrium, everyone's relative holdings of risky assets are the same as in the market portfolio.
- The size of the risk premium of the market portfolio is determined by the risk aversion of investors and the volatility of the return.
- The risk premium on any asset is equal to its beta times the risk premium on the market portfolio.

Whether or not the CAPM is strictly true, it provides a rationale for a very simple passive portfolio strategy:

- Diversify your holdings of risky assets according to the proportions of the market portfolio, and
- Mix this portfolio with the risk-free asset to achieve a desired risk-reward combination.

The CAPM is used in portfolio management primarily in two ways:

- to establish a logical and convenient starting point in asset allocation and security selection, and
- to establish a benchmark for evaluating portfolio-management ability on a risk-adjusted basis.

In corporate finance, the CAPM is used to determine the appropriate risk-adjusted discount rate in valuation models of the firm and in capital-budgeting decisions. The CAPM is also used to establish a "fair" rate of return on invested capital for regulated firms and in cost-plus pricing.

Today few financial scholars consider the CAPM in its simplest form to be an accurate model for fully explaining or predicting risk premiums on risky assets. However, modified versions of the model are still a central feature of the theory and practice of finance.

The APT gives a rationale for the expected return–beta relation that relies on the condition that there be no arbitrage profit opportunities; the CAPM requires that investors be mean-variance portfolio optimizers. The APT and CAPM are not incompatible; rather, they complement each other.

Key Terms

- capital asset pricing model   344
- market portfolio   344
- capital market line   345
- beta   348
- security market line   348
- indexing   350
- alpha   350

Answers to Quick Check Questions

Quick Check 13-1   *Investor 3 has a $100,000 portfolio with nothing invested in the risk-free asset. How much is invested in GM and how much in Toyota?*

ANSWER: $75,000 is invested in GM stock and $25,000 in Toyota stock.

Quick Check 13-2   *According to the CAPM, what is a simple way for investors to form their optimal portfolios?*

ANSWER: According to the CAPM, a simple way for investors to form their optimal portfolios is to combine the market portfolio with the risk-free asset.

Quick Check 13-3   *What would the slope of the CML be if the average degree of risk aversion increased from 2 to 3?*

ANSWER: If risk aversion increased from 2 to 3, the risk premium on the market portfolio would increase from .08 to .12, and the slope of the CML would increase from .4 to .6.

Quick Check 13-4   *Suppose you are examining a stock that has a beta of 0.5. According to the CAPM, what should be its expected rate of return? Where should the stock be located in relation to the CML and the SML?*

ANSWER: A stock with a beta of 0.5 should have an expected risk premium equal to half the risk premium on the market portfolio. If the market risk premium is .08, then the stock's expected rate of return should be the risk-free rate plus .04. The stock would be located on the SML at a point halfway between the vertical axis and point M. It would be located on or below the CML at a latitude corresponding to its expected rate of return of $r_f + .04$.

Quick Check 13-5   *If the CAPM were empirically accurate, then what should be the alpha of all portfolios?*

ANSWER: According to the CAPM, all portfolios should have an alpha of zero.

Quick Check 13-6   *What would be the estimated value of Steadygrowth stock if its beta was 2 instead of 1.5?*

ANSWER: If Steadygrowth's beta is 2, then $k = .19$, and $P_0 = 5/(.19 - .10) = \$55.56$ per share.

Questions and Problems

1. ***Composition of the Market Portfolio***
   Capital markets in Flatland exhibit trade in four securities, the stocks X, Y, and Z, and a riskless government security. Evaluated at current prices in U.S. dollars, the total market values of these assets are, respectively, $24 billion, $36 billion, $24 billion, and $16 billion.
   a. Determine the relative proportions of each asset in the market portfolio.
   b. If one trader with a $100,000 portfolio holds $40,000 in the riskless security, $15,000 in X, $12,000 in Y, and $33,000 in Z, determine the holdings of the three risky assets of a second trader who invests $20,000 of a $200,000 portfolio in the riskless security.

2. ***Implications of CAPM***
   The riskless rate of interest is .06 per year, and the expected rate of return on the market portfolio is .15 per year.
   a. According to the CAPM, what is the efficient way for an investor to achieve an expected rate of return of .10 per year?
   b. If the standard deviation of the rate of return on the market portfolio is .20, what is the standard deviation on the foregoing portfolio?
   c. Draw the CML and locate the foregoing portfolio on the same graph.
   d. Draw the SML and locate the foregoing portfolio on the same graph.

e. Estimate the value of a stock with an expected dividend per share of $5 this coming year, an expected dividend growth rate of 4% per year forever, and a beta of 0.8. If its market price is less than the value you have estimated (i.e., if it is underpriced), what is true of its mean rate of return?

3. If the CAPM is valid, which of the following situations is possible? Explain. Consider each situation independently.

a. *Portfolio*   *Expected Return*   *Beta*

Portfolio	Expected Return	Beta
A	.20	1.4
B	.25	1.2

b. *Portfolio*   *Expected Return*   *Standard Deviation*

Portfolio	Expected Return	Standard Deviation
A	.30	.35
B	.40	.25

c. *Portfolio*   *Expected Return*   *Standard Deviation*

Portfolio	Expected Return	Standard Deviation
Risk free	.10	0
Market	.18	.24
A	.16	.12

d. *Portfolio*   *Expected Return*   *Standard Deviation*

Portfolio	Expected Return	Standard Deviation
Risk free	.10	0
Market	.18	.24
A	.20	.22

4. If the Treasury bill rate is currently 4% and the expected return to the market portfolio over the same period is 12%, determine the risk premium on the market. If the standard deviation of the return on the market is .20, what is the equation of the capital market line?

5. ***Determinants of the Market Risk Premium***
Consider an economy in which the expected return on the market portfolio over a particular period is .05, the standard deviation of the return to the market portfolio over this same period .25, and the average degree of risk aversion among traders is 3. If the government wishes to issue riskless zero-coupon bonds with a term to maturity of one period and a face value per bond of $100,000, how much can the government expect to receive per bond?

6. Norma Swanson has invested 40% of her wealth in MGM stock and 60% in Industrial Light and Magic stock. Norma believes the returns to these stocks have a correlation of .6 and that their respective means and standard deviations are:

	MGM	ILM
Expected return	10%	15%
Standard deviation	15%	25%

a. Determine the expected value and standard deviation of the return on Norma's portfolio.
b. Would a risk-averse investor such as Norma prefer a portfolio composed entirely of only MGM stock? Of only ILM stock? Why or why not?

7. Consider a portfolio exhibiting an expected return of 20% in an economy in which the riskless interest rate is 8%, the expected return to the market portfolio is 13%, and the standard deviation of the return to the market portfolio is .25. Assuming this portfolio is efficient, determine:
   a. Its beta.
   b. The standard deviation of its return.
   c. Its correlation with the market return.

8. **Application of CAPM to Corporate Finance**
   The Suzuki Motor Company is contemplating issuing stock to finance investment in producing a new sports-utility vehicle, the Seppuku. The annual return to the market portfolio is expected to be 15% and the current riskless interest rate is 5%. The analysts further believe that the expected return to the Seppuku project will be 20% annually. What is the maximum beta value that would induce Suzuki to issue the stock?

9. Roobel and Associates, a firm of financial analysts specializing in Russian financial markets, forecasts that the stock of the Yablonsky Toy Company will be worth 1,000 roubles per share one year from today. If the riskless interest rate on Russian government securities is 10% and the expected return to the market portfolio is 18%, determine how much you would pay for a share of Yablonsky stock today if:
   a. The beta of Yablonsky is 3.
   b. The beta of Yablonsky is 0.5.

10. **Application of CAPM to Portfolio Management**
    Suppose that the stock of the new cologne manufacturer, Eau de Rodman, Inc., has been forecast to have a return with standard deviation .30 and a correlation with the market portfolio of .9. If the standard deviation of the yield on the market is .20, determine the relative holdings of the market portfolio and Eau de Rodman stock to form a portfolio with a beta of 1.8.

11. The current price of a share of stock in the Vo Giap Clothing Company of Vietnam is 50 dong and its expected yield over the year is 14%. The market risk premium in Vietnam is 8% and the riskless interest rate 6%. What would happen to the stock's current price if its expected future payout remains constant while the covariance of its rate of return with the market portfolio falls by 50%?

12. Suppose that you believe that the price of a share of IBM stock a year from today will be equal to the sum of the price of a share of General Motors stock plus the price of a share of Exxon, and further that you believe that the price of a share of IBM stock in one year will be $100 whereas the price of a share of General Motors today is $30. If the yield on 91-day T-bills (the riskless rate you use) is 5%, the expected yield on the market is 15%, the variance of the market portfolio is 1, and the beta of IBM is 2, what price would you be willing to pay for one share of Exxon stock today?

13. Ascertain whether the following quotation is true or false, and state why: "When arbitrage is absent from financial markets, and investors are each concerned with only the risk and return to their portfolios, then each investor can eliminate all the riskiness of his investments through diversification, and as a consequence the expected yield on each available asset will depend only on the covariance of its yield with the covariance of the yield on the diversified portfolio of risky assets each investor holds."

14. **Application of CAPM to Measuring Portfolio Performance**
    During the most recent five-year period, the Pizzaro mutual fund earned an average annualized rate of return of 12% and had an annualized standard deviation of 30%. The average risk-free rate was 5% per year. The average rate of return in the market index over that same period was 10% per year and the standard deviation was 20%. How well did Pizzaro perform on a risk-adjusted basis?

Challenge Problem

15. *CAPM with Only Two Risky Assets*

    There are only two risky assets in the economy: stocks and real estate, and their relative supplies are 50% stocks and 50% real estate. Thus, the market portfolio will be half stocks and half real estate. The standard deviations are 0.20 for stocks, 0.20 for real estate, and the correlation between them is 0. The coefficient of relative risk aversion of the average market participant (A) is 3. r_f is .08 per year.

    a. According to the CAPM what must be the equilibrium risk premium on the market portfolio, on stocks, and on real estate?

    b. Draw the capital market line. What is its slope? Where is the point representing stocks located relative to the CML?

    c. Draw the SML. What is its formula? Where is the point representing stocks located relative to the SML?

C H A P T E R

14

Forward and Futures Prices

OBJECTIVES

- To learn how to use forward and futures contracts for hedging, speculating, and arbitrage.
- To understand the relations among spot, forward, and futures prices of commodities, currencies, and securities.
- To learn what kinds of useful information can be inferred from the relations among spot and forward prices.

CONTENTS

We introduced forward and futures contracts in chapter 11 and showed how they are used to hedge against risks. In this chapter, we explain how their prices are determined and how to extract information from them.

We begin with commodities such as wheat and show how forward and futures prices guide decisions about how much wheat to store from one growing season to the next. Next, we examine the relation between the spot and forward prices of gold and show how one can infer from them the implicit cost of carrying gold from one period to another. We then turn to the prices of **financial futures,** that is, stocks, bonds, and foreign currencies for future delivery.

14.1 DISTINCTIONS BETWEEN FORWARD AND FUTURES CONTRACTS

As we saw in chapter 11, any agreement between two parties that calls for delivery of an item on a specified future date for an agreed-upon price that is paid in the future is called a **forward contract.** We can summarize the main features of a forward contract as follows:

- Two parties agree to exchange some item in the future at a delivery price specified now.
- The *forward price* is defined as the delivery price that makes the current market value of the contract zero.
- No money is paid in the present by either party to the other.
- The *face value* of the contract is the quantity of the item specified in the contract times the forward price.
- The party who agrees to buy the specified item is said to take a *long* position, and the party who agrees to sell the item is said to take a *short* position.

A simple way to remember who pays what to whom is the following rule:

> If the spot price on the contract maturity date is higher than the forward price, the party who is long makes money. But if the spot price on the contract maturity date is lower than the forward price, the party who is short makes money.

Futures contracts serve many of the same purposes as forward contracts, but they differ in several respects. We briefly discussed these differences in chapter 11. Here we consider them in greater detail.

Forward contracts are negotiated between two parties (usually business firms) and, therefore, can have unique specifications that depend on the demands of those parties. This "customization" is a disadvantage if one of the parties wants to terminate the contract before the delivery date because it makes the contract illiquid.

By contrast, futures contracts are standardized contracts that are traded on exchanges. The exchange specifies the exact commodity, the contract size, and where and when delivery will be made. It is, therefore, easy for parties to a futures contract to "close out"—that is, to terminate—their positions before the specified delivery date. Indeed, the vast majority of futures contracts are terminated before the final contract delivery date.

To illustrate, the wheat futures contract traded on the Chicago Board of Trade (CBT) specifies a quantity of 5,000 bushels of a specific grade of wheat. Table 14.1 shows a listing of CBT wheat futures contracts and prices from *The Wall Street Journal.*

The futures contracts in Table 14.1 differ from each other only in their delivery months. The first three columns show the day's opening price and the day's high and low. The next column shows the settlement price, which is usually an average of the prices of the last few trades of the day. The next column shows the

TABLE 14.1   Wheat Futures Contracts and Prices

Monday Aug. 5, 1991

WHEAT (CBT) 5,000 bu.; cents per bu.

	Open	High	Low	Settle	Change	Lifetime High	Lifetime Low	Open Interest
Sept	292	294½	289	290¾	−7¼	326	258½	16,168
Dec				304¼				
Mr92				310				
May				307½				
July	301	303	298½	299¾	−6¼	311	2798½	3,561

Est. volume 16,000; vol Fri 11,126; open int. 54,588, −1,101

change from the previous day's settlement price. The next two columns show the contract's lifetime high and low prices. The last column shows the number of contracts outstanding at the end of the day.

The parties who are long and short on these wheat futures have contracts with the CBT rather than with each other, although the exchange is careful to exactly match the number of long and short positions outstanding. Orders are carried out through brokers who have seats on the exchange.

To make sure that the parties to a futures contract do not default, the exchange requires that there be enough collateral (called the *margin requirement*) posted in each account to cover any losses. All accounts are marked to market at the end of each trading day based on that day's settlement price.

Let us illustrate how futures contracts work using the prices in Table 14.1. You place an order to take a long position in a September wheat futures contract on August 4, 1991. The broker requires you to deposit money in your account—say, $1,500— to serve as collateral.[1]

On August 5, the futures price closes 7¼ cents per bushel lower. Thus, you have lost 7¼ cents × 5,000 bushels or $362.50 that day, and the broker takes that amount out of your account even though you may not have made any trades. The money is transferred to the futures exchange, which transfers it to one of the parties who was on the short side of the contract.

If the collateral in your account falls below a prespecified level, you will receive a **margin call** from the broker asking you to add money. If you do not respond immediately, then the broker liquidates your position at the prevailing market price and returns any leftover collateral.

This process of daily *realization* of gains and losses minimizes the possibility of contract default. Another consequence of daily marking to market of futures contracts is that no matter how great their face value, their market value is always zero at the beginning of each day.

At any time during the contract's life, you can decide to close out your position. The open interest indicates the total number of futures contracts still outstanding at the end of each trading day. In Table 14.1, open interest for each contract delivery month is reported in the last column. As the contract delivery date approaches, the open interest declines. Open interest for all delivery months combined is reported at the bottom of the table.

---

[1]The collateral can be in the form of interest-bearing government securities, and you receive the interest earned.

Because of their careful procedures to protect against the risk of contract default by requiring the posting of margin, futures markets are used by individuals and firms whose credit ratings may be costly to check. Forward contracts, on the other hand, tend to be used when the credit rating of the contracting parties is high and easy to verify. Thus, forward contracts are common in the foreign currency market when the contracting parties are two banks or a bank and one of its corporate customers.

The pricing relations to be discussed later in this chapter that apply to forward prices apply with minor modification to futures prices. They may differ because of the daily marking-to-market feature of futures contracts. In practice, however, for most assets the futures and forward prices hardly differ at all.[2]

Quick Check 14-1
What would happen in your futures trading account if you take a long position in wheat futures and instead of going down by 7¼ cents per bushel, the futures price went up by that amount?

14.2 THE ECONOMIC FUNCTION OF FUTURES MARKETS

The most obvious function of commodity futures markets is to facilitate the reallocation of exposure to commodity price risk among market participants. However, commodity futures prices also play an important informational role for producers, distributors, and consumers of commodities who must decide how much wheat to sell (or consume) now and how much to store for the future. *By providing a means to hedge the price risk associated with storing a commodity, futures contracts make it possible to separate the decision of whether to physically store a commodity from the decision to have financial exposure to its price changes.*

For example, suppose that it is one month before the next harvest and a wheat distributor has a ton of wheat in storage from the last harvest. The spot price of wheat is $2 per bushel, and the futures price for delivery a month from now (after the new crop has been harvested) is F. The distributor can hedge its exposure to price changes by either (1) selling the wheat in the spot market for $2 per bushel and delivering it immediately, or (2) selling short a futures contract at a price of F and delivering the wheat a month from now. In either case, he has complete certainty about the price he will receive for his wheat.

Suppose that a distributor's cost of physically storing the wheat—the "cost of carry," which includes interest, warehousing, and spoilage costs—is 10 cents per bushel per month. This distributor will choose alternative (2) and carry the ton of wheat for another month (i.e., past the next harvest) only if F is greater than $2.10. For example, if the futures price is $2.12 per bushel, then the distributor will choose to carry the wheat in storage for another month.

Now suppose that there is another distributor whose cost of carry is 15 cents per bushel per month. At $2.12, this "high-storage-cost" distributor will choose alternative (1) and sell his wheat immediately in the spot market rather than carry it and hedge by taking a short futures position. Thus, a distributor will choose to carry

---

[2]See Bradford Cornell and Marc R. Reinganum, "Forward and Futures Prices: Evidence from the Foreign Exchange Markets," *Journal of Finance,* 36 (December 1981).

the wheat for another month only if his cost of carrying it is less than the difference between the futures and spot prices of wheat.

Letting S be the spot price of wheat and C_j be the cost of carry for distributor j, we can generalize from our example to say that distributor j will choose to carry the wheat in storage for another month only if $C_j < F - S$. Thus, the difference between the futures and the spot price, called the **spread,** governs how much wheat will be stored in aggregate and by whom:

> The futures and forward markets contribute to economic efficiency by creating a structure in which the least-cost distributors will do the necessary physical storage.

Suppose that the next wheat harvest is expected to be an especially bountiful one, and, therefore, it would be socially desirable to consume all of the wheat currently available in storage. The forward market makes it possible to hedge the price risk without physically storing the wheat. The forward price carries the message not to store to all producers and distributors of wheat by trading below the current spot price, so that it would not pay for anyone to store wheat from now until after the harvest, even if it were costless to do so (i.e., $C = 0$).[3]

Quick Check 14-2

Suppose you are a distributor of corn and you observe that the spot price is $3 per bushel and the futures price for delivery a month from now is $3.10. If your cost of carrying corn is $0.15 per bushel per month, what should you do?

14.3 THE ROLE OF SPECULATORS

Producers, distributors, and consumers of wheat may be in the best position to forecast future wheat prices (perhaps because they have low costs of gathering the relevant information), but others are not banned from the market. Anyone using a futures contract to reduce risk is called a **hedger.** But much of the trading of futures contracts is carried on by **speculators,** who take positions in the market based on their forecasts of the future spot price.

Because speculators are not trying to reduce their risk exposure, their motivation for participating in the futures market is to make a profit on their futures trades. Speculators typically gather information to help them forecast prices, and then buy or sell futures contracts based on those forecasts.

The same party can be both a hedger and a speculator. Indeed, one might say that if a farmer, baker, and a distributor choose *not* to hedge their price risk in the futures market, then they are speculating on the price of wheat. Competition among active forecasters in the futures markets will encourage those who have comparative advantage in forecasting wheat prices to specialize in it.

For example, suppose you are a wheat speculator. You gather information on all the supply and demand factors that determine the price of wheat, such as total

---

[3]Furthermore, this price structure would induce arbitrageurs to find any holders of physical wheat who might plan to store and try to borrow their wheat, sell it in the spot market, and hedge their "short" exposure by going long a forward contract. Thus, in seeking arbitrage profits, the arbitrageurs increase the quantity of wheat that is delivered for current consumption.

acreage planted, rainfall, production plans of major baked goods producers, and so on, and come up with a forecast of next month's spot price of wheat. Say it is $2 per bushel. If the current futures price for delivery a month from now is less than $2 per bushel, you buy the futures contract (take a long position) because you expect to make a profit from it.

To see this, suppose the current futures price for wheat to be delivered a month from now is $1.50 per bushel. By taking a long position in this futures contract, you lock in a buying price of $1.50 per bushel for wheat to be delivered a month from now. Because you expect the spot price to be $2 at that time, your expected gain is $0.50 per bushel.

On the other hand, suppose that the current futures price for delivery a month from now is greater than $2 per bushel (your forecast); say it is $2.50 per bushel. Then to earn an expected profit, you sell the futures contract (take a short position). By taking a short position in this futures contract, you lock in a selling price of $2.50 per bushel for wheat to be delivered a month from now. You expect to be able to buy wheat at a spot price of $2 per bushel at that time. You, therefore, expect a gain of $0.50 per bushel.

As a speculator, you take whatever position gives you an expected profit. Of course, because you do not know for sure what the spot price will be a month from now, you could lose money on your futures contract. But you accept that risk in pursuit of what you believe to be expected profit.

Speculative activity in futures markets is sometimes perceived by critics as having no social value. Indeed, it is often portrayed as being the economic equivalent of gambling. However, there are at least two economic purposes served by the activity of speculators that differentiate it from gambling in sports or at the casino.

First, commodity speculators who consistently succeed do so by correctly forecasting spot prices. Their activity, therefore, makes futures prices better predictors of the direction of change of spot prices. Second, speculators take the opposite side of a hedger's trade when other hedgers cannot readily be found to do so. Thus, the activity of speculators makes futures markets more *liquid* than they would otherwise be. Indeed, if only hedgers bought and sold futures contracts, there might not be enough trading to support an organized futures exchange. Thus, the presence of speculators may be a necessary condition for the very existence of some futures markets.

14.4 RELATION BETWEEN COMMODITY SPOT AND FUTURES PRICES

As we saw in section 14.2, distributors can completely hedge their inventory exposure to wheat price changes by either (1) selling wheat in the spot market for $2 per bushel and delivering it immediately, or (2) selling short a futures contract at a price of F, storing the wheat, and delivering it a month from now.

By buying wheat now and following (2), arbitrageurs could lock in a sure arbitrage profit if the futures price were too far above the spot price. This consideration establishes an upper bound on the spread between the spot and futures prices:

The futures price cannot exceed the spot price by more than the cost of carry:

$$F - S \leq C \tag{14.1}$$

Because the cost of carry can vary both over time and across market participants, the upper bound on the spread is not constant.

14.5 EXTRACTING INFORMATION FROM COMMODITY FUTURES PRICES

It is sometimes said that futures prices can provide information about investor expectations of spot prices in the future. The reasoning is that the futures price reflects what investors expect the spot price to be at the contract delivery date and, therefore, one should be able to retrieve that expected future spot price.

What information can one extract from the forward price of wheat?

We must distinguish between two conditions: (1) no wheat is in storage, and (2) wheat is in storage.

1. If there is no wheat in storage—a condition called a *stock out*—then equation 14.1 holds as a strict inequality, and the spot and forward prices are not linked precisely through an arbitrage-pricing relation. In this case, the forward price will provide information about the expected future spot price that is not extractable from the current spot price.[4]

2. If wheat is being stored, then no further inference about the future expected spot price is possible beyond that extractable from the current spot price. The reason is that, because by the force of arbitrage, equation 14.1 must hold as an equality. Hence, the forward price is completely specified by knowing the spot price and the cost of carry, independently of what the assessments are about the future expected spot price. Therefore, if we observe that a commodity, an asset, or a security is being stored, then the forward price provides no additional information about the expected future spot price. However, the forward price, when combined with the current spot price, can be used to extract an estimate of the cost of carry.[5]

> **Quick Check 14-3**
> When does the forward price provide no additional information about expected future spot prices than can be extracted from the current spot price?

14.6 FORWARD-SPOT PRICE PARITY FOR GOLD

Just as the force of arbitrage establishes the spread between the futures and spot prices of wheat when it is being stored, so it establishes the spread in the case of gold. The resulting relation between the futures and spot prices is called the **forward-spot price-parity relation.**

Suppose you are contemplating investing in an ounce of gold for the next year. There are two ways for you to do it. The first is to buy gold at the current spot price, S, put it into storage, and at the end of the year sell it at a price of S_1. Let s be the cost of storing the gold for the year as a fraction of the spot price. Your rate of return is, therefore,

$$r_{gold} = \frac{S_1 - S}{S} - s \qquad (14.2)$$

---

[4]But even in this case when it does provide information, it is not necessarily an unbiased forecast of the future spot price. We discuss this issue in greater detail in section 14.9.

[5]If storage occurs and the forward and spot prices imply a negative cost of carry, then almost surely there are benefits to holding the physical commodity, asset, or security that are not being taken into account in the analysis. The magnitude of these implied benefits is called the *convenience yield* (for owning the physical).

For example, if the spot price of gold is $300 and storage costs are 2% per year, your rate of return is

$$r_{gold} = \frac{S_1 - 300}{300} - .02$$

Another way to invest in gold for the year is to take the same $300 and instead of investing it in gold, invest it in *synthetic* gold. You create synthetic gold by investing $300 (i.e., the spot price) in the risk-free asset and at the same time taking a long position in a gold forward contract with a delivery date a year from now and a forward price of F. The rate of return on this investment in synthetic gold will be

$$\hat{r}_{gold} = \frac{S_1 - F}{S} + r \qquad (14.3)$$

For example, if the risk-free rate is 8%, your rate of return on synthetic gold will be

$$\hat{r}_{gold} = \frac{S_1 - F}{300} - .08$$

By the Law of One Price, these two equivalent investments must offer the same return, so by equating 14.2 and 14.3 we get

$$\frac{S_1 - F}{S} + r = \frac{S_1 - S}{S} - s$$

Rearranging terms we get the forward-spot price-parity relation for gold:

$$F = (1 + r + s)S \qquad (14.4)$$

In our example, the forward price for delivery of gold in one year should be $330 per ounce:

$$F = (1 + r + s)S = 1.10 \times 300 = 330$$

If, in violation of equation 14.4, the forward price exceeds $330 per ounce, it would pay an arbitrageur to buy gold at the spot price and simultaneously sell it for future delivery at the forward price. If on the other hand, the forward price were less than $330 per ounce, an arbitrageur would sell gold short in the spot market (i.e., borrow it and sell it immediately), invest the proceeds of the short sale in the risk-free asset, and go long the forward contract.

In practice, the parties who maintain the forward-spot price-parity relation are gold dealers. This is because they typically have the lowest storage and transaction costs.

Table 14.2 shows the arbitrage opportunity that would be available if the forward price were $340 per ounce instead of $330. A dealer would borrow, use the funds to buy gold for $300 per ounce, and simultaneously sell gold forward at $340 per ounce. After paying off the loan and the storage costs a year from now, there would be $10 left over *regardless of what the spot price turns out to be at that time.*

Now consider the situation if the forward price of gold were only $320 per ounce. Table 14.3 shows the arbitrage opportunity that would be available to a gold dealer if the forward price were $320 per ounce instead of $330. The dealer would

TABLE 14.2	Arbitrage Opportunity When Forward Price of Gold Is Too High	
Arbitrage Position	*Immediate Cash Flow*	*Cash Flow 1 Year From Now*
Sell a forward contract	0	$340 - S_1$
Borrow $300	$300	-$324
Buy an ounce of gold	-$300	S_1
Pay storage costs		-$6
Net cash flows	0	$340 - $330 = $10

TABLE 14.3	Arbitrage Opportunity When Forward Price of Gold Is Too Low	
Arbitrage Position	*Immediate Cash Flow*	*Cash Flow 1 Year From Now*
Sell short an ounce of gold	$300	$-S_1$
Buy a forward contract	0	$S_1 - $320
Invest $300 in 1-year pure discount bonds	-$300	$324
Receive storage costs		$6
Net cash flows	0	$330 - $320 = $10

sell gold short in the spot market at $330 per ounce, invest the funds in the risk-free asset, and simultaneously sell gold forward at $320 per ounce. After paying off the loan and collecting the storage costs a year from now, there would be $10 left over *regardless of what the spot price turns out to be at that time.*[6]

The forward-spot price-parity relation does not carry any causal implications. It does not say that the forward price is determined by the spot price and the cost of carry. Rather, the forward and spot prices are jointly determined in the market. If we know one of them, then by the Law of One Price we know what the other must be.

Quick Check 14-4
Suppose that $r = .06$, $S = $400, and $s = .02$. What must the forward price of gold be? Show how, if it is not, there would be an arbitrage opportunity.

14.6.1 The "Implied" Cost of Carry

A consequence of the forward-spot price-parity relation for gold is that one cannot extract any additional information about the expected future spot price from the forward price than can be gotten from the spot. In the case of wheat discussed in

---

[6]When a gold dealer sells short gold in the spot market, he in effect borrows it from a customer for whom he is storing it in inventory. In principle, any stored commodity can be sold short in a similar fashion.

section 14.4, we saw that when there is no storage, the forward price contains information about the expected future spot price that is not embodied in the current spot price. Because gold is stored, no such information about expected future prices can be extracted from the forward price.

The only information one can infer from the observed spot and forward prices of gold is the *implied cost of carry,* defined as the spread between the futures and the spot price:

$$\text{Implied Cost of Carry} = F - S$$

It represents the implied marginal carrying cost for an investor who is at the point of indifference between investing in physical gold or in synthetic gold.

From the forward-spot price-parity relation in equation 14.4, we know that the carrying cost as a fraction of the spot price is the sum of the risk-free interest rate and storage costs:

$$F = S(1 + r + s)$$
$$\frac{F - S}{S} = r + s$$

Thus, by subtracting the observed risk-free interest rate from the implied cost of carry, one can infer the implied cost of storing gold:

$$s = \frac{F - S}{S} - r$$

For example, suppose we observe that the spot price of gold is $300 per ounce, the one-year forward price is $330, and the risk-free interest rate is 8%. What are the implied cost of carry and the implied storage cost?

$$\text{Implied Cost of Carry} = F - S = \$330 - \$300 = \$30 \text{ per ounce}$$

$$\text{Implied Storage Cost} = (F - S)/S - r = .10 - .08 = .02 \text{ or } 2\% \text{ per year}$$

Quick Check 14-5
Suppose the spot price of gold is $300 per ounce and the one-year forward price is $324. What is the implied cost of carrying gold? If the risk-free interest rate is 7% per year, what is the implied storage cost for gold?

14.7 FINANCIAL FUTURES

E-BOOK

14.7

We now focus on the prices of *financial futures*—that is, stocks, bonds, and foreign currencies for future delivery. Unlike commodities such as wheat or gold, financial securities have no intrinsic value. They are not consumed, used as inputs to physical production, or held for their own sake. Rather, they represent claims to streams of income in the future.

Securities can be produced and stored at very low cost, and this is reflected in the relation between their spot and futures prices. Indeed, to a first approximation, we can ignore those costs completely in deriving parity relations between spot and forward prices.

Consider a hypothetical stock called S&P, which is a share in a mutual fund that invests in a broadly diversified portfolio of stocks. It reinvests all dividends received and pays no dividends. A forward contract on a share of S&P is the promise to deliver a share at some specified delivery date at a specified delivery price. Let us denote this forward price by F. The party who is long the forward contract agrees to pay F dollars at the delivery date to the party who is short. We denote the stock price on the delivery date by S_1.

Rather than actually delivering the stock, the contract is usually settled in cash. This means that no delivery of stock takes place; only the *difference* between F and S_1 is paid at the contract maturity date. For example, suppose the forward price is $108 per share. Then if the stock price at the delivery date turns out to be $109, the party who is long receives $1 from the party who is short. However, if the spot price turns out to be $107, the party who is long must pay $1 to the party who is short.

Now let us consider the relation between the forward and spot prices of S&P stock. Assume that the spot price of S&P is $100, that the risk-free interest rate is 8% per year, and that the delivery date is one year from now. What must the forward price be?

Note that we can replicate the share of S&P by buying a pure discount bond with face value F and simultaneously taking a long position in a forward contract for a share of S&P. At the maturity date of the forward contract, we cash in the bond at its face value of F and use the money to buy a share of S&P at the forward price.

Thus, the forward contract plus the pure discount bond constitute a synthetic share of S&P with exactly the same probability distribution of payoffs as S&P stock itself. By the Law of One Price, the two equivalent securities must have the same price.

Table 14.4 shows the transactions and payoffs involved in replicating the stock with a pure discount bond and a forward contract. Note that the S&P stock and its replicating portfolio have the same payoff a year from now, namely S_1.

TABLE 14.4 Replication of Non-Dividend-Paying Stock Using a Pure Discount Bond and a Stock Forward Contract

Position	Immediate Cash Flow	Cash Flow 1 Year From Now
Buy a share of stock	−$100	S_1
Replicating Portfolio (Synthetic Stock):		
Go long a forward contract on stock	0	$S_1 - F$
Buy a pure discount bond with face value of F	$-F/1.08$	F
Total replicating portfolio	$-F/1.08$	S_1

Setting the cost of the synthetic stock equal to the cost of the actual stock, we get:

$$S = \frac{F}{1 + r} \tag{14.5}$$

which says that the spot price equals the present value of the forward price discounted at the risk-free interest rate.

Rearranging equation 14.5, we find the formula for the forward price, F, in terms of the current spot price, S, and the risk-free interest rate, r:

$$F = S(1 + r) = \$100 \times 1.08 = \$108$$

More generally, when the maturity of the forward contract and the pure discount bond are equal to T years, we get the following forward-spot price-parity relation:

$$F = S(1 + r)^T \tag{14.6}$$

which says that the forward price equals the future value of the spot price compounded at the risk-free interest rate for T years.

This relation is maintained by the force of arbitrage. Let us illustrate by imagining that it is violated. First, suppose that given the risk-free rate and the spot price, the forward price is too high. For example, suppose that $r = .08$, $S = \$100$, and the forward price, F, is \$109 instead of \$108. Thus, the forward price is \$1 higher than the parity relation implies.

Provided that there is a competitive market for S&P stock and S&P forward contracts, then there is an arbitrage opportunity. To exploit it, an arbitrageur would buy the stock in the spot market and simultaneously sell it forward. Thus, the arbitrageur would buy S&P stock, finance that purchase by borrowing 100% on margin, and simultaneously hedge it by going short an S&P forward contract. The result of this would be a zero net cash flow at the beginning of the year and a positive net cash inflow of \$1 per share at the end of the year. If the quantity of shares involved were 1 million, then the arbitrage profit would be \$1 million.

Table 14.5 summarizes the transactions involved in carrying out this arbitrage. Arbitrageurs would attempt to carry out these transactions in very large amounts. Their buying and selling activities in the spot and forward markets will cause the forward price to fall and/or the spot price to rise until the equality in equation 14.6 is restored.

TABLE 14.5   Arbitrage in Stock Futures

Arbitrage Position	Immediate Cash Flow	Cash Flow 1 Year From Now
Sell a forward contract	0	$\$109 - S_1$
Borrow \$100	\$100	-108
Buy a share of stock	$-\$100$	S_1
Net cash flows	-0	\$1

As we saw with gold, the forward-spot price-parity relation does not imply any causal implications. It does not say that the forward price is determined by the spot price and the riskless interest rate. Instead, all three of the variables—*F, S,* and *r*—are jointly determined in the market. If we know any two of them, then by the Law of One Price, we know what the third must be.

14.8 THE "IMPLIED" RISKLESS RATE

Just as one can replicate the stock using the riskless asset and a forward contract, one can replicate a pure discount bond by buying a share of stock and simultaneously taking a short position in a forward contract. We assume that F is $108, S is $100, and T is one year. We can replicate a one-year pure discount bond with a face value of $108 by buying a share of stock for $100 and simultaneously taking a short forward position in a share for delivery in one year at the forward price of $108.

The initial outlay is $100, and the payoff a year from now will be $108 no matter what the spot price of the stock (S_1) turns out to be. Therefore, if you can buy a synthetic one-year pure discount bond with a face value of $108 for a total cost of $100, the implied risk-free interest rate is 8%. Table 14.6 summarizes the transactions involved.

More generally, the implied risk-free interest rate obtainable by buying the stock and going short the forward contract is

$$\hat{r} = \frac{F - S}{S} \tag{14.7}$$

Quick Check 14-6

Suppose the spot price of S&P is $100 and the one-year forward price is $107. What is the implied riskless rate? Show that if the actual risk-free rate were 8% per year, there would be an arbitrage opportunity.

TABLE 14.6   Replication of a Pure Discount Bond Using a Stock and a Forward Contract

Position	Immediate Cash Flow	Cash Flow 1 Year From Now
Buy a T-bill with face value $108	$-\$108/(1 + r)$	$108
Replicating Portfolio (Synthetic T-Bill):		
Buy a share of stock	−$100	S_1
Go short a forward contract	0	$108 - S_1$
Total replicating portfolio	−$100	$108

14.9 THE FORWARD PRICE IS NOT A FORECAST OF THE FUTURE SPOT PRICE

In the case of a stock that pays no dividend and offers a positive risk premium to investors, it is straightforward to show that the forward price is *not* a forecast of the expected future spot price. To see this, assume that the risk premium on S&P stock is 7% per year and the riskless interest rate is 8%. The expected rate of return on S&P is, therefore, 15% per year.

If the current spot price is $100 per share, then the expected spot price one year from now is $115. This is because to earn an expected rate of return of 15% on S&P in the absence of any dividends, the ending spot price must be 15% higher than the beginning spot price:

$$\text{Expected Rate of Return on S\&P} = \frac{\text{Ending Price} - \text{Beginning Price}}{\text{Beginning Price}}$$

$$\overline{r}_{SP} - \frac{\overline{S}_1 - S}{S} = .15$$

$$\overline{S}_1 = 1.15S = 1.15 \times 100 = 115$$

But the forward-spot price-parity relation tells us that the forward price of the S&P for delivery in one year must be $108. An investor who buys the synthetic stock (a pure discount bond plus a long forward position) is expected to earn the same 7% per year risk premium as one who buys the stock itself.

Quick Check 14-7

Suppose the risk premium on S&P stock is 6% per year instead of 7%. Assuming the riskless rate is still 8% per year, how does this affect the expected future spot price? How does it affect the forward price?

14.10 FORWARD-SPOT PRICE-PARITY RELATION WITH CASH PAYOUTS

In the previous section, we derived the forward-spot price-parity relation on the assumption that the stock would not pay any cash dividends during the term of the forward contract. Let us consider how the existence of cash dividends causes us to modify the forward-spot price-parity relation for stocks in equation 14.6.

Suppose that everyone expects the stock to pay a cash dividend of D per share at the end of the year. It is not possible to replicate the payoff from the stock with certainty because the dividend is not known with certainty. But it is possible to determine a forward-spot relation in terms of the expected dividend. The replicating portfolio will now involve buying a pure discount bond with a face value of $F + D$ and going long a forward contract, as shown in Table 14.7.

TABLE 14.7   Replication of a Dividend-Paying Stock Using a Pure Discount Bond and a Stock Futures Contract

Position	Immediate Cash Flow	Cash Flow 1 Year From Now
Buy stock	$-S$	$D + S_1$
Replicating Portfolio (Synthetic Stock):		
Go long a futures contract on a share of stock	0	$S_1 - F$
Buy a pure discount bond with face value of $D + F$	$\dfrac{-D + F}{(1 + r)}$	$D + F$
Total replicating portfolio	$\dfrac{-D + F}{(1 + r)}$	$D + S_1$

Setting the price of the stock equal to the cost of the replicating portfolio, we get:

$$S = \frac{D + F}{(1 + r)}$$
$$F = S(1 + r) - D$$
$$F = S + rS - D \tag{14.8}$$

The forward price will be greater than the spot price if and only if D is less than rS, or equivalently, if the stock's dividend yield (D/S) is less than the riskless interest rate. Because D is not known with complete certainty, the full force of arbitrage cannot be relied on to maintain the forward-spot price-parity relation. In such cases, we say that there is a *quasi-arbitrage* situation.

> **Quick Check 14-8**
> Compare the forward-spot price-parity relation for gold to the one for stocks. What is the cost of carry for stocks?

14.11 "IMPLIED" DIVIDENDS

We saw in section 14.8 that for a stock that pays no dividends, one can infer an implied risk-free rate from the spot and forward prices. In the case of a stock that does pay dividends, we can infer an **implied dividend.** By rearranging equation 14.8 we find that:

$$\overline{D} = S(1 + r) - F$$

Thus, if we know that $S = \$100$, $r = .08$, and $F = \$103$, then the implied value for the expected dividend is $5:

$$\overline{D} = 100 \times 1.08 - 103 = 5$$

14.12   THE FOREIGN-EXCHANGE PARITY RELATION

Now let us consider the relation between the forward price of a foreign currency and its spot price. Let us take U.S. dollars and yen as the two currencies and express the forward and spot prices in dollars per yen.

The forward-spot price-parity relation involves two riskless interest rates:

$$\frac{F}{(1 + r_\$)} = \frac{S}{(1 + r_¥)} \tag{14.9}$$

where F is the forward price of the yen, S is the current spot price, $r_¥$ is the yen interest rate, and $r_\$$ is the dollar interest rate. The maturity of the forward contract and the interest rates is one year.

For example, suppose we know three of the four variables: $S = \$0.01$ per yen, $r_\$ = .08$ per year, and $r_¥ = .05$ per year. By the Law of One Price, the fourth variable, F, must be $\$0.0102857$ per yen:

$$F = 0.01 \times \frac{1.08}{1.05} = 0.0102857$$

This is because one can replicate a yen-bond using dollar-bonds and a yen-forward contract. This is done by entering a forward contract for ¥1 at a forward price of F and simultaneously buying a dollar bond with a face value of F. The dollar cost today of this synthetic yen-bond is $F/(1 + r_\$)$. Both the yen-bond and the replicating portfolio have a sure payoff of ¥1 a year from now, which will be worth exactly S_1 dollars. Table 14.8 summarizes this information.

Because they are equivalent securities, by the Law of One Price the current dollar price of the yen-bond must be equal to the current dollar cost of the synthetic yen-bond. We, therefore, have the forward-spot price-parity relation for dollars and yen:

$$\frac{F}{(1 + r_\$)} = \frac{S}{(1 + r_¥)} \tag{14.10}$$

The expression on the right side of equation 14.10 is the current dollar price of a yen-bond (that pays ¥1 with certainty at maturity), and the expression on the left side is the current dollar cost of replicating the yen-bond's payoff with dollar-bonds and yen-forward contracts.

TABLE 14.8   Replication of a Yen-Bond Using Dollar-Bonds and a Yen-Forward Contract

Position	Immediate Cash Flow in $	Cash Flow 1 Year From Now in $
Buy a yen-bond	$-S/(l + r_¥)$	S_1
Replicating Portfolio (Synthetic Yen-Bond):		
A long position in a forward contract on ¥1	0	$S_1 - F$
Buy a dollar bond with face value of F	$-F/(l + r_\$)$	F
Total replicating portfolio	$-F/(l + r_\$)$	S_1

Like the forward-spot price-parity relations for stocks and for bonds, the foreign-exchange parity relation does not carry any causal implications. It simply implies that given any three of the four variables, the fourth is determined by the Law of One Price.

Quick Check 14-9

Suppose that $r_\$ = .06$, $r_¥ = .03$, and $S = \$0.01$. What must the forward price of a yen be? Show how, if it is not, there would be an arbitrage opportunity.

14.13 THE ROLE OF EXPECTATIONS IN DETERMINING EXCHANGE RATES

A popular theory of the determination of exchange rates is the **expectations hypothesis,** which holds that the forward price of a currency is equal to its expected future spot price.

Applied in the example of the preceding section, if S_1 denotes the spot dollar price of the yen one year from now and $E(S_1)$ is the expected future spot price, then the expectations hypothesis can be expressed as

$$F = E(S_1) \tag{14.11}$$

To illustrate, Table 14.9 shows *The Wall Street Journal* listing of spot and forward prices of the Japanese yen on January 9, 1991. If the expectations hypothesis is correct, then from the fact that the forward prices of the yen decline as the contract maturity lengthens, we can infer that the dollar price of the yen is expected to rise in the future. For example, from the ratio of the 180-day forward price to the current spot price of the yen—0.007289/0.007302 = 0.99822—we can infer that the dollar price of the yen is expected to fall over the next 180 days by 0.178%.

If equation 14.11 is valid, then the foreign-exchange parity relation equation (14.10) tells us that the same information is reflected in the other three variables:

$$S \, \frac{(1 + r_\$)}{(1 + r_¥)} = E(S_1) \tag{14.12}$$

If the expected future price of the yen rises, that causes both the forward price (on the left side of equation 14.11), and the expression on the left side of equation 14.12 to rise. In other words, if the expectations hypothesis is true, there are two equally valid ways of using market information to derive an estimate of the future spot price: (1) Look at the forward price, or (2) look at the expression on the left side of equation 14.12.

Empirical studies of the currency markets do not seem to provide much support for the expectations hypothesis. Furthermore, the theory has the unfortunate feature that if it applies in one currency, it cannot in another, and this follows as a matter of mathematics.[7] That is, if equation 14.11 applies for the dollar price of the yen, then it

---

[7]To see this, note that $1/S$ is the spot yen price of the dollar one year from now, and $1/F$ is the forward price of the dollar in terms of yen. If equation 14.11 applies to yen-dollar as well, then $1/F = E(1/S_1)$. For this and $F = E(S_1)$ to both apply, it must be that $E(1/S_1) = 1/E(S_1)$. But, by a mathematical theorem called Jensen's inequality, this is false because $E(1/S_1) > 1/E(S_1)$.

TABLE 14.9	Selected Exchange Rates
Country	*Price in $U.S.*
Japan (yen)	0.007302
30-day forward	0.007299
90-day forward	0.007291
180-day forward	0.007289

Notes: These are New York foreign-exchange selling rates that apply to trading among banks in amounts of $1 million and more, as quoted at 3 P.M. Eastern time by Bankers Trust Co.

cannot apply for the yen price of the dollar. Hence, if it held empirically for dollar-yen, then it *must* fail empirically for yen-dollar. Despite its lack of theoretical robustness across currencies and the lack of empirical support, the expectations hypothesis continues to be cited as a model for determining exchange rate expectations.

Summary

Futures contracts make it possible to separate the decision of whether to physically store a commodity from the decision to have financial exposure to its price changes.

Speculators in futures markets improve the informational content of futures prices and they make futures markets more liquid than they would otherwise be.

The futures price of wheat cannot exceed the spot price by more than the cost of carry:

$$F - S \leq C$$

The forward-spot price-parity relation for gold is that the forward price equals the spot price times the cost of carry:

$$F = (1 + r + s)S$$

where F is the forward price, S is the spot price, r is the riskless interest rate, and s are storage costs. This relation is maintained by the force of arbitrage.

One can infer the implied cost of carry and the implied storage costs from the observed spot and forward prices and the riskless interest rate.

The forward-spot price-parity relation for stocks is that the forward price equals the spot price times 1 plus the riskless rate less the expected cash dividend:

$$F = S(1 + r) - D$$

This relation can, therefore, be used to infer the implied dividend from the observed spot and forward prices and the riskless interest rate.

The forward-spot price-parity relation for the dollar/yen exchange rate involves two riskless interest rates:

$$\frac{F}{(1 + r_\$)} = \frac{S}{(1 + r_¥)}$$

where F is the forward price of the yen, S is the current spot price, $r_¥$ is the yen interest rate, and $r_\$$ is the dollar interest rate.

Key Terms

- financial futures   361
- forward contract   361
- margin call   362
- spread   364
- hedger   364

- speculators   364
- forward-spot price-parity relation   366
- implied dividend   374
- expectations hypothesis   376

Answers to Quick Check Questions

Quick Check 14-1   *What would happen in your futures trading account if you take a long position in wheat futures and instead of going down by 7¼ cents per bushel, the futures price went up by that amount?*

ANSWER: You gain 7¼ cents × 5,000 bushels or $362.50 that day, and the broker adds that amount to your account even though you may not have made any trades. The money is transferred from one of the parties who was on the short side of the contract.

Quick Check 14-2   *Suppose you are a distributor of corn and you observe that the spot price is $3 per bushel and the futures price for delivery a month from now is $3.10. If your cost of carrying corn is $0.15 per bushel per month, what should you do?*

ANSWER: You should sell any corn you are storing for delivery a month from now and enter into a long futures contract to take delivery a month from now.

Quick Check 14-3   *When does the forward price provide no additional information about expected future spot prices than can be extracted from the current spot price?*

ANSWER: When there is storage of the commodity, asset, or security and equation 14.1 holds as an equality.

Quick Check 14-4   *Suppose that $r = .06$, $S = \$400$, and $s = .02$. What must the forward price of gold be? Show how, if it is not, there would be an arbitrage opportunity.*

ANSWER: The forward price for delivery of gold in one year should be $424 per ounce:

$$F = (1 + r + s)S = 1.06 \times 400 = 424$$

If the forward price exceeds $424 per ounce, it would pay an arbitrageur to buy gold at the spot price and simultaneously sell it for future delivery at the forward price. If, on the other hand, the forward price was less than $424 per ounce, an arbitrageur would sell gold short in the spot market (i.e., borrow it and sell it immediately), invest the proceeds of the short sale in the riskless asset, and go long the forward contract.

Quick Check 14-5   *Suppose the spot price of gold is $300 per ounce and the one-year forward price is $324. What is the implied cost of carrying gold? If the riskless interest rate is 7% per year, what is the implied storage cost for gold?*

ANSWER:

Implied Cost of Carry $= F - S = \$324 - \$300 = \$24$ per ounce

Implied Storage Cost $= (F - S)/S - r = .08 - .07 = .01$ or 1% per year

Quick Check 14-6 *Suppose the spot price of S&P is $100 and the one-year forward price is $107. What is the implied risk-free rate? Show that if the actual riskless rate were 8% per year, there would be an arbitrage opportunity.*

ANSWER: The implied riskless interest rate obtainable by buying the stock and going short the forward contract is

$$\hat{r} = \frac{F - S}{S} = \frac{107 - 100}{100} = .07$$

If the actual riskless rate is 8%, arbitrage profits can be made by selling short the stock at $100, investing the proceeds at the riskless rate of 8%, and taking a long position in the forward contract at a forward price of $107. The riskless arbitrage profit is $1 per share to be received a year from now.

Quick Check 14-7 *Suppose the risk premium on S&P stock is 6% per year instead of 7%. Assuming the riskless rate is still 8% per year, how does this affect the expected future spot price? How does it affect the forward price?*

ANSWER: The expected rate of return on S&P is 14% per year. If the current spot price is $100 per share, then the expected spot price one year from now must be $114. This is because in order to earn an expected rate of return of 14% on S&P in the absence of any dividends, the ending spot price must be 14% higher than the beginning spot price. But the forward-spot price-parity relation tells us that the forward price of the S&P for delivery in one year must still be $108.

Quick Check 14-8 *Compare the forward-spot price-parity relation for gold to the one for stocks. What is the cost of carry for stocks?*

ANSWER: The cost of carry for stocks is the negative of the dividend because the holder of the stock receives the dividend paid during the carrying period.

Quick Check 14-9 *Suppose that $r_\$ = .06$, $r_\yen = .03$, and S = $0.01. What must the forward price of a yen be? Show how, if it is not, there would be an arbitrage opportunity.*

ANSWER: The forward price must be 0.0102913 yen per dollar:

$$F = .01 \times \frac{1.06}{1.03} = 0.0102913$$

If the forward price is too high, then arbitrage profits can be made by borrowing in dollars at 6%, lending in yen at 3%, and hedging the exchange risk at the delivery date by selling the yen for future delivery at the current forward price. If the forward price is too low, then arbitrage profits can be made by borrowing in yen at 3%, lending in dollars at 6%, and hedging the exchange risk at the delivery date by buying yen for future delivery at the current forward price. In either case the arbitrage profit will be the absolute value of the difference between the expressions on the two sides of equation 14.10.

$$\frac{F}{(1 + r_\$)} = \frac{S}{(1 + r_\yen)} \tag{14.10}$$

The expression on the right of equation 14.10 is the current dollar price of a yen-bond (that pays ¥1 with certainty at maturity), and the expression on the left is the current dollar cost of replacing the yen-bond's payoff with dollar-bonds and yen-forward contracts.

Questions and Problems

TEMPLATE

14.1–14.3, 14.6–14.10

1. **Forward Contracts and Forward-Spot Parity**
   Suppose that you are planning a trip to England. The trip is a year from now, and you have reserved a hotel room in London at a price of £50 per day. You do not have to pay for the room in advance. The exchange rate is currently $1.50 to the pound sterling.
   a. Explain several possible ways that you could completely hedge the exchange rate risk in this situation.
   b. Suppose that $r_£ = .12$ and $r_\$ = .08$. Because $S = \$1.50$, what must the forward price of the pound be?
   c. Show that if F is $0.10 higher than in your answer to part b, there would be an arbitrage opportunity.

2. **Forward-Spot Price-Parity Relation with Known Cash Payouts**
   Suppose that the Treasury yield curve is flat at an interest rate of 7% per year (compounded semiannually).
   a. What is the spot price of a 30-year Treasury bond with an 8% coupon rate assuming coupons are paid semiannually?
   b. What is the forward price of the bond for delivery six months from now?
   c. Show that if the forward price is $1 lower than in your answer to part b, there would be an arbitrage opportunity.

3. **Forward-Spot Price-Parity Relation with Uncertain Dividends**
   A stock has a spot price of $100; the riskless interest rate is 7% per year (compounded annually), and the expected dividend on the stock is $3, to be received a year from now.
   a. What should be the one-year futures price?
   b. If the futures price is $1 higher than your answer to part a, what might that imply about the expected dividend?

4. **Storage Costs versus Dividend Yield**
   Compare the forward-spot price-parity relation for gold to the one for stocks. Is it fair to say that stocks have a negative storage cost equal to the dividend yield?

5. Suppose you are a distributor of canola seed and you observe the spot price of canola to be $7.45 per bushel whereas the futures price for delivery one month from today is $7.60. Assuming a $0.10 bushel carrying cost, what would you do to hedge your price uncertainty?

6. **Inferring the Spot Price**
   Infer the spot price of an ounce of gold if you observe the price of one ounce of gold for forward delivery in three months is $435.00, the interest rate on a 91-day Treasury bill is 1%, and the monthly carrying cost per ounce of gold is $0.002.

7. **Inferring the Interest Rate**
   You are a dealer in kryptonite and are contemplating a trade in a forward contract. You observe that the current spot price per ounce of kryptonite is $180.00, the forward price for delivery of one ounce of kryptonite in one year is $205.20, and annual carrying costs of the metal are 4% of the current spot price.
   a. Can you infer the annual return on a riskless zero-coupon security implied by the Law of One Price?
   b. Can you describe a trading strategy that would generate arbitrage profits for you if the annual return on the riskless security is 5%? What would your arbitrage profit be per ounce of kryptonite?

8. **Inferring Carrying Cost**
   Calculate the implicit cost of carrying an ounce of gold and the implied storage cost per ounce of gold if the current spot price of gold per ounce is $425.00, the forward

price of an ounce of gold for delivery is 273 days is $460.00, the yield over 91 days on a zero-coupon Treasury bill is 2%, and the term structure of interest rates is flat.

9. The forward price for a share of stock to be delivered in 182 days is $410.00, whereas the current yield on a 91-day T-bill is 2%. If the term structure of interest rates is flat, what spot price for the stock is implied by the Law of One Price?

10. You observe that the one-year forward price of a share of stock in Kramer, Inc., a New York tour-bus company and purveyor of fine clothing, is $45.00 whereas the spot price of a share is $41.00. If the riskless yield on a one-year zero-coupon government bond is 5%:
   a. What is the forward price implied by the Law of One Price?
   b. Can you devise a trading strategy to generate arbitrage profits? How much would you earn per share?

11. Infer the yield on a 273-day, zero-coupon, Japanese government security if the spot price of a share of stock in Mifune and Associates is 4,750 yen whereas the forward price for delivery of a share in 273 days is 5,000 yen.

12. On your first day of trading in Vietnamese forward contracts, you observe that the share price of Giap Industries is currently 54,000 dong whereas the one-year forward price is 60,000 dong. If the yield on a one-year riskless security is 15%, are arbitrage profits possible in this market? If not, explain why not. If so, devise an appropriate trading strategy.

13. The share price of Schleifer and Associates, a financial consultancy in Moscow, is currently 10,000 roubles whereas the forward price for delivery of a share in 182 days is 11,000 roubles. If the yield on a riskless zero-coupon security with term to maturity of 182 days is 15%, infer the expected dividend to be paid by Shleifer and Associates over the next six months.

14. The spot rate of exchange of yen for Canadian dollars is currently 113 yen per dollar but the one-year forward rate is 110 yen per dollar. Determine the yield on a one-year, zero-coupon, Canadian government security if the corresponding yield on a Japanese government security is 2.21%.

A P P E N D I X

Pricing of Swap Contracts

As we saw in chapter 11, a swap contract consists of two parties exchanging (or "swapping") a series of cash flows at specified intervals over a specified period of time. The swap payments are based on an agreed principal amount (the notional amount). There is no immediate payment of money and, hence, the swap agreement itself provides no new funds to either party.

The pricing of swap contracts is an extension of the principles for pricing forward contracts already covered in this chapter. This is because a swap can always be decomposed into a series of forward contracts.

For example, consider a yen-dollar currency swap. Suppose it is a contract extending over two years, with a notional principal of ¥100 million. At the end of each of the next two years, one of the two counterparties will have to pay the other the difference between the prespecified rate of exchange between dollars and yen and the actual spot rate of exchange at that time multiplied by ¥100 million.

The one- and two-year forward rates of exchange between dollars and yen are observable in the forward market. For example, suppose that the one-year forward price of the yen is $0.01 and the two-year forward price is $0.0104. If instead of a swap the two counterparties entered a series of two forward contracts for delivery of ¥100 million each, we can compute the dollar amounts that would have to be paid in each year in exchange for ¥100 million. In the first year it is $1 million, and in the second it is $1.04 million.

But a currency swap calls for a single swap exchange rate to apply in both years. How can the swap rate be determined?

Assume that the riskless dollar interest rate is 8% per year, and is the same for one- and two-year maturities. Let F be the swap rate in dollars per yen. The swap contract can be seen as the obligation for one of the counterparties to pay $100,000,000F$ dollars this year and next year in return for a prespecified quantity of yen in each of those years.

As we just saw, if the quantities to be paid were set in accordance with the separate one- and two-year forward prices of $0.01 per yen and $0.0104, then the amounts would be $1 million in the first year and $1.04 million in the second year. By the Law of One Price, the present value of those payments discounted at the risk-free rate has to be the same as the present value of the payments under the actual swap agreement calling for a single swap rate of F. Thus, F is found by solving

$$\$1 \text{ million}/1.08 + \$1.04 \text{ million}/1.08^2 = 100,000,000F(1/1.08 + 1/1.08)^2$$

$$F = \frac{\$1 \text{ million}/1.08 + \$1.04 \text{ million}/1.08^2}{100,000,000(1/1.08 + 1/1.08^2)}$$

$$F = \$0.010192307 \text{ per yen}$$

CHAPTER

15

Options and Contingent Claims

OBJECTIVES

- How to use options to modify one's exposure to investment risk.
- To understand the pricing relationships that exist among calls, puts, stocks, and bonds.
- To explain the binomial and Black-Scholes option-pricing models and apply them to the valuation of corporate bonds and other contingent claims.
- To explore the range of financial decisions that can be fruitfully analyzed in terms of options.

CONTENTS

Any contract that gives one of the contracting parties the right to buy or sell something at a prespecified exercise price is an option. There are as many different kinds of option contracts as there are items to buy or sell. Stock options, interest-rate options, foreign-exchange options, and commodity options are traded both on and off organized exchanges all around the world. This chapter explains how these options are used to manage risks and how they are priced.

Options are an example of a broader class of assets called contingent claims. A **contingent claim** is any asset whose future payoff is contingent on (i.e., depends on) the outcome of some uncertain event. For example, corporate bonds are contingent claims because if the issuing corporation goes bankrupt, the bondholders will receive less than the full interest and principal promised by the issuer. This chapter shows how the same methods developed to value options can be applied to the valuation of corporate bonds and other contingent claims.

The most familiar model for the pricing of options is the Black-Scholes model, discovered in the early 1970s. The Chicago Board Options Exchange (CBOE), the first public options exchange, began its operations in April 1973, and by 1975, traders on the CBOE were using the Black-Scholes formula to both price and hedge their option positions. Such a rapid transition from theory to practice on such a large scale was unprecedented in the history of finance.

Since then, option-pricing technology has been applied to the pricing of other contingent claims, and it has played a fundamental role in supporting the creation of new financial products and markets around the globe. A knowledge of option-pricing principles has become essential for the serious student of finance.

We begin this chapter by explaining how options work and how they can be used to create a variety of payoff patterns from an underlying risky asset. We then apply the Law of One Price to derive parity relations among the prices of calls, puts, stocks, and bonds, and we explain the binomial and Black-Scholes option-pricing models. Then we show how corporate debt and equity securities may be described in terms analogous to options and priced accordingly. We conclude the chapter by discussing the range of applications to which contingent-claims pricing technology has been applied.

15.1 HOW OPTIONS WORK

An option is a contract that gives its owner the *right* to buy or to sell some asset at a prespecified price. It differs from a forward contract, which *obliges* the long holder to buy and the short holder to sell.

There is a special terminology associated with options:

- An option to *buy* the specified item at a fixed price is a **call;** an option to *sell* is a **put.**

- The fixed price specified in an option contract is called the option's **strike price** or **exercise price.**

- The date after which an option can no longer be exercised is called its **expiration date** or *maturity date.*

- An **American-type option** can be exercised at any time up to and including the expiration date. A **European-type option** can only be exercised on the expiration date.

Exchange-traded options have standard terms defined by the options exchange. The exchange matches buyers and sellers of options and guarantees payment in the event of default by either party. Options not traded on an exchange are called **over-the-counter options.**

TABLE 15.1 Listing of IBM Option Prices

IBM (IBM)					Underlying stock price: 120$\frac{1}{16}$			
		Call			Put			
Strike	Expiration	Volume	Last	Open Interest	Volume	Last	Open Interest	
115	Jun	1372	7	4483	756	1$\frac{3}{16}$	9692	
115	Oct	. . .	. . .	2584	10	5	967	
115	Jan	. . .	. . .	15	53	6$\frac{3}{4}$	40	
120	Jun	2377	3$\frac{1}{2}$	8049	873	2$\frac{7}{8}$	9849	
120	Oct	121	9$\frac{5}{8}$	2561	45	7$\frac{1}{8}$	1993	
120	Jan	91	12$\frac{1}{2}$	8842	. . .	. . .	5259	
125	Jun	1564	1$\frac{1}{2}$	9764	17	5$\frac{3}{4}$	5900	
125	Oct	91	7$\frac{1}{2}$	2360	. . .	. . .	731	
125	Jan	87	10$\frac{1}{2}$	124	. . .	. . .	70	

Prices at close Thursday, May 28, 1998

Source: The Wall Street Journal Interactive Edition, May 29, 1998. Reprinted by permission of *The Wall Street Journal,* © 1998 Dow Jones & Company, Inc. All Rights Reserved Worldwide.

In addition to its type (call or put) and the name of the underlying security, an option is identified by its strike price and its expiration date. For exchange-traded options, these are determined by the rules of the exchange. Thus, on the Chicago Board Options Exchange (CBOE), a single call-option contract gives its owner the right to buy 100 shares of the underlying stock and is of the American type. Original maturities of CBOE options vary from three months to three years, and they all expire on the third Friday of the month in which they mature.[1] Table 15.1 shows a list of the prices of IBM stock options traded on the CBOE.

The right-hand column of the second row of Table 15.1 shows that the closing price of IBM stock on Thursday, May 28, 1998 was 120$\frac{1}{16}$. Look at the fifth row, which is the first row containing numbers. It starts with the strike price, 115, and expiration month, June. On May 28, the June IBM call options had about three weeks left to go before expiration. The entry in the column labeled "Volume" gives the number of contracts traded on the CBOE that day. This was 1,372 contracts in the case of the June IBM 115 call. A glance down at the next two rows in that same column shows that there were no October or January IBM 115 calls traded. The column to the right of "Volume" shows that the last price at which the June IBM call traded was 7, which means $700 per contract.[2] The next column, which is labeled "Open Interest," is the total number of CBOE contracts of that type in existence on May 28. The next three columns give the daily trading volume, closing price, and open interest for the June IBM 115 put.

The hypothetical value of an option *if it were expiring immediately* is called its **intrinsic value** (or **tangible value**). If the June IBM 115 call were expiring immediately,

---

[1]CBOE options with maturities of one year and longer are called LEAPS®, an acronym that stands for long-term equity anticipation securities.

[2]An option contract is for 100 shares.

how much would it be worth? Because the price of IBM stock is 120$\frac{1}{16}$ per share and the option's exercise price is 115, the value of the call if exercised immediately is 5$\frac{1}{16}$ per share of stock. The option's price of 7, therefore, exceeds its intrinsic value by 1$\frac{15}{16}$. This difference is called the option's **time value.**

An American option's time value is greater, the longer it has to go before expiration. For example, in Table 15.1 look at the prices of IBM 120 calls expiring in June, October, and January. All three have the same intrinsic value of $\frac{1}{16}$, but their prices are 3$\frac{1}{2}$, 9$\frac{5}{8}$, and 12$\frac{1}{2}$, respectively. Similar patterns hold for IBM 115 puts.

When an option's intrinsic value is zero, it is said to be **out of the money.** For example, the IBM 115 put options are out of the money. The IBM 115 calls, on the other hand, are said to be **in the money.** Whenever a call is in the money, then the corresponding put is out of the money, and vice versa. An option whose exercise price is equal to the price of the underlying stock is said to be **at the money.**

There is an inverse relation between the price of a call and its strike price. For puts this relation is reversed. To see this, look at the options in Table 15.1 that expire in June. As the strike price goes from 115 to 120 to 125, the prices of the calls go from 7 to 3$\frac{1}{2}$ to 1$\frac{1}{2}$, and the prices of the puts go from 1$\frac{3}{16}$ to 2$\frac{7}{8}$ to 5$\frac{3}{4}$.

Quick Check 15-1
Using Table 15.1, compute the intrinsic value and the time value of the June IBM 125 call. Do the same for the put.

15.1.1 Index Options

In addition to options on individual securities such as IBM stock, there are also **index options.** For example, the CBOE offers trading in calls and puts on the S&P 500 stock index under the symbol SPX. SPX options are effectively calls or puts on a hypothetical index fund that invests in a portfolio composed of the stocks that make up the S&P 500 index, each of the 500 companies in proportion to the total value of its shares outstanding.

Table 15.2 shows a listing of the prices and trading activity for these options on Friday, June 5, 1998. SPX options are of the European type and can, therefore, only be exercised at expiration.[3]

The SPX contract specifies that if the call option is exercised, the owner of the option will receive a cash payment of $100 times the difference between the index value and the strike price. For example, assume that when the June 1110 call option listed in Table 15.2 expires on June 19, 1998, the value of the index is 1115. Upon expiration its owner will receive $500, which is:

$$\$100 \times (1115 - 1110) = \$500$$

This process of **cash settlement** differs from what happens in the case of CBOE options on individual stocks. For example, assume IBM's stock price is $120, and an owner of an IBM call with a strike price of 115 exercises her option. She pays $11,500

---

[3]Information about the contract specifications is available at the CBOE's Internet site, http://www.cboe.com/products/cs/cs114.html.

TABLE 15.2 Listing of Index Option Prices						

S&P 500 INDEX-AM			**Chicago Exchange**			
Underlying Index	**High**	**Low**	**Close**	**Net Change**	**From Dec. 31**	**% Change**
S&P500 (SPX)	1113.88	1084.28	1113.86	+19.03	+143.43	+14.8
Strike			**Volume**	**Last**	**Net Change**	**Open Interest**
Jun	1110 call		2,081	17¼	+8½	15,754
Jun	1110 put		1,077	10	−11	17,104
Jul	1110 call		1,278	33½	+9½	3,712
Jul	1110 put		152	23⅜	−12⅛	1,040
Jun	1120 call		80	12	+7	16,585
Jun	1120 put		211	17	−11	9,947
Jul	1120 call		67	27¼	+8¼	5,546
Jul	1120 put		10	27½	−11	4,033

Prices at close Friday, June 5, 1998

Source: The Wall Street Journal Interactive Edition, June 6, 1998. Reprinted by permission of *The Wall Street Journal,* © 1998 Dow Jones & Company, Inc. All Rights Reserved Worldwide.

and receives 100 shares of IBM stock worth $12,000. If the IBM call option were settled in cash as in the case of index options, the seller would pay the owner of the call $500 (i.e., $12,000 − $11,500) instead of delivering the shares of IBM stock and receiving $11,500 in cash.

Quick Check 15-2

Suppose you bought an SPX June 1120 call on June 5, 1998 for the price listed in Table 15.2. If the value of the index at expiration on June 19, 1998 turned out to be 1200, what would be your rate of return?

15.2 INVESTING WITH OPTIONS

Options make it possible for investors to modify their risk exposure to the underlying assets. The kind of modifications possible can be described using **payoff diagrams** that depict the relation between the value of an option (measured on the vertical axis) and the price of the underlying asset (on the horizontal axis). Figure 15.1 shows the payoffs on the expiration date for a call option on a stock whose current value is 100. The strike price is 100.

At expiration the payoff from the call is max $(S_T - 100, 0)$, where S_T is the stock price on the expiration date of the option. In Figure 15.1, the value of the call increases one for one with the stock price to the right of 100. But to the left of 100, the call is worthless.

Now consider the payoffs from the put, which is max $(100 - S_T, 0)$. The put payoff diagram is shown in Figure 15.2. If the stock price at expiration is less than the exercise price, then the value of the put *increases* one for one (to a maximum of

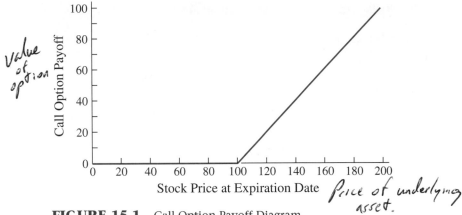

FIGURE 15.1   Call Option Payoff Diagram

Note: The exercise price is 100 for the call.

100) as the price takes on lower values. If, on the other hand, the stock price exceeds the exercise price, then the put expires worthless.

In addition to using options to modify risk exposure as just described, buying or selling options is an alternative way for a person who does not own the underlying asset to take a position. Let's see how this works. Because the price of a call option is only a fraction of the price of the underlying stock, investing the same amount of money in calls as in the stock provides leverage. For example, suppose that you are bullish on stocks and have $100,000 to invest. Assume that the riskless interest rate is 5% per year and that the stock pays no dividends. Compare your portfolio's rate of return for three alternative investment strategies over a one-year holding period:

1. Invest all $100,000 in the stock.
2. Invest all $100,000 in calls.
3. Invest $10,000 in calls and the rest in the risk-free asset.

Assume that the price of a share of stock is 100, and the price of a call is 10. This means that under strategy 1 you buy 1,000 shares of stock, and under strategy 2

FIGURE 15.2   Put Option Payoff Diagram

Note: The exercise price is 100 for the put.

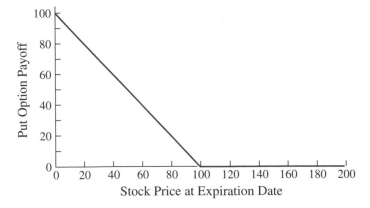

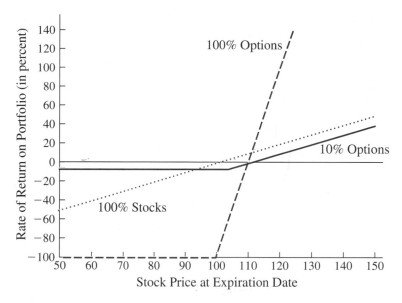

FIGURE 15.3   Payoff Diagrams for Alternative Bullish Stock Strategies

you buy calls on 10,000 shares. Now consider your payoffs, which are depicted in Figure 15.3.

Figure 15.3 plots the stock price along the horizontal axis and your portfolio's rate of return along the vertical axis. For strategy 1—the dotted line in Figure 15.3—the payoff graph is a straight line with a break-even price of 100. At that index value, your rate of return will be zero. If the price turns out to be higher than 100, your rate of return will increase by 1% for every one-point increase. If the price is lower than 100, your rate of return will fall by 1% for every one-point decrease in stock price.

Under strategy 2—the dashed line in Figure 15.3—the break-even price is 110. To the right of the kink point, its slope is 10 times the slope of strategy 1. This is because a call provides the same dollar upside potential as a share of stock, and under strategy 2 you have 10 times as many calls as stocks under strategy 1. If, however, the stock price is less than 100, the solid line shows that you lose your entire investment under strategy 2, and your rate of return is -100%.

Your payoff graph for strategy 3 is the kinked solid line in Figure 15.3. To the right of the strike price of 100 it has the same slope as the 100% stock strategy (the dotted line), but to the left of the stock price it is flat at -5.5%. This is because if the stock price falls, the worst that can happen is that you will lose your $10,000 investment in calls. The $90,000 that you invested in the riskless asset will grow to $94,500 and, therefore, your minimum portfolio rate of return will be -5.5%.[4]

---

[4]Under strategy 3, the formula for the total rate of return on your portfolio is:

$$\text{Portfolio Rate of Return} = \frac{\text{Value at End of Year} - \text{Value at Beginning of Year}}{\text{Value at Beginning of Year}}$$

$$= \frac{\$90,000(1.05) + 1,000\max(S_T - 100, 0) - \$100,000}{\$100,000}$$

$$= -.055 + .01\max(S_T - 100, 0)$$

Strategy 3, thus, provides an example of how options are used to provide minimum-return-guarantee products.[5]

All three of the strategies under consideration are bullish in that you would only choose them if you believe that the stock price is likely to rise. But to determine which of the three is best for you, you must define more precisely your expectations about the stock price and your tolerance for risk.

For example, suppose that you have scenario forecasts for three possible states of the economy as shown in Table 15.3. You believe there is a probability of .2 that there will be a boom and the stock price will rise by 50% during the year, a probability of .6 that the economy will be normal and the market will rise by 10%, and a probability of .2 that there will be a recession and the stock will fall by 30%.

Table 15.3 shows the rate of return for each strategy in each scenario. Look at the row corresponding to a boom. Under strategy 1 (100% stocks), your rate of return would be 50%. Under strategy 2 (100% call options), your options will be worth $500,000 at expiration, and your rate of return will be 400%. Under strategy 3 (10% call options), your options would be worth $50,000 and your bonds $94,500, so your rate of return would be:

$$\frac{\$50,000 + \$94,500 - \$100,000}{\$100,000} = .445 \text{ or } 44.5\%$$

Let us compare the probability distributions for the three strategies across all three scenarios. Notice that none of the strategies outperforms the others in all three scenarios. Strategy 2 (100% call options) performs best in a boom and worst in the other scenarios. Scenario 3 performs best in a recession and worst in the other scenarios. Scenario 1 performs best in a normal scenario, but comes in second in the other two scenarios.

Thus, none of the strategies dominates the others. Depending on an investor's tolerance for risk, he or she might choose any one of them. Indeed, a very risk-averse investor might rationally prefer the strategy of investing all $100,000 in the risk-free asset to earn 5% for sure.

TABLE 15.3   Probability Distribution of Returns for Bullish Strategies

| | | | Rate of Return on Portfolio | | |
| | | | *Strategy 1* | *Strategy 2* | *Strategy 3* |
State of Economy	*Probability*	*Riskless*	*100% Stocks*	*100% Calls*	*10% Calls*
Boom	.2	5%	50%	400%	44.5%
Normal	.6	5%	10%	0	4.5%
Recession	.2	5%	−30%	−100%	−5.5%

[5]In an early real-world application, Merton and Scholes developed the first options-strategy mutual fund in the United States, Money Market/Options Investments, Inc., in February 1976. The strategy invested 90% of its assets in money market instruments and 10% in a diversified portfolio of stock call options.

> **Quick Check 15-3**
> Strategy 4 is to invest $96,000 in the riskless asset and $4,000 in options. What is the minimum guaranteed rate of return? What is the slope of the payoff graph to the right of the exercise price?

15.3 THE PUT-CALL PARITY RELATION

In the previous section, we saw that a strategy of investing some of your money in the riskless asset and some in a call option can provide a portfolio with a guaranteed minimum value and an upside slope equal to that of investing in the underlying stock. There is another way of creating that same pattern of payoffs: Buy a share of stock and a put option.

Table 15.4a and Figure 15.4a describe the payoffs from the two separate components of this "protective put" strategy and show how they add up to an insured position in the stock. The minimum value of this portfolio is the exercise price of 100. Table 15.4b and Figure 15.4b describe the payoffs from the two separate components of the bond plus call strategy and show how they add up to an insured position in the stock. Thus, a portfolio consisting of a stock plus a European put option (with exercise price E) is equivalent to a pure discount default-free bond (with face

TABLE 15.4a   Payoff Structure for Protective Put Strategy

	Value of Position at Maturity Date	
Position	If $S_T < \$100$	If $S_T > \$100$
Stock	S_T	S_T
Put	$\$100 - S_T$	0
Stock plus put	$\$100$	S_T

FIGURE 15.4a   Payoff Diagram for Protective Put Strategy

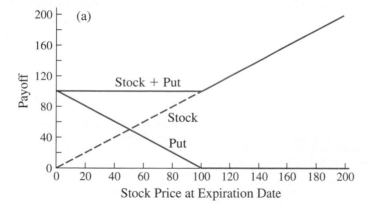

	TABLE 15.4b	Payoff Structure for a Pure Discount Bond Plus a Call	

	Value of Position at Maturity Date	
Position	*If $S_T < \$100$*	*If $S_T > \$100$*
Pure discount bond with face value of $100	$100	$100
Call	0	$S_T - \$100$
Pure discount bond plus call	$100	S_T

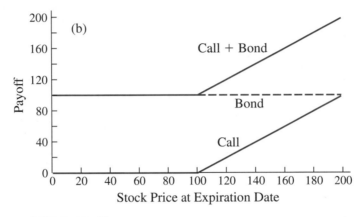

FIGURE 15.4b   Payoff Diagram for Pure Discount Bond Plus Call

value *E*) plus a European call option (with exercise price *E*).[6] By the Law of One Price, they must have the same price.

Equation 15.1 expresses this price relation:

$$S + P = \frac{E}{(1 + r)^T} + C \tag{15.1}$$

where *S* is the stock price, *E* represents the exercise price, *P* the price of the put, *r* the riskless interest rate, *T* the maturity of the option, and *C* the price of the call.[7]

Equation 15.1 is known as the **put-call parity relation.** In addition to its use in determining the price of any one of the four securities from the values of the other

---

[6]This equivalence must be modified for American-type options, which can be exercised prior to the expiration date.

[7]To this point in the discussion, we have assumed that no dividends are paid on the stock during the life of the option. In general, the possibility of dividends complicates the put-call parity relation. However, one case in which adjusting the parity relation is straightforward is if the dividend yield paid per year, *d,* is known for certain and constant. Then the relation is:

$$S(1 - d)^T + P = \frac{E}{(1 + r)^T} + C$$

three, equation 15.1 can be used as a "recipe" for *synthesizing* any one of the four from the other three. For example, by rearranging equation 15.1, we find that a call is equivalent to holding a share of the stock, borrowing the present value of the exercise price (i.e., selling short a pure discount default-free bond with face value E), and buying a put:

$$C = S - \frac{E}{(1 + r)^T} + P \qquad (15.2)$$

Equation 15.2 gives us some insight into the nature of a call option. In effect, it says that the characteristics of a call option can be broken into three components:

1. Buying the stock.
2. Borrowing part of the money to do so (leverage).
3. Buying insurance against downside risk (the put).

Equation 15.2 can also be regarded as a formula for *converting* a put into a call and vice versa. For example, suppose that the values on the right side of equation 15.2 are:

$$S = \$100, E = \$100, T = 1 \text{ year}, r = .08, \text{ and } P = \$10$$

Then the price of the call, C, would have to be $17.41, computed as:

$$C = 100 - 100/1.08 + 10 = 17.41$$

To see why, suppose that C is $18 and that there are no barriers to arbitrage. Then the call's price is too high. It will pay an arbitrageur to sell calls and buy the equivalent of the calls by using a replicating strategy. In other words, sell dear and buy cheap. The outlay on the stock is $100 less $92.59 borrowed. The net outlay on the levered position in the stock is, thus, $7.41. The insurance against downside risk (the put) costs $10, so the total cost of the synthetic call is $17.41. The arbitrageur would sell calls at a price of $18 and pocket the $0.59 difference between the price of the call and the $17.41 cost of synthesizing it. Table 15.5 shows the transactions involved.

TABLE 15.5   Put-Call Arbitrage

Position	Immediate Cash Flow	Cash Flow at Maturity Date	
		If $S_T < \$100$	*If $S_T > \$100$*
Sell a call	$18	0	$-(S_T - \$100)$
Buy Replicating Portfolio (Synthetic Call)			
Buy a stock	-$100	S_T	S_T
Borrow the present value of $100	$92.59	-$100	-$100
Buy a put	-$10	$100 - S_T$	0
Net cash flows	$0.59	0	0

We can gain some additional insight into the nature of the relation among puts, calls, stocks, and bonds by rearranging the terms in equation 15.2 as follows:

$$C - P = S - \frac{E}{(1 + r)^T}$$

In this form, the put-call parity relation implies that:

- If the stock price *equals* the present value of the option's exercise price, then the price of the call equals the price of the put.

- If the stock price *exceeds* the present value of the option's exercise price, then the price of the call exceeds the price of the put.

- If the stock price *is less than* the present value of the option's exercise price, then the price of the put exceeds the price of the call.

Quick Check 15-4
Show how one can synthesize a share of the stock using a put, a call, and a pure discount bond with a face value of *E*.

15.4 VOLATILITY AND OPTION PRICES

The higher the volatility of a stock's price, the higher the prices of *both* puts *and* calls on that stock. To see why, consider the case in which the stock price can take only one of two values a year from now—either $120 or $80—each with a probability of .5.

	Low-Volatility Scenario	
Now		*In 1 Year*
Stock Price	*Stock Price*	*Call Option Payoff*
	$120	$20
$100		
	$80	0
Expected Value:	$100	$10

The expected value of the end-of-year stock price is, therefore, .5 × $120 + .5 × $80 = $100.

Now consider a call option on the stock with an exercise price of $100 expiring in one year. At expiration, the call will pay either $20 if the stock price is $120, or it will pay nothing if the stock price is $80. The expected payoff on the call is, therefore, .5 × $20 + .5 × 0 = $10.

Suppose the stock becomes more volatile with no change in its expected end-of-year price. For example, suppose the two possible values for the end-of-year stock price are now $200 and 0, each with probability .5.

High-Volatility Scenario		
Now	*In 1 Year*	
Stock Price	*Stock Price*	*Call Option Payoff*
	$200	$100
$100		
	$0	0
Expected Value:	$100	$50

The expected value of the end-of-year stock price is still $100 (.5 × $200 +.5 × 0), but the volatility is much greater. The expected value of the payoff on the call option, however, is now $50 (.5 × $100 + .5 × 0), higher by $40. Clearly, the price of the call option will increase. Thus, we see that an increase in volatility (holding constant the current price of the stock) causes the expected value of the payoffs on a call option on the stock to increase and, therefore, raises its current price. The same is true with a put.

The same reasoning applies in the more general case of a continuous probability distribution for the underlying stock price. The payoff from an option at expiration cannot be negative. At worst, the option will be worthless and not be exercised. Therefore, the probability distribution for the option's payoff is truncated at zero. This truncation makes the expected payoff on the option an increasing function of the underlying stock's price volatility, holding fixed the expected payoff on the stock.

In summary, an increase in a stock's volatility, holding constant the current price and expected rate of return on the stock, will cause the expected returns on puts and calls on that stock to rise. Consequently, the prices of puts and calls increase with the volatility of the stock. Moreover, the put-call parity relation implies that an increase in stock-price volatility will result in the exact *same* increase in the price of both the call and the corresponding put (i.e., the put with the same maturity and exercise price as the call).

> **Quick Check 15-5**
> Suppose that at a given stock-price volatility, $S = \$100$, $E = \$100$, $T = 1$ year, $r = .08$, $C = \$17.41$, and $P = \$10$. Now volatility goes up and the price of the call rises to $20. What must be the new price of the put if S, E, T, and r remain unchanged?

▷15.5   TWO-STATE (BINOMIAL) OPTION PRICING

As we saw in equation 15.2, the put-call parity relation allows us to express the price of a call in terms of the price of the underlying stock, the riskless rate of interest,

(Δ) exempt from final

and the price of the corresponding put. But we would like to have a way of computing the price of a call without knowing the price of the put. To do so, we have to make some assumptions about the probability distribution of future stock prices.

In this section we assume that the stock price can take only one of two possible values at the expiration date of the option. Although this assumption is unrealistic, the *two-state model* forms the basis for a more realistic option-pricing model known as the *binomial model,* which is widely used in practice. The intuitive understanding one can derive from the two-state model also carries over to the Black-Scholes model.

The method is similar to the one we used to derive the put-call parity relation. We construct a synthetic call using only stocks and riskless borrowing. Then by the Law of One Price, we know that the price of the call must equal the cost of the synthetic call that we have constructed.

Consider a one-year call with an exercise price of $100. We assume that the underlying stock price is now $100 and it can either rise or fall by 20% during the year. Thus, at the option expiration date one year from now, the stock price can be either $120 or $80. The riskless interest rate is 5% per year.

The payoffs to the stock and to the call can be described by the following "tree":

Now	*In 1 Year*	
Stock Price	*Stock Price*	*Call Option Payoff*
	$120	$20
$100		
	$80	0

Now compare the call option payoffs to the payoffs on a portfolio consisting of a share of the stock, financed in part by riskless borrowing. Because the collateral for the loan will be the stock itself, the most that the investor can borrow at the riskless rate is the present value of the stock's minimum price a year from now. The minimum price is $80, so the amount borrowed today is $80/1.05 = $76.19. The payoffs on this portfolio depend on the stock price a year from now as follows:

		Cash Flow at Maturity Date	
Position	*Immediate Cash Flow*	*If $S_1 = \$120$*	*If $S_1 = \$80$*
Buy 1 share of stock	−$100	$120	$80
Borrow $76.19	+$76.19	−$80	−$80
Total portfolio	−$23.81	$40	0

Now	*In 1 Year*	
Cost of Portfolio	*Stock Price*	*Portfolio Payoff*
	$120	$40
$23.81		
	$80	0

Next, we need to find what fraction of a share of stock is needed to replicate the payoffs from the call option. This fraction of a share of stock is called the option's **hedge ratio.** More generally, an option's hedge ratio in the two-state model is the difference between the two possible payoffs of the option divided by the difference in the two possible terminal prices of the underlying stock. In our case this is:

$$\text{Hedge Ratio} = \frac{\text{Range of Option Values}}{\text{Range of Stock Values}}$$

$$= \frac{\$20 - 0}{\$120 - \$80} = .5$$

Thus, if we were to buy ½ a share of the stock and borrow only $38.095, we would have a synthetic call. The amount to borrow is the maximum amount that can be paid back with interest at the expiration date with complete certainty. Because in our example the worst possible outcome for the half share of stock is a value of $40, the amount to borrow is the present value of $40 discounted at the riskless rate of 5%, which is $38.095.

Table 15.6 summarizes the payoffs from the call itself and the synthetic call created by this replicating portfolio.

By the Law of One Price, the call and its replicating portfolio (the synthetic call) must have the same price, so the call's price must be:

$$C = .5S - \$38.095$$

$$= \$50 - \$38.095$$

$$= \$11.905$$

Quick Check 15-6

Suppose that the underlying stock is more volatile than in the previous example. It can rise or fall by 30% during the year. Use the two-state model to derive the price of the option.

TABLE 15.6   Creating a Synthetic Call through Replication

Position	Immediate Cash Flow	Cash Flow at Maturity Date	
		If $S_1 = \$120$	If $S_1 = \$80$
Call option		$20	0
Synthetic Call			
Buy ½ share of stock	-$50	$60	$40
Borrow $38.095	$38.095	-40	-40
Total portfolio	-$11.905	$20	0

◢ 15.6 DYNAMIC REPLICATION AND THE BINOMIAL MODEL

E-BOOK

15.6

The assumption that there are only two possible prices that the stock can have a year from now is clearly unrealistic. To move in the direction of greater realism, therefore, we subdivide the one-year period into two sixth-month periods and assume that the stock price can either go up or down by $10 over each subperiod. Thus, the maximum amount the price can change during the year is $20 up or down. There will now be three possible stock prices at the end of the year ($120, $100, or $80) and the corresponding payoffs for the call option are $20, 0, and 0.

The method now consists of finding a **self-financing investment strategy** that replicates the call option payoff structure. The strategy is a *dynamic* one that calls for adjusting the number of shares of stock and the amount of borrowing after six months according to the stock price that materializes at that time. Subsequent to the original cash outlay, no additional funds are added or withdrawn by the investor.

At each point in time, the replication strategy boils down to the one we already considered in the two-state model of the previous section. Figure 15.5 shows what is involved in the form of a **decision tree.**

The stock price starts out at $100 (point *A*). Initially, you buy ½ share of stock for $50, borrowing $45. Your net cash outlay is, therefore, $5. At the end of the first sixth-month subperiod, the stock price is either $110 (point *B*) or $90 (point *C*). If you find yourself at point *B,* you borrow $55 more to buy another half share of stock. If, however, you are at point *C,* you sell your half share of stock and pay off your debt of $45 with the proceeds. This strategy produces exactly the same payoffs at the end of the year as does the option.

The strategy is completely self-financing subsequent to the original cash outlay. That is, no additional funds are added or withdrawn prior to the option expiration date by the investor. The conclusion is that because the initial cost of the

FIGURE 15.5   Decision Tree for Dynamic Replication of Call Option

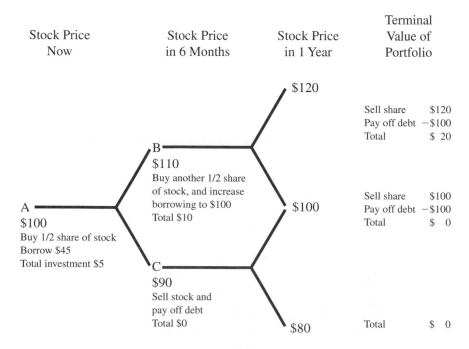

dynamic self-financing portfolio strategy that replicates the payoffs from the call is $5, by the Law of One Price, $5 must be the call price.

The option-pricing model we have just derived improves on the two-state model. It is called a **binomial option-pricing model.**[8] Greater realism and accuracy can be achieved with this binomial model by subdividing the one-year period into shorter and shorter time intervals. Binomial option-pricing models are widely used in practice. The number of time intervals used depends on the degree of accuracy required in any particular application.

15.7 THE BLACK-SCHOLES MODEL

A more realistic model frequently used by practitioners to price stock options is the **Black-Scholes model.**[9] Its derivation follows a similar line of reasoning to the one we just presented but assumes that one *continuously* adjusts the replicating portfolio over time.

The original Black-Scholes formula for the price of a European call option on stock has five parameters, four of which are directly observable: S, the price of the stock, E the exercise price, r the riskless interest rate (the annualized continuously compounded rate on a safe asset with the same maturity as the option), and T the time to maturity of the option.

The formula is:

$$C = N(d_1)S - N(d_2)Ee^{-rT}$$

$$d_1 = \frac{\ln(S/E) + (r + \sigma^2/2)T}{\sigma\sqrt{T}} \tag{15.4}$$

$$d_2 = d_1 - \sigma\sqrt{T}$$

where:[10]

C = price of the call

S = price of the stock

E = exercise price

r = riskless interest rate (the annualized continuously compounded rate on a safe asset with the same maturity as the option)

T = time to maturity of the option in years

σ = standard deviation of the annualized continuously compounded rate of return on the stock

$\ln$ = natural logarithm

e = the base of the natural log function (approximately 2.71828)

$N(d)$ = the probability that a random draw from a standard normal distribution will be less than d

---

[8]For a development of the binomial model, see Cox, Ross, and Rubinstein, "Option Pricing: A Simplified Approach," *Journal of Financial Economics,* 7 (1979), 229–263.

[9]Fischer Black, and Myron Scholes, "The Pricing of Options and Other Corporate Liabilities," *Journal of Political Economy,* 81 (May/June 1973).

[10]The continuously compounded rate of return is equal to the natural logarithm of (1 + the rate of return).

We can derive the formula for the value of a put by substituting for C in the put-call parity condition that $P = C - S + Ee^{-rT}$. The resulting formula for the value of the put is:

$$P = (N(d_1) - 1)S + (1 - N(d_2))Ee^{-rT}$$

In deriving their formula, Black and Scholes assumed that no dividends are paid during the life of the option. The model was generalized by Merton to allow for a constant continuous dividend yield, d.[11] That dividend-adjusted option-pricing formula is:

$$C = N(d_1)Se^{-dT} - N(d_2)Ee^{-rT}$$

$$d_1 = \frac{\ln(S/E) + (r - d + \sigma^2/2)T}{\sigma\sqrt{T}} \qquad (15.5)$$

$$d_2 = d_1 - \sigma\sqrt{T}$$

Note that the expected return on the stock does not explicitly appear in the option-pricing formula. Its effect comes through the stock price: Any change in expectations about the future stock price or in the expected return required on the stock will cause the stock price to change and thereby change the price of the call. But at any *given* stock price, the option price can be derived without knowing the expected return on the stock. Analysts who disagree about the expected return on the stock will nevertheless agree about the right price for the option, *given* the current observed price of the stock.

In the real world, neither volatility (σ) nor the dividend yield (d) are known with certainty, and empirical evidence suggests that both vary stochastically over time. Models that incorporate these stochastic variations have been developed and are used in practice. The dividend-adjusted option pricing formula in equation 15.5 is easily computed using an electronic spreadsheet. We have included one in the supplements to this text.

For convenience we organize the information in a tabular form similar to the one we used for present value calculations in chapter 4. For example, suppose that we want to compute the price of a six-month call option with a strike price of $100 whose underlying stock price is $100, dividend yield 3% per year, and volatility .20. The riskless rate is 8% per year. The inputs and outputs of the option-pricing program are presented in Table 15.7.

Table 15.8 summarizes the effects of the six input parameters on the prices of calls and puts as reflected in equation 15.5.

The table should be interpreted as follows:

- An increase in the price of the underlying stock results in an increase in the price of the call and a decrease in the price of the put.

TABLE 15.7   Option Price Calculation Table

S	E	r	T	d	σ	Result	
100	100	.08	.5	.03	.2	$C = \$6.79$	$P = \$4.35$

[11]Robert C. Merton, "Theory of Rational Option Pricing," *Bell Journal of Management Science,* 4 (Spring 1973).

TABLE 15.8 Determinants of Option Prices

Increase in	Call	Put
Stock Price, S	Increase	Decrease
Strike Price, E	Decrease	Increase
Volatility, σ	Increase	Increase
Time to Expiration, T	Increase	Increase
Interest Rate, r	Increase	Decrease
Cash Dividends, d	Decrease	Increase

- An increase in the strike price results in a decrease in the price of the call and an increase in the price of the put.
- An increase in volatility results in an increase in the prices of both the call and the put.
- An increase in the time to expiration results in an increase in the price of the call and an increase in the price of the put.[12]
- An increase in the interest rate results in an increase in the price of the call and a decrease in the price of the put.
- An increase in the dividend yield results in a decrease in the price of the call and an increase in the price of the put.

For the special case in which the price of the underlying stock equals the present value of the strike price (i.e., $S = Ee^{-rT}$), there is a convenient approximation that one can use to calculate option prices:

$$\frac{C}{S} \approx .4\sigma\sqrt{T}$$

This approximation is also valid for the price of the put. Thus, if the stock price is $100, the strike price is $108.33, the maturity is one year, the riskless interest rate is 8%, dividend yield zero, and volatility .20, then the approximate price of the call and of the put is .08 of the stock price or $8.[13]

If we use the exact formula (equation 15.5) to calculate these option prices, we find that the approximation is not bad:

S	E	r	T	d	σ	Result	
100	108.33	.08	1	0	.2	$C = \$7.97$	$P = \$7.97$

Quick Check 15-7

Suppose that the volatility of the underlying stock is .3 instead of .2 in the previous example. What is the approximate price of the call?

---

[12]This applies only for American-type options.

[13]Note that the interest rate does not appear in the approximation formula.

15.8 IMPLIED VOLATILITY

E-BOOK

15.8

Implied volatility is defined as the value of σ that makes the observed market price of the option equal to the value computed using the option-pricing formula. Thus, in the previous example, suppose that we observe the values on the left side of the table (including a price of $7.97 for the call).

S	E	r	T	d	C	σ
100	108.33	.08	1	0	7.97	?

If we substitute these values into equation 15.6 and solve for σ, we have found the volatility implied by this option's price. In this case the implied volatility is .2.

The CBOE has constructed an implied volatility index for the S&P 100 stock price index to be used as the basis for creating new futures and options contracts on implied volatility itself.[14] This implied volatility index (VIX) has been designed to minimize statistical bias while using information from the prices of eight S&P 100 index options with a maturity of approximately 30 days.

Figure 15.6 shows the value of the VIX index over the period from 1986 to 1993. It is evident that the implied volatility of the stock price index has fluctuated quite a bit over the period. There was a huge spike increase at the time of the October 1987 stock market crash. Thereafter, implied volatility returned to its former level.

FIGURE 15.6 Implied Volatility, 1986–1993

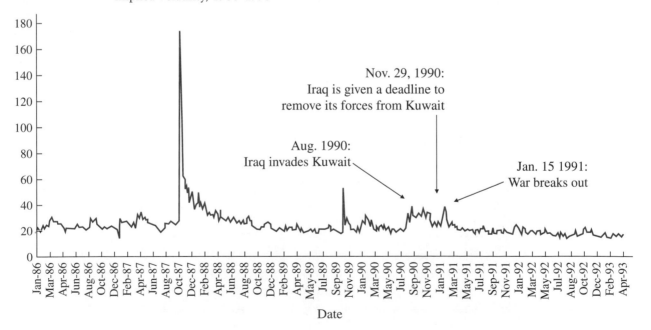

_____

[14]For a detailed description of the construction of the CBOE's VIX index, see R. E. Whaley, "Derivatives on Market Volatility: Hedging Tools Long Overdue," *Journal of Derivatives* (Fall 1993), pp. 80–82.

15.9 CONTINGENT CLAIMS ANALYSIS OF CORPORATE DEBT AND EQUITY

E-BOOK

15.9

Contingent claims analysis (CCA) is the application of the replication methodology used in option pricing to the valuation of other securities. In this section we will show how it is used to value the debt and equity of a firm, given information about the firm's total value.

Our hypothetical firm, Debtco, is in the real estate business. It has issued two types of securities: common stock (1 million shares) and zero-coupon bonds with an aggregate face value of $80 million (80,000 bonds each with a face value of $1,000). Debtco's bonds mature one year from now. If we know that the total market value of Debtco is $100 million, what are the separate market values of its stocks and bonds?

Let:

V be the current market value of Debtco's assets ($100 million)

E be the current market value of Debtco's equity

D be the current market value of Debtco's debt

We know that the combined market value of the firm's debt and equity is $100 million:

$$V = D + E = \$100 \text{ million}$$

We want to find the values of each separately: E and D.

Consider the possible payoffs to the holders of Debtco's securities when the bonds mature a year from now. The payoff diagrams are shown in Figures 15.7 and 15.8. If the value of the firm's assets exceeds the face value of its debt (i.e., if $V_1 > \$80$ million), the stockholders receive the difference between the two (i.e., $V_1 - \$80$ million). However, if the value of the assets falls short of $80 million, then the company will default on the debt, and the stockholders will get nothing. The bondholders will receive all of the firm's assets.[15]

FIGURE 15.7   Payoff Diagram for Debtco's Bonds

Note: For values of the firm less than $80 million, the bondholders receive all the firm's assets, and for values greater than $80 million, the bondholders receive $80 million.

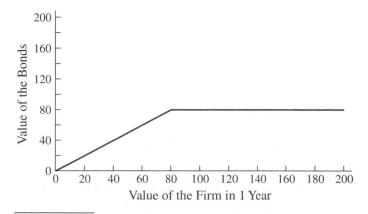

---

[15]This applies when bankruptcy is costless and the rules of seniority among the firm's liabilities are followed strictly. In real-world bankruptcy, there are costs and negotiated solutions.

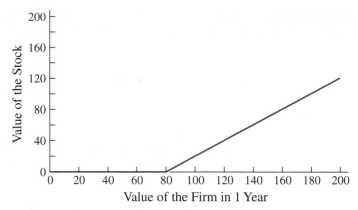

FIGURE 15.8   Payoff Diagram for Debtco's Stock

Note: For values of the firm less than $80 million, the stockholders receive nothing, and for values greater than $80 million, they receive the value of the firm less $80 million.

Figure 15.7 shows that for values of the firm less than $80 million, the bondholders receive the value of all the assets, and for values greater than $80 million, the bondholders receive $80 million. Figure 15.8 shows that for values of the firm less than $80 million, the stockholders receive nothing, and for values greater than $80 million, they receive the value of the firm minus $80 million.

Note that the payoff diagram for Debtco's equity is identical to that of a call option in which the underlying asset is the firm itself, and the exercise price is the face value of its debt. We can, therefore, apply formula 15.5 with a change of symbols. The resulting formula for the value of the firm's equity is:

$$E = N(d_1)V - N(d_2)Be^{-rT}$$

$$d_1 = \frac{\ln(V/B) + (r + \sigma^2/2)T}{\sigma\sqrt{T}} \tag{15.6}$$

$$d_2 = d_1 - \sigma\sqrt{T}$$

where

V = value of the firm

E = value of the equity in the firm

B = face value of the pure discount debt

r = riskless interest rate

T = time to maturity of the debt in years

σ = standard deviation of the annualized continuously compounded rate of return on the firm's assets

ln = natural logarithm

e = the base of the natural log function (approximately 2.71828)

$N(d)$ = the probability that a random draw from a standard normal distribution will be less than d

The value of the debt, *D,* is by definition equal to $V - E$. The continuously compounded *promised* rate of interest on the debt, *R,* is therefore equal to:

$$R = \frac{\ln(B/D)}{T}$$

In implementing equation 15.6, we can use the same programs as we did in pricing options according to equation 15.5. We simply have to change the interpretation of the inputs and the output. Let the riskless interest rate be 8% per year, and the volatility of the firm's asset value be .3. Then Table 15.7 becomes 15.7a.

The value of the debt is equal to $V - E$:

$$D = \$100 \text{ million} - \$28.24 \text{ million} = \$71.76 \text{ million}$$

The continuously compounded *promised* rate of interest on the debt, *R,* is therefore equal to:

$$R = \ln(80/71.76) = .1087 \text{ or } 10.87\% \text{ per year}$$

So we find that Debtco's bonds must offer a promised yield to maturity of 10.87% when the riskless interest rate is 8% per year.

Now consider the special case in which the value of the firm's assets equals the present value of the face value of the debt evaluated using the riskless interest rate; that is,

$$PV = 80e^{-.08}$$

The approximate value of the corporation's equity in this case is:

$$\frac{E}{V} \approx .4\sigma\sqrt{T}$$

Let $V = 100$, $B = 108.33$, $\sigma = .3$, $T = 1$, and apply the approximation to get:

$$E = \$12 \text{ million}$$

If we apply the exact formula, we find:

V	B	r	T	σ	Result
100	108.33	.08	1	.3	E = $11.92

TABLE 15.7a Corporate Equity Calculation Table

V	B	r	T	σ	Result
100	80	.08	1	.3	E = $28.24

Quick Check 15-8
What would be the yield to maturity on Debtco's debt in the special case just examined?

15.10 CREDIT GUARANTEES

Guarantees against credit risk pervade the financial system and play an important role in corporate and public finance. Parent corporations routinely guarantee the debt obligations of their subsidiaries. Commercial banks and insurance companies offer guarantees in return for fees on a broad spectrum of financial instruments ranging from traditional letters of credit to interest rate and currency swaps.

The largest providers of financial guarantees are almost surely governments and governmental agencies. Even in the United States, where the prevailing philosophy is one of limited government involvement in the private sector, the federal and local governments provide a wide range of financial guarantees. The most important of these, both economically and politically, is deposit insurance. However, guarantees are also used extensively elsewhere. In the corporate sector, the government has guaranteed the debt of small businesses and on occasion it has done so for very large businesses. The Pension Benefit Guarantee Corporation (PBGC) provides limited insurance of corporate pension plan benefits. Residential mortgages and farm and student loans are examples of noncorporate obligations that the government has guaranteed. The U.S. government has also given guarantees of other sovereigns' debt as a form of foreign aid.

But guarantees are even more pervasive than this list of *explicit* guarantees would suggest. Anytime a loan is made, an *implicit* guarantee of that loan is involved. To see this, consider the fundamental identity, which holds in both a functional and a valuation sense:

$$\text{Risky Loan} + \text{Loan Guarantee} = \text{Default-Free Loan}$$

$$\text{Risky Loan} = \text{Default-Free Loan} - \text{Loan Guarantee}$$

Thus, whenever lenders make dollar-denominated loans to anyone other than the U.S. government, they are implicitly also selling loan guarantees. The lending activity, therefore, consists of two functionally distinct activities: pure default-free lending and the bearing of default risk by the lender.

To see this point more clearly, it will perhaps be helpful to think of the lending activity taking place in two steps: (1) the purchase of a guarantee and (2) the taking of a loan. Suppose that the guarantor and the lender are two distinct entities. In the first step, the borrower buys a guarantee from the guarantor for $10. In the second step, the borrower takes this guarantee to the lender and borrows $100 at a default-free interest rate of 10% per year. The borrower winds up receiving a net amount of ($100 − $10 =) $90 in return for a promise to pay back $110 in a year.

Of course, often the lender and the guarantor are the same entity—for example, a commercial bank—and the borrower simply receives the net $90 from the bank in return for a promise to repay $110 in a year. The promised interest rate on the loan is then stated as 22.22%, that is, ($110 − $90)/$90. This promised rate reflects both the riskless interest rate and the charge for the guarantee. To see that the two are separable activities, note that the holder of the risky debt could buy a third-party guarantee for $10. The holder would then be making a total investment of $90 + $10 = $100 and would receive a sure payment of $110.

The purchase of any real-world loan is, thus, functionally equivalent to the purchase of a pure default-free loan and the simultaneous issue of a guarantee of that loan. In effect, the creditor simultaneously pays for the default-free loan and receives a "rebate" for the guarantee of that loan. The magnitude of the value of the guarantee relative to the value of the default-free loan component varies considerably. A high-grade bond (rated AAA) is almost an all default-free loan with a very small guarantee component. A below-investment-grade or "junk" bond, on the other hand, typically has a large guarantee component.

Guarantees are also involved in other financial contracts besides loans. In swap contracts, for example, guarantees of performance by both parties to the swap agreement are often provided by a third-party financial intermediary. If such a guarantee is not purchased, then each of the parties is providing de facto a guarantee of its counterparty's performance. As nonfinancial firms increasingly use such contracts, their managers need to better understand how to efficiently manage the explicit and implicit guarantees associated with them.

Options theory can be used to analyze the efficient management of such guarantees. Guarantees are like put options. The guarantor must make the promised payment on a financial contract if the issuer fails to do so. The loss to the guarantor is equal to the difference between the promised payment on the guaranteed contract and the price received from the sale of the assets that are available from the issuer as collateral for this obligation.[16] This difference is called the *shortfall*. It is generally assumed that the issuer will only default if the shortfall is nonnegative.

For example, consider the profit from the sale of a single guarantee. If the value of collateral assets, V, exceeds the promised payments, E, the guarantor keeps the premium and pays nothing. But if the value of assets is less than the promised payments, the guarantor must pay the difference, $E − V$. The guarantor's maximum profit is equal to the premium plus interest earned from investing the premium prior to payment of losses or expiration of the guarantee. This maximum profit is diminished by the shortfall or loss experience from issuer defaults. The maximum loss exposure is the promised payment. The guarantor's profit function is, thus, given by $P − \max[0, E − V]$, where P is the premium plus the interest earned from investing it.

15.10.1 A Hypothetical Example

We return to the example of Debtco Corporation introduced in the previous section. Suppose that a bank, insurance company, or the government undertakes to guarantee the debt of Debtco against default. What is the fair market value of this guarantee? One way to compute its value is to take the difference between the

---

[16]We use the term *collateral* to refer to all assets of the liability issuer that the guarantor has recourse to seize, even if they are not formally pledged and segregated.

present value of riskless bonds promising the same cash flows as Debtco bonds and the value of Debtco bonds without the guarantee.

Because the riskless interest rate is .08 per year continuously compounded, and the debt promises $80 million at maturity a year from now, its value as risk-free debt is

$$PV = 80e^{-.08} \text{ million} = \$73.849 \text{ million}$$

Because its value without the guarantee is $71.759 million, the value of the guarantee must be the difference:

Value of guarantee = Value with guarantee − Value without guarantee

= $73.849 million − $71.759 million

= $2.09 million

But there is another way to compute the value of the guarantee. The credit guarantee is equivalent to writing a put option on Debtco's assets with a strike price equal to the face value of the debt. The guarantee's value can, therefore, be computed using the adjusted put-option-pricing formula:

$$G = (N(d_1) - 1)V + (1 - N(d_2))Be^{-rT}$$
$$d_1 = \frac{\ln(V/B) + (r + \sigma^2/2)T}{\sigma\sqrt{T}}$$
$$d_2 = d_1 - \sigma\sqrt{T}$$

V	B	r	T	σ	Result
100	80	.08	1	.3	G = $2.09

15.11 OTHER APPLICATIONS OF OPTION-PRICING METHODOLOGY

Many financial contracts contain embedded options.[17] Examples from household finance are the prepayment right that gives the homeowner the right to renegotiate the interest rate paid to the lender if rates fall; a car lease that gives the customer the right, but not the obligation, to purchase the car at a prespecified price at the end of the lease.

Many option-pricing applications do not involve financial instruments. The family of such applications is called *real options*. The most developed area for real-

---

[17]For extensive references, see R. C. Merton, "Applications of Option-Pricing Theory: Twenty-Five Years Later," *American Economic Review* (June 1998), pp. 323–349, from which this section was drawn.

option application is investment decisions by firms. However, real-options analysis has also been applied to real estate investment and development decisions. The common element for using option-pricing here is the same as in the preceding examples: The future is uncertain (if it were not, there would be no need to create options because we know now what we will do later), and in an uncertain environment, having the flexibility to decide what to do after some of that uncertainty is resolved definitely has value. Option-pricing theory provides the means for assessing that value.

The major categories of options within project-investment valuations are the option to initiate or expand, the option to abandon or contract, and the option to wait, slow down, or speed up development. There are growth options, which involve creating excess capacity as an option to expand, and research and development as creating the opportunity to produce new products and even new businesses, but not the obligation to do so if they are not economically viable.

An example of an application of the real options technology is in the generation of electric power, the power. A power plant can be constructed to use a single fuel such as oil or natural gas or it can be built to operate on either. The value of that option is the ability to use the least-cost fuel available at each point in time and the cost of that option is manifest in both the higher cost of construction and less efficient energy conversion than with the corresponding specialized equipment.

Another example comes from the entertainment industry and involves the decision about making a sequel to a movie. The choices are either to produce both the original movie and its sequel at the same time, or wait and produce the sequel after the success or failure of the original is known. One does not have to be a movie production expert to guess that the incremental cost of producing the sequel is going to be less if the first path is followed. Although this is done, more typically the latter is chosen, especially with higher-budget films. The economic reason is that the second approach provides the option not to make the sequel (if, for example, the original is not a success). If the producer knew (almost certainly) that the sequel will be produced, then the option value of waiting for more information is small and the cost of doing the sequel separately is likely to exceed the benefit. Hence, once again, we see that the amount of uncertainty is critical to the decision, and the option-pricing model provides the means for quantifying the cost-benefit trade-off.

The individual's decision as to how much vocational education to acquire can be formulated as an option-valuation problem in which the optimal exercise conditions reflect when to stop training and start working. In the classic labor-leisure trade-off, one whose job provides the flexibility to increase or decrease the number of hours worked and, hence, his or her total compensation, on relatively short notice, has a valuable option relative to those whose available work hours are fixed. Wage, welfare, and pension plan floors that provide for minimum compensation have an option-like structure.

Health care insurance contains varying degrees of flexibility, a major one being whether the consumer agrees in advance to use only a prespecified set of doctors and hospitals (HMO plan) or retain the right to choose an out-of-plan doctor or hospital. In making the decision on which to take the consumer solves an option-pricing problem as to the value of that flexibility. Much the same structure of valuation occurs in choosing between pay-per-view and flat-fee payment for cable television services.

Option value can be a significant proportion of the total value of government-granted offshore drilling rights and pollution rights. Option-pricing analysis quantifies the government's economic decision whether to build roads in less populated areas depending on whether it has the policy option to abandon rural roads if they are not used enough.

Various legal and tax issues involving policy and behavior have been addressed using the option model. Among them is the valuation of plaintiffs' litigation options, bankruptcy laws including limited-liability provisions, tax delinquency on real estate and other property as an option to abandon or recover the property by paying the arrears, tax evasion, and valuing the tax timing option for the capital-gains tax in a circumstance when only realization of losses and gains on investments triggers a taxable event.

Option theory has proven to be a fruitful framework for the analysis of strategic decisions. Early strategic applications are in energy- and power-generation industries that need long-term planning horizons and have major fixed-cost components on a large scale with considerable uncertainty. Because energy and power generation are fundamental in every economy, this use for derivatives offers mainline applications in both developed and developing countries. Eventually, option models may become standard tools for implementing strategic objectives.

Summary

- Options can be used to modify an investor's exposure to investment risk. By combining the risk-free asset and stock-index call options, an investor can achieve a guaranteed minimum rate of return plus substantial upside participation in the stock market.

- A portfolio consisting of a stock plus a European put option is equivalent to a riskless bond with a face value equal to the option's exercise price plus a European call option. Therefore, by the Law of One Price, we get the *put-call parity relation:*

$$S + P = \frac{E}{(1 + r)^T} + C \tag{15.1}$$

  where S is the stock price, P the price of the put, r the riskless interest rate, T the maturity of the option, and C the price of the call.

- One can create a *synthetic option* from the underlying stock and the riskless asset through a dynamic replication strategy that is self-financing after the initial investment. By the Law of One Price, the option's price is given by the formula:

$$C = N(d_1)Se^{-dT} - N(d_2)Ee^{-rT}$$
$$d_1 = \frac{\ln(S/E) + (r - d + \sigma^2/2)T}{\sigma\sqrt{T}} \tag{15.5}$$
$$d_2 = d_1 - \sigma\sqrt{T}$$

where:

C = price of the call

S = price of the stock

E = exercise price

r = riskless interest rate (the annualized continuously compounded rate on a safe asset with the same maturity as the option)

T = time to maturity of the option in years

σ = standard deviation of the annualized continuously compounded rate of return on the stock

d = continuous dividend yield on the stock

ln = natural logarithm

e = the base of the natural log function (approximately 2.71828)

$N(d)$ = the probability that a random draw from a standard normal distribution will be less than d

- The same methodology used to price options can be used to value many other contingent claims, including corporate stocks and bonds, loan guarantees, and the real options embedded in investments in research and development and flexible manufacturing technology.

Key Terms

- contingent claim   384
- call   384
- put   384
- strike price   384
- exercise price   384
- expiration date   384
- American-type option   384
- European-type option   384
- exchange-traded option   384
- over-the-counter option   384
- intrinsic value   385
- tangible value   385
- out of the money   386
- in the money   386

- at the money   386
- time value   386
- index option   386
- cash settlement   386
- payoff diagram   387
- put-call parity relation   392
- hedge ratio   397
- self-financing investment strategy   398
- decision tree   398
- binomial option-pricing model   399
- Black-Scholes model   399
- implied volatility   402

Answers to Quick Check Questions

Quick Check 15-1   *Using Table 15.1, compute the intrinsic value and the time value of the June 125 call. Do the same for the put.*

ANSWER: Because the IBM 125 call is currently out of the money, its intrinsic value is zero, and its time value equals its price (1½). The June IBM 125 put has an intrinsic value of $4^{15}\!/_{16}$ (= 125 − $120^{1}\!/_{16}$). Since its price is 5¾, its time value is $^{13}\!/_{16}$.

Quick Check 15-2   *Suppose you bought an SPX June 1120 call on June 5, 1998 for the price listed in Table 15.2. If the value of the index at expiration on June 19 turned out to be 1200, what would be your rate of return?*

ANSWER:
$$\text{Rate of return on the call} = \frac{1200 - 1120}{12} = 6.67\%.$$

Quick Check 15-3   *Strategy 4 is to invest $96,000 in the riskless asset and $4,000 in options. What is the minimum guaranteed rate of return? What is the slope of the payoff graph to the right of the exercise price?*

ANSWER: By investing the $4,000 in one-year call options at a price of $10, you can buy 400 options. Your payoff from the options will be $400 \max(S_T - 100,0)$. If the options expire worthless, you will have $100,800 from your investment in the riskless asset. This is a rate of return of 0.8% on your $100,000. The slope of the upward-sloping part of the payoff graph is .004. The formula for the total rate of return on your portfolio is:

$$\text{Portfolio Rate of Return} = \frac{\text{Value at End of Year} - \text{Value at Beginning of Year}}{\text{Value at Beginning of Year}}$$

$$= \frac{\$96,000(1.05) + 400\max(S_T - 100, 0) - \$100,000}{\$100,000}$$

$$= .008 + .004\max(S_T - 100, 0)$$

Payoff Diagram for Stock Market Strategies

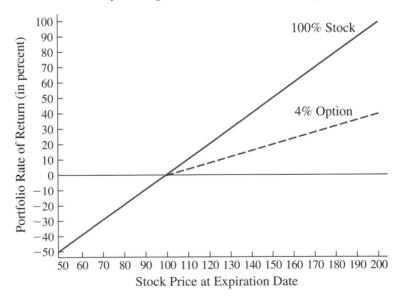

Quick Check 15-4   *Show how one can synthesize a share of the stock using a put, a call and a pure discount bond with a face value of E.*

ANSWER: By rearranging equation 15.1 so that the stock price is on the left we get:

$$S = \frac{E}{(l + r)^T} + C - P$$

This implies that one can create a synthetic share of stock by purchasing a pure discount bond with a face value of E, purchasing a call, and selling a put.

Payoff Structure for a Pure Discount Bond Plus a Call Minus a Put		
Position	*Value of Position at Maturity Date*	
	If $S_T < E$	If $S_T > E$
Pure discount bond with face value of E	E	E
Long a call	0	$S_T - E$
Short a put	$S_T - E$	0
Pure discount bond plus call minus put	S_T	S_T

Quick Check 15-5 *Suppose that at a given volatility, $S = \$100$, $E = \$100$, $T = 1$ year, $r = .08$, $C = \$17.41$, and $P = \$10$. Now volatility goes up and the price of the call rises to $\$20$. What must be the new price of the put if S, E, T, and r remain unchanged?*

ANSWER: The price of the put has to increase by exactly the same amount as the price of the call, which in this case is $2.59. So the put price will be $12.59.

Quick Check 15-6 *Suppose that the underlying stock is more volatile than in the previous example. It can rise or fall by 30% during the year. Use the two-state model to derive the price of the option.*

ANSWER:

$$\text{Hedge Ratio} = \frac{\text{Range of Option Values}}{\text{Range of Stock Values}} = \frac{\$30 - 0}{\$130 - \$70} = .5$$

The amount to borrow is the maximum amount that can be paid back with interest at the expiration date with complete certainty. Because in our example the worst possible outcome for the half share of stock is a value of $35, the amount to borrow is the present value of $35 discounted at the riskless rate of 5%, which is $33.33.

The price of the call equals the cost of the replicating portfolio, which is equal to the hedge ratio times the current stock price minus the amount borrowed. By the Law of One Price this is the price of the call option:

$$C = .5S - \$33.33$$
$$= \$50 - \$33.33$$
$$= \$16.67$$

Quick Check 15-7 *Suppose that the volatility of the underlying stock is .3 instead of .2 in the previous example. What is the approximate price of the call?*

ANSWER: $C = .4 \times .3 \times \$100 = \$12$

Quick Check 15-8 *What would be the yield to maturity on the corporation's debt in this special case?*

ANSWER: Using the approximate value of $12 million for the value of the equity,

$$D = \$100 \text{ million} - \$12 \text{ million} = \$88 \text{ million}$$

The continuously compounded *promised* rate of interest on the debt, *R*, is therefore equal to:

$$R = \ln (108.33/88) = .2078 \text{ or } 20.78\% \text{ per year}$$

Questions and Problems

TEMPLATE

15.9–15.11

1. *Payoff Diagrams*
   Graph the payoff for a European put option with exercise price *E*, written on a stock with value *S*, when:
   a. You hold a long position (i.e., you buy the put).
   b. You hold a short position (i.e., you sell the put).

2. Graph the payoff to a portfolio holding one European call option and one European put option, each with the same expiration date and each with exercise price E, when both options are on a stock with value *S*.

3. *Investing with Options*
   The riskless one-year rate of interest is 4%, and the Globalex stock index is at 100. The price of one-year European call options on the Globalex stock index with an exercise price of 104 is 8% of the current price of the index. Assume that the expected dividend yield on the stocks in the Globalex index is zero. You have $1 million to invest for the next year. You plan to invest enough of your money in one-year T-bills to insure that you will at least get back your original $1 million and you will use the rest of your money to buy Globalex call options.
   a. Assuming that you can invest fractional amounts in Globalex options, show the payoff diagram for your investment. Measure the Globalex index on the horizontal axis and the portfolio rate of return on the vertical axis. What is the slope of the payoff line to the right of an index value of 104?
   b. If you think that there is a probability of .5 that the Globalex index a year from now will be up 12%, a probability of .25 that it will be up 40%, and a probability of .25 that it will be down 20%, what is the probability distribution of your portfolio rate of return?

4. *Put-Call Parity*
   a. Show how one can replicate a one-year pure discount bond with a face value of $100 using a share of stock, a put, and a call.
   b. Suppose that $S = \$100, P = \$10,$ and $C = \$15.$ What must be the one-year interest rate?
   c. Show that if the one year, risk-free interest rate is lower than in your answer to part b, there would be an arbitrage opportunity. (Hint: The price of the pure discount bond would be too high.)

5. A 90-day European call option on a share of stock of Toshiro Corporation is currently trading at 2,000 yen whereas the current price of the share itself is 2,400 yen. Ninety-day zero-coupon securities issued by the government of Japan are selling for 9,855 yen per 10,000 yen face value. Infer the price of a 90-day European put option on this stock if both the call and put have a common exercise price of 500 yen.

6. Gordon Gekko has assembled a portfolio consisting of ten 90-day U.S. Treasury bills, each having a face value of $1,000 and a current price of $990.10, and 200 90-day European call options, each written on a share of Paramount stock and having an exercise price of $50.00. Gekko is offering to trade you this portfolio for 300 shares of Paramount stock, which is currently valued at $215.00 a share. If 90-day

European put options on Paramount stock with a $50.00 exercise price are currently valued at $25.00,

  a. Infer the value of the calls in Gekko's portfolio.

  b. Determine whether you should accept Gekko's offer.

7. The stock of Kaukonen, Ltd., a hot tuna distributor, currently lists for $500.00 a share, whereas one-year European call options on this stock, with an exercise price of $200.00, sell for $400.00 and European put options with the same expiration date and exercise price sell for $84.57.

  a. Infer the yield on a one-year, zero-coupon, U.S. government bond sold today.

  b. If this yield is actually at 9%, construct a profitable trade to exploit the potential for arbitrage.

8. ***Two-State Option Pricing***

  Derive the formula for the price of a put option using the two-state model.

9. The share value of Drummond, Griffin and McNabb, a New Orleans publishing house, is currently trading at $100.00 but is expected, 90 days from today, to have risen to $150.00 or to have declined to $50.00, depending on critical reviews of its new biography of Ezra Pound. Assuming the riskless interest rate over the next 90 days is .01, can you value a European call option written on a share of DGM stock if the option carries an exercise price of $85.00?

10. ***The Black-Scholes Formula***

  a. Use the Black-Scholes formula to find the price of a three-month European call option on a non-dividend-paying stock with a current price of $50. Assume the exercise price is $51, the continuously compounded riskless interest rate is 8% per year, and σ is .4.

  b. What is the composition of the initial replicating portfolio for this call option?

  c. Use the put-call parity relation to find the Black-Scholes formula for the price of the corresponding put option.

11. As a financial analyst at Yew and Associates, a Singaporean investment house, you are asked by a client if she should purchase European call options on Rattan, Ltd. stock, which are currently selling in U.S. dollars for $30.00. These options have an exercise price of $50.00. Rattan stock currently exhibits a share price of $55.00, and the estimated variance of the stock is .04. If these options expire in 25 days and the riskless interest rate over that period is 5%, what do you advise your client to do?

12. ***Valuation of Corporate Securities with the Two-State Model***

  Lorre and Greenstreet, Inc., a purveyor of antique statues, currently has corporate assets valued at $100,000 and must repay $40,000, the aggregate face value of zero-coupon bonds sold to private investors, in 90 days. An independent appraisal of a newly acquired antique falcon from Malta will be publically released at that time, and the value of the firm's assets is expected to increase to $170,000 if the falcon is certified as genuine, but to decline to a mere $45,000 if the antique is found to be a fake. The firm will declare bankruptcy in this latter circumstance and shareholders will surrender the assets of the firm to its creditors.

  a. Can you express the current aggregate value of equity in Lorre and Greenstreet as a contingent expression of the value of the firm's assets and the face value of its outstanding debt?

  b. Is there a relation between the expression you have derived for equity and a 90-day European call option written on the aggregate value of the firm's assets?

  c. Can you express the current aggregate value of the bonds issued by Lorre and Greenstreet in terms of the value of the firm's assets and the face value of its outstanding debt?

   d. Is there a relation among the current value of the bonds the firm has issued, the current value of riskless bonds with the same term to maturity and face value, and a European put option written on the aggregate value of the firm's assets? What would the implication of such a relationship be for expressing the value of risky debt in terms of riskless debt and collateral?

13. Gephardt, Armey and Gore, a vaudeville booking agency, has issued zero-coupon corporate debt this week, consisting of 80 bonds, each with a face value of $1,000 and a term to maturity of one year. Industry analysts predict that the value of GAG assets will be $160,000 in one year if Rupert Murdoch succeeds in purchasing and converting the Washington Press Club to a comedy venue, $130,000 if Murdoch buys the club but retains its current scheduling, and $20,000 if Murdoch builds an alternative comedy venue in Washington. Industry analysts also predict that the aggregate value of the assets of a second firm in the field of comedy entertainment, Yeltsin Yuks, Ltd., will have the values of $100,000, $100,000, and $40,000, in these respective circumstances. Assuming that investors can purchase portfolios comprised of shares of the assets of GAG and YY Ltd., as well as buying or short-selling one-year, zero-coupon, government bonds at the riskless annual rate .10, then:

   a. Infer the three alternative values for aggregate equity in GAG, one year from today.

   b. Devise a portfolio that is a perfect substitute for the payoffs given by a portfolio composed only of equity in GAG.

   c. Determine the current market value of a share of equity in GAG, assuming 10,000 shares of GAG stock are outstanding, the current market value of GAG assets is $120,000, and the current market value of YY Ltd. assets is $85,725.

   d. Determine the current market value of a bond issued by GAG, assuming 80 bonds are issued, under these circumstances. What is the yield to maturity on each such bond?

CHAPTER

16

Capital Structure

OBJECTIVES

- To understand how a firm can create value through its financing decisions.
- To show how to take account of a firm's financing mix in evaluating investment decisions.

CONTENTS

This chapter deals with decisions regarding a firm's capital structure, that is, its mix of debt, equity, and other financing instruments. The central question is how to determine an *optimal* capital structure for the firm assuming that the objective is to maximize the wealth of its existing shareholders. In capital structure decisions the unit of analysis is the firm *as a whole*.

The starting point for analyzing corporate capital structure is a frictionless financial environment, defined as one in which there are no taxes or transaction costs, and contracts are costless to make and enforce. In such an environment the value of the firm is not affected by its financing mix and, therefore, the wealth of existing shareholders cannot be increased by policies that change only the firm's capital structure, such as borrowing to repurchase stock or issuing new stock to retire debt.

In the real world, however, there are many different frictions that make capital structure matter very much. Because contract law, taxes, and regulations differ from place to place and change over time, we will find that there is no single optimal financing mix that applies to all firms. Rather, finding the optimal capital structure for a corporation involves making trade-offs that depend on the particular legal and tax environment in which the corporation finds itself.

The chapter begins with an overview of the major types of financing available to firms. It then presents the reasons why in a frictionless economic environment the total value of a firm is determined only by the earning power of its assets and is not affected by its capital structure. Then the chapter considers the most important frictions that exist in the real world of finance and how they influence a firm's capital structure. Finally, we show how to take account of a firm's capital structure in evaluating investment decisions, such as whether to expand the size of the business.

16.1 INTERNAL VERSUS EXTERNAL FINANCING

In analyzing capital structure decisions, it is important to distinguish between *internal* and *external* sources of funds. **Internal financing** arises from the operations of the firm. It includes sources such as retained earnings, accrued wages, or accounts payable. For example, if a firm earns profits and reinvests them in new plant and equipment, this is internal financing. **External financing** occurs whenever the corporation's managers must raise funds from outside lenders or investors. If a corporation issues bonds or stocks to finance the purchase of new plant and equipment, it is external financing.

The decision processes that take place within a corporation are usually different for internal and external financings. For a corporation that is well established and not undertaking any major expansions that would require extraordinarily large amounts of funds, financing decisions are routine and almost automatic. Financing policy consists of deciding on a dividend policy (e.g., to regularly pay out one-third of its earnings as cash dividends to shareholders) and maintaining a line of credit with a bank. The amount of managerial time and effort required to make these internal financing decisions and the degree of scrutiny of planned expenditures are usually less than for external financing.

If a corporation raises funds from external sources, as it might if it needs to finance a major expansion, the process is more complicated and time consuming. In general, outside providers of funds are likely to want to see detailed plans for the use of the funds and will want to be convinced that the investment project will produce sufficient future cash to justify the expenditure. They will scrutinize the plans and are likely to be more skeptical about the prospects for success than the corporation's own managers. External financing, therefore, subjects the corporation's plans more directly to the discipline of the capital market than internal financing does.

Quick Check 16-1

How does the need for external financing impose market discipline on a corporation?

16.2 EQUITY FINANCING

The defining feature of equity financing is that equity is a claim to the residual that is left over after all debts have been paid. As explained in chapter 2, there are three major types of equity claims: *common stock, stock options,* and *preferred stock.* Common stocks are also called *shares,* so when we refer to the corporation's shareholders, we mean the holders of its common stock. Common stock confers on its holder the **residual claim** to the corporation's assets. In other words, after all other parties with a claim on the corporation have been paid, whatever is left goes to the holders of the common stock. Each share of stock is entitled to a *pro rata* share of the residual assets.

The managers of the corporation owe their primary allegiance to the shareholders. Indeed, in many legal jurisdictions, managers and boards of directors can be held liable for failure to fulfill their fiduciary responsibilities to the shareholders.

Often there is more than one class of common stock. Classes of common stock can differ in terms of their voting rights and the ability of the holder to sell them to other parties. For example, some corporations issue Class A common stock that has voting rights and Class B common stock that does not. Restricted stock is often issued to the founders of a corporation, and it usually constrains them not to sell their shares for a certain number of years. Stock options give their holders the right to buy common stock at a fixed exercise price in the future. Thus, suppose a firm with assets worth $100 million has only two types of claims outstanding—10 million shares of common stock, and 10 million stock options expiring a year from now with an exercise price of $10 per share. Because the holders of the options can convert them into common stock by paying $10 per share, they share ownership of the firm with the holders of the common stock. Often managers and other employees of a corporation will receive part of their compensation in the form of stock options. This is especially true in the United States in the start-up phase of a business.

Preferred stocks differ from common stock in that they carry a specified dividend that must be paid before the firm can pay any dividends to the holders of the common stock. It is in this sense that they are *preferred* over common stocks. However, preferred stocks receive only their promised dividends and do not get to share in the residual value of the firm's assets with the holders of the common stock. Failure to pay preferred dividends does not trigger a default.

> **Quick Check 16-2**
> In what way is preferred stock like debt, and in what way is it like equity?

16.3 DEBT FINANCING

Corporate debt is a contractual obligation on the part of the corporation to make promised future payments in return for the resources provided to it. Debt financing in its broadest sense includes loans and debt securities, such as bonds and mortgages, as well as other promises of future payment by the corporation, such as accounts payable, leases, and pensions. For many corporations, long-term lease and pension liabilities may be much larger than the amount of debt in the form of loans, bonds, and mortgages.

The main features of corporate debt securities were already explained in chapter 8. In the next three sections we describe three important forms of corporate debt not discussed previously: secured debt, long-term leases, and pension liabilities.

16.3.1 Secured Debt

When a corporation borrows money, it promises to make a series of payments in the future. In some cases, the corporation pledges a particular asset as security for that promise. The asset pledged as security is called **collateral** and the debt is called *secured*.

Collateralized borrowing by corporations is similar to an individual taking a mortgage loan to buy a house. The house serves as collateral for the loan. If the homeowner defaults, the lender is paid from the proceeds of the sale of the house. If there is any money left over, it reverts to the homeowner. However, if the proceeds from the sale of the house are not sufficient to pay off the balance of the mortgage loan, the lender can try to recoup the rest from the homeowner's other assets.

When a borrowing corporation secures a loan by designating specific assets as collateral, the secured lender gets first priority on those assets in the event of non-payment. For example, an airline might borrow money to finance the purchase of airplanes and pledge the airplanes as collateral for the loan. If the airline subsequently goes bankrupt before the secured loan is completely paid off, the secured lenders are paid out of the proceeds from the sale of the airplanes. Lenders who made unsecured loans to the airline may not get paid anything.

Quick Check 16-3
Would you expect the interest rate on a secured loan to be higher or lower than the rate on an otherwise identical unsecured loan? Why?

16.3.2 Long-Term Leases

Leases were briefly considered in the appendix to chapter 10. Leasing an asset for a period of time that covers much of the asset's useful life is similar to buying the asset and financing the purchase with debt secured by the leased asset.

For example, suppose an airline signs a contract to lease an airplane for 30 years. The airline gets the exclusive use of the plane in return for the promise to make fixed lease payments each year. Alternatively, the airline might buy the plane and issue 30-year bonds secured by the airplanes to raise the money needed to make the purchase.

Table 16.1 compares the market-value balance sheets for two hypothetical airlines: Airbond and Airlease. In both cases the main corporate asset is a fleet of airplanes with a market value of $750 million. Both companies have equity with a market value of $250 million and debt of $750 million. The difference between the companies is that for Airbond Corporation the debt takes the form of 30-year secured bonds and for Airlease it takes the form of a 30-year lease.

The main difference between the secured bonds and the lease as a form of debt financing is in who bears the risk associated with the residual market value of the

TABLE 16.1   Market-Value Balance Sheets of Airbond
and Airlease Corporations

a. Airbond Corporation

Assets		Liabilities and Shareholders' Equity	
Fleet of airplanes	$750 million	30-year bonds	$750 million
Other assets	$250 million	Equity	$250 million
Total	$1 billion	Total	$1 billion

b. Airlease Corporation

Assets		Liabilities and Shareholders' Equity	
Fleet of airplanes	$750 million	30-year lease	$750 million
Other assets	$250 million	Equity	$250 million
Total	$1 billion	Total	$1 billion

leased asset at the end of the term of the lease.[1] Because Airbond Corporation has bought its planes, it bears this risk. In Airlease's case, however, it is the *lessor*—the firm that has leased the plane to Airlease Corporation—that bears this residual-value risk.

Quick Check 16-4
Should a long-term lease be considered debt financing or equity financing?

16.3.3 Pension Liabilities

Pension plans were briefly discussed in chapter 2. Pension plans are classified into two types: defined contribution and defined benefit. In a *defined-contribution* pension plan, each employee has an account into which the employer and usually the employee too make regular contributions. At retirement, the employee receives a benefit whose size depends on the accumulated value of the funds in the retirement account.

In a *defined-benefit* pension plan, the employee's pension benefit is determined by a formula that takes into account years of service for the employer and, in most cases, wages or salary. A typical benefit formula would be 1% of average preretirement salary for each year of service. For corporations with defined-benefit pension plans, promises to pay future pension benefits to employees are a significant part of the firm's total long-term liabilities, and differences across countries in corporate pension-funding practices produce different patterns of corporate capital structure. For example, in the United States and the United Kingdom the law requires firms to establish a separate pension trust with a pool of assets sufficient to pay those promised benefits. This is called funding the pension plan. The

[1]There are possibly tax and accounting differences, depending on the type of lease and its term.

pension liabilities are, therefore, a form of corporate debt secured by the pension assets as collateral.

However, in many countries pension liabilities are not funded in this way. In Germany, for example, corporations do not set aside a separate pool of assets to serve as collateral for their pension liabilities. The obligation to pay pension benefits is, therefore, an *unsecured* debt of the corporation.[2]

To clarify, consider Table 16.2, which contrasts the economic balance sheets of AmeriPens Corporation and DeutschePens Corporation.

AmeriPens has a fully funded pension plan, which means that the market value of the pension assets ($400 million) equals the present value of its pension liability. The pension assets consist of securities (stocks, bonds, mortgages, etc.) issued by other entities such as businesses, governments, and individuals. AmeriPens has also issued bonds with a market value of $400 million. Its shareholders' equity is worth $600 million.

Like AmeriPens, DeutschePens Corporation has operating assets worth $1 billion, a pension liability of $400 million, and shareholders' equity worth $600 million. DeutschePens, however, has no separate pool of securities serving as collateral securing its pension liability. Its pension plan is, therefore, said to be *unfunded*.

Quick Check 16-5

Suppose AmeriPens Corporation's pension assets were worth only $300 million. If its pension liability still had a present value of $400 million, what would be its shareholders' equity?

TABLE 16.2   Balance Sheets of AmeriPens and DeutschePens Corporations

a. AmeriPens Balance Sheet

Assets		Liabilities and Shareholders' Equity	
Operating assets: plant, equipment, etc.	$1 billion	Bonds	$400 million
		Pension liability	$400 million
Pension assets: stocks, bonds, etc.	$400 million	Shareholders' equity	$600 million
Total	$1.4 billion	Total	$1.4 billion

b. DeutschePens Balance Sheet

Assets		Liabilities and Shareholders' Equity	
Operating assets: plant, equipment, etc.	$1 billion	Pension liability	$400 million
		Shareholders' equity	$600 million
Total	$1 billion	Total	$1 billion

---

[2]Corporate accounting rules in Germany do require the corporation to show the present value of its pension obligations on its balance sheet as a form of corporate indebtedness.

16.4 THE IRRELEVANCE OF CAPITAL STRUCTURE
IN A FRICTIONLESS ENVIRONMENT

We have seen that there is a wide array of possible corporate capital structures. We now turn our attention to the factors that determine why a firm chooses one rather than another.

To understand how a firm's management can enhance shareholder wealth through its capital structure decisions, a good way to start is by clarifying what does *not* matter. Modigliani and Miller (M&M) showed that in an economist's idealized world of frictionless markets the total market value of all the securities issued by a firm would be governed by the earning power and risk of its underlying real assets and would be independent of how the mix of securities issued to finance it was divided.[3]

Merton Miller has explained the M&M capital-structure proposition in terms of a pie: "Think of the firm as a gigantic pizza, divided into quarters. If now, you cut each quarter in half into eighths, the M&M proposition says that you will have more pieces, but not more pizza."

M&M's frictionless environment assumes the following conditions:

1. No income taxes.
2. No transactions costs of issuing debt or equity securities.
3. Investors can borrow on the same terms as the firm.
4. The various stakeholders of the firm are able to costlessly resolve any conflicts of interest among themselves.

In this frictionless environment, the total market value of the firm is independent of its capital structure. To see why, let us compare the values of two firms with identical assets differing only in their capital structures: Nodett Corporation, which issues only stock, and Somdett Corporation, which issues bonds and stock.

Nodett Corporation currently has total earnings of $10 million per year, which we will refer to as *EBIT* (earnings before interest and taxes). Nodett pays out all $10 million per year of its *EBIT* as dividends to the holders of its 1 million shares of common stock.

Let us assume that the market capitalization rate on Nodett's expected dividends is 10% per year. Then the firm's total value would be the present value of the $10 million perpetuity or

$$\frac{\$10 \text{ million}}{.1} = \$100 \text{ million}$$

and its price per share would be $100.

Somdett is identical to Nodett in its investment and operating policies. Therefore, its *EBIT* has the same expected value and risk characteristics as Nodett's. Somdett differs from Nodett only in its capital structure, in that it is partially debt financed. Somdett has issued bonds that have a face value of $40 million at an interest rate of 8% per year. Thus, the bonds promise to pay a coupon of $3.2 million per year (.08 × $40 million). We assume the bonds are in perpetuity.[4]

Let us assume that Somdett's bonds are default free and that the riskless rate of interest is 8% per year. The interest payments will be the same $3.2 million per

---

[3]Prior to their path-breaking work, finance theorists and practitioners just assumed that capital structure did matter, but for the wrong reasons. See Franco Modigliani and Merton Miller, "The Cost of Capital, Corporation Finance, and the Theory of Investment," *American Economic Review* (June 1958), pp. 261–297.

[4]Alternatively, we assume that the bonds are simply "rolled over," that is, replaced with new bonds, as they mature.

year regardless of the realized value of *EBIT*. The formula for the earnings available to Somdett's shareholders after the payment of interest on the bonds is:

$$\text{Somdett's Net Earnings} = EBIT - \$3.2 \text{ million}$$

The total cash payments made to Somdett's bondholders and stockholders *combined* is:

$$\text{Somdett's Total Payments} = \text{Somdett's Net Earnings} + \text{Interest Payments}$$

$$\text{Somdett's Total Payments} = EBIT - \$3.2 \text{ million} + \$3.2 \text{ million} = EBIT$$

The intuition behind the M&M capital structure irrelevance proposition is that because Somdett offers exactly the same future cash flows as Nodett, the market value of Somdett should be $100 million, which is the same as Nodett's. Because the interest payments on Somdett's bonds are assumed to be riskless, the bonds will have a market value equal to their $40 million face value. Thus, the market value of Somdett's equity should be $60 million ($100 million total firm value less $40 million of debt). Assuming that the number of shares of Somdett stock is 600,000 (60% of the number of Nodett shares), the price of a share should be $100. We can prove it by means of an arbitrage argument.

Suppose that the price of Somdett stock was less than the price of Nodett stock. For example, suppose that Somdett's price was $90 per share instead of $100. This would violate the Law of One Price. To see this, note that one can replicate or "synthesize" Nodett stock by buying proportional amounts of the stock and bonds of Somdett. For example, holding 1% of the shares of Nodett stock (10,000 shares) has exactly the same future cash flows as holding 1% of the shares of Somdett (6,000 shares) and 1% of the bonds of Somdett. An arbitrageur could therefore make an immediate $60,000 in arbitrage profits with no outlay of his own money by selling short 1% of the total amount of Nodett stock for $1 million and simultaneously buying 1% of the stock and bonds of Somdett for $940,000. Table 16.3a summarizes the relevant cash flows.

Now suppose that the price of Somdett stock was greater than the price of Nodett stock. For example, suppose that Somdett's price was $110 per share rather than $100. This too would violate the Law of One Price. To see this, note that one can replicate Somdett stock by buying a certain proportion of the stock of Nodett and borrowing to finance its purchase using the same personal debt-to-equity mix as Somdett. For example, buying 1% of the shares of Nodett stock (10,000 shares for $1,000,000) financed by borrowing 40% of the purchase price ($400,000), produces exactly the same future cash flows as holding 1% of the shares of Somdett (6,000 shares for $660,000). Table 16.3b summarizes the relevant cash flows.

Although a share of stock in each of the companies has the same price, the expected returns to shareholders and the risks of the stock investments differ. Let us flesh out the numerical example a bit in order to highlight these differences. Suppose the probability distribution of future *EBIT* is as shown in Table 16.4.

The columns labeled *EPS* show the earnings per share (and, therefore, dividends per share because we assume no reinvestment of earnings) corresponding to each value of *EBIT*. The formula for Nodett's *EPS* is:

$$EPS_{Nodett} = \frac{EBIT}{1,000,000 \text{ shares}}$$

The interest payments will be the same $3.2 million per year (.08 × $40 million) regardless of the realized value of *EBIT*. Somdett's *EPS* is, therefore:

$$EPS_{Somdett} = \frac{\text{Net Earnings}}{600,000 \text{ shares}} = \frac{EBIT - \$3.2 \text{ million}}{600,000 \text{ shares}}$$

TABLE 16.3a   Arbitrage When Somdett Sells for $90 per Share

Position	Immediate Cash Flow	Cash Flow in the Future
Sell short 1% of the shares of Nodett stock at $100 per share	$1,000,000	−1% of *EBIT*
Buy Replicating Portfolio (Synthetic Nodett):		
Buy 1% of the shares of Somdett at $90 per share	−$540,000	1% of (*EBIT* − $3.2 million per year)
Buy 1% of the bonds of Somdett	−$400,000	1% of $3.2 million per year
Total replicating portfolio	−$940,000	1% of *EBIT*
Net cash flows	$60,000	0

TABLE 16.3b   Arbitrage When Somdett Sells for $110 per Share

Position	Immediate Cash Flow	Cash Flow in the Future
Sell short 1% of the shares of Somdett stock at $110 per share	$660,000	−1% of (*EBIT* − $3.2 million per year)
Buy Replicating Portfolio (Synthetic Somdett):		
Buy 1% of the shares of Nodett at $100 per share	−$1,000,000	1% of *EBIT*
Borrowing $400,000 in perpetuity	$400,000	−$32,000 per year
Total replicating portfolio	−$600,000	1% of (*EBIT* − $3.2 million per year)
Net cash flows	$60,000	0

Comparing the *EPS* of Nodett with Somdett in Table 16.4, it is clear that the effect of increased financial leverage (changing only the financing mix and not the assets) is to increase both the mean *EPS* and the risk of *EPS*. Somdett's *EPS* is higher in the good state when *EBIT* = $15 million and lower in the bad state when *EBIT* = $5 million.

In the case of Nodett, the total risk of uncertain *EBIT* is spread among 1 million shares. In Somdett's case the same total risk exposure is spread among only 600,000 shares because the debtholders have a riskless claim. Somdett's stock, therefore, has a higher expected return and higher risk than Nodett's stock, yet the total values of the two *firms* are equal.

> The implication of the M&M analysis in a frictionless environment is that capital structure does not matter. The wealth of existing shareholders will not be affected by either reducing or increasing the firm's debt ratio.

If Nodett Corporation (with 1 million shares of stock outstanding) were to announce an issue of $40 million of debt to be used to repurchase and retire common stock, what would be the effect on the share price? After the stock repurchase how many shares of stock would be outstanding?

The answer is that the price of the common stock would remain unchanged at $100 per share. The $40 million debt issue would be used to repurchase and retire 400,000 shares of stock, thus leaving 600,000 shares outstanding with a total market value of $60 million.

TABLE 16.4   Probability Distribution of *EBIT* and *EPS* for Somdett and Nodett

		Nodett	Somdett	
State of the Economy	EBIT	EPS (1 million shares)	Net Earnings	EPS (600,000 shares)
Bad business	$5 million	$5	$1.8 million	$3.00
Normal business	10	10	6.8	11.33
Good business	15	15	11.8	19.67
Mean	10	10	6.8	11.33
Standard deviation		4		6.81
Beta	1.0	1.0		1.67

Note: Each state of the economy is equally likely.

Quick Check 16-6

Mordett is a firm with assets identical to Nodett and Somdett, but with $50 million of risk-free debt outstanding (interest rate of 8% per year) and 500,000 shares of stock. What is Mordett's probability distribution of *EPS*? What is the price of a share? If Nodett Corporation (with 1 million shares of stock outstanding) were to announce an issue of $50 million of debt to be used to repurchase and retire common stock, what would be the effect on its share price? After the stock repurchase, how many shares of stock would be outstanding?

16.5 CREATING VALUE THROUGH FINANCING DECISIONS

We have established that in a frictionless economic environment capital structure does *not* affect the value of the firm. In the real world there are frictions of many sorts. For both investors and firms, the tax treatment of interest income and expense from debt and equity securities may be different from payments on equity securities. And it is costly to make and enforce contracts specifying the allocation of the firm's cash flows to the holders of different classes of securities under all possible circumstances. Moreover, laws and regulations differ from place to place and change over time. Finding the optimal capital structure for a corporation involves making trade-offs that depend on the particular legal and tax environment the corporation finds itself in.

In view of the frictions that exist in the real world of corporate financing, let us now consider the ways that management might be able to add value through its capital structure decisions. They fall into three categories:

- By its choice of capital structure the firm can reduce its costs or circumvent burdensome regulations. Examples of such costs are taxes and bankruptcy costs.
- By its choice of capital structure the firm may be able to reduce potentially costly conflicts of interest among various stakeholders in the firm: for example, conflicts between managers and shareholders or between shareholders and creditors.
- By its choice of capital structure the firm may be able to provide stakeholders with financial assets not otherwise available to them. The firm, therefore, expands

the opportunity set of financial instruments available and earns a premium for doing so. To the extent that the firm engages in this activity, it is performing the functions of a financial intermediary.

16.6 REDUCING COSTS

By its choice of capital structure the firm can reduce its costs. Examples are taxes, subsidies, and the costs of financial distress. Let us consider each separately.

16.6.1 Taxes and Subsidies

In addition to shareholders and creditors, there is an additional claimant to the *EBIT* generated by a firm, namely, the government tax authority. Some taxes are paid at the corporate level (the corporate income tax) and some at the level of the individual shareholder (personal income taxes on cash dividends and realized capital gains).

A firm's capital structure matters in the presence of corporate income taxes in the United States because interest expense is deductible in computing a firm's taxable income whereas dividends are not. Therefore, by using debt financing the firm can reduce the amount of its cash flow that must be paid to the government tax authority.

For example, consider the two firms of section 16.4, Nodett and Somdett corporations. In the case of Somdett Corporation the *EBIT* flow will be divided among three classes of claimants in order of priority:

- creditors (interest payments)
- government (taxes)
- shareholders (residual)

To illustrate this tax effect, let us consider the case in which there is a corporate tax rate of 34% and *no* personal taxes. The formula for Somdett's total after-tax cash flow to shareholders and creditors combined is:

$$
\begin{aligned}
CF_{Somdett} &= \text{Net Earnings} + \text{Interest} \\
&= .66(EBIT - \text{Interest}) + \text{Interest} \\
&= .66EBIT + .34\text{Interest} \\
&= CF_{Nodett} + .34\text{Interest}
\end{aligned}
$$

Somdett's total market value is maximized by having as much debt as possible. To see why, look at the after-tax cash flows to shareholders and creditors of the firm presented in Table 16.5. It shows that in every possible scenario the after-tax cash flow from Somdett exceeds that from Nodett by $1.088 million.

The market value of Somdett should, therefore, *exceed* the value of Nodett by the present value of the tax savings created by the interest payments on the debt:

Market Value of Somdett = Market Value of Nodett + *PV* of Interest Tax Shield

Under the assumption that Somdett's debt is free of default risk, the present value of the tax shield is equal to the tax rate of 34% times the value of the debt:

PV of Somdett's Interest Tax Shield = .34 × $40 million = $13.6 million

Comparing Somdett to Nodett illustrates the effect of debt financing on the distribution of the firm's value between the shareholders and bondholders on the one hand and the government tax authority on the other. Table 16.6 shows the breakdown.

TABLE 16.5   Probability Distribution of After-Tax Cash Flow for Nodett and Somdett

	Nodett	Somdett	
Possible Levels of EBIT ($ million)	After-Tax Cash Flow ($ million)	Net Earnings ($ million)	After-Tax Cash Flow ($ million)
$5	$3.3	$1.188	$4.388
10	6.6	4.488	7.688
15	9.9	7.788	10.988

TABLE 16.6   Breakdown of Values of Claims for Nodett and Somdett

Claimant	Nodett	Somdett
Creditors	0	$40 million
Shareholders	$66 million	$39.6 million
Government Tax Authority	$34 million	$20.4 million
Total	$100 million	$100 million

For both Somdett and Nodett, the total value of *all* claims (including the government's) is $100 million. In the case of Nodett, the value of the equity is $66 million and the value of the government's tax claim is $34 million. In the case of Somdett, the value of the equity is $39.6 million, the value of the debt is $40 million, and the value of the government's tax claim is only $20.4 million.

If Nodett Corporation (with 1 million shares of stock outstanding) were to announce an issue of $40 million of debt to be used to repurchase and retire common stock, what would be the effect on its share price? After the stock repurchase how many shares of stock would be outstanding?

With all-equity financing the price of a share of Nodett common stock would be $66. If management announced that it was issuing $40 million worth of bonds to retire stock, the stock price would rise to reflect the $13.6 million present value of the interest tax shield. The value of the 1 million shares would rise to $79.6 million or $79.6 per share. The number of shares repurchased and retired would be 502,513 shares ($40 million/$79.6 per share), thus leaving 497,487 shares outstanding. The original owners of the 1 million shares, thus, experience a gain of $13.60 per share. Those who sell shares take the gain in cash; those who keep their shares have an unrealized capital gain. Under these assumptions, management would want to maximize the proportion of debt in the firm's capital structure.

Quick Check 16-7

Mordett is a firm with assets identical to Nodett and Somdett, but with $50 million of risk-free debt outstanding. Assuming a corporate tax rate of 34%, what is Mordett's total value and how is it divided among the equity, the debt, and the government's tax claim? If Nodett Corporation (with 1 million shares of stock outstanding) were to announce an issue of $50 million of debt to be used to repurchase and retire common stock, what would be the effect on the share price? After the stock repurchase, how many shares of stock would be outstanding?

Subsidies

Sometimes *subsidies* are available for a particular form of financing, thus making it advantageous for firms to tilt their capital structure in that direction. An example would be when a governmental body offers to guarantee the debt of a firm that invests in an economically depressed area. For instance, suppose that if Hitek Corporation invests $100 million in Eldesealand, the World Bank will guarantee the debt at no cost to Hitek. Because the guarantee is only available if Hitek uses debt to finance its investment, the wealth of Hitek's shareholders is enhanced by choosing to finance with debt. One would, therefore, expect Hitek to choose debt rather than equity financing.

> **Quick Check 16-8**
> Besides a free government guarantee, what other forms might a subsidy to debt financing take?

16.6.2 Costs of Financial Distress

As the proportion of debt in a firm's capital structure increases, so too does the likelihood that it might default on that debt should future cash flow be less than expected. Firms that are in imminent danger of defaulting on their debt obligations are said to be in *financial distress.* In such circumstances firms usually incur significant costs that reduce the firm's total value below what it would be if there were no debt. These costs include the time and effort of the firm's managers in avoiding bankruptcy and fees paid to lawyers specializing in bankruptcy proceedings. Most important, business can be lost because customers, suppliers, and employees become greatly concerned by the threat of bankruptcy followed by the possibility of a liquidation of the firm.

Taking the costs of financial distress into consideration as well as the tax savings associated with higher levels of debt financing produces a trade-off. To illustrate this trade-off, consider Nodett Corporation again.

We showed in section 16.3.1 that the tax saving associated with issuing debt would lead Nodett's management to want to issue debt to retire shares. If the firm issued $40 million in debt, the stock price would rise from $66 to $79.60; and if it issued $50 million in debt, the stock price would rise to $83 per share. Now suppose that for higher levels of debt, there is a substantial probability that the firm could go bankrupt and incur substantial bankruptcy costs. In that case, if it announced that it was going to issue $60 million in debt to repurchase shares of its common stock, the stock price would fall rather than rise.

Figure 16.1 illustrates the possible effect of higher and higher debt ratios on the price of the firm's stock. The optimal debt ratio is at the point at which the stock price is maximized.

One could imagine a corporation announcing various levels of debt that it intends to issue to repurchase shares, observing the effect of its announcements on the firm's stock price, and then choosing the amount of debt that maximizes the share price. This rarely (if ever) happens in practice. In practice it is very difficult to find the precise mix of debt and equity financing that maximizes the firm's value. Nonetheless, the direction of improvement might be clear for a firm that has far too little or far too much debt.

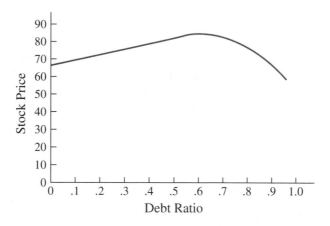

FIGURE 16.1   Effect of the Debt Ratio on Stock Price

Quick Check 16-9

How would a decrease in the costs of financial distress affect corporate capital structure?

16.7 DEALING WITH CONFLICTS OF INTEREST

A second path by which capital structure decisions can create wealth for shareholders is by reducing potentially costly conflicts of interest among various stakeholders in the firm: for example, conflicts between managers and shareholders or between shareholders and creditors. These costs are generally referred to as **agency costs.**[5] Let us consider each separately.

16.7.1 Incentive Problems: Free Cash Flow

In chapter 1 we discussed the problem of conflicts of interest between the managers and shareholders of corporations. When managers have a lot of discretion about how to allocate a firm's cash flows, there is a temptation to use the cash to invest in projects that do not increase the wealth of shareholders. Examples include investments with negative *NPV* that increase the power, prestige, or perks of the managers. In order to mitigate this incentive problem created by free cash flow, a certain amount of debt may be a good thing.

Debt forces management to distribute cash to the firm's debtholders in the form of prescheduled payments of interest and principle. Issuing debt to repurchase shares can, therefore, be a way of creating value for the shareholders by reducing the amount of free cash flow available to managers.

Quick Check 16-10

What incentive problem is created by free cash flow and how does issuing debt help deal with the problem?

---

[5]This term comes from the principal-agent problem discussed in chapter 2, section 3.

16.7.2 Conflicts between Shareholders and Creditors

We have already discussed the costs of financial distress and showed how they limit the optimal amount of debt in a firm's capital structure. But there is also a problem of incentive alignment between shareholders (and managers acting in the interest of shareholders) and creditors in firms with significant amounts of debt. The incentive problem arises because shareholders have little incentive to limit the firm's losses in the event of a bankruptcy. Managers acting in the best interests of shareholders will, therefore, choose to undertake more volatile investments that have the effect of increasing the wealth of shareholders at the expense of the debtholders.

For example, suppose the firm's current assets are worth $100 million. The firm has debt with a face value of $104 million maturing a year from now. Management has the choice of investing all $100 million in riskless T-bills maturing in one year that pay an interest rate of 4%, or investing in a venture that will either be worth $200 million or nothing a year from now.

Even if the probability of the new venture's succeeding is quite small, management (acting in the best interests of shareholders) will choose to undertake the risky venture. The reason is that if management invests in T-bills, then the value of the firm's shares will fall to zero. If the firm has some chance, no matter how small, of being worth more than $104 million a year from now, then the shares will have some value now. The creditors in this example bear all the downside risk of the risky venture, and the shareholders get all of the incremental upside potential for gain.

Thus, creditors face a potential moral hazard problem when they lend to certain firms. In firms with large amounts of debt, *managers might have an incentive to redeploy the firm's assets in a way that actually reduces the firm's total value (the size of the whole pie) in order to increase share price* (the size of the equity piece). Because creditors are aware that under certain adverse circumstances managers might be tempted to do them in, they will limit their lending in the first place.

Quick Check 16-11

What kind of investments might increase the wealth of a firm's shareholders at the expense of the firm's creditors?

16.8 CREATING NEW OPPORTUNITIES FOR STAKEHOLDERS

The third path by which capital structure decisions can create value is by creating opportunities for some of the firm's stakeholders that otherwise would be available to them at greater cost or not at all. The idea is that by altering the claims it issues to stakeholders, the firm can create value without any change in the size or composition of its operating assets.

An example of creating opportunities for stakeholders is the use of pension promises as a form of corporate financing. This may create value for the employees of the firms sponsoring the pension plans by providing a type of retirement benefit not otherwise available to them. By sponsoring a pension plan, the firm's shareholders might gain by obtaining labor services at a lower total present-value cost than otherwise possible. However, the creation of new financial instruments for investors is generally more efficiently done by specialized financial-service firms instead of the typical nonfinancial firm.

> **Quick Check 16-12**
> How might offering a pension plan to its employees increase the wealth of a firm's shareholders?

16.9 FINANCING DECISIONS IN PRACTICE

Financing decisions always involve trade-offs that depend on the specific circumstances of the firm. For example, a firm that pays no corporate income tax because it has been losing money will evaluate the trade-off between tax benefits and costs of financial distress quite differently from a firm that does have to pay taxes. Having considered some of the main ways that financing decisions can generally matter to the owners and to the managers of a firm, let us now consider some specific cases.

Next we describe five different company situations and five different financing methods. We ask the reader to suggest the financing method that seems most appropriate for each situation. Our answers are summarized in Table 16.7.

16.9.1 The Five Companies

Orr Oil Company

Orr Oil Company needs $10 million to finance the test drilling of some land it owns in New Guinea. If the tests are favorable, the company will need an additional $10 million to develop the site. Orr Oil common stock is currently selling at $10 per share, and earnings are $2 per share. Other firms in the oil industry sell at from 10 to 12 times earnings. Orr Oil's debt ratio is 25% compared to an industry average of 40%. Total assets at the last balance sheet date were $105 million.

TABLE 16.7   Match of Financing Methods to Company Circumstances

Company	Financing Method	Reasons
Orr Oil Company	Debt with warrants	If oil is found, then the price of Orr stock will rise and new equity financing will be forthcoming to finance the additional investment needed.
Gormeh Foods, Inc.	Leasing arrangement	No more debt capacity. Leasing provides debt financing secured by the leased equipment.
Bombay Textile Company	Factoring	Rather than having to carry and finance receivables that might be costly to monitor and collect, it is more efficient to sell them to an institution that specializes in collecting receivables.
Holey's Burger Queen	Loans from friends or relatives	Cannot borrow from any institutional lender unless he has more capital of his own. Only those who know him and trust him would provide the capital to him.
Lee Productions	Common stock	Agency costs of debt financing would be very high.

Gormeh Foods, Inc.

This company operates a chain of gourmet food stores in the southeastern United States. It is owned by the five Gormeh sisters, each of whom holds one-fifth of the outstanding stock. The company is profitable, but rapid growth has put it under severe financial strain. The real estate is all heavily mortgaged, the inventory is being used to secure a bank line of credit, and the accounts receivable are being factored. With total assets of $15 million, the company now needs an additional $2 million to purchase equipment for the shipping department.

Bombay Textile Company

Bombay Textile Company manufactures cotton cloth in India and exports about half of it to small clothing companies operating in Singapore. The company's plant and equipment have been financed in part by a loan from the government, and this is its only long-term debt. It pays cash for its inputs, and offers 60 days' credit to its customers in Singapore. Recent growth in its export sales to $5 million per year has created the need for an additional $500,000 in financing.

Holey's Burger Queen

Jarvis Holey has been driving a cab in Philadelphia for five years, and has saved up $50,000 toward the purchase of a Burger Queen franchise. Burger Queen Corporation (BQC) requires that each of its franchisees invest at least $100,000 of equity capital, and then BQC arranges debt financing for the remainder. Holey has just learned that the owner of an existing Burger Queen franchise in his neighborhood wants to sell out for $250,000, and Holey wants to buy the business from him.

Lee Productions

Lee Productions is a small independent movie production company that has recently attracted attention because of the unexpected success of its film, *Red Tide Rising*. There are currently 10 owners, and they want to double the number of new movies the company produces. The company recently incorporated and now wants to raise $10 million from outside investors.

16.9.2 The Five Financing Methods

Loans from Friends or Relatives

This "family" institutional form of financing is appropriate when a business is starting out as a small enterprise, and its future prospects are very uncertain. The success of the business will depend largely on the determination and character of the entrepreneur(s). Only people who know the owners of the firm personally and trust them will lend them money.

Leasing Arrangement

In a leasing arrangement, the lessor provides some real asset—an office, a warehouse, equipment—to the lessee in return for contractually fixed payments over a set period of time. Functionally, leasing is essentially no-recourse debt financing secured by the leased asset. (Check the discussion in section 16.3.2.)

Common Stock

Issuing common stock is a method of financing that is used when the firm is organized as a corporation. It is typically used either when the firm goes public for the first time or when it wants to undertake a major expansion.

Debt with Warrants

Warrants are call options giving their owners the right to buy shares of the issuing company's stock at a fixed price. Warrants are attached to a debt issue when the company envisions a need for raising new equity capital some time before the debt has to be repaid. The debt bears a lower interest rate than it would if it had no warrants attached.

Factoring Receivables

When a company factors its receivables, it sells its accounts receivable (at a discount) to a **factor,** which is a firm that specializes in investing in receivables. Factoring is raising cash by selling a company asset rather than by borrowing or issuing new equity.

16.10 HOW TO EVALUATE LEVERED INVESTMENTS

E-BOOK

16.10

In chapter 6 we studied how to use discounted cash flow concepts to analyze investment decisions such as whether to enter a new line of business or to automate production.[6] We concluded that a firm should accept any project that has a positive net present value. In this section we extend that analysis to show how to take into account a company's capital structure in evaluating investment projects.

We will examine three alternative methods used in practice:

- adjusted present value (*APV*)
- flows to equity (*FTE*)
- weighted average cost of capital (*WACC*)

In principle, all three methods should result in the same estimate of the *NPV* of an investment project. In the following example we will illustrate how this is possible.

16.10.1 Three Valuation Methods Compared

To explain the three methods, let us look at a specific project. The Global Connections Corporation (GCC), which provides satellite communications services to customers around the world, is considering investing in a new satellite to increase its capacity. The current market capitalization of GCC (debt plus equity) is $1 billion. The new investment requires an initial outlay of $100 million, and it is expected to result in increased revenue of $20 million per year. Annual maintenance expense on the new satellite is estimated to be $5 million, and it is expected to last indefinitely. The effective tax rate on GCC's profits is 30%. Its capital structure is 20% debt and 80% equity, based on the market value of the firm. GCC expects to maintain these proportions if the new project is done. The GCC debt is riskless with an interest rate of 8% per year. If the required rate of return on unlevered investments in the satellite communications business is 10% per year, what is the project's *NPV*?

The point of departure is to compute the project's *NPV* if it were financed with 100% equity. Then we will compare how each of the three valuation methods accounts for the impact of the debt financing.

The project's expected after-tax incremental cash flow is the expected revenue of $20 million less maintenance of $5 million multiplied by 1 minus the tax rate:

---

[6]Before proceeding further, the reader is urged to review chapter 6.

$$\text{Unlevered Expected Cash Flow} = (1 - .3) \times (\$20 \text{ million} - \$5 \text{ million})$$
$$= .7 \times \$15 \text{ million} = \$10.5 \text{ million}$$

Using 10% as the market discount rate, we find that the present value of the project is:

$$PV \text{ of Unlevered Investment} = \frac{\$10.5 \text{ million}}{.1} = \$105 \text{ million}$$

Subtracting the initial outlay of \$100 million, we find that the *NPV* of the project is:

$$NPV \text{ without Leverage} = \$105 \text{ million} - \$100 \text{ million} = \$5 \text{ million}$$

Now let us consider the three different methods of adjusting for the effect of debt financing.

The Adjusted Present Value (*APV*) Method

The **adjusted present value** (*APV*) method is based directly on the tax-shield valuation method we used in section 16.6.1. The *APV* of the project is equal to the project's unlevered *PV* plus the present value of the interest tax shields from additional debt financing created by taking the project. By the assumed financing policy for GCC, the amount of new debt created by taking the project is 20% of the increase in the market value of the firm, or $.20 \times APV$ of the project. Because the new debt is perpetual, the present value of the additional tax shield created equals the tax rate times the amount of new debt, or $.30 \times .20 \times APV = .06 \times APV$. So the project's *APV* is:

$$APV = \text{Unlevered } PV + PV \text{ of Incremental Tax Shield}$$
$$= \$105 \text{ million} + .06 \times APV$$
$$= \$105 \text{ million}/.94 = \$111.70 \text{ million}$$

Multiplying .06 times *APV*, we have that the *PV* of the incremental interest tax shield is \$6.70 million. The increase in value to GCC shareholders given by the adjusted net present value (*ANPV*) of the project is:[7]

$$ANPV = \text{Unlevered } NPV + PV \text{ of Incremental Tax Shield}$$
$$= \$5.00 \text{ million} + \$6.70 \text{ million} = \$11.70 \text{ million}$$

The Flows to Equity (*FTE*) Method

In the *FTE* method we calculate the incremental expected after-tax cash flows to the firm's shareholders and then compute *NPV* by discounting using the cost of *equity* capital, k_e, which can be computed using the formula:[8]

$$k_e = k + (1 - t)(k - r)d \tag{16.1}$$

---

[7]In situations where the dollar amount of new debt to be issued as a result of doing the project is specified, one can compute the *PV* of the incremental tax shield, and thus *ANPV*, directly without computing *APV* first as done here. It is common terminology to shorten *ANPV* as used here to *APV*, but the context should make the meaning unambiguous.

[8]This formula applies only if the debt of the firm is riskless in terms of default. It is not correct to extend it to risky debt by simply applying the formula using either the *promised* or the *expected* debt rate as a substitute for the riskless rate. The correct valuation of the tax shield when the debt has default risk is complex and beyond the level of this book.

where

k = the cost of capital with no leverage

t = the tax rate

r = the rate of interest on the debt, which is assumed to be default free

d = market debt-to-equity ratio

Since GCC maintains a capital structure with a debt-to-equity ratio, $d = .20/.80 = .25$, we have by substitution into equation 16.1 that the cost of equity capital in our case is:

$$k_e = .10 + (1 - .30) \times (.10 - .08) \times .25 = 0.1035.$$

The expected incremental after-tax cash flow to GCC's *shareholders* from the satellite project, *CFS*, is:

$$CFS = \text{Unlevered Expected Cash Flow} - \text{After-tax Interest Expense}$$
$$= \$10.5 \text{ million} - (1 - t) \times r \times D = \$10.5 \text{ million} - .70 \times .08 \times D$$
$$= \$10.5 \text{ million} - .056D$$

where D denotes the increase in GCC debt outstanding after the project is undertaken. We find that the increase in the present value of equity outstanding, E, is:

$$E = CFS/k_e = \$101.45 \text{ million} - .5411D$$
$$= \$101.45 \text{ million} - .5411 \times .25 \times E = \$101.45 \text{ million} - .1353E$$
$$= \$101.45 \text{ million}/1.1353 = \$89.36 \text{ million}$$

and $D = \$22.34$ million because GCC financing policy has $D = .25E$. The amount of new equity to be issued to finance the project is $100.0 million – $22.34 million = $77.66 million. Therefore, the *NPV* to the shareholders from undertaking the project is $89.36 million – $77.66 million = $11.70 million, the same amount derived in the adjusted present value method.

The Weighted Average Cost of Capital (WACC) Method

With this method, we estimate the project's *PV* by discounting the expected *unlevered* after-tax cash flow using a **weighted average cost of capital** (*WACC*), and then we subtract the full $100 million investment outlay.

The formula for *WACC* is:

$$WACC = k_e \frac{1}{1+d} + (1 - t)r \frac{d}{1+d} \tag{16.2}$$

In words, the *WACC* is a weighted average of the cost of equity capital and the after-tax cost of debt. The weights are the market values of equity and debt as a fraction of the present value of the project. Thus, in the satellite project, the *WACC* is:

$$WACC = .1035 \times .80 + .7 \times .08 \times .20 = 0.094$$

The *NPV* of the project is computed as the expected unlevered after-tax annual cash flow discounted at the *WACC* less the $100 million initial investment outlay:

$$NPV = \frac{\$10.5}{0.094} - \$100 = \$111.7 - \$100.0 = \$11.7 \text{ million}$$

Quick Check 16-13
Assume that GCC has a market debt-to-firm-value ratio of 30% instead of 20%, and that this is the ratio for the satellite project to be financed. Assuming all else is the same as in the text, use the *APV* method to find the satellite project's *NPV*. Then use the *FTE* and *WACC* methods to verify that you get the same estimate of *NPV* as when you use the *APV* method.

Summary

- External financing subjects a corporation's investment plans more directly to the discipline of the capital market than internal financing does.

- Debt financing in its broadest sense includes loans and debt securities, such as bonds and mortgages, as well as other promises of future payment by the corporation, such as accounts payable, leases, and pensions.

- In a frictionless financial environment in which there are no taxes or transaction costs, and contracts are costless to make and enforce, the wealth of shareholders is the same no matter what capital structure the firm adopts.

- In the real world there are a number of frictions that can cause capital structure policy to have an effect on the wealth of shareholders. These include taxes, regulations, and conflicts of interest between the stakeholders of the firm. A firm's management might, therefore, be able to create shareholder value through its capital structure decisions in one of three ways: (1) by reducing tax costs or the costs of burdensome regulations, (2) by reducing potential conflicts of interest among various stakeholders in the firm, and (3) by providing stakeholders with financial assets not otherwise available to them.

- There are three alternative methods used in estimating the net present value of an investment project to take account of financial leverage: the adjusted present value method, the flows to equity method, and the weighted average cost of capital method.

Key Terms

- internal financing   418
- external financing   418
- residual claim   419
- collateral   420

- agency costs   430
- factor   434
- adjusted present value   435
- weighted average cost of capital   436

Answers to Quick Check Questions

Quick Check 16-1 *How does the need for external financing impose market discipline on a corporation?*

ANSWER: Outside providers of funds are likely to want to see detailed plans for the use of the funds and will want to be convinced that proposed investments will produce sufficient future cash to justify the expenditure.

Quick Check 16-2 *In what way is preferred stock like debt, and in what way is it like equity?*

ANSWER: Preferred stock is like debt in that there is a contractually specified fixed payment that must be made before the holders of common stock can be paid anything. It is like equity in that failure to pay the promised dividends on preferred stock does not trigger a default.

Quick Check 16-3 *Would you expect the interest rate on a secured loan to be higher or lower than the rate on an otherwise identical unsecured loan? Why?*

ANSWER: Lower. The risk of loss to the lender in the event of default is lower.

Quick Check 16-4 *Should a long-term lease be considered debt financing or equity financing?*

ANSWER: It has elements of both. The fixed payments are like debt. But because the residual value of the asset stays with the lessor, a lease might also be considered a form of equity financing.

Quick Check 16-5 *Suppose AmeriPens Corporation's pension assets were worth only $300 million. If its pension liability still had a present value of $400 million, what would be its shareholders' equity?*

ANSWER: Shareholders' equity would be only $500 million. Total assets would be $1.3 billion and total liabilities $800 million.

Quick Check 16-6 *Mordett is a firm with assets identical to Nodett and Somdett, but with $50 million of risk-free debt outstanding (interest rate of 8% per year) and 500,000 shares of stock. What is Mordett's probability distribution of EPS? What is the price of a share? If Nodett Corporation (with 1 million shares of stock outstanding) were to announce an issue of $50 million of debt to be used to repurchase and retire common stock, what would be the effect on the share price? After the stock repurchase, how many shares of stock would be outstanding?*

ANSWER: The expected *EPS* of Mordett is $12, its standard deviation $8.165, and its beta 2. The price of a share of Mordett will be $100. Although its expected *EPS* is higher than Somdett's and Nodett's, its risk is higher too. The increase in riskiness exactly offsets the increase in expected *EPS*. If Nodett issued $50 million of debt to repurchase shares, it would have no effect on the stock price. It would use the $50 million to repurchase 500,000 shares, thus leaving 500,000 shares outstanding.

		Nodett	Mordett	
State of the Economy	EBIT	EPS (1 million shares)	Net Earnings	EPS (500,000 shares)
Bad business	$5 million	$5	$1 million	$2.00
Normal business	10	10	6	12.00
Good business	15	15	11	22.00
Mean	10	10	6	12.00
Standard deviation		4		8.165
Beta	1.0	1.0		2.0

Probability Distribution of *EBIT* and *EPS* for Mordett

Quick Check 16-7 *Mordett is a firm with assets identical to Nodett and Somdett, but with $50 million of risk-free debt outstanding. Assuming a corporate tax rate of 34%, what is Mordett's total value and how is it divided among the equity, the debt, and the govern-*

ment's tax claim? If Nodett Corporation (with 1 million shares of stock outstanding) were to announce an issue of $50 million of debt to be used to repurchase and retire common stock, what would be the effect on the share price? After the stock repurchase, how many shares of stock would be outstanding?

ANSWER: Mordett's $50 million debt creates an interest tax shield with a present value of $17 million. The total market value of Mordett's debt plus equity will, therefore, be $83 million ($66 million + $17 million). Mordett's debt will have a value of $50 million, its equity $33 million, and the government's tax claim $17 million. By issuing $50 million in debt, Nodett's management could increase the wealth of shareholders by $17 million. The price of a share would increase from $66 to $83. The number of shares repurchased would be 602,410 ($50 million/$83 per share), leaving 397,590 shares of stock outstanding.

Quick Check 16-8 *Besides a free government guarantee, what other forms might a subsidy to debt financing take?*

ANSWER: Government might offer to pay part of the interest on the debt or to forgo part of the repayment of principal.

Quick Check 16-9 *How would a decrease in the costs of financial distress affect corporate capital structure?*

ANSWER: Corporations would make greater use of debt financing.

Quick Check 16-10 *What incentive problem is created by free cash flow and how does issuing debt help deal with the problem?*

ANSWER: When managers have a lot of discretion about how to allocate a firm's cash flows, they may be tempted to use the cash to invest in projects that do not increase the wealth of shareholders. Debt forces management to distribute cash to the firm's debtholders in the form of prescheduled payments of interest and principle.

Quick Check 16-11 *What kind of investments might increase the wealth of a firm's shareholders at the expense of the firm's creditors?*

ANSWER: Risky investment projects. The creditors bear much of the downside risk of such projects, whereas most of the upside potential goes to the shareholders.

Quick Check 16-12 *How might offering a pension plan to its employees increase the wealth of a firm's shareholders?*

ANSWER: By fulfilling a need of the employees, it might lower the present value of the firm's labor costs.

Quick Check 16-13 *Suppose that GCC had a market debt-to-firm-value ratio of 30% instead of 20%, and that this is the ratio for the satellite project to be financed. Assuming all else is the same, use the APV method to find the satellite project's NPV. Then use the FTE and WACC methods to verify that you get the same estimate of NPV.*

ANSWER: Using the *APV* method, we add to the project's unlevered *NPV* the value that is created through the debt financing. Because 30% of the *APV* of the project will be new debt, there will be an additional tax shield created with a value equal to the amount of new debt times the tax rate of .3, or .09 *APV*. So the project's *APV* and A*NPV* are

$$APV = \$105 \text{ million}/.91 = \$115.4 \text{ million}$$

$$ANPV = \text{Unlevered } NPV + PV \text{ of Incremental Tax Shield}$$

$$= \$5.0 \text{ million} + \$10.4 \text{ million} = \$15.4 \text{ million}$$

In the *FTE* method with $d = .30/.70 = .429$, we calculate $k_e = 0.1060$.

$$CFS = (\text{Unlevered Expected Cash Flow} - \text{After-tax Interest Expense})$$
$$= \$10.5 \text{ million} - .056D$$

The increase in the *PV* of equity is computed by discounting the expected cash flow to shareholders using the cost of equity capital:

$$E = CFS/k_e = \$99.06 \text{ million} - .5283D$$
$$= \$99.06 \text{ million} - .5283 \times .429E$$
$$= \$99.06 \text{ million} - .2264E$$
$$= \$80.77 \text{ million}$$

and $D = .429E = \$34.63$ million.

When we subtract the additional $65.37 million of equity capital to be invested in the new project by shareholders, we find that the *NPV* is the same $15.4 million that we estimated using the *APV* method. To use the *WACC* method, we first compute:

$$WACC = .106 \times .70 + .7 \times .08 \times .30 = 0.0910$$

The *NPV* of the project is computed as the expected unlevered after-tax annual cash flow discounted at the *WACC* less the $100 million initial investment outlay:

$$NPV = \frac{\$10.5}{0.0910} - \$100 = \$115.4 - \$100 = \$15.4 \text{ million}$$

Questions and Problems

TEMPLATE

16.7–16.8

1. ***Debt-Equity Mix***
   Divido Corporation has decided to issue $20 million of bonds and to repurchase $20 million worth of its stock.
   a. What will be the impact on the price of its shares and on the wealth of its share-holders? Why?
   b. Assume that Divido's *EBIT* has an equal probability of being either $20 million, $12 million, or $4 million. Show the impact of the financial restructuring on the probability distribution of earnings per share in the absence of taxes. Why does the fact that the equity becomes riskier not necessarily affect shareholder wealth?

2. ***Leasing***
   Plentilease and Nolease are virtually identical corporations. The only difference between them is that Plentilease leases most of its plant and equipment whereas Nolease buys its plant and equipment and finances it by borrowing. Compare and contrast their market-value balance sheets.

3. ***Pension Liabilities***
   Europens and Asiapens are virtually identical corporations. The only difference between them is that Europens has a completely unfunded pension plan, and Asiapens has a fully funded pension plan. Compare and contrast their market-value balance sheets. What difference does the funding status of the pension plan make to the stakeholders of these two corporations?

4. Comfort Shoe Company of England has decided to spin off its Tango Dance Shoe Division as a separate corporation in the United States. The assets of the Tango Dance Shoe Division have the same operating risk characteristics as those of Comfort. The capital structure of Comfort has been 40% debt and 60% equity in terms of market values and is considered by management to be optimal. The required return on Comfort's assets (if unlevered) is 16% per year, and the interest rate that the firm (and the division) must currently pay on their debt is 10% per year.

   Sales revenue for the Tango Shoe Division is expected to remain indefinitely at last year's level of $10 million. Variable costs are 55% of sales. Annual depreciation is $1 million, which is exactly matched each year by new investments. The corporate tax rate is 40%.
   a. How much is the Tango Shoe Division worth in unlevered form?
   b. If the Tango Shoe Division is spun off with $5 million in debt, how much would it be worth?
   c. What rate of return will the shareholders of the Tango Shoe Division require?
   d. Show that the market value of the equity of the new firm would be justified by the earnings to the shareholders.

5. Based on the foregoing problem, suppose that Foxtrot Dance Shoes makes custom-designed dance shoes and is a competitor of Tango Dance Shoes. Foxtrot has similar risks and characteristics as Tango except that it is completely unlevered. Fearful that Tango Dance Shoes may try to take over Foxtrot in order to control its niche in the market, Foxtrot decides to lever the firm to buy back stock.
   a. If there are currently 500,000 shares outstanding, what is the value of Foxtrot's stock?
   b. How many shares can Foxtrot buy back and at what value if it is willing to borrow 30% of the value of the firm?
   c. What if it is willing to borrow 40% of the value of the firm?
   d. Should Foxtrot borrow more?

6. Hanna-Charles Company needs to add a new fleet of vehicles for its sales force. The purchasing manager has been working with a local car dealership to get the best value for the company dollar. After some negotiations, a local dealer has offered Hanna-Charles two options: (1) a three-year lease on the fleet of cars or (2) 15% off the top to purchase outright. Option 2 would cost Hanna-Charles company about 5% less overall versus the lease option.
   a. What are the advantages and disadvantages of leasing?
   b. Which option should the purchasing manager at Hanna-Charles pursue and why?

7. Havem and Needem companies are exactly the same, differing only in their capital structures. Havem is an unlevered firm issuing only stocks whereas Needem issues stocks and bonds. Neither firm pays corporate taxes. Havem pays out all of its yearly earnings in the form of dividends and has 1 million shares outstanding. Its market capitalization rate is 11% and the firm is currently valued at $180 million. Needem is identical except that 40% of its value is in bonds and has 500,000 shares outstanding. Needem's bonds are risk free and pay a coupon of 9% per year and are rolled over every year.
   a. What is the value of Needem's shares?
   b. As an investor forecasting the upcoming year, you examine Havem and Needem using three possible states of the economy that are all equally likely: normal, bad, and exceptional. Assuming the earnings will be the same, one-half, and one and one-half respectively, draw out a distribution table that shows the earnings and the earnings per share for both Havem and Needem.

8. Using the foregoing example, let us now assume that Havem and Needem must pay taxes at the rate of 40% annually. Given the same possible outcomes as previously,

a. What are the possible after tax cash flows for Havem and Needem?

b. What are the possible values of the shares?

c. If one was not risk averse, which company would that person invest in?

9. The Griffey-Lang Food Company faces a difficult problem. In management's effort to grow the business, it accrued a debt of $150 million whereas the value of the company is only $125 million. Management must come up with a plan to alleviate the situation in one year or face certain bankruptcy. Also upcoming are labor relations meetings with the union to discuss employee benefits and pension funds. Griffey-Lang at this time has three choices it can pursue: (1) Launch a new, relatively untested product that if successful (probability of .12) will allow G-L to increase the value of the company to $200 million. (2) Sell off two food production plants in an effort to reduce some of the debt and the value of the company, thus making it even (.45 probability of success), or (3) do nothing (probability of failure = 1.0).

a. As a creditor, what would you like Griffey-Lang to do and why?

b. As an investor?

c. As an employee?

17

Finance and Corporate Strategy

OBJECTIVE

■ To show how to use finance theory to analyze strategic decisions, such as acquiring or merging with another firm, spinning off a business unit as a separate firm, and investing in real options.

CONTENTS

This chapter shows how to apply finance theory to strategic decision making in firms. In chapter 1 we concluded that both in theory and in practice the criterion for the managers of a firm in evaluating strategic decisions should be the maximization of the wealth of the company's owners. In chapters 6 and 16, we showed how to apply discounted cash flow analysis to estimate an investment's contribution to the wealth of a firm's owners. In this chapter we extend that analysis in two ways to examine two basic aspects of corporate strategy. First, we analyze corporate decisions regarding mergers, acquisitions, and spinoffs. Then we show how option theory can be applied to evaluate management's ability to time the start of an investment project, to expand it, or to abandon it after it has begun.

17.1 MERGERS AND ACQUISITIONS

When one firm acquires a controlling interest in another it is called an **acquisition;** when two firms join to form a new firm, it is called a **merger.** Under the criterion for good management of maximizing current shareholders' wealth, there are essentially three reasons for considering acquiring or merging with another company: synergy, taxes, or bargains. Let us consider each.

Synergy is said to exist if: by combining two companies, the value of the operating assets of the combined firm will exceed the sum of the values of the operating assets of the two companies taken separately. Such synergy will occur if there are economies of scale in the production or distribution of the products of two or more firms. It can also occur through the elimination of duplicate efforts in management, in technology, or in research and development. In essence, the value goes up because the factors of production are more efficiently organized in the combined firm.

For example, in 1995 in the United States there was a wave of mergers among banks. The mergers were largely explained by the executives involved and by outside analysts as attempts to realize cost savings through consolidation of various banking activities and elimination of expensive duplicative technology. This interpretation was corroborated by the postmerger closing of many branch offices and the elimination of many jobs in the merged banks.

Another potential source of increased value to shareholders from mergers and acquisitions is a *reduction in the taxes paid to the government* by the companies involved in the merger. Even in the absence of opportunities to reduce production and distribution costs through true operating synergies, corporations can sometimes reduce the combined present values of their tax payments through a merger. For example, under certain conditions, a profitable firm may acquire an unprofitable firm and thereby reduce its taxes by exploiting the unprofitable firm's tax-loss carryforwards.

Unlike mergers motivated by synergies, solely tax-motivated business reorganizations add no net value to society at large. The market value of a firm reflects its value to the private sector. Because the firm pays taxes (or may pay taxes in the future), there is an additional value of the firm to society in the form of the present value of its tax payments. The sum of the market value in the private sector and this "shadow" value is the total value of the firm to society.

In the case of synergy, the value of the firm to society is increased with a corresponding increase in both the market and shadow social values of the firm. However, where a reduction in taxes is the sole reason for a merger, the value of the combined firm to society is just equal to the sum of the values to society of the two firms. This combination does not increase the total value to society, but it does redistribute the total between the shareholders of the firms and the tax-paying public.[1]

A third reason for mergers and acquisitions is to take advantage of *bargains* in the stock market. If the firm to be acquired has a market value that is less than its intrinsic value, then by acquiring the firm, the management of the acquiring firm can increase its stockholders' wealth.

There are two distinct reasons why a firm could be selling for less than intrinsic value. The first is that *relative to the acquiring firm's information set,* the stock market is not *efficient* in the sense discussed in chapter 7. That is, the management of the acquiring firm believes that it has information such that if this information were widely known, the market value of the firm to be acquired would be higher than its acquisition cost. If this is the principal reason for the acquisition, then the management's behavior is identical to that of a security analyst whose job it is to identify mispriced securities.

A second reason why a firm could be selling for less than its intrinsic value is that the firm to be acquired is currently being mismanaged. That is, through either incompetence or malevolence, the current management is not managing the firm's

---

[1]Recent changes in U.S. tax laws have greatly limited the use of a firm's net operating losses to offset profits in entities that acquire the firm after the losses occurred.

resources so as to maximize the market value of the firm. Unlike the first reason, this reason is completely consistent with an efficient capital market.

Quick Check 17-1
What are three value-increasing reasons for mergers or acquisitions?

Notable by its absence among the three valid reasons for acquisitions is *diversification*—the acquisition of another firm for the sole purpose of reducing the volatility (variance) of the firm's operations. Although diversification is a frequently cited reason for an acquisition, it is often not the real reason. More often than not, it will be for one of the three reasons already given.

However, if diversification *is* the real reason, then the acquisition route will in general be an *inefficient* way to achieve it. Finance theory and a large amount of empirical evidence lead to the following conclusion:

> The combined market value of two firms that merge solely in order to achieve diversification of risks is no more than the sum of the market values of the two separate firms.

In other words, in the area of corporate diversification the whole is worth no more than the sum of its parts.

The argument in favor of corporate diversification is often presented by analogy with an individual investor where we have seen in chapter 12 that diversification is quite important. However, this type of argument simply illustrates the pitfalls of treating the firm as if it were an individual household with its own preferences rather than as an economic organization designed to serve specific economic functions.

An intuitive explanation of why the market values of two firms will not be increased through a merger even though the combined firm may have a smaller total risk (variance) than the individual firms is as follows: In order for investors to be willing to pay a higher price for the combined firm than they were willing to pay for the two firms separately, *the act of combining the two firms must provide a service to the investors that they were previously unable to obtain.*

However, prior to the combination, investors could purchase shares of either or both firms in any mix they want. In particular, in the case of a merger, investors can purchase the shares of both firms in the same ratio implicit in the combined firm. Hence, investors could achieve for themselves (prior to the merger) the same amount of diversification (of the risks of both firms) as is provided by the combined firm. Therefore, the merger provides no new diversification opportunities to investors. For that reason, investors would not pay a premium for the combined firm. Indeed, in the absence of diversification benefits, the combined firm should sell for *less* than the sum of the values of the two separate firms simply because there are costs to doing the merger.

Firm diversification can also *hurt* market value by reducing the investment choices available to investors and by reducing the amount of information available to investors. After consolidation of the two firms, investors have fewer choices for portfolio construction than they did before consolidation. For example, prior to a merger, investors could hold any amounts of each of the two merging firms. After the merger, the only way that investors can hold firm 1 is to invest in the combined firm, which means they must *also* invest in firm 2. Indeed, they can only invest in firm 1 if they are willing to invest in firm 2 in the relative proportions of the post-merger firm. The consolidated accounting and other public statements of the merged firm will typically contain less total information than was provided to investors in the individual filings when the companies were separate. Unless this increase in "opaqueness" permits the firm to improve its profitability, the reduction in information is likely to cause a reduction in firm value.

Note that this negative aspect of firm diversification applies even in a frictionless world of no transactions costs and where the merger takes place on terms where no premium above market value is paid for the acquired firm by the acquiring firm. In the real world, the acquiring firm must usually pay a premium above the market value to acquire a firm. The premium can range from 5% to more than 100% with an average somewhere around 20%. A natural question to ask is: Why do the owners of the firm to be acquired demand a premium for their shares?

Although there are several possible explanations, one that is consistent with our previous analyses is as follows: If the acquiring firm's management is behaving optimally, then the reason for its making a takeover attempt must be one of the three reasons discussed at the outset of this section. Because any one of these three reasons will increase the value of the acquiring firm's shares, the acquired firm's shareholders are demanding compensation for providing the means for this increase in value.

How this potential increase in value is shared between the acquiring and acquired firms' shareholders cannot be determined in general (as is the usual case for bilateral bargaining), but almost certainly, the acquired firm's shareholders will receive some positive share. Of course, the acquired firm's shareholders do not know what the acquiring firm's management believes the value of the acquired firm is. Hence, it might appear that no consolidation could be consummated because whatever price is offered, clearly, the acquiring firm's management believes it is worth more and, therefore, the acquired firm's shareholders should demand more.

However, the fact that the acquiring firm shareholders believe it is worth more does not mean that it is, indeed, worth more. Their beliefs may be wrong. Hence, at a high enough price above market, the acquired firm's shareholders will take the sure premium, and let the acquiring firm take the risk (and earn the possible reward) that its information is sufficiently superior to the market's that the acquired firm is still a "bargain."

Whether or not the acquired firm's shareholders or the acquiring firm's shareholders come out ahead on these takeovers is still an open empirical question. However, it is clear that acquiring another firm for the *sole purpose of diversification* is a losing proposition for the acquiring firm because it must pay a premium for a firm whose acquisition promises no increase in market value even if it is purchased without paying a premium over the market price prior to the announcement of the takeover.

Although the premium paid over market value for the acquired firm is usually the principal cost of an acquisition, there are other costs as well that can frequently be substantial. In an uncontested merger, there are legal costs and management's time that could be spent on other activities. There are uncertainties created for the acquired firm's management, employees, suppliers, and customers that could affect the operations of that firm during the negotiations and subsequent transition. Of course, if the merger is contested, then litigation costs will be substantial.

Even if it is decided that firm diversification is warranted, then achieving this diversification through acquisition is very costly. If it is costly for your shareholders to diversify their portfolios by direct purchase of individual firms' shares, then this service almost surely can be provided at less cost by mutual funds, investment companies, and other financial intermediaries. If, because of management risk aversion or debt capacity or supplier concerns, it is decided that the volatility or total risk of the firm should be reduced, then this can be achieved much more efficiently (i.e., at lower cost) by simply purchasing a portfolio of equities and fixed-income securities in which no premium is paid over market and no significant transactions costs are incurred. In general, the risk management objectives of a firm can be implemented more efficiently by using a growing array of financial technologies and specialized products provided by financial-service firms.

If diversification is desired simply to provide cash flow from these operations to fund growth investments in current operations, then it is almost certainly less costly to issue securities and raise the funds in the capital markets. Don't pay $12 to $20 to acquire $10 in cash!

In summary, there are three types of reasons for a firm to consider the acquisition of another firm:

1. synergy
2. taxes
3. the firm to be acquired is a bargain

They all have in common that the acquisition should increase the value of the acquiring firm's current stockholders' wealth.

The possibility of a takeover of one firm by another is an important check that serves to force managements of publicly owned firms to pursue policies that are (at least approximately) value maximizing.

Simple diversification by the firm is, in general, *not* an important objective for the management of the firm. Hence, if pursued, then a minimum of resources should be used to achieve it. Specifically, the acquisition of another firm is a costly way to achieve diversification.

Beware: Diversification is frequently given as the reason for acquiring a firm by the acquiring firm's management. If carefully investigated (most of the time), the meaning of *diversification* as used is not the one described here, and the real reasons will be one or more of the three (proper) reasons for making an acquisition.

Quick Check 17-2
Why is diversification of risk a poor reason for two firms to merge?

17.2 SPIN-OFFS

A spin-off occurs when a corporation divests itself of one or more of its business units and creates a separate company with assets, liabilities, and stock of its own. For example, in 1997 Pepsico spun off its restaurant division, giving it $1 billion (at book value) in assets and $1.2 billion (at book value) in liabilities.[2] What reasons might there be for a corporation to spin off a business unit?

From the perspective of value maximization it pays to spin off a business unit if the sum of the expected market values of the separate businesses—often called the firm's "breakup" value—exceeds the firm's value as a single entity. The reasoning

---

[2]This implies a negative book net worth, which is possible in an accounting sense, but not in the market-value sense.

is identical to the reasoning behind a merger or acquisition discussed in section 17.1. If there is *no* synergy between the business units comprising a multidivisional firm, then the business units are more valuable as separate firms.

There is another possible reason for a multidivisional firm to spin off business units into separate firms, even if the sum of the value of the assets after the breakup does *not* exceed the value of the firm as a single entity. If the firm has a lot of long-term, fixed-income liabilities, then it may be possible for management to increase the wealth of shareholders at the expense of the firm's creditors by breaking the firm up into two or more separate firms.

To see how this is possible, let us consider Multicorp, a firm with two divisions, each of which has assets worth $1 billion. Assume that the returns on each of the separate divisions are quite risky, but that they are perfectly negatively correlated, so that in combination Multicorp has a riskless return. The riskless rate of interest is 5% per year, and that is also the expected equilibrium rate of return on each of the two divisions. Assume that Multicorp has $1 billion of long-term debt, which also bears an interest rate of 5% per year.

Before the spin-off, the market value of the debt is $1 billion because there is no uncertainty about the firm's earning a risk-free 5% rate of return. However, suppose that Multicorp spins off one of its divisions as a new firm, Unicorp, with $1 billion in assets and $0.5 billion of Multicorp's debt. The combined market value of the two separate firms is still $2 billion, but the debt will fall in market value because there is now a possibility of default for each of the separate firms. The decline in the value of the debt accrues to the shareholders of Multicorp, who are now the shareholders of both Multicorp and Unicorp.

Note that the transfer of wealth from Multicorp's creditors to its shareholders is only with respect to the existing debt. After the spin-off, lenders would require an interest-rate premium that is large enough to compensate them for the risk of default.

> **Quick Check 17-3**
> Suppose that instead of being perfectly negatively correlated, Multicorp's two business units were uncorrelated. Would it still increase shareholder wealth to spin off Unicorp as a separate firm?

17.3 INVESTING IN REAL OPTIONS

E-BOOK

17.3

To this point we have ignored an extremely important aspect of many (if not most) corporate investment opportunities—the ability of managers to delay the start of a project, or once started, to expand it or to abandon it. Failure to take account of these *real* options (as contrasted with financial options) will cause an analyst evaluating the project to underestimate its *NPV*.

The movie industry provides a good example of the importance of real-option values in evaluating investment projects. Often a movie studio will buy the rights to a movie script and then wait to decide if and when to actually produce it. Thus, the studio has the option to wait. Once production starts, and at every subsequent step in the process, the studio has the option to discontinue the project in response to information about cost overruns or changing tastes of the movie-going public.

Another very important managerial option in the movie business is the option of the film studio to make sequels. If the original movie turns out to be a success, then the studio has the exclusive right to make additional movies with the same title and characters. The option to make sequels can be a significant part of a movie project's total value.

There is a fundamental similarity between the options in investment projects and call options on stocks: In both cases the decision maker has the *right* but not the *obligation* to buy something of value at a future date.

Recognizing the similarity between call options and managerial options is important for three reasons:

- It helps in structuring the analysis of the investment project as a sequence of managerial decisions over time.
- It clarifies the role of uncertainty in evaluating projects.
- It gives us a method for estimating the option value of projects by applying the quantitative models developed for valuing call options on stocks.

17.3.1   An Example

An example may help to clarify how the analogy between call options and managerial options can help in analyzing an investment project. Consider a film studio's decision about whether to purchase the movie rights to a book currently being written by a best-selling author.

Assume the author charges $1 million for the exclusive right to make a movie out of her novel that is scheduled for publication a year from now. If the novel is a success as a book, then the film studio will make a movie out of it, but if the book is a commercial failure the studio will not exercise its right to make it into a movie. Figure 17.1 shows this investment project as a *decision tree*.

The studio's current decision is whether to pay the $1 million price the author demands. This is represented by a decision box at the bottom of the tree. The top branch coming out of the first decision box corresponds to a decision to pay the $1 million for the movie rights and the right branch to a decision not to pay the $1 million.

The circle attached to the upper decision branch represents an event not under the control of management: whether the book is a commercial success. There are two branches coming out of this event circle: The upper branch corresponds to the possibility that the novel is a success, and the lower branch to the possibility that the novel is a failure. Each has a probability of .5. Analysts at the studio estimate that if the book is a success, then the *NPV* of the movie a year from now will be $4 million. If, however, the book is a failure then the *NPV* of the movie a year from now will be -$4 million.

Note that attached to the right side of each branch extending from the event circle is another decision box representing the decision management must make about whether to actually produce the movie. If the project were analyzed without taking account of management's ability to abandon it a year from now, then the project would be rejected. This is because the project's expected present value today would be zero at *any* cost of capital no matter how low. Management would surely not spend $1 million to buy the rights to make a movie that has an expected present value of zero.

But this is a misspecification of the investment opportunity. Because management has the *right* and not the *obligation* to make the movie, the possible payoffs a year from now are an *NPV* of $4 million if the book turns out to be a success and an *NPV* of 0 if the novel is a failure. This payoff distribution has an expected value of $2 million. As long as the cost of capital used to discount this $2 million expected *NPV* to the present is less than 100% per year, the project's expected present value will exceed the $1 million cost of the movie rights to the book. Thus, we see that it

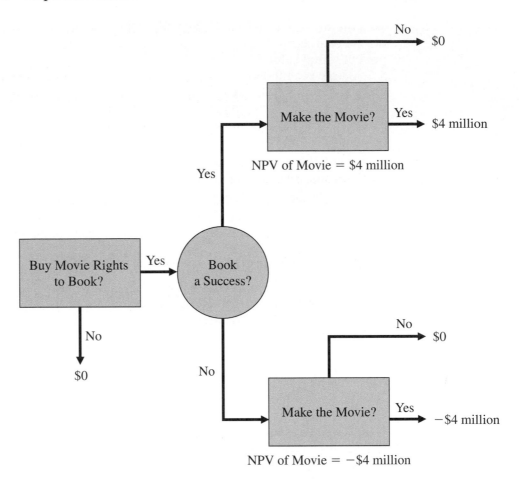

FIGURE 17.1   Decision Tree for Movie Project

is extremely important in structuring the analysis of the project to take account of management's ability to change course in the future.

  We also learn something about the impact of uncertainty on the project's *NPV* from thinking about it in terms of options. For example, suppose the range of possible future *NPV*s doubled whereas the expected value remained 0: $8 million if the book is a success and –$8 million if it is a failure. Because management will not make the movie if the book is a failure, the worst possible outcome is still only 0 and not –$8 million. Because management will choose to abandon the project if the book turns out to be a failure, the expected *NPV* a year from now increases from $2 million to $4 million. Thus, the project's expected *NPV* doubles as a result of the doubling in the range of possible future outcomes. In this sense, an increase in the uncertainty about the project's future payoffs increases its value.

  How important is the value of managerial options as a component of an investment project's total value? The answer depends on the type of project, but it is difficult to think of any investment project where management has *no* discretion to alter its plans once the project has begun. It is especially important to take option value into account when considering investments in research and development. The use of the financial theory of options in capital budgeting has been adopted by at least one large pharmaceutical company (see Box 17.1). In general, the greater the uncertainty about future outcomes of the project, the greater the need to account explicitly for any options.

> ### BOX 17.1
>
> ### *Option Analysis at Merck*
>
> In an interview with the editors of the *Harvard Business Review* in 1994, Judy Lewent, the CFO of the pharmaceutical firm Merck, described her company's extensive use of option analysis in capital budgeting. As just one example, Merck frequently enters into business relationships with universities in order to gain access to early-stage research projects. The contractual agreements are often structured so that Merck will make an initial payment to the university followed by a series of progress payments that are contingent on the outcome of the research. Merck analyzes these contracts using the tools of option-pricing theory.

> ### Quick Check 17-4
>
> Recognizing the similarity between call options and managerial options is important for three reasons. What are they?

17.3.2 Applying the Black-Scholes Formula to Value Real Options

Now that we have recognized the importance of taking account of the option value in investment opportunities, how do we quantify that value? One way is to apply the Black-Scholes formula.

For example, suppose that a firm, Rader Inc., is considering acquiring another firm, Target Inc. Let us assume they are both 100% equity-financed firms; that is, neither firm has any debt outstanding. Each firm has 1 million shares of common stock outstanding that can be freely bought and sold in a competitive market. The current market value of Target's assets is $100 million and the standard deviation of the proportional change in its value is .20. Suppose that Target's management offers Rader an option to acquire 100% of Target's shares a year from now for $106 million. The riskless interest rate is 6% per year.

If the option costs $6 million, is the investment worthwhile?

From Rader's perspective this is a capital budgeting decision. The initial outlay is the $6 million cost of the option to acquire Target's assets a year from now. To determine the value of this option we can use the same valuation models developed in chapter 15 to price a European call option on a stock. Applying the Black-Scholes formula:[3]

$$C = N(d_1)S - N(d_2)Ee^{-rT}$$

$$d_1 = \frac{\ln(S/E) + (r + \sigma^2/2)T}{\sigma\sqrt{T}}$$

$$d_2 = d_1 - \sigma\sqrt{T}$$

---

[3]Because in this case the exercise price of the option equals the future value of the underlying firm compounded at the riskless interest rate, we can use the linear approximation to the Black-Scholes formula:

$$\frac{C}{S} \approx .4\sigma\sqrt{T}.$$

where

C = price of the option

S = price of the stock

E = exercise price

T = time to maturity of the option in years

σ = standard deviation of the annualized continuously compounded rate of return on the stock

			Option Price Calculation Table			
S	*E*	*r*	*T*	*d*	*σ*	*Result*
100	106	.05	1	0	.2	C = $8 million

The value of the option is approximately $8 million. The *NPV* of the investment opportunity is $2 million—the option's value to Rader less its $6 million cost—so it is worthwhile.

Now let us consider how option theory can help to evaluate an investment opportunity that does not involve the *explicit* purchase of an option but does contain a managerial option. Suppose Electro Utility has the opportunity to invest in a project to build a power-generating plant. In the first phase an initial outlay of $6 million is required to build the facility to house the equipment. In the second phase, one year from now, equipment costing $106 million must be purchased. Suppose that viewed from today's perspective the value of the completed plant a year from now is a random variable with a mean of $112 million and a proportional standard deviation of .2.

Suppose that we do a conventional DCF analysis of this investment opportunity. At a discount rate of *k,* the present value of the completed plant is $112 million/ $(1 + k)$. Because the $106 million investment outlay for power-generating equipment is known for certain, its present value is computed by discounting at the riskless rate. If that rate is 6%, then the present value of the outlay is $100 million. In addition, the initial outlay to build the facility is $6 million. Thus, the project's *NPV* is given by

$$NPV = \$112 \text{ million}/(1 + k) - \$100 \text{ million} - \$6 \text{ million}$$
$$= \$112 \text{ million}/(1 + k) - \$106 \text{ million}$$

The *NPV* of the project so computed will be negative for any *k* greater than 5.66%, which is even less than the riskless rate of interest. For example, if the *k* is 12%, then the present value of the completed plant is $100 million, and the project's computed *NPV* is −$6.0 million.

But to do this is to ignore the important fact that management has the right to abandon the project a year from now. In other words, management will invest an additional $106 million in the second stage of the project *only if* the value of the plant turns out to be more than $106 million.[4]

How can we evaluate this investment taking management's flexibility into account? The answer is that we can apply the same method we just applied in evaluating Rader Inc.'s option to buy Target Inc. Although the circumstances are somewhat different, the two situations have the same structure and even the same payoffs.

To see this, note that by undertaking the first phase of the project, Electro Utility would in effect be paying $6 million to "buy an option" that will mature in one

---

[4]We assume for simplicity that the $6 million initial outlay is lost completely if the plant is not completed. That is, the salvage value is zero.

year. The option is to undertake phase two of the project, and its "exercise price" is $106 million. The present value of the completed project is $100 million.

The Black-Scholes formula says that this option is worth approximately $8 million. The project, therefore, has a positive *NPV* of $2 million instead of the negative *NPV* computed when we ignored management's option to discontinue the project after the first year.

Our conclusion is that taking management's flexibility explicitly into account increases a project's *NPV.* Moreover, from the theory of option pricing, we know that the value of flexibility increases with the volatility of the project.

Again, consider the example of Electro Utility. Suppose that the value of the power-generating plant is actually more volatile than was at first thought. Instead of the standard deviation being .20, suppose it is .40. This makes the investment project *more* attractive. Applying the Black-Scholes formula, we find that the option value is now $16 million. The project's *NPV* is, therefore, $10 million, rather than the $2 million computed earlier.

Virtually *all* future investment opportunities can be viewed as call options because firms can almost always wait before making their initial outlay and can decide *not* to proceed with it. The amount of time the firm can wait is analogous to the option's time to expiration; the initial outlay is analogous to the exercise price; and the present value of the project's expected future cash flows is analogous to the price of the underlying stock. The project's conventionally computed *NPV* is, thus, analogous to the option's intrinsic value, that is, what it would be worth if it were expiring immediately. Conventional *NPV* understates the value of the project because it ignores the option's time value.

Quick Check 17-5

What is the option value of the Electro Utility investment project if the volatility of the power-generating plant is .3 instead of .2?

Summary

- There are three valid reasons for a merger or acquisition: (1) to reduce operating costs through synergies, (2) to reduce taxes, and (3) to take advantage of bargains in the stock market.

- Diversification of risk is a poor reason for two firms to merge, because in general shareholders can diversify their portfolios on their own; they do not need the firm to do it for them.

- An extremely important feature of investment projects is the ability of managers to delay the start of a project, or once started, to expand it or to abandon it. Failure to take account of these management options will cause an analyst evaluating the project to underestimate its *NPV.*

- Recognizing the similarity between financial options and real managerial options is important for three reasons: (1) It helps in structuring the analysis of the investment project as a sequence of managerial decisions over time, (2) it clarifies the role of uncertainty in evaluating projects, and, (3) it gives us a method for estimating the option value of projects by applying the quantitative models developed for valuing call options on stocks.

Key Terms

- acquisition   443
- merger   443
- synergy   444

Answers to Quick Check Questions

Quick Check 17-1   *What are three value-increasing reasons for mergers or acquisitions?*

ANSWER: There are three valid reasons for a merger or acquisition:
- to reduce operating costs through synergies
- to reduce taxes
- to take advantage of bargains in the stock market

Quick Check 17-2   *Why is diversification of risk a poor reason for two firms to merge?*

ANSWER: Diversification of risk is a poor reason for two firms to merge, because shareholders can diversify their portfolios on their own or through financial-service firms; they do not need the firm to do it for them.

Quick Check 17-3   *Suppose that instead of being perfectly negatively correlated, Multicorp's two business units were uncorrelated. Would it still increase shareholder wealth to spin off Unicorp as a separate firm?*

ANSWER: Yes. When the two units are combined, the creditors face less risk of default than when they are separate entities. Therefore, the debt has a higher market value and the equity a lower market value when the business units are combined. Spinning off Unicorp would transfer wealth from the creditors to the shareholders of Multicorp.

Quick Check 17-4   *Recognizing the similarity between call options and managerial options is important for three reasons. What are they?*

ANSWER:
- It helps in structuring the analysis of the investment project as a sequence of managerial decisions over time.
- It clarifies the role of uncertainty in evaluating projects.
- It gives us a method for estimating the option value of projects by applying the quantitative models developed for valuing call options on stocks.

Quick Check 17-5   *What would happen to the net present value of the investment project if the standard deviation of the value of the power-generating plant is .3 instead of .2?*

ANSWER:

$$\frac{C}{S} \approx .4\sigma\sqrt{T}$$

The inputs to the model are:

$$S = \$100 \text{ million}, T = 1 \text{ year}, \sigma = .3$$

The value of the option is, therefore, approximately $12 million. The *NPV* of the investment is $6 million (the option's value to Rader less its $6 million cost), and it is worthwhile.

Questions and Problems

1. Hampshire-Cathaway (H-C), a large established corporation with no growth in its real earnings, is considering acquiring 100% of the shares of Trilennium Corporation, a young firm with a high growth rate of earnings. The acquisitions analysis group at H-C has produced the following table of relevant data:

	Hampshire-Cathaway	*Trilennium*
Earnings per share	$3.00	$2.00
Dividend per share	$3.00	$0.80
Number of shares	200 million	10 million
Stock price	$30	$20

   H-C's analysts estimate that investors currently expect growth of about 6% per year in Trilennium's earnings and dividends. They assume that with the improvements in management that H-C could bring to Trilennium, its growth rate would be 10% per year with no additional investment outlays beyond those already expected.
   a. What is the expected gain from the acquisition?
   b. What is the *NPV* of the acquisition to H-C shareholders if it costs an average of $30 per share to acquire all of the outstanding shares?
   c. Would it matter to H-C's shareholders whether the shares of Trilennium stock are acquired by paying cash or H-C stock?

2. A film studio, Nadir Productions, has to decide whether to make a movie out of the book *Planetary Wars,* to which it has acquired the rights. The studio's experts estimate that the production costs for the film will be $30 million and the subsequent cash flows net of distribution costs and taxes to be received a year later have an expected present value of $35 million with a volatility of .5. The studio uses a discount rate of 20% in deciding whether to accept such projects.
   a. What is the conventionally computed *NPV* of the project?
   b. At this point a new MBA on the CFO's staff suggests that they have not taken account of the option to produce a sequel to the movie. If the movie succeeds at the box office, then surely they will want to make *Planetary Wars II* the following year.
   c. Draw a decision tree for the project.
   d. Assuming that the cost estimates and the distribution of future cash flows for the sequel are the same as for the original movie, how does taking account of the option to make a sequel affect the desirability of the project?
   e. Suppose that Nadir's executives believe that a successful film of this genre can have as many as three sequels. What is the *NPV* of the project taking account of this?

3. Suppose Microstuff Corporation has the opportunity to invest in a new computer technology that would use television sets to connect to the Internet. In the first phase an initial outlay of $100 million is required for a pilot project to determine the feasibility of the technology. In the second phase, one year from now, an additional investment of $1 billion would be required. Suppose that viewed from today's perspective the value of the project a year from now is a random variable with a mean of $1.1 billion and a standard deviation of .20. The required rate of return on the project is 10% per year. Use the Black-Scholes option-pricing model to help determine if this is a worthwhile investment.

Suggested Readings

Chapter 2

Allen, F., and D. Gale. *Financial Innovation and Risk Sharing.* Cambridge: MIT Press, 1994.

Bodie, Z., and D. Crane. "The Transformation of Banking: A Functional Perspective." *Harvard Business Review,* March–April 1996.

Crane, D., K. Froot, S. Mason, R. C. Merton, A. Perold, Z. Bodie, E. Sirri, and P. Tufano. *The Global Financial System: A Functional Perspective.* Boston: Harvard Business School Press, 1995.

Ibbotson, R. G., and G. P. Brinson. *Global Investing: The Professional's Guide to the World Capital Markets.* New York: McGraw-Hill, 1993.

Logue, D. E. *The WG & L Handbook of Financial Markets.* Cincinnati: Warren, Gorham & Lamont, 1995.

Mason, S. C., R. C. Merton, A. F. Perold, and P. Tufano. *Cases in Financial Engineering: Applied Studies of Financial Innovation.* Upper Saddle River, N.J.: Prentice-Hall, 1995.

Merton, R. C., "A Functional Perspective of Financial Intermediation." *Financial Management* 24, Summer 1995.

Miller, M. *Financial Innovations & Market Volatility.* Cambridge: Blackwell, 1991.

Chapter 3

Fraser, L. M., and A. Ormiston. *Understanding Financial Statements.* 5th Ed. Upper Saddle River, N.J.: Prentice-Hall, 1998.

Lee, C. F. *Financial Analysis and Planning: Theory and Application.* Reading, Mass.: Addison-Wesley, 1985.

Rappaport, A. *Creating Shareholder Value: The New Standard for Business Performance.* New York: Free Press, 1986.

Vander Werde, J., and S. F. Maier. *Managing Corporate Liquidity: An Introduction to Working Capital Management.* New York: John Wiley & Sons, 1985.

Chapter 4

Fisher, I. *The Theory of Interest: As Determined by Impatience to Spend Income and Opportunity to Invest It.* 1930. New York: Augustus M. Kelley, 1965.

Hishleifer, J. "On the Theory of Optimal Investment Decision." *Journal of Political Economy* 66, August 1958.

Chapter 5

Bodie, Z., and D. Crane. "Personal Investing: Advice, Theory, and Evidence." *Financial Analysts Journal,* January–February 1998.

Hirshleifer, J. *Investment, Interest and Capital.* Englewood Cliffs, N.J.: Prentice-Hall, 1970.

Modigliani, F., and R. Brumberg. "Utility Analysis and the Consumption Function: An Interpretation of Cross-Section Data." *Post Keynesian Economics.* Ed. K. Kurihara. New Brunswick, N. J.: Rutgers University Press, 1954.

Winger, B. J., and R. R. Frasca. *Personal Finance: An Integrated Planning Approach.* 4th Ed. Upper Saddle River, N.J.: Prentice-Hall, 1997.

Chapter 6

Bierman, H., and S. Smidt. *The Capital Budgeting Decision.* 8th Ed. New York: Macmillan, 1992.

Chapter 7

Fama, E. F. "Efficient Capital Markets: A Review of Theory and Empirical Work." *Journal of Finance* 25, May 1970.

Fama, E. F. "Efficient Capital Markets II." *Journal of Finance* 46, December 1991.

Meulbroek, L. K. "An Empirical Analysis of Insider Trading." *Journal of Finance* 47, December 1992.

Samuelson, P. A. "Proof That Properly Anticipated Prices Fluctuate Randomly." *Industrial Management Review* 6, Spring 1965.

Chapter 8

Bodie, Z., A. Kane, and A. Marcus. *Investments,* 4th Ed. Boston: Irwin/McGraw-Hill, 1999.

Fabozzi, F. J., and T. D. Fabozzi, eds. *The Handbook of Fixed Income Securities.* 4th Ed. Burr Ridge, Ill.: Irwin, 1995.

Sundaresan, S. *Fixed Income Markets and Their Derivatives.* Cincinnati: Southwestern College Publishing, 1997.

Chapter 9

Bodie, Z., A. Kane, and A. Marcus. *Investments.* 4th Ed. Boston: Irwin/McGraw-Hill, 1999.

Copeland, T., T. Koller, and J. Murrin. *Valuation: Measuring and Managing the Value of Companies.* 2nd Ed. New York: John Wiley & Sons, 1994.

Miller, M., and F. Modigliani. "Dividend Policy, Growth, and the Valuation of Shares." *Journal of Business* 34, October 1961.

Miller, M., and M. S. Scholes. "Dividends and Taxes." *Journal of Financial Economics* 6, December 1978.

Chapter 10

Arrow, K. J. "The Role of Securities in the Optimal Allocation of Risk Bearing." *Review of Economic Studies* 31, April 1964. Trans. of 1953 article in French.

Beaver, W. H., and G. Parker, eds. *Risk Management: Problems and Solutions.* Stanford: Stanford University Press, McGraw-Hill, 1995.

Bodie, Z., A. Kane, and A. Marcus. *Investments.* 4th Ed. Boston: Irwin/McGraw-Hill, 1999.

Merton, R. C., and Z. Bodie. "On the Management of Financial Guarantees." *Financial Management* 21, Winter 1992.

Shapiro, A. C., and S. Titman. "An Integrated Approach to Corporate Financial Management." *Midland Corporate Finance Journal* 3, Summer 1985.

Chapter 11

Bodie, Z., A. Kane, and A. Marcus. *Investments.* 4th Ed. Boston: Irwin/McGraw-Hill, 1999.

Breeden, D. T. "Futures Markets and Commodity Options: Hedging and Optimality in Incomplete Markets." *Journal of Economic Theory* 32, April 1984.

Figlewski, S., with K. John and J. Merrick. *Hedging with Financial Futures for Institutional Investors: From Theory to Practice.* Cambridge: Ballinger, 1986.

Smithson, C. H., and C. W. Smith with D. S. Wilford. *Managing Financial Risk,* Burr Ridge, Ill.: Irwin, 1995.

Chapter 12

Bodie, Z. "On the Risk of Stocks in the Long Run." *Financial Analysts Journal,* May–June 1995.

Bodie, Z., R. C. Merton, and W. Samuelson. "Labor Supply Flexibility and Portfolio Choice in a Life-Cycle Model." *Journal of Economic Dynamics and Control* 15, 1992.

Markowitz, H. "Portfolio Selection." *Journal of Finance* 7, March 1952.

Markowitz, H. *Portfolio Selection: Efficient Diversification of Investments.* New York: John Wiley & Sons, 1959.

Merton, R. C. "An Analytical Derivation of the Efficient Portfolio Frontier." *Journal of Financial and Quantitative Analysis* 10, September 1972.

Merton, R. C. *Continuous-Time Finance* Rev. ed. London: Basil Blackwell, 1992.

Tobin, J. "Liquidity Preference as Behavior Towards Risk." *Review of Economic Studies* 25, February 1958.

Chapter 13

Bodie, Z., A. Kane, and A. Marcus. *Investments.* 4th Ed. Boston: Irwin/McGraw-Hill, 1999.

Lintner, J. "The Valuation of Risk Assets and the Selection of Risky Investments in Stock Portfolios and Capital Budgets." *Review of Economics and Statistics* 47, February 1965.

Merton, R. C. "An Intertemporal Capital Asset Pricing Model." *Econometrica* 41, September 1973.

Merton, R. C. "A Reexamination of the Capital Asset Pricing Model." *Studies in Risk and Return.* Eds. J. Bicksler and I. Friend. Cambridge: Ballinger, 1977.

Mossin, J. "Equilibrium in a Capital Asset Market." *Econometrica* 35, October 1966.

Ross, S. A. "Arbitrage Theory of Capital Asset Pricing." *Journal of Economic Theory* 13, December 1976.

Sharpe, W. "Capital Asset Prices: A Theory of Market Equilibrium." *Journal of Finance* 19, September 1964.

Chapter 14

Brown, K. C., and D. J. Smith. *Interest Rate and Currency Swaps: A Tutorial.* Charlottesville, Va.: Institute of Chartered Financial Analysts, 1995.

Hull, J. C. *Options, Futures, and Other Derivatives.* 3rd Ed. Upper Saddle River, N.J.: Prentice-Hall, 1997.

Jarrow, R., and S. Turnbull. *Derivative Securities.* Cincinnati: Southwestern College Publishing, 1996.

Stoll, H., and R. E. Whaley. *Futures and Options.* Cincinnati: Southwestern College Publishing, 1993.

Chapter 15

Black, F., and M. S. Scholes. "The Pricing of Options and Corporate Liabilities." *Journal of Political Economy* 81, May–June 1973.

Merton, R. C. "Theory of Rational Option Pricing." *Bell Journal of Economics and Management Science* 4, Spring 1973.

Merton, R. C. "An Analytic Derivation of the Cost of Loan Guarantees and Deposit Insurance: An Application of Modern Option Pricing Theory." *Journal of Banking and Finance* 1, June 1977.

Merton, R. C. "On the Pricing of Contingent Claims and the Modigliani-Miller Theorem." *Journal of Financial Economics* 5, November 1977.

Merton, R. C. "Applications of Option-Pricing Theory: Twenty-Five Years Later." *Les Prix Nobel 1997.* Stockholm: Nobel Foundation. Rpt. in *American Economic Review,* June 1998.

Scholes, M. S. "Derivatives in a Dynamic Environment." *Les Prix Nobel 1997.* Stockholm: Nobel Foundation. Rpt. in *American Economic Review,* June 1998.

Chapter 16

Chew, D. *The New Corporate Finance: Where Theory Meets Practice.* New York: McGraw-Hill, 1993.

Harris, M., and A. Raviv. "The Theory of Capital Structure." *Journal of Finance* 46, March 1991.

Merton, R. C. "On the Pricing of Corporate Debt: The Risk Structure of Interest Rates." *Journal of Finance* 29, May 1974.

Miles, J., and R. Ezzel. "The Weighted Average Cost of Capital, Perfect Capital Markets and Project Life: A Clarification." *Journal of Financial and Quantitative Analysis* 15, September 1980.

Modigliani, F., and M. Miller. "The Cost of Capital, Corporation Finance, and the Theory of Investment." *American Economic Review* 48, June 1958.

Myers, S. C. "Interactions of Corporate Finance and Investment Decisions: Implications for Capital Budgeting." *Journal of Finance* 29, March 1974.

Taggart, R. "Secular Patterns in the Financing of U.S. Corporations." Ed. B. Freedman. *Corporate Capital Structure in the United States.* Chicago: University of Chicago Press, 1985.

Chapter 17

Coase, R. H. "The Nature of the Firm." *Economica* 4, 1937.

Coase, R. H. *The Firm, the Market, and the Law.* Chicago: University of Chicago Press, 1988.

Dixit, A., and R. Pindyck. *Investment under Uncertainty.* Princeton: Princeton University Press, 1994.

Jensen, M. "Agency Costs of Free Cash Flow, Corporate Finance and Takeovers." *American Economic Review* 76, May 1986.

Jensen, M., and W. H. Meckling. "Theory of the Firm: Managerial Behavior, Agency Costs, and Ownership Structure." *Journal of Financial Economics* 3, October 1976.

Kester, W. C. "Today's Options for Tomorrow's Growth." *Harvard Business Review,* March–April 1984.

Merton, R. C., and S. C. Mason. "The Role of Contingent Claims Analysis in Corporate Finance." *Recent Advances in Corporate Finance.* Ed. E. I. Altman and M. G. Subrahmanyam. Homewood, Ill.: Richard D. Irwin, 1985.

Myers, S. C. "Finance Theory and Financial Strategy." *Interfaces* 14, January–February 1984.

Scholes, M. S., and M. A. Wolfson. *Taxes and Business Strategy: A Planning Approach.* Englewood Cliffs, N.J.: Prentice-Hall, 1992.

Trigerorgis, L. *Real Options: Managerial Flexibility and Strategy in Resource Allocation.* Cambridge: MIT Press, 1996.

Glossary

acquisition The acquiring by one firm of a controlling interest in another.

actuaries Professionals trained in mathematics and statistics who gather and analyze data and estimate the probabilities of illness, accidents, and other such risks.

adjusted present value A method of calculating a project's net present value that takes into account the value that is created by the project's debt financing.

adverse selection A type of incentive problem in which those who purchase insurance against risk are more likely to be at risk than the general population.

after-tax interest rate The interest rate earned after paying income taxes.

alpha The difference between the average rate of return on a security or portfolio of securities and the rate predicted by the Capital Asset Pricing Model.

amortization The process of paying off a loan's principal gradually over time.

amortization schedule A table that shows the portions of loan payments that go toward principal and interest over the period of the loan.

annual percentage rate The annualized rate of interest on loans and savings accounts, with a certain frequency of compounding (contrast with effective annual rate).

annualized capital cost The annual cash payment that has a present value equal to the initial outlay.

arbitrage The purchase and immediate sale of equivalent assets in order to earn a sure profit from a difference in their prices.

asset Anything that has economic value.

asset allocation Choosing how much to invest in major asset classes such as stocks, bonds, and cash.

at-the-money The state of an option whose exercise price is equal to the current price of the underlying security.

before-tax interest rate The interest rate earned without taking into account income taxes.

beta A measure of a security's market-related risk, showing how much a security's rate of return tends to change when the return on the market portfolio changes; risk as measured in the CAPM.

binomial option pricing model A widely used model for pricing options that assumes that in each period the underlying security can take only one of two possible values.

Black-Scholes formula The most widely used option pricing model, named for its developers, Fischer Black and Myron Scholes. It assumes a lognormal distribution and continuous adjustment of the replicating portfolio.

book value The value of an asset as listed on its company's officially recognized balance sheet.

break-even point The sales volume at which either net profit or the net present value of a project is zero.

call option An instrument that gives its holder the right to buy some asset at a specified price on or before some specified expiration date. Sometimes shortened to *call*.

capital asset pricing model An equilibrium theory based on the mean-variance theory of portfolio selection.

capital gain The gain in the market price of an asset over the period it is held.

capital loss The loss in the market price of an asset over the period it is held.

CAPM The capital asset pricing model.

capital market The market for long-term debt and equity securities.

capital market line In the capital asset pricing model, the risk–return trade-off line between standard deviation and expected return which represents the best risk–reward combinations available to all investors.

caps Upper limits placed on compensation under an insurance contract.

cash budget A short-term plan to forecast cash outflows and inflows.

cash cycle time The number of days between the date a firm must start to pay cash to its suppliers and the date it begins to receive cash from its customers.

cash dividend A distribution of cash to the shareholders of a corporation.

cash settlement The settlement of a forward or option contract in cash rather than by delivery of the underlying commodity or security.

collateral The asset pledged as security for a debt.

collateralization Giving the lender the right to seize specific business assets in the event of default. It is widely used to reduce the incentive problems associated with lending.

commercial banks Financial intermediaries that perform two functions: taking deposits and making loans.

commercial loan rate The rate charged by banks on loans made to businesses.

compound interest Interest paid on interest earned in previous periods.

compounding The process of going from present value to future value.

confidence interval A certain range of values for a random variable with a specified probability of occurrence.

continuous probability distribution A random variable has such a distribution when it can take any numerical value within its range.

copayments A fraction of a loss that an insured party must cover from his or her own resources.

corporation A firm that is a legal entity distinct from its owners.

correlation A statistical measure of the degree to which two random variables tend to move together.

cost of capital The capitalization rate used to discount a project's cash flows in computing its net present value.

counterparty Also called *counterpart*. The party on the other side of a contract.

coupon bond A bond that obligates the issuer to make periodic payments of interest (called *coupon payments*) to the bondholder for the life of the bond.

credit risk The risk that the counterparty to a contract will default.

current yield A bond's annual coupon divided by its price.

decision tree A graphic representation of the sequence of decisions and possible consequences involved in making a strategic decision.

deductible An amount of money that the insured party must pay out of his or her own resources before receiving any compensation from the insurer.

default risk The possibility that some portion of the interest or the principal on a fixed-income instrument will not be paid in full.

defined-benefit pension plan A type of pension plan in which the employee's pension benefit is determined by a formula that takes into account years of service and, in most cases, wages or salary.

defined-contribution pension plan A type of pension plan in which the employer and usually the employee too make regular contributions and the beneficiary receives the value of the assets plus the accumulated earnings.

derivatives Financial instruments whose payoffs are defined in terms of the prices of other assets.

discounted cash flow analysis Making decisions based on the calculation of net present value of future cash flows.

discounted dividend model Any model that computes the value of a share of stock as the present value of its expected future cash dividends.

diversifiable risk The part of a security's risk that can be eliminated by combining it with other risky assets.

diversification principle The theory that by diversifying across risky assets investors can sometimes achieve a reduction in their overall risk exposure with no reduction in their expected return.

diversifying A method of reducing risk by holding small amounts of many risky assets instead of concentrating in only one or a few risky assets.

dividend policy A corporation's policy regarding paying out cash to its shareholders.

dividend yield A stock's annualized dollar dividend divided by its price, expressed as a percentage.

effective annual rate An equivalent interest rate on a loan or savings account if interest were compounded only once per year (contrast with APR).

efficient markets hypothesis The proposition that an asset's current price fully reflects all publicly available information about future economic fundamentals affecting the asset's value.

efficient portfolio A portfolio that offers the investor the highest possible expected rate of return at a specified level of risk.

efficient portfolio frontier A graph showing the best combinations of portfolio risk and return than an investor can attain by diversifying. See also *capital market line.*

exchange rate The price of one currency in terms of another.

exclusions Losses that might seem to meet the conditions for coverage under the insurance contract but are specifically excluded.

exercise price The price that must be paid for the underlying asset in an option contract. Also called *strike price.*

expectations hypothesis The theory that the forward price of an asset equals its expected future spot price.

expected rate of return The sum over all possible outcomes of each possible rate of return multiplied by its probability.

expiration date The last date by which an option can be exercised.

external financing Funding that originates from outside a firm, usually from lenders or investors.

face value The promised cash payment on a bond's maturity date.

feasible consumption plan A life-cycle spending plan that has a present value less than or equal to the present value of the household's lifetime resources.

finance The study of how people allocate resources over time in an uncertain environment.

financial futures Futures contracts in which the underlying asset is a stock, bond, or other financial asset.

financial guarantees Insurance against credit risk.

financial system The set of markets and other institutions used for financial contracting and the exchange of assets and risks.

fixed-income instruments Also called *debt instruments*. They promise to pay fixed sums of cash in the future.

flow of funds The flows of saving, investment, and external financing among different economic sectors over a period of time.

forward contract An agreement between two parties to exchange some item in the future at a prearranged price.

forward price The delivery price of an item specified at the time a forward contract is entered into that makes the value of the contract equal to zero.

fundamental value The price well-informed investors would pay for an asset in a free and competitive market.

future value The amount of money an investment will grow to at some date in the future by earning interest at a compound rate.

futures contract A standardized forward contract that is traded on some organized exchange.

growth annuity An annuity in which the cash flows from an investment grow at a constant rate.

growth stocks Stocks that have relatively high price/earnings ratios because their future investments are expected to earn rates of return in excess of the market capitalization rate.

hedge ratio The fraction of one unit of an asset needed in a portfolio designed to replicate the payoffs from a derivative security (such as a call option) on that asset.

hedgers Parties who reduce their exposure to risk by giving up part of the potential for gain.

hedging A method of transferring risk in which an action taken to reduce one's exposure to loss also causes one to give up possible gains.

human capital The present value of one's future labor income.

immediate annuity A periodic cash flow that starts immediately, as in a savings plan or a lease.

implied dividend A dividend that can be inferred from the futures price of a stock index.

implied volatility The value of volatility that makes the observed market price of the option equal to the value computed using the option pricing formula.

index options Calls and puts on a stock index or any other economic index.

indexing An investment strategy of matching the performance of some index.

index-linked bonds Bonds whose interest and principal are denominated in terms of the basket of goods and services used to compute the cost of living in a particular country.

insuring Paying some amount for sure to avoid the possibility of incurring larger losses.

intangible assets Assets whose physical embodiment is irrelevant to their value.

interest-rate arbitrage Borrowing at a lower rate and lending at a higher rate when default risk is held constant.

interest-rate cap An interest-rate insurance policy in which the maximum interest rate is guaranteed.

interest-rate floor A guarantee of a minimum interest rate on a loan.

internal financing Funding that originates within a firm, including retained earnings, accrued wages, and accounts payable.

intertemporal budget constraint The restriction that the present value of one's lifetime consumption spending cannot exceed present value of one's lifetime resources.

in-the-money The state of an option that would have positive value if the current time were its expiration date.

intrinsic value Also called *tangible value*. The hypothetical value of an option if it were exercised immediately.

investment banks Firms whose primary function is to help businesses, governments, and other entities raise funds to finance their activities.

Law of One Price The idea that, in a competitive market, if two assets are equivalent, they will have the same market price.

liability Any claim on the assets of an entity other than owner's equity.

life annuities Contracts that promise periodic payments for as long as the purchaser lives.

limited liability A feature of common stock whereby if a firm is liquidated and the proceeds from the sale are insufficient to pay off all the firm's debts, the creditors cannot assess the common stockholders for more money to meet this shortfall.

liquidity The relative ease and speed with which an asset can be converted into cash.

long position In a financial contract, the term used to describe the position of the buyer.

margin call A demand from a broker or a counterparty for an investor to add more collateral.

market capitalization rate Also called *risk-adjusted discount rate*. The expected rate of return that anonymous investors require in order to be willing to invest in the specified risky asset.

market portfolio A portfolio that holds all assets in proportion to their outstanding total market values.

market-weighted stock indexes A type of index that represents the price performance of a portfolio that holds each stock in proportion to its total market value.

maturity For fixed-income instruments, the length of time until the repayment of the entire amount borrowed.

mean   In probability distribution, the sum over all possible outcomes of each possible rate of return multiplied by its probability.

merger   The joining of two firms into a single firm.

minimum-variance portfolio   The portfolio of risky assets with the lowest possible variance.

money market   The market for short-term debt (less than one year).

moral hazard   A situation in which having insurance against some risk causes the insured party to take greater risk or to take less care in preventing the event that gives rise to the loss.

mortgage rate   The interest rate that home buyers pay on the loans they take to finance their homes.

mutual fund   A portfolio of stocks, bonds, or other assets purchased in the name of a group of investors and managed by a professional investment company or other financial institution.

net present value   The amount by which a project is expected to increase the wealth of a firm's current shareholders.

net worth   The value of an entity's assets minus liabilities.

nominal future value   The future value of a sum not adjusted for inflation.

nominal interest rate   An interest rate not adjusted for inflation (contrast with real interest rate).

nominal prices   Prices in terms of some currency not adjusted for inflation.

nondiversifiable risk   The portion of a portfolio's risk that cannot be eliminated by diversification.

normal distribution   The most widely used continuous probability distribution, typified by its bell-shaped curve.

opportunity cost of capital   The rate that could be earned on capital if it were invested elsewhere in assets of the same risk.

optimal combination of risky assets   The portfolio of risky assets that is mixed with a riskless asset to achieve the most efficient portfolio.

option   The right to purchase or sell something at a fixed price in the future.

ordinary annuity   An annuity in which the cash flows start at the end of the current period rather than immediately.

out-of-the-money   The state of an option that would be worthless if the current time were its expiration date.

over-the-counter markets   Also called *off-exchange markets*. Networks for trading assets that have no central location.

par bonds   Coupon bonds with a market price equal to their face value.

partnership   An unincorporated firm with two or more owners who share the equity in the business.

payoff diagram   A chart that shows the relation between the value of a derivative at expiration and the price of its underlying asset.

percent-of-sales method   A planning forecast that assumes that most of the items on a company's income statement and balance sheet will maintain the same ratio to sales in the next year as in the previous year.

permanent income   The constant level of consumption spending that has a present value equal to one's human capital.

perpetuity   A stream of cash flows that lasts forever.

portfolio selection   The process of making choices about how to invest one's wealth.

portfolio theory   Quantitative analysis for risk management.

precautionary saving   Saving that is motivated by the desire to have enough wealth to cover unanticipated expenses in the future.

premium bond   A bond whose market price is higher than its face value.

present value   The sum in hand today that would be equivalent in value to some specified future payments.

price/earnings multiple   The ratio of a firm's stock price to its earnings per share.

principal-agent problem   A situation arising when agents do not make the same decisions that the principals would have made if the principals knew what the agents knew and were making the decisions themselves.

probability distributions   The statistical term for a random variable's set of possible values and associated probabilities.

purchasing-power parity   The theory that exchange rates adjust so as to maintain the same inflation-adjusted price of a representative basket of goods and services in different currency areas.

pure discount bonds   Also called *zero-coupon bonds*. Bonds that promise a single payment of cash at some date in the future, called the maturity date.

put   The option to sell a specified item at a fixed price.

put option   An instrument that gives its holder the right to sell some asset at a specified price on or before some specified expiration date.

put-call parity relation   The price relation among the price of the put, the price of the call, the price of the underlying security, and the present value of the exercise price.

rate of return on capital   Capital's productivity expressed as a percentage per year.

real future value   The future value adjusted for inflation.

real interest rate   The interest rate corrected for inflation.

real interest-rate parity   The theory that the expected real interest rate on riskless loans is the same all over the world.

real prices   Prices corrected for inflation.

reinvestment rate   The interest rate at which funds invested for more than a single period can be reinvested.

residual claim   The type of claim represented by common stock, in which the owners of common stock are entitled to any assets of the firm left over after meeting all the firm's other financial obligations.

risk aversion   A measure of one's willingness to pay to reduce one's exposure to risks.

risk exposure   The degree to which an entity's welfare is affected by a source of risk.

risk management   The process of formulating the benefit-cost trade-offs of risk reduction and deciding on the course of action to take.

risk-adjusted discount rate   Also called *market capitalization rate*. The expected rate of return that investors require in order to be willing to invest in a project.

risk-management process   A systematic attempt to analyze and deal with risk.

security market line   In the capital asset pricing model, the relation showing that the risk premium on any asset is equal to its beta multiplied by the risk premium on the market portfolio.

self-financing investment strategy   An investment strategy that requires only an initial cash outlay with no subsequent cash infusions.

sensitivity analysis   A method of testing a project's worthiness even if some of the underlying variables turn out to be different from what was originally assumed.

share repurchase   A method of cash distribution by a corporation to its shareholders in which the corporation pays cash to buy shares of its stock in the stock market, thereby reducing the number of shares outstanding.

short position   In a financial contract, the term used to describe the position of the seller.

simple interest   The interest rate times the original principal, not including interest on interest.

sole proprietorship   A firm in which the assets and liabilities of the firm are the personal assets and liabilities of the proprietor.

speculators   Investors who take positions that increase their exposure to risks in the hope of increasing their wealth.

spot price   The price specified for immediate delivery of an item in a forward contract.

spot-futures price-parity relation   The relation among the futures price, the spot price, and the riskless interest rate.

spread   The difference between two asset prices or rates of return.

standard deviation   The statistic that is most widely used to measure the volatility of a stock's probability distribution of returns. The larger the standard deviation, the greater the volatility of the stock.

strategy   A plan that takes into account future decisions in making current decisions.

strike price   The fixed price specified in an option contract. See also *exercise price*.

sustainable growth rate   The rate of growth in a firm's owners' equity. A firm cannot grow any faster than its sustainable growth rate.

swap contract   An agreement between two parties to exchange a series of cash flows at specified intervals over a specified period of time.

synergy   The combination of two companies that results in the value of the operating assets of the combined firm exceeding those of the two companies taken separately.

time line   A diagram used for analyzing the timing of cash flows.

time value (of an option)   The difference between an option's price and its value if the current time were its expiration date.

time value of money   The concept that a given amount of money in hand today is worth more than the claim to the same amount to be received in the future.

transaction costs   Costs that accompany a sale, including the costs of shipping, handling, insuring, and broker fees.

triangular arbitrage   An arbitrage transaction that involves three currencies.

unit of account   The medium in which payments are denominated, usually a currency (e.g., dollars, francs, and yen), sometimes a commodity such as gold or silver or some standard basket of goods and services.

volatility   A commonly used measure of an asset's riskiness, related to the range of possible rates of return and to their likelihood of occurring. In options trading, used synonymously with standard deviation, as in *implied volatility*.

weighted average cost of capital   A method of calculating a project's net present value using a weighted average of the cost of equity capital and the after-tax cost of debt. The weights are the market values of equity and debt as a fraction of the present value of the investment.

working capital   The difference between a firm's current assets and current liabilities.

yield curve   A curve depicting the relation between the promised interest rates (yields) on fixed-income instruments of a given risk and the maturity of the instrument.

yield spread   The difference in yields between two instruments.

yield-to-maturity   The discount rate that makes the present value of a bond's stream of promised cash payments equal to its price; the internal rate of return of a bond.

Index